FROM ECLIPSE TO APOCALYPSE  STAR WISDOM, VOL. 6

VOLUMES IN THE STAR WISDOM SERIES

Cosmology Reborn

Star Wisdom, vol 1
With Monthly Ephemerides and Commentary for 2019

Saturn - Mary - Sophia

Star Wisdom, vol 2
With Monthly Ephemerides and Commentary for 2020

As Above, So Below

Star Wisdom, vol 3
With Monthly Ephemerides and Commentary for 2021

Cosmic Communion

Star Wisdom, vol 4
With Monthly Ephemerides and Commentary for 2022

The Turning Point

Star Wisdom, vol 5
With Monthly Ephemerides and Commentary for 2023

From Eclipse to Apocalypse

Star Wisdom, vol 6
With Monthly Ephemerides for 2024

From Eclipse to Apocalypse

Star Wisdom, volume 6
2024

EDITOR
JOEL MATTHEW PARK

ADVISORY BOARD

Lindisfarne Books

LINDISFARNE BOOKS
An imprint of Steinerbooks/Anthroposophic Press, Inc.
834 Main Street PO Box 358, Spencertown, NY 12165
www.steinerbooks.org

With grateful acknowledgment to Peter Treadgold (1943–2005), who wrote the Astrofire program (available from the Sophia Foundation), with which the ephemeris pages in *Star Wisdom* are computed each year. DISCLAIMER: The views expressed by the contributors in *Star Wisdom* do not necessarily reflect those of the editorial board of *Star Wisdom* or Anthroposophic Press, Inc.

The chapter "Individual Spirit Beings and the Constant Foundation of the Universe" is reprinted from lecture 7 (Nov. 25, 1917) in *Secret Brotherhoods and the Mystery of the Human Double,* Rudolf Steiner Press, Sussex, UK, 2011, by kind permission of the publisher. All rights reserved.

This final edition of *Star Wisdom* is dedicated to the memory of Ian Clyne

aka Norm D. Feather—September 17, 1956 – July 14, 2023

A Grail Knight on both sides of the Threshold

ISBN: 978-1-58420-883-9

CONTENTS

ASTROSOPHY

The Sophia Foundation was founded and exists to help usher in the new age of Sophia and the corresponding Sophianic culture, the Rose of the World, prophesied by Daniel Andreev and other spiritual teachers. Part of the work of the Sophia Foundation is the cultivation of a new star wisdom, *Astro–Sophia* (*astrosophy*), now arising in our time in response to the descent of Sophia, who is the bearer of Divine Wisdom, just as Christ (the Logos, or the Lamb) is the bearer of Divine Love. Like the star wisdom of antiquity, astrosophy is sidereal, which means "of the stars." Astrosophy, inspired by Divine Sophia, descending from stellar heights, directs our consciousness toward the glory and majesty of the starry heavens, to encompass the entire celestial sphere of our cosmos and, beyond this, to the galactic realm—the realm that Daniel Andreev referred to as "the heights of our universe"—from which Sophia is descending on her path of approach into our cosmos. Sophia draws our attention not only to the star mysteries of the heights, but also to the cosmic mysteries connected with Christ's deeds of redemption wrought two thousand years ago. To penetrate these mysteries is the purpose of the annual volumes of *Star Wisdom*.

For information about Astrosophy/Choreocosmos/Cosmic Dance
workshops
Contact the Sophia Foundation:
4500 19th Street, #369, Boulder, CO 80304
Phone: (303) 242-5388; sophia@sophiafoundation.org;
www.sophiafoundation.org

PREFACE

Robert Powell, PhD

This is the sixth volume of the annual *Star Wisdom* (formerly *Journal for Star Wisdom*), intended to help all people interested in the new star wisdom of astrosophy and in the cosmic dimension of Christianity, which began with the Star of the Magi. The calendar comprises an ephemeris page for each month of the year, computed with the help of Peter Treadgold's *Astrofire* computer program, with a monthly commentary by Joel Matthew Park. The monthly commentary relates the geocentric and heliocentric planetary movements to events in the life of Jesus Christ.

Jesus Christ united the levels of the earthly personality (*geocentric* = Earth-centered) and the higher self (*heliocentric* = Sun-centered) insofar as he was the most highly evolved earthly personality (Jesus) embodying the higher self (Christ) of all existence, the Divine "I AM." To see the life of Jesus Christ in relation to the world of stars opens the door to a profound experience of the cosmos, giving rise to a new star wisdom (astrosophy) that is the Spiritual Science of Cosmic Christianity.

Star Wisdom is scientific, resting on a solid mathematical–astronomical foundation and a secure chronology of the life of Jesus Christ, while it is also spiritual, aspiring to the higher dimension of existence, expressed outwardly in the world of stars. The scientific and the spiritual come together in the sidereal zodiac that originated with the Babylonians and was used by the three magi who beheld the star of Bethlehem and came to pay homage to Jesus a few months after his birth.

In continuity of spirit with the origins of Cosmic Christianity with the three magi, the sidereal zodiac is the frame of reference used for the computation of the geocentric and heliocentric planetary movements that are commented upon in the light of the life of Jesus Christ in *Star Wisdom*.

Thus, all zodiacal longitudes indicated in the text and presented in the following calendar are in terms of the sidereal zodiac, which needs to be distinguished from the tropical zodiac widely used in contemporary astrology in the West. The tropical zodiac was introduced into astrology in the middle of the second century AD by the Greek astronomer Claudius Ptolemy. Prior to this, the sidereal zodiac was used. Such was the influence of Ptolemy on the Western astrological tradition that the tropical zodiac replaced the sidereal zodiac used by Babylonian, Egyptian, and early Greek astrologers. Yet the astrological tradition of India was not influenced by Ptolemy, and the sidereal zodiac is still used to this day by Hindu astrologers.

The sidereal zodiac originated with the Babylonians in the sixth to fifth centuries BC and was defined by them in relation to certain bright stars. For example, Aldebaran (the "Bull's Eye") is located in the middle of the sidereal sign–constellation of the Bull at 15° Taurus, while Antares ("the Scorpion's Heart") is in the middle of the sidereal sign–constellation of the Scorpion at 15° Scorpio. The sidereal signs, each 30° long, coincide closely with the twelve astronomical zodiacal constellations of the same name, whereas the signs of the tropical zodiac—since they are defined in relation to the vernal point—now have little or no relationship to the corresponding zodiacal constellations. This is because the vernal point, the zodiacal location of the Sun on March 20–21, shifts slowly backward through the sidereal zodiac at a rate of 1° every seventy-two years ("the precession of the equinoxes"). When Ptolemy introduced the tropical zodiac into astrology, there was a nearly exact coincidence between the tropical and the sidereal zodiac, as the vernal point, which is defined as 0° Aries in the tropical zodiac, was at 1° Aries in the sidereal zodiac in the middle of the second century AD. Thus, there was only 1° difference between the two zodiacs. Thus, it made hardly any difference to Ptolemy or his contemporaries to use the tropical zodiac instead of the sidereal zodiac. Now, however—the vernal point having shifted back from 1° Aries to 5° Pisces owing to precession—there is a 25° difference, and thus there is virtually no correspondence between the two. Without going into further detail concerning the complex issue of the zodiac (as shown in the *Hermetic Astrology* trilogy), the sidereal zodiac is the zodiac used by the three magi, who were the last representatives of the true star wisdom of antiquity. For this reason, the sidereal zodiac is used throughout the texts in *Star Wisdom*.

Readers interested in exploring the scientific (astronomical and chronological) foundations of Cosmic Christianity are referred to the works listed here under "Literature." The *Chronicle of the Living Christ: Foundations of Cosmic Christianity* (listed on the following page) is an indispensable reference source (abbreviated *Chron.*) for *Star Wisdom*. The chronology of the life of Jesus Christ rests upon Robert Powell's research into the description of Christ's daily life by Anne Catherine Emmerich in her three-volume work, *The Visions of Anne Catherine Emmerich* (abbreviated *ACE*).

Further details concerning *Star Wisdom* and how to work with it on a daily basis may be found in the general introduction to the *Christian Star Calendar*. The general introduction explains all the features of *Star Wisdom*. The new edition, published in 2003, includes sections on the megastars (stars of great luminosity) and on the 36 decans (10° subdivisions of the twelve signs of the zodiac) in relation to their planetary rulers and to the extra-zodiacal constellations, or the constellations above or below the circle of the twelve constellations–signs of the zodiac.

Further material on the decans, including examples of historical personalities born in the various decans, as well as a wealth of other material on the signs of the sidereal zodiac, can be found in *Cosmic Dances of the Zodiac* (listed below). Also foundational is *History of the Zodiac,* published by Sophia Academic Press (listed under "Works by Robert Powell").

LITERATURE

See also "Cited Works and Related Reading" section.

General Introduction to the Christian Star Calendar: A Key to Understanding, 2nd ed. Palo Alto, CA: Sophia Foundation, 2003.

Bento, William. Robert Schiappacasse, and David Tresemer. *Signs in the Heavens: A Message for Our Time.* Boulder: StarHouse, 2000.

Emmerich, Anne Catherine. *The Visions of Anne Catherine Emmerich* (new edition, with material by Robert Powell). Kettering, OH: Angelico Press, 2015.

Paul, Lacquanna, and Robert Powell. *Cosmic Dances of the Planets.* San Rafael, CA: Sophia Foundation Press, 2007.

———. *Cosmic Dances of the Zodiac.* San Rafael, CA: Sophia Foundation Press, 2007.

Smith, Edward R. *The Burning Bush: Rudolf Steiner, Anthroposophy, and the Holy Scriptures* (3rd ed.). Great Barrington, MA: SteinerBooks, 2020.

Steiner, Rudolf. *Astronomy and Astrology: Finding a Relationship to the Cosmos.* Forest Row, UK: Rudolf Steiner Press, 2009.

Sucher, Willi. *Cosmic Christianity and the Changing Countenance of Cosmology: An Introduction to Astrosophy.* Hudson, NY: Anthroposophic Press, 1993. *Isis Sophia* and other works by Willi Sucher are available from the Astrosophy Research Center, PO Box 13, Meadow Vista, CA 95722.

Tidball, Charles S., and Robert Powell. *Jesus, Lazarus, and the Messiah: Unveiling Three Christian Mysteries.* Great Barrington, MA: SteinerBooks, 2005. This book offers a penetrating study of the Christ mysteries against the background of *Chronicle of the Living Christ* and contains two chapters by Robert Powell on the Apostle John and John the Evangelist (Lazarus).

Tresemer, David (with Robert Schiappacasse). *Star Wisdom and Rudolf Steiner: A Life Seen Through the Oracle of the Solar Cross.* Great Barrington, MA: SteinerBooks, 2007.

WORKS ON ASTROSOPHY BY ROBERT POWELL, PhD

Starcrafts
(formerly Astro Communication Services, or ACS):

History of the Houses (1997)
History of the Planets (1989)
The Zodiac: A Historical Survey (1984)
www.acspublications.com
www.astrocom.com
Business Address:
Starcrafts Publishing
334 Calef Hwy.
Epping, NH 03042
Phone: 603-734-4300
Fax: 603-734-4311
Contact maria@starcraftseast.com

SteinerBooks:

Orders: (703) 661-1594; www.steinerbooks.org

The Astrological Revolution: Unveiling the Science of the Stars as a Science of Reincarnation and Karma, Kevin Dann, coauthor (Great Barrington, MA: Lindisfarne Books, 2010). After reestablishing the sidereal zodiac as a basis for astrology that penetrates the mystery of the stars' relationship to human destiny, the reader is invited to discover the astrological significance of the totality of the vast sphere of stars surrounding the Earth. This book points to the astrological significance of the entire celestial sphere, including all the stars and constellations beyond the twelve zodiacal signs. This discovery is revealed by the study of megastars, illustrating how they show up in an extraordinary way in Christ's healing miracles by aligning with the Sun at the time of those events. This book offers a spiritual, yet scientific, path toward a new relationship to the stars.

Christian Hermetic Astrology: The Star of the Magi and the Life of Christ (Hudson, NY: Anthroposophic Press, 1998). Twenty-five discourses set in the "Temple of the Sun," where Hermes and his pupils gather to meditate on the Birth, the Miracles, and the Passion of Jesus Christ. The discourses offer a series of meditative contemplations on the deeds of Christ in relation to the mysteries of the cosmos. They are an expression of the age-old hermetic mystery wisdom of the ancient Egyptian sage, Hermes Trismegistus. This book offers a meditative approach to the cosmic correspondences between major events in the life of Christ and the heavenly configurations at that time 2,000 years ago.

Chronicle of the Living Christ: Foundations of Cosmic Christianity (Hudson, NY: Anthroposophic Press, 1996). An account of the life of Christ, day by day, throughout most of the 3½ years of his ministry, including the horoscopes of conception, birth, and death of Jesus, Mary, and John the Baptist, together with a wealth of material relating to the new star wisdom focused on the life of Christ. This work provides the chronological basis for *Christian Hermetic Astrology* and *Star Wisdom*.

Elijah Come Again: A Prophet for Our Time: A Scientific Approach to Reincarnation (Great Barrington, MA: Lindisfarne Books, 2009). By way of horoscope comparisons from conception–birth–death in one incarnation to conception–birth–death in the next, this work establishes scientifically two basic astrosophical research findings. These are: the importance 1) of the sidereal zodiac and 2) of the heliocentric positions of the planets. Also, for the first time, the identity of the "saintly nun" is revealed, of whom Rudolf Steiner spoke in a conversation with Marie von Sivers about tracing Novalis's karmic background. The focus throughout the book is on the Elijah individuality in his various incarnations, and is based solidly on Rudolf Steiner's indications. It also can be read as a karmic biography by anyone who chooses to omit the astrosophical material.

Star Wisdom (Great Barrington, MA: Lindisfarne Books, 2019–); *Journal for Star Wisdom* (Lindisfarne Books, 2010–2018), edited by Joel Matthew Park, Robert Powell, and others engaged in astrosophic research. A guide to the correspondences of Christ in the stellar and etheric worlds. Includes articles of interest, a complete geocentric and heliocentric sidereal ephemeris, and an aspectarian. According to Rudolf Steiner, every step taken by Christ during his ministry between the baptism in the Jordan and the resurrection was in harmony with, and an expression of, the cosmos. The journal is concerned with these heavenly correspondences during the life of Christ. It is intended to help provide a foundation for Cosmic Christianity, the cosmic dimension of Christianity. It is this dimension that has been missing from Christianity in its 2,000-year history. A starting point is to contemplate the movements of the Sun, Moon, and planets against the background of the zodiacal constellations (sidereal signs) today in relation to corresponding stellar events during the life of Christ. This opens the possibility of attuning to the life of Christ in the etheric cosmos in a living way.

Sophia Foundation Press and Sophia Academic Press Publications

Books available from Amazon.com
JamesWetmore@mac.com
www.logosophia.com

History of the Zodiac (San Rafael, CA: Sophia Academic Press, 2007). Book version of Robert Powell's PhD thesis, *The History of the Zodiac*. This penetrating study restores the sidereal zodiac to its rightful place as the original zodiac, tracing it back to fifth century BC and the Babylonians. Available in paperback and hardcover.

Hermetic Astrology: Volume 1, Astrology and Reincarnation (San Rafael, CA: Sophia Foundation, 2007). This book seeks to give the ancient science of the stars a scientific basis. This new foundation for astrology based on research into reincarnation and karma (destiny) is the primary focus. It includes numerous reincarnation examples, the study of which reveals the existence of certain astrological "laws" of reincarnation, on the basis of which it is evident that the ancient sidereal zodiac is the authentic astrological zodiac, and that the heliocentric movements of the planets are of great significance. Foundational for the new star wisdom of astrosophy.

Hermetic Astrology: Volume 2, Astrological Biography (San Rafael, CA: Sophia Foundation, 2007). Concerned with karmic relationships and the unfolding of destiny in seven-year periods through one's life. The seven-year rhythm underlies the human being's astrological biography, which can be studied in relation to the movements of the Sun, Moon, and planets around the sidereal zodiac between conception and birth. The "rule of Hermes" is used to determine the moment of conception.

Sign of the Son of Man in the Heavens: Sophia and the New Star Wisdom (San Rafael, CA: Sophia Foundation, 2008). Revised and expanded with new material, this edition deals with a new wisdom of stars in the light of Divine Sophia. It was intended as a help in our time, as we were called on to be extremely wakeful up to the end of the Maya calendar in 2012.

Cosmic Dances of the Zodiac (San Rafael, CA: Sophia Foundation, 2007), coauthor Lacquanna Paul. Study material describing the twelve signs of the zodiac and their forms and gestures in cosmic dance, with diagrams. Includes a wealth of information on the twelve signs and the 36 decans (the subdivision of the signs into decans, or 10° sectors, corresponding to constellations above and below the zodiac).

Cosmic Dances of the Planets (San Rafael, CA: Sophia Foundation, 2007), coauthor Lacquanna Paul. Study material describing the seven classical planets and their forms and gestures in cosmic dance, with diagrams, including much information on the planets.

American Federation of Astrologers (AFA) Publications (currently not in print)

www.astrologers.com

The Sidereal Zodiac, coauthor Peter Treadgold (Tempe, AZ: AFA, 1985). A *History of the Zodiac* (sidereal, tropical, Hindu, astronomical) and a formal definition of the sidereal zodiac with the star Aldebaran ("the Bull's Eye") at 15° Taurus. This is an abbreviated version of *History of the Zodiac.*

Rudolf Steiner College Press Publications
9200 Fair Oaks Blvd., Fair Oaks, CA 95628

The Christ Mystery: Reflections on the Second Coming (Fair Oaks, CA: Rudolf Steiner College Press, 1999). The fruit of many years of reflecting on the Second Coming and its cosmological aspects. Looks at the approaching trial of humanity and the challenges of living in apocalyptic times, against the background of "great signs in the heavens."

The Sophia Foundation
4500 19th Street, #369, Boulder, CO 80304; distributes many of the books listed here and other works by Robert Powell.
Tel: (303) 242-5388
sophia@sophiafoundation.org
www.sophiafoundation.org

Computer program for charts and ephemerides, with grateful acknowledgment to Peter Treadgold, who wrote the computer program *Astrofire* (with research module, star catalog of over 4,000 stars, and database of birth and death charts of historical personalities), capable of printing geocentric and heliocentric–hermetic sidereal charts and ephemerides throughout history. The hermetic charts, based on the astronomical system of the Danish astronomer Tycho Brahe, are called "Tychonic" charts in the program. This program can:

- compute birth charts in a large variety of systems (tropical, sidereal, geocentric, heliocentric, hermetic);
- calculate conception charts using the hermetic rule, in turn applying it for correction of the birth time;
- produce charts for the period between conception and birth;
- print out an "astrological biography" for the whole of lifework with the geocentric, heliocentric (and even lemniscatory) planetary system;
- work with the sidereal zodiac according to the definition of your choice (Babylonian sidereal, Indian sidereal, unequal-division astronomical, etc.);

- work with planetary aspects with orbs of your choice.

The program includes eight house systems and a variety of chart formats. The program also includes an ephemeris program with a search facility. The geocentric–heliocentric sidereal ephemeris pages in the annual volumes of *Star Wisdom* are produced by the software program *Astrofire,* which is compatible with Microsoft Windows.

Those interested in obtaining the *Astrofire* program should contact:

The Sophia Foundation
4500 19th Street, #369
Boulder, CO 80304
Tel: (303) 242-5388
sophia@sophiafoundation.org
www.sophiafoundation.org

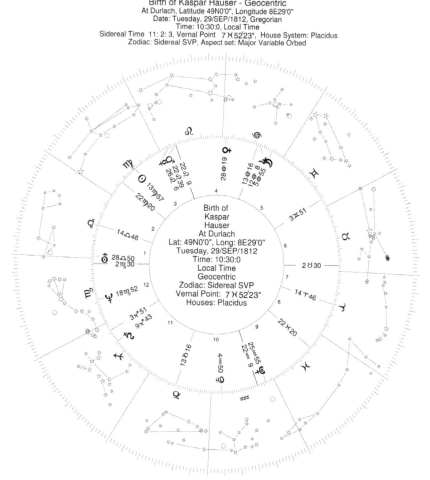

Birth of Kaspar Hauser - Geocentric
At Durlach, Latitude 49N0'0", Longitude 8E29'0"
Date: Tuesday, 29/SEP/1812, Gregorian
Time: 10:30:0, Local Time
Sidereal Time 11: 2: 3, Vernal Point 7♓52'23", House System: Placidus
Zodiac: Sidereal SVP, Aspect set: Major Variable Orbed

Birth of
Kaspar
Hauser
At Durlach
Lat: 49N0'0", Long: 8E29'0"
Tuesday, 29/SEP/1812
Time: 10:30:0
Local Time
Geocentric
Zodiac: Sidereal SVP
Vernal Point: 7♓52'23"
Houses: Placidus

A horoscope generated by the Astrofire *program*

THE SEVEN IDEALS OF THE ROSE OF THE WORLD

Robert Powell, PhD

In gratitude to Daniel Andreev (1906–1959), the Russian prophet of the Rose of the World as the coming world culture, inspired by Sophia—a culture based on Love and Wisdom.

Alla and Daniel Andreev
(1959)

The Rose of the World is arising through the approach of Divine Sophia toward the Earth. Her approach is calling forth the following basic qualities or attributes of the new world culture that She is creating and inspiring:

1. First and foremost: *interreligion*. For Sophia all true religious and spiritual traditions are different layers of spiritual reality, which She seeks to weave together as petals of the Rose of the World. Sophia is not founding a new world religion as She approaches, descending from cosmic heights, and drawing ever closer to our solar system. On Her path of descent, approaching our planet to incarnate into the Earth's aura during the Age of Aquarius, She is bestowing insight concerning each religion and spiritual tradition, thus awaking interreligiosity, signifying a heartfelt interest in religious and spiritual traditions other than one's own. This signifies the blossoming and unfolding of the petals of the Rose of the World, creating brother–sisterhood between all peoples.

2. Sophia's approach toward our planet is bringing about an awaking of social conscience on a global scale, inspiring active compassion combined with unflagging practical efforts on behalf of social justice around the world.

3. Through Sophia a framework for understanding the higher dimension of historical processes is coming about: metahistory, illumining the meaning of historical processes of the past, present, and future in relation to humankind's spiritual evolution. This entails glimpses into the mystical consciousness of humanity such as may be found in the book of Revelation.

4. On the national sociopolitical level, Sophia's inspiration is working to transform the state into a community. The community of Italy, the community of France, etc., is the ideal for the future, rather than the political entity of the state representing (or misrepresenting) the people. And on the global scale Sophia is seeking to bring about the unification of the planet as a world community through bringing the different country communities into a harmonious relationship with one another on a religious, cultural, and economic level.

5. This world community, the Rose of the World, inspired by Sophia, will seek to establish the economic wellbeing of every man, woman, and child on the planet, to ensure that everyone has a roof over their heads and sufficient food to live on. Here it is a matter of ensuring a decent standard of living for all peoples of the Earth.

6. A high priority of the Rose of the World will be the ennobling of education. New methods of education are being inspired by Sophia to help bring out everyone's creative talents. To ennoble education so that each person's creativity can unfold is the goal here.

7. Finally, Sophia is working for the transformation of the planet into a garden and, moreover, for the spiritualization of nature. Humanity and nature are to live in cooperation and harmony, with human beings taking up their responsibility toward nature, which is to work for the spiritualization and redemption of the kingdoms of nature.

EDITORIAL FOREWORD: FROM ECLIPSE TO APOCALYPSE

Joel Matthew Park

I. A MEMORY: REFLECTIONS ON THE GREAT CONJUNCTION AS A TURNING POINT (*written December 2020*)

On August 21, 2017, thousands of people gathered together across the United States to witness an event that had not occurred since 1918: a total solar eclipse whose pathway crossed from coast to coast of the contiguous United States. With well-deserved hype emerging throughout digital media, this eclipse came to be called the "Great American Solar Eclipse."

I can remember this eclipse quite vividly. At this point in time, I was still living at Plowshare Farm in Greenfield, New Hampshire. Since 2014, I had become increasingly involved with a local group of Sophians and Hermeticists, some of whom might be known to some readers, as they have been long-time friends and facilitators of Sophianic work: Richard Reho, Gail Dupre, and James Wetmore, to name a few. All told, there were nine of us locally who had been working together.

Specifically, our work centered on the Grail Knight's Practice, a mantric distillation of Valentin Tomberg's *Lord's Prayer Course*, to which Robert Powell had given eurythmic movement. We also focused on a new form of working with the Tarot of Marseilles, which came to be called "Hermetic Conversation." Eventually, I would present something of the work with Hermetic Conversation at the Sophia Foundation's Annual Meditation Retreat in Santa Fe, New Mexico, in 2019.[1]

In both 2014 and 2015, this New Hampshire group had periodic retreats facilitated by Robert Powell and/or Estelle Isaacson. However, after 2016, Robert Powell began a much less intense travel and workshop schedule.[2] He has not traveled to the United States since then. Our group had a weekend intensive with Estelle Isaacson in the summer of 2016, and as we looked to the summer

---

1   See the-unknown-friends.com for more information.

2   See https://sophiafoundation.org/wp-content /uploads/2017/04/Choreocosmos _ConsiderationsEaster_2016.pdf.

Image: https://www.space.com/35171-great-american-solar-eclipse-coming-in-2017.html

of 2017, we decided we wanted to have another intensive with Estelle.

This was not to be, however—the weekend we chose to have our event was centered around the Great American Solar Eclipse. This happened to be at exactly the same time as the Sophia Foundation's Annual Meditation Retreat in Idaho—and Estelle had already made the commitment to jointly facilitate this retreat with Karen Rivers. Due to health reasons, as well as massive shifts in her spiritual life, this was to be the last year that Estelle was able to attend a Sophia Foundation event, at least up through the present time.

So, undaunted, we decided to carry on and co-create a retreat of our own. We invited friends, including Kevin Dann and Ian Clyne.[3] We left the evenings open-ended, during which Ian (a professional jazz pianist) guided us through musical experiences of our birth horoscopes. In the mornings we had Hermetic Conversation on the The Devil, Temperance, and Death. In the afternoons we experimented with more improvisational forms of Choreocosmos, and entered deeply into the Grail Knight's Practice. The weekend culminated with experiencing the Solar Eclipse, the cosmic configuration of which created the foundation for our improvisational Choreocosmos. All the while, we kept in consciousness that we had another group of Sophians actively engaged in complementary spiritual work on the other side of the country—like the two pillars of the 4th Apocalyptic Seal.

It was an incredibly rejuvenating weekend. We had begun to engage in content and processes that felt new, yet were also natural continuations of the work with which we had all become so deeply familiar. Unexpectedly—although it felt like a new beginning—it proved in reality to be the fruition of what we had been cultivating together for the past three years. By the year's end, five of our nine would move—four to Ecuador, where Robert Powell and Lacquanna Paul had found their new home. Two of them would become more heavily involved

in their external vocations, making it difficult to meet further with regularity. In hindsight, it feels as though this particular group of people was meant to gather to bring something to full expression at the time of this Solar Eclipse, and then go their separate ways. By the summer of 2019, I and my family moved away from New Hampshire to Copake, New York, to join Camphill Village—and yet the work that had begun in New Hampshire carried on, with my spiritual brother Phillip Malone and me continuing our work on Hermetic Conversation up to the present day.

And why do I write all of this? Because I wonder if others, too, perhaps feel as though they entered a different *realm* as of this Great American Solar Eclipse—particularly, but not limited to, my friends, known and unknown, here in the United States. It may be that we stand in the midst of— yes, right now [Dec. 2020] *exactly* in the midst of—a 6⅔-year long period.

In an extremely rare turn of events, the total solar eclipse that was visible from coast to coast of the United States on August 21, 2017, will be followed by *another* total solar eclipse on April 8, 2024. This eclipse will be visible not just across the United States, but all the way from Mexico to Canada.[4]

---

3 Known to our readers as Norm D. Feather—God rest his soul. He passed away on July 14, 2023; this final edition of *Star Wisdom* is dedicated to him.

4 See https://www.greatamericaneclipse.com/april -8-2024.

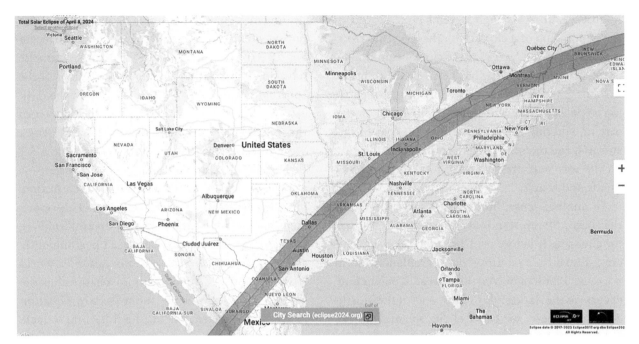

The map above shows the path of the 2024 eclipse, which might be called "The Great *North* American Solar Eclipse." Below shows the intersecting point of the two paths, from 2017 and 2024.

Notice that the midpoint of these two American Eclipses is December 14 and 15, 2020, less than one week before the Great Conjunction of Saturn and Jupiter on the Winter Solstice (Dec. 21). In

fact, there is a total solar eclipse visible in *South* America, in Chile and Argentina, at the exact midpoint.[5] From this we can see that the third week of Advent leading up to the Great Conjunction is a kind of turning point or pivot in this 6⅔-year time period. We might imagine the 3⅓ years from

---

5   See https://www.greatamericaneclipse.com/2020 -dec-14.

Image: https://www.wlky.com/article/cities-that-will-have-a-total-solar-eclipse-in-2017-and-2024/10378429

August 21, 2017 through December 21, 2020, as the winding up of a clock, with the 3⅓ years from now until April 8, 2024, as the clock beginning to mark the time—of what has been seeded to begin sprouting and revealing itself. The image of entering a *vortex*, of traveling one spiraling arm on the way in; entering the center point (the "eye of the storm"); and then traveling the other spiraling arm on the way out, presents itself to the eyes of our minds and hearts.

In another sense, humanity at large (certainly the United States) stands at a crossroads. The time for choosing is before us: Christ or Ahriman. Liberty, Equality, Fraternity or Surveillance, Technocracy, Plutocracy. As this Great Conjunction occurs on the darkest day of the year in the Northern Hemisphere, we can feel the spiritual world holding its breath as humanity enters into the time of deepest darkness, wondering if they will choose for the Light to be reborn. Indeed, there are historical indications that are quite encouraging in this regard; for those who would wish to read further about these indications, turn to my "Editorial Foreword" to 2019's *Saturn—Mary—Sophia: Star Wisdom,* volume 2.

By turning our hearts and our thoughts to the cosmic memories of the configurations of these two eclipses and the Great Conjunction, we make ourselves more receptive to the intentions of the spiritual world for this time. The Great American Solar Eclipse from August 21, 2017, was monumental in this regard: the occultation of the Sun by the Moon occurred at 3° Leo, conjunct Eta Leonis. This very closely recalled the seventh healing miracle of Christ from the Gospel of John, the Raising of Lazarus from the Dead. This miracle also occurred during a New Moon (every solar eclipse is a New Moon) conjunct Eta Leonis, one of the most powerful megastars, on July 26 AD 32 (all of the dates from the life of Christ in this article are drawn from the work of Robert Powell in *Chronicle of the Living Christ* and *Christian Hermetic Astrology*).

Looking to the Great Conjunction, this meeting of Saturn and Jupiter occurs at 5° Capricorn. This is only 3° shy of the Sun's position at the *first*

healing miracle, the Changing of Water into Wine, during which the Sun was 8° Capricorn, on December 28 AD 29. Notice that both of these miracles have an emphasis on drawing the cold light of the spiritual heights of the Father down into the darkest, warmest depths of the Mother in the heart of the Earth—the fusion of the furthest extremes. We can feel, then, that the time period from 2017 through 2020—the first spiral of the vortex—is a movement in reverse through the seven healing miracles from the Gospel of John. This movement backward is taken up by Valentin Tomberg in one of his final works, published posthumously as *Lazarus: The Miracle of Resurrection in World History,* in which he brings into relationship the healing miracles and the seven days of Creation in the Book of Genesis. The final healing miracle of the Raising of Lazarus is a recapitulation of the first day of Creation—"Let there be light!"—while the first healing miracle of the Changing of Water into Wine is a recapitulation of the seventh day of Creation, during the primal Sabbath, when the Elohim declared all of Creation to be "very good." During these past three years, therefore, we have had the opportunity to become a new Creation through Christ.

The Great Conjunction is even more closely related to another event in the life of Jesus—the Adoration of the Magi. While the Solomon Jesus was born on March 5, 6 BC, it took the Magi over nine months after his birth for them to arrive at the house of Jesus and his family. The three Magi bestowed their gifts of gold, frankincense, and myrrh on December 26, 6 BC, to the 9-month-old child they knew to be the reincarnation of their great spiritual teacher from prior incarnations, Zoroaster (Zarathustra). On this day, the Sun was 6° Capricorn, only 1° away from the alignment of Saturn and Jupiter in this year's Great Conjunction.

And what about the Great North American Solar Eclipse that we look forward to on April 8, 2024? On this day, the Sun and Moon will conjoin at 24° Pisces. This, too, recalls the incarnation of the Solomon Jesus. The year 7 BC also saw a Great Conjunction of Saturn and Jupiter—but this year was special; as sometimes happens due to retrograde motion, the two of them were conjunct not once but *three* times. It was this series of conjunctions that woke the Magi to the reality of Zarathustra's descent once again into an earthly body. In particular, it was the first of these conjunctions, which occurred on May 27, 7 BC, at 24° Pisces—the same position as the Sun and Moon on April 8, 2024. It was shortly after this Great Conjunction that Zarathustra was conceived and began his descent to Earth, on June 7, 7 BC.

And so this second 3⅓ year period, leading out of the vortex of 2020, draws our gaze to the individuality of Zoroaster or "Radiant Star," yet again moving backward through time, from the Adoration of the Magi when he was nine months old, to the time just before his conception. We might imagine this, on the one hand, to indicate a resurrection of the ancient Star Wisdom of Babylonian Astrology—a "moving back" to the Solomon Jesus's incarnation as Zoroaster in the 6th century BC. The April 8, 2024, solar eclipse also very closely recalls the miracle of the Feeding of the Four Thousand (March 15 AD 31; Sun 25° Pisces); Peter receiving the Keys to the Kingdom of Heaven (March 19 AD 31; Sun 28° Pisces); and the Triumphant Entry to Jerusalem on "Palm Sunday" (March 19 AD 33; Sun 29° Pisces). All of these star memories combine to give the strong impression of the "Return of the King"—of true Authority overcoming false authority, putting things into their proper order.

II. THE AGE OF ECLIPSE

I begin this article with the above piece, which I wrote in December 2020, in order to give the reader a sense of my inner orientation at that time, the mid-point of what I have come to consider the "Age of Eclipse." The perspective I came to then—that we entered a particularly hazardous twilight zone in August 2017 and would remain wandering there until April 2024, with December 2020 as the turning point in the vortex—has only been reinforced by my experiences since. Am I the only one who feels that the past six years have witnessed a total eclipse of values, of logic, of orientation, of social health?

There is an old legend concerning Zarathustra, that he incarnated seven times, accumulating all the wisdom the world could offer in each of those lives through his conscious clairvoyance and perception of the spiritual world. Then, in an eighth life he was born blind inwardly and outwardly—without perception of the physical world or the spiritual world. He was put to the test as to how much of what he had gained of his prior experience had truly united itself with his eternal spirit, and could be reborn as though out of nothing—out of his own inner resources alone, without any help from the spiritual world.[6] Perhaps during these years, humanity as a whole has been confronted with a similar trial—when left completely to our own resources, with no help from the benevolent spirits, and in the face of the incarnation of Ahriman in human form, are we able to draw the necessary forces seemingly out of nothing? Much of what we have been given over the past century and a half from guides such as Rudolf Steiner, Beinsa Douno (Peter Deunov), and Valentin Tomberg has taken root and come to life in a totally individualized way in each of us?

To this day I still worry and wonder if we passed our examination—perhaps better said, if *I* passed *my* examination!

In addition to the perspective that 2017 to 2024 was an age of eclipsed sanity on the part of humanity, the part that the Great Conjunction had to play as a midpoint or a pivot has also been greatly reinforced for me, even down to small details. The group of Sophians who gathered in 2017 only to split apart shortly afterward has begun to regroup in the region of Copake, New York, over the past year and a half. The work on the Minor Arcana of the Tarot that I began with Phillip Malone around 2017 is coming to its completion.

Most pertinent of all in this regard has to do with my editorship of this publication. I first became involved with the *Journal for Star Wisdom* in 2017, right around the time of the solar eclipse. As the years have gone by, I have felt

---

6 Cf. "The Letter to the Angel of the Church of the Laodiceans" in Valentin Tomberg's *Christ and Sophia*.

increasingly taxed by the amount of time, effort, and inner resources I need to pour out each year to make this publication possible—particularly in regards to the commentaries. This past year, Julie Humphreys began to share a weekly stargazing commentary on *Starlight*, the Substack of the Sophia Foundation.[7] They have been immensely popular and successful (there are no commentaries in this present volume—they will be found on *Starlight* weekly throughout 2024). It made me realize that this is a much more flexible way for me to share articles on astrosophy: I can post them to *Starlight* all year round, with no deadlines for publication. And so, I do intend for this edition of *Star Wisdom* to be the last; as of 2024 what would otherwise be published in these volumes will become a part of *Starlight*. I would like to extend my deep gratitude to all of the contributors, as well as everyone at SteinerBooks (Jens Jensen in particular) who helped bring this publication to the world over the years.

Returning to the main theme of this article: my intention now (in the summer of 2023), as we look toward the gateway leading out of the "Age of Eclipse" on April 8, 2024, is to look more deeply not only at the astrological signatures of the Solar Eclipses of 2017 and 2024 and the Great Conjunction in their midst, but also beyond these events. We will also investigate the Annular Eclipse of October 14, 2023, whose path also moves from the West to East Coast of the United States, as well as another American Solar Eclipse in the far future—August 12, 2045.

My hope is that out of a multiplicity of details—hatchmarks on the page so to speak—an image will begin to arise for me and for you of the cosmic intentions, possibilities, and results of this Age of Eclipse, such that we can unveil what is veiled, and move from Eclipse to Apocalypse.

III. THE PAST: THE GREAT AMERICAN SOLAR ECLIPSE OF 2017 AND THE GREAT CONJUNCTION OF 2020

The Age of Eclipse began, as noted above, with a total solar eclipse visible across all of the contiguous United States, moving from the West to the East Coast on August 21, 2017. This had not occurred since 1918; and the eclipse itself was 100 years since 1917. The years 1917 to 1918 were centered on World War I, the Bolshevik Revolution, and the outbreak of the Spanish Flu. In one form or another, these three calamities found themselves reborn throughout the nearly seven years of the Age of Eclipse: the nationalistic perils of World War I have found themselves renewed in the proxy war that NATO and Russia have fought in Ukraine; Bolshevism has morphed into an elitist cultural monster in the form of mass censorship, cancel culture, and woke ideology; and the Spanish Flu returned from the grave as a kind of zombie in the form of Covid-19. In terms of the latter, we can imagine this not so much in terms of the disease itself, but in terms of the incredibly irresponsible, sociopathic responses to it on the part of so-called leaders and experts.

But there were other events happening in 2017 that were of greater significance in the realm of *depth*, i.e. esoterically rather than exoterically. Primary amongst these was the 100-year anniversary of the apparitions of Our Lady of Fátima. Amongst the many Marian apparitions that have occurred over the years, perhaps those that continue to have the most relevance to contemporary humanity's spiritual struggle are the appearances of Our Lady to three peasant children in Portugal over one hundred years ago. Toward the end of World War I, she appeared to them six times between May 13 and October 13, 1917. Notably, these apparitions took place precisely between the February and October Revolutions that led to the Bolshevik takeover of the Russian Empire, which led five years later to the formation of the USSR.

In Our Lady's third appearance to the children of Fátima, she implored the Holy See to consecrate Russia to her Immaculate Heart. In her instructions, she indicated that if this were to be done, Russia would be converted, leading to an era of world peace.

Among those who have faith in the visionary experiences of Fátima, there is not a consensus as to whether or not the request of Our Lady has been properly fulfilled. From the point of view of the Holy See, when Pope John Paul II consecrated the world to the Immaculate Heart on March 25, 1984, he inwardly directed this consecration to Russia specifically. Others point even earlier, to the papal bull "Sacro Vergente," written by Pope Pius XII on July 7, 1952, to the people of Russia, in which he consecrated them specifically to Her Immaculate Heart. The evidence that these were effective consecrations is witnessed in the fall of the USSR in 1991, and the re-emergence of Russia as a Christian nation in the years since then (albeit Russian Orthodox and not Roman Catholic).

There are some (such as Fathers Malachi Martin and Nicholas Gruner, and Archbishop Carlo Maria Viganò) who argue that the consecration was never done in the way that Our Lady specified. They argue that the consecration needs to be given specifically to the Russian *nation*, and that all bishops must be involved in this consecration along with the Pope. They see the work of the conversion of Russia in order to inaugurate a time of world peace as not yet fulfilled.

How can we understand this from an anthroposophical and Christian Hermetic point of view? From anthroposophy, we understand that in years to come, Russia and the Slavic nations will be the center of a truly Christian and Sophianic world culture. The seeds of this culture can and must be planted in our time, but they will take more than 2,000 years to come to fruition: the Russian epoch is not destined to flourish until the year 3574, according to the spiritual research of Rudolf Steiner.

Perhaps we can understand the consecration of Russia to Our Lady's Immaculate Heart not as a one-time event that must be done exactly right, leading to an immediate period of world peace. From a Goethean and Hermetic perspective, we can understand this as a process of development and growth: a gradual nurturing of Russia to take up her spiritual mission. Perhaps each time Russia is consecrated to Mary—regardless whether this consecration is done "correctly" or not—catalyzes the next stage on the path of her spiritual evolution.

For example, the years following the consecration of the Russian people by Pope Pius XII saw the death of Stalin and the leadership of Nikita Krushchev, who "de-Stalinized" Russia and aimed to decrease Cold War tensions with John F. Kennedy. And in the years after Pope John Paul II's consecration of the whole world (specifically Russia), the world witnessed the fall of communism in the Pope's home country of Poland, as well as the fall of the Berlin Wall in 1989.

In Valentin Tomberg's *Lazarus: The Miracle of Resurrection in World History*, he presents a unique picture of the Pope's role in the Church as the mouthpiece of Peter. Regardless as to whether the human being who has become the Pope is a "good person" or not—in other words, regardless of the relative "fitness" of the vessel (we can think for example of Pope Alexander VI)—from the Tombergian perspective there are times when the Pope can do nothing other than be the vessel through which the eternal spirit of Peter speaks on behalf of Christ "above" and the whole of Christianity "below." Hypothetically, even if we were to have an "evil Pope" in the Holy See, he would be at times "possessed by the Good"—overwhelmed by the moral force of St. Peter, and compelled to speak the Truth.

From this perspective, we can understand that 1) Russia is in a gradual process of becoming the cultural center of Christianity; 2) the consecration of Russia to the Immaculate Heart of Mary is integral to this process; and 3) over time, the eternal spirit of Peter is able to "speak through" various Popes in order to bring these consecrations about. It is Peter, from Rome, who accomplishes the gradual union of Mary-Sophia with Russia.

And now in this Age of Eclipse, when the messages of Our Lady of Fátima are being emphasized by the stellar configurations, a third consecration has occurred. On March 25, 2022, Pope Francis consecrated both Ukraine and Russia to the Immaculate Heart of Mary. This was requested of him by Ukrainian Catholic bishops on Ash Wednesday, just over a week after the sudden escalation of the Russo-Ukraine conflict that began eight years previously. He did so on the Feast of the

Annunciation, one of the principal Marian Feasts of the Christian year. Just as Gabriel brought to Mary the holy tidings that would lead to the birth of Jesus in nine months' time, we can hold in our hearts a hope and expectation that at some point soon, the world can experience a new level of peace born of this consecration, just as it did in the 1950s and 1980s. Beyond this, we can hold the picture that this consecration is not simply for the sake of relieving and resolving the current conflict between Ukraine and Russia; its deeper significance lies in the fact that this is one more step in the path to Russia's spiritual destination.

As noted above, the eclipse of August 21, 2017, occurred in alignment with the Sun's position at Christ's raising of Lazarus (i.e., John the Apocalyptist) from the dead. But in the Catholic tradition, August 21 is important for an additional reason: it is the feast day of Our Lady of Knock. On August 21, 1879, the Virgin Mary, along with John the Apocalyptist, St. Joseph, and Christ in the form of the Lamb from the Book of Revelation appeared to villagers from Knock, Ireland. Some believers understand this vision to indicate the opening of the seven seals of the Book of Revelation, and the start of a time of trial for the Church and the world.[8]

It is noteworthy that this vision occurred in 1879; according to Rudolf Steiner's occult research, this is both the start of the Age of Michael, as well as the end of the War in Heaven described in Revelation 12, at which point Ahriman was cast down from the spiritual to the earthly realm, working within the human psyche very powerfully since then. And so, the intuition of the Catholic faithful is in alignment with the results of spiritual scientific research. The years 1917 and 1879 will continue to appear as two of the strongest "memories" called up by the alignments of the Age of Eclipse. We will also see the alignments of this time repeatedly directing us back to our spiritual guides: the Virgin Mary; John the Apocalyptist; St. Michael; Zarathustra; and most of all, Christ.

One final star memory of August 21, 2017: while the children in Portugal were experiencing their fourth apparition of Our Lady of Fátima, Rudolf Steiner was delivering a series of lectures on the *Karma of Materialism* (CW 176), a prelude to his lectures on *The Fall of the Spirits of Darkness* (CW 178), a series to which we will return later in this article.

Three years and four months after this eclipse, there occurred the Great Conjunction of Jupiter and Saturn in Capricorn on December 21, 2020. We have considered this Great Conjunction to some degree already in the first part of this article, emphasizing its position (along with the South American eclipse of December 14, 2020), occupying the mid-point of the Age of Eclipse (2017–2024)—the center of the vortex, the eye of the storm.

These two stellar events took place almost exactly 100 years after Rudolf Steiner's lectures on *Universal Spirituality and Human Physicality* (CW 202). Over the course of these lectures, Rudolf Steiner builds a clear conceptual bridge between the physical and spiritual aspects of the world and humanity. He emphasizes that theoretical ideas destroy this connection, while it is only moral ideas that can build up both the human being and nature. These lectures culminate in Steiner's Christmas lectures on "The New Isis and the Search for the Divine Sophia," in which he describes the transformed role of "Kings" and "Shepherds" in our time.

The shepherds that visited the nativity of the Nathan Jesus represented a stream that had revelatory experiences of the spiritual hierarchies in a direct, childlike way—out of heart forces. In contrast, the magi who visited the Solomon Jesus had developed a clairvoyant understanding of the science of the stars in conjunction with a rigorous development of their thinking. Rudolf Steiner proposes that what is needed in our time is a transformation of each stream. The shepherd stream must develop a relationship to nature akin the magi, but directed to the earthly rather than cosmic realms. They must cultivate a clairvoyance for elemental

---

8   See http://unveilingtheapocalypse.blogspot.com /2017/03/our-lady-of-knock-and-opening-of -sealed.html?m=1.

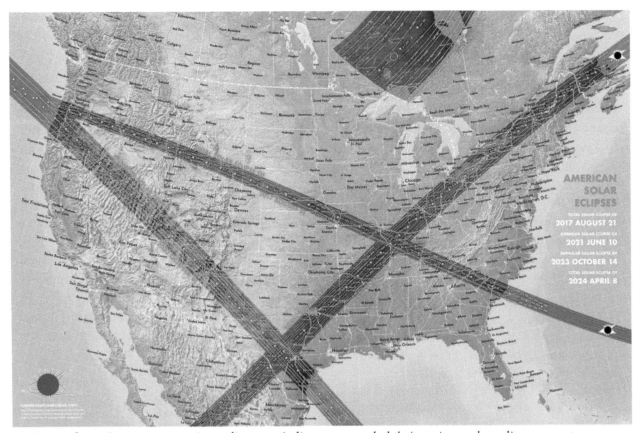

Image: https://www.greatamericaneclipse.com/eclipse-maps-and-globe/american-solar-eclipses-2017-to-2024

forces and beings, nature spirits. On the other hand, the kingly stream must look inwardly rather than outwardly, coming to a clear perception of cosmic and planetary evolution through reading the akashic record. These are the paths to the Divine Sophia in our time.

We can also keep in mind two feasts from December. The Feast of Santa Lucia takes place on December 13 every year. At the time when this feast was inaugurated in the 14th century, due to the use of the Julian calendar, December 13 was the darkest day of the year, the Winter Solstice. Similarly, the Feast of Our Lady of Guadalupe is on December 12. The visions of Our Lady of Guadalupe took place between December 9th and 13th in 1531, which would be the equivalent in the Gregorian calendar to December 19th and 23rd. And so, both of these festivals honoring the Divine Feminine are related to this time period during the third and fourth weeks of Advent, a time when both the eclipse and Great Conjunction occurred in 2020. They are especially related in terms of

the rebirth of the light of Wisdom (Sophia) in the midst of the deepest darkness.

IV. THE PRESENT: ANNULAR SOLAR ECLIPSE OF OCTOBER 14, 2023 AND TOTAL SOLAR ECLIPSE OF APRIL 8, 2024

On October 14, 2023, the United States experienced the second of three eclipses that would travel across the entire United States. The three of them together form a triangular shape over the country. If August 21, 2017, was the gateway leading *into* the Age of Eclipse, and the Great Conjunction was the turning point in the journey, then we can consider the event of October 14, 2023, as a kind of prelude or preparation for the gateway leading *out of* the Age of Eclipse properly and completely on April 8, 2024.

What is fascinating about this event is its strong resonance with the August 21, 2017 event. The eclipse of 2017 occurred 100 years after the visions of Our Lady of Fátima. These visions culminated with the Miracle of the Sun on October

13, during which thousands of people witnessed the Sun (at 26° Virgo) dance across the sky for about ten minutes. And so the Sun at 26° Virgo on October 14, 2023 is remembering the culmination of the miracle of Our Lady of Fátima in 1917!

From the perspective of Catholicism, it is also significant that on October 13, 1884—exactly 33 years prior to the Miracle of the Sun—Pope Leo XIII was given a vision of a century of temptation on the part of the Catholic Church akin to the testing of Job.[9] As a protection against it, he was given the following prayer to St. Michael, which became a part of the Low Mass from 1886 to 1964 (its removal was bound up with the results of Vatican II):

> St. Michael the Archangel, defend us in battle. Be our defense against the wickedness and snares of the Devil. May God rebuke him, we humbly pray, and do thou, O Prince of the heavenly hosts, by the power of God, thrust into hell Satan, and all the evil spirits, who prowl about the world seeking the ruin of souls. Amen.

In the autumn of 1884, Rudolf Steiner had just published the first volume of Goethe's scientific writings, and had moved in with the Sprecht family to tutor their boys.

On the other hand, nearly simultaneously with the Miracle of the Sun, it was on October 14, 1917, that Rudolf Steiner delivered the central lecture of his series *The Fall of the Spirits of Darkness*: "The Battle between Michael and 'The Dragon.'" Over the course of this lecture, Steiner laid out for the first time in explicit terms the expression of this battle over the course of the 19th to 20th centuries. He described how this image of Archangel Michael slaying the Dragon is an eternal image with manifold meanings at different points in human history, the most recent battle taking place over the course of the 19th century, during which time human culture had the least access to spiritual thinking, and materialistic thoughts infected the minds of human beings in a way analogous to bacterial infection. This battle in the spiritual world between Michael and the Dragon took place

between 1841 and 1879, at which point in time the Age of Michael began, and the ahrimanic spirits were cast down into the earthly sphere, into the thoughts and will of human beings.

He indicates that the year 1879 is a pivot point: the War in Heaven lasted for 38 years *prior* to 1879; 38 years *after* 1879 would see the full expression of the fall of the spirits of darkness on Earth. That year was 1917, the year he was giving these lectures. It was also the year of the Bolshevik revolution, which took place less than a month after this lecture was given. And so again, very strongly, our gaze is drawn by the star memories of the October 14, 2023, eclipse to the years 1879 and 1917, as years heavily related to our current Age of Eclipse.

Rudolf Steiner makes astounding claims in this lecture that might bring to mind the events of the past years (emphasis mine):

> The deepest impulse that has been living in many human souls since 1879 is therefore one that was cast down into the human realms; before that, it lived as ahrimanic power in the world of the spirit. It is helpful to look for other ways of strengthening the idea in our minds by using concepts from the material world, using them essentially as symbolic images. What happens today more at the level of soul and spirit had more of a material bias in very early times. The world of matter is also spiritual; it is merely a different form of spirituality.
>
> If you were to go back to very early times in evolution, you would find a battle similar to the one I just described. As mentioned, these battles have recurred over and over again, but always over different issues. In the distant past, the crowd of ahrimanic spirits were also cast down from the spiritual worlds into the earthly realm when they had lost such a battle. You see, they would return to the attack again and again. After one of these battles, for example, the crowd of ahrimanic spirits populated the earth with the earthly life forms that the medical profession now calls bacilli. Everything that has the power to act as a bacillus, everything in which bacilli are involved, is the result of crowds of ahrimanic spirits being cast down from heaven to earth at a time when the dragon

---

9   See https://ucatholic.com/vision-of-pope-leo.

had been overcome. In the same way the ahrimanic, Mephisphophelean way of thinking has spread since the late 1870s as the result of such a victory. Thus, we are able to say that tubercular and bacillary diseases come from a similar source as the materialism that has taken hold of human minds.

We can also compare the occurrences of the last century with something else. We can point to something that you know already from *An Outline of Esoteric Science:* the withdrawal of the Moon from the sphere of Earth evolution. The Moon was once part of the Earth; it was cast out from the Earth. As a result, certain Moon influences took effect on Earth, and this, too, followed a victory won by Michael over the dragon. We are therefore also able to say that everything connected with certain effects relating to the phases of the Moon, and all impulses that reach the Earth from the Moon, have their origin in a similar battle between Michael and the dragon.

These things really do belong together, in a way, and it is extremely useful to consider this, for it has profound significance. Some individuals develop an irresistible hankering for the intellectual materialism that arises from being in league with the fallen Ahriman. They gradually come to love the impulses that Ahriman raises in their souls and, indeed, consider them to be of a particularly noble and sublime way of thinking. Once again, it is necessary to be fully and clearly aware of these things. Unless they are in our conscious awareness and we have clear insight, we cannot make head or tail of events. The danger inherent in all this must be looked at with a cool eye, as it were, and a calm heart. We have to face them calmly. We shall only do so, however, if we are quite clear about the fact that a certain danger threatens human beings from this direction. This is the danger of preserving what should not be preserved. Everything that happens within the great scheme of things does also have its good side. It is because the ahrimanic powers entered into us when Michael won his victory that we are gaining in human freedom. Everything is connected with this, for the crowd of ahrimanic spirits has entered into all of us. We gain in human freedom, but we must be aware of this.

We should not allow the ahrimanic powers to gain the upper hand, as it were, and we should not fall in love with them.

This is tremendously important. There always is the danger of people continuing in materialism, in the materialistic, ahrimanic way of thinking, and carrying this on into ages when, according to the plan of things, it should have been overcome. The people who do not turn away from the ahrimanic, materialistic way of thinking and want to keep it, would then be in league with everything that has come about through similar victories won over the dragon by Michael. They therefore would not unite with spiritual progress in human evolution but with material progress. *And a time would come in the sixth post-Atlantean age when the only thing to please them would be to live in something that will have been brought about by bacilli, those microscopically small enemies of humanity.*

Something else also needs to be understood. Exactly because of its logical consistency, and indeed its greatness, the scientific way of thinking, too, is in great danger of sliding into the ahrimanic way of thinking. Consider how some scientists are thinking today in the field of geology, for instance. They study the surface formation of the earth and the residues and so on, to determine how certain animals live, or have lived, in the different strata. Empirical data are established for certain periods. Scientists use these as a basis for their views as to what the earth looked like thousands and millions of years ago, arriving, for instance, at the nebular hypothesis of Kant and Laplace. They also develop ideas as to the future evolution of the earth, and from the physical point of view these are quite correct. They are often utterly brilliant, but they are based on a method where the evolution of the earth is observed for a time and then conclusions are drawn: millions of years before, and millions of years afterward.

What is really being done in this case? It is the same as if we were to observe a child when it is seven, eight or nine years old, taking note of how its organs gradually change, or partly change, and calculate how much these human organs change over a period of two or three years. We then multiply this to work out how much these organs will change over a period of centuries. So, we can work out what this child looked like a hundred years ago, and going in the other direction we can also work out what it will look like in a hundred and fifty years. It is a method that can be quite brilliant and is, in fact, the method used by geologists today to work out the primeval conditions of the earth; it was also used to produce the hypothesis of Laplace. Exactly the same method is used to visualize what the world is going to be like according to the physical laws that can now be observed. But I think you will admit that such laws do not signify much when applied to a human being, for example. A hundred years ago the child did not exist as a physical human being; neither will it exist as a physical human being in 150 years' time.

The same applies to the earth with reference to the time-scale used by geologists. The earth came into existence later than Tyndall, Huxley, Haeckel and others reckon. Before the time comes when you can simply paint the walls of a room with protein and have enough light to read by, the earth will be nothing but a corpse. It is quite easy to work out that one day it will be possible to use physical means to put protein on a wall where it will shine like electric light, so that one can read the paper. This is bound to happen as part of the physical changes, no doubt. But, in fact, the time will never come, just as it will never happen that in a hundred and fifty years' time a child will show the changes calculated from successive changes seen in its stomach and liver in the course of two or three years between the ages of seven and nine.

Here you gain insight into some very strange things we have today. You can see how they clash. Think of a conventional scientist listening to what I have just been saying. He will say this is sheer foolishness. And then think of a spiritual scientist; he will consider the things the conventional scientist says to be foolish. All the many hypotheses concerning the beginning and the end of the earth are indeed nothing but foolishness, even though people have been utterly brilliant in establishing them.

You see from this how unconsciously human beings are in fact being guided. But we are now

in an age when such things must be perceived and understood. It is necessary to link such an idea with the other ideas we have characterized today. A time will come when we must have transformed our materialistic ideas to such an extent that we can progress to a more spiritual form of existence, but by then the earth will have become a corpse for a long time. It will no longer support us, and incarnations in the flesh such as we seek today will no longer be sought. *But the individuals who have become so tied up with the materialistic way of thinking that they cannot let go of it will still sneak down to that earth and find ways of involving themselves in the activities of bacilli—the tubercle bacillus and others—bacillary entities that will be rummaging through every part of the earth's corpse. Today's bacilli are merely the prophets, let us say, of what will happen to the whole earth in future. Then a time will come when those who cling to the materialistic way of thinking will unite with the moon powers and surround the earth, which will be a burnt-out corpse, together with the moon. For all they want is to hold on to the life of the earth and remain united with it; they do not want to take the right course, which is to progress from the earth's corpse to what will be the future soul and spirit of the earth.*[10]

During this Age of Eclipse the world has witnessed quite publicly the transhumanist motivations of individuals attempting to bring about the so-called Fourth Industrial Revolution, primarily through the vehicle of the World Economic Forum. On the other hand, the experimentation with live attenuated viruses in bioweapons research, as well as in mRNA technologies to combat them, has also risen to the surface of collective consciousness. Rudolf Steiner's indications shine a new light on this unholy union of the military, pharmaceutical industry, technology, economics, and politics: it would seem that the transhumanist

10 These quotations are from Rudolf Steiner, *The Fall of the Spirits of Darkness* (CW 177), lect. 9, pp. 139–143. Note that in other contexts Steiner indicated that reunion of the Moon with the Earth will occur around AD 5734 (the start of the Anglo-American Age), and that this event would coincide with the loss of the ability for sexual procreation in human beings.

(i.e., ahrimanic) urge to overcome death by uniting completely with the machine world will find its fulfillment in the form of microscopic organisms that help to break down the "earth's corpse."

It should be noted that precisely at the time of the fall of the spirits of darkness—the autumn of 1879—the possibility of live attenuated vaccination was discovered due to Louis Pasteur's assistant forgetting to administer cholera samples to the chickens upon which they were experimenting. The development of live attenuated vaccinations—which invariably deattenuate, eventually coming back stronger and more virulent than before, demanding a new vaccination to confront them—opened up the path to the techno-pathogenic development Steiner alludes to above.

At the same time that Steiner was delivering the lectures on the Fall of the Spirits of Darkness, he began publishing a series of articles on *The Chymical Wedding of Christian Rosenkreuz*. This again points to Lazarus-John, the Apocalyptist, as a guide through this time (we will return to *The Chymical Wedding* later on).

When we look at what was happening 100 years prior to the October 14, 2023, eclipse, Rudolf Steiner was delivering the fifth and final lecture of his series *The Four Seasons and the Archangels*. Once again, the Michael imagination is highlighted here, but brought into relationship with the other three Archangels—Gabriel, Raphael, and Uriel—as well as natural processes throughout the seasons. In a way, it was a precursor to the Agricultural Course he would give in Koberwitz eight months later. Perhaps we can bring Gabriel into relationship with Mary-Sophia; Raphael into relationship with Christ; and Uriel with the impulses of the so-called Great Teachers of Humanity—in particular Christian Rosenkreuz and the Master Jesus in terms of our present study.

More than a hundred years ago, Rudolf Steiner began speaking about the reappearance of Christ in our time. Just as Christ incarnated into a physical body almost 2,000 years ago, on September 23 AD 29, Rudolf Steiner indicated that around

the 1930's, it would become clear to some people that Christ had incarnated into an elemental body, a body of life forces ("etheric" in theosophical/anthroposophical parlance).

While a physical body experiences itself as limited to taking up a certain amount of space for a limited time, an elemental body experiences fluidity; it is a body *of* Time rather than *in* time. The early Christians referred to this second coming of Christ as the *Parousia*—or "advent," "appearance," "arrival (especially of royalty)," "presence"—indicating that Christ, during this second coming, could be present for all peoples everywhere, simultaneously.

Rudolf Steiner saw this Parousia beginning around the 1930s, and this indeed came to pass, although not perhaps in the way that the Anthroposophical Society suspected or noticed. In 1931, Christ appeared to Sister Maria Faustina of the Blessed Sacrament, a simple 26-year-old nun of little education, at a convent in Płock, Poland. From Wikipedia:

> On the night of Sunday, February 22, 1931, while she was in her cell in Płock, Jesus appeared wearing a white garment with red and pale rays emanating from his heart. In her diary, she wrote that Jesus told her to "paint an image according to the pattern you see, with the signature: 'Jesus, I trust in You.' I desire that this image be venerated, first in your chapel, and then throughout the world. I promise that the soul that will venerate this image will not perish." Three years later, after her assignment to Vilnius (then in Poland, now in Lithuania), the first artistic rendering of the image was performed under her direction. In the same February 22, 1931, message about the Divine Mercy image, Kowalska also wrote in her diary that Jesus told her that he wanted the Divine Mercy image to be "solemnly blessed on the first Sunday after Easter; that Sunday is to be the Feast of Mercy."
>
> In late May 1933, Sister Faustina was transferred to Vilnius to work as the gardener, completing tasks including growing vegetables. Shortly after arriving in Vilnius, Faustina met Father Michael Sopoćko, the newly appointed confessor to the nuns. When Faustina went to

Sopoćko for her first confession, she told him that she had been conversing with Jesus, who had a plan for her. After some time, in 1933 Sopoćko insisted on a complete psychiatric evaluation of Faustina by Helena Maciejewska, a psychiatrist and a physician associated with the convent. Faustina passed the required tests and was declared of sound mind.

Thereafter, Sopoćko began to have confidence in Faustina and supported her efforts. Sopoćko also advised Faustina to begin writing a diary and to record the conversations and messages from Jesus that she was reporting. Faustina told Sopoćko about the Divine Mercy image, and in January 1934, Sopoćko introduced her to the artist Eugene Kazimierowski who was also a professor at the university. By June 1934, Kazimierowski had finished painting the image based on the direction of Faustina and Sopoćko. That was the only Divine Mercy painting Faustina saw. A superimposition of the face of Jesus in the Image of the Divine Mercy upon that in the already well-known Shroud of Turin shows great similarity.

Faustina wrote in her diary that, on Good Friday, April 19, 1935, Jesus told her that he wanted the Divine Mercy image publicly honoured. A week later, on April 26, 1935, Sopoćko delivered the first sermon ever on the Divine Mercy, and Faustina attended the sermon. The first Mass during which the Divine Mercy image was displayed occurred on April 28, 1935, the first Sunday after Easter, and was attended by Faustina. This day was also the celebration of the end of the Jubilee of the Redemption by Pope Pius XI. Sopoćko obtained Archbishop Jałbrzykowski's permission to place the Divine Mercy image within the Gate of Dawn church in Vilnius during the Mass that Sunday and celebrated the Mass himself. On September 13, 1935, while still in Vilnius, Faustina wrote of a vision about the Chaplet of Divine Mercy in her diary. The chaplet is about a third of the length of the Rosary. Faustina wrote that the purpose for chaplet's prayers for mercy are threefold: to obtain mercy, to trust in Christ's mercy, and to show mercy to others.

Later, in 1936, Faustina became ill, since speculated to be tuberculosis. She was moved to the sanatorium in Prądnik, Kraków. She

continued to spend much time in prayer, reciting the chaplet and praying for the conversion of sinners. The last two years of her life were spent praying and keeping her diary. On March 23, 1937, Faustina wrote in her diary that she had a vision that the feast of the Divine Mercy would be celebrated in her local chapel and would be attended by large crowds and also that the same celebration would be held in Rome attended by the Pope. In July 1937, the first holy cards with the Divine Mercy image were printed. In August, Sopoćko asked Kowalska to write the instructions for the Novena of Divine Mercy, which she had reported as a message from Jesus on Good Friday 1937.

As her health deteriorated at the end of 1937, Faustina's reported visions intensified, and she was said to be looking forward to an end to her life. In April 1938, her illness had progressed, and she was sent to rest in the sanatorium in Prądnik for what was to be her final stay there. In September 1938, Sopoćko visited her at the sanatorium and found her very ill but in ecstasy as she was praying. Later in the month, she was taken back home to Kraków to await her death there. Sopoćko visited her at the convent for the last time on September 26, 1938. Faustina died at the age of 33 on October 5, 1938, in Kraków. She was buried on October 7 and now rests at Kraków's Basilica of Divine Mercy.[11]

During exactly the same time period that Faustina was bringing about devotion to the second coming of Christ, the Anthroposophical Society, which was intended to be the vehicle for experiencing Christ "in the Etheric," was tearing at the seams. In April 1935, two key members of the first executive council of the Society (Ita Wegman and Elizabeth Vreede) were expelled, and along with them thousands of members of the Dutch and English Free Anthroposophical Groups. While interpersonal conflicts, jealousy, and drama were absorbing the attention of anthroposophists, the Parousia was taking place and going unnoticed! Unfortunately, the ten virgins had not kept their lanterns lit.

On the other hand, devotion to the elemental Christ exists now as a long-standing tradition in the Catholic Church. Notice that this devotion is in the form of an image. The elemental Christ exists in the sphere of living imaginations, of archetypes. It is only fitting that He be portrayed as a living image, an icon that can speak to the heart of virtually anyone, regardless of language or soul capacities.

The core of this path to experiencing Christ in his second coming is that of praying the Novena of the Divine Mercy, referenced above, keeping in mind the words of the anonymous author of Meditations on the Tarot, in his 19th Letter-Meditation on The Sun (p. 551, brackets my editorial):

> Now, the mystery of the number nine, that of the development of the Trinity [Father, Son, and Holy Spirit] into the luminous Trinity [Father and Mother, Son and Daughter, Holy Spirit and Holy Soul], also lives in the practice of prayer and ritual within the Church.
>
> I have in mind the practice, universally diffused in the Catholic Church, of the novena—the most practiced form of which is the act of prayer consisting of one Pater Noster and three Ave Marias, to which one devotes oneself for nine days. One makes a novena by appealing to the paternal love of the Father (Pater Noster) and to the maternal love of the Mother (the three Ave Marias) simultaneously for nine days, for the sake of a person or cause. What depth there is underlying this practice that is so simple! In truth—in any case for the Hermeticist—the direction of the superhuman wisdom of the Holy Spirit is manifested here!
>
> So with the novena, we are entering into one of the highest and most effective forms of sacred magic. The Novena to the Divine Mercy is practiced every day from Good Friday (this year on March 29) until the eve of the Divine Mercy (Saturday, April 6), ideally at 3 p.m., the hour of Christ's death (local time; what is important here is the position of the Sun in the sky relative to the one praying, and not so much that "everyone pray at the same time").[12]

---

11 There is of course, much more to this amazing story, involving the spread of popularity of devotion to the Divine Mercy, as well as its rocky road to official approval from the Papacy—a road that was trod primarily by Pope John Paul II, who himself died on the eve of Divine Mercy Sunday (April 2, 2005). See https://en.wikipedia.org/wiki/Faustina_Kowalska.

---

12 Here is a link to a relatively simple version of the Novena to the Divine Mercy: https://www.shrineofdivinemercy.org/novena-prayer/46; and in greater depth: https://www.thedivinemercy.org/message/devotions/novena. For more information on novenas in general, see here: https://www.shrineofdivinemercy.org/what-are-novenas.

Of even greater importance for Sister Faustina was the praying of the Chaplet of the Divine Mercy, which is a specific version of the Rosary prayer. In the same section of the Letter-Meditation on the Sun (pp. 551–552, brackets my editorial), the anonymous author states:

> Similarly, it is so with the rosary prayer, where appeal to the two aspects of divine paternal love in the prayer addressed to the Father and the Mother is made during meditation on the mysteries of the Joy, Suffering…Glory [and Light] of the Blessed Virgin. The rosary prayer is—in any case for the hermeticist—again a masterpiece of simplicity, containing and revealing things of inexhaustible profundity…a masterpiece of the Holy Spirit![13]

We must not fall into the same trap as the Anthroposophical Society in 1935. Something is happening, right under our noses, and we are distracted from it by pettiness, drama, jealousy, and indolence. We react to it out of hysteria and panic, because we do not yet know how else to react. For truly these are apocalyptic times—and apocalypse means nothing other than "uncover, reveal, disclose." Apocalypse does not mean "the end of the world" in the sense of, for example, the mutually assured destruction of the Cold War; rather, it means "the end of an old world, and the beginning of a new one." Unfortunately, we react as though it meant only "the end of the world altogether"!

This new world calls for our active spiritual participation. And, as indicated before, traditional prayer is the most potent and accessible means to this participation. As the anonymous author points out in the 21st Letter-Meditation on the Fool (pp. 618–19):

> Prayer—which asks, thanks, worships and blesses—is the radiation, the breath and the warmth of the awakened heart: expressed in formulae of the articulated word, in the wordless inner sighing of the soul, and, lastly, in the silence, both outward and inward, of the breathing of the soul immersed in the element of divine respiration and breathing in unison with it…. Thus, it is never in vain and without effect. Even a prayer-formula pronounced rapidly in a detached and impersonal manner has a magical effect, because the sum-total of ardor put into this formula in the past—by believers, saints and Angels—is evoked solely through the fact of pronouncing the prayer-formula. Every prayer-formula consecrated by use has a magical virtue, since is it collective. The voices of all those who have ever prayed it are evoked by it and join the voice of he who pronounces it with serious intention. This applies above all to all the formulae of liturgical prayer. Each phrase of the Roman Catholic Mass or Greek Orthodox Liturgy, for example, is a formula of divine sacred magic. There is nothing astonishing about this, since the Mass and the Liturgy consist only of the prayers of prophets, saints and Jesus Christ himself. But what is truly astonishing is that there are—and always have been—esotericists…who improvise cults, prayer-formulae, new "mantras," etc., as if something is gained through novelty! Perhaps they believe that the formulae taken from Holy Scripture or given by the saints are used up through usage and have lost their virtue? This would be a radical misunderstanding. Because usage does not at all deplete a prayer-formula, but rather, on the contrary, it adds to its virtue….
>
> One should know, dear Unknown Friend, that one never prays alone, i.e. that there are always others—above, or in the past on earth—who pray with you in the same sense, in the same spirit and even in the same words. In praying, you always represent a visible or invisible community together with you…. For this reason the Lord's prayer is not addressed to "my Father in heaven," but rather to "our Father in heaven," and asks the Father to "give us this day our daily bread," that he "forgive us our trespasses," that he "delivers us from evil." Thus, whatever the particular intention of the one who prays the Lord's prayer may be, it is in the name of the whole of mankind that he prays.

And so through these powerful and uncompromising words of the anonymous author, we can see that the most potent and accessible spiritual activity in which we can engage is to pray

---

13 Here is a link to detailed instructions for praying the Chaplet, which is possible to do even if one does not have Rosary beads: https://www .thedivinemercy.org/message/devotions/pray -the-chaplet.

traditional prayers in unison with devotees of the past and present, on Earth and in Heaven. We need not even set aside a special time or special place in which to say these prayers as "even a prayer-formula pronounced rapidly in a detached and impersonal manner has a magical effect," as attested to above.

Now, looking to the central event of 2024, the total solar eclipse of April 8—our gateway *out* of the Age of Eclipse and *into* Apocalypse—what strikes us immediately is that it takes place the day after this year's Divine Mercy Sunday, the Catholic Feast Day of Christ in his Second Coming. Divine Mercy Sunday occurred close to this year's date on April 8, 1934. This was at the heart of the time period that Sister Faustina was receiving the messages from the Etheric Christ concerning the honoring of the Divine Mercy. In fact, it was that year that the first image of Christ of the Divine Mercy was created, by Eugeniusz Kazimirowski (1873–1939).

At the same time that this image was being created, Valentin Tomberg was publishing his work on the significance of Abraham, Isaac, and Jacob as the founders of Israel (see *Christ and Sophia*). If we look back a hundred years from April 8, 2024, we come to April 1924, when Rudolf Steiner was delivering his karma lectures.[14] His focus at this point in time was on the incarnation of the stream in opposition to the School of Michael—the Academy of Gondishapur. He points to the incarnation of the individuality Hārūn al-Rashīd, around the time of Parzival (8th–9th centuries), as the leader of the anti-Grail stream of Arabism. This individual then reincarnated in the 16th to 17th centuries as Francis Bacon, the father of modern empirical scientific materialism.

Now, it is interesting to look at these two time periods in relation to the three patriarchs of Israel mentioned above. According to the research of Robert Powell, these three individualities were active once again at the time of Parzival: the Abraham individuality in connection with Charibert de Laon, grandfather of Charlemagne and the

initiator of the mysteries of the Holy Grail at the turn of the 7th to 8th centuries; Isaac in connection with Anfortas, the wounded Grail King; and Jacob in connection with Kyot, paladin of Charlemagne, founder of the monastery Saint-Guilhem-le-Désert, and Eschenbach's spiritual source for his telling of *Parzival*. These were the roles they played as part of the Grail stream as the counterforce to the Arabism of Gondishapur.

These individualities were active again close to the time of Francis Bacon. Kyot returned as Johannes Kepler, the great astronomer who was active primarily in the 17th century; Anfortas preceded him as Paracelsus, the father of modern holistic medicine in the 16th century; and the Abraham being was active through Christian Rosenkreuz himself in the 15th century, who delved into the mysteries of nature as a path to Christ. This brings us back to the *Chymical Wedding of Christian Rosenkreuz*, the initiation of the Lazarus individuality, which takes place around Easter in the year 1459. This would have been around April 3rd (Gregorian date—at the time, under the Julian calendar, it would have been March 25). The Sun on that day was at 25° Pisces, while on April 8, 2024 it will be 24° Pisces. And so here again, we have a strong resonance of the eclipses with Christian Rosenkreuz. (As well as Zarathustra, as once again we have a memory of the birth of the Solomon Jesus—the Great Conjunction that announced his birth took place at this same degree in Pisces).

Perhaps we can consider these three individuals and their respective realms of focus—Kepler in the stars above, Paracelsus amongst humanity, and Rosenkreuz in the earth below—as the "patriarchs" of our modern stream of "Eternal Israel," the stream of the Holy Grail.

Robert Powell indicates that Francis Bacon reincarnated as Bertrand Russell. It may be that these three patriarchs returned during the twentieth century as well, to continue their work in contrast to the analytical philosophy of individuals like Russell. Indeed, Robert Powell considers Willi Sucher to have been the reincarnation of the Isaac individuality, while Abraham worked through Valentin Tomberg.

---

14 See Steiner, *Karmic Relationships,* vol. 2 (CW 236) and *Karmic Relationships,* vol. 6 (CW 240).

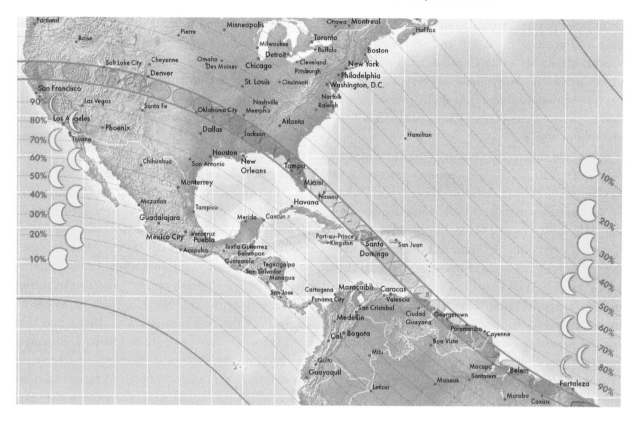

V. THE FUTURE: TOTAL SOLAR ECLIPSE OF AUGUST 12, 2045

Now, we can consider the Age of Eclipse as a seven-year period in isolation, but we can also connect it into a larger period of development. There will be a third total solar eclipse that passes all the way across the contiguous United States, and then down into South America, on August 12, 2045, almost exactly 28 years after the solar eclipse of 2017.

We could hope that the crisis we have experienced during these seven years is much like the first seven years of childhood, whereas 2045 could represent achieving egohood around the age of 28. Note that the midpoint between these two is in 2031, during which time humanity has a great potential to experience the Parousia, Christ's presence in the etheric, as this will be 100 years after his appearance in the 1930s, and 100 years before his resurrection from the sub-earthly spheres in 2135.

The year 2045 is close to the year 2040, Christ's deepest descent into the sub-earthly spheres, at which point he starts his process of re-ascending and returning to humanity (leading up to 2135). It is also close to the year 2047, the end of humanity's collective repetition of Christ's 40 days in the wilderness—a time that began in AD 869, and has reached a fever pitch ever since 1929.

In terms of star memories, August 12, 2045 is almost exactly 100 years after the bombings of Hiroshima and Nagasaki at the end of World War II. This is a dire warning—akin to those related to the fall of the spirits of darkness in reference to prior eclipses—of the disastrous results of technocracy.

On the other hand, August 13, 1905, was the 40th birthday of Ida Peerdeman (1905–1996), a Dutch Catholic who began to experience visions of Mary in the form of The Lady of All Nations—beginning in 1945! These visions lasted from 1945 to 1959; over the course of them, The Lady of All Nations asked for an image to be made of her; for the rosary to be prayed daily for the salvation of the world; and for a particular prayer to be directed to her (given on February 11, 1951, just over 33 years after the apparitions of Our Lady of Fátima):

Lord Jesus Christ, Son of the Father,
Send now Your Spirit over the earth,
Let the Holy Spirit live in
the hearts of all nations,
That they may be preserved
From degeneration, disasters and war.
May the Lady of All Nations,
who once was Mary,
Be our Advocate, Amen.

She also emphasized that there must come about the proclamation of the fifth Marian Dogma. The four Marian dogmas that have been proclaimed thus far by the Catholic Church are: 1) Mary as the Mother of God, proclaimed at the Council of Ephesus in AD 431; 2) her Perpetual Virginity, recognized since at least the 3rd century; 3) her Immaculate Conception, proclaimed by Pope Pius IX on December 8, 1854; 4) her assumption into Heaven, proclaimed by Pope Pius XII on

November 1, 1950.[15] It is noteworthy that these last two are the only *ex cathedra* (i.e., infallible) proclamations made by the Pope since the dogma of papal infallibility was established by Pope Pius IX. Statements *ex cathedra* are thus far reserved for the Virgin Mary!

The Lady of All Nations requested that Mary officially be proclaimed in a threefold way: as Co-redeemer, Mediator, and Advocate. We might imagine that this threefold recognition is in some way related to Valentin Tomberg's description of the Holy Trinosophia as a feminine triad that, as united with the masculine Holy Trinity, radiates as a "Luminous Holy Trinity" in the form of a six-pointed star. Perhaps we can consider the Daughter as Co-redeemer with the Son; the Mother as Mediator of all graces; and the Holy Soul as the eternal Advocate for humanity.

Now, it is very interesting to note that it was the summer of 1945 that Valentin Tomberg became a Catholic. During this time period he was hard at work on his second volume on jurisprudence, which has recently been published in English for the first time by Angelico Press as *Jus Humanitatis: The Right of Humankind as Foundation for International Law*. This work was, in a way, Tomberg's diagnosis and prescription for working toward world peace in the aftermath of the two World Wars.

As the years went on, the Catholic Valentin Tomberg became interested in the visions of Ida Peerdeman. She lived in Amsterdam, where he and his family had lived from 1938 to 1944; her two public visions took place in the St. Thomas Aquinas Church, where Tomberg's son, Alex, had been baptized. He eventually traveled back to Amsterdam himself to investigate the validity of these messages, and found them to be authentic.

There is a deeper significance to all of this, which we can bring into relationship with the cosmic rhythm associated with the birth of Kalki Avatar. Valentin Tomberg brings into relationship the path of the Avatars and the path of the Buddhas. From his perspective, the Avatars are beings

---

15 See https://www.catholicnewsagency.com/resource /55423/the-four-marian-dogmas.

of revelation and grace from above. They are the semi-archangelic beings who inspire the bodhisattvas on their paths to enlightenment, whereas the bodhisattvas themselves represent the stream of human effort and experience. The eventual attainment of Buddhahood, in the final incarnation of a bodhisattva, represents the final and complete union between the inspiring Avatar being above (on a path of descent) and the striving human bodhisattva below (on a path of ascent). He specifically refers to the eventual union of Maitreya Buddha and Kalki Avatar as one being on the historical plane. For those of us who consider Valentin Tomberg to be an incarnation of the Maitreya Bodhisattva, it makes sense to take his characterization seriously—"from the horse's mouth," so to speak!

Rudolf Steiner indicated that for a bodhisattva, between the ages of 30 to 33 a great change comes over the individual. The "normal" ego of the individual leaves completely and a transcendent ego is able to descend (what Tomberg would characterize as the Avatar). Steiner indicates that in the final incarnation of Maitreya Buddha, rather than the personal ego needing to leave to make room for the transcendent one, when this inspiring ego descends it finally unites completely with the personal ego of the Maitreya, the culmination of a 5,000 year process (he indicates this Buddhahood will be achieved approximately 2,400 years from now). This is essentially the same picture as that given by Valentin Tomberg.

Now, my own perspective, using Tomberg's language and based out of his perspective, is something a bit more nuanced and fluid. In what follows I will refer to the transcendent, archangelic aspect of the Buddha-in-becoming as Kalki Avatar, and the reincarnating human individuality as Maitreya Bodhisattva. Please, do not let there be any confusion that when I refer to Maitreya I mean anything transcendent. I am writing in Tomberg's own terms, according to which Maitreya is a "mere man" going through many, many lifetimes of struggle in order to—through a Faustian effort, so to speak—attain to Buddhahood.

In any given lifetime, around the ages of 30 to 33, the Kalki Avatar makes a partial descent toward Maitreya. He can only come into as close a contact as this vessel is prepared to allow, through destiny and through his own efforts. And this "touching in" of Kalki Avatar into the life of Maitreya may or may not last for the remainder of the incarnation, in spite of what Rudolf Steiner indicates. It is by no means a linear path to Buddhahood. All that can be sure is that in the final incarnation, the Avatar is able to approach *completely*, and to merge *completely* with the struggling ego of Maitreya. In the meantime, and as a preparation, we must think of this struggling Maitreya as a kind of gestating child in a womb. He is surrounded and formed by a karmic community that radiates its impulses into him in his various incarnations. This karmic community is inspired and guided by Kalki Avatar (let us remember that archangelic beings find their expression on the material plane in communities, nations, languages, peoples). And so it also depends—up until the final incarnation—to what extent the karmic community surrounding the focal point of Maitreya is prepared, by destiny and by their own efforts, to receive the guiding impulses of Kalki Avatar.

We can carry this image of Kalki working through a karmic circle, radiating his forces and guidance into Maitreya in the center, as akin to the incarnation of Christian Rosenkruez in the 13th century, when as a child he was surrounded by the "circle of twelve" who radiated into his being their particular experiences, wisdom, and capacities acquired over the ages. We can then imagine the final incarnation of Maitreya Buddha as akin to the reincarnation of Christian Rosenkreutz who was active in the 15th century as the founder of the Rosicrucian Brotherhood—all of the capacities that had been radiated into him in his prior life could now operate through him completely naturally, as a gift of grace.

This "touching in" or "birth" of the Kalki Avatar is related to certain cosmic phenomena. According to an ancient Hindu prophecy, Kalki Avatar will appear among men as the restorer of true religion at the close of Kali Yuga (which ended in 1899), when the Sun, Jupiter and the Moon stand together in Cancer (specifically in the Lunar

Mansion Pushya, 4°–17° Cancer). We can imagine that each time this configuration occurs, an opportunity is given for the overlighting Kalki Avatar to influence the life of the Maitreya individuality and his or her community. When we bring this cosmic indication into connection with the earthly lives of Maitreya Bodhisattva, this individuality's relationship to the Catholic Church, and developments within the Catholic Church herself, we are guided to a particular imagination around the year 2045.

According to the karmic research of Robert Powell, Valentin Tomberg incarnated in the 19th century as Princess Marie Amelie of Baden, born October 11, 1817. She was the younger sister of Kaspar Hauser, and perhaps would have been of great support to him had he lived. The Kalki Avatar alignment took place on July 30, 1848, when she was 30 years of age: Jupiter was 10° Cancer, Sun was 14° Cancer, and the Moon travelled through them. No later than 1853 had she converted to Catholicism (it was only in 1853 that it was first publicly reported). In 1854, Pope Pius IX pronounced the 3rd Marian Dogma, that of the Immaculate Conception (as noted above). Pope Pius IX was also known for organizing the First Vatican Council in the 1860s—it was held from 1868 to 1870 after four years of planning. The hallmark of this Council was to reinforce the tradition of the Catholic Church in the face of rising materialism and liberalism. It resulted in the official dogma of papal infallibility (applied retroactively to the Marian Dogma pronounced by Pius IX sixteen years prior).

When we look 95 years later, we come once again to this Kalki Avatar configuration: on August 1, 1943, Jupiter was 12° Cancer, Sun was 14° Cancer and the Moon travelled through them. Valentin Tomberg was 43 years of age. Shortly after this time period (the summer of 1945, as noted above) he converted to Catholicism— approximately 95 years after Princess Marie Amelie of Baden. Exactly 95 years after the proclamation of the 3rd Marian Dogma, Pope Pius XII proclaimed the 4th Marian Dogma—that of the Assumption. And exactly 95 years after the First Vatican Council was the Second Vatican

Council (popularly referred to as "Vatican I and Vatican II"). It was prepared 1959 to 1962, and took place from 1962 to 1965; in sharp contrast to Vatican I, which was highly traditional and conservative, Vatican II saw the Church attempting to expand their horizons, keep up with the times, and become more inclusive—what many (including Valentin Tomberg) perceived as a radically progressive Council as opposed to the traditionalism of the first.

Now, when we look to our own time, we see that another Kalki Avatar configuration will occur, again with the rhythm of 95 years. On August 1, 2038, Jupiter will be 15°, Sun will be 13° Cancer, and the Moon will travel through them. (Note that here we have four significant seven year cycles: 2017–2024; 2024–2031; 2031–2038; and 2038–2045). Perhaps, if he is once again incarnated, the Maitreya individuality will find him or herself drawn back to the Catholic Church in the years following this alignment? Time will tell. More importantly, however, we can see that exactly 95 years after the proclamation of the 4th Marian Dogma by Pope Pius XII is the year 2045! It is "written in the stars" and in a sense incumbent on us, that we inwardly and outwardly work toward the official proclamation of the 5th Marian Dogma in the year 2045. This would in a certain sense enshrine the threefold Mary (the Most Holy Trinosophia—an esoteric reality) as official doctrine of the exoteric church.

Beyond this, perhaps we can imagine and pray into being a Third Vatican Council, sometime around 2054 to 2060; perhaps this Vatican III could find the middle path that is truer and deeper than the hardness of traditionalism to the right and the dissolution of progressivism to the left. Can the Church (and thereby the world) be renewed—regenerated—through Mary in the 21st century?[16]

In last year's editorial foreword to *The Turning Point*, I highlighted the fact that we are

---

16 It is well outside the scope of this article, but perhaps worth pointing out that 95 years after 2038, there will be another Kalki Avatar alignment, on August 1, 2133, very close to the time of Christ's re-emergence from the sub-earthly spheres.

currently in the midst of a "4th Turning," a collective crisis point that lasts from approximately 2010 to 2030. By the year 2045, we will be well into the culmination of a "1st Turning," a time period of renewal and reconstruction (the 2030s and 2040s). Let us pray and work to contribute in anyway that we are able, to realize the mandate of The Lady of All Nations, and to bring to reality Tomberg's vision of world peace and international order as described in his *Jus Humanitatis*. Indeed, between the years 1917 to 1924, Rudolf Steiner laid out his vision for social renewal in the form of his Threefold Social Organism. It was around the year 1945 (specifically between the years 1944 to 1952) that Valentin Tomberg focused almost entirely on the regeneration of jurisprudence as informed by his newfound devotion to Catholicism. Social renewal born out of spiritual perception and inspiration is a key hallmark of this time from Eclipse to Apocalypse.

In summary, then, the key points of focus that emerge from the star memories of all of these cosmic events revolve around:

The Virgin Mary (Our Lady of Knock; Our Lady of Fátima; The Lady of All Nations; The New Isis and the Search for the Divine Sophia; Our Lady of Guadalupe)

Archangel Michael (The Fall of the Spirits of Darkness; The Four Seasons and the Archangels; the Prayer of Pope Leo XIII)

Christ in His Second Coming (The Divine Mercy)

Christian Rosenkreuz (The Raising of Lazarus; Our Lady of Knock; the Chymical Wedding of Christian Rosenkreuz; the Three Patriarchs)

Zarathustra (The Star of the Magi and the Visitation of the Magi)

Social Renewal in opposition to Bolshevism (Rudolf Steiner's threefold social organism; Valentin Tomberg's Regeneration of Jurisprudence)

Catholicism and the Kalki Avatar

VI. A Final Perspective

In Valentin Tomberg's *Christ and Sophia*, he indicates that Christ's second coming unfolds in reverse order to Christ's first coming. Two thousand years ago, Christ united with Jesus in the River Jordan; then came his ministry; then the Mystery of Golgotha; then the Ascension and Whitsun; and finally, the preaching of the Gospel. In our time, claims Tomberg, it will occur the other way around: first will be the preaching of Christ in the etheric; then comes the Pentecostal event; then Ascension, and so on.

If the time period of the Second Coming lasts for 2,500 years, as indicated by Rudolf Steiner, we could imagine that this moving backward through time is related to the rhythm of Mars. Mars takes 1.881 years to circle the Sun; if each day in the life of Christ plays itself out in one Mars year, this would be the equivalent of 2,500/1.881 = 1,329.08 days. This is exactly the amount of time from the Baptism in the Jordan (September 23 AD 29) to Ascension (May 14 AD 33). The Whitsun event of the Second Coming, then, would have occurred 18 or 19 years (10 x 1.881 = 18.81) prior to the start of this 2,500-year period.

It is difficult to say precisely when the starting point of this 2,500-year period is. We could certainly think of the work of both Rudolf Steiner and Peter Deunov as "preaching the Gospel" of the Second Coming. For Peter Deunov, March 22, 1914 was the return of Christ to Earth; whereas we might see from the work of Robert Powell that Ascension Day (May 25) 1933 marked the start of the Second Coming.[17] Note that these two dates are 19 years apart—perhaps the first was the Whitsun event, and the second was the Ascension, the "true start" of 2,500 years?

On the other hand, the external presentation of these events seems to have a bit of a lag. For

17 On the date March 22, 1914, see https: //sophiafoundation.org/wp-content/uploads /2020/06/Prophecy-of-Peter-Deunov-Beinsa-Douno .pdf. Also, see Robert Powell, *The Christ Mystery*, for more on the date May 14, 1933, as well as earlier references to the passage of Christ's ego through the sub-earthly spheres and the recapitulation of the Forty Days of Temptation.

example, we might look to the event of the burning of the first Goetheanum (and the subsequent Foundation Stone Meditation the following year) on December 31, 1922, as an outer expression of this Whitsun event—around nine years after March 22, 1914. And we could look to the teaching of the Our Mother Prayer by Valentin Tomberg during the Lord's Prayer Course in March, 1942, as the outer expression of the Ascension event—again, around nine years after May 25, 1933. This would place the end of the 2,500-year period sometime between 4433 and 4442—perhaps around the time period of the final incarnation of Maitreya. This would place the modern equivalent of the Mystery of Golgotha somewhere in the years between 2006 and 2019; if we take March 22, 1914, as the moment of Whitsun, then the time period from the Resurrection until the Last Supper is from May 2006 until early 2011. If instead we use the burning of the Goetheanum as the Whitsun event, then this time period from Resurrection to Last Supper is from March 2015 through the end of 2019. This aligns fairly well with the time period of the incarnation of Ahriman, and the start of our current 4th Turning.

But perhaps this recurrence of the life of Christ in reverse order occurs on different scales and at different time periods in the midst of this 2,500-year period. This certainly seems to be the case in the years surrounding our current Age of Eclipse. On Easter Sunday, April 20, 2014, Jupiter at 18° Gemini opposed Pluto at 18° Sagittarius, whereas on the original Easter Saturday, they opposed at 17° Gemini and Sagittarius respectively. Then there is the strong resonance with the Raising of Lazarus on August 21, 2017—a New Moon at 3° Leo. There were 252 days between Holy Saturday and the Raising of Lazarus, whereas there are 1,219 days from April 20, 2014, to August 21, 2017. This would indicate each day of the life of Christ became 4.84 (1,219/252) days in our time. The April 8, 2024, eclipse is 2,422 days after August 21, 2017—this points to a date 500 (2,422/4.84) days prior to the Raising of Lazarus on July 26 AD 32: March 14 AD 31. Remarkably,

this is only one day shy of March 15 AD 31: the Feeding of the Four Thousand, when the Sun was at 25° Pisces—the same degree as the eclipse on April 8, 2024!

According to this timing, Whitsun would align with August 2013; Ascension with October 2013; and the Mystery of Golgotha with April 2014. The time period equivalent to Christ's journeys into Egypt would then align with the years 2015 to 2017. The Raising of Lazarus in our time was signified by the August 21, 2017 eclipse. Shortly after that, we began to journey through the "eclipsed portion" of Anne Catherine Emmerich's visions (May AD 32 and July AD 31). This is the time period from 2018 to 2022. At the heart of this time period is the Jupiter-Saturn conjunction, which could signify for us the sixth miracle of the Healing of the Man Born Blind. We can now look forward to a kind of Transfiguration event occurring between the October 14, 2023, and April 8, 2024, eclipses; and shortly after the 2024 eclipse, the equivalent of the fourth and third healing miracles.

Moving ahead, the equivalent of the Baptism in the Jordan would occur around May 2031—around the midpoint of the 2017 and 2045 eclipses, and seven years after the eclipse of 2024. This gives us a time period from August 2013 through May 2031 as a kind of recapitulation in reverse of the ministry of Christ—a time that aligns very well with the crisis period of the 4th Turning! The start of this period also aligns with the time of the Mystery of Golgotha in the larger time period of 2,500 years, between 2006 and 2019. This would indicate that this miniature time period embedded within the larger is analogous to the Mystery of Golgotha, which itself was the miniature expression of the entirety of Christ's ministry, embedded within it. Somehow, through the tragic events of the past ten years and throughout the next seven, we are being shaped into the proper vessel to receive the Etheric Christ—we are being made whole.

LETTER TO THE EDITOR

Cale Brandley

Dear Mr. Park,

Greetings. As a reader of *Star Wisdom* journals for the past twelve years, I am deeply appreciative of you sharing your work in developing and evolving the Christian Sophianic rituals.

After reading and rereading your article in this year's journal on the Johannine communions and service, I hear that there may be a need to integrate music and dance into the service. As a composer who is interested in sacred and community-sculpting works, I'd like to humbly share a small piece with you, which I can imagine being sung outside as part of the new communion service.

The text is the Venusian words from the cross, from John's Gospel and, therefore, may fit the mood of the service. "Behold thy mother, Behold thy son." The melody is very earth-directed, after beginning in a higher range. It should be sung as a two-part round, repeated many times (perhaps with vowels replacing the text on some repetitions), and I would love to dream a choreography to it!

I've had some success in the past singing this with beginning singers in community gatherings.

Take or leave it as you will.

And Blessings on your Work!

In gratitude,
Cale Brandley

From the editor:

Now, as fate would have it, I received this wonderful handwritten letter from Cale on my birthday in March. I did not get the chance to properly reply to him until much later—as it turned out, just before his birthday in June! Cale and his family live very close to Plowshare Farm in New Hampshire, where I and my family lived for eight years. And so, we made the plan to visit him while we were vacationing in New Hampshire and perform the Foot-washing ritual together. Nine of us gathered there in July and got to experience the service with the song he wrote.

As I introduced the background to the service to those of us who were gathered, some of whom were unfamiliar with the details, I frequently brought up Natalia Haarahiltunen, as this ritual is our co-creation. Incredibly, I got a text from Natalia—who lives in Finland—the next week, that she had just met Cale! He had traveled to Finland for a music conference, which Natalia also happened to be part of! And it was just a few days after her birthday.

I feel very blessed and a bit awestruck that I've gotten to know Cale and his family in this magical, serendipitous way! And I look forward to future collaboration.

Holy Kannon

Mulier, ecce filius tuus

John XIX. 26-27

CFB 2021

IN SERVICE FOR NATURE

Natalia Haarahiltunen

In the last two volumes of *Star Wisdom,* Joel Park has shared articles in which he gave a background for the Foot-washing service. In a nutshell, it has four parts in connection with the four kingdoms of nature—mineral, human, plant, and animal—for each of which is offered what is lacking in them. In its center it has the Our Mother prayer by Valentin Tomberg and several parts are read from the Gospel of John. Milk and honey are the essential ingredients together with frankincense and spikenard oil, and these are the ingredients that are needed to be able to hold this service. The detailed steps, one can find from the article "The Sacrifices of Jesus and Christ, Part II," in *The Turning Point: Star Wisdom,* vol 5.

When I first read about the idea of this service in the blog of Joel Park, I felt a deep resonance to it and an inner call to try it out. I wanted to make an experience of the Foot-washing ritual because it seemed so profound that I was sure it held much to be explored. To have an actual experience for yourself is giving you also such an inner certainty that cannot be given otherwise. I decided to share glimpses of these experiences I have had to give encouragement to those who have been thinking about doing the Foot-washing ritual but have not yet made it happen. I hope this can inspire all of us who are looking for ways to heal nature, places, communities (and who look for an experience of the power of milk and honey the way one can have in this service).

September 2020, the Island of Capri, Italy

It was in the summer of 2020 that I asked Joel to formulate this service into a form that could be tried out on our vacation to Capri, Italy. I chose to do it there because somehow going to a distant place and enjoying the nature there gives one a special opportunity to introduce some healing to those places as well. I found out that doing the Foot-washing service actually makes one's travels more special as you bring there something deep, and the location will answer you back. This same Capri, where many film stars like to go and to which others go for a quick daytime visit and buy the lovely Carthusian perfumes made with Capri's wonderful wildflowers…now they may have been receiving some milk and honey prep on them! There are many authentic parts of this rocky island that hardly any tourists visit, but where you can be welcomed by some sweet wild goats, real "capricorns," of these mountains. We chose our "Mother service" (that´s how I called this ritual at that time) to happen in Anacapri, on top of Monte Solaro, behind the chapel called Cetrella, behind the backs of Mary and the people! Actually, it was just a cliff but the view ahead of us was the amazing panorama: Gulf of Naples, Sorrento, Vesuvius. In Capri there exists also a cave called Grotta di Matermania, where an ancient Mother ritual has been celebrated.

Out of that first experience of the Foot-washing I would like to share a few things. First of all, I would encourage people to try out such "travel versions," as you can do it anywhere in the world where you can buy milk and honey and have a bowl to shake the prep for 20 minutes. It is such a wonderful contribution to nature in the places where you have arrived, probably by car or plane. Our solution was to prepare the milk and honey in the morning in our rented apartment's kitchen and bottle it. Later we made little holes into those bottles when we started to sprinkle them during the third part of the plant kingdom. As there were not many plants on that cliff where we sat, except one flower, and a butterfly that guided us there, it was a natural choice to walk the pathway from the mountain down and sprinkle the prep for wild plants while singing for animals, too. It is always such a sweet joyous mood at the end!

The next night after this "prototype" Foot-washing ritual (as all the parts were not yet there in their fullness) I had a very beautiful spiritual dream of a golden light shining from below in which I was hovering, my hands being in the prayer eurythmy gesture. As I woke up, I felt this golden light flowing around me, and I took it as an answer for this ritual from the Mother Earth.

First Foot-washing ritual in Finland, August 2021

This time we gathered with a group of friends at a cottage close to Helsinki, Espoo. This was a day when the Sophia Foundation had an annual meeting close to Copake, and we wanted to join our efforts and timing from a distance. It was a day when we were doing the Foot-washing ritual for the first time with a bigger group. In our Finnish group we started by doing the prep together while singing as one of our friends played the accordion, which created a nice friendly atmosphere before we actually started the ritual itself. Preparing the prep seems to draw animals closer while they are getting interested in what is happening! A small cat was there with us, too, and naturally she wanted to taste a bit of the milk and honey. The first part is about honoring the stone world and earth, and from the owner of the cottage we got a dagger from the Second World War, which was a very symbolic item to be transformed through the warmth of an oil, which is the way to heal the coldness of the mineral realm.

My most precious memory from this Foot-washing was how I felt the presence of Christ in me growing strong, like being one with him while doing the Foot-washing for others. It was such a Christian brotherly-sisterly mood we came to celebrate that day. At the end of the ritual, we also had a little drizzling soft rain, which felt like a blessing on top. It was also a good idea to sit down for a coffee and tea after the ritual to share what lived in our hearts concerning this ritual as it was our first time, and I asked to have some feedback about it. One friend shared with me that she had experienced Christ through me and my eyes, and she was deeply moved. This same friend hosted the next Foot-washing ritual in her cottage.

May 2022, Ascension Day, Finland, The Fool and Fire of Love!

If one reads Joel's ideas behind the Foot-washing ritual, we find that the ideal time for the Foot-washing would be after Pentecost or the Holy Trinity Day. When I have been asked to do Foot-washing in the spring, I have had an experience that it can embrace well the Christian calendar festivals, too. To most of the Finnish people the saying "the forest is my church" is a reality. I think we are always in a mood of Foot-washing ritual here in the north. Actually, Ascension for us is a celebration with a strong connection to nature as we feel Christ already strongly "outside" in nature. The clouds of Ascension surrounded us as well as the first warm weather. In a spirit of "The Fool," which is the Tarot card in the esoteric part in Foot-washing for this time of the year, we experienced the Fire of Love from the Sun on us brightly. From this Foot-washing day one can't forget a young Lapland dog who almost drank all the milk and honey prep, and that we had with us our young friend ready to give birth to her first child after one week. This time I asked volunteers to join for doing Foot-washing, as it had been such a beautiful experience for me to wash the feet of others. The owner of the cottage gladly participated with me, and it really gives another level of communal experience as more people do the Foot-washing for each other. The dog, who was fully energized by prep, was barking just in the middle of the animal part and stood in the center of the circle! This time we had a ritual where fresh young life forces and joy were strongly present.

Midsummer 2022, inside our living room, Helsinki, Finland

My husband had got strong Covid illness while traveling, and when he came back I also got ill. We had an intuition to do the Foot-washing to support ourselves while feeling very weak. As we could not really go outside, I gathered some of our pot flowers in the middle of our living room and left the balcony door open for elementals to join in and hear it. Later I went around our house and close by trees with milk and honey prep. Doing the Foot-washing in those circumstances gave us light in the darkness we were in.

September 2022, Herzberg Hill, Austria

On our first visit to Budapest to see our Hungarian friends, I suggested that we would do the Foot-washing while being there. Finally, it seemed right to do it on our short visit to the Austrian side, to visit the Templar castle Lockenhaus and its nearby location called the Herzberg Hill. We decided to do it on this "Heart hill," which has an interesting historical background since Gilgamesh. Rudolf Steiner visited there, and Ita Wegman went there several times. We arrived there with the family of Krisztina Cseri and one of her friends. There was rain in the weather forecast, which made me quite nervous. But I knew from earlier that when we get started, nature and heaven support us. So, it happened also this time that the Sun shone on our faces between the clouds on the Our Mother part! As there were two kids with us, I invited them to prepare the right amount of water and milk and to add honey to this mixture. It was great to see the alchemical magic that surrounded our silent work of preparing the prep. As we usually collect some stones and flowers in the middle of the Foot-washing circle the kids were happy to assist in that, too. Also, during the last part when we danced pan eurythmy, they came to join, as everybody likes the spreading of milk and honey. It is a very joyful mood always! Nature answered us by sending many dragonflies around our circle. We all felt that Foot-washing really united us as a community and its memory stayed with us for a long time.

May 2023, Budapest, Hungary

On our second visit to Budapest all of us were already familiar with this ritual. We decided to do it with a special intention to also ask mercy for a very difficult health situation of one participant.

Because of it, we stayed inside the house. Outside it was raining until we went there to sprinkle the prep! The kids of the household were already familiar with all this preparation and joined in even more than the last time. All the crystals and our favorite stones were gathered together with plants, children's toy camel and horses. When we reached the actual Foot-washing part, we were surprised as the kids started to wash our feet (as in the fall they had only watched this part and played around with nature instead). It was a touching and joyful Foot-washing! Also some of the horses feet got washed as well! In the animal part of this ritual, we were singing all possible children's animal songs that we knew in different languages. Kids also asked a few questions of why we were doing certain things, and we explained how we wanted to sing for the animals because they are not able to speak like we do, and we offer our voice for them by singing. It is very natural and beautiful to have children involved with the Foot-washing ritual, I must say. So far everything has gone with a flow of taking people and situations as they are and integrating them and so having new experiences arise out of this lovely service.

May 22, 2023, Ascension Day, Gulf of Naples, Capri, Italy

It was a beautiful Ascension Day in May when we headed for a small, rocky beach. There used to be a bathhouse of Emperor Augustus, which had long since fallen into water, leaving behind only some ruins. Already in the morning we had prepared the milk and honey mixture, which we brought down in our bottles. Behind a huge rock we were quite unseen by others on the beach. There we first cleaned up all the plastic that had gathered from the sea, and then we gathered a few rocks and flowers to be our tiny center for this ritual. It was our first time by the sea with clouds on the horizon, which were so well suited for the Ascension Day mood of Christ disappearing into the light of the sun and clouds. Now He is back with us again in these manifold etheric realms surrounding our Earth, bringing healing for the earthly kingdoms.

It was also very healing for us to have again milk and honey, as we had come down with a flu during several rainy days. The joyous mood of spreading the prep on plants along the public roadside and in people's gardens while walking away from the beach finally led us to the oldest church in Capri, where the patron saint Costanzo was celebrated during that week. People were reciting the Rosary as we briefly stepped in. We smiled a little for the Star of the Sea and San Costanzo for this little farewell at the end of the day.

June 17, 2023, Helsinki, Island of Suomenlinna, Finland

On this day there was a Sun-Moon-Earth alignment pointing toward the central Sun, the Source of the Creation, at 2° Sagittarius.

Together with my husband we wanted to go to see the sunset by the sea and the best place to have it is a former fortress island outside Helsinki. We decided to do the ritual at the same time as the Sun sets, which is at 11 p.m. in midsummer. Late evening gave a very different, more inward and tranquil mood, even though here in the north you can hardly call the nights of summer "nights," as even stars are not to be seen as sunset and sunrise interchange in a few hours' time. Throughout the "white nights," one is able to experience nature in a bit of a magical way. I think this Foot-washing became a tribute for the whole creation starting from the Central Sun via our Sun, which kisses especially this part of the world so abundantly during these special days of the year.

July 9, 2023, Sandefjord, Norway

For a while, I'd had a wish to do the Foot-washing service on the new farm of our friends Are and Lizz in southern Norway. As I introduced the Foot-washing ritual for Are Thoresen, a healer and a clairvoyant, he started to wonder if this would be a ritual that would help to Christianize the elemental beings!

I asked him to observe how the elemental world was reacting while we are doing the different parts in the Foot-washing service. It was a hot summer day, and we gathered under a big tree in a wonderful flowery garden in the grounds of the old Viking center of Norway. As I started to shake the milk and honey prep, Are made an observation that the Finnish elemental beings were flowing into the prep. He said that we always put our etheric imprint to the things we do. Then English-born Lizz Daniels continued with the prep, and from her there came the elemental beings of English origin. Are said that the Finnish and English elementals were opposite types of beings and created some disharmony to the prep. We pondered that it is socially very nice to give everyone the opportunity to stir the prep, but it seemed it could be more harmonious if people from only one nationality would stir the prep. These are things one needs to consider oneself and be intuitive to the circumstances I would say.

As we moved to the second part of the ritual and did the actual Foot-washing for each other, Are did observe that there were many elemental beings laying on the ground, and that they had put up their feet! This was a clear sign for us that they also wanted their feet to be washed! We sprinkled the prep to the grass and spontaneously decided to say the same words of Christ as for humans: "If your feet are clean, you are entirely clean. If I have washed your feet, you are to wash each other's feet."

This is also something one can consider doing more consciously from now on. I think the question about Christianizing the elementals was given an answer this way; some of them hear the call and want voluntarily to join the ritual. We humans are the doorway for Christ to continue to work on earth.

As we are always at the mercy of nature while doing this ritual it must be said that there have usually been lovely responses from nature, as I have already pointed out: soft rains like blessings, animals reacting, Sun coming out behind the clouds at beautiful moments, stormy weathers changing their ways, etc. This ritual has a free "aura," even if it is essentially Christian in its mood and touches the hearts of the churchgoers as well as those who do not join the official Christian ceremonies. I personally feel a special bond with people with whom

I have shared the Foot-washing. Others have also noticed this community-building force.

So far, I have been under a variety of circumstances while doing the Foot-washing service, and many times some adaptation to the situation has been needed. But this is what I so like in this ritual, too; it is so deep and full that it can carry all these changes naturally; like nature, it can embrace life's different circumstances without losing its essence.

I hope you feel more inspired to try out this service and connect with its healing forces. Let´s all help one way or another the Mother Earth on her way of becoming a shining star!

At the turn of time,

cosmic spirit light descended

into the Earth's stream of being.

Night's darkness

had run its course.

Day-bright light

streamed into human souls—

light that warms

poor shepherds' hearts,

light that illumines

the wise heads of kings.

Divine light,

Christ Sun,

warm through our hearts;

illumine our heads,

so that what

we would create

from our hearts

and guide from our heads,

in sure willing,

may be good.

—RUDOLF STEINER
Start Now! pp. 241–42
Trans. Christopher Bamford

THE SACRIFICES OF JESUS AND CHRIST, PART III

Joel Matthew Park

And a great sign was seen in heaven: a woman garbed with the sun, and the moon beneath her feet, and on her head a chaplet of twelve stars, and she was pregnant, and she cries out, enduring birth-pangs, and in an agony to give birth. And another sign was seen in heaven, and look: a great flame-hued dragon who had seven heads and ten horns and on his heads seven diadems. And his tail drags along one third of the stars of heaven, and he cast them onto the earth. And the dragon stood before the woman who was about to give birth so that, when she should give birth, he might devour her child. And she bore a son, a male child, who is about to shepherd all the gentiles with a rod of iron, and her child was seized away to God and to his throne. And the woman fled into the wilderness, there where she has a place prepared by God, so that they might nourish her for twelve hundred and sixty days. And war broke out in heaven: that of Michael and his angels waging a war with the dragon. And the dragon and his angels waged war, and did not prevail, nor was any place still found for them in heaven. And the great dragon was cast down, the ancient serpent, the one that is called Slanderer and Accuser, the one that leads the whole inhabited world astray—it was cast down into the earth and its angels were cast down with it. And I heard a loud voice in heaven saying, "Now has come about the salvation and the power and the Kingdom of our God, and the authority of his Anointed, because the persecutor of our brothers, the one prosecuting them before our God, day and night, has been cast down. And they conquered him by the blood of the suckling lamb and by the word of their testimony, and they did not love their own soul all the way to death. For this reason, be glad, O heavens and those tabernacling therein; alas for the earth and sea, because the Slanderer has descended into you with a great rage, knowing that he has little time." And, when the dragon saw that he had been cast down into the earth, he pursued the woman who had given birth to the male child. And the two wings of the great eagle were given to the woman so that she might fly to the wilderness, to her place, there where she is nourished—for a season, and for seasons, and for half a season—away from the serpent's face. (Rev. 12:1–14)

A great deal of history is condensed—and foreseen—in these first fourteen verses of the twelfth chapter of the Book of Revelation, if only we know how to read the images that are written there.

There are any number of ways to "accurately" date the events described in the Book of Revelation, since this is a multivalent work of sacred art akin to the Tarot of Marseilles. One could think of the Book of Revelation as a description of *Archetypal Time*, analogous to Goethe's *Archetypal Plant*. The forms, gestures, and movements of the text will be consistent across different literal lengths of linear time, but those lengths of time are specific embodiments of the overarching *timing* (emphasis on the verb aspect of this word) of Revelation.

How can we clarify these ideas?

Let's look together at a few of the different ways this text unfolds in time, with one motive being to find out where we are in that timing. In one of Rudolf Steiner's earliest lecture cycles on the Apocalypse, he describes the various levels of the Book of Revelation in relation to anthroposophical cultural epochs.[1] Specifically, he refers to the seven letters as related to the seven post-Atlantean cultural epochs; the seven seals as related to

---

1 See Steiner, *The Apocalypse of St. John: Lectures on the Book of Revelation* (CW 104).

the seven cultural epochs in the Sixth Age (after the War of All Against All and the reunion of the Earth and Moon); the seven trumpets as related to the seven cultural epochs of the Seventh Age (during which the Sun will reunite with the Earth, and our cosmos as we know it will come to an end); and the seven vials of wrath as related to the "small Pralaya" in between this fourth stage of Earth evolution and the fifth, which will be a kind of proto-Jupiter evolution. He brings this preliminary experience of Future Jupiter into relation with the descent of the New Jerusalem at the end of the Book of Revelation.

This is a vast and sprawling time scale, which specifically brings our time—that of the fifth cultural epoch—into relation with the letter to the Church in Sardis. There is much that can be and has been said about what this letter to Sardis expresses about the trials and mission of our time, but I will leave the readers to discover that on their own. Look to the lecture series above, but also to the fourth lecture from Steiner's very different cycle on the Apocalypse from 1924.[2] I also highly recommend Valentin Tomberg's meditations on this fifth letter to the Churches in the penultimate section of *Christ and Sophia*.[3]

Now, in the lecture cycle from 1924 (mentioned above), Rudolf Steiner brings in a very different form of timing the Apocalypse, and places modern humanity at a different moment in the course of its unfolding versus the letter to the Church in Sardis. In the thirteenth lecture, he brings the seven seals into relationship with the time period between the Mystery of Golgotha and the Crusades; the blowing of the trumpets began with the Crusades, and has carried on into our own time. During the War in Heaven between Michael and the Dragon—he specifically points to the years 1843 and '44 as the height of materialism—the sixth trumpet began to blow. Rudolf Steiner indicated that the seventh trumpet would blow around the time of the rise of the Sorathic impulse in the year 1998.

2 See Steiner, *The Book of Revelation: And the Work of the Priest* (CW 346).

3 See pp. 333–341.

Based on Rudolf Steiner's indications, we can calculate a more exact rhythm for the unfolding of the four series of seven (letters, seals, trumpets, vials) in the Book of Revelation. The Mystery of Golgotha marks the time of the first seal, while the turn of the year 1843 to '44 marks the time of the start of the blowing of the sixth trumpet. Therefore, the time between April 3 AD 33 and December 31, 1843, can be divided into twelve (seven seals and five trumpets): 1810.74/12 = 151.58 years. If we multiply this number by seven, we come to the length of time covered by each of the four groups of seven: 151.58×7 = 1061.06.

From this we can see that:

The age of seven letters lasted from 1029 BC to AD 33
The age of seven seals lasted from 33 to 1094 (the first Crusade began in 1095)
The age of seven trumpets began in 1094 and will last until 2155
And the age of seven vials will last from 2155 to 3216

It is perhaps worth noting that the first King of Israel, Saul, was crowned in 1026 BC. From this perspective, the unfolding of the Book of Revelation shows us the journey from Jerusalem as an earthly royal city to the New Jerusalem, the "kingdom of heaven." It is also worth noting that the end year of the Apocalypse from this perspective corresponds to the year 6977 of the Hebrew Calendar—very close to the end of a "week" of millennia (the year 7000, which corresponds to the year AD 3239). According to some traditions, the last "day" of this week of millennia will be the Messianic Age, a grand Sabbath and day of rest. This "day" would correspond to the years 2239 to 3239, the heart of the period during which the Etheric Christ appears to humanity. For some scholars, we have already reached the "eve" of the Sabbath in the 20th century, and have technically already entered this Sabbath millennium.

In terms of where we are right now in apocalyptic, historical unfolding, we are in the midst of the seventh trumpet blowing, which lasts from 1994 through 2155. In the Book of Revelation, the seventh trumpet blows at the end of chapter 11, and the first vial of wrath is not poured out until the start of chapter 16. The events of chapters 12, 13, 14, and 15 are therefore all part of our contemporary apocalyptic story from this point of view.

Now, there is a third point of view that is born more from my own research, based on some indications from Robert Powell and Rudolf Steiner. They have both indicated that the War in Heaven described in chapter 12 took place between 1841 and '79. Powell points out that the appearance of the woman clothed with the sun at the start of this chapter took place around the turn of the 18th and 19th centuries, indicating Sophia's union with our portion of the Milky Way galaxy in her gradual path of incarnation into a human etheric body (more on this later). Steiner indicates that the incarnation of the "Beast from the Earth" (Sorat) in chapter 13 is related to the year 1998, whereas Powell tells us that this chapter has to do with the current incarnation of Ahriman in human form.

It seems to me that chapter 12 is describing the fate of Europe in the 19th century. First of all, who exactly is the woman crowned with stars, clothed with the sun, standing on the moon? She is Sophia, yes, but in what role specifically? She is Sophia as the Soul of Europe, the Divine Ideal of Europe. Her threefold garment of stars, sun and moon are the threefold social organism of Europe: Liberty for the individual, Equality under the law, and Fraternity in our work. She is Columbia, the guiding light of the revolutions of the late 18th and early 19th centuries, the heritage of which could have been taken up in a new way through the impulses of Goethe, Schiller and Novalis. We could say that she is intimately bound up with the Goethean enlightenment that flourished during this time period in the Germanic Austro-Hungarian region of Europe.

This woman is in labor, bearing a son who is to "shepherd all the Gentiles with a rod of iron." And this is no mere image or symbol, but quite literally this child existed. For who was the "Child of Europe"? None other than Kaspar Hauser; and as

Rudolf Steiner described to Count Ludwig Polzer-Hoditz in November 1916:

> South Germany should have become the new Grail Castle of the new Knights of the Grail and the cradle of future events. The spiritual ground had been well prepared by all those personalities whom we know of as Goethe, Schiller, Hölderlin, Herder, and others. Kaspar Hauser was to have gathered around him, as it were, all that existed in this spiritual ground thus prepared.[4]

And so this Goethean culture that developed during the late 18th and early 19th century was the earthly expression of this Sophia-Europa, as the vessel for a new Knighthood of the Grail led by Kaspar Hauser, the Child of Europe. But just as it is written in Revelation, the dragon waited by the lady's feet in order to consume this child. Let's look at the rest of the quotation of Rudolf Steiner from November 1916, of which only a portion has already been quoted:

> Those circles that conceal everything and today still try to conceal what happened in connection with Kaspar Hauser's destiny, are those members of Western Lodges and Jesuits who have worked together in their leading organizations for more than 150 years, but demonstrably since January 1802. The latter, therefore, do not want to have exposed what they have staged as an experiment, as an elaborate attempt to separate the individual in question from his mission and to hold him in a twilight zone, not completely spirit and not altogether a man on earth, but diverted from his mission and kept as though in spiritual exile; that is to say, to build a body, but not be able to take hold of it as an individual ego. This experiment, however, did not succeed and that is the reason why Kaspar Hauser had to die. The people concerned were forced to experience that their experiment achieved just that which they had tried to avoid: the awakening of the individuality, yes, even that he became conscious of reincarnation and karma.

---

4 This and the following quotation are from Tradowsky, *Kaspar Hauser: The Struggle for the Spirit,* appendix 1.

But that was just what should not have been. South Germany should have become the new Grail Castle of the new Knights of the Grail and the cradle of future events. The spiritual ground had been well prepared by all those personalities whom we know of as Goethe, Schiller, Hölderlin, Herder, and others. Kaspar Hauser was to have gathered around him, as it were, all that existed in this spiritual ground thus prepared. But that was not wanted by those circles (the Western Lodges and the Jesuits). They could not tolerate a center that was awakening to consciousness if they were not to relinquish their power and designs for power. A spirit such as Goethe's frightened them. Napoleon forced them to unite and form a league for the aspired-to world domination in the spheres of ideology and commerce. Napoleon had already thwarted their effort; it was he who fundamentally forced the two currents into union. From that time onward the tasks allotted to each were clearly circumscribed. But for that their clearly defined goal of world domination became all the more effective. The ideological and spiritual affairs were given exclusively into the hands of the Jesuits; the commercial ones into the hands of the Anglo-American Lodges of the West. These plans, however, will lead to ever more tragic catastrophes, because none of them take human development into account. What was intended to happen through Kaspar Hauser was overthrown by mankind. On these "planned" ruins the black-and-white principle gained ascendancy. The black-and-white principle, however, is something constructed, something exclusive. This is also the tragedy of Bismarck himself, who was quite well able to construct the model for a Federal State, the constructive idea of a true Central Federation, but could not supply the supporting idea, that which would have made a state construction of this kind appear necessary and justified. It was that which Bismarck was seeking in Frankfurt, too, the Goethean spirit, that which could have developed in the region of southern Germany through Kaspar Hauser but did not come about. It was in Frankfurt, actually, where Bismarck encountered the principle of black-and-white and all that then

bound him to the King of Prussia. It was from then on that the era of the lawyer began, but politics is not a legal problem.

It is fascinating to realize that in 1832—the year before the assassination of Kaspar Hauser—the Rothschilds (Western lodges) made a donation the equivalent of $70,000,000 in modern value to the Holy See (Jesuits).[5]

Kaspar Hauser was born in 1812 and was murdered in 1833—and so, indeed, the Child was "seized up to God and his throne." What follows this in chapter 12 is the War in Heaven between Michael and the Dragon. We might wonder if Kaspar Hauser himself was a part of this war in the spiritual world? The War in Heaven lasted from 1841 to '79, during which Europe was completed eclipsed by materialistic thinking. At the end of this time the Slanderer [*Satan* in Hebrew, *Ahriman* in Persian] was thrown down to Earth. This corresponds closely with the birth in December 1878 of Joseph Stalin, who in his subsequent incarnation would become the vessel for the incarnation of Ahriman [this is alluded to in chapter 13 of Revelation, with the first beast who rises from the sea representing Joseph Stalin, and the "image of the beast" as his reincarnation, the vessel for Ahriman]. The casting down of the spirits of darkness in 1879 led to the dragon releasing the deluge to drown the woman: this is the rise of Marxism, Darwinism, and Bolshevism at the turn of the 19th and 20th centuries, centered on World War I and the Bolshevik Revolution.

The Slanderer pursues Sophia-Europa, and she is given the wings of an eagle to go into the wilderness for 1260 days (or, "a season, seasons, and half a season"). We can understand this to indicate that sometime after 1879—and throughout the 20th century—the Soul of Europe disappeared. More precisely, she entered the "wilderness" in order to be protected from the destructive forces of the Slanderer, the dragon, until the allotted time period has passed.

In his "Course on the Lord's Prayer," Valentin Tomberg describes the seven archetypal countries

---

5 See https://en.wikipedia.org/wiki/Rothschild_loans _to_the_Holy_See.

of Europe in relation to the seven lotuses of the astral body.[6] He gives brief descriptions of the spiritual tasks of each of these countries, and the nature of their guiding archangel or folk spirit. These countries are:

Saturn	Crown — Poland
Jupiter	Brow — Germany
Mars	Larynx — France
Sun	Heart — Italy
Mercury	Solar Plexus — Spain/Portugal (according to Robert Powell; Tomberg does not specify)
Venus	Sacral — Netherlands
Moon	Root — England

In the next section, Valentin Tomberg makes an interesting statement regarding Germany and America.

Germany–Jupiter:

Germany—here the Archangel works through the element of warmth, both inner and outer warmth.

Warmth is bound up with two sources: digestion and the blood (one warms oneself at the fire or through eating); and through the ideals which the human being has.

The mission of Germany was to make the self (the source of ideals) so strong that it masters the digestive system.

However, the contrary took place.

Digestion and the blood rose up and created their own ideals, which had the consequence of driving the Archangel away.

This refers to Nazi Germany, where the ideal of pure, Aryan blood was promulgated, and the Archangel of Germany was obliged to withdraw its field of activity to America.

The highest warmth from the human being is in the Word from the Cross: "My God, my God, why hast thou forsaken me?"

Human beings must develop a warmth from within in order to seek the highest: God. Then, through the initiative of the two-petalled lotus

flower, all the other lotus flowers also come into vibration by way of resonance.

The loneliest warmth is bound up with the mission of the self.

And so, we see, due to the consequences of the rise of the Dragon (Nazism), the Archangel of Germany—which is meant to be the leading culture of the Age of the Consciousness Soul in Europe—fled to America. The "woman fled into the wilderness" indicates on one level the Germanic Archangel fleeing to America (the wilderness indeed!).

Now the Nazism that drove Sophia-Europa into America was not an isolated being, but rather the external, militant branch of the cooperation between the Western Lodges and the Jesuits (dark powers of commerce and ideology). The true source for both the Nazi and the Bolshevist disruptions in the 20th century comes from the "mastermind" of England, where the Western Lodges have operated for centuries. Indeed, they left their signature, as the Nazis chose the swastika (traditionally related to the root chakra) as their icon—and England is the "root chakra" of Europe.

The occultism of England suffers an identity crisis, a kind of "Cain" jealousy for the "Abel" of true European (Germanic, Goethean) culture. Rudolf Steiner makes the following relationships clear throughout his lectures in the 1910s:

- Italy is a recapitulation of the sentient soul culture of Ancient Egypt
- France is a recapitulation of the intellectual soul culture of Ancient Greece/Rome
- *England is the first experience proper of the consciousness soul culture*
- The Germanic/Austro-Hungarian nations are the Ego of Europe
- Finland is the threefold soul and conscience of Europe
- The Slavic/Russian countries are the still-gestating Spirit Self of Eurasia

Occultists of England have understood this role as consciousness soul for centuries, and therefore from the very beginning of the Age of the Consciousness Soul have attempted to rule Europe

---

6 I am using the translation available from the Sophia Foundation for this section. There will soon be a single volume edition of *The Lord's Prayer Course* available.

and determine her destiny (see for example the events surrounding Joan of Arc). At first, they did this more overtly through the British Empire, but through blackmail and subterfuge (i.e., primarily through intelligence agencies) they have maintained a stranglehold on world culture. The United States of America may seem as though they are the primary culture of modern times, but ever since the end of World War II they have been playing a very similar role to Nazi Germany before them: the attack dog, the external arm of the Western Lodges originating in England.

However, this is all a great misunderstanding, for England is not, in another sense, properly part of Europe at all, at least not the current mission of Europe. For England's mission will not come about for thousands of years, during the Anglo-American epoch from 5734 to 7894. England and America are meant to work together, and be the leading culture in the world—but not for a very long time. We can even see this astrogeographically, as the projection of Taurus covers virtually the entirety of Europe except for the U.K., which is under the projection of Aries.

In misperceiving themselves as the cultural leader of the current time period, British occultists have facilitated to a great degree the incarnation of Ahriman, as they have attempted to subvert the development of both the 5th and 6th cultural epochs (European and Russian respectively) and are wittingly or unwittingly attempting to bring about the Anglo-American cultural era 4,000 years too soon. And this era is the time period when "mechanical occultism" will face off against "transhumanism"; when the Moon reunites with the Earth and sexual reproduction will become impossible; when the "white magic" of those who have cultivated the resurrection body (and therefore only incarnate physically, not materially) will attempt to rescue those who will become increasingly enmeshed in matter and sub-matter. This time period culminates with the "War of All Against All," a war fought primarily in the elements of the air (just as Lemuria was destroyed by fire, and Atlantis submerged in water, our age is destroyed by the polluting, poisoning and

weaponizing of the air). Do we not see all of these future events attempting to rear their heads too soon, in our own age?

This fleeing of Sophia-Europa to the wilderness of America was also expressed in the gesture of the guiding light of true occultism throughout the 20th century. It began in the Germanic countries with the Anthroposophical Society; Valentin Tomberg (as well as Walter Johannes Stein, Willi Sucher, and Karl König, among many others) transferred this activity to the U.K. over the course of the 1930s and '40s. Then individuals like Willi Sucher and Carlo Pietzner made the leap to the U.S. (following in the footsteps of individuals such as Ehrenfried Pfeiffer) in the 1960s.

So this middle period of the 20th century was a transition, a migration west. This reached its apotheosis in the 1990s, when a British anthroposophist—Robert Powell—founded the Sophia Foundation with Karen Rivers in California. The true spirit of Goethean culture could—and still can—be found in the Sophia Grail celebrations cultivated there for the past twenty-five years. Perhaps more than anywhere else, it was the American Camphill communities and the Sophia Foundation that protected the seed of true European culture, the Sophia-Europa, from the encroachment and attacks of the Slanderer.

Overall, we might bring this time in the wilderness into relation with the period of humanity's experience of the Temptations in the Wilderness, which according to Robert Powell began in 1929 and will last until 2047.[7] It is this period of time that corresponds more or less to chapter 13, whereas chapter 12 lasted from the turn of the 18th to 19th centuries until around 1929.

Chapter 14 shows us the return of Christ in the etheric. This image, like all the others in the Book of Revelation, is multivalent. It could refer to 1933, when Christ became available to human beings in elemental guise for the first time; or it could refer to the year 2375, when the Sun will enter Aquarius at the spring equinox (the Sign of the Son of Man in the Heavens). It could also refer

---

7   Robert Powell discusses this in many of his works, including *The Christ Mystery*.

to Christ's presence in the astral and devechanic planes (around the years 4000 and 6000 respectively). The image of Christ coming in the clouds bears all of these events within it in a seed form.

In terms of the timing we are working with in this case, we can bring this appearance of Christ in chapter 14 into relation with the years 2133 to 2135. Robert points to AD 2133 to 4233 as the unfolding of the Ego of Christianity (after the unfolding of its physical body between AD 33 and 733; its etheric body between 733 and 1433; and its astral body between 1433 and 2133).[8] He also points to Christ's appearance in the etheric as related to a journey into the underworld; yes, Christ appeared in the Earth's etheric aura between 1933 and 1945, but then began a journey into the sub-earthly spheres (demarcated by the exploding of the atomic bomb in the Trinity Test of July 16, 1945). By and large, Christ has descended below the level of our conscious awareness during this time. He will descend all the way to the Mother below the nine sub-earthly spheres in 2040, and then will begin his re-ascent. He will return to the etheric aura of the Earth—as he was between 1933 and 1945—in the year 2135.

So, we have chapter 12 lasting from the turn of the 18th to 19th centuries until about 1929; chapter 13, lasting from about 1929 to 2047; and chapter 14, centered on the reappearance of Christ in the etheric in 2135.

We can find a more specific timing for the unfolding of each chapter of the Book of Revelation by taking the year 3216 referred to above as an "end point," and taking as our starting point September 30 AD 395. Why this date? In an esoteric lesson from 1911, Rudolf Steiner claims that the Apocalyptist time-traveled to that specific date in order to write the Apocalypse.[9]

Now, between 3,216.44 and 395.75, there are 2,820.69 years. When we divide this by the 22 chapters of the Book of Revelation, we come to: 2,820.69/22 = 128.21 years per chapter. Based on

this timing, chapter 12 corresponds to the years 1806 to 1934; chapter 13 corresponds to 1934 to 2062; and chapter 14 corresponds to 2062 to 2190. Note that, according to this timing, chapter 16—during which all of the vials of wrath are poured out—would take place between 2318 and 2447. While from the perspective Steiner set out from in 1924 the entire time period from 2155 to 3216 is an outpouring of the vials of wrath (see above), when we incorporate this other perspective, it would seem that the 24th to 25th centuries will be of particular intensity in this regard. This aligns very much with Steiner's indications regarding Archangel Oriphiel, the Saturnine archangel whose rulership extends from 2234 to 2588.[10] It becomes quite clear from Rudolf Steiner's indications that, rather than the "dawning of the Age of Aquarius" announcing itself as a time of peace, love and harmony, it is rather a time when the "Waterbearer" pours out vials of Divine Wrath upon a humanity that struggles to awaken from materialistic somnambulism. According to Steiner, it is only in the Venusian Age of Anael, which comes after the Age of Oriphiel, that a culture of love and beauty will truly be able to manifest itself (around 2588–2943). Our task as modern Michaelites is to train ourselves during this incarnation to "hold the line" through the coming times of darkness, when we reincarnate in the Age of Oriphiel—a time compared with which our modern dilemmas are only bootcamp.

In terms of locating ourselves in time, we find ourselves in the second half of chapter 13 of the Book of Revelation. In the first half of this chapter, the beast from the waters arises. Note that he rises up from the waters that were meant to drown Ideal Europe at the end of chapter 12. We could relate this to the rise of both Hitler and Stalin in the 1930s, but in particular this is in reference to

---

8 See Powell, *Hermetic Astrology*, vol 1, appendix 2.

9 See Steiner, *Esoteric Lessons 1910–1912* (CW 266/2), lesson 26, Mar. 5, 1911.

10 Steiner makes several references to the darkness of this coming age: *Esoteric Lessons 1904–1909* (CW 266/1), lessons 10, 20, 22, 25, and 38. He also describes this time in *Esoteric Lessons 1910–1912*, lesson 24; in *The Fall of the Spirits of Darkness*, lect. 9, "The Battle between Michael and 'the Dragon'"; and in *Secret Brotherhoods and the Mystery of the Human Double* (CW 178), lect. 4.

Stalin, who prepared himself to become the vessel for Ahriman in his next incarnation. The beast that was slain, and yet lived, and was worshipped by all the Earth refers to the militant form of Bolshevism that flowed through Stalin dying and resurrecting as a more cosmopolitan cultural Marxism in his next incarnation: Bolshevism presenting itself as kindness, openness, and progressivism, and therefore much more insidious.

According to Robert Powell's research, Stalin reincarnated on February 5, 1962.[11] Based on my own research, Ahriman entered the vessel of this individuality sometime in his "Parzival years"—ages 15 to 21 (somewhere between 1977 and 1983), and had the greatest degree of free reign around 33 years later—centered on April 20, 2014, an Easter Sunday during which the exact same Jupiter-Pluto opposition occurred as the original Easter Sunday on April 5 AD 33. The "beast from the earth," Sorath, arose in the year 1998. It has been largely his activity since that time—and for the coming decades—to bring about the rise of the "image of the first beast," to which all must bow down.

Notice that the second beast arises from the earth, which came to the aid of the woman at the end of chapter 12 by swallowing all the water. The Western powers were able to stop Hitler and Stalin only through the elaboration of increasingly draconian forms of technology (beginning with Alan Turing's invention of the first computer and Oppenheimer's development of the atomic bomb), which have since infiltrated every aspect of our cultural life. These powers wish to create an "image of the beast"—in other words, make it possible for the reign of Ahriman to extend beyond the lifetime of any one incarnation, and become a structural component of an increasingly technocratic culture. A prime example of this is the social credit system of communist China, in which one's ability to buy and sell is predicated on whether one's behavior and speech aligns with what the almighty State has decided is wrong and right. Modern so-called woke and cancel culture; the collusion of government with big tech to censor "mis" and "dis" information—these

conscious and unconscious alliances tend to lead us ever closer to an apparently decentralized and pervasive worldwide governance, spearheaded by institutions such as the World Economic Forum and World Health Organization, that will manage the behavior, speech, and even thoughts of everyone on the planet through economic incentives. In other words: global slavery of the masses of "deplorables" who need to be managed by a self-appointed aristocracy of experts who "know better." Resisting the mark of the beast: this is the struggle of our age, up through the year 2062 or thereabout.

So, if we want to locate our time within the events of the Book of Revelation, we will find it in the letter to the Church in Sardis; in the time of the seventh trumpet (chapters 11–15); and most specifically of all, in the latter half of chapter 13, during the implementation of the mark of the beast and the worship of his image by the beast from the earth.[12]

Now, it is indicated that Sophia-Europa enters the wilderness only for a transitional time (as pointed out by Friedrich Weinreb in his excellent *Roots of the Bible*, "three-and-a-half" is a number used in the Bible consistently to indicate a transition, specifically through the Sabbath to the "eighth day" of the Promised Land), one that we have proposed lasts from 1929 to 2047.[13] We can trust in the spiritual world that at some point, perhaps quite gradually, it will be the right time for Sophia-Europa to return to her homeland—to leave the United States. But when she returns, it will not be to the same regions. We can think of the seven archetypal countries of Europe laid out above by Valentin Tomberg as prototypes, in a way, of the true Europe to come. We could say those are the seven archetypal countries of the *Pisces* time period of the Consciousness Soul Age (1414–2375), whereas during the *Aquarian* time period of that

---

11 Powell, *Prophecy, Phenomena, Hope*, p. 12.

12 See the addendum at the end of this article for further indications regarding our time in relation to the Book of Revelation.

13 See in Friedrich Weinreb, *Roots of the Bible: The Key to Creation in Jewish Tradition*, pp. 263–67; available from Angelico Press.

Age (2375–3574) seven different regions may take on a leading or archetypal role.

In 1914, Rudolf Steiner described the relationship between the forms on the columns of the first Goetheanum and the different European cultures.[14] He indicates here that the second column relates to southwestern Europe (Italy), the third column to France, the fourth to England, and the fifth to the Germanic countries. But he goes on to address the question: what about the northern countries, like Norway, Denmark, Sweden?

He then makes the interesting claim that the more southerly and westerly European cultures are simpler in comparison to those of the northern and eastern nations. He points out that Norway is like England transformed by Germany; Denmark like France transformed by Germany; and Sweden like Italy transformed by Germany. We might think of the original seven (Poland, Germany, France, Italy, Spain, Netherlands, England) as all more-or-less still under the strong influence of the Roman system from the prior, Greco-Roman cultural era—cultures in between the Age of the Intellectual Soul and the Age of the Consciousness Soul, due to the Age of Pisces bridging these two cultural eras. A new group of seven will begin to arise, perhaps centered around the Baltic Sea: Norway, Denmark, Sweden, and possibly Finland, Lithuania, Latvia, and Estonia? These nations will be "in between" in the opposite sense: they will build the bridge to the sixth cultural epoch of the Slavic-Russian peoples (the Age of Aquarius is the bridge between the Age of the Consciousness Soul and the Age of the Spirit Self). They would be the seven prior archetypal European nations transformed by the Germanic spirit—by Sophia-Europa.

In my own astrogeographical research, which appeared in As Above, So Below: Star Wisdom, vol 3, I elaborated on the following map of stellar projections onto Europe.[15]

We can imagine Europe as someone being raised from the dead (e.g. Martialis, the Youth of

Nain). We can imagine the regions along line A (totally horizontal) to be of particular importance during the Greco-Roman era (747 BC–AD 1414); those along line B to be of particular significance during the Age of Pisces (215–2375); and those along line C to be of particular importance during the European-Germanic era (1414–3574).

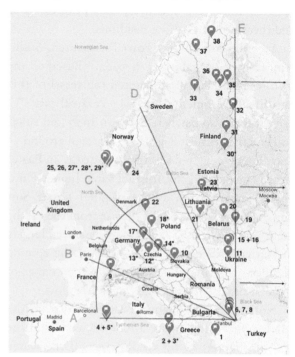

Then line D is of particular significance during the Age of Aquarius, from 2375 to 4535. Now, in the previous sections of this article series (see volumes IV and V of Star Wisdom), I pointed out that in the biography of Philosophia, at the start of her third life cycle during the last third of the Age of Aries (506 BC–AD 215), there arose the philosophers Plato and Aristotle. Their worldviews blossomed rapidly, and just as rapidly died away. But it had been as though they planted seeds for the future Pisces culture, that could only blossom again after the gift of the Ego during the Mystery of Golgotha: Platonism came to inspire the entirety of the first third of the Age of Pisces (215–935), whereas Aristotelianism came to inspire the entirety of the second third (935–1655). These time periods correspond to the life cycles equivalent to ages 21 to 28 (sentient soul) and 28 to 35 (mind soul) in the biography of the Archangelic Philosophia.

14 See, for example, Steiner, *Architecture as Peacework* (CW 287), lect. 4.

15 See "Finding Future Grail Sites: An Astrogeographical Investigation."

Now we are in the final third of the Age of Pisces, and similarly in our time, new impulses have arisen which blossomed rapidly, only to seemingly fade away, just as it was in the final third of the Age of Aries. The modern Platonism is Goetheanism; the modern Aristotelianism is Anthroposophy. They may die away externally, and only return to flourish after the gift of the *manas* consciousness has been poured out on humanity through the Second Coming, the fifth sacrifice of Christ in the etheric. It may be in between lines C and D on the map—in northern Germany, Poland, Norway, and Denmark—that the "Neo-Goethean" culture will arise, after Sophia-Europa returns to her homeland, over the course of the 3rd millennium (from approximately 2375 to 3095). Line E becomes of significance at the start of the Slavic-Russian era, from 3574 to 5734. We can imagine this totally vertical line as the Youth of Nain risen from the dead, ready to walk—heading east, through the Russian territory. Here we see that it would be in the nations between lines D and E that the "Neo-Anthroposophy" could arise—Lithuania, Latvia, Finland, Sweden—in the 4th millennium, transitioning into the Slavic-Russian culture (approximately 3095–3815).

And so, these are the regions that ask for a "christening" through the Foot-washing ritual described in Part II in order to prepare them for their future missions over the course of the next 2,000 years (the Age of Aquarius), leading up to the appearance of Christ in the astral realm (the sixth sacrifice of Jesus and Christ)—just as Joseph of Arimathea prepared the southern and western regions of Europe for the Age of Pisces in preparation for our current moment in human history.

We can also consider the fact that there are three key individualities now and into the future—each of them raised from the dead by Christ. Salome, the daughter of Jairus, will be the guiding individuality for the Age of Capricorn, bridging the Slavic-Russian cultural epoch with that of the Anglo-American. We can imagine Salome to be in close relationship with the Skythianos individuality and impulse—the protector of the Atlantean mysteries of "mechanical occultism," of working

with nature forces. Lazarus will be the guiding individuality of the Age of Aquarius—he is in close relationship with the Maitreya Boddhisatva, bridging the Germanic-European culture with the Slavic-Russian through the Rosicrucian impulse. And in our time, in the Age of Pisces, it is the Youth of Nain (Martialis) who is the guiding individuality, building the bridge from the Greco-Roman to the Germanic-European culture through the Manichaean impulse.

This individuality's incarnation stream, according to the research of Robert Powell, was 1) Mani in the 3rd century; 2) Parzival in the 8th to 9th century; and 3) Kaspar Hauser in the 19th century—the "Child of Europe" we spoke of earlier! Rudolf Steiner indicated that this individuality would incarnate in our time. Considering that we are approaching the threshold of the Age of Pisces, heading into the Age of Aquarius (2375), perhaps the time is at hand for this individuality to realize that which could not be achieved in the 19th century—to found a new Knighthood of the Holy Grail, not in southern Germany, but in the region of the Baltic Sea.

Keeping these indications in mind, we can also look to the individuality with the incarnation lineage of Abel—Solomon—Mary Magdalene—Repanse de Schoye.

In *Through the Eyes of Mary Magdalene*, volume 2, Estelle Isaacson writes of Magdalene's three-day initiation in the cave by Christ just prior to the Passion (bold emphasis mine):

The three days of initiations were also a preparation, a seed-planting, both for her future and for that of humanity as a whole. The three days' initiations corresponded to the following **three and a half millennia** of her incarnations, as well as the incarnations of humanity as a whole.

The *Friday initiation* prepared the soil and planted the seeds for her incarnations during the *first* thousand [approximately 1,181] years. This initiation corresponded to the trial, scourging, crowning with thorns, bearing of the cross, crucifixion, death, descent into hell, overcoming of Satan, and everything these events encompassed—every action, every feeling, every word, spoken and unspoken.

The *Saturday initiation* was a preparation for the *second* thousand years of her incarnations [ending around the year 2394]. This corresponded to the washing and anointing of the body of Christ, the enshrouding, the visiting of the souls imprisoned in the underworld, the ascent to the souls in paradise, and the entombment—as well as everything these events encompassed.

And the *Sunday initiation* had to do with the *third* thousand years [ending approximately 3575]. This corresponded—and corresponds still in our day—to the opening of the tomb, angelic vigil, emergence from cosmic midnight, resurrection, reunion, and ascension to the Father; to walking, partaking, communing, and touching through the resurrection body—and to everything these events encompassed, including the ability to transcend time and space.

I understood that the three days of initiations, in addition to their correspondence with the three days of the Passion and the ensuing three [and a half] millennia of incarnations, corresponded also to the three and half years of Christ's ministry. If we take the three and half years of his ministry and correlate it to the millennia of Magdalene's incarnations, we arrive somewhere near the year AD 3500 [3575].

At the conclusion of these three millennia of incarnations I saw the individuality of Magdalene become a new kind of human being, surrounded with light as was Jesus at the Transfiguration, although I do not know if that is the proper term to describe the transformation I beheld. I cannot say that the individual I saw was a *woman*—but the incarnation was primarily of a *divine feminine* nature.

I was shown that the Word, or the seeds planted in the individuality of Magdalene during her initiations, would come to manifestation toward the close of her "Sunday night" of incarnations! She appeared in that coming time as an *angelic human being*.[16]

Robert Powell writes in *Christ and the Maya Calendar: 2012 and the Coming of the Antichrist* of the gradual incarnation of Sophia into an etheric body, building on the visions and indications of the Russian mystic and visionary Daniel Andreev (contained in his magnum opus, *The Rose of the World*). This is the incarnation of the very being of Revelation, chapter 12, the woman clothed with the Sun, with the Moon under her feet, a chaplet of twelve stars on her head.[17]

For the journey of Sophia into incarnation takes place gradually from the far reaches of the cosmos. She descended from the Central Sun, the heart of our Milky Way galaxy, and united herself with the starry heavens of our local Sagittarius Arm of the galactic spiral ("chaplet of stars"). This occurred in 1775, around the time of the cultural renaissance and revolution mentioned above—the time of Goethe, Novalis, Schiller, etc. She will descend to the level of the Sun sphere and unite spiritually with our Sun 600 years later in 2375, at the dawn of the Age of Aquarius ("clothed with the Sun"), inaugurating the "Neo-Goethean" culture centered around Norway. A further 600 years later she will enter the lunar sphere, uniting with our Moon, in the year 2975 ("the Moon under her feet"), inaugurating the "Neo-Anthroposophical" culture centered around Finland. Finally—virtually coinciding with the transition to the Slavic-Russian cultural epoch—in 3575 she will incarnate in an etheric body here within the Earth herself, as a being Daniel Andreev calls "Sventa Zventana" the "brightest of the bright and the holiest of holies."

It is my intuition that the vessel for the incarnation of Sophia into an etheric body around the year 3575 will be provided by the individuality of Mary Magdalene. It is this event that will bring about a Transfiguration-like event for this individual, transforming her into an angelic being. She will work very closely with the reincarnated Lazarus in order to bring about the fulfillment of European culture in the Baltic/Scandinavian regions, setting the stage for the Slavic-Russian culture which will be inaugurated by this transformative incarnation in 3575.

This clarifies to some degree what we may be looking at when we see the Book of Revelation

16 Isaacson, *Through the Eyes of Mary Magdalene*, vol 2, pp. 39–40.

17 See Powell and Dann, *Christ and the Maya Calendar*, chap. 9, "The Rose of the World."

as culminating in the year 3216 (both from Steiner's perspective and from my own). Perhaps we can consider the Book of Revelation as the Cain individuality's vivid description of the process of preparation for the Abel individuality to prepare herself to be the vessel for the incarnation of Sophia on Earth. The culmination of this process of preparation is described in the Book of Revelation as the descent of the New Jerusalem, the Bride of the Lamb. This would indicate that her final incarnation in a physical body would be sometime around 3216, at which point she achieves the transformation that allows her etheric body to be the vessel for Sophia's incarnation around 3575 when the Abel individuality has become a more-or-less angelic being.

Let's remember that the goal of the Age of Aquarius is to fully engage *manas* cognition, just as the goal of the Age of Pisces was to fully engage ego-consciousness. The year 3575 will be comparable to the year 1414, inasmuch as Northern Europe will be prepared to undergo a "Spiritual Scientific Revolution" equivalent to the scientific revolution of the 16th century. Increasingly, spiritual visionary activity could become commonplace, as this time is right in the heart of the potential age of Finnish "Neo-Anthroposophy" between 3095 and 3815. This is the cultural milieu in which the Magdalene spirit will be active—indeed, it is just for this that she has been preparing herself.

Rudolf Steiner's words from January 17, 1915, are important to remember in this context:

> What we see there in Goethe himself is a character trait of the German people. It can give an indication as to the mission given to human beings. The mission is, and we can present this very clearly to our souls, that true benefit for the progress of mankind will arise only if within a certain group of people, a harmonious relationship is established between Central Europe and Eastern Europe.
>
> It is possible to visualize Eastern Europe expanding westward, across Central Europe, by brute force. It is possible to visualize this happening. That, however, would be equivalent to a situation where Joan of Arc had not done her deed in the 15th century and England had annexed France in those days. If it had come to that, and I state this emphatically, something would have come about that would not only have brought calamity to France but would have meant calamity also for England. And if German culture were now to suffer through what may come from the East, this would be to the detriment not only of German culture but also of the East. The worst that can happen to the East is that it might expand for a time and have an adverse effect on German culture. For as I said, the souls formerly incarnated in Western Europe or on the Italian peninsula and now growing up in the East unite with the Christ impulse as though instinctively, in the unconscious depths of the astral body. Yet the Christ impulse that is to grow within them can never arise through linear progression of the instinctive element that lives in their souls under the name of orthodox Catholicism which, on the whole, is Byzantine of course, for this is a name, not an impulse. It is just as impossible for this to evolve into what it is predestined to become as it is impossible for a woman without a man to have a child. What is preparing in the East can only come to something if Central Europe strongly and consciously—that is, in a state of full awareness—unites the force of the human ego and human powers of insight with the Christ impulse, out of what souls are striving for out of egoic nature.
>
> What has to come about for the civilization and culture of the future will only come about if the German folk spirit finds souls that transplant the Christ impulse into their astral body and ego the way it can indeed be implanted there in a state of full conscious awareness. It has to come about through harmony being established, by uniting with that which is consciously achieved in Central Europe—more and more consciously.
>
> This will need not just one or two centuries, but a very long time. The time needed will be so long that we may reckon on about two thousand years, I would say, counting from the year 1400. Adding two thousand years to 1400 we get the approximate time when something will emerge in the evolution of the earth that has had its seeds in the German life of the spirit, ever since there has been such a life of

the spirit. We therefore realize that we have to consider a future lying not just centuries ahead but more than a thousand years. And the mission of the Central European, the German folk spirit, a mission already before us, is that there will have to be more and more of that nurturing of the life in the spirit through which men take up in conscious awareness—right into the astral body and ego—a comprehension of the Christ impulse that in earlier times moved through the peoples of Europe as a living but unconscious impulse. Once evolution takes this course then the East, too, will gradually, by twining upward, reach the level reached in Central Europe because of what is already inherent there. That is the intention of the cosmic intelligence. We only interpret the intention of the cosmic intelligence rightly when we say to ourselves: It would be the greatest misfortune also for the East of Europe to harm the very spiritual power it needs to use as a support in twining upward, a power the East should indeed revere, revere in friendship, foster and cherish. It will have to come to this. For the moment the East is very far indeed from achieving this.[18]

Hand in hand with the gradual incarnation of Sophia is the gradual establishment of the Rose of the World. One way in which this could present itself is an increasing rapprochement of the Roman Catholic and Eastern Orthodox Churches. Just as the past 500 years leading up to Christ's fifth sacrifice have seen a rapprochement between the Catholic Church and the Oriental Orthodox Churches in the Eastern Catholic confessions, so the years 3300 to 3800 may see the even greater reconciliation of Catholicism with Russian Orthodoxy. It is this reconciliation, along with the integration and dissolution of the foot-washing rite of the Age of Aquarius, that would facilitate the emergence of the Rose of the World. This, too, is precisely what the individuality of Magdalene has been preparing for, and will continue to prepare for over the next 1,300 years.

The Age of Aquarius—and the overall biography of Philosophia—will culminate in the year 4535. Sometime around the year 3833 will see the sixth sacrifice of Archangel Jesus and Christ. The Archangel Jesus will offer up his *manas* body in order to create a vessel for *budhi*, for Life-Spirit to enter Spirit-Self. It is at this point that there will no longer be a necessity for the Sophianic communion—the Church of the Mother, the milk and honey, the foot-washing of the Johannine service, will have done its work. With the attainment of *budhi*, what will gradually dawn on humanity is not just *spirit vision*, but actual dialogue, conversation, and active collaboration with hierarchical spirits, elemental beings, and humans on the other side of the threshold.

Six members of the human being will then have fully precipitated out of the spiritual potentiality held by the Higher Self and the Guardian Angel—with only the Resurrection Body still gestating, which it has been doing ever since the fourth sacrifice of the Mystery of Golgotha.

The year 4443, approximately, will witness the last incarnation of Maitreya Boddhisatva, as

18 Steiner, *The Destinies of Individuals and of Nations* (CW 157), lect. 4.

Maitreya Buddha. From this point onward, the work of Skythianos will be of key importance. Among other tasks this will entail the struggle to reintegrate the Anglican/Protestant communions back into the Catholic Church (the Rose of the World). To be sure, by this point the Catholic Church will be transfigured—on its way to becoming a New Jerusalem—having reintegrated into herself the Oriental and Eastern Orthodox Churches, as well as the Aquarian/Sophianic Church of the Mother. It will be akin to the difference between the primal sacrifice of Abel's best lamb to Yahweh versus the fully elaborated rituals of the Ancient Hebrews at the time of Moses.

We already have a prefiguring of this reintegrated Anglican/Protestant Church in the Christian Community developed by Lutheran anthroposophists under the guidance of Steiner a century ago. A Christian Community service can give one a presentiment of a future Church that has integrated Roman Catholicism, Oriental Orthodoxy, Eastern Orthodoxy, Anglicanism, Protestantism, the Johannine service of the Aquarian Age, and even Freemasonry. Like the agape feast of Melchizadek and Abraham, it is a necessary cultivation for the sake of a future time.

In summary, the following is a possible timeline heading into the future:

Current time–2375 (Completion of the "Sun Years" of Philosophia, 35–42): The culmination of the mission of Mani/Parzival. The appearance of the Etheric Christ. The confrontation with the incarnation of Ahriman. Humanity dimly feels the birth of Manas-cognition (imaginative clairvoyance). Sophia descends to the sphere of the Sun from the realm of fixed stars. The Age of Michael/Vidar (1879–2234) prepares the way for the darkness of the Age of Oriphiel (2234–2589).

2375–3095 ("Mars Years" of Philosophia, 42–49): The Age of Aquarius begins in the midst of the Age of Oriphiel, a "pouring out of the vials of wrath" by the Water Bearer. This is followed by the Venusian Age of Anael, an age of beauty and renewal: Neo-Goetheanism arises in the northern regions of Europe.

The Johannine/Aquarian Church of the Foot-washing is wedded to this movement. Manas-cognition comes to the point of the metamorphic consciousness of Goethe becoming relatively commonplace. Sophia descends to the sphere of the Moon. The Lazarus individuality (Rosicrucianism) comes to the fore after the Mani-Parzival individuality (Manichaeism).

3095–3815 ("Jupiter Years" of Philosophia, 49–56): Neo-Anthroposophy arises along the European/Russian border, in Finland in particular. Manas-cognition comes to the point of the fully visionary clairvoyance of Rudolf Steiner becoming relatively commonplace. Sophia unites with the Earth, and incarnates into the etheric body of the Magdalene individuality, who transfigures into an angelic being. The reunion of the Eastern Orthodox and Catholic Churches begins in earnest.

3815–4535 ("Saturn Years" of Philosophia, 56–63): Both the Manas-cognition exercised over the past 2,000 years as well as the Johannine (Sophianic) Mass culminate in the sixth appearance of Christ, around the year 3833. The Archangel Jesus offers up his perfected Manas-cognition as the vehicle for Christ to offer his *Budhi* or life-spirit to human beings as a whole, which has been gestating for the entirety of the Aquarian age. The human being will now have six fully elaborated members and one that remains in gestation—the Resurrection Body, the transformed physical body whose seed was planted at the Mystery of Golgotha. The final incarnation of the Maitreya Buddha takes place around 4443; the Sophianic Mass and Eastern Orthodoxy are subsumed into the Catholic Church. This is the end of the biography of Philosophia, which lasted from 1945 BC to AD 4535: nine life cycles of 720 years each rather than seven years.

The Age of Capricorn will begin in 4535, whereas the Anglo-American cultural epoch begins 1199 years later, in 5734. This is the time of Skythianos, who is the guardian of ancient Atlantean mysteries in terms of *moral technology:* the sub-natural (technological) forces of the Earth by this time will be responsive to the power of the *moral word* or *moral ether* bestowed on humanity by the Maitreya Buddha. Skythianos will lead the charge of the "white magicians" of moral technology against the "black magicians," the Sorathic foes who attempt to enslave humanity in a transhumanist state of permanent mineral attachment. The Sorathic impulse is to escape the wheel of death and rebirth by permanently affixing the soul to the mineral world (i.e., the Singularity of the transhumanists), whereas the impulse of the white magician is to demineralize or dematerialize the physical body through Christ (i.e., the Eucharist), in order to return to the pre-Lemurian state of continual transformation and metamorphosis.

This goal will be accomplished to some degree by the year 5734, at which time the Moon will reunite with the Earth. The body of the human being at this point will mature only to about the age of 14; sexual reproduction will no longer be a possibility. One will either have developed oneself to be able to "put on the Resurrection Body" of alchemically wedded life and death, or one will have to rely on science and technology in order to create new (materially incarnated) human beings.[19]

By this point, the Church will have become truly Catholic, having reintegrated the Anglican Communion. When the seventh appearance of Christ occurs around 5734, the Archangel Jesus will offer up the perfected Budhi, and the Resurrection Body (or "Atma") which had been gestating since the Mystery of Golgotha will become fully available to humanity. The human being will, at last, fully engage with other spiritual beings in intuitive union; it will be a sevenfoldness that can withstand being absorbed by and

absorbing—co-inhering—an eighth (i.e., another spiritual being) in full consciousness.

The Catholic Church will begin to transform into the New Jerusalem, finding its home—under the guidance of Mani-Parzival, who will have by this point ascended to the position of *Manu*—in the etheric region of what is currently the Pacific Ocean. The untransfigured portion of humanity will destroy itself in the "War of All against All," a global Trial by Air (juxtaposed to the Trial by Water of the Great Flood that destroyed Ancient Atlantis and the Trial by Fire that destroyed Ancient Lemuria).

It will be the mission of this transfigured portion of humanity over the course of the Sixth Age, after the War of All against All, not only to redeem and rescue fallen humanity, but to transform (i.e., dematerialize) all of Nature. By the end of the Sixth Age, the Sun will have reunited with the Earth—and the whole Earth will have become the New Jerusalem in her entirety.

---

19 See Steiner, *Materialism and the Task of Anthroposophy* (CW 204); *The Karma of Materialism* (CW 176), lect. 14; *Ancient Myths and the New Isis Mystery* (CW 180) lect. 1 and 5; and *How Can Mankind Find the Christ Again?* (CW 187), lect. 3.

ADDENDUM: THE BOOK OF REVELATION, THE TAROT, AND THE AGE OF ECLIPSE

We can consider the 22 chapters of the Book of Revelation in relation to the 22 Major Arcana of the Tarot of Marseilles. There are different ways of going about this, but for our purposes here we will be straightforward: chapter 1 with the Magician, chapter 2 with the High Priestess, and so on.

On the other hand, Robert Powell has brought the 22 Major Arcana into relation with the twelve signs of the zodiac and the ten planets (seven classical planets plus Uranus, Neptune, and Pluto). We can consider the zodiacal positions of the eclipses over the past seven years (and into 2045, see the Editorial Foreword), and some striking arcane imagery arises.

The eclipse on August 21, 2017, took place in the sign of Leo, which Powell brings into relation with the 10th Arcanum, the Wheel of Fortune. The eclipse of December 14, 2020, was in Scorpio and is brought into relation with the 13th Arcanum, Death. The October 14, 2023, eclipse was in the sign of Virgo, which Powell brings into relation with the 11th Arcanum, Force. And the April 8, 2024, eclipse is in Pisces and brought into relation with the 12th Arcanum, the Hanged Man.

These images themselves paint quite a picture, of the 10th through the 13th Arcana:

They also tell the story of the 10th through the 13th chapters of the Book of Revelation. According to Rudolf Steiner's timing, chapters 10 and 11 (which take place between the blowing of the sixth and the seventh trumpets) describe events that took place between 1843 and 1994. Note that the 10th chapter describes the 4th Apocalyptic Seal, the red pillar and the blue pillar united by the Sun:

This is in direct relationship to the events of chapter 11, during which the two prophets are martyred and resurrected. These two prophets are the two pillars—the red pillar is Moses, who was one prophet of our time as Rudolf Steiner; and the blue pillar is Elijah, who is also present in our time in a veiled way, working through public figures.

Chapter 12 (which describes the 5th Seal) and chapter 13, on the other hand, are part of the events between the blowing of the seventh trumpet and the pouring out of the first vial of wrath in chapter 16. They are directly related to our time, as described in the "Editorial Foreword."

Now, looking into the future, we have the August 12, 2045, eclipse, during which the Sun and the Moon will be in the sign of Cancer. This is represented in the Tarot of Marseilles in the 18th Arcanum, the Moon. The archetypal and spiritual content of this Arcanum is centered around passing through the trial of an eclipse. It is the ideal depiction of humanity's impasse during the years 2017 to 2024.

Now, each of these stellar events involved the Sun and the Moon. They are represented in the Arcana by the 1st and 3rd—the Magician and the Empress, who show to us the paths of Mysticism and Sacred Magic. On the other hand, the turning point of the Age of Eclipse was the Great Conjunction of Saturn and Jupiter. These two are represented to us by the 2nd and 4th Arcana—the High Priestess, who shows the path of Gnosis, and the Emperor, who shows the path of Hermeticism. It is they who add the element of consciousness to the super-conscious activities of Mysticism and Sacred Magic. And so the turning point in

December of 2020 created the circumstances by which humanity could bring to consciousness that through which it was passing.

This alignment occurred in the sign of Capricorn, represented in the Arcana by the 17th image, The Star, who pours out the living waters of tradition. When brought into relation with the Book of Revelation, we now see chapters 10 to 13, 17, and 18 being focused upon. While chapters 10 to 13 describe the confrontation of the two prophets and Sophia with the three beasts, in Chapters 17 and 18 is described the fall of the Whore of Babylon, the defeat of the system created by the beasts. Perhaps we have the opportunity of overcoming the Babylonian slavery that has been unleashed from 2017 to 2024 as we head toward the time of the future eclipse, on August 12, 2045?

There is of course much more that could be said in regard to the relationship between the positions of the stellar events, the Arcana, and the Book of Revelation. I leave these here as indications for readers to take up on their own.

"In the twentieth century, there began for humanity the vision of Christ in the etheric realm.... Now the etheric Christ walks among human beings the whole world over. This event must not pass by unnoticed by humanity. Human beings must awake to Christ, so that a sufficient number of people may behold him in the etheric realm. He is already present.... It is possible today, if we only seek him, to be very near to Christ, to find him in a quite different way than has been possible hitherto.

Christ spoke some words that should be deeply engraved into the human soul: 'I am with you always, until the end of time.' This is a truth, a reality. He is here. He is now making his presence felt in a new way

Christ is not a ruler of human beings, but our brother. He wishes to be consulted on all the details of life. In everything we undertake, we ought to ask Christ, 'Should we do this or not?' Then human souls may have the experience of Christ standing by them as the beloved companion, and they will then not only obtain consolation and strength from Christ, but will also receive instructions from him as to what should be done. The figure of Christ Jesus is now able to draw near to us and give us the strength and force with which we can live more fully here on Earth. If we seek him, Christ is able to guide us, to stand beside us as a brother, so that our hearts and souls may be strong enough to grow in our further development."

RUDOLF STEINER, February 6, 1917

THE BULL HURLS A THUNDERBOLT

Julie Humphreys

Uranus will make its way across the Aries-Taurus cusp in June of this year, marking the end of its sojourn before the stars of the Ram. As Uranus crosses the starry threshold from one zodiacal sign to another, as it will in June, it follows a rhythm that is known deep within our souls: the seven-year period. Each period of seven years—within the unfolding of the human biography, or the time spent by Uranus in each zodiacal constellation—announces the possibility of a new level of spiritual growth.

The tempo of Uranus represents a unique intersection of time and space. For within the number seven dwells the mystery of time—the seven zodiacal epochs within the seven Great Epochs within the seven *manvantaras* of Earth evolution, the seven days of the week, and the seven days that separate each phase of the Moon. The number twelve bears the mystery of space: the twelvefold division of the zodiac, which is eternal in nature, unchanging over time. Thus does Uranus signify a link between the temporal and the eternal.

First identified by telescope in March 1781, Uranus leads us outward beyond the confines of the seven classical planets (i.e., those visible to the naked eye). Steiner connected the stages of Earth evolution to the planetary spheres of those planets known in antiquity. Whether Uranus, Neptune, and Pluto existed *prior to* the start of Earth evolution—or whether, as Steiner said,[1] they attached themselves to our planetary system at a later time, we know for certain that they represent something *completely different*.

An intimate experience of the influence of Uranus can be known when we compare its movement at any given time to a birth chart. (This is called a *transit*.) As Uranus moves counterclockwise around the zodiac over the course of our lives—its orbit takes 84 years—it spends seven years in each of the twelve, equal, astrological houses. Experiencing the influence of Uranus this way is *very personal*. For example, when Uranus transits the 1st house, we feel driven to free ourselves of "old" expectations, whether self-imposed or not. However, this transit can affect one person decades before it affects another. For two individuals to be "in sync" vis-à-vis the transiting house placement of Uranus, they must share (or nearly share) the same Ascendant degree at birth.

Yet, we know that there exists a *collective* experience of Uranus as well, an experience that can be felt by way of its zodiacal sign. While we cannot describe this influence of Uranus as "generational" (in the way that slow-moving Pluto's is), we might characterize it as a sort of "cultural pulse." As Uranus moves through the signs, it calls forth something within us—and within our culture—that might draw us closer to the spiritual world. For Uranus, like Neptune and Pluto, is part of the *transcendental realm*.

The transcendental planets call us toward cosmic intelligence (Uranus), cosmic harmony (Neptune), and cosmic life (Pluto). But to get there, we must first cross three abysses that could be characterized as aspects of the Antichrist. As such, they are, by their very nature, evil. Robert Powell describes them as *electrified thinking* (Uranus), *magnetized feeling* (Neptune), and *uncontrolled or "atomic" willing* (Pluto).

Unlike the classical planets (which are linked to earthly metals, human organs, and the human chakra system), vestiges of the transcendental planets are trapped in *sub*earthly realms. Robert Powell describes them as *trapped light* (Uranus), *trapped sound* (Neptune), and *trapped life* (Pluto).

---

1 Steiner, *Astronomy and Astrology*, p. 181.

When we doubt the supremacy of the spiritual world over the material, we create an affinity for the fallen Uranus forces, which seek to sever our connection to the World Thoughts. Hence, the *thinking* aspect of the antichrist can gain entry to our souls. When our *feeling* nature lacks love and compassion for our fellows in suffering, we attract the forces of fallen Neptune, which bring to our hearts the black seeds of hatred and cynicism for which the antichrist is known. And when we substitute "Thy will be done" with "My will be done," fallen-Pluto forces can gain a foothold within our souls. The antichrist leaves no one in freedom—it must coerce!

While the movements of the transcendentals can (and do) bring us to our knees, they do so with spiritual purpose: to challenge our attachment to the material world. When we fail to live up to this challenge, transcendental "anvils" seem to rain from the sky. The "thunderbolt" of Uranus renders into rubble human thoughts that stand in violation of divine law, including "coming in our own name." Such thoughts *will* encounter divine reality. If we do not humble ourselves from *within*, it shall be achieved from *without*. The "raging flood" of Neptune has the potential to sweep away even what we feel is most secure. When we are obedient only to our feelings—what we like and don't like—we abandon our conscience, which makes us vulnerable to drowning in Neptune's illusions. Following the eruption of the "volcano" of Pluto, we are offered new, transformative life—but the destruction that precedes this transformation can be very painful indeed. Uranus, Neptune, and Pluto have the power to separate us from what we hold dear. Will we wallow in self-pity, or begin to reorient our whole souls toward spiritual heights?

Planets act as interpreters of the holy living creatures of the zodiac. Each planet allows us a unique glimpse into the mysteries of the zodiacal signs, whose lofty qualities would otherwise be beyond our understanding—much like the way that the nine hierarchies of Angels "step down" the radiance of the Godhead to make it knowable to humankind.

Uranus gives us a heightened sense of what is reaching toward us from the future, and it engenders imaginative, revelatory visions of that future. As it reveals the falsehoods that dwell in the dusty corners of the soul, it awakens us to Truth. It demands (and ultimately gets) *humility*. When understood as the bearer of an aspect of the antichrist, Uranus leads us to the *thinking* nature of this loveless being. Evil thoughts share an electric quality. And in the same way that electric light mimics the light of the Sun, Uranus can draw us into the misapprehension that earthly intelligence surpasses whatever thoughts—if any!—might exist in the cosmos.

The Uranian temptation for humankind is *the urge to seek recognition and adulation*, whereby we set ourselves above others. Whether or not this temptation will find fertile soil within our souls is entirely up to us. We are free to resist it, or to give in to its allure.

To better understand the influence and power of Uranus, our finest guide lies within the sixteenth letter-Arcanum of the Tarot, which bears two names "La Maison Dieu" (The House of God) and "The Tower of Destruction." Tomberg described its study as a *school of humility*.[2] He wrote: "[He] who builds a 'tower' to replace revelation from heaven by what he himself has fabricated, will be blasted by a thunderbolt—i.e., he will undergo the humiliation of being reduced to his own subjectivity and to terrestrial reality."[3]

When we doubt (or are unaware of) the reality of cosmic law—which reveals us to be the fools that we are—we essentially claim that to find wisdom, we need look no further than a human intellectual construct or system, known esoterically as a "tower." The tower depicted in the card was constructed as a *representation* of truth (a "house of God"). Whether its creators simply believed in their false promises, or intended to lead others astray, we don't know. Its crenellated top (which is being upset by the "fire from above") resembles a crown—one that is *not* representative of divine authority, but, instead, of *self-aggrandizement*.

---

2 Anon., *Meditations on the Tarot*, p. 447.

3 Ibid., p. 444.

The thunderbolt is the consequence of seeking to conquer heaven by means of forces acquired and developed on the Earth.[4] In doing so, *it liberates us from lies.*

URANUS AND THE ZODIAC

What does it mean to cross this cusp?[5] Through the forces of Aries we become upright, intelligent beings, which gives us dominion over the rest of creation. Taurus bestows upon us the ability to listen and to speak—thereby allowing us to exchange our ideas with others.

In terms of the various parts of the human body that are built up by way of archetypes that dwell within the zodiacal stars, we move from the head (Aries) to the throat (Taurus). Aries is set aflame by ideals (the highest of which is the creative fire of love) and, like Uranus, demands independence. Taurus, bearing a deep connection to nature, is the builder of the zodiac and determines (by way of rational thinking) the stable structures here on Earth on which these ideals might be "built." Aries, ruled by Mars, is prone to impulsiveness, while Taurus (ruled by Venus) does not like to be hurried—knowing as it does that the digestion of ideas requires time. Aries is particularly attuned to what is *right;* Taurus responds most strongly to *beauty.* Lastly, the creative, active Sun finds its exaltation in fiery Aries, whereas the reflective, contemplative Moon does so when in earthy Taurus.

We might imagine that Uranian "lightning" finds a greater affinity for the fire signs (Aries, Leo, Sagittarius) and air signs (Gemini, Libra, Aquarius) of the zodiac—those deemed "masculine"—than it does for the earth signs (Taurus, Virgo, Capricorn) and water signs (Cancer, Scorpio, Pisces)—the "feminine" signs. Jacques Dorsan, the great French sidereal astrologer, went so far as to characterize Uranus's passage through the masculine signs as the seven fat cows of the Pharaoh's dream, and its passage through the feminine signs as the seven gaunt cows of the same dream (Gen. 41:17–21). His thesis is supported by the remarkably disproportionate number of wars that have occurred when Uranus was moving before the stars of the earth and water constellations of the zodiac.[6] I cannot refute it.

We'll turn now to the last three passages of Uranus across this cusp. The first occurred in 1772; the second in 1856; and the third in 1940. (This means that, during the seven years prior to these dates, Uranus was in Aries; during the subsequent seven years, it was in Taurus.) Regarding the current cycle, Uranus first moved before the stars of Aries in April 2017, and will move before the stars of the Bull in June 2024. Our theme is an American one, for the dates shed light upon the beginnings of three grave military conflicts in the United States: The Revolutionary War, the Civil War, and World War II. Uranus thus leads us through the life stages of the constitutional republic of the Unites States—*creation* (Revolutionary War), *consolidation* (Civil War), *expansion* (World War II), and *likely demise* (currently).

Keep in mind that the *archetypes* of the zodiacal signs present us with a perfect unity (the "circle of twelve"), whereas the *qualities* of each sign plant seeds that might be nurtured in the others. If we are set afire by love and individual freedom, and thus devote ourselves to its cultivation (Aries), our conscience might be awakened (Taurus) to all that bears *eternal value.* Alternatively, if we feed our own narcissism (which has no regard for others), "Thy will" won't be done on Earth as it is in heaven. Lastly, we might say that the cynicism that so aptly characterizes the fallen forces of the Ram—whether such cynicism reflects an absence of ideals or, instead, the presence of evil ones—encourages in turn the apathy that so effectively diminishes the nobility of the Bull.

---

4 Ibid., p. 442.

5 The transcendentals cross any zodiacal cusp three times: when moving forward (direct), when moving backward (retrograde), and when resuming forward motion. For simplicity and clarity, all dates of these crossings will hereafter refer to Uranus's *first* entry to Taurus.

6 Dorsan, *Retour au Zodiaque des Étoiles: Vous n'êtes pas né sous le signe que vous croyez* [*Return to the Stellar Zodiac: You're not the sign you think you are*], pp. 231–237.

This article examines the historical impact of Uranus's passage across the Aries-Taurus cusp, which can be characterized as a transition from a period of enlivened idealism to one of the execution of these ideals. Unfortunately, such execution has brought the United States to war time and time again. We have, as of yet, proven ourselves unable to find another way.

Additionally, we'll be exploring the significance of Uranus's alignment with the two stellar standouts in the constellation of Taurus—the star cluster known as the Pleiades, and *Aldebaran* (the "star-eye" of the Bull). Let's begin!

1772: CREATION

Uranus in Aries: 1765–1772

Uranus in Taurus: 1772–1779

Conjunct the Pleiades: Boston Tea Party

Conjunct *Aldebaran*: The Declaration of
Independence

Only a virtuous people are capable of freedom. As nations become more corrupt and vicious, they have more need of masters.

— BENJAMIN FRANKLIN

The French and Indian War (1754–1763) raged between New France (now part of Canada) and the British North American territory (the colonies as well as part of what it now known as the Maritimes). The prize was the great North American continent, and the French and the British, each aided by their numerous Native American allies, fought savagely to maintain and expand their presence there. Although the British forces outnumbered those of the French by a factor of 300, the latter garnered far greater support from the Native Americans and, as such, posed an existential threat to the colonies themselves.

The "Join, or Die" cartoon of 1754 (attributed to Benjamin Franklin) that rallied for shared purpose among the colonies against the French-Indian threat, assumed a new meaning in the decade that followed: independence from the British Crown.

Once the war was behind them, the colonists began to chafe under British rule, whose grip tightened in the 1760s. Parliament passed various

JOIN, or DIE.

revenue-raising measures (the Townshend Acts and the Stamp Act, to name a few) that required the colonists to fund the administration of their oppressors in the colonies—while, of course, denying them representation in their Parliament. The Quartering Act (1765) was a particular indignity because it demanded the housing and feeding of British soldiers. Boycotts were somewhat successful, but they ultimately resulted in a greater presence of the British soldiers whom they so resented. As the British increasingly lacked the "consent of the governed," resistance grew. The year 1770 brought the Boston Massacre, when British soldiers fired into a mob that had surrounded one of their own. When British reinforcements came, the mob began hurling snowballs, then stones. Five were killed in retaliation, after which the soldiers were ultimately acquitted of any crime.

The colonial pot was near a full boil! And although the colonists shared the Aries virtue of independence and a deep respect for the sovereign freedom of the individual, they were yet to find an effective strategy for the realization of these ideals.

The movement of Uranus into Taurus in June of 1772 brought change. It coincided with the burning of the British customs schooner *Gaspee* in Narragansett Bay, Rhode Island. After the *Gaspee* had run aground in the tidal shallows, Rhode Island citizens overpowered the crew and set fire to the ship. Its destruction was one of the first violent uprisings by the colonists, and it served to unite the colonies in a shared purpose: they'd had enough. When, in 1773, British Parliament passed the Tea Act (its dual objective being to support the troubled British East India Company as well as to reduce the quantity of cheaper, smuggled, tea in the colonies), the response was definitive. As Uranus passed before the stars of the Pleiades, hundreds of crates of British tea were dumped into Boston Harbor.

The Boston Tea Party is commonly regarded as the event that set the Revolutionary War in motion. Thereafter, the colonial assembly called for local militia to train and prepare for hostilities, should they occur. The Battles of Lexington and Concord (April 1775) were precipitated by a British effort to capture and destroy colonial gunpowder and armaments stored at Concord. As it happened, through the successful gathering of intelligence, the Patriots were able to move their stores and (as immortalized by Longfellow) alert others to the British plan of attack.

While resisting subjugation is as old as the origin of humanity, the moral foundation upon which the rebellion stood—God-given rights, the consent of the governed—was as broad and as solid as a pyramid's. There also existed among the colonists an undeniable self-interest: a longing to know what they could accomplish as a self-governing people, and an urge for westward expansion that would only be inhibited by the British.

The principles of the founding of the United States are sanctified in the Declaration of Independence (1776), which, like the ideal of resurrection, was "as light coming from the east and shining as far as the west"(Matt. 24:27).[7] It marked the beginning of a glorious pilgrimage that began when the superlative intellectuality of the Founders found inspiration in spiritual ideals. The Declaration was the work of Fools. Howsoever short we've fallen from our original principles, the Declaration of Independence has hung like a blessing over the land for over two centuries, sustaining hope for a better future:

…Mankind are more disposed to suffer, while Evils are sufferable, than to right themselves by abolishing the Forms to which they are accustomed. But when a long Train of Abuses and Usurpations, pursuing invariably the same

Object, evinces a Design to reduce them under absolute Despotism, it is their Right, it is their Duty, to throw off such Government, and to provide new Guards for their future Security.

Drafted by Thomas Jefferson, the Declaration was signed on July 4, 1776, when Uranus was aligned with *Aldebaran,* the Bull's brightest star. Britain demanded its revocation, to no avail: a country was born two months later, when the thirteen colonies became the United States. The first American flag was flown in 1777, the same year that the Articles of Confederation and Perpetual Union became the supreme law of the land until its replacement by the United States Constitution in 1789.

1856: Consolidation

Uranus in Aries: 1849–1856
Uranus in Taurus: 1856–1863
  Conjunct the Pleiades: Bleeding Kansas
    (ongoing)
  Conjunct *Aldebaran*: Lincoln becomes
    President; Rudolf Steiner is born

America will never be destroyed from the outside. If we falter and lose our freedoms, it will be because we destroyed ourselves.
— Abraham Lincoln

The movement of a planet completing cycle after cycle around the zodiac is ideally imagined not as *circular,* but as *helical*—for at the conclusion of each cycle, we have ideally achieved a higher level of understanding and consciousness. Thus, by 1856, the issue of slavery forced the United States to confront its failures in acknowledging the "unalienable rights" of African-born slaves. The "perpetual union" of the United States was plunged into uncertainty, as well it should have been. While a handful of states abolished the practice of slavery during or soon after the Revolutionary War—and while the Northern states had long defied the fugitive slave laws[8]— slavery was a wound that would not heal without moral redress.[9]

7 See Anon., *Meditations on the Tarot,* p. 556.

8 These laws required the return of slaveholders' "property."

9 Britain had abolished the practice in 1833.

Until the Civil War, the matter of slavery was left to the states. Many, like democrat James Buchanan (elected president in 1856) favored keeping it that way. Should the federal government be granted the power to weigh in, however, the number of free states in comparison to that of the slave states would be of great consequence. The westward expansion of the country raised more concerns in the South. Would a transcontinental railroad establish a bond between the Northern states and the West? How would the new territories regard the issue of slavery when they eventually *became* states?

More dry tinder and a lighted match were thrown on the debate in March 1857, when the Supreme Court ruled against Dred Scott, a slave petitioning for his freedom. Indignation in the North matched relief in the South as the soundness of the decision was called into question.

The first battleground for America's soul was Kansas Territory, the geographical "heart" of the continental United States. Known as the *first* American war over slavery, Bleeding Kansas—so-named because of its savage violence—began in 1854. Abolitionists and pro-slavery "border ruffians" alike regarded Kansas Territory as critical to their cause: Whether Kansas would become a free state or a slave state would affect the balance of power in the Senate. Settlers poured into Kansas Territory from both camps.[10] Uranus was conjunct the Pleaides as Bloody Kansas reached its midpoint.

The election of Abraham Lincoln in 1860 brought further unease to the South, whose agricultural economy could not thrive without a large labor force. Lincoln had already expressed his opposition to slavery in the territories outside the states of the Union. Uranus stood before *Aldebaran* as Lincoln was elected to the presidency; one month later, South Carolina seceded from the union, citing a President whose opinions and purposes were "hostile to slavery." Ten states followed suit in 1861, the same year that the confederate States elected Jefferson Davis as their President. The war would soon begin. The words spoken by Lincoln in 1858 foreshadowed the bloodshed to come:

A house divided against itself, cannot stand.

I believe this government cannot endure permanently half slave and half free.

I do not expect the Union to be dissolved—I do not expect the house to fall — but I do expect it will cease to be divided.

It will become all one thing or all the other.

Either the opponents of slavery will arrest the further spread of it, and place it where the public mind shall rest in the belief that it is in the course of ultimate extinction; or its advocates will push it forward, till it shall become lawful in all the States, old as well as new—North as well as South.[11]

The conscience of the country was awakened by an Angel's trumpet that served to restore our memory of *what we had done*. Thus, too, will the conscience of the whole of humanity be resuscitated at the last judgment. Valentin Tomberg (fluent in Greek, Hebrew, and Latin, as well as other languages) points out that the Greek word for judgment is *krisis*. He notes: "Friedrich Schiller said rightly that "the history of the world is the judgment of the world"—i.e., it is a continual crisis, the stages of which are "historical epochs."[12]

On New Year's Day 1863, at the end of this Uranus-Taurus period, Lincoln issued the Emancipation Proclamation, offering perpetual freedom to slaves—but the war was far from over. Exactly six months later, the Union achieved a solid victory at Gettysburg, which was generally regarded as a great turning point in the Union's favor.

10 John Brown was the leading voice in favor of using violence in the abolitionist movement. He fought in Kansas Territory and, after attempting to incite an armed slave rebellion at Harper's Ferry (now West Virginia), was hanged in 1859.

11 Lincoln, "A House Divided," June 16, 1858, Springfield, Illinois.
12 Anon., *Meditations on the Tarot*, p. 585.

1940: Expansion

Uranus in Aries: 1933–1940
Uranus in Taurus: 1940–1947
  Conjunct the Pleiades: Pearl Harbor
  Conjunct *Aldebaran*: D-Day

Men occasionally stumble over the truth, but most of them pick themselves up and hurry off as if nothing ever happened.
  —Winston Churchill

Another level of our American "Uranus spiral" takes us to 1933, when Uranus began its journey through Aries—whereby the idealism that is characteristic of the Ram streamed to Earth by way of our first transcendental planet. Many "towers of destruction" were underway at this time. This was the year that Hitler became Chancellor of Germany, at the head of the Nazi party—a party whose empire (*Reich*) would be built upon their certainty in their racial superiority. Although Hitler's power was tenuous at that time, he had an innate sense of opportunities for the enrichment of his authority. The Reichstag fire that occurred one month after his ascendancy afforded him the ideal occasion to suspend civil rights and to place political enemies under arrest. Before year's end, Jews began to be excluded from civic life, and the doors of Dachau—the first Nazi concentration camp—opened wide.

And yet, something else was happening at the same time: The etheric body of Christ began to surround and permeate the Earth. This is the true "second coming" of Christ. Although this subject is beyond the scope of this article, it can readily be imagined that the rise of Hitler (as well as the concurrent consolidation of Stalin's power) represented a *counteroffensive* to the new presence of Christ. Thus, the set of ideals that we might call "love, mercy, and forgiveness" grew alongside those known by "hatred, and tolerance for human suffering."

Jews, of course, were not the only group in the Reich's crosshairs. The Reich actively pursued the elimination of those with various forms of disability. Furthermore, the eastward expansion of the Reich—a dream dear to Hitler—would require the exportation, extermination, or enslavement of the majority of the non-Aryan populations of Central and Eastern Europe.

Weary from World War I, the British wanted—above all—to avoid another war. In any case, aside from Winston Churchill, there was little evidence that those in the British ruling class could foresee—or had the will to resist—Hitler's plans.

Initially, it was the hope of the United States to stay well out of the war brewing in Europe. The Great Depression slogged on, and there remained a deep imprint of the futility of the last World War—even though American casualties in WWI were dwarfed by those of France and Britain.[13] Common sense revolted against trench warfare and the inability of anyone (save Rudolf Steiner) to explain the reason for the war with any clarity.

During Uranus's final months in Aries, the United States maintained its neutrality as Hitler invaded Poland in 1939, and Paris in May 1940. It remained neutral still throughout most of the German air assaults over Britain. The British had made it through the Blitz with the pluck and "stiff upper lip" that were characteristic of them at that time. Although the physical damage wrought by the Germans was enormous, the British lost neither their willingness nor their ability to fight.

With the passage of the Lend-Lease Act in 1941, Congress agreed to provide the Allies, including the Soviet Union, with huge amounts of materiel—but the United States would not go to war in Europe. A more immediate threat lay across the Pacific.

Following its victory in the Spanish-American War in 1898, the United States acquired Spain's Pacific territories. (These included the Philippines and Guam. Concurrently, the United States claimed Hawaii as an American territory under quite different circumstances.) This westward expansion across the sea brought the Americans into direct conflict with the colonial dreams of

---

13 By a factor of 35.

Japan. Already in possession of Taiwan, Korea, and Manchuria, Japan's intention was to unify and dominate a large bloc of Asian states that could withstand Western interference as well as provide Japan with the critical natural resources (such as oil) that it lacked. Known as the Greater East Asia Co-Prosperity Sphere (GEACPS), Japan proposed to rule its occupied territories. Achievement of this "co-prosperity" depended upon aggressive expansion into the Pacific; therefore, it was essential for Japan to create a large buffer between Asia and the United States.

And there was another American matter that had bothered Imperial Japan. In 1937, during the Japanese invasion of Nanking (now Nanjing), three American tankers navigated the Yangtze River to rescue Americans and Chinese fleeing the savage atrocities of what was known as the Rape of Nanking. The *USS Panay*, a gunboat accompanying the tankers, was bombed by the Japanese; survivors treading water were strafed. The Japanese were forced to apologize publicly.

The United States was not at war in the early hours of December 7, 1941—at which time Uranus was aligned with the Pleiades. Shortly after sunrise, Japanese Zeroes, dive bombers, and torpedo bombers flew over Pearl Harbor, hoping to destroy the American fleet. (Before another day had passed, Japan would attack Midway Island, the Philippines, Guam, Wake Island, and Hong Kong.) The imperial hope was to damage the American fleet so severely that capitulation would quickly follow. Instead, the attack on Pearl Harbor was the event that found the United States— perhaps buoyed by the miraculous absence of their aircraft carriers from the harbor that morning—enthusiastically picking up the gauntlet thrown down by Imperial Japan. America had avoided war until it could do so no longer. Once Germany declared war on the United States four days later, the American military had been called to duty across the two greatest oceans of the world. Their military presence would span a full two-thirds of the longitudes of the globe.

Despite the shroud of death, the period of the war *before* the US dropped atomic bombs on

Hiroshima and Nagasaki (August 1945) remains an uplifting period of its history. Clarity of purpose and reports of extraordinary acts of bravery and sacrifice heartened the American soul. The Battle of Midway (June 1942) and the music of Aaron Copland's ballet, *Rodeo*—which debuted a few months later—arouse similar feelings in the author, for one: pride in their unique *Americanness*, optimism, a willingness to do what's needed when under duress. The passage of Uranus across the Aries-Taurus cusp in 1940 represents a pivotal year in the destiny of the United States—one that is an echo of the previous two cycles. During these Aries years (1933–1940), America had to come to terms with what it stood for; once Uranus reached the stars of the Bull, what needed to be done and what must be sacrificed in service of these ideals was revealed. To end Hitler's genocidal campaign, and to restore self-government to those deprived of it, they had to fight. When Uranus reached Aldebaran, the Allies stormed the beaches at Normandy (June 6, 1941), thereby turning the war in their favor.

How did the notion of expansion creep into the American psyche in the years leading up to the German invasion of Poland in September 1939? Had American expansion been a gleam in FDR's eye all along? Opinions differ. By 1945, the war had taken a heavy toll on Britain, whose citizens suddenly seemed to stop believing in themselves. Britain lost Singapore to Japan in 1942; there were revolts and unrest in African colonies; and India, the jewel in Britain's imperial crown, would gain independence in 1947.

After World War II, the imperial void left by Britain was filled by the United States. Morale in America at that time was very high. In 1947, the first "Levittown" appeared on the American landscape, just in time for the publication of Benjamin Spock's guide to baby and child care. This expansive mood allowed the United States to assume a more influential role worldwide, for good or ill. Wars have since expanded in number and scope. Indeed, they seem never to end. Perhaps (as Robert Powell has suggested) the release of atomic bombs—"Little Boy" and

"Fat Man"—over mainland Japan so damaged the Earth's crust that the evil, subearthly forces therein began rise and engulf humanity.

2024: LIKELY DEMISE

Uranus in Aries: 2017–2024
Uranus in Taurus: 2024–2031
   Conjunct the Pleiades: Jul-Nov/2025
   Conjunct *Aldebaran*: May/2029–Jan/2030

The ceremony of innocence is drowned:
The best lack all conviction, while the worst
Are full of passionate intensity.

                  —W. B. YEATS

In *The Fate of Empires* (1913), British author Sir John Glubb presented a theory that the average life of an empire is 250 years. (The United States will turn 250 years in 2026.) His conclusion was supported by historical examples that span nearly three millennia. Perhaps decadence will always nip at the heels of prosperity.

The current Uranus-Aries cycle began in 2017 and is bookended by the two great American solar eclipses (Aug. 21, 2017 and Apr. 8, 2024). This seven-year period bears an especially eerie quality. These eclipses have been so named because their totality will have been experienced *only* in the continental United States. Furthermore, the paths of the two eclipses form a foreboding "X" across the American landmass. It is no coincidence that during the intervening years we experienced the egregious suspension of human rights in the name of "public health."

Robert Powell, consistent with indications by Steiner and others, has advanced the compelling idea that the United States is where the unique incarnation of the antichrist would occur. This event, which was destined to last three and a half years (Rev. 13:5)—nearly equal to the 1,290 days between Christ's Baptism and his crucifixion—is not an "incarnation" in the sense of a birth into the world. Instead, it signifies the temporary *entry of the antichrist into a human vessel.* It is the estimation of this author that this unholy incarnation has come and gone, and that the whirlwind we

see around us—cultural, economic, political—is its inescapable consequence.

The symbolism inherent in a solar eclipse is the darkening our higher nature (Sun) by materialism and intellectualism (the Moon). Steiner was quite clear. During a solar eclipse, humanity's unbridled will-instincts flow into the cosmos in an abnormal way; instead of meeting the purifying light of the Sun, they are *scattered.* Therefore, during a solar eclipse, it is incumbent upon us to summon our own Sun consciousness (our "I") in order to "burn" what the eclipsed Sun cannot.

The higher nature of the United States has indeed been darkened during this Uranus-Aries period. Consistent with Benjamin Franklin's quote regarding the link between virtue and freedom, America lost a terrifying amount of both between 2017 and 2024. We are, as Lincoln warned, being destroyed from within. We don't yet know if the rot can be expunged—or if trying to do so will mean war.

The revolutionaries of the past decades, who wanted to "stick it to the Man," have *become* "the Man." Indeed, those who used to demand peace now demand war. In little more than a decade, they have transformed government agencies into departments of terror, accountable to no one. Inequal application of the law, disregard of the law altogether, persecution or imprisonment of political enemies, censorship—the U.S. as a whole is now a police state. Every imaginable diversity is promoted except the one on which our freedom depends: diversity of thought.

As Lenin and Stalin knew well, when there is no God, there can be no God-given rights, no right and wrong. Hence those who prey upon our children today are given a "voice" in the culture. We are not only failing to protect our children from this demonic culture—we offer them as sacrifices upon its godless altar. Those parents who want only to raise and educate their children as they see fit are labeled domestic terrorists. Because the state worships no God that *we* know, the American culture has abandoned virtue entirely. The arts no longer uplift; they intentionally debase.

Late-14th-century French tapestry:
Satan giving power to the Beast

The ideals engulfing the United States (and much of the world) are ideals of evil—subjugation, coercion, violence, hatred, and defilement. As Uranus crosses the Aries-Taurus cusp this year, those who name this evil will be forced to separate from those who refuse to do so.

Do not be disheartened! Let us remember that hatred and indifference are not creative forces in the world—love is. Let us remember what is of *eternal value*: devotion, inner balance, perseverance, self-sacrifice, compassion, courtesy, contentment, patience, self-discipline, courage, discretion, magnanimity. Let us love the future as much as we love the past! Divine will is not done on Earth as it is in heaven *unless we pray for it*.

"The mission to which his birth called him [the birth of Jacob, the Old Testament patriarch] was revealed to him through the realm of the angels...conscious perception of the angels came to him.... The first stage...is attained when one enters conscious interaction with the beings of the angelic hierarchy.... [This] does not involve knowledge of universal laws, but entering conscious interaction with the beings who know the mysteries of birth. The true horoscope will not be reached by a path of calculation but through a path of interaction with suprasensory beings. What angels have imparted to humankind, that is the 'horoscope' in the true sense."

VALENTIN TOMBERG, *Christ and Sophia*, p. 47

INDIVIDUAL SPIRIT BEINGS
AND
THE CONSTANT FOUNDATION OF THE UNIVERSE

Rudolf Steiner

In order to expand on them, I shall today refer back to some of the points we have been considering.[1] For long ages human beings have had thoughts, feelings and impulses to help them find whatever they needed to make progress. But now the signs of the times are telling us that these thoughts, feelings and impulses no longer give us what we require to help us go toward the near future.

Yesterday one of our members showed me last Wednesday's issue of the *Frankfurter Zeitung*. In it there is an article by a very learned gentleman; indeed, he must be exceedingly learned, for his name is preceded by the letters denoting not only doctor of philosophy but also those denoting doctor of theology, and these are in turn preceded by the title of professor. So, this man is very smart indeed. His essay is about all kinds of modern spiritual needs, and it contains the following passage:

> The experience of the beingness that lies behind everything requires neither pious solemnity nor religious evaluation, for it is, in itself, religion. It is not one's own individual content that must be sensed and grasped, but the grand irrationality that lies hidden behind all existence. Those who touch it and cause the divine spark to flash across will undergo an experience that is primeval and prototypical. This unites the one who is having the experience with all that moves in the same stream of life; he is vouchsafed a cosmic sense of life—to use a favorite phrase of recent times.

Forgive me, dear friends. I am not reading this to you in order to awaken any great ideas that might be contained in these wishy-washy sentences but in order to demonstrate a sign of the times: "A cosmic religiosity is in the making among us, and the strength of people's longing for it is demonstrated by the perceptible growth of the theosophical movement that is attempting to discover and reveal the gyrations of that hidden life." It isn't easy to stumble through all these wishy-washy concepts, but they are, are they not, remarkable as signs of the times! The writer continues: "This cosmic piety is not a matter of quietistic mysticism that begins with a rejection of the world and ends in contemplation for it is received among the rolling waves of events and arouses ever new commotion"—and so on.

It really is not possible to make any sense of all this! But since it is preceded by "Professor, DD and PhD," we must surely regard it as something smart; otherwise, we should have to see in it the stammerings and unclear ramblings of a learned gentleman who cannot discern the way forward on the path he is following but nonetheless feels obliged to hint at something that does exist and that appears to him to be not entirely without hope.

We ought not to find anything pleasing in such outpourings, for such outpourings must above all not be allowed to lull us to sleep in the pleasant notion that here, once again, is someone who has noticed that there is, after all, something worthwhile behind the spiritual science movement. It would be very damaging if this were to happen. For those who express such outpourings are sometimes the very ones who feel satisfied by them but who do not press on. In their wishy-washy way they point to something that wants to enter into

---

1 This lecture is part 3 of "Individual Spirit Beings and the Constant Foundation of the Universe," reprinted (with minor revisions) from lecture 7 (Nov. 25, 1917) of the illuminating lecture course, *Secret Brotherhoods and the Mystery of the Human Double* (Rudolf Steiner Press, Sussex, 2011); used by kind permission of the publisher. All rights reserved.

the world yet they remain much, much too idle to embark on any serious study of spiritual science and of what it is that must take hold of human hearts and souls if these realities are to enter the stream of coming existence in ways that will be beneficial. It is of course easier to talk of "rolling waves" and "cosmic feelings" than it is to go more seriously into things that—as the signs of the times demand—must be told to humanity just now. That is why it seems necessary to me to say here what I said and will continue to say in the public lectures, while emphasizing the difference between what is dead and gone with no life left in it but that has led us into the present catastrophic times, and what the human soul must really grasp if any kind of forward step is to be taken.

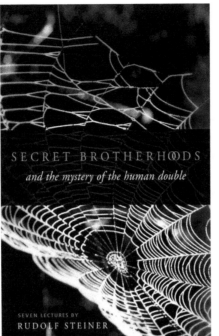

SECRET BROTHERHOODS
and the mystery of the human double

SEVEN LECTURES BY
RUDOLF STEINER

You could hold thousands of congresses, world congresses and peoples' congresses or whatever, involving the old wisdom that has brought humanity thus far; and thousands and thousands of societies could be founded. But it must be clearly understood that these thousands of congresses and thousands of societies will achieve nothing if the spiritual life-blood of the science of the spirit does not flow through them.

What people lack today is the courage to embark properly on researching the spiritual world. Strange though it may sound, it has to be said that a next step could simply be to spread the booklet *Approaches to Anthroposophy* in the widest circles. That would be another way of bringing forward knowledge about the links between human beings and the cosmic order. The booklet draws attention to this knowledge. Attention is drawn to actual facts, such as the way in which the earth changes its states of consciousness year by year. What is said in the lecture and in the booklet is said expressly with the needs of our time in mind. To absorb this would mean more

than all that wishy-washy talk of cosmic feelings or mingling with some "rolling waves" of whatever kind. I have just read these things aloud to you and I cannot repeat them because they are too meaningless in the way they are formulated.

This does not mean that we must not pay attention to these things, for they are important and real. I want to make it clear, though, that we must not create our own fog but should always retain the utmost clarity if we want to work for the spiritual science of anthroposophy.

Once again, I want to remind you that during this fifth post-Atlantean period the time is approaching when humanity will be having to deal very carefully with certain great life questions that have thus far been hidden, in a way, by the wisdom of former times. I have already pointed this out. One of these great life questions can be described as follows. Endeavors are to be undertaken to place the spiritually etheric element in the service of external, practical life. I have already pointed out that the fifth post-Atlantean period will have to solve the problem of how the temper of the human soul, the flow of human moods, can be transmitted to machines in wavelike movements. The human being must be linked with something that has to grow more and more mechanical. A week ago, I spoke of the external way in which a certain part of our earth is taking this mechanization. I gave the example of how the American way of thinking is trying to spread mechanical principles to include human life itself. I spoke of the rest-breaks that are to be used to enable a specific number of workers to load not fewer tons but up to fifty tons. All that is needed for this is to introduce Darwin's principle of selection into life.

At such places there is the will to harness human energy with mechanical energy. It would be quite wrong to think that we should try to prevent these things, for they will happen, they will come about. The only question is whether they will be brought about as a part of human evolution by people who are selflessly familiar with the great goals of earthly evolution and will do them in ways that are beneficial to humanity, or whether they will be brought about by those groups of people who only want to make use of them egoistically or solely for the sake of their own group. It is not *what* is done that matters in this instance; the *what* will happen anyway. The important thing here is the *how*—how these things are tackled. The *what* will happen in any case, because the *what* is intrinsic in earthly evolution. Welding together human nature with mechanical nature will be a great and significant ongoing problem for the remainder of earthly evolution.

Recently I have often very deliberately pointed out, also in public lectures, that human consciousness is linked with the forces of destruction. Twice in public lectures in Basle I have said, "We die into our nervous system." These forces, these forces of dying away will grow ever stronger and stronger. Connections will be created between the human being's forces of dying away—which are related to electrical, to magnetic forces—and external mechanical forces. People will be able in a certain way to steer their intentions and their thoughts into the mechanical forces. As yet undiscovered forces in the human being will be discovered, forces that work on external electrical and magnetic forces.

That is the one question—linking the human being with mechanisms, this being something that will gain ground more and more in the future. Another problem is the matter of calling on spiritual conditions for help. This will only be possible when the time is ripe and when a sufficient number of individuals will have been prepared for this in the right way. But it must happen eventually that the spiritual forces are mobilized to have control over life in relation to sickness and death.

Medicine will be made spiritual, very, very spiritual. But caricatures of this will also be created by a certain quarter. These caricatures, however, will only serve to show what must actually come about in reality. Once again, as with the other problem,

this matter will be taken up in an external, egoistic way by individuals or groups.

A third matter is the introduction of human thinking into how the human race comes into being through birth and conception. I have pointed out that congresses about this have already been set up, and also that in future there will be a materialistic elaboration of the science concerned with conception and how man and woman are harnessed together. All these things point to significant developments. Today, it is still all too easy to ask why those who know about these things in the right way do not put them into practice.

In future it will be possible to reach an understanding of what is involved in the practical application of these things and to see what forces are still at work just now putting obstacles in the way of developing a spiritualized science of medicine, for example, or of economics. One cannot do more today than speak about these things until people have understood them sufficiently, those individuals, namely, who will want to take them up in a selfless way. Many believe they can already do these things; but many life factors still prevent such a thing, and these can only be overcome by allowing an ever deeper understanding to gain ground and by renouncing, for a while at least, any direct efforts at practical application on a larger scale.

In all these matters it has to be said that not much remains now of whatever existed behind the old, atavistic endeavors carried on up to the fourteenth or fifteenth centuries. Today people talk a lot about ancient alchemy, remembering the process of producing the homunculus and so on. Most of what is said misses the mark. A time will come when people will understand what is meant by the Homunculus scene in Goethe's Faust. But since the sixteenth century these things have been shrouded in mist; awareness of them has receded.

The law governing these things is the same law that determines the rhythmical alternation of waking and sleeping in the human being. Just as a human being cannot disregard sleep, so could humanity, where spiritual development is concerned, not avoid the sleep in matters of spiritual science that characterizes the centuries since the sixteenth century. Humanity had to go to sleep spiritually so that spirituality could reappear in a new form. One simply has to come to terms with such necessities. But we must not be downcast about them. We must realize that the time has now come to wake up, that we can participate in working at this awakening, that events often precede knowledge, and that we will fail to comprehend the events going on all around us if we do not make the effort to gain the knowledge.

I have repeatedly mentioned that certain groups of people working in egoistically occult ways are making efforts in certain directions. Initially it was necessary for a specific kind of knowledge to retire into the background for humanity—knowledge nowadays given incomprehensible names such as alchemy or astrology and so on. This knowledge had to disappear, be slept through, so that people no longer had the possibility of drawing soul qualities out of their observations of nature but were instead more thrown back on themselves. So that human beings could awaken the forces of their own being it was necessary for certain matters to appear first in an abstract form that must now take on a concrete spiritual form.

Three ideas have gradually been given form over the course of recent centuries, ideas that are abstract in the way they have come among human beings. Kant wrongly called them: God, freedom and immortality. Goethe rightly called them "God, virtue and immortality."

What is encompassed by these three words is now rather abstract, whereas in the fourteenth or fifteenth century it was more concrete, but in the old atavistic sense also more physical. People experimented in the old way, endeavoring in alchemical experiments to observe processes that revealed the working of God. They tried to produce the philosophers' stone.

There is something concrete behind all these things. The philosophers' stone was supposed to help the human being become virtuous, although this was thought of in a more material sense. It was also intended that it should make people able to experience immortality by placing themselves

in a relationship with the cosmos that would let them experience what lies beyond birth and death. All the wishy-washy ideas people use today in their effort to grasp these things no longer fit with what was striven for in those days. Things have become abstract, and modern humanity talks about abstract ideas. People try to comprehend God by means of abstract theology, and virtue, too, as something wholly abstract. The more abstract the idea, the more does modern humanity like talking about these things. The same goes for immortality. People speculate about what could be immortal in the human being. In the first Basle lecture I spoke of today's science of philosophy being a starved science, an undernourished science in the way it deals with questions such as immortality. This is only a different description of the abstract way in which these things are striven for nowadays.

Certain brotherhoods of the West, however, have preserved the connection with the old traditions and are trying to apply it in ways that will place it at the service of a kind of group egoism. These things must be pointed out. Of course, when this quarter in the West mentions these things in public, exoteric literature it also talks of God, virtue or freedom, and immortality in the abstract sense. But those in the circles of initiates know that all this is speculation and that it is all abstract. Among themselves, they look for something much more concrete in the abstract formulations of God, virtue and immortality. So, in the schools in question these words are translated for the initiates.

God is translated as gold, and they seek to fathom the question of the mystery of gold. For gold—the representative of what is sunlike within the earth's crust—is indeed something that embodies an important secret. In the material sense, gold relates to other substances as the thought of God relates to other thoughts. The crucial thing is how this mystery is interpreted.

This is connected with the way these groups egoistically make use of the mystery of birth. They try to attain a genuinely cosmic understanding. But in recent times human beings have replaced this cosmic understanding with an understanding that is totally earthly. If they want to study how, for example, the embryo of an animal or human being develops, they point their microscope at what is present at the location on the earth where they are looking through that microscope. They regard this as the thing they should be studying. But this cannot be the case. They will discover—and certain circles are very near to making this discovery—that the forces at work are not to be found in what they are examining through their microscope but that these forces come in from the cosmos, from the constellation in the cosmos. When an embryo comes into being, it comes into being because cosmic forces streaming from all the directions of the cosmos are at work in the living creature inside of which the embryo is forming. What will arise when fertilization takes place will depend on which cosmic forces are active during the fertilization.

Something will have to be understood that is not understood as yet. Suppose you have a living creature, a hen, shall we say. When a new life arises within this living creature, the biologist focuses his observation on how the egg is growing out of the hen. He investigates the forces that he supposes are making the egg grow out of the hen herself. This is nonsense. The egg does not grow out of the hen for she is merely the foundation. Forces ray in from the cosmos and generate the egg on the ground prepared for it within the hen. But the biologist imagines that the forces in question are situated at the spot he is examining through his microscope, whereas what he is seeing is something that depends on the forces of the stars working together in a specific constellation at a certain spot. The truth of the matter will only be discovered when the cosmic forces are discovered, namely, that it is the cosmos that conjures the egg into the hen.

All these things are connected above all with the mystery of the sun, and from the earthly point of view with the mystery of gold. What I am putting forward today is no more than a schematic hint, but as time goes on these matters will become much clearer.

In the schools that have been mentioned virtue is not spoken of as virtue but as health. Here the

endeavor is to find out what cosmic constellations are involved when human beings recover their health or fall ill. By getting to know the cosmic constellations one also finds out about the different substances in the earth's surface, fluids and so on, that are in their turn linked to health and sickness. From a particular quarter a more material form of health science will be developed that will, however, rest on a spiritualistic foundation.

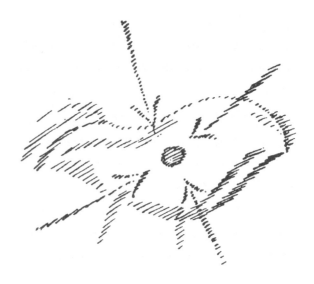

The concept to be disseminated from that quarter is that people do not become good through learning all kinds of ethical principles in the abstract but through taking, let us say, copper under a specific constellation, or arsenic under another constellation. You can imagine how these things can be utilized for the egoistic intentions of certain groups to gain power! Simply by not disseminating such knowledge to others, who are then prevented from participating, one has at one's disposal the best means of controlling great masses of the population. Without making any mention of something like this one could, for example, introduce a new kind of snack. This new snack, duly adulterated, could then be marketed. Such things can be done when one conceives of these matters in a materialistic way. One must simply be aware that everything material is filled with the workings of spirituality. Only those who know that in the true sense of the word nothing material exists, but only what is spiritual, can plumb the mysteries of life.

In a similar vein there is the matter of bringing the question of immortality into materialistic channels. This matter of immortality can be brought into materialistic channels in similar ways, by utilizing the cosmic constellations. This does not lead to the attainment of what is often speculated to be immortality, but it does bring about another kind of immortality. Since it is not yet possible to work on the physical body as a way of artificially extending life, one prepares to undergo certain experiences in the soul that will enable one to remain within the lodge of brothers even after death when one can help out with the forces that are then at one's disposal. So in those circles, immortality is referred to simply as life-extension.

Outward signs of all this are already to be seen. Perhaps some of you noticed the book *Der Unfug des Sterbens* (Death is a nonsense) that came over from the West and made quite a sensation for a time. Such things are all pointing in that direction, but they are only a beginning, for anything that reaches beyond the beginning is still being stored up for egoistic group activities and kept as something very esoteric. These things are possible if they are brought into materialistic channels, if the abstract ideas of God, virtue and immortality are turned into the concrete ideas of gold, health and life-extension, if the great questions of the fifth post-Atlantean period I mentioned earlier are used to further the purposes of group egoism.

What that professor and doctor of theology and doctor of philosophy termed "cosmic feeling" in a wishy-washy way is already being presented by many—also unfortunately in many cases in an egoistic sense—as the cosmic knowledge of the human being. Whereas for centuries science has paid attention only to things that work side by side on the earth and has avoided any glance toward the most important element that comes in from outside the earth, what will happen now in the fifth post-Atlantean period is that specifically those forces that come in from the cosmos will be put to use. And just as the most important thing for biology professors now is to have microscopes that provide the greatest possible degree of enlargement and laboratory procedures

that are most appropriate, in future, when science has become spiritual, the important thing will be whether certain processes are put in train in the morning or the evening, or at midday; or whether what one has done in the morning can be further influenced by what works in the evening or whether it excludes or paralyses the cosmic influence of the morning until the evening.

Of course, much water will still flow down the Rhine before the purely materialistic platforms, laboratories and suchlike are handed over to spiritual scientists. But if humanity wants to avoid sinking into complete decadence the work of these laboratories will have to be replaced by another kind of work. For example, in the case of the good that should be attained in the immediate future, certain processes take place in the morning and are then interrupted during the rest of the day. Then in the evening the cosmic streams flow through them again, and the result is then rhythmically preserved until the next morning. In this way, processes take place in which certain cosmic effects are always interrupted during the day and introduced during the morning and the evening. This will call for all kinds of different ways of doing things.

From all this it will be obvious to you that if one is not in a position to take part publicly in these things then all one can do is to speak about them. Those quarters that want to replace God, virtue and immortality with gold, health and life-extension are the very quarters that strive to work with forces that are quite different from the forces of morning and evening processes. I mentioned last time that a certain quarter seeks to remove the impulse of the Mystery of Golgotha from the world by bringing in another impulse from the West, a kind of Antichrist, and that coming from the East the Christ-impulse as it appears in the twentieth century is to be paralyzed by distracting people's attention from the coming of Christ in the etheric realm.

From the quarter that will put forward the Antichrist as the Christ will come endeavors to make use of something that can work through the most material of forces, something that can work spiritually through the most material of forces. More than anything else, that quarter will strive to make use of electricity, especially the earth's magnetism, to bring about effects all over the world. I have shown you how the forces of the earth rise up in what I have termed the human double. People will discover this secret. It will be an American secret to use the earth's magnetism in its duality, the northern and southern magnetism, in order to send controlling forces across the whole earth, forces that work spiritually. Look at the magnetic map of the earth and compare the magnetic map with what I am about to say, namely, the magnetic line where the needle deflects to the east and to the west, and where it does not deflect at all. I cannot now give more than hints about these things.

Spiritual beings are incessantly working in from a specific point of the compass. All that needs to be done is to get these spiritual beings to work in the service of earth existence; and then, since those beings working in from the cosmos are able to mediate the secret of the earth's magnetism, one will be able to fathom that secret. Thereafter, with regard to those three things—gold, health and life-extension—one will be able to work very effectively in the direction of group egoism. It will be a matter of mustering the dubious courage to do these things. And within certain circles this courage will surely be mustered!

Coming from the direction of the east it will be a matter of strengthening what I have already described by also placing in the service of the earth those beings who are streaming down from the opposite direction of the cosmos. There will be a great struggle in the future. Human science will turn to cosmic influences, but it will endeavor to do so in various ways. The task of good, beneficial science will be to find certain cosmic forces that can come into being on the earth through the working together of two cosmic streams arriving from different directions. These two cosmic streams from different directions will be Pisces and Virgo. It will above all be a matter of discovering how what works as sun forces from the cosmos coming from Pisces can combine with what works from the direction of Virgo. This is what

will be good: to discover how from two directions of the cosmos morning and evening forces can be placed in the service of humanity, those coming from the direction of Pisces and those coming from the direction of Virgo.

These forces will be of no interest to those who endeavor to achieve everything by means of the dualism of polarity, through positive and negative forces. The spiritual secrets that on earth can cause the spirit to stream through from the cosmos—with the help of the dual forces of positive and negative magnetism—these spiritual secrets derive from the direction of Gemini. They are the forces of midday. Even in ancient times it was known that this is something cosmic, and scientists today know exoterically that behind Gemini in the zodiac positive and negative magnetism exists in some way.

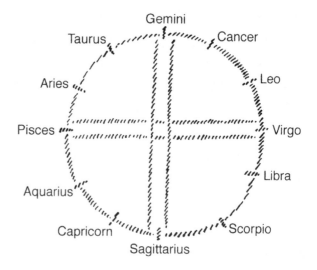

Here it will be a matter of paralyzing what should be won from the cosmos through the revelation of duality, a matter of paralyzing this in a materialistic, egoistic way through the forces that stream to humanity especially from Gemini, forces that can be put to work entirely in the service of the double.

Then there are the brotherhoods who want to bypass the Mystery of Golgotha. They will make use of the human being's dual nature that, now in the fifth post-Atlantean period, contains on the one hand the human being and on the other the lower, animal nature. The human being truly is a centaur in a certain way, for he contains the lower animal nature astrally, and in a way the human part is simply grafted onto this animal nature. Here again we have a duality of forces in the way these two aspects work in the human being. This is a duality of forces that certain egoistic brotherhoods in a more easterly, Indian direction will use to lead also the eastern part of Europe astray, the part of Europe that has the task of preparing for the sixth post-Atlantean period. This dualism makes use of the forces coming from Sagittarius.

What lies in store for humanity is that the cosmic forces will be won for humanity in a dual way that is wrong or a single way that is right. This will bring a genuine renewal to astrology, which is atavistic in its old form—a form in which it cannot continue to exist. Those who know about the cosmos will struggle against one another. Some will make use of the morning and evening processes in the way I have suggested; in the West the midday processes will mostly be used while the morning and evening processes are excluded, and in the East the midnight processes will be used. It will no longer be a matter of making substances only according to the chemical processes of attraction and repulsion, for people will know that the substance will be different depending on whether it is produced by means of morning and evening processes or by midday and midnight processes. They will know that such substances work quite differently on the trinity of God, virtue and immortality, or gold, health and life-extension.

It will not be possible to achieve anything bad by means of a collaboration between what comes from Pisces and Virgo. What will be achieved through these will, it is true, detach the mechanism of life somewhat from the human being, but it will not be a foundation for any kind of power or dominion of one group over another. The cosmic forces brought in from this direction will produce machines that are remarkable—machines that can be labor-saving for people because they will contain a degree of intelligence. And it will be the task of a science of the spirit concerned with the cosmos to ensure that all the great temptations emanating from these machine-animals created by

human beings themselves will be unable to have any damaging influence on them.

Something important must be said in connection with all this. It is essential to prepare for it all by no longer assuming that realities are illusions and by really entering into a spiritual view of the world and gaining a spiritual grasp of the world. Much depends on seeing things for what they are! But we can only see them for what they are if we are able to apply to reality the concepts and ideas given to us by the spiritual science of anthroposophy.

For the remainder of earthly existence, the dead will collaborate with us to a high degree. But how they collaborate will be what matters, for there will be great differences. It will be important that people on the earth behave in such a way that collaboration in a good way with the dead can be allowed, so that the impulse coming from them is also the starting point coming from the spiritual world that the dead themselves experience after death.

There will also, on the other hand, be many attempts to introduce the dead into human life by artificial means. The dead will be brought into human life via a detour through Gemini, which in quite a specific way will cause human vibrations to continue resonating in the machines. The cosmos will then move the machines via the detour I just mentioned.

If these problems arise it will be important to use nothing improper but only those elemental forces derived from nature itself; one must not introduce any improper forces into the life of these machines. In this occult field one must not harness the human being to the mechanism in any way that makes use of the Darwinian theory of selection in connection with human labor as in the example I gave last time.

I am giving you all these hints, which cannot of course exhaust the subject in such a short time, because I am sure you will continue to mull them over and endeavor to build a bridge between them and your own life experiences, especially those we are gaining today in these difficult times. You will see how much clarity you will gain when you look at things in the light of these ideas. It is not a matter now of a confrontation between forces and constellations of forces about which so much is being said in external, exoteric life, for it is a matter of quite other things. What is happening now is that a kind of veil is being drawn over the true impulses we are concerned with. Human forces are at work trying to garner something for themselves. What do they want to garner? Certain human forces are at work defending the impulses that were justifiable impulses up to the time of the French Revolution and were then also represented by certain secret schools; but now the endeavor is to represent them in a retarded, ahrimanic and luciferic form in a way that would maintain a social order thought to have been overcome by humanity since the end of the eighteenth century.

In the main, there are two camps in opposition to each other—representatives of the principle that had been overcome by the end of the eighteenth century and representatives of the present time. Of course, a great number of people instinctively represent the impulses of the present time. So those who are supposed to represent the old impulses of the eighteenth, seventeenth, sixteenth centuries will have to be harnessed by artificial means emanating from certain brotherhoods working to promote their group egoism. The most effective principle of modern times that can be used to extend one's power over the number of people one wishes to use is the economic principle, the principle of economic dependence. But this is merely the tool. The real concern is something quite different. The real concern is what you will have surmised from all the hints I have been giving. The economic principle is connected with all that can be used to make a huge number of people across the earth into a kind of army for these principles.

These are the matters that confront one another, the ones that are really doing battle in the world today. Rooted in the West there is the principle of the eighteenth, seventeenth, sixteenth centuries that makes itself invisible by clothing itself in the phrases of the Revolution, the phrases of democracy, the principle that dons this mask and

is striving to gain as much power as possible. It is advantageous for this principle if as many individuals as possible make no effort to see things as they really are and constantly allow themselves to be lulled by maya, the maya that is expressed in the words: There is a war going on between the Entente and the Central Powers.

In reality there is no such war, and our concern should be for quite other things that are the true reality behind the maya. The battle of the Entente with the Central Powers is merely an illusion. We can reach a conclusion about what is really doing battle if we look behind things and illumine them in the way I am, for certain reasons, only hinting at. One must at least try for oneself not to mistake illusion for reality, and then the illusion will gradually dissolve as far as is necessary. One must try above all to see things as they show themselves to a realistic and unprejudiced view.

If you look at all the things I have been unfolding here, you will find that even a remark I made on the side during these lectures was not as unimportant as it might have seemed. When I said that a remark made by Mephistopheles to Faust, "I see that thou the Devil knowest," would not have been made by him to Woodrow Wilson, this was not an unimportant observation. It was in fact intended to throw light on the situation! One must be able to look at these things without either sympathy or antipathy; they must be seen objectively. One must consider what constellations signify in something that is at work, and what a person's own forces signify. Frequently something entirely different lies behind a person's own forces than what lies behind the mere constellation. Ask yourselves objectively what the value of Woodrow Wilson's brain would be if this brain did not happen to be seated upon the presidential chair of the North American Union. Assume that this brain was situated in a different constellation; that is where it would reveal its own personal force! So, it is the constellation that matters.

Let me put it in the abstract and radically, although not to illustrate the instance I have just mentioned, for I would not do such a thing in this very neutral country. Apart from that instance, consider the important insight that would be revealed if one were to ask whether a certain brain attained its value through being illuminated spiritually in a special way, in the sense I have been describing in these lectures, or whether its value scarcely exceeded the result obtained by placing it in a scale and balancing it against weights in the other scale.

The moment you penetrate fully into all the secrets of the double, whom I mentioned last time, you will find yourself able to assess the value of brains that are merely lumps that you have placed on a scale, lumps that can be brought to life solely by the double.

All these things appear grotesque to people today, but everything that is grotesque about them must come to be seen as perfectly ordinary if certain matters are to be guided from harmful into beneficial channels. There is no point in constantly talking round them! You must come to realize that all the wishy-washy talk of "cosmic religiosity' or "how powerful the yearning for it is" or "the movement that is undertaking to discover and unveil the circulations of life not accessible to the senses" and so on is also nothing other than a means of spreading fog over these matters that ought actually to be entering the world in clarity, which can only work in clarity and that, above all, ought only to be carried in clarity into human life as practical moral and ethical impulses.

I can bring you only certain isolated hints. So I now leave it to your own meditation to build further in these matters. Much is aphoristic but, if you take summaries such as the zodiac I have drawn here and really use them as material for meditation, you will be able to derive a great deal from them.

"Why does a feeling of grandeur, of reverent awe, come over us when we look up into the starry heavens? It is because without our knowing it the feeling of our soul's home awakes in us. The feeling awakens: Before you came down to earth to a new incarnation, you yourself were in those stars, and out of the stars have come the highest forces that are within you. Your moral law was imparted to you when you were dwelling in the world of stars. When you practice self-knowledge, you can behold what the starry heaven bestowed upon you between death and a new birth—the best and finest powers of your soul. What we behold in the starry heavens is the moral law that is given to us from the spiritual worlds, for between death and a new birth we live in these starry heavens. One should contemplate the starry heavens with feelings such as these.... If we then raise our eyes to the starry heavens, we will be filled with a feeling of reverence and will know that this is the memory of the human being's eternal home."

RUDOLF STEINER, *Life between Death and Rebirth*, Nov. 18, 1912

RETURNING TO THE ORIGIN OF THE HOUSES, PART IV
PRACTICAL APPLICATION AND SUMMARY

Joel Matthew Park

One of the occasions on which Rudolf Steiner implicitly makes reference to a clockwise house system was on November 25, 1917, during a lecture published in *Secret Brotherhoods and the Mystery of the Human Double*. During that lecture, he brings this clockwise arrangement of the signs of the zodiac into direct connection with Earth forces, specifically the magnetic fields that emanate from the core and run from pole to pole.[1]

The perceptive reader will notice, however, that there is a slight difference between the arrangement of the signs in relation to north, south, east, and west in the context of this lecture in comparison to other occasions. Normally, Steiner associates east with Aries, west with Libra, north with Capricorn, and south with Cancer. However, in the lecture referring to magnetic currents, he associates east with Pisces, west with Virgo, north with Sagittarius, and south with Gemini—that is, one sign back, in the mutable rather than cardinal signs. Why might this be so?

It is my understanding that it has to do with the focus he puts on magnetism in this article. There are two ways to determine the four directions: true north and magnetic north. True north is constant, and is in relation to the axis of the Earth. Currently we use the Pole Star to find true north; as long periods of time go on, eventually a different star will be the indicator of true north.[2]

On the other hand, magnetic north has to do with the magnetic field of the Earth, which is determined by the magnetism of the Earth's core. As changes occur in the core, the magnetic field also changes. These changes can be so drastic as to flip the magnetic poles of the Earth; scientists currently believe the poles have reversed hundreds of times over long periods of time. According to the spiritual-scientific research of Judith von Halle, there was only one point in time during which the north and south magnetic poles were exactly aligned with true north and south—during the life of Christ.[3] Since that time, they have gradually drifted apart once again, so that now magnetic north is not exactly the same as true north. A compass will point north but not precisely in the direction of Polaris.

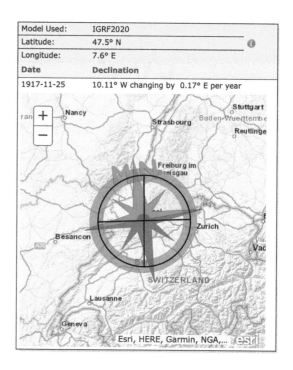

This image indicates the difference between magnetic north and true north at the time and place Rudolf Steiner gave his lecture on November 25,

---

1 This lecture is reprinted in this volume (see the previous article).

2 For a thorough explanation of this, please refer to Powell and Bowden, *Astrogeographia,* chap. 4, "The Foundations of Astrogeographia."

---

3 She indicates this in her recently published work *Das Wort*, not yet translated into English.

1917, in Dornach, Switzerland.[4] We can see here that magnetic north is somewhat to the west of true north; therefore, magnetic south is somewhat to the east of true south. In the normal clockwise house circle, Capricorn is aligned with true north; moving one sign west of Capricorn brings us to Sagittarius—this is the sign of magnetic north, therefore, at that particular time and place. Similarly, this would make Gemini magnetic south, Pisces magnetic east, and Virgo magnetic west.

In order, therefore, to make use of the indications that Steiner gives in the lecture—in terms of taking advantage of the Sun's position in Pisces and Virgo, while avoiding making use of its position in Gemini and Sagittarius—we must understand that he is referring to a clockwise house system specifically in relation to the magnetic poles.

Here at Camphill Village Copake, there are substances being developed using these indications. Our Healing Plant Garden grows ingredients that are then used in anthroposophical medicines; some are treated in relation to the Sun's rising and setting:

> In the Healing Plant in Camphill…we make tinctures for the pharmacy Uriel, and as we know if we want to preserve something there, you…can go the way of preserving, say, arnica root in alcohol, but alcohol has in a way this deadening effect. [But] through Dr. Haushka and a few lectures from Steiner we developed [an alternative] method—for instance harvesting, say, arnica root, and then adding some distilled water, honey and lactose [milk and honey] and then only exposing the substance for two hours at sunrise and two hours at sunset, and then closing it or putting it in a closed peat moss space enduring the other hours of the day. Because we know that Ahriman is most active during the day and Lucifer more at night, and somehow Christ in the morning and evening. So, with this, when you expose the substances for seven days, fourteen times to sunrise and sunset, you can experience that the substance becomes lighter or more ethereal, and also you

can preserve it for several years without adding any preservative. So, you in a way lift this plant substance out of…I don't know how to describe it…but I feel like it has to do with lifting it into the etheric maybe? I don't know…but anyway, this is the rhythm we work with and it seems to work. (personal communication from Andreas Fontein, Aug. 2021)

So, we have in Camphill Village a concrete example of biodynamic gardeners putting Steiner's indications about the clockwise house system to a very effective use in the production of healing remedies for humanity. My intuition tells me that much more could be developed in every realm of culture—religion, art, medicine, economics, agriculture—if we began to engage with the houses in a more conscientious way. I have referred to this way of working with the "inner zodiac" and "inner planets" of the clockwise house system as *ecosophy*.

In this section we look more closely at indications from Manilius regarding each of the twelve houses, including which of the planets finds its home in certain of them.[5] We will keep in mind that, from the perspective I have outlined in the past three sections of this article series,[6] there is an "inner zodiac" radiating from the center of the Earth, whose exact determination is based in large part on the location of the individual human being experiencing it at any given moment in time. This "inner zodiac" of twelve houses has within it "inner planets" moving through the houses; this inner movement is mirrored in the movement of the outer planets from the eastern horizon, to the zenith, to the western horizon, to the nadir, and back to the eastern horizon. And so, in what follows, whenever we refer to a sign of the Zodiac, what we mean in reality is a certain domain of the sky above us in relation to east, west, above and below that is mirroring a reality in the interior of the Earth. Similarly, whenever we refer to planets in what follows, we are

---

4 Generated using the following website: https://www.ngdc.noaa.gov/geomag/calculators/magcalc.shtml.

5 All of these are taken from Manilius, *Astronomica* (Harvard University ed.), pp. 151–158.

6 See *Star Wisdom*, vols. 2–4.

referring to the external planets' positions in relation to east, west, above and below as indicators of the movements of the inner planets within (or perhaps better said, around) this inner zodiac (the core of the Earth). This is the essence of ecosophy in contrast to astrosophy.

To alleviate confusing the inner planets with the outer, or the houses with the zodiac, I propose using the arcane language of the Tarot of Marseilles to designate the names of the twelve houses and ten inner planets. In what follows, I point out these Arcana in relation to Manilius' indications. Additionally, I refer to Rudolf Steiner's indications regarding the twelve worldviews (to which he gives a clockwise arrangement) and the seven "soul moods" that move through them, as well as the indications of Jacques Dorsan, an astrologer I consider to be the authority on the clockwise house system.[7] At times it will seem as though the indications of Manilius, Steiner, and Dorsan have little to do with one another when taken as abstract concepts at face value. However, my hope is that the reader can begin to see the value of using Arcana as designations for the twelve houses and the inner planets that move through them. An Arcanum is multivalent—that is, it can contain a whole variety of meanings within itself, rather than a single, linear interpretation. The Arcanum The Fool, for example, is able to contain within itself all three at once—the indications of Manilius, Steiner, *and* Dorsan regarding the 1st House, as different as they may be once they have been fully crystallized into specific concepts and viewpoints.

We begin with the words of Manilius:

In any geniture, every sign is affected by the sky's division into temples [houses]; position governs the stars, and endows them with the power to benefit or harm; each of the signs, as it revolves, receives the influences of heaven and to heaven imparts its own. The nature of the position prevails, exercises jurisdiction within its province, and subjects to its own character the signs as they pass by, which now are enriched with distinction of every kind and now bear the penalty

of a barren abode. The temple that is immediately above the horoscope and is the next but one to heaven's zenith is a temple of ill omen, hostile to future activity and all too fruitful of bane; nor that alone, but like unto it will prove the abode that with confronting star shines below the occident and adjacent to it. And so that this temple should not outdo the former, each alike moves dejected from a cardinal point with the spectacle of ruin before its eyes. Each shall be a portal of toil; in one you are doomed to climb, in the other to fall.

Here he describes what we would refer to as the 2nd House (above the orient) and 8th House (below the occident) in a clockwise house system—each one a *Porta laboris* (portal of toil). The Arcana symbolizing these two are The Judgement (analogous to Taurus) and Death (analogous to Scorpio).

Rudolf Steiner describes these two as the regions of the worldviews of Rationalism (2nd House) and Dynamism (8th House). Jacques Dorsan describes these two Houses as such:

SECOND HOUSE

Finance and fortune in general, banking, nourishment, material possessions, wealth, income, salaries and remunerations, real estate, agriculture, goods acquired through the subject's personal labors and initiatives; management as well as the qualifications and circumstances that come together to bring about the acquisition of material goods. The subject's financial position as

---

7 Steiner's indications will come from *Human and Cosmic Thought* (CW 151), lectures 3 and 4.

seen from the outside. Possessions and aptitudes that cause them to fructify. Behavior with regards to material goods. Buying power. Personal gains and, consequently, also loss in the case of affliction due to exaggerated overspending or bad management....

EIGHTH HOUSE

Represents profound changes, the main one being death, the circumstances surrounding death and by extension serious illnesses, injuries, and accidents. The world beyond, life after death, spheres that are invisible to the eyes of mortals, the esoteric sciences, and all that is mysterious. Criminology, inasmuch as it is concerned with these matters.

Regeneration, life, and sexual instincts.

The partner's finances, financial clauses in contracts, the marriage partner's fortune, the state of the patrimony after marriage. Inheritances, legacies, wills. Possible advantages arising out of the deaths of those around the subject. Earnings easily procured, hardly without working; annuities, monopolies, privileges, royalties, exclusive commercial rights, private means of income.

Antiques and, generally speaking, all dead things, archaeology, numismatics, philately, and so on.[8]

Note that the Eighth House is the house of death, and bears Death (the 13th Arcanum) as its sigil.

Manilius continues:

Not more fortunate is the portion of heaven above the occident or that opposite it below the orient; suspended, the former face downward, the latter on its back, they either fear destruction at the hands of the neighboring cardinal or will fall if cheated of its support. With justice are they held to be the dread abodes of Typhon, whom savage Earth brought forth when she gave birth to war against heaven and sons as massive as their mother appeared. Even so, the thunderbolt hurled them back to the womb, the collapsing mountains recoiled upon them, and Typhoeus was sent to the grave of his warfare and his life alike. Even his mother quakes as he blazes beneath Etna's mount.

Here Manilius describes the 6th House (above the occident) and 12th House (below the orient), each of them a *Typhonis Sedes,* an Abode of Typhon. The 6th House is represented by the 11th Arcanum (Force, analogous to Virgo) and the 12th House by the 12th Arcanum (the Hanged Man, analogous to Pisces).

Steiner brings these regions into relation with the worldviews of Phenomenalism (6th House) and Psychism (12th House). Dorsan describes these two Houses as such:

SIXTH HOUSE

Sickness and disabilities, notably those contracted through work, hygiene, especially nutrition and all that is related to diet. Worries and the wounds inflicted on one's pride during the course of one's professional life. The psychosomatic troubles that follow on from this.

Professional tasks, all that is ungrateful and imposed therein, carried out without one's own initiative and under the constraints of others, the situation of the officer below the rank of captain. Employees, domestic servants, that is to say, being a part of the house, as well the nature of the relations that are maintained with them. The capacity to serve. Harvests, fruits, savings, and things that have been accumulated. Small animals, especially familiar ones and household pets.

---

8 Dorsan, *The Clockwise House System,* pp. 67–70.

The spouse, be it a man or a woman, and the dominant factors concerning him or her. The best friend and confidant.[9]

TWELFTH HOUSE

Obscurity. The secret and hidden life. Mysterious things and the research that leads to their discovery. Bad habits and vices. Drugs. Worries, hardships, problems, and discontentment. Criminal actions, murder. Despair, self-destructive characteristics that could lead to suicide. However, with the accompanying influence of the spiritual life, there is the courage to react and to surmount the most unfavorable conditions.

Here the two fish of the corresponding twelfth sign are found, one of which lets itself be drawn along by the current, while the other struggles against it and overcomes it.

Detachment from material things, sacrifices and renunciation. Personal evolution, which is acquired either through trials and tribulations or through wisdom, studies, and meditation.

The mystical life, occult sciences, the arts of divination, metaphysics, and their practice.

Obscure occupations, ambushes, snares, and plots. Solitude and exile. Secret enemies. Intrigues, imposters, and treachery. Obstacles and impediments, constraints, and hindrances of all types that could hamper the subject. Lack of liberty, fatality, and free will. People, actions, events, and circumstances that are unfavorable to the subject's destiny. All that is opposed or unknown to one, at least temporarily.

Childbirth. Large animals and ferocious beasts.

The material difficulties of existence, notably unemployment, poverty, restrictions, limitations and deprivations, the reduction of purchasing power, and the string of consequences arising from this, the effects of which are felt within the family circle.

Places where a certain number of people are brought together and where there reigns either a rigid discipline or a sense of the loss of liberty, as in the case of mental asylums, hospitals, clinics, sanctuaries, retreats, boarding schools, certain hostels, convents, and prisons.

Invalidity and accidents. Illnesses that act in an underhanded way and still remain undiagnosed and, consequently, untreated, so that they drain the vital sources. Serious illnesses, which are often chronic and require periods of hospitalization or surgery, thus often leading along the slow path to death, which fully justifies the fact that astrologers call this house "the hell of the horoscope."

Note that there also exists a trap for the interpreter. One has to be extremely skillful, in certain cases, in order to differentiate between the subject who knowingly acts maliciously versus the subject who passively suffers acts of wickedness, which are directed against the person.

Also note that one could find the above list a little long. I do not deny this fact. However, there is not one iota that does not have its basis in the purest tradition as far as the house is concerned. Practice teaches that one of the luminaries or Mercury (the mentality) in a favorable aspect, or one of the benefics placed in this house, brings very great satisfaction and success in the areas that are within its sphere of influence. Men and women of science who have spent their lives in laboratories for the benefit of humankind, great surgeons, and the most gifted sleuths who have saved human lives through their activity, as well as famous esotericists, all owe their success to what they are able to draw from this sector of the horoscope.[10]

Manilius then carries on:

The temple immediately behind the summit of bright heaven, and (not to be outdone by its neighbor) of braver hope, surges ever higher, being ambitious for the prize and triumphant over the earlier temples: consummation attends the topmost abode, and no movement save for the worse can it make, nor is aught left for it to aspire to. There is thus small cause for wonder, if the station nearest the zenith, and more secure than it, is blessed with the lot of Happy Fortune. So most closely does our language approach the richness of Greek and render name for name. In this temple dwells Jupiter: let its ruler convince you that it is to be reverenced.

9 Ibid., pp. 68–69.

10 Ibid., pp. 71–73.

This is his characterization of the 3rd House (the House of *Felix Fortuna* or Happy Fortune) in the clockwise system, represented by the 19th Arcanum (The Sun, analogous to Gemini). Rudolf Steiner brings the 3rd House into relationship with the worldview of Mathematism. Note that Manilius claims that Jupiter is well placed in this House—for Rudolf Steiner, Jupiter is the "mood" of Logicism. It makes total sense that Logic would find its home in the Mathematical understanding of the world, as math is the language of pure logic. In terms of the language of ecosophy (the stars and planets in the center of the Earth), the "planet" in question here is The Emperor, the 4th Arcanum, analogous to cosmic Jupiter; an ideal placement in this case is The Emperor in the House of The Sun.

This is how Dorsan describes the 3rd House:

Intelligence, concrete intellect, common sense, characteristics and preferences of studies, intellectual pursuits and the power of understanding. The desire to be upwardly mobile, the ability to satisfy ambitions, and the professional vocation. Writings, correspondence, paperwork, documents, general meetings and advertising. Transportation, short journeys, and postings. Conferences, exchanges and communications. Blood relatives, brothers, sisters, cousins, as well as neighbors, colleagues and professional associates. Professional and family surroundings. Relationships more of an intellectual than an affectionate nature. Assistance (or lack of) from those who are close.[11]

And how he describes Jupiter in the 3rd House:

The subject is capable of coordinating ideas with actions. A spirit of synthesis allows one to grasp a wide range of matters. One has a sense of hierarchy or natural order—hence, a sense of values. Jupiter bestows good judgment, a broad mind, and an enthusiastic and optimistic character. It is often the sign of high moral values and a careful education. Mental faculties are favored and lead to the pursuit of further studies. Sincerity and courtesy are prevalent, not only in oral expression, but also in written works. One could earn an income through writing; in any case, the heavens promise success through communication.

Success is achieved through the practice of a professional activity corresponding to the chosen vocation. So, if natives of this house follow their dreams and aspirations, their work situation will evolve easily. The result of this will be brilliant social success.

Great profit will be gained during travels, notably those undertaken in lands bordering on the place of birth. A member of the family, possibly a brother, could play a fortunate role in one's career.

As though by a miracle, one could escape unharmed from a car, train, or airplane accident.[12]

Jupiter was in the 3rd house at the time of Christ's crucifixion (from around 12:30 until 3:00 in the afternoon of Good Friday).

Manilius continues in describing the 9th House, opposite the 3rd:

Like this temple, but with an inverse likeness, is that which is thrust below the world and adjoins the nadir of the submerged heaven, and which shines in the opposite region: wearied after completion of active service it is again marked out for a further term of toil, as it waits to shoulder the yoke of the cardinal temple and its role of power: not as yet does it feel the weight of the world, but already

11 Ibid., p. 67.
12 Ibid., p. 120.

aspires to that honor. This seat the Greeks call Daemonie: a rendering of the name in Roman speech is wanting. Lay carefully in your mind the region and the divinity and appellation of the puissant deity, so that hereafter the knowledge may be put to great use. Here largely abide the changes in our health and the warfare waged by the unseen weapons of disease, wherein are engaged the two powers of chance and godhead affecting this region of uncertainty on either side, now for better, now for worse.

Manilius calls this 9th House the House of the Daemonie; it is represented by the 9th Arcanum (The Hermit, analogous to Sagittarius). Steiner brings this region into relationship with the worldview of Monadism.

This is how Dorsan characterizes the 9th House:

Long-distance travel, foreign lands, and all that the native draws from these. Tools and armaments.

Well-thought-out social action. Apostolate and social works.

Long voyages of thought, abstract superior intellect, intellectual speculations, scholarly works, and scientific research. Philosophy, idealism, and law. High aspirations, possible adhesion to moral principles or moral isolation, religious dispositions. Slumber and dreams, contacts with the beyond, astral projection, spiritual experiences, and spiritual evolution.

Above all, it is the father's house, whatever the sex of the subject, whether one is born during the day or at night; it is also the house of the possible spiritual master, of the Guru.[13]

Manilius continues:

The stars that follow midday, where the height of heaven first slopes downward and bows from the summit, these Phoebus nourishes with his splendor; and it is by Phoebus's influence that they decree what ill or hap our bodies take beneath his rays. This region is called by the Greek word signifying God.

And so, the 5th House is the House of God, represented in arcane language by the 10th Arcanum, the Wheel of Fortune (analogous to Leo). Rudolf Steiner brings this region into relation with the worldview of Sensationalism. By Phoebus, Manilius means the Sun, and that the Sun finds its home in the 5th House. In Steiner's terms, the Sun is the mood of Empiricism. Again, it is no surprise that the activity of empiricism would find its home in the realm of sensation. In Arcane imagery, the Sun is the 1st Arcanum, the Magician. And so, we find the Magician at home in the Wheel of Fortune.

Dorsan characterizes the 5th House as such:

Attachments at birth, sentimental relationships, love life, children and relationships we enjoy

---

13 Page 70 of *The Clockwise House System*.

and cultivate. Vital energy prolonged into the following generation. Pleasures, hobbies, personal creations, artistic, literary and scientific works. Speculation, games of chance, lotteries, strokes of luck, the stock market (securities, commodity exchanges, and so on). Gifts, gains and losses other than those earned through labor. School, university and education.[14]

And the Sun in the 5th House:

The Sun in the fifth house increases vitality, even into the following generation. It promises satisfaction in theaters, concert halls, amusements, social games, toys, leisure activities, and vacations. The same goes for all that touches education, schools, universities, the fine arts, and the publishing business. Furthermore, professional success often incites the native to teach what one has acquired. Success is promised in personal business ventures and initiatives that make this individual stand out, and even put one into the limelight. Sudden windfalls or prosperity through speculation are possible.

A flattering liaison may bring a certain amount of prestige. One is likely to have few children; an only child is likely to be a boy. The birth of children might lead to problems. Children may need careful education. This person has a tendency toward pride and jealousy in love. One should take care that excessive behavior does not harm one's reputation or strike a blow against one's esteem.[15]

The Sun was in the 5th House during the Crucifixion of Christ—just as Jupiter was in the 3rd House. Manilius carries on:

Shining face to face with it [the 5th House] is that part of heaven which rises first from the bottom-most regions and brings back the sky once more: it controls the fortunes and fate of brothers; and it acknowledges the Moon for its mistress, who behold her brother's realms shining on her from the other side of heaven and who reflects human mortality in the dying edges of her face. Goddess is the name in Roman speech to be given to this region, whilst the Greeks call it by the same word in their language.

Here Manilius is describing the 11th House (the House of the Goddess), opposite the 5th, with the Moon as its ruler. In the arcane language, this would be the House of Temperance (the 14th Arcanum, analogous with Aquarius), with The Empress (the 3rd Arcanum, analogous to the Moon) as its ruler.

For Steiner, this was the region of the world-view of Pneumatism, while the Moon was the soul mood of occultism. Just as logic belongs with mathematics, and empiricism with sensation, occultism belongs with pneumatology.

Dorsan characterizes the 11th House in this way:

Friendships, including those of a secret or intimate nature. Relationships, masters, protectors, educators, and counselors. Customers, clients, pupils, and disciples. Associations, groups, clubs, cooperatives, and unions that are frequented. People who contribute to development. Conciliators. To sum up, all that is brought to bear on the native from the outside, from surrounding people and the nature of relationships and behavior toward those one encounters.

Hopes, desires, and projects. The profitable use of friends, protectors, and benefactors. The subject's ability to take advantage of favorable circumstances and to lessen, through diplomacy or the intervention of powerful and helpful relations, all that is negative and thus opposed to his objectives.[16]

14 Ibid., p. 68.
15 Ibid., pp. 80–81.

16 Ibid., p. 71.

And he describes the Moon in the 11th House as such:

> Progress and improvement will be realized through relationships and friendships, which will be numerous, varied, and unstable, but continually renewed. The subject has the gift to fraternize, to mix easily with people, and to understand their problems, while looking for and obtaining their friendship and drawing the best from relationships to favor personal goals. One's fertile imagination impels work at many projects. There is an aptitude for all that involves waves, rhythms, vibrations, electricity, and aviation, as well as psychology. The native is very sociable and could play an active and useful role in community groups and collectives such as unions, cooperatives, or friendly societies concerned with community welfare. Among one's relationships will be many women. However, a judicious selection will be warranted. At first, there will be a great deal of satisfaction, but disagreements may be unavoidable. The resulting complications will be detrimental to one's emotional health. This is an excellent configuration for a public career. In the case of a merchant, a feminine clientele is favored. It is a sign of many children and, in certain cases, indicates that one's partner will have a child from a previous union.[17]

Once again, during the Crucifixion, the Moon was in the 11th House. Manilius then describes the 4th House:

> But in the citadel of the sky, where the rising curve attains its consummation, and the downward slope makes its beginning, and the summit towers midway between orient and occident and holds the universe poised in its balance, here does the Cytherean claim her abode among the stars, placing in the very face of heaven, as it were, her beauteous features, wherewith she rules the affairs of men. To the abode is fittingly given the power to govern wedlock, the bridal chamber, and the marriage torch; and this charge suits Venus, the charge of plying her own weapons. Fortune shall be this Temple's name; and mark it well, that I may take a short route in my lengthy song.

The 4th House is the House of Fortune, and is ruled by Venus. In Arcane imagery, this is the House of The Moon (the 18th Arcanum, analogous to Cancer) and is ruled by The Lover (the 6th Arcanum, analogous to Venus).

Steiner assigns the worldview of Materialism to this region, while Venus is the soul-mood of Mysticism. A "mystical materialism" may sound paradoxical, but interestingly enough, he goes out of his way to describe this exact combination and its potentials:

> Again, one can be a mystic through all the twelve mental constellations. It would certainly not be especially favorable if one were a mystic of materialism—i.e. if one experienced inwardly not the mental, the spiritual, but the material. For a mystic of materialism is really he who has acquired an especially fine perception of how one feels when one enjoys this or that substance. It is somewhat different if one imbibes the juice of this plant or the other, and then waits to see what happens to one's organism. One thus grows together with matter in one's experience; one becomes a mystic of matter. This can even become an "awakening" for life, so that one follows up how one substance or another, drawn from this or that plant, works upon the organism, affecting particularly this or that organ. And so, to be a Mystic of Materialism is a precondition for investigating individual substances in respect of their healing powers.[18]

---

17 Ibid., pp. 91–92.

18 Steiner, *Human and Cosmic Thought* (CW 151), lect. 3.

Dorsan describes the 4th House as such:

Career, professional activity, the place of employment, the employer, the degree of authority within the professional field; professional occupations but more so, those that are imposed by circumstances and independent events over which one has no control. This can be favorable or unfavorable. The struggle to obtain and keep one's social position, in other words, *le panier de crabes* (the basket of crabs), as Dr. Libert-Chatenay said in *Les cahiers astrologiques* [Astrological notebooks] (March 1954), not without humor, as he attached, as we do, this house to the sign of the Crab.

Public life, reputation, popularity, prestige, honors, titles, dignities and public office. The name, the well-known and respected brand, the work that will be remembered. Relationships with authority. Glory and celebrity but also total reversal and the fall from power.

The mother and to a lesser degree, family life, but only what is known and visible from the outside.

The MC, radical or progressed and if the hour of birth is absolutely exact, takes on primordial importance through aspects and transits in order to fix the stations of destiny.[19]

Here is Dorsan's characterization of Venus in the 4th House:

Social success is easily achieved, whether through the practice of a Venusian profession or simply through the charm that the personality exudes, through the excellence of relationships (especially feminine ones) or at the beginning of one's career through the mother's influence. Working conditions will be pleasant, but will not depend necessarily on a Venusian occupation, such as artistic activities, luxury trades, or body care.

Thanks to good fortune, happy events could occur without any effort. These natives benefit from the corroboration of influential women and from beneficial and powerful relationships that will often depend on their love life. They will know how to draw satisfaction from any situation, thanks to the feelings of sympathy that they awake in others.

Often, this configuration brings about an advantageous marriage, from which sentiments will not be absent. It is often the promise of a happy and peaceful family life.

If the planet is afflicted, there is the danger of one's reputation being stained by a scandal or affair.[20]

Venus traveled through the 4th House during the crowing with thorns and sentencing of Christ on Good Friday, around 9:00 a.m.

Manilius describes the 10th House, opposite the 4th:

Where at the opposite pole the universe subsides, occupying the foundations, and from the depths of midnight gloom gazes up at the back of the Earth, in that region Saturn exercises the powers that are his own: cast down himself in ages past from empire in the skies and the throne of heaven, he wields as a father power over the fortunes of fathers and the plight of the old. Daemonium is the name the Greeks have given it, denoting influences fitting the name.

The House of Daemonium is ruled by Saturn; in arcane imagery, this is the House of The Star (the 17th Arcanum, analogous to Capricorn), ruled by the High Priestess (the 2nd Arcanum, analogous to Saturn).

For Rudolf Steiner, this region was the worldview of Spiritism, while Saturn is the world

---

19 Dorsan, *The Clockwise House System,* p. 68.

20 Ibid., p. 103.

outlook of Gnosis. And so, we have Gnostic Spiritism as an ideal:

A man can be so attuned in his soul—for the present it is immaterial by which of these twelve "mental-zodiacal signs" his soul is illuminated—that the soul mood expressed in the whole configuration of his world-outlook can be designated as *Gnosis*. A man is a Gnostic when his disposition is such that he gets to know the things of the world not through the senses, but through certain cognitional forces in the soul itself. A man can be a Gnostic and at the same time have a certain inclination to be illuminated by, e.g., the mental-zodiacal-sign that we have here called "Spiritism." Then his Gnosticism will have a deeply illuminated insight into the relationships of the spiritual worlds.[21]

It is worth noting that it is baleful when Saturn is placed opposite this position—i.e., Gnosis in Materialism. This was the aspect that held sway on the day Parzival failed to ask the Grail Question during his first visit to Munsalvaesche. Both Saturn and Sun were overhead: gnostic, empirical materialism leads to ignorance.

Dorsan describes the 10th House:

Heredity, profound and faraway origins, atavistic tendencies, easy or difficult destiny imposed at birth, and the support or impediments, which could eventuate from this. Heritage, if by this we mean the environment, goods, and chattels available right from the cradle. Ancestors and the influence of a birth into rich or poor circumstances. The many different places of residence commencing with the birth place. Real estate, property, inheritances, mineral wealth, hidden treasures.

Intimate home life, attitudes toward family members living under the same roof. Comfort and the embellishment of the home, as well as the attacks it could sustain either from human beings (burglary, fire, acts of war) or from acts of nature (weather, earthquakes, cataclysms). Shelter and refuge.

Ripe old age and conditions of existence in the latter years of life. Ultimate realizations. The tomb.

Note: Above all in horary astrology, the end of the matter.[22]

And Saturn in the 10th House as such:

This configuration is often an indication of a severe, austere heredity, a strict, rigid education, a monotonous, melancholic life, or of an unhappy childhood. This is often due to the fact that the parents are too old or too traditional. These natives often suffer from the burden of too much responsibility. They have to make every effort possible to exercise their free will.

This configuration underlines the importance of inherited possessions and the role that these will play in life. There are possible wrangles within the family over inherited property or real estate. They will probably be involved in a profession related to architecture and construction and sideline occupations that may include real estate.

Life could be saddened by the early loss through death of male family members. These natives should take every precaution to ensure their old age by setting aside at least the bare minimum needed to avoid a painful environment or an unpleasant residence.[23]

Saturn passed through the 10th House when Christ was before Pilate early on Good Friday, but also at the moment of the Resurrection on Easter Sunday morning.

Next, Manilius describes the 1st House:

Turn now your gaze upon heaven as it climbs up from the first cardinal point, where the rising signs commence afresh their wonted courses, and a pale Sun swims upward from the icy waves and begins by slow degrees to blaze with golden flame as it attempts the rugged path where the Ram heads the procession of the skies. This temple, Mercury, son of Maia, men say is yours, marked for its bright aspect with a designation which writers also give you for name. The one wardship is commissioned with two charges; for in it nature has placed all fortunes of children and has made dependent on it the prayers of parents.

21 Steiner, *Human and Cosmic Thought*, lect. 3.

22 Dorsan, *The Clockwise House System*, pp. 70–71.
23 Ibid., p. 132.

The 1st House is expressed in Arcana by The Fool (the Arcanum without number, analogous to Aries) and is ruled by Mercury, expressed by the Pope (the 5th Arcanum).

For Steiner, this region is devoted to the world-view of Idealism, while Mercury is the soul mood of Transcendentalism. We are reminded of transcendental idealism, the philosophical stream of Immanuel Kant.

Dorsan describes the 1st House:

> The temperament, the potential vital energy, health, the preferred physical activity, outer appearance, the physical body, hereditary tendencies and predispositions, environment and general conditions of existence, especially during childhood. Character and, notably, reactions to outer circumstances, deep hopes and aspirations that produce behavior patterns.
>
> Note that all of the former reveals itself to be valid only in practice, through the sign or the two signs of the zodiac in question, in the case where this first house is empty of planets. In the opposite case, the presence of luminaries or planets exercises a preponderant influence. The planets are very near to us; the fixed stars, which make up the zodiacal signs, are very far away. Their apparent diameter and their luminosity are both greatly reduced in relation to the planets.
>
> Note, too, that the point of the Ascendant, radical or progressed, assumes considerable importance in matters of health, through

aspects and transits, right throughout the life up until death.[24]

Mercury in the 1st House according to Dorsan:

> This influence is quick to make itself felt and we notice it right from the earliest age onward. The mind is forever alert, lively, subtle, adroit, and ingenious. Such subjects can easily express themselves both through the spoken and written word. Written works show originality and invention. They love public speaking, though sometimes a little nervously. They are gifted with quick wit and easy elocution. Impassioned by studies, these subjects are fascinated by a wide range of topics. With inquisitive minds, they are always eager to acquire new information. They are extremely adaptable and supple. Lively and developed intellectual faculties assist them in drawing the maximum profit from circumstances. They have business and commercial sense and an aptitude to play the role of intermediary.
>
> In the case of affliction, the subject could become the victim of criticism, gossip, and exaggeration, and, above all, be very nervous and high strung. If the weak points are kept under control, one appears younger than his age.
>
> Health depends greatly upon the family and professional surroundings, to which such a one is highly sensitive. The native is always moving and completes a great quantity of short, frequent journeys.[25]

Mercury was in the 1st House when Peter denied Christ three times, early on Good Friday. Finally, Manilius describes the 7th House:

> There remains one region, that in the setting heaven. It speeds the falling sky beneath the Earth and buries the stars. Now it looks forth on the back of the departing Sun, yet it once beheld his face; so wonder not if it is called the portal of somber Pluto [i.e., Hell] and keeps control over the end of life *and death's firm-bolted door.* Here dies even the very light of day, which the ground beneath steals away from the world and locks up captive in the dungeon of night. This temple also claims for itself the guardianship of

---

24 Ibid., pp. 66–67.
25 Ibid., p. 93.

good faith and constancy of heart. Such is the power that dwells in the abode which summons to itself and buries the Sun, thus surrendering that which it has received, and brings the day to its close.

This is the House of the Portal of Pluto (i.e., Gates of Hell), shown in Arcana by the 8th, Justice, analogous to the sign of Libra. Rudolf Steiner places the worldview of Realism in relation to this region.

Dorsan describes the 7th House in this way:

Alliances, associations, groups, and parties to which one belongs, partnerships, marriage, and the marriage contract if there is one. Contracts of all types, and the possible breach of same. Rivalries, declared adversaries, and competitors. Theft and robberies. Trials, lawsuits, and the adversary's barrister or lawyer. Problems and obstacles. The struggle for survival.

Owing to the fact that this house is in opposition to the Ascendant, it informs us about relationships with others, more especially with regard to those who openly oppose the subject or his course of action. One of two things can happen: either one comes to an agreement, or one begins to do battle, which results either in reconciliation or in a conflict of interests. The magnitude of the conflict will generally depend upon the situation of the subject.

Note: The cusp of the seventh is also known as the "point of death" for obvious

reasons, since it is diametrically opposed to the Ascendant, which is the life source. The importance given to it by the astrologer, while conducting research into the periods that are dangerous for the health, will be in direct relation to the degree of exactitude attributed to the hour of birth.[26]

My hope is that the reader can come to a clearer impression of the multivalency of the Major Arcana of the Tarot of Marseilles. Indeed, each of the meanings of the Houses described here is contained within the Arcanum in potential, but each of the Arcana is not exhausted by these descriptions. My hope would not be that the reader attempt to memorize a rote formula for what each House indicates according to Steiner, Dorsan, etc.; rather, I would encourage the reader to meditate on the images of the Arcana themselves, in order to thereby discover additional characteristics and implications of the houses and the inner planets that have not been indicated by Rudolf Steiner, Manilius, or Jacques Dorsan, yet emerge from the same arcana source.

This is the path of ecosophy: allowing the inner earth to guide and inspire us in our economic and ecological activity via the elemental language of Arcana—and a concrete, increasingly ever-present perception of *where I am* and *when I am*.

As an inspiration for further research, I will also clarify here that the association of Arcana with Sign and Planet comes from the intuitive research of Robert Powell. I consider myself to be in harmony with that research, but I cannot say that it is absolute. A method of association that would be more in line with tradition would be inspired by the Kabbalah. In the *Sepher Yetzirah*, the author divides the Hebrew Alphabet into three parts: three mother letters (*Aleph, Mem,* and *Shin*); seven doubles (*Bet, Gimmel, Dalet, Kaf, Pet, Resh,* and *Tau*); and twelve singles (*Heh, Vau, Zayin, Chet, Tet, Yod, Lamed, Nun, Samech, Ayin, Tzadeh, Qof*). The three mothers were associated with the three horizontal lines on the Sephiroth Tree; the seven doubles with the seven vertical lines; and the twelve singles with

---

26 Ibid., pp. 69–70.

the twelve diagonal lines. The three mothers were associated with the three elements Air (*Aleph*), Water (*Mem*), and Fire (*Shin*)—which we might bring into relationship with Pluto (Chaos = Gas), Neptune (Gaia = Water), and Uranus (Celestial Fire). The seven doubles were associated with the seven classical planets, and the twelve singles with the twelve signs of the zodiac.

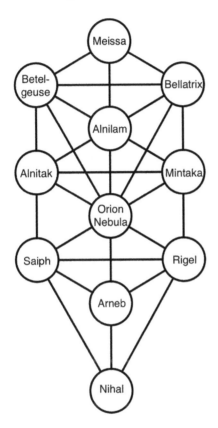

Aleph	א	Magician
Bet	ב	High Priestess
Gimmel	ג	Empress
Dalet	ד	Emperor
Heh	ה	Pope
Vau	ו	Lover
Zayin	ז	Chariot
Chet	ח	Justice
Tet	ט	Hermit
Yod	י	Wheel of Fortune
Kaf	כ	Force
Lamed	ל	Hanged Man
Mem	מ	Death
Nun	נ	Temperance
Samech	ס	Devil
Ayin	ע	Tower of Destruction
Peh	פ	Star
Tzadeh	צ	Moon
Qof	ק	Sun
Resh	ר	Judgment
Shin	ש	Fool
Tav	ת	World

In this case, there would be different Arcana associated with the different ecosophical entities; for example, inner Pluto would be the Magician rather than the Devil; inner Neptune would be Death instead of The World; and inner Uranus would be The Fool instead of the Tower of Destruction. The seven planets would be associated with the High Priestess, Empress, Emperor, Force, Star, Judgement, and the World. The twelve houses would be associated with the Pope, Lover, Chariot, Justice, Hermit, Wheel of Fortune, Hanged Man, Temperance, Devil, Tower of Destruction, Moon, and Sun.

Again, while this designation is entirely different from that indicated by Robert Powell; it is more in line with Kabbalistic and Hermetic tradition. I leave it to the reader to play with such an alternate designation to see if they come to any fruitful insights in the "interior forum."

Now, there is also an association between the Hebrew Alphabet and the Tarot of Marseilles. Indeed, as I pointed out in part 3 of this article series (see *Star Wisdom* vol. 4), the Hebrew Alphabet emerged directly from the *spiritual reality* of the Tree of Life in its descent toward humanity and the center of the Earth; whereas the Tarot of Marseilles are that same *spiritual reality* as it emerges from the center of Mother Earth. In this sense, the Tarot are identical with the Hebrew Alphabet, at a later stage of their metamorphosis. They are the holy language of our time.

Relationships between the Tarot and the Hebrew alphabet is as follows:

ONE HUNDRED YEARS AFTER
THE KARMA LECTURES BY RUDOLF STEINER

Karmic Relationships from an Astrological Point of View

Krisztina Cseri

One hundred years have passed since Rudolf Steiner held his lectures on the esoteric study of karmic relationships in 1924. However, this article was not inspired directly by Steiner's lectures, but by Steffen Hartmann's article published in last year's edition of *Star Wisdom*, Elisabeth Vreede's letter to the members (May 21, 1929), and the work I started with Natalia Haarahiltunen in the winter of 2021/22.

Last year's article by Steffen Hartmann made a deep impression on me. On the one hand, I can identify with his ideas regarding reincarnated anthroposophists to a great extent, and on the other hand, with his thoughts on community work, he gave me new stimulation to continue the work that I have been doing for a few years, and which seems to be developing more and more in our collaboration with Natalia. For those who have not read the article published in last year's edition of *Star Wisdom*, I would like to quote a line of thoughts from it here.

> Rudolf Steiner also called it "putting karma in order"—and even the angels can learn something from this. Here we encounter the power of Christ presently in the etheric realm, in the realm in which networks of destiny weave between and among people. There we can silently and yet clearly hear HIS word: "Behold, I make everything new" (Rev. 21:5).
>
> It is an experience of the heart: Today many things between people can be seen and healed much more directly and quickly, more openly and freely than ever before in human history.

On the next page, Steffen explains that, according to his perception, 2012 is the year from which the students of Michael have been able to encounter one another more directly in the earthly world and to recognize each other in their true essence, and he writes that he perceives the unconditional intention/impulse to work together—despite all karmic difficulties and challenges. He directs our attention to the fact that, in addition to Kaspar Hauser's quality of pure perception and pure soul being, the requirement of our time is pure thinking, which is inseparable from the recognition and deep experience of destiny—an experience ultimately only possible in community with other people and in interaction and encounter with others.

Turning to the basic approach of this publication (i.e., the point of view of star wisdom), I take a big detour to return to this starting point again afterward. I will first try briefly to review the astrological efforts to research individual karma and reincarnation, as well as karmic communities, in my own interpretation, keeping in mind the karmic and non-karmic factors that underlie community life.

After Rudolf Steiner, Elisabeth Vreede was the first to state concretely that astrology should become a *social science* in the future. The fundamental basis of this idea is that a person leaves the circle of self-observation and takes into account the system of relationships with one's companions. One does all this, of course, not on the basis of intellectual curiosity, but with the aim of getting to know and identify with the destiny of the other person, and thus also with the destiny that becomes common: we go beyond our own characteristics, and we understand our own destiny together with the destiny of the other person, or even *within* the destiny of the other person—when we talk about a smaller community.

The idea is also supported by Steiner's published knowledge of occult faculties,[1] of which *eugenic occultism* plays a prominent role from the point of view of a community astrological viewpoint.

Steiner spoke of three such occult faculties: mechanical, hygienic, and eugenic faculties. In my understanding, each ability requires astrological background knowledge, but each in a different way according to the character of the occult faculty. In mechanical occultism, the object of the faculty is not the human being, but some other object on which one intends to have an effect. Here, the presence of astrological knowledge seems to be the most remote and limited to the relationship between the Earth and the Sun, although the star constellation of the given time and the individual relationship of the given person with the stars can contribute to the completion of special tasks. In hygienic occultism, the object of the faculty is the human being him- or herself, but preferably in isolation, not in one's social connections—here the role of astrology grows considerably. In eugenic occultism, however, both the human being and one's human relationship system play a role in the necessity of an astrological view, which in this case requires the highest degree of knowledge and revelation. So, the complex *cognitive* and *intuitive* activity of the astrological approach is fulfilled to the highest degree in eugenic occultism, although its deeper knowledge is also required for the development of the other two occult faculties.

Based on the literature I have read,[2] after Elisabeth Vreede, the cosmological-astrological view that focuses on *the human being*—the individual human being and the relationship of the individual human being to the community, thus practically the basis of eugenic occultism—has gone to the periphery of the activities of the anthroposophic movement. In anthroposophic literature, the description of the path and functioning of the human being remained general, and the views often try to draw conclusions about the human being from the perspective of the plant world (or specifically on the basis of the plant world), which approach can also aim only at a general characterization of the human being. The examination of *space* and at the same time the light ether appears with extraordinary force (see the application of projective geometry from a spiritual point of view), while *time* either remains "organic time" in relation to the heat ether, which defines an entire lifetime for a living being, or finds expression in rhythms referring to the chemical ether. These rhythms, however, do not reach the level of sophistication (related to the individual human being) of the planetary rhythms and rhythmic encounters, especially not the etheric body fixations and projections that work specifically in humans, and which mechanisms reach the realm of the life ether and the Akasha ether.

At the core of the anthroposophic movement, the focus on the how, on the *mechanism,* seems to have remained, basically keeping in mind the natural world and the general human being, and an intuitive approach referring to *the unique content* of things appeared on the "periphery,"[3] basically focusing on the individual human being. It seems to me that the scientism of researching the mechanism (and scientism measured by its own criteria) does not dare to move toward the subjective approach of astrology, which is based on intuition to a large extent, and thus toward the *full* examination of the individual human being *carrying karma;* at the same time, the subjective approach often seems not to be interested in how what happens is possible (with the intervention of what beings and forces, and with what concrete mechanisms), and the mode of performance remains revelatory. There is a lack of communication and thus a lack of an organic interweaving between the two approaches, which then leads to serious problems. Such an initial basic problem is the issue of the sidereal vs. tropical zodiac, which is still present and affects almost all areas of life.

1   Steiner, *The Challenge of the Times* (CW 186), lect. 3: "The Mechanistic, Eugenic and Hygienic Aspects of the Future," Dornach, Dec 1, 1918.

2   In recent years, I have started to engage with the works of George Adams, Ernst Marti, Nick Thomas, Paul Emberson, Lawrence Edwards, and Olive Whicher.

3   I use the word *periphery,* because of the approach from the perspective of the anthroposophic movement.

Of course, *karma* is a key word here, since there is a huge difference between examining a being that does not carry karma (a member of the natural kingdoms) or a being that currently carries karma (a human being). And so, the strange situation exists, that even though Steiner gave lectures on karma in his last years and at the same time at the peak of his life, and the importance of this is acknowledged by everyone without exception, *the factors and insights necessary for a comprehensive examination of karmic necessities were put on the "periphery"*—from the perspective of the general anthroposophic movement and literature.

THE INDIVIDUAL HUMAN BEING AND ONE'S RELATIONSHIP SYSTEM (KARMIC CIRCLE)

We can thank Willi Sucher, Robert Powell, and the StarFire Research Group[4] for delving deeply into the astrological regularities that apply to *the individual human being and his relationship system*, and the results have greatly sophisticated the general approach of the human being.

Sucher basically expanded the studies directed at the birth horoscope—i.e., a static, and moreover, a single static situation and at the same time character drawing—by including the other two threshold points (i.e., conception and death) into the studies. By researching the hermetic rule, he focused on the coordination of conception and birth, and by taking into account the embryonic period, he also opened up the possibility of investigating etheric projections. With this, the general biographical characterization that can be described on the basis of the seven-year rhythm characteristic of all people (which has become so general and fashionable in the field of anthroposophy) has acquired a new layer specific to the individual human being. He also introduced the heliocentric view alongside the geocentric one, although he did so mainly—but not exclusively—with respect to the Earth and all of humanity (see his work *The Drama of the Universe*). With these new aspects, in terms of the human being, Sucher essentially remained *within*

the research of one human life (including deep researches on the periods before and after earthly life), but he significantly expanded the research fields of the human being's life carrying karma, and at the same time shed new light on the extent of the *freedom-degree*, which is inherent in physical laws (the astronomical determinacy of the orbiting of the planets) and is examined from the point of view of the arranging of karma. By "freedom-degree" I mean that the soul can switch between two lives to a heliocentric and geocentric planetary position in its threshold charts, and several threshold points (conception, birth, and death) are involved in the coordination of lives—as it turns out from the later research by Robert Powell—which makes the astronomically determined possibilities *expand* in terms of karmic alignment between lives (and karmic partners).

On the one hand, Robert Powell further expanded or modified[5] the same knowledge, and on

---

4   I apologize to all those who are left out of the list whose activities I do not know.

5   The consideration of the arriving soul as a being of body-members by the two researchers seems to me fundamentally different, although no summary work by Willi Sucher has survived. Sucher considered three stages that could still be grasped by the intellect to be important for the formation of the four body members. He believed that the birth horoscope belonged most to a person's physical body, because that is when one fully enters the physical world. The formation of the etheric body is best suggested by the conception horoscope, and the whole period in which the etheric body forms the physical body—i.e., the embryonic period. And the astral body is best characterized by the *philosophical constellation* that is formed when the soul enters from the Sun-sphere into the Moon-sphere. He considered the conception horoscope to be identifiable by the hermetic rule, the philosophical constellation by the connections between the Moon and the lunar node. In the work of Robert Powell, we do not find the philosophical constellation for which there is no clear rule for calculating it, or at least intuition is needed to find it. Taking into account the heliocentric viewpoint and the geocentric viewpoint together, he creates the so-called hermetic, or "tychonic," horoscope. According to him, the conception horoscope provides information about the physical body from the tychonic perspective, about the etheric body from the geocentric point of view, the birth-chart about the astral body from the geocentric point of view, and about the higher intentions of our "I" from the tychonic point of view.

the other hand, he left the field of investigation of the single life of the human being, and by focusing on the research of *life chains, he clearly separated the destiny of the individual human being and the destiny of the whole of humanity.* With his research results, he pointed out that the individual human being and the participation of the human being in humanity—i.e., one's group soul in the broadest sense (and the group activity arising from it)—are two different things. By bringing to the fore the problems of the sidereal zodiac and the tropical zodiac and presenting the reincarnation mechanism of the individual human being linked to the sidereal zodiac, Powell actually not only rejected the technique of the tropical zodiac—or rather the tropical ring—applied to the individual human being, but also pointed out that humanity can be said to have an independent "soul," which is like a slowly and constantly moving river, to which individual souls (as group souls or as individualized egos) are connected by a chain-of-life mechanism. This river currently contains a tropical dimension appearing in slowly changing, rhythmic returns—*unifying* the individual souls and promoting group activity—due to the necessity of humanity's coexistence with the natural world, while its other layer remains sidereal in accordance with the sidereal connection of the souls of the individual human beings who built it, and is exposed to the sidereal influences transferred in rapidly changing and complex rhythms provided by the planets—*helping individualization and at the same time preserving the individual germs* (as can be seen from historical events, as well, which are not linked to seasons).[6]

With his research, Robert Powell thus *separated* the destiny mechanism of the individualizing human being and one's karmic circle from the—soul-unifying—psychical and physical cradle of humanity connected to the natural world, all the way to the circle of karmic circles, to the widest community. With his research results, the general characterization of the human being not only gained sophistication, but also received a special place in the characteristics of the *river* of humanity. The detachment of the tropical ring effect also draws attention to the fact that the separation of the Sun and the Earth resulted not only in this "ring of life" for the evolution of humanity, but also in the presence of the two internal focuses of the human self—i.e., helio/geo (space) and the phenomenon of solar progression (time).

Meanwhile, we see from the point of view of examining the relationship system (karmic circle) of the individual human being that Powell strongly maintains the point of view of the individual human being. Although he wrote many times about the life of a given person in a small community (together with a karmic partner) and the timing of their meeting, the astrological examination of the *two-sided* relationship of the individual human beings (and the timing of their birth relative to each other) is not in his focus on the basis of his books; nor was it in Willi Sucher's.[7]

---

6 Of course, the change in the culture of humanity involves the displacement of the tropical points in the sidereal background (e.g., we are currently living in the Age of Pisces). And in the case of the greatest historical events, the slow-moving river shakes together with all the natural kingdoms, and this is usually indicated by the position of the apsides present in the Sun-Earth relationship (similar to the tropical corner points, also a phenomenon resulting from the separation of Sun and Earth).

7 Robert Powell does not see any regularities in the chart comparisons of karmic partners that would justify their karmic connection. In *Hermetic Astrology,* vol. 2 (p. 59), he writes about a "shift in emphasis" regarding the goal of the hermetic astrologer in the direction of independent investigation of the individuality, where karmic partners can be reached by examining the previous life or lives of the individuality and not on an astrological basis. This latter statement is not disputed by those described here, and this latter statement is actually also valid for the determination of the previous life or lives of the individuality. So, we do not use the tools of astrology (at least not exclusively) to determine past lives or karmic partners of someone. The *already known* karmic circles—similarly to the *already known* previous lives of the individuality—can show whether there was intention, and what kind, to fit in for the sake of karmic tasks. In the case of Richard Wagner and Ludwig II, I consider the birth Sun-Moon conjunction (in addition to the ASC-Moon conjunction) and the Saturn-Moon-lunar node conjunction to be a very strong connection factor, even if it cannot be elevated to the level of a single law and extended to all [*cont. next page*]

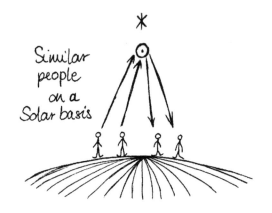

It is in the work of David Tresemer and Robert Schiappacasse where I saw the point of view emerging in which the astrological aspect of communication with the destiny of "similar companions" (sometimes solar karmic companions)—that can be raised to the level of regularities and introduced into astrological practice—does manifest. That is, here the examining of *the human relationship system of the individual human being* does appear, in the dimension between the individual human being and the "general environment" of humanity. In his book on the Solar Cross,[8] Tresemer explains in detail the significance of the "Images" connected to the human being cross-wise and on a solar basis—through the Sun position of conception, birth or death—in which the human being shares a common energy pattern, common spiritual gestures and even common tasks with those who also chose these Images for their transition between the Earth and the spiritual world. The most powerful factor of the cross is the Gate or Solar Image (for which the simple drawing here was made), against which the cross is set up. At the same time, the house system (which, recalling the hermetic rule, is related to the position of the Moon at conception) becomes secondary. The

approach is based on a mechanism (as explained by David Tresemer) that also enables identification with the spiritual essence of the events during the life of Christ. In other words, human activities (similarly to the life events of Jesus Christ) leave an etheric imprint on the degrees of the zodiac in the Akasha chronicle through the mediation of the Sun, and we can connect to them afterward.

With this approach, we get closer to the individual human being's *solar soul community* with other people, but most of these "similar people" are not so closely related to the individual (there is not even a Sun-karma level task between them) to have a concrete physical contact with them on Earth, or one person is in incarnation, the other is not, and thus physical contact cannot be realized. Of course, the physical relationship is not the measure of the joint spiritual work, but here I will try to focus primarily on the groups that are on Earth at the same time and thus get to the general characteristics of the *karmic groups*. ("At the same time" of course means an overlap in the presence of people when physical contact may occur.)

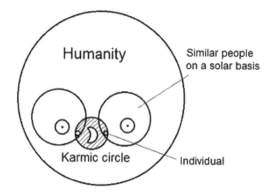

So, if we move on to the karmic groups, we can see that we need to supplement our participation in the solar community. The figure shows that the individual human being is located in the common section of two circles. Standing as part of one of the circles ("Similar people on a solar basis"), one is influenced by the Akasha Images from one's Sun positions and is in constant interaction with them. This is how one is connected to both the Christ events and the heritage of "similar people" (possibly one's own heritage: see Robert Powell's expanded first astrological rule of

_____

karmic relationships. I also consider the Lilith-lunar node conjunction between them to be particularly important. In addition, there was a square between the two birth Suns, which seems significant based on the Solar Cross theory.

8   Tresemer with Schiappacasse, *Star Wisdom and Rudolf Steiner: A Life Seen through the Oracle of the Solar Cross.*

reincarnation)—insofar as the connection through the Sun is concerned. At the same time, the individual is also included in another circle, which I call the "karmic circle." This is where one connects with all those with whom one is in relation, either through the Sun or through other planetary positions. In the area of intersection, there are people who are both "similar people on a solar basis" and part of one's "karmic circle." This is the rarest case for anyone to be included here. In the part outside the area of intersection, the "Sun-identity" is not realized with regard to the karmic circle, but the connecting role of the Moon comes to the fore. Here I also include the lunar nodes, Moon's apogee (Lilith) and the ASC/DESC axes, the latter of which I consider to be a "gate" in the same way as the lunar nodes, albeit not between the Sun-sphere and the Moon-sphere, but between the Moon-sphere and the Earth-sphere. So, in fact, all of these elements are *lunar* in some sense. Thus, to the planetary sphere elements residing in one human being, or to one's Sun, the other human being is connected through a lunar element. One [this other human being] can of course connect to planetary sphere elements [of the previous human being] with one's Sun or other planetary elements as well, but these connections seem additional/secondary to the lunar entanglement.

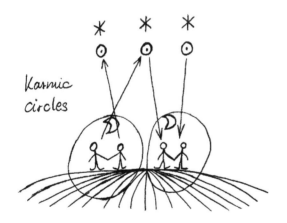

Karmic circles

The research results of contemporary astrology and the results of my own research equally support that the most common planetary connection among people in a karmic relationship occurs with the *participation* of the Sun, the Moon, the lunar nodal axis, the ASC/DESC and the Moon's apogee. Participation means that other planets are closely related to these positions, especially Saturn. In the case of the closest relationships, however, these positions *themselves* also meet each other for the most part. Here, of course, contemporary astrology takes only birth charts into account, but if conception charts and the embryonic period are also taken into account, then this solar *and* lunar connection becomes even more grounded.

In the Lemurian period, the Moon's separation from the Earth brought a new dimension to human life. Physical incarnation began and the human reproductive system was formed. In this peculiar reproductive system, the Moon is of particular importance, since in the ten lunar months of the embryonic period, a special layer is formed in the human etheric body for unfolding one's destiny on Earth, and conception and birth themselves become connected by the Moon (see the hermetic rule). However, according to experience, this lunar environment not only leads to the completely unique nature of the individual human being, but also participates in the relationship system of the human being with one's karmic partners. This is actually not surprising, since a human being can unfold one's destiny only through companions, with their help.[9]

9   For my part, I am sure that the Moon and ASC/DESC, which is strongly dependent on the Moon (due to the previously mentioned Moon-Earth gate nature and hermetic rule-based coordination for conception and birth), are also involved in the rules that coordinate the reincarnation of the individual human being, but this cannot become obvious; only in the rarest of cases is the hour-by-minute timing of the threshold points known. ASC/DESC rotates in one day in front of the background of the zodiac, but even in the case of the Moon, the daily distance traveled is about 12 degrees (which can mean a difference of at least 6-6 degrees if the 12-hour noon threshold is assumed to be crossed) in the assumed Moon position, which makes it difficult to raise it to the level of a law. However, we have to ask the question: does it matter at which hour and minute the soul leaves the Earth at death? Is it not possible that the karmic map of a subsequent life—for example, a Sun, Saturn or Moon position—results in the time of departure within the day for the death of the previous life?

Here it seems important to highlight Willi Sucher's line of thought, according to which the entry of the soul from the solar sphere into the lunar sphere is related to the movement of the lunar nodes and the Moon's position appearing at birth. This approach brings up to an extraordinary extent the lunar dimension alongside the solar nature in the human being, which also becomes connected with the sphere of the zodiac (i.e., with Akasha Images), as it indicates a direction of *cosmic entry*. I don't think we can talk about a "Lunar Cross" (as a counterpart to the Solar Cross), but here we can probably speak about a similar, but lunar-determined karmic map ("karmic Akasha Image"), which is closely related through the Moon to the cross of the "earthly" house system, as well, which is also a frequent fitting point in the community of individual human beings.

Regarding these lunar elements, it is important to see that it is as if the soul comes through a triple gate, if we believe Willi Sucher's standpoint to be true. According to him, when the soul enters the Moon sphere from the Sun sphere, the lunar node is at the same place as the ASC/DESC at the time of conception and the Moon at the time of birth. The corridor of the soul refers to a specific zodiacal segment through three factors and in an extended time period. Probably, this triple gate phenomenon creates a karmic corridor—in addition to the approximate 11° to 14° karmic windows of the lunar nodes between their conception and birth positions—where images and tasks left in the spiritual world can be seen by one person through the other person, and this accumulated debt and opportunity brings together karmic couples and communities.

I would like to deal with the Moon's apogee (one of the Moon's apsides) only briefly here. The apsides of the Moon—similarly to the apsides of the Sun—are structural points, that are not "gates," or at least they are "closed gates," where the planet (here the Moon) cannot run out of its slightly elliptic orbit. In my experience, these points of the Moon are not primarily related to the sphere of the zodiac (i.e., with common memories of people) but take a role in the deep psychic world

of the individual human being that is unfolding in relation with the astrological houses. I would say, they seem to be a "sub-dimension" or secondary regularity regarding astrological fitting points among people. The frequent appearance of the Moon's apogee (Lilith) in challenging relationships of karmic couples, however, calls the attention to the necessity for further research in community astrology. (See, e.g., the Sun-Lilith conjunction at 6–7° Aries at the deaths of Alfonso X and Abu Yusuf Ya'kub, and the Lilith-Sun conjunction at 20° Capricorn in a reversed condition at the birth in their later incarnations as Joseph von Spaun and Franz Schubert. Through his being, Schubert probably shed light to Spaun's own inner uncertainties, false expectations and fantasies, and "apogee swings," a central life theme that can also be seen in his occupation as a lottery director.)

MY TRANSIT IS MY KARMIC PARTNER

The connecting of people is actually a "transit phenomenon" from one person's point of view—if we leave out causal time, then from both sides. The threshold chart of one person is a transit interpreted to the threshold chart of the other person.

The most common situation is the following: Another person is born at a certain moment of time that is important to us, with whom we come into contact later, but usually many years after the transit, and so during the transit we do not know about and probably do not perceive anything about that person. Here, a lot depends on how old we are and where we are at the time of the transit, and therefore how well the spiritual beings controlling karma can—if at all they want to—bring the subject of the transit into our view. The transit, therefore, also means the threshold chart of another person, as well as the karmic legacy and solar potential inherent in the two threshold charts interact after the contact, which is connected to another transit—i.e., independent of the two threshold charts. (For example, someone is born in 1950, another person is born in 1970, and then they meet in 2000.) It is like a delayed transit effect by a person who embodies the transit—i.e., the person brings something important from the transit constellation (1970) for us, for the time of the connection, the later transit (2000), which works continuously from then on (so long as we have some kind of relationship with the person).

The special version of this general situation occurs in the case of a *blood relationship*, during reproduction itself—i.e., in the parent-child relationship. The birth of the child and the meeting with that child (the two transits just mentioned) coincide; their constellation is one and the same. (For example, the mother is born in 1950, her child in 1970.) This special transit can also be called an "integrating transit," since the threshold chart for one person (child) is *the same* as the transit of the "meeting" for the other person (parent), and the *two threshold charts* go through a kind of *unification* owing to the spiritual-psychical-physical mechanism of reproduction and child-care—because of the mother-child or perhaps father-child relationship. For example, at the time of the birth of my own two children, one had the Moon at my birth lunar node, and the other had the lunar node at my birth Moon. I have been continuously perceiving the effect of these qualities—carried by their being as an anchor (i.e., appearing in a threshold chart)—since their birth, and this will probably be the case for a long time to come. The etheric essence or karmic map carried in their being *is integrated into* my own etheric quality.

Here, of course, it arises that we often do not perceive our own child as our karmic partner in our spiritual development, but the general situation is—at least with regard to our lunar karma—that we are in some kind of close destiny relationship with our children, and out of the meeting of our karmic maps some common etheric essence is formed and exerts attraction in both directions.

The connection to the cosmos through the other person's threshold chart is always of special significance, and opens the door through and beyond the transit constellation of the encounter to the karmic constraints and possibilities that the given person carries, which is *more* than what lies in the effect of the constellation of the encounter on us. This is also true for the birth of one's own child. A person leaves the "anchor position" of ones' own soul and

takes into account the qualities of another person's being. In an astrological sense, a person is connected to another person's somewhat important factor(s) through the somewhat important factor(s) of one's own threshold chart, but beyond that, one is also immersed in factors of the macrocosm and factors of karmic heritage carried by the other person, with which that person is not so related (some of the threshold chart elements of the other person are not directly related to the elements of his or her own threshold chart). Through the other person, in addition to the experience of karmic compulsions, the realm of possibilities is also revealed, as if the other person were an "extended hand" of the person. The common elements carry a great power and attraction to take on the tasks of karma for the past and the future, but it is the realm of otherness outside of this (beyond the common elements) that really brings the completely objective vision to the understanding of the other person and, at the same time, to the understanding of the "generally human." This placement in, empathy with, and acceptance of the other person's destiny can result in the creation of a *common etheric body*, in which at the same time the "I" and other parts of the person's being are retained. A classic case can be a marital community or the parent-child community, but it can also be created in spiritual communities. In spiritual literature, we can read about the formation of etheric oases, in which people going together on the spiritual path create a common etheric body and operate their daily lives out of the resurrection powers of Christ up to the nutritional level. This could be the way for the *fraternal communities* of the future.

In fact, what I am writing here is not new; the issue of karmic encounters and astrological synastry has become a prime issue in contemporary astrology these days. However, what contemporary astrology does not take into account are the transits of the embryonic period (a) and the transits to the etheric patterns projected from the embryonic period (b)—which is important for us here in terms of the viewpoint of karmic encounters and communities of destiny. These cases are therefore the following:

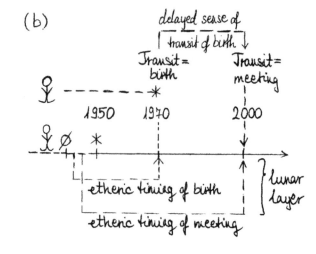

(a) When we talk about the transit during embryonic life, we are actually talking about "almost simultaneous" birth: the transit of the general situation interpreted at the beginning of the chapter "slips into" the period before birth. For example, someone is born in December 1950, and someone is born in November 1950. In fact, the two births can take on any variation in relation to each other in the time span between conception and birth. (Here we cannot speak of a parent-child relationship.)

(b) In the case of transits to the etheric patterns projected from the embryonic period, someone is born during an important projection. For example, one's birth Moon (conception ASC/DESC axis) is reached by the Sun in July 1950 during the embryonic period, which in projection activates in 1970, at which time a karmic partner is born. (This can also be a parent-child relationship.)

These transits show a special connecting *in the lunar layer*, as they refer to the embryonic period. The transit itself (the time of the other person's birth) is therefore not only examined from the point of view of the birth chart, but also for the embryonic period state (a) or projected embryonic state (b). Here, the connection between the two people's threshold charts can take on an even deeper significance due to the *special timing of birth*. I also call this form of connection "etheric programming," because here the "transit" (the birth of the other person) is connected to an unfolding karmic seed as a result of an etheric internal time algorithm, *not* or *not only* to the threshold chart for life. Case

(a) is actually the "zero" level of etheric programming, because the other person is born at the time of planting the karmic seed, not at the time of its projection. The transit of the meeting itself must of course be examined separately—in the case of a non-parent-child relationship—and the meeting may also be connected to an etheric projection in the background of the current transit.

In the drawings above, you can see that I have also indicated the lunar layer under the transit constellations of births and encounters, in which the etheric timing of birth/conception and the etheric timing of encounter are marked with separate arrows. In case (a), "Transit = birth" can also be conception, only I did not want to describe and depict every case here. The significance of the projection of such a birth/conception transit in the embryonic period requires further investigations.

What could this special connection mean? I think of karmic circles like skydivers or paratroopers jumping out of an airplane. Although they cross the threshold differently in space and/or time, they still carry "signs" that later lead them to each other. The etheric maps carried in their being exert a kind of simultaneous attraction on each other (through some connection of the constellations) that helps to keep them together for the duration of the tasks. To find this attraction, however, transits are necessary, when the meeting can be brought about with the help of some aligning celestial constellation. A special timing of births is not unconditionally necessary for the revival or creation of karmic relationships, but when it also comes into being, the relationship seems even more meaningful. In the cases I have seen so far, the Sun reached the position of the lunar node or the position of the birth Moon during the embryonic period, and this (in projection or immediately) was accompanied by the birth or conception of the karmic partner. So, one could say that the "karmic route of the soul" was crossed by the course of the Sun, when the karmic partner also "jumped out of the plane."

Here I would mention the relationship between Rudolf Steiner and Ita Wegman as an example. Steiner's lunar node axis was crossed by the Sun on July 26, 1860, which in projection falls on March 26, 1875, when Wegman could have been conceived. If we take into account the projection of ca. 93.5 days related to the Sun traveling one degree, then the period of April–May–June may have included the time of conception. Since Wegman was born on February 22, 1876, she could have been conceived in May–July 1875. (May 31, 1875, can be found in the Astrofire program.)

It should be added that, according to the solar progression associated with the newborn period (one degree = one year according to solar time counting), such etheric timings for conception/birth and/or meeting may also occur. It also happens that the lunar etheric projection of one party and the solar etheric projection of the other party are connected. The same applies to the case when, after the encounter, the start of substantive work falls on a later date, which is actually a case of a "third transit." However, we will not go further into the complexity of the topic here.

KARMIC CIRCLE IN THE SOPHIA FOUNDATION

Coming back after the general discussion to the original questions, such as the opportunity for community work perceived by Steffen Hartmann (which has probably been increasingly present since 2012 and has an effect on putting karma in order), the expectations regarding reincarnated anthroposophists, and Elisabeth Vreede's letter about the future of astrology (in which the sociality of astrology and the development of the eugenic

occult faculty are in focus), we can ask ourselves the question: where do we stand in terms of the settling of our karma among ourselves and where do we stand in the socialization of astrology, which simultaneously supports this settling of karma and the knowledge of the communal incarnation of the human being, which grows into an occult faculty?

In the winter of 2021/2022, Natalia Haarahiltunen and I (with the encouragement of Kevin Dann and with the help of James Wetmore and Joel Matthew Park, as well as direct inquiries) collected the birth and conception data of a few people belonging to the Sophia Foundation to see if there are common elements in our conception-birth intentions, which can create the force and attraction mentioned in the previous section between us in order to settle our karma and facilitate our solar tasks. And in general, we wanted to see how people are connected to the relatively well-known sidereal positions that we know mainly in their connection to the life of Christ.

I cannot disclose the names and data of the participants in the research here, because they are living persons. At the same time, this would not be appropriate, because we do not want to exclude anyone from this study just because we did not reach him/her for some reason. Likewise, I don't want to share personal conclusions; I try to remain as objective as possible.

Since the amount of data is too large, we had to decide how to take aspects into account. Finally, in the research, we only considered a narrower perspective (at least in this first phase), namely the geocentric view, but we indicated both the positions of conception and birth. At first, we only displayed the Sun, the Moon, and the lunar nodes in one diagram. (Lilith was not taken into account here, it is the subject of a separate research.) Next we added Mercury and Venus, then Mars, Jupiter and Saturn, and lastly the planets beyond Saturn. Here we present the first and the last figure. The data of one-to-one person are written on the concentric circles (on the original paper, the data of conception in red and the data of birth in black).

Of course, this provided an opportunity for a narrow-minded analysis, since the lack of a

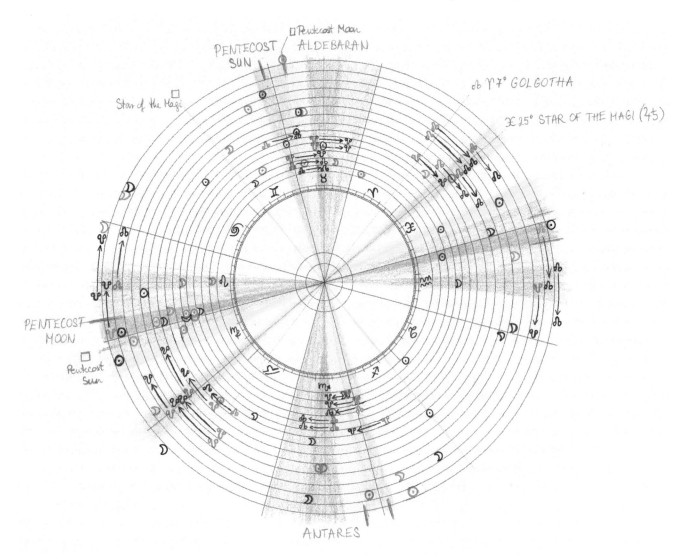

heliocentric point of view and a process perspective limits comprehensiveness. (By process perspective, I mean the special etheric timing of birth and the etheric projection related to the physical encounter, which are linked to embryonic and newborn life, and the examination of the transit of the encounter.) Nevertheless, I saw and still see that even in this form there are some striking phenomena, which we will cover here.

It is also clear that at the Sophia Foundation (as with other karmic groups) there are little twigs on a tree with a main trunk. We are looking for a main trunk, but we may have to stay on our own small branch, which does not necessarily reflect the "common spirit" and mission of the entire

Sophia Foundation. So, it is possible that we got a picture typical of a smaller karmic branch branching off from a main trunk, which readers can now expand with their own characteristics, and thus will get a somewhat different picture.

The overall picture reminds me of a Chladni dust figure, in which the vibrations created on the plate produce specific figures. Of course, the dots on it are much more disordered, but still there are discernible patterns. The characteristic of Chladni's figures is that two-dimensional waves are created with the help of a sound generator, which result in standing waves. This leads to the fact that when the disc vibrates, the dust is thrown from the "swelling points" (places of vibration of maximum

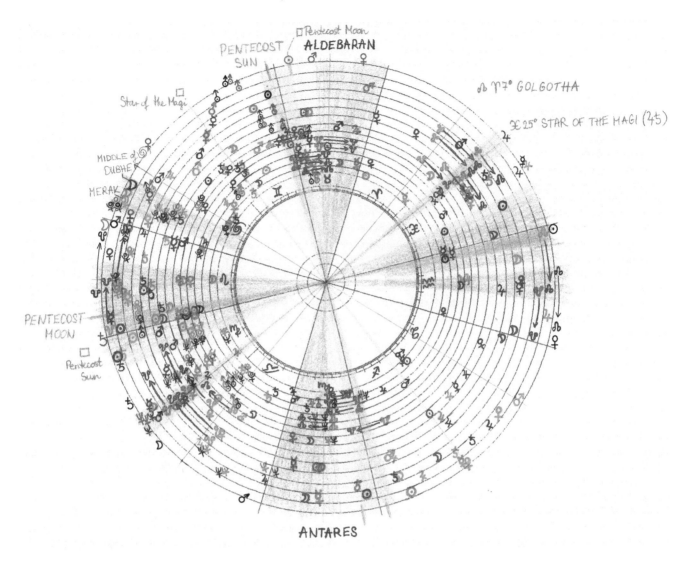

amplitude) and gathers on the "nodal lines" (places of vibration of minimum amplitude)—as it can be read in the scientific descriptions of physics. In an astrological approach, the plane of the ecliptic may represent this "plate."

We noticed in this overall picture, too, that the most striking phenomenon is the coincidence of the lunar *nodes* and then the ASC/DESCs ("earthly *nodes*"). These are accompanied by the presence of the Sun to a greater or lesser extent.

In the first figure, we can clearly see that two basic lines are drawn by the nodes. One is the Aldebaran-Antares axis; the other is the Star of the Magi axis at 25° Pisces. Specifically: out of fifteen people, four people have an Aldebaran-Antares lunar nodal line or ASC/DESC line and

six people have a Star of the Magi lunar nodal line or ASC/DESC line at the time of conception or birth (within 2° orb). If we take into account all the lunar nodal axes, everyone has either the lunar nodes of conception or birth, or both, in one of the signs of Taurus, Leo, Scorpio and Aquarius, in addition to the six people having the lunar nodal axis of Virgo-Pisces, basically focused on the Star of the Magi. It should also be noted that two people have an exact Pleiades lunar nodal line within the Taurus/Scorpio signs.

The other axis of densification is also clearly visible in the first figure. Here, the coincidence is created with the help of the Moon and the Sun. (It should be noted here that according to the hermetic rule, the Moon and the ASC/DESC are in a close, mutually presupposing relationship, so the ASC/DESC axes are also indicated by the Moon positions.) This comes into being in the immediate vicinity of the position of the Pentecost Moon (24°59' Leo) or opposite to it (24°59' Aquarius). Six people have their conception or birth Sun and five people have their conception or birth Moon (one person has his conception lunar node) between 24°-30° Leo/Aquarius. It should also be noted here that, according to Willi Sucher, the position of the Moon at birth is also related to the lunar node, as I have already written above: the lunar node is at the same place, during the transition of the soul from the Sun sphere to the Moon sphere, where the birth Moon is. If we accept this, the lunar node appears latently again in the "background" of the birth Moons.

The position of the Pentecost Sun also appears in a relatively weaker way, indicated by two lunar nodes and two Sun positions.

As the diagram was enlarged to include the other planets, these initial emphases were further amplified by the planets. In addition, a Leo-Aquarius middle line, a line on the Cancer/Leo border and a general Cancer emphasis (scattered in the sign) became more prominent. In this latter Cancer emphasis Pluto takes a large part, which was here for several people at the time of their birth, but it is also striking that eight people had the conception or birth Venus in this sign. Here it is important to recognize that the ecliptic meridians of the two Pointer stars of the Great Bear, Dubhe and Merak, are also here (at 20°28' and 24°42' Cancer).

During the enlargement, it was also revealed that at the end of Taurus, especially between 25° and 30°, but already a few degrees earlier, a lot of planets are "congested." Likewise, planets appear in the first degrees of Virgo/Pisces. These new developments led us to the conclusion of a "diluted/scattered" Pentecostal cross. Here we can also consider that on the day of Pentecost the Moon moved forward a total of 12° and thus a larger zodiacal region can also be "Pentecostal Moon-spirited." At the same time, the square of the Pentecost Moon at 25° Taurus and the square of the

Pentecost Sun at 2° Virgo arise, which stretch a cross-based attunement through the square.

In summary, looking at the zodiacal positions, a Taurus/Leo/Scorpio/Aquarius cross appears to emerge, with a mid-sign emphasis, and a similar cross with an emphasis on the cusps (leading to Gemini/Sagittarius, Virgo/Pisces) giving the impression of a "Pentecostal cross." In addition, the Star of the Magi axis is extraordinarily prominent, and as I mentioned above, the planets scattered in Cancer.

I don't want to list the factors on both "crosses" and the Star of the Magi axis, so I chose the "Pentecostal cross," also only in relation to the Sun, Moon, and lunar nodal line. The factors at 10° of Virgo/Pisces and Gemini/Sagittarius can be taken as not strictly belonging here, but as promoting social connection. (In the case of eleven people, the given person is included in both lists.)

It should be noted that two of the fifteen people have their birthdays on the same month and day, and two people were conceived within the same year, month and day.

It should be emphasized that by examining the other planets, the picture becomes even stronger, but we will not go into that here.

If we have a closer look at the special etheric timing of birth that we cannot see from this static viewpoint of concentric circles, we see the following: One person was born during the embryonic period of another person (case (a) above), when the Sun transited the other person's conception ASC/DESC axis. Related to the same situation, in

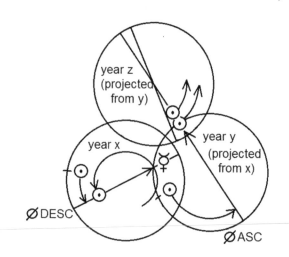

Sun, Moon, Lunar Node Conjunctions
and Oppositions along the "Pentecostal Cross"

(∅ *indicates conception, and* ∗ *indicates birth*)

1) ∅ Sun: 27°34' Leo,
   ∗Moon: 27°03' Leo

2) ∅ Sun: 28°26' Leo,
   ∅ Moon: 27°47' Leo

3) ∅ Sun: 27°45' Leo

4) ∗Sun: 29°12' Leo

5) ∅ Moon: 24°11' Leo

6) ∗Moon: 29°35' Leo

7) ∗Moon: 28°21' Leo   ∗Sun: 10°46' Pisces

8) ∗Sun: 27°42' Aqua

9) ∗Sun: 29°45' Aqua

10) ∅ lunar node: 27°57' Leo/Aqua ∗Sun: 8°52' Virgo

11) ∅ Sun: 3°1' Virgo

12) ∅ Sun: 6°13' Virgo

3) ∗Moon: 3°13' Pisces

13)   ∗Sun: 10°42' Pisces

1) ∗Sun: 25°45' Taurus

2) ∗Sun: 22°58' Taurus

3) ∅ Sun: 24°9' Taurus

4) ∅ Sun: 25°6' Taurus

5) ∅ Sun: 27°24' Scorp

6) ∗Moon: 25°45' Scorp,
   ∅ lunar node: 27°19' Taur/Scorp

7) ∗lunar node: 26°48' Taur/Scorp ∅ lunar node: 11°1' Gem/Sag

8) ∗Sun: 0°13' Gemini

9) ∗Sun: 5°35' Gemini

3) ∅ lunar node: 0°35' Gemini/Sag

10) ∅ lunar node: 2°18' Gem/Sag

11)   ∅ Moon: 9°38' Sag

12)   ∅ Sun: 11°38' Sag

13)   ∅ Sun: 11°14' Gemini

etheric projection, another person was conceived in the projection range (case (b) above). At that time, Mercury was on the conception ASC/DESC axis, while the Sun was only in the projection range. In addition, two people were conceived according to the etheric projection of the embryonic transit of the latter person, when the Sun passed through this person's conception ASC/DESC axis (case (b) above). Here in the projection range, a special situation is that on the day of conception of the two people, the Sun was in alignment exactly with this conception ASC/DESC axis (so the day of conception did not fall only in the "dilution" range of ca. 3-months). Among the two people one has the same conception ASC/DESC axis (within 1.5° orb), the other has a slightly different one (within 12° orb but in the same sign). It may be important to note that none of these people are spouses or children of the other, and some have never even met each other in person.

In addition, we should examine (as I wrote above) the etheric projections and transits related to encounters and possible joint work, in order to get closer to the nature of karmic relationships. We will not go into this here not only because of the scope, but also because we partly do not know the relationships between the fifteen people, and partly we do not want to disturb the intimate sphere of the fifteen *living* people.

CONCLUSIONS

I realize that this study and the entire article raise several questions. For my part, I am convinced that sooner or later, when examining the karmic circles (including the aspects of the embryonic and newborn period), it will be revealed that there are significant connections along the solar *and* lunar elements from an astrological point of view. Since individual human beings want to adjust to both their own previous life and to karmic companions during their lifetime, and karmic companions only *partially* carry the same characteristics and tasks as the individual person, it is not expected that individuals are better suited to their karmic companions than to their own lives. If we add to this the fact that individuals cannot choose a perfect

constellation, even for themselves, due to the determinism of physical laws, then it becomes even more of a questionable area whether they shift their center of gravity from themselves to a karmic partner for the sake of the common task.

At the same time, I consider it important *to turn toward each other* and take stock of how much we tune our own reincarnation journey to each other's for the sake of our common goals. After all, fitting in with one another, the karmic situations created by each other affect what a person "dies into" and "is born with." Human beings seem to fit in only with themselves, but this fit is largely based on the situations experienced with one's peers. We unfold the karma together. In this sense, community participation can become even more important and at the same time a reason in the reincarnation mechanism of the individual human being, and in its laws(!).

In this examined circle, the Sun, the Moon, and the other lunar elements are quite clearly grouped together on few zodiacal lines. I don't know if it is possible to talk about an ideal community in the karmic sense, where, for example, all twelve signs are equally represented. Perhaps this would be conceivable at the level of the Sun positions, and perhaps only the lunar elements would carry "stellar cohesion" and entry directions from the cosmos (from the solar sphere). But it is also possible that the "karmic group" *always* includes some narrower zodiacal segments through the Sun positions as well, and this also gives it a marked tone compared to the other karmic groups.

Of course, karmic connection to ourselves and others can be made using the same zodiacal Akasha stores that others use. For example, if we mapped the entire anthroposophic movement, the same zodiacal/star emphases still might be characteristic, yet we know that there are smaller karmic circles within the movement. This is equally true for the individual person, where up to fifty people are born in a big city in a few minutes, yet they are not reincarnations of the same person (and it is also not certain that these people died at the same time previously). So, it is clear that *intuition* is always primary in determining who has what relationship with their own past (and future) lives and the present and past (and future) lives of others.

Despite all questions and reservations, I would be glad if I had aroused the reader's curiosity to turn to the other person, taking into account astrological aspects, and notice the healing possibilities of the karmic situation underlying the relationship and the signs of joint creative work. As Steffen Hartmann pointed out, and as I think we all already know, the presence of Christ in the etheric world is a huge help if people make efforts to get to know one another more deeply. For me, doing this research, and especially our work with Natalia, led to karmic-reincarnation realizations and healing of a particular physical weakness. In addition, through correspondence with a few people, it became clear to me how much power lies in such a spiritually based community, where the *resonances* preserved by common zodiacal and planetary positions can increase the intensity of the connection with each other and with the spiritual world. Achieving and maintaining the appropriate balance in this intensity can provide a great sustaining power for small communities operating on a fraternal basis and creating a common etheric body, such as this community could become or will become in the future(?).

Human synastry, whereby several people are connected to one another, is a large fabric, for the creation of which it is difficult to establish an astrological rule, or at least to give a simple astrological rule instead of a complex one. This applies also for the case of only two people involved. However, I say that since individuals unfold their karma in karmic relationships, they are also astrologically aligned with companions in their reincarnation decisions. I can also imagine that in the coordination one *gives up* an individual element of attunement for the sake of the effectiveness of the common destiny—and/or because of astronomical laws including few or low freedom-degrees—and receives this "given up" element through the other person.[10] I think that in the

future individual human beings must be approached more and more from the perspective of their karmic environment, especially if we also keep in mind the eugenic occult faculty and the formation of fraternal communities.

If we want to delve further in this direction, it is worth asking the following questions:

> Why did I incarnate at that time when I did? In other words, what are the key points in my birth horoscope? When would these key points have been given in the same way (if they could have been at all), e.g., considering the entire twentieth century?

> If I had been born with the key points at a different time, how would I have adjusted to the birth charts of my karmic companions? Even then, would I have been able to develop the potential inherent in each planetary position?

> What does the horoscope comparison of my blood family look like? What is my family's astrological attunement? How does this look for my other karmic partners? (Here the "Chladni figures" can be created using concentric circles, as in the example.)

Of course, these questions should be extended to conception and death constellations, too, if possible.

Erin Sulllivan's book *The Astrology of Family Dynamics* can also be helpful for making analysis, if one is willing to prescind from the tropical-sidereal problem and focus on the planetary positions and angles accumulated in the family.

I consider the research of the lunar node to be an important issue that can be of great importance

---

10 For example, in the previously mentioned case, Abu Yusuf Ya'kub died with h-Venus at 27° Gemini, and not his later incarnation, Franz Schubert, but Joseph von Spaun, his karmic partner, was born later with h-Venus at 27° Gemini—in addition with h-Jupiter at 27° Gemini, meaning, as it were, "the

rich patron of Art." In their case, it is interesting to see that at their deaths, Spaun died with h-Mercury at ca. 17° Capricorn and Schubert died with h-Venus at 16° Cancer, patterning again the so called "second astrological rule of reincarnation" between them in another way; in addition, Spaun died with g-Venus at 18° Libra and Schubert died with g-Mercury at ca. 23° Libra which may give further emphasis to this special connection through Mercury and Venus. At their previous deaths, they had g-Mercury conjunction, with g-Venus conjunction on Alfonso's part, in Aries. It would be interesting to see more incarnations in order to follow up on this theme between them.

in three phases during the descent of the soul: during the transition from the Sun-sphere to the Moon-sphere, at conception, and at birth. Contemporary astrology only tries to infer the "past" and "future" and the quality of karmic relationships from the position of the descending and ascending lunar nodes at birth.

If we want to research the special etheric timing of conception/birth, the Astrofire program is of great help. The Moon, due to its rapid movement, naturally has a high chance of creating special etheric timing in relation to the Sun, lunar nodes and ASC/DESC, and the more planets involved, the greater the chance there is. It may therefore be worthwhile to focus more on the situations created by the Sun. The case of Richard Wagner, Cosima Wagner and Ludwig II drew my attention to an interesting situation within this approach. Here, I took into account the embryonic period from birth to the time of conception (i.e., backward) in the projection, and this is how interesting projections were shown. In the etheric projection of Richard Wagner, the Sun crossed the lunar node of conception on January 10, 1837, and Cosima Wagner was born on December 24, 1837; the Sun crossed the birth Moon position on February 22, 1845, and Ludwig II was born on August 25, 1845. These cases may represent new research challenges for us.

Finally, I would like to make a few subjective comments regarding the "Michael circle." I experience the karmic circle in the Sophia Foundation as part of the wider Michael karmic circle, and I write about the *potential power* of this part, which I could experience. It is potential, because it is not certain that the tasks of the settling of karma and the solar-type work will be realized to the maximum extent, even though the elements of common attunement are visible also astrologically—sometimes statically, sometimes in a process approach, sometimes both. In other circles within the wider Michael circle, the tendency to cooperate and the

help from the spiritual world are probably given to the same extent—as Steffen Hartmann writes.

Regarding the cooperation between the karmic circles within the Michael circle, however, I perceive a different situation. The tragic situation regarding the anthroposophist "exclusions" still persists, which may also make the situation of the excluded anthroposophists, who have been incarnated for the second time, difficult further on in terms of effective communication, since it is as if they should defend themselves again and again, which involves a lot of effort and leads to a quiet retreat. At the same time, intensive cooperation between other karmic circles began, and thus "reformed circles" are created. Here in Hungary, for example, this summer a small Judith von Halle reading circle was formed for the translation of Judith's new book (*Das Wort* [The word]) into Hungarian, where five people also come from a well-known Rosicrucian circle. So, I see a "karmic realignment" going on—mainly involving independently thinking, open minded people.

In our relationship with Natalia, the year 2012 was a special preparation before we met in person in 2018 at a Kaspar Hauser seminar held by Robert Powell. Both of us, without knowing each other, invited Powell to the anthroposophic circle of our own country, where he visited for the first time, and exactly one after the other (he flew from Helsinki to Budapest). It was also this year and the following when both of us (together with our husbands) were forced to withdraw from our local "official" anthroposophic life. These situations represented a serious spiritual-psychical challenge for us. So, the openness to cooperation that Hartmann writes about, 2012 began for us with this radical situation showing that working within the Society was not possible. I definitely felt, and still feel to this day, that those were the years when the definitive separation of the mainstream of anthroposophy and the circles "excluded" for some reason took place as for the cooperation in the time of Covid and today.

"We stand today at a transitional point.... The attempt had to be made to create a group [Theosophical/Anthroposophical Society] in which people find themselves together without the differentiation of the ancient group soul's nature, and there will be many such associations in the future. Then we shall no longer have to speak of racial connections but of intellectual, ethical, and moral aspects with regard to the associations that are formed. The individuals voluntarily allow their feelings to stream together, and this again causes the forming of something that goes beyond the merely emancipated human. An emancipated human being possesses an individual soul that is never lost once it has been attained. But when people find themselves together in voluntary associations, they group themselves round centers. The feelings streaming to a center in this way once again give beings the opportunity of working as a kind of group soul, though in quite a different sense from the early group souls.... The more that people are divided, the fewer lofty souls will descend into the human sphere. The more that associations are formed in which feelings of fellowship are developed with complete freedom, the more lofty beings will descend, and the more rapidly the earthly planet will be spiritualized."

RUDOLF STEINER, *Good and Evil Spirits*, June 1, 1908

CLASSICS IN ASTROSOPHY, PART VII:
LUNAR CALENDAR FOR FARMERS AND GARDENERS

Robert Powell, PhD, and Fred Gettings

The foregoing experiment to test the effect of the Moon on the growth of potatoes is one in a series planned by Nick Kollerstrom in collaboration with a market gardener. These experiments will be analyzed as the results come in and will be reported in the *Mercury Star Journal*. The editor of the *Mercury Star Journal* is compiling statistical reports of the experiments for those who are interested.[1]

The results obtained so far are promising, and support Maria Thun's biodynamic research work. She has reported her observations, made over many years, of the cosmic influences on plants in the German biodynamic periodical *Lebendige Erde* (Living Earth).

The spiritual-scientific foundation for Maria Thun's work is based on an understanding of how the etheric formative forces are related to the zodiac. The four ethers are described by Guenther Wachsmuth[2] and related to the signs of the zodiac, as in table 1.[3]

state. The maintenance of a particular condition is effected by the activity of etheric forces. There are four different cosmic etheric forces to maintain the four types of terrestrial condition—e.g., all air is permeated with light ether. The activity of these cosmic etheric forces is stimulated by the astral forces emanating from the zodiac. Moreover, the celestial signs of the zodiac each activate one particular ether more powerfully than any other. This was known in antiquity and was expressed in the doctrine of "elements," in which the four elements—earth, water, air, and fire—are assigned to the twelve zodiacal signs (see table 1).

The ancient expression "element" is simply an expression of the recognition that the whole earth sphere is compounded of four conditions, the fiery, the airy, the watery, and the earthly, which in the modern terminology of spiritual science are designated heat-state, gaseous, liquid, and solid. This is the basis for table 1. For example, the liquid condi-

TABLE 1

ETHER	SIGNS OF THE ZODIAC	CONDITION	ELEMENT
life ether	Taurus, Virgo, Capricorn	solid	earth
chemical ether	Cancer, Scorpio, Pisces	liquid	water
light ether	Gemini, Libra, Aquarius	gaseous	air
warmth ether	Aries, Leo, Sagittarius	heat state	fire

Everything in terrestrial existence is in one of four conditions: solid, liquid, gaseous, or heat

tion, maintained by the activity of chemical ether, corresponds to the element of water, which is related to the zodiacal signs Cancer, Scorpio, and Pisces. What does this signify? It means that the astral forces of Cancer, Scorpio, and Pisces stimulate the chemical ether and consequently activate everything in the terrestrial realm that is in a liquid condition.

1   This article first appeared in the *Mercury Star Journal,* June 1977.
2   Wachsmuth, *The Etheric Formative Forces in Cosmos, Earth and Man*, p. 44.
3   Wachsmuth, *Kosmische Aspekte von Geburt und Tod*, p. 11.

Maria Thun and members of the Biodynamic Association have applied this spiritual-scientific theory to the growth of plants and have achieved encouraging results. The basis for this application consists in the observation of the fourfold nature of all plants. Maria Thun discovered that all plants can be classified into one of four types: root, leaf, flower, and fruit seed.[4] The classification is made according to which aspect of the plant is predominant. For example, potatoes, carrots, and turnips are representative of the root type, since the root is predominant. Similarly, cabbages and lettuces are of the leaf type. The flower types are self-evident, and the fruit-seed types are, notably, beans, peas, tomatoes, etc.

It was Guenther Wachsmuth who first postulated (in a lecture) that since a certain element predominated in each of the four types, then the signs of the zodiac are likely to exert a corresponding influence. For example, the watery element is predominant in cabbages, therefore the growth of cabbages should be enhanced by the signs of Cancer, Scorpio, and Pisces. Maria Thun proceeded to test this hypothesis.

It is evident that of all the cosmic bodies the Sun and Moon exert the most powerful influence upon the earth. The rate of motion of the Sun, taking a whole month to pass through one sign of the zodiac, is too slow to allow the farmer to plan his sowing and planting by the Sun.[5] It is quite different, however, in the case of the Moon. In 27 1/3 days the Moon passes through each of the twelve signs of the zodiac, spending a little over two days in each sign. Hence the influence exerted by the Moon can be readily harnessed by the farmer. According to the type of plant he wishes to grow, he can wait for the planting of it until the Moon is in an appropriate sign. Since the natural forces of Cancer, Scorpio, and Pisces

stimulate the chemical ether, he will wait until the Moon is in one of these signs conducive to the growth of cabbages, for example, before he plants his cabbages (see table 2).

TABLE 2

MOON SIGN	FOR PLANTING
Taurus, Virgo, Capricorn	root type crops
Cancer, Scorpio, Pisces	leaf type crops
Gemini, Libra, Aquarius	flower type crops
Aries, Leo, Sagittarius	fruit-seed type crops

Maria Thun has made observations over many years to test the theory summarized in table two. She has conducted experiments using certain vegetables, e.g. potatoes, carrots, beans, etc., to try and assess the validity of the theory. The method she had adopted in such experiments is to plant crops of a given type with the Moon in successive signs (and therefore associated with a different element) and observing the growth. The observations she has made and the experiments she has conducted confirm that the Moon signs listed in table two are indeed conducive to the growth of the corresponding type of crop. Nick Kollerstrom and others, following similar procedures, have also obtained results in conformity with the theory expressed in table two.[6]

One important point to notice is that the Moon signs employed are sidereal, i.e. they are defined with respect to the fixed stars. The use of the sidereal zodiac by biodynamic farmers and research workers can be traced back to the year 1912, when Rudolf Steiner's *Calendar of the Soul* was published. However, the *Calendar of the Soul* and its successor, the *Sternkalender*, employ sidereal divisions of unequal length. The unequal-length sidereal divisions, known as *constellations*, are based on Ptolemy's "Catalogue of Stars," in books 7 and 8 of the *Almagest*, compiled in the first half of the second century AD. However, the sidereal *signs*, are equal-length

---

4   Maria Thun's report, "Nine Years Observation of Cosmic Influences on Annual Plants," originally appeared in English in *Star and Furrow* (spring 1964). See also Koepf, Pettersson, and Schaumann, *Biodynamic Agriculture*, pp. 203–206.

5   Apart from the obvious fact of sowing in a given season of the year, which is determined by the zodiacal location of the Sun.

6   Cf. Ulf Abele, *Vergleichende Untersuchungen zum Konventionellen und biol. dyn. Pflanzenbau*, PhD Thesis, University of Giessen, 1973.

divisions, each 30° in length, marked out by certain fixed stars. Whereas the constellations were not defined until the second century AD,[7] the sidereal signs were used by the Babylonians as early as the fifth century BC.[8] A comparison of the two divisions (constellations and signs) of the sidereal zodiac shows that there are only minor differences between them, with the exception of the boundary between Virgo and Libra. The practical consequence for farmers is that whether the signs or constellations of the sidereal zodiac are used, in general the results should be more or less the same. Why, then, should the sidereal signs be used in preference to the constellations?

At the present time, until further tests have been made, no assessment of the comparative efficacy of the signs or constellations in the effect on plant growth can be made. The reason biodynamic farmers use the constellations is primarily historical (i.e., the constellations during the first half of this century), handed down from Greek astronomy, whereby only the sidereal divisions generally known. It is only in the second half of the twentieth century that widespread knowledge of the signs, originating from Babylonian astronomy, was acquired. Even now, to a large extent the signs are unknown, but thanks to the painstaking work of a number of science historians, especially Otto Neugebauer (1899–1990), the highly sophisticated Babylonian astronomy of the final centuries BC has been reconstructed in some detail.[9]

The importance of Babylonian astronomy as the foundation for the future development of astronomical science cannot be too strongly emphasized. Without Babylonian astronomy it is difficult to envisage how a work like the Almagest could have been written. Owing to the universal acknowledgment of the Almagest as the ultimate authority in astronomical science, Ptolemy's definition (vols. 7 and 8) of the constellations became accepted by astronomers as the definitive version of the sidereal zodiac. Apart from minor modifications, Ptolemy's sidereal zodiac is used by almost all modern astronomers. The earlier Babylonian division became forgotten everywhere, with the single exception of India. The rediscovery in the twentieth century of the division of the sidereal zodiac into signs, originally defined by astronomer-priests in Babylon, means that there are now two alternative divisions of the sidereal zodiac.

We have on the one hand the division into constellations (unequal-length) belonging to the Greek tradition of astronomy, and on the other hand we have the division into signs (equal-length) of Babylonian origin. In the spirit of scientific enquiry, so that comparative studies of the two sidereal divisions may be made, the *Mercury Star Journal* is taking the radical step of departing from the tradition biodynamic sowing calendar based on constellations in order to tabulate a calendar based on the equal-length sidereal signs.

The sidereal signs are 30° arcs in celestial space marked out by certain fixed stars. For example, the sign of Gemini extends from the end of the Bull's horns (marked by Elnath and Alhecka, and Tauri) to the head of the Twins (marked by Castor and Pollux, and Gemini). The Moon signs are delineated by the actual fixed stars that the 30° arcs in celestial space encompass—e.g., the sign of Leo is delineated by Denebola, Zosma, and Regulus (see fig. 1, page 114). The fixed-star signs are literally "signs" in celestial space.

7 The constellations were referred to earlier than this—e.g., by Hipparchus (second century BC)—but they did not acquire a scientific definition until Ptolemy.

8 The first recorded use of the sidereal zodiac with twelve equal fixed-star signs is in a Babylonian list of solar eclipses, preserved on cuneiform tablets for the years from 475 to 457 BC; cf. Aaboe, Asger-Sachs, Abraham, "Two Lunar Texts of the Achaemenid Period from Babylon," *Centaurus* 14 (1969), p. 17. From Babylon the sidereal zodiac was transmitted to Greece and thence to Egypt during the early Hellenistic period. With the rampageous spread of astrology from Alexandria the sidereal zodiac became transmitted to India, where it is still in use to this present day.

9 Cf. Neugebauer, *A History of Ancient Mathematical Astronomy*, 3 vols., for a masterly exposition of ancient astronomy.

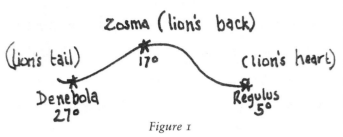

Figure 1

The modern sidereal signs are identical with those used in antiquity by the Babylonians, Egyptians and Greeks, and with those that are used to this present day by Hindu astronomers and astrologers. The historical background to the sidereal signs has already been discussed in this *Journal*. From such considerations it is evident that the signs, originally defined by the Babylonian priest, became metamorphosed into the constellations specified by Ptolemy. The phenomena discovered by Maria Thun show that the astronomer-priests of Babylon did not divide the stars comprising the zodiacal belt into twelve signs arbitrarily but did so out of some comprehension of the differentiated nature of the fixed stars belonging to the zodiacal belt. Thereby they laid the foundations for a true cosmic science, the fruits of which will surely prove to be of substantial benefit to modern humanity. The rediscovery through spiritual science of the significance of the ancient doctrines has practical consequences, as demonstrated here, which enable humanity to live in harmony with nature and with the spiritual world that supports and sustains nature.

Lunar Calendar

The lunar year 1977–78 commenced with the new Moon of Aries on March 19. In the lunar year there are twelve lunar months corresponding to the twelve signs of the zodiac (if there are thirteen lunar months, e.g., in the lunar year 1978–79, a second month of Pisces is usually intercalated). Each lunar month comprises four lunar weeks corresponding to the four quarters of the Moon.

Rainfall and weather changes appear to be correlated with the lunar weeks. In particular, new Moon and full Moon tend to precipitate rain.[10] On this basis farmers are justified in planting shortly before the new or full moon in order to take advantage of precipitated rainfall. Comparatively little research has been made into the effect of the lunar phases on plant growth, but special mention can be made of the research of Lili Kolisko. She tested the traditional belief that leaf crops are best sown during the waxing moon while root crops benefit most from being sown under the waning Moon. In the case of all kinds of vegetables she found invariably that the best growth is obtained by sowing two days prior to the full Moon.[11] Even for those vegetables that, according to tradition, should grow best by being sown at (or shortly before) new Moon, e.g., radishes, beetroot, carrots, and kohlrabi, she obtained maximum growth by sowing two days prior to the full Moon. However, this "Kolisko effect" has not been duplicated experimentally (as far as I know), primarily because of lack of research. Nevertheless, the lunar phases are tabulated here in order that the foregoing may at least be considered, even if not followed.[12]

EDITORIAL FOREWORD
(ROBERT POWELL; MARCH 1978)

In years to come astrology will occupy an increasingly important position in Western cultural life. Already a rapidly growing interest in astrology is apparent. Yet will modern astrology (which is actually Greek astrology handed down with some additions and modifications) satisfy the hearts and minds of future generations? Does astrology need

---

10 Cf. Bradley, Woodbury, and Brier, "Lunar Synodical Periods and Widespread Precipitation," *Science* 137 (1962).

11 Kolisko, *The Moon and the Growth of Plants*.

12 ED. NOTE: in the original article, Robert Powell included the phases of the lunar months of Cancer, Leo, Virgo, and Libra in the summer of 1977, as well as the date and time of ingress of the Moon into a new sign of the zodiac throughout those lunar months, so that readers who were also biodynamic gardeners could experiment with the indications of the article. The ephemerides included in this volume for the year 2024 provide this information for the entire growing season, and could be used for that purpose by interested readers.

to undergo a metamorphosis before it will be of real service to humanity?

Apart from a number of traditionalists most will answer "yes" to this latter question. Few people who have made a serious study of astrology would deny that they have experienced some degree of dissatisfaction with modern astrology. The fact that only a few present-day scientific thinkers take astrology seriously is itself a cause for dissatisfaction, giving rise to the question: "Why is it that modern science finds astrology unacceptable?" Even when faced with incontrovertible scientific evidence that there *is* a reality to the ancient belief in a relationship between humankind and the stars, few scientists are willing to accept astrology as a science. All of this might signify that something is lacking in astrology, which causes it to be excluded from the domain of modern science.

Alternatively, it could indicate that there is something missing from the modern scientific outlook. Perhaps it is a transformation of the scientific world-view that is needed, rather than a reformation of astrology?

In fact, there is a degree of truth in each of these viewpoints. Not only is astrology in need of a reformation but also, if astrology is to become scientifically acceptable, science will need to expand its horizon of consciousness to include a greater reality than what is perceptible to the physical senses or measurable with physical instruments. For it is by taking into consciousness that a cosmic (non-earthly) element is present in every human being that astrology can begin to have a cognitive foundation. It was an assumption inherent in the original formulation of astrology that the human being is born from the cosmos and, with the loss of this assumption coinciding with the advent of modern science, the science of horoscopes lacks any solid basis.

As I have endeavored to show in my contribution, "The Astrological Paradigm and the Origin of Horoscopic Astrology," horoscopic astrology (the general form of astrology today) originated within an esoteric circle of the Chaldean priesthood and based on occult experience gained

through initiation practiced by its members. The doctrines underlying astrology evolved from these Chaldean mysteries and were later elaborated in conceptual form primarily by Greek practitioners of the celestial science. The astrological teachings that have been transmitted down through the centuries, since the days of ancient Greece, form the corpse of what was once a living practice, an esoteric science. As Fred Gettings shows in his contribution, "The Sigils for Pisces and Spica," even astrological details such as the symbols used for stars and for the signs of the zodiac are intelligible only in the light of the esoteric background from which astrology has evolved.[13]

Thus, in order for astrology to progress, to become astrosophy (to use Steiner's term for what he envisaged the future science of the stars to be), it must become living and it must become progressively more esoteric—i.e., concerned with invisible realities. Perhaps the most comprehensive and complete source of modern esoteric teaching is to be found in Anthroposophy (which originated with Rudolf Steiner), and it is from this source that a number of dedicated astrologers have found a well-spring of esoteric truths capable of yielding a renewed, revitalized astrology (or astrosophy) worthy of the name "celestial science."

Anthroposophy builds a bridge from modern scientific thought, which is concerned with earthly realities, to esoteric thought, which is occupied with higher realities. In this respect Anthroposophy is justifiably called "spiritual science." Astrology, also, has the potential to be a "spiritual science"—i.e., a science embodying a spiritual conception of humanity and the universe. But in order for this potential to unfold, a transformation of consciousness is necessary in which a "seeing" of a higher reality in each

13 Fred Gettings refers to the Magian origin of astrology. This may appear to contradict the results of my research pinpointing the origin of astrology to Babylon in the sixth century BC. However, since Zaratas the Chaldean (the initiate-teacher of the Babylonian priesthood) was the reincarnation of Zarathustra the Persian and was also known as Zoroaster the Mage, it is equally correct to refer to a Magian origin of astrology.

human being takes place. One who looks at a horoscope with this kind of (new) awareness will awaken to the realization that he is concerning himself with something divine, of celestial origin. Out of this transformed consciousness, scientists of the future will be able to recognize that indeed astrology is a science, a science that is concerned not with earthly but with heavenly realities. Then astrology will come into its own as the royal science, the science of the human being's divinity. In this sense it may be said that astrology will become of increasing importance in Western cultural life, as consciousness begins to undergo a transformation and begins to awaken to the divinity within each and every human being. We may look toward a New Age (one that is already making its way into the world in an increasing number of human forms of consciousness) in which the sublime potential of astrology will begin to be realized, when human beings are able to say to themselves: "I live not just in a physical reality but in a spiritual and moral universe the foundation of which is Love and Truth, which dwell also in me in heart and mind, and which radiate forth from the planets and stars who are co-creators with me of my pathway through earthly life."

THE ASTROLOGICAL PARADIGM AND THE ORIGIN OF HOROSCOPIC ASTROLOGY (ROBERT POWELL; MARCH 1978)

In the Michaelmas 1977 issue of the *Mercury Star Journal* (pp. 81–84), the "astrological paradigm" was outlined as an alternative to the generally held modern biological and psychological theories about the nature of humankind. The astrological paradigm embodies a conception of the human being that extends back in time to a remote antiquity. Knowledge of it has been transmitted from century to century over the ages, often among only a small number of people, and is emerging once again in the twentieth century, having been virtually lost to Western culture. Within it is the fundamental conception underlying horoscopic astrology, namely that the human being is a living soul who unites with the

body at the moment of birth. Thus, according to Professor van Der Waerden in his excellent discussion of horoscopic astrology: "The soul comes from the heavens, where it partook of the circulation of the stars. It unites itself with a body and forms with it a living being. This explains how human character comes to be determined by the heavens."[14]

This conception underlying horoscopic astrology can be traced back to Chaldean priests in Babylon.

> The notion that the soul descending from heaven takes on the characteristics of the planetary spheres through which it passes, before it enters into corporeal existence, and that after death it makes its journey through the heavens in reverse direction and with opposite effect— this derives from the same religious circles as those in which the doctrine of the voyage of the soul through the spheres had developed: the later Babylonian astral theology.[15]

The first horoscopes, i.e. astronomical calculations of the celestial configuration at the moment of birth, were computed by Babylonian priests.[16] All that remains now of these first horoscopes is for the most part the actual computation inscribed in cuneiform; how the celestial configurations were considered or interpreted is barely indicated in the cuneiform texts. Yet we may deduce from the Chaldean Oracles,[17] the mystery teachings transmitted from Babylon by two Hellenized Orientals, Julian the Chaldean and his son Julian the Theurgist, that the Chaldeans in some way had actual knowledge of the soul's descent through

---

14 Van der Waerden, *Science Awakening*, p. 147.

15 Lewy, *Chaldean Oracles and Theurgy*, p. 146.

16 Cf. Abraham Sachs, "Babylonian Horoscopes," *Journal of Cuneiform Studies* vi (1952), pp. 49–75, where the world's first horoscopes are discussed. The earliest horoscope dates from the fifth century BC.

17 The Chaldean Oracles were known to many members of the Neoplatonic school and most of the extant texts of the Oracles have been preserved in the writings of Proclus. C. Wilhelm Kroll, "De Oraculis Chaldaicis," *Breslau Philologische Abhandlungen* vii (1894), pp. 76ff.

the planetary spheres into incarnation.[18] Thus we may surmise that the reason why the Chaldean priest computed the celestial configuration at the moment of an individual's birth was because they regarded the horoscope as an expression of the living soul.

To comprehend the astrological paradigm and thereby understand what astrology is, clearly one of the foremost requirements is to acquire insight into the nature of the human soul. However, genuine knowledge of the soul, such as that possessed by the Chaldean priests, hardly exists in contemporary Western civilization. Indeed, for most brought up in twentieth-century Western culture it is difficult to experience and bring to conscious realization that the human being is anything more than a "body." For by far the greater part of contemporary life is oriented toward the body and its needs. Even psychology, the "science of the soul," hardly deals with the soul.

> It may seem somewhat frivolous to say that psychology does not deal with its own subject—the human soul; yet it is true. Psychology deals, on the one hand, with the conscious human mind, and on the other hand it tries to enter the vast realm of the unconscious. But the soul itself, this very being of humankind, is left out.[19]

In modern astrology, too, as in psychology, the soul remains a vague concept and there is consequently a tendency to neglect the essential element with which astrology is concerned. To counterbalance this tendency, it is helpful to become aware

of the roots of astrology, of its birth in the circle of the Babylonian priestly caste, and to think about their conception of astrology.

From the Chaldean Oracles it is apparent that the Babylonian priests divided the realms beyond the earth into three zones: (1) the Empyrean, the abode of the Supreme Father enthroned above the revolving starry spheres; (2) the Ethereal World reaching up to the fixed stars and containing the seven planetary spheres (with the spheres arranged in the order of speed of rotation—Saturn, Jupiter, Mars, Sun, Venus, Mercury, Moon); and (3) the Hylic World comprising the sub-lunar region. Aion, or Chronos-Saturn, was considered to be the ruler of the highest zone, the sun was held to be ruler of the ethereal world, while the moon rules over the hylic world. To acquire knowledge of the three worlds beyond the earth was the aim of the aspirant in the Chaldean mysteries, and the moon, sun, and Aion were known as the "Rulers of the initiation." To be initiated by the sun, for example, the candidate for initiation passed through purification and magical rituals enabling his soul to separate from the body and, ascending through the planetary spheres, "to rush to the center of the sounding light," i.e. to the Sun, which is at the center of the planetary spheres.[20] Thus even during his earthly life the initiate in these ancient mysteries was able to experience the journey that every soul undergoes after its final departure from the body at the moment of death. The initiate in the Chaldean mysteries could thereby gain direct knowledge of the hidden life of the soul, of its journey through the cosmic realms after death. The sun was of special importance in the Chaldean initiation, being considered the "heart" of the planetary spheres. The significance of this initiation was that, from it, knowledge could be acquired that would serve as the basis for the fundamental conception underlying astrology. That is to say, within the initiation knowledge transmitted in conceptual form by the esoteric doctrines of the Chaldeans is contained the conception that during the descent from its super-celestial place of origin the soul acquires a vesture or garment formed out

18 Julian the Chaldean and his son appeared in Rome during the reign of the Emperor Marcus Aurelius. Concerning the term "Chaldeans" Hans Lewy (op. cit., p. 427) says it "...referred primarily to the members of the priestly caste of Babylon and to their Hellenistic disciples.... The name always remained attached to the esoteric knowledge of the science of the heavenly bodies and of the theology based on it. If therefore the two founders (Julian and Julian) of Theurgy in the period of the general high estimation of all Oriental wisdom appeared in Rome before both the educated and common people with the name Chaldeans, they thereby gave expression to their claim to be regarded as descendants and spiritual heirs of the priestly sages of Babylon."

19 König, *The Human Soul*, p. 1 (rev.).

20 Lewy, op. cit., p. 175.

of the substance of the planetary spheres that it traverses. Computing the planetary positions for the moment of birth, the horoscope thus gives a picture or representation of this celestial garment or "astral body" acquired by the soul during the descent through the planetary spheres en route to birth. The horoscope may be considered, then, as a kind of map of the "astral body" that clothes the soul, according to the esoteric doctrines of the originators of astrology. But at what period in Babylonian history, and with whom did horoscopic astrology originate?

In endeavoring to answer this question we are confronted by the fact that there is virtually nothing written on this subject. The material concerning horoscopic astrology from cuneiform sources is exceedingly fragmentary. Yet by following a careful, historical approach it is possible to gain some insight into the obscure origins of astrology. Professor Abraham Sachs' remarkable paper on the birth of horoscopic astrology in Babylonia provides a broad outline of the development over the two millennia before the Christian Era from general, omen astrology in Assyria and Babylonia to the birth of horoscopic astrology—i.e., the prediction of individual human destiny from the positions of the sun, moon and planets at the moment of birth.[21] As he points out, the collection of Babylonian texts from the extensive library of the Assyrian king Assurbanipal contains not the slightest indication of horoscopic astrology, although thousands of astrological omens have been recovered from this great library, which was destroyed when the Medes sacked Nineveh in 612 BC.[22] Therefore the existence of horoscopic astrology prior to the sixth century BC can be safely ruled out.

After the collapse of the Assyrian empire, Babylon became restored as the world's leading cultural center during the reign of the Chaldean kings— Nabopolassar, Nebuchadnezzar II, Amel-Marduk, Nergal-Shar-Usar, Labashi-Marduk and Nabunaid. The last-named king's seventeen-year reign terminated in 539 BC, when the Persian king Cyrus the Great captured Babylon. The Persian dynasty inaugurated by Cyrus continued to rule Babylon until 331 BC, when Alexander the Great made his entry into the city. Since the oldest extant horoscope has been dated by Abraham Sachs to the year 410 BC, during the reign of the Persian king Darius II, it may be concluded that horoscopic astrology originated at some time in Babylon in the sixth or in the fifth century BC—either during the reign of the Chaldean kings, prior to 539 BC, or under the Persian kings, between 539 and 410 BC.

In my opinion, and I admit that the evidence is circumstantial, the impulse for the development of horoscopic astrology is to be traced to the time of the last of the Chaldean kings, Nabunaid (or Nabonidus), who acceded to the throne of Babylon in 556 BC. The period of Nabunaid's reign covers the last part of the Jewish captivity in Babylon, which lasted for almost fifty years, and includes the time when the prophet Daniel was active.[23] It includes also the last years of Zaratas the Chaldean, the great teacher of the priesthood in Babylon.[24] Zaratas had among his pupils a young

---

23 Cf. Daniel I, 21: "And Daniel continued until the first year of King Cyrus." Note that King Nebuchadnezzar, as he is named in the book of Daniel, is actually Nabunaid. This has been established by evidence from cuneiform sources, cf. Wiseman et al, *Notes on Some Problems in the Book of Daniel*.

24 According to Rudolf Steiner's karma research, Zaratas was the reincarnation of Zarathustra, the founder of the Zoroastrian religion (cf. his lecture course *Acccording to Matthew*). This discovery of Steiner's accounts for the confusion among scholars concerning Zarathustra (or Zoroaster). Cf. Henning, *Zoroaster: Politician or Witch-doctor?* p. 13: "Any student who contemplates the figures of Zoroaster drawn by Herzfeld (in *Zoroaster and his World*) on the one hand, by Nyberg (in *Die Religionen des alten Iran*) on the other, will be willed with perplexity. How is it possible, one is bound to ask, that two scholars of renown who work with precisely the same material, use exactly the same sources, arrive at results that are diametrically opposed to each other? The answer lies in a knowledge of reincarnation. Herzfeld's Zoroaster lived at the time of Cyrus, in the sixth century BC, while Nyberg's Zoroaster was a prehistoric man. Both scholars describe the same individual, but in different incarnations. [*Cont. next page*]

---

21 Abraham Sachs, "Naissance de l' astrologie horoscopique en Babylonie", *Archeologia* 15 (Paris, mars/avril, 1967), pp. 13–19.

22 Ibid., p. 17.

Greek, who later founded his own esoteric school. This was Pythagoras. "At Babylon Pythagoras associated with the Chaldeans and visited Zaratas by whom he was cleansed of the pollutions of his earlier life."[25] Undoubtedly the influence of Zaratas played an important part in Pythagoras' school, and such astrological leanings as may be discerned in Pythagorean teachings may well have stemmed originally from Zaratas' esoteric school into which Pythagoras was initiated. This circumstantial evidence could well point to Zaratas as a primary source for the origin of the teachings that later became encapsulated in the form of horoscopic astrology.

In addition to Zaratas, however, it is possible that his contemporary, Nabunaid, the last of the Chaldean kings, was also an important source for the impulse that led toward the development of horoscopic astrology. As is evident in the Book of Daniel, the interpretation of astrological dreams was practiced at Nabunaid's court. From other sources it is known that Nabunaid had an interest in astrological matters surpassing that of all other Eastern kings.[26] Unlike his predecessors on the throne, Nabunaid did not depend upon the priesthood (who were professional star-gazers) for the interpretation of the stars. He regarded himself as more competent than the priesthood, and claimed to have been initiated directly by the Moon god Sin (or I'teri) from whom he gained his knowledge of the mysteries (concerning the stars). "I am wise, I have knowledge; I can see the se(cret things); though I do not know how to impress the stylus on a tablet, I can see the my(stery); the god I'teri made me perceive a vision (whereby) He made k(nown to me) everything…every wisdom (I possess)."[27]

An example of an astrological dream (or initiation experience) is given by Nabunaid himself.

[The Moon, the star] Venus, the planet Saturn, the star Arcturus, the star Vindemiatrix, [the planet] Jupiter, the inhabitants of heaven, I made them [i.e., these stars] the exalted [ar]biters [of my destiny]. For long days of life, stability of the throne, duration of the dynasty, favorable presentation of my affairs before Marduk, my Lord, I implored them. [Then] I laid down [to sleep]. During the midnight watch I saw Cyula [=Vega], my Lady, the reviver of the dead, the giver of a long life, and for eternal life of my soul, for turning the countenance [toward me] I implored her. And she turned her countenance toward me; with her shining face she faithfully looked at me and actually caused [him, i.e., Marduk] to show mercy.[28]

This text shows clearly that astrology in its origins was not merely conceptual but was a matter of experience—experience obtained through revelation (in dreams) or through initiation. Two great initiates were present contemporaneously in Babylon in the sixth century BC—Nabunaid and Zaratas the Chaldean. Both were initiates into the world of stars. It is to these two great individuals that available evidence points, leading me to consider them as the likely originators of esoteric doctrines that subsequently led to the development of horoscopic astrology. Thus, the fundamental doctrine underlying horoscopic astrology, that the human being is a living soul who unites with the body at the moment of birth (the essence of the astrological paradigm) can be traced back in all probability to Babylon in the sixth century BC, to the time of Zaratas and Nabunaid, the last of the Chaldean kings.

The Sigils for Pisces and Spica (Fred Gettings; March 1978)

I have been asked to write an article on an aspect of esoteric astrology in order to give my impression of how this form of astrology differs from ordinary, exoteric astrology. This I do with pleasure, even though such an attempt is thwart with

The incarnation as Zarathustra was in prehistoric times, somewhere in the region of Oxus and Jaxarted, while the incarnation as Zaratas was in the time of Nabunaid and Cyrus (Herzfeld maintains that (his) Zoroaster was actually related by marriage to Cyrus).

25 Cf. Porphyry, The Life of Pythagoras (see bibliography).

26 Cf. Hildegard Lewy, "The Babylonian Background of the Kay Kaus Legend," Archiv Orientalni 17 (1949), pp. 28–109.

27 Ibid., p. 68.

28 Ibid., p. 52.

difficulties—the main difficulty being one of communication, in that so many esoteric truths are so subtle, so out of the ordinary, that it is extremely hard to express them (even to those with a knowledge of esoteric astrology) in a clear and intelligible form. I have come to the conclusion that the most reasonable way of presenting the delicate truths of esoteric astrology is to base one's work on a structure of sound research, by which one's ideas may be defended, and by means of which supportive arguments may be followed by those interested in the truth.

First of all, then, I must record my conviction that exoteric astrology (that is, the kind practiced and studied in most circles these days) is not only a shadow of esoteric astrology, but actually depends for its life, such as it is, on the vast spiritual energies that were (perhaps even *are*) at the command of those who give form to esoteric astrology. Both exoteric and esoteric astrology are fundamentally philosophical schema that may be used for a variety of purposes. I make this accurate generalization in order to disassociate myself from the specific use to which exoteric astrology is so frequently put—that is, for "ego aggrandizement" and emotional manipulation. The stars deserve better of humankind. If in earlier centuries astrology could be described as the princess daughter of Urania, then I feel that today her virtue being lost, her corpus being misused, she might now be described as a whore.

In order that this whore might be saved, and made fit to be treated as a princess, much work has to be done—yet this work cannot even be started without the development of a new morality, and a true understanding of the original truths of esoteric astrology. The research into esoteric astrology is something akin to the work of the genealogist, seeking to reveal to this poor creature the truth of her royal and celestial origin. After much review of the situation, I have come to the conclusion that the new astrology must be founded not only upon a moral and imaginative approach to humankind, but also on a reliable approach to the past, on an examination of the

esoteric tradition, which will prove capable of regenerating the present form.

It is the nature of esoteric astrology that the deeper truths are well hidden, so that each individual must—through meditation, reflection, and archival research—gain a personal picture of the sublime nature of true astrology. I doubt that anyone can actually *teach* esoteric astrology, though it may be learned. It is probably for this reason that so few astrologers have actually attempted to write about esoteric astrology.[29] An exception to this general rule is Rudolf Steiner, who has spoken at great length and with supreme clarity on many aspects of esoteric astrology. Following his lines of thought I have been able to discover esoteric astrological truths that, when apprehended in their full power, have the potential of transforming and vitalizing even the dead letter of modern astrology.

Perhaps I should at this point be specific, and make some record of how Steiner's indications have fructified my personal research.

As an example, I will take certain lines of thought connected with the single sigil for the zodiacal sign Pisces: ♓. If we take any ordinary exoteric astrological text, we find always the claim that the glyph for Pisces expresses a variety of ideas concerning "duality." Such a duality runs through the ancient tradition, and was admirably set down in a fairly wholesome exoteric way by Pagan at the beginning of our century, so that little of the voluminous literature since that time has added much to what this theosophist had to say.[30] In regard to the dual nature of the sigil,

---

29 In name, if not in fact, three books spring to mind: A. Leo, *Esoteric Astrology*, c. 1900; A. E. Thierens, *Elements of Esoteric Astrology*, 1931; and A. A. Bailey, *Esoteric Astrology*, 1951. While each of these books no doubt contributes something of value, each is personal to a point where the system propounded breaks contact with the past, and thus with the roots of genuine esoteric astrology, which in itself is not a personal thing. One gets the impression, especially with the last two titles, that "complex, systematized and theosophical" equals "esoteric," while in my experience esoteric ideas are often remarkably simple ones. It is difficult to bring the material in either of these books down to earth in a useful way.

30 Pagan, *From Pioneer to Poet*, p. 183ff.

most writers on astrology pay lip-service to the association so frequently drawn between Pisces and Christ. For example, M. E. Hone says "...the two fishes with their link...is representative of man's physical and spiritual sides, joined yet separate," and with reference to the rulership of Pisces over the feet, continues that this is an aspect of "Christian symbolism when Jesus abased Himself to wash the *feet* of His disciples. These were men whose work was to catch *fish*."[31] Again, J. Mayo is equally specific, for after referring to the common idea that the symbol represents two fishes joined together and pulling in reverse directions, "typical of the dual and vacillating nature of the Piscean type," he points to the New Testament, and suggests that "the positive Piscean characteristics are embodied in the teachings of Jesus, essentially universal love, self-renunciation, service."[32] Similar examples could be given from other sources.

Now, my aim is not to criticize such approaches to the sign and sigil for Pisces, but to point out that they are merely a shadow of the esoteric truth hidden behind the sign and sigil.

So far as I know, Steiner has nothing to say about the sigil for Pisces, but he did talk at length about the imagery of the fish, and why it is linked with the human feet as a solar symbol.[33] Additionally, in a little known series of lectures, he spoke about the origin of the names for the constellations Pisces, Virgo and Gemini, giving the demarcation of the fixed stars into these asterisms, as well as the zodiacal associations relevant to them, to the Magian school. He says that these pre-Christian adepts chose and located the constellation patterns in order to express the idea of the coming of the birth of Christ (Pisces), from the Virgin Mother (Virgo) by means of the two Jesus Children (Gemini). In these lectures we find a sublime explanation for the origin of these signs and symbols, connected with an account of how the spiritual world transmits its meanings into

everyday experience.[34] Thus, the essence of what Steiner says about Pisces is that it is an image connected with the solar evolutionary forces, linked with humanity's first physical incarnation, and at the same time prophetic of the solar force that will redeem humankind: we may see in the sigil the idea of the two Jesus children yoked together by the one incarnating Christ.

Of course, esoteric explanation on this level is too extraordinary to receive a ready hearing. For most people, the idea of two Jesus children is hard enough to accept, let alone the further complication that pre-Christian adepts were supposed to know about the coming Incarnation, and its peculiar form. Even more difficult to accept is the idea that an esoteric school attempted to encapsulate the idea in a single graphic sigil. It is much easier to think otherwise, even if one's thinking leads to contradictions.

Actually, for all the heresy attached to the idea of the two Jesus children in relation to Pisces, several expressions of the connection have filtered through various art forms, even into esoteric astrology. The most sublime example is the entire basilican church of San Miniato, in Florence, for anyone who is prepared to experience the range of Piscean imagery within this lovely basilica cannot fail to be converted to the idea of esoteric astrology. A fairly ordinary example is still to be found in the south ambulatory of Christchurch in Hants; on one of the floor memorial stones, there is an epitaph that includes the word *Christchurch*, in a short form, ♓-church, linking *Christ* with *Pisces*. Between these two extremes lie a whole gamut of Piscean imagery yoked into the service of Christian esoteric symbolism.

Thus far, we have pointed to the Magian tradition, as set out by Steiner, and have then leapt millennia to draw conclusions regarding the nature

---

31 Hone, *The Modern Text-Book of Astrology*, p. 84.

32 Mayo, *Astrology*, 1964 ed., p. 70.

33 Steiner, *Occult Signs and Symbols* (British ed.), p. 25, for example.

34 Steiner, *The Search for the New Isis, Divine Sophia*, four lectures in Dec. 1920 (now in *Universal Spirituality and Human Physicality* (CW 202). These astrological ideas should be studied in relation to the idea of the two Jesus Children set out by Steiner in these lecture courses: *From Jesus to Christ* (CW 131); *According to Luke* (CW 114); and *According to Matthew* (CW 123).

of the modern sigil for Pisces, which we take as a vestigial drawing of two natures united by a single line—a superior symbol of the Incarnation of the solar Christ. The truth is that this sigil is no older than the thirteenth century.

Prior to the thirteenth century, the texts that used the astrological sigils appear to have been influenced by either the Egyptian demotic tradition, or by the Greek-Byzantine, as transmitted by Arabian astrology. The glyph for Pisces had no settled form, though the element of "duality" was generally contained within the sigils used to express its nature. Then, suddenly, in the thirteenth century, the modern form of the sigil emerges, alongside the other sigils that are still in use. This fact leaves me in no doubt that during the thirteenth century an esoteric school (presumably attached to the Masonic schools concerned with cathedral construction) reformed the astrological sigils that have come down to us. There were two elements that allowed the "new" forms to become "traditional"—first, there was the Masonic influence of the cathedral designers, and secondly, there was the stabilizing influence of the introduction of printing to the West, in the fifteenth century.

There is no space here to deal with the sublime esoteric astrology of the cathedrals, but we may see a touch of the esoteric force if we consider the earliest printed books in which certain astrological sigils are recorded.[35]

In relation to Pisces, it is possible to show that its present sigil had been formed by the thirteenth century, and, while competing for attention with other variants, it reigned supreme by the fifteenth century. It has been possible to trace and date these developments through manuscripts in English libraries.[36] Thus, it is no accident that in

his 1510 manuscript of *De occulta philosophia*, Agrippa gives two variant sigils for Aries, three for Taurus, two for Leo, two for Virgo, three for Scorpio, three for Sagittarius, and two for Capricorn: he gives one sigil each for the remaining five, including Pisces.[37] The example he gives for Pisces is the familiar modern one.

In fact, Agrippa is the earliest known example of an astrologer setting down in writing the *intellectual* reasons why a sigil should have a particular shape or form. Unfortunately, his account is not an esoteric one, and for Pisces he derives the sigil from fishes.[38] In theory, then, we should not be able to find a clue in Agrippa's text to any esoteric knowledge concerning Pisces. This is perhaps surprising, for *De occulta* (in spite of its appearance as a monumental, if low-key, exoteric work) has proved to be of esoteric origin, as well as being a useful compendium of medieval occult and astrological lore. Within its pages, therefore, we may legitimately seek to find a trace of a link between the Piscean sigil and the two Jesus Children tradition, which is reflected in its duality.

Agrippa lists fifteen sigils for fixed stars, which he has derived from medieval astrological traditions.[39] With certain variations, these forms given by Agrippa have entered the stream of Western occultism, even though in one case at least Agrippa copied one traditional sigil wrongly.[40] Thus, it is not surprising to find that the fixed star sigils recorded by the modern Robson, are, with minute variations (and with the inclusion of Agrippa's mistake), those set out by Agrippa in the early sixteenth century.[41]

Several manuscripts of the thirteenth century preserve the fifteen fixed star sigils used by

---

35 Perhaps one day an astrologer will do for Chartres and Notre Dame in Paris what Fulcanelli has done in regard to their alchemical symbolism. See Fulcanelli, *The Mystery of the Cathedrals*.

36 The following two manuscripts (in the British Museum Manuscript Dept.) give samples of the modern Pisces sigil: Add. 10,362 *Opuscula Varia astronomica et astrologica* [Astronomical and astrological variation]: Add. 23,770 *Introductorius ad iudicia astrologie* [Introduction to Yudhisthira's astrology] by Andalò del Negro of Genoa. The

earliest printed work with the modern sigil is probably the 1482 edition of Hyginus' *Poeticon astronomicon* [Poetic Astronomy].

37 See Nowotny *De occulta philosophia,* appendix 1, p. 552.

38 Ibid., 1531, II, Cap. LII, cxcvi.

39 Ibid., cxcvii.

40 Agrippa copied *Hircus* (the modern *Capella*) wrongly: as a sigil it may now be confused with *Aldebaran*.

41 Robson, *The Fixed Stars and Constellations in Astrology*, p. 233.

Agrippa—one of these is in the Bodleian Library, in Oxford.[42] A comparison of these sigils with those given by Agrippa reveals that he was copying fairly accurately, and so it is interesting to note the important variation he recorded for the fixed star *Spica* (now the binary *alpha* Virginis):

Figure 2

This variation is sufficiently important to warrant our attention, for the resultant sigil closely resembles on one side the modern form of the sigil for Pisces. The line connecting the two curves terminates in one single circle. Thus, with the framework of the "thought-out" system such as Agrippa favored (standing as he did at the beginning of the Age of the Consciousness Soul), one might be tempted to see the sigil as an expression of the idea of the two separate Jesus children uniting in the single Christ.

Spica is, of course, the ear of corn in the hand of the Virgin constellation. In certain rare examples of astrological manuscripts, Virgo is presented as the Virgin Mary, holding the ear of corn, the fruit from the earth that will bring life once more to the earth.[43] It is perhaps such pictures, and certainly this Marian tradition, which encouraged some scholars to trace the origin of the Virgo glyph (♍) to the letters *MV*, or *Maria virgo*.[44]

As Steiner indicated, the constellation Virgo was placed opposite to Pisces in order to prefigure the coming of this dual fruit that would bring life to humankind: Christ is held in the arms of the Virgin as the *epiousios* Bread of Life.[45]

Consideration of this rich tradition concerning *Spica*, and its known link with Pisces within the esoteric tradition, supports the argument that Agrippa was familiar with the esoteric doctrine concerning the two Jesus children, and that he incorporated it as a powerful trace into his version of the sigil for *Spica*.

There is no academic argument that Agrippa knew of the esoteric truth of the two Jesus children. Indeed, there is virtually no academic argument for that esoteric truth itself, in spite of its persistence in art, and its recent rediscovery in the Gospels and in the Dead Sea Scrolls.[46] However, the fact is that the evidence of art alone—especially in the works of the Milanese Borgognone, Leonardo and Raphael, to name but three—shows that this ancient idea, which found expression in early Christian art, and then later in heretical forms, had been reintroduced into esoteric Renaissance circles—possibly through the same esoteric school that gave rise to the humanist Neoplatonic circles.[47] Agrippa, with his vast knowledge and his penchant for eclectic esotericism, would no doubt have been familiar with such an important tradition. This hypothesis would at least explain certain of the mysteries concerned with the emergence of the Piscean sigil during the period prior to the Renaissance. As a hypothesis it differs from academic methodology in that it presents the history of ideas as the history of periodic inseminations from esoteric schools. It is clear to me that only the acceptance of such an idea—albeit contrary to the general academic view—will account for the fact that civilization, working within a framework of something akin to a spiritual

---

42 Bodleian Library manuscript: *Ashmole* 341, 13th century.

43 An example is reproduced in F. Boll, C. Bexold, W. Gundel, *Sternglaube und Sterndeutung* (Star faith and astrology), 1966, plate 17.

44 Allen, *Star-Names and Their Meanings*, 1899, p. 463.

45 *Epiousios*, the untranslatable word that gave

St. Jerome so much trouble and perhaps reminds us that *Spica* is a binary. Cf. Fletcher, *The Aramaic Sayings of Jesus*, 1967, p. 20.

46 Few serious attempts have been made to introduce the idea in England, other than through translations of Steiner. The articles by C. Sturm in *The Modern Mystic*, Feb., 1944, etc. "The Double Jesus," are seriously marred by bad scholarship. In his valuable *A New Chronology of the Gospels*, 1972, O. Edwards provides original material, though the duality of the Jesus children is not his main concern.

47 See Hella Krause-Zimmer, *Die Zwei Jesusknaben* (The two Jesus boys), 1969.

second law of thermodynamics, had not relapsed entirely into barbarism many centuries ago.[48]

My attempt in this short article has been to point the way to an understanding of the relationship that esoteric astrology holds to the exoteric form—which is essentially a role of supportive vitalization. The force of my argument rests not on the incidentals of historic parallels I draw (that is, on Agrippa and his glyph for *Spica*) but on the fact that such historic parallels *could have occurred*. Were the full spiritual nature of the Christ-filled

sigil for Pisces fully appreciated, then I feel sure that each time we intend to write the word, or scrawl down the sigil on a horoscope, we would experience the same impulse as those medieval monks in their scriptoria, when faced with writing the Holy name—we would wish to clean our hands with water in a humble grace, before marking down the sigil forever into the material world.

Only the development of something akin to such an attitude will enable us to regenerate and revitalize this corpse of the princess Divine Sophia.

---

48 Naturally, all serious histories of esotericism presuppose this approach: see, for example, Collins, *The Theory of Celestial Influence.*

"All the stars are colonies of spiritual beings in cosmic space, colonies that we can learn to know when, having passed through the gate of death, our own soul lives and moves among these starry colonies…with the beings of the hierarchies…. To understand karma, therefore, we must return once more to a wisdom of the stars. We must discover spiritually the paths of human beings between death and a new birth in connection with the beings of the stars…. There has come forth a certain stream of spiritual life that makes it very difficult to approach, with an open mind, the science of the stars and the science of karma…. We can nevertheless go forward with assurance and approach the wisdom of the stars and the real shaping of karma."

RUDOLF STEINER
Karmic Relationships, vol. 4, Sept. 18, 1924

ODE TO DENEB

Natalia Haarahiltunen

Your starry shining is so perfect

so perfect in its calling

for transformation

and transubstantiation.

Your being, such a crystal shining clearness of higher grounds

your name, like a drop falling from swan's eye in the winter's night

"De neb."

We call you

to purify us,

cleanse us from our earthly dust,

from this valley of tears

to a mountain top lead us.

Make us ready for a perfect state

of transcendental peace,

may all waters be calmed in us

let every teardrop left in our eyes

cry only for perfection

to a growing harmony

with stellar connections

in our destiny-bodies.

May honey-milk of stars flow through us

and touch our inner being.

Oh, perfect peace, dwell in our veins, in our hearts

that we may bring forwards future times

that long to be born amidst us

though, still like a tender premonition,

like a touch of swanfeathers, soft wind in treetops high

We do believe, once rainbows will cross the skies

and every child of God is called peacemaker of their times.

WORKING WITH THE
STAR WISDOM CALENDAR

Robert Powell, PhD

In taking note of the astronomical events listed in the Star Calendar, it is important to distinguish between long- and short-term astronomical events. Long-term astronomical events—for example, Pluto transiting a particular degree of the zodiac—will have a longer period of meditation than would the five days advocated for short-term astronomical events such as the New and Full Moon. The following describes, in relation to meditating on the Full Moon, a meditative process extending over a five-day period.

Sanctification of the Full Moon

As a preliminary remark, let us remind ourselves that the great sacrifice of Christ on the Cross—the Mystery of Golgotha—took place at Full Moon. As Christ's sacrifice took place when the Moon was full in the middle of the sidereal sign of Libra, the Libra Full Moon assumes special significance in the sequence of twelve (or thirteen) Full Moons taking place during the cycle of the year. In following this sequence, the Mystery of Golgotha serves as an archetype for *every* Full Moon, since each Full Moon imparts a particular spiritual blessing. Hence the practice described here as *Sanctification of the Full Moon* applies to every Full Moon. Similarly, there is also the practice of *Sanctification of the New Moon*, as described in *Hermetic Astrology, Volume 2: Astrological Biography*, chapter 10.

During the two days prior to the Full Moon, we can consider the focus of one's meditation to extend over these two days as *preparatory days*, immediately preceding the day of the Full Moon. These two days can be dedicated to spiritual reflection and detachment from everyday concerns as one prepares to become a vessel for the in-streaming light and love one will receive at the Full Moon, something that one can then impart

further—for example, to help people in need, or to support Mother Earth in times of catastrophe. During these two days, it is helpful to hold an attitude of dedication and service and try to assume an attitude of receptivity that opens to what one's soul will receive and subsequently impart—an attitude conducive to making one a true *servant of the spirit*.

The day of the Full Moon is itself a day of *holding the sacred space*. In doing so, one endeavors to cultivate inner peace and silence, during which one attempts to contact and consciously hold the in-streaming blessing of the Full Moon for the rest of humanity. One can heighten this silent meditation by visualizing the zodiacal constellation–sidereal sign in which the Moon becomes full, since the Moon serves to reflect the starry background against which it appears.

If the Moon is full in Virgo, for example, it reminds us of the night of the birth of the Jesus child visited by the three magi, as described in the Gospel of St. Matthew. That birth occurred at the Full Moon in the middle of the sidereal sign of Virgo, and the three magi, who gazed up that evening to behold the Full Moon against the background of the stars of the Virgin, witnessed the soul of Jesus emerge from the disk of the Full Moon and descend toward Earth. They participated from afar, via the starry heavens, in the Grail Mystery of the holy birth.

By meditating on the Full Moon and opening oneself to receive the in-streaming blessing from the starry heavens, we can exercise restraint by avoiding the formulation of what will happen or what one might receive from the Full Moon. Moreover, we can also refrain from seeking tangible results or effects connected with our attunement to the Full Moon. Even if we observe only the date but not the exact moment when the Moon is full, it is helpful to find quiet time to reflect alone or to use the opportunity for deep meditation on the day of the Full Moon.

We can think of the two days following the Full Moon as a *time of imparting* what we have received from the in-streaming of the Moon's full disk against the background of the stars. It is now possible to turn our attention toward humanity and the world and endeavor to pass on any spiritual blessing we have received from the starry heavens. Thereby we can assist in the work of the spiritual world by transforming what we have received into goodwill and allowing it to flow wherever the greatest need exists.

It is a matter of *holding a sacred space* throughout the day of the Full Moon. This is an important time to still the mind and maintain inner peace. It is a time of spiritual retreat and contact with the spiritual world, of holding in one's consciousness the archetype of the Mystery of Golgotha as a great outpouring of Divine Love that bridges Heaven and Earth. Prior to the day of the Full Moon, the two preceding days prepare the sacred space as a vessel to receive the heavenly blessing. The two days following the day of the Full Moon are a time to assimilate and distribute the spiritual transmission received into the sacred space we have prepared.

One can apply the process described here as a meditative practice in relation to the Full Moon to any of the astronomical events listed in *Star Wisdom,* especially as most of these *remember* significant Christ Events. Take note, however, whether an event is long-term or short-term and adjust the period of meditative practice accordingly.

> "The stars are the expression of love in the cosmic ether.... To see a star means to feel a caress that has been prompted by love.... To gaze at the stars is to become aware of the love proceeding from divine spiritual beings.... The stars are signs and tokens of the presence of gods in the universe."
>
> RUDOLF STEINER, *Karmic Relationships,*
> vol. 7, June 8, 1924

SYMBOLS USED IN CHARTS

PLANETS		ZODIACAL SIGNS		ASPECTS	
⊕	Earth	♈	Aries (Ram)	☌	Conjunction 0°
☉	Sun	♉	Taurus (Bull)	✳	Sextile 60°
☽	Moon	♊	Gemini (Twins)	☐	Square 90°
☿	Mercury	♋	Cancer (Crab)	△	Trine 120°
♀	Venus	♌	Leo (Lion)	☍	Opposition 180°
♂	Mars	♍	Virgo (Virgin)		
♃	Jupiter	♎	Libra (Scales)		
♄	Saturn	♏	Scorpio (Scorpion)		
♅	Uranus	♐	Sagittarius (Archer)		
♆	Neptune	♑	Capricorn (Goat)		
♇	Pluto	♒	Aquarius (Water Carrier)		
		♓	Pisces (Fishes)		

OTHER

☊	Ascending (North) Node	☉'	Sun Eclipse
☋	Descending (South) Node	☽'	Moon Eclipse
P	Perihelion–Perigee	☌'	Inferior Conjunction
A	Aphelion–Apogee	☌'	Superior Conjunction
N	Maximum Latitude	⚷	Chiron
S	Minimum Latitude		

TIME

The information relating to daily geocentric and heliocentric planetary positions in the sidereal zodiac is tabulated in the form of an ephemeris for each month, in which the planetary positions are given at 0 hours Universal Time (UT) each day.

Beneath the geocentric and heliocentric ephemeris for each month, the information relating to planetary aspects is given in the form of an aspectarian, which lists the most important aspects—geocentric and heliocentric–hermetic—between the planets for the month in question. The day and the time of occurrence of the aspect on that day are indicated, all times being given in Universal Time (UT), which is identical to Greenwich Mean Time (GMT). For example, zero hours Universal Time is midnight GMT. This time system applies in Britain; however, when summer time is in effect, one hour must be added to all times.

In other time zones, the time must be adjusted according to whether it is ahead of or behind Britain. For example, in Germany, where the time is one hour ahead of British time, an hour must be added; when summer time is in effect in Germany, two hours have to be added to all times.

Using the calendar in the United States, do the following subtraction from all time indications according to time zone:

- Pacific Time subtract 8 hours
- Mountain Time subtract 7 hours
- Central Time subtract 6 hours
- Eastern Time subtract 5 hours

This subtraction will often change the date of an astronomical occurrence, shifting it back one day. Consequently, since most of the readers of this calendar live on the American Continent, astronomical occurrences during the early hours of day x are sometimes listed in the Commentaries as occurring on days x–$1/x$. For example, an eclipse occurring at 03:00 UT on the 12th is listed as occurring on the 11–12th since in America it takes place on the 11th.[1]

SIMPLIFYING THE PROCEDURE

The preceding procedure can be greatly simplified. Here is an example for someone wishing to know the zodiacal locations of the planets on Christmas Day, December 25, 2018. Looking at the December ephemeris, it can be seen that Christmas Day falls on a Tuesday. In the upper tabulation, the geocentric planetary positions are given, with that of the Sun indicated in the first column, that of the Moon in the second column, and so on. The position of the Sun is listed as 8°07' Sagittarius.

For someone living in London, 8°07' Sagittarius is the Sun's position at midnight, December 24–25, 2017—noting that in London and all of the United Kingdom, the Time Zone applying there is that of Universal Time–Greenwich Mean Time (UT–GMT).

For someone living in Sydney, Australia, which on Christmas Day is eleven hours ahead of UT–GMT, 8°07' Sagittarius is the Sun's position at 11 a.m. on December 25.

For someone living in California, which is eight hours behind UT–GMT on Christmas Day, 8°07' Sagittarius is the Sun's position at 4 p.m. on **December 24**.

For the person living in California, therefore, it is necessary to look at the entries for **December 26** to know the positions of the planets on December 25. The result is:

For someone living in California, which is eight hours behind UT–GMT on Christmas Day, the Sun's position at 4 p.m. on December 25 is 9°08' Sagittarius and, by the same token, the Moon's position on Christmas Day at 4 p.m. on December 25 is 24°08' Pisces—these are the positions

---

1 See *General Introduction to the Christian Star Calendar: A Key to Understanding* for an in-depth clarification of the features of the calendar in *Star Wisdom,* including indications about how to work with it.

alongside December 26 at midnight UT–GMT—and eight hours earlier equates with 4 p.m. on December 25 in California.

From these examples it emerges that the **planetary positions as given in the ephemeris** can be utilized, but that according to the Time Zone one is in, **the time of day is different** and also for locations West of the United Kingdom **the date changes** (look at the date following the actual date).

Here is a tabulation in relation to the foregoing example of December 25 (Christmas Day).

UNITED KINGDOM, EUROPE, AND ALL LOCATIONS WITH TIME ZONES EAST OF GREENWICH

Look at what is given alongside December 25—these entries indicate the planetary positions at these times:

- 12:00 a.m. (midnight December 24–25) in London (UT–GMT)
- 01:00 a.m. in Berlin (CENTRAL EUROPEAN TIME, which is one hour ahead of UT–GMT)
- 11:00 a.m. in Sydney (AUSTRALIAN EASTERN DAYLIGHT TIME, which is eleven hours ahead of UT–GMT)

CANADA, USA, CENTRAL AMERICA, SOUTH AMERICA, AND ALL LOCATIONS WITH TIME ZONES WEST OF GREENWICH

Look at what is given alongside December 26—these entries indicate the planetary positions at these times:

- 7:00 p.m. in New York (EASTERN STANDARD TIME, which is five hours behind UT–GMT)
- 6:00 p.m. in Chicago (CENTRAL STANDARD TIME, which is six hours behind UT–GMT)
- 5:00 p.m. in Denver (MOUNTAIN STANDARD TIME, which is seven hours behind UT–GMT)
- 4:00 p.m. in San Francisco (PACIFIC STANDARD TIME, which is eight hours behind UT–GMT)

- **IF SUMMER TIME IS IN USE**, add **ONE HOUR**—FOR EXAMPLE:
- 8:00 p.m. in New York (EASTERN DAYLIGHT TIME, which is four hours behind UT–GMT)
- 7:00 p.m. in Chicago (CENTRAL DAYLIGHT TIME, which is five hours behind UT–GMT)
- 6:00 p.m. in Denver (MOUNTAIN DAYLIGHT TIME, which is six hours behind UT–GMT)
- 5:00 p.m. in San Francisco (PACIFIC DAYLIGHT TIME, which is seven hours behind UT–GMT)

Note that Daylight Time in the U.S. becomes permanent in 2023. Note, too, that in the preceding tabulation, the time given in Sydney on Christmas Day, December 25, is Daylight Time. Six months earlier, on June 25, for someone in Sydney they would look alongside the entry in the ephemeris for June 25 and would know that this applies (for them) to

- 10:00 a.m. in Sydney (AUSTRALIAN EASTERN TIME, which is ten hours ahead of UT–GMT)

In these examples, it is not just the position of the Sun that is referred to. The same applies to the zodiacal locations given in the ephemeris for *all* the planets, whether geocentric (upper tabulation) or heliocentric (lower tabulation). *All that is necessary to apply this method of reading the ephemeris is to know the Time Zone in which one is and to apply the number of hours difference from UT–GMT.*

The advantage of using the method described here is that it greatly simplifies reference to the ephemeris when studying the **zodiacal positions of the planets**. However, for applying the time indications listed under "Ingresses" or "Aspects" it is still necessary to add or subtract the time difference from UT–GMT as described in the above paragraph denoted.

EPHEMERIDES FOR 2024
AND FOR THE MINISTRY OF CHRIST
Joel Matthew Park

INTRODUCTION

This year, *Star Wisdom* provides the ephemerides for 2024. Weekly commentaries and Starwatch are available from Julie Humphreys through the Starlight Substack, the newsletter of the Sophia Foundation: https://starlightnewsletter.substack.com.

We are also making available the planetary positions and alignments during the ministry of Christ. You will find the monthly ephemerides from April to December AD 29; January to December 30; January to July and November 31; May to December 32; and January to June 33. These ephemerides correspond more or less to the visions of Anne Catherine Emmerich.[1] They begin in April 29, when John the Baptist begins preparing the way for Christ through his preaching and baptizing. There is a break in her visions that lasts from July 31 until May 32. I have included the month of November 31, as the research of Robert Powell indicates that the sixth healing miracle (that of the man born blind) took place on November 23, 31.[2] The ephemerides end in June, 33, during the founding of the original church by Peter and the disciples.

For the past few decades, this publication and its predecessors, *Journal for Star Wisdom* and *Christian Star Calendar,* have provided readers with commentaries that point out the correspondences between contemporary positions and alignments of the planets and those occurring during the life of Christ. Now, with the publication of the visions of Anne Catherine Emmerich, combined with the availability of the ephemerides found here, readers are enabled to determine for themselves the stellar resonances of any given day. In 2024, for example, there is a Full Moon in Libra on April 23. If we want to find the correspondence with the life of Christ, we could look to the ephemeris for April AD 33, and find that the Full Moon in Libra occurred on April 4. When we turn to the visions of Anne Catherine Emmerich, we find that this was on Holy Saturday of the Mystery of Golgotha. It is therefore my hope that the ephemerides of the ministry of Christ can be an ongoing reference and resource for fellow astrosophers. In future years, I plan to post the ephemerides on a monthly basis to Starlight, so that interested readers can continue to find the current stellar correspondences.

Obviously, these ephemerides are not comprehensive, inasmuch as they do not contain the stellar configurations for important dates, such as the birth of the Solomon or Nathan Jesus, the Assumption of Mary, and so on (for which the dates have also been determined by Robert Powell). An excellent resource for many of these other important dates in the lives of the two Jesus individualities and the two Mary individualities can be found in Julie Humphreys' *Awakening to the Spiritual Archetypes in the Birth Chart* (appendices 2 and 3). If readers are interested in a horoscope for a particular day, simply reach out to me by email at joelmpark77@gmail.com, and I will post the chart on the Starlight Substack.

---

1   Available as *The Visions of Anne Catherine Emmerich,* vols. 1–3.

2   See the article by Robert Powell, "The Healing of the Man-Born-Blind and the Central Sun: Foundations of Star Wisdom (*Astrosophy*)," *Journal for Star Wisdom 2016*, pp. 24–40.

EPHEMERIDES FOR 2024

SIDEREAL GEOCENTRIC LONGITUDES : JANUARY 2024 Gregorian at 0 hours UT

DAY	☉	☽	☊	☿	♀	♂	♃	♄	♅	♆	♇
1 MO	14 ♐ 58	10 ♌ 56	26 ♓ 0R	27 ♏ 12R	7 ♏ 32	2 ♐ 14	10 ♈ 30	8 ♒ 10	24 ♈ 18R	0 ♓ 0	4 ♑ 17
2 TU	15 59	22 45	25 56	27 6	8 45	2 59	10 31	8 15	24 17	0 1	4 19
3 WE	17 0	4 ♍ 33	25 53	27 10D	9 58	3 43	10 31	8 21	24 16	0 2	4 20
4 TH	18 1	16 26	25 53	27 22	11 11	4 28	10 32	8 26	24 15	0 3	4 22
5 FR	19 2	28 29	25 53	27 42	12 25	5 12	10 33	8 32	24 14	0 4	4 24
6 SA	20 4	10 ♎ 47	25 52	28 8	13 38	5 57	10 34	8 37	24 12	0 5	4 26
7 SU	21 5	23 27	25 50	28 42	14 51	6 42	10 35	8 43	24 11	0 6	4 28
8 MO	22 6	6 ♏ 31	25 45	29 21	16 4	7 27	10 37	8 49	24 10	0 7	4 30
9 TU	23 7	20 2	25 37	0 ♐ 5	17 18	8 11	10 39	8 55	24 9	0 8	4 32
10 WE	24 8	4 ♐ 1	25 27	0 54	18 31	8 56	10 40	9 1	24 9	0 10	4 34
11 TH	25 9	18 24	25 15	1 48	19 45	9 41	10 43	9 6	24 8	0 11	4 36
12 FR	26 11	3 ♑ 4	25 2	2 45	20 58	10 26	10 45	9 12	24 7	0 12	4 38
13 SA	27 12	17 55	24 51	3 45	22 12	11 11	10 48	9 18	24 6	0 13	4 40
14 SU	28 13	2 ♒ 47	24 41	4 48	23 25	11 56	10 50	9 25	24 5	0 14	4 42
15 MO	29 14	17 32	24 35	5 54	24 39	12 41	10 53	9 31	24 5	0 16	4 44
16 TU	0 ♑ 15	2 ♓ 3	24 31	7 2	25 52	13 26	10 56	9 37	24 4	0 17	4 45
17 WE	1 16	16 18	24 29	8 12	27 6	14 11	11 0	9 43	24 4	0 18	4 47
18 TH	2 17	0 ♈ 14	24 29	9 25	28 20	14 57	11 3	9 49	24 3	0 20	4 49
19 FR	3 19	13 53	24 29	10 39	29 33	15 42	11 7	9 56	24 3	0 21	4 51
20 SA	4 20	27 16	24 28	11 54	0 ♐ 47	16 27	11 11	10 2	24 2	0 23	4 53
21 SU	5 21	10 ♉ 24	24 24	13 12	2 1	17 12	11 15	10 8	24 2	0 24	4 55
22 MO	6 22	23 20	24 17	14 30	3 15	17 58	11 19	10 15	24 1	0 26	4 57
23 TU	7 23	6 ♊ 4	24 7	15 50	4 28	18 43	11 24	10 21	24 1	0 27	4 59
24 WE	8 24	18 38	23 54	17 11	5 42	19 28	11 28	10 28	24 1	0 29	5 1
25 TH	9 25	1 ♋ 2	23 40	18 33	6 56	20 14	11 33	10 35	24 1	0 30	5 3
26 FR	10 26	13 17	23 26	19 56	8 10	20 59	11 38	10 41	24 1	0 32	5 5
27 SA	11 27	25 22	23 13	21 20	9 24	21 45	11 44	10 48	24 1	0 33	5 7
28 SU	12 28	7 ♌ 19	23 3	22 45	10 38	22 30	11 49	10 55	24 1D	0 35	5 9
29 MO	13 29	19 11	22 55	24 11	11 52	23 16	11 55	11 1	24 1	0 37	5 11
30 TU	14 30	0 ♍ 58	22 50	25 38	13 6	24 2	12 0	11 8	24 1	0 38	5 13
31 WE	15 30	12 46	22 47	27 6	14 20	24 47	12 6	11 15	24 1	0 40	5 15

INGRESSES :

- 2 ☽ → ♍ 14:45
- 5 ☽ → ♎ 2:59
- 7 ☽ → ♏ 12: 8
- 8 ☿ → ♐ 21:12
- 9 ☽ → ♐ 17:10
- 11 ☽ → ♑ 19: 0
- 13 ☽ → ♒ 19:29
- 15 ☉ → ♑ 18: 1
- ☽ → ♓ 20:34
- 17 ☽ → ♈ 23:34
- 19 ♀ → ♐ 8:42
- 20 ☽ → ♉ 4:58
- 22 ☽ → ♊ 12:31
- 24 ☽ → ♋ 21:59
- 27 ☽ → ♌ 9:16
- 29 ☽ → ♍ 22: 1

ASPECTS & ECLIPSES :

- 1 ♀ □ ♄ 13:25
- ☽ ☌ A 15:12
- 2 ☽ ☍ ♆ 14:49
- 4 ☉ □ ☽ 3:29
- ☽ ☌ ☋ 18:51
- 5 ☽ ☍ ♃ 23:34
- 7 ☽ ☍ ♅ 1:23
- 8 ☽ ☌ ♀ 18:43
- 9 ☿ □ ♆ 1:35
- ☽ ☌ ☿ 18:23
- 10 ☽ ☌ ♂ 8:44
- 11 ☉ □ ☊ 1:45
- ☽ □S ☊ 11: 5
- ☉ ☌ ☽ 11:56
- 12 ☽ ☌ ♇ 2:31
- 13 ☽ ☌ P 10:24
- 14 ☽ ☌ ♄ 10:49
- 15 ☽ ☌ ♆ 21: 2
- 17 ☽ ☌ ☊ 14: 2
- 18 ☉ □ ☽ 3:51
- ☽ ☌ ♃ 19: 3
- 19 ♀ □ ♆ 15:55
- ☽ ☌ ♅ 18:10
- 20 ☉ ☌ ♇ 13:39
- 22 ☽ ☍ ♀ 20:38
- 23 ☽ ☍ ☿ 20:52
- 24 ☽ ☍ ♂ 1:42
- ☽ N□ ☊ 9:58
- 25 ☽ ☍ ♇ 7:51
- ☉ ☍ ☽ 17:52
- 27 ☉ □ ♃ 7:17
- ☿ ☌ ♂ 14:58
- 28 ☿ □ ☊ 4:24
- ☽ ☍ ♄ 7:19
- ♂ □ ☊ 14:20
- 29 ☽ ☌ A 7:57
- ☽ ☍ ♆ 23:19
- 31 ☽ ☌ ☋ 20:16

SIDEREAL HELIOCENTRIC LONGITUDES : JANUARY 2024 Gregorian at 0 hours UT

DAY	Sid. Time	☿	♀	⊕	♂	♃	♄	♅	♆	♇	Vernal Point
1 MO	6:40:37	29 ♋ 8	11 ♍ 22	14 ♊ 58	23 ♏ 49	20 ♈ 46	12 ♒ 49	26 ♈ 32	1 ♓ 50	4 ♑ 49	4 ♓ 55'30"
2 TU	6:44:33	4 ♌ 12	12 59	15 59	24 23	20 51	12 51	26 32	1 50	4 50	4 ♓ 55'30"
3 WE	6:48:30	9 7	14 36	17 1	24 56	20 57	12 53	26 33	1 51	4 50	4 ♓ 55'30"
4 TH	6:52:26	13 52	16 13	18 2	25 29	21 2	12 55	26 34	1 51	4 50	4 ♓ 55'30"
5 FR	6:56:23	18 29	17 50	19 3	26 3	21 7	12 57	26 34	1 51	4 50	4 ♓ 55'30"
6 SA	7: 0:19	22 56	19 26	20 4	26 36	21 13	12 58	26 35	1 52	4 51	4 ♓ 55'30"
7 SU	7: 4:16	27 15	21 3	21 5	27 9	21 18	13 0	26 36	1 52	4 51	4 ♓ 55'30"
8 MO	7: 8:13	1 ♍ 25	22 40	22 6	27 43	21 24	13 2	26 36	1 52	4 51	4 ♓ 55'29"
9 TU	7:12: 9	5 28	24 17	23 8	28 16	21 29	13 4	26 37	1 53	4 51	4 ♓ 55'29"
10 WE	7:16: 6	9 24	25 53	24 9	28 50	21 34	13 6	26 38	1 53	4 52	4 ♓ 55'29"
11 TH	7:20: 2	13 13	27 30	25 10	29 24	21 40	13 8	26 38	1 54	4 52	4 ♓ 55'29"
12 FR	7:23:59	16 56	29 7	26 11	29 58	21 45	13 10	26 39	1 54	4 52	4 ♓ 55'29"
13 SA	7:27:55	20 32	0 ♎ 43	27 12	0 ♐ 31	21 51	13 12	26 40	1 54	4 53	4 ♓ 55'29"
14 SU	7:31:52	24 3	2 20	28 13	1 5	21 56	13 14	26 40	1 55	4 53	4 ♓ 55'29"
15 MO	7:35:48	27 29	3 56	29 14	1 39	22 2	13 16	26 41	1 55	4 53	4 ♓ 55'28"
16 TU	7:39:45	0 ♎ 51	5 33	0 ♋ 16	2 13	22 7	13 18	26 42	1 55	4 53	4 ♓ 55'28"
17 WE	7:43:42	4 7	7 9	1 17	2 47	22 12	13 20	26 43	1 56	4 54	4 ♓ 55'28"
18 TH	7:47:38	7 20	8 45	2 18	3 21	22 18	13 22	26 43	1 56	4 54	4 ♓ 55'28"
19 FR	7:51:35	10 29	10 22	3 19	3 55	22 23	13 24	26 44	1 56	4 54	4 ♓ 55'28"
20 SA	7:55:31	13 34	11 58	4 20	4 30	22 29	13 25	26 45	1 57	4 55	4 ♓ 55'28"
21 SU	7:59:28	16 37	13 34	5 21	5 4	22 34	13 27	26 45	1 57	4 55	4 ♓ 55'28"
22 MO	8: 3:24	19 36	15 10	6 22	5 38	22 39	13 29	26 46	1 58	4 55	4 ♓ 55'27"
23 TU	8: 7:21	22 33	16 46	7 23	6 12	22 45	13 31	26 47	1 58	4 55	4 ♓ 55'27"
24 WE	8:11:17	25 28	18 22	8 24	6 47	22 50	13 33	26 47	1 58	4 56	4 ♓ 55'27"
25 TH	8:15:14	28 21	19 58	9 25	7 21	22 56	13 35	26 48	1 59	4 56	4 ♓ 55'27"
26 FR	8:19:11	1 ♏ 11	21 34	10 26	7 56	23 1	13 37	26 49	1 59	4 56	4 ♓ 55'27"
27 SA	8:23: 7	4 1	23 10	11 27	8 31	23 7	13 39	26 49	1 59	4 57	4 ♓ 55'27"
28 SU	8:27: 4	6 49	24 46	12 28	9 5	23 12	13 41	26 50	2 0	4 57	4 ♓ 55'27"
29 MO	8:31: 0	9 36	26 22	13 29	9 40	23 17	13 43	26 51	2 0	4 57	4 ♓ 55'26"
30 TU	8:34:57	12 22	27 58	14 30	10 15	23 23	13 45	26 51	2 0	4 57	4 ♓ 55'26"
31 WE	8:38:53	15 7	29 34	15 31	10 49	23 28	13 47	26 52	2 1	4 58	4 ♓ 55'26"

INGRESSES :

- 1 ☿ → ♌ 4: 3
- 7 ☿ → ♍ 15:44
- 12 ♂ → ♐ 1:45
- ♀ → ♎ 13:15
- 15 ⊕ → ♋ 17:51
- ☿ → ♎ 17:55
- 25 ☿ → ♏ 13:56
- 31 ♀ → ♏ 6:37

ASPECTS (HELIOCENTRIC +MOON(TYCHONIC)) :

- 1 ☽ ☍ ♄ 3:50
- 2 ☽ □ ♂ 3:29
- ☽ ☍ ♆ 18:30
- 3 ☿ ☍ ♄ 19: 2
- ☽ ☌ ♀ 23:29
- 4 ⊕ ☌ P 5:47
- 5 ☽ □ ♇ 12:28
- 6 ☽ ☍ ♃ 19:57
- ☿ □ ♂ 23:25
- 7 ♀ □ ⊕ 1:20
- ☽ ☍ ♅ 5:51
- 8 ☿ ☍ ♆ 2:38
- ☽ □ ♄ 11:42
- 9 ☽ ☌ ♂ 14:49
- ☽ □ ♆ 20:23
- 10 ☽ □ ☿ 12:22
- 11 ☽ □ ♀ 16:46
- 12 ☽ ☌ ♇ 2:55
- 13 ☽ □ ♃ 6:22
- ☽ □ ♅ 14: 6
- 14 ☽ ☌ ♄ 17: 0
- 15 ♂ □ ♆ 11:21
- ♀ □ ♇ 14:13
- ☿ □ ⊕ 17:56
- ☽ ☌ ♆ 23:46
- 16 ☽ □ ♂ 0:16
- 17 ☿ □ ♇ 5:45
- 18 ☽ □ ♇ 8: 8
- ☽ ☍ ☿ 16: 9
- ☽ ☍ ♀ 16:54
- ☿ ☌ ♀ 22: 6
- 19 ☽ ☌ ♃ 15:18
- ☽ ☌ ♅ 23: 3
- 20 ⊕ ☍ ♇ 13:39
- 21 ☽ □ ♄ 5:39
- 22 ☽ □ ♆ 16:13
- 23 ☽ ☍ ♂ 0:16
- ☿ ☍ ♃ 1:38
- ☿ ☌ ☋ 8: 6
- 24 ☿ ☍ ♅ 11: 2
- 25 ☽ ☍ ♇ 7:36
- 26 ☽ □ ♀ 18:57
- ☽ □ ♃ 19:28
- ♀ ☍ ♃ 22:59
- 27 ☽ □ ♅ 2:54
- ☽ □ ☿ 22:39
- 28 ☽ ☍ ♄ 12:53
- 29 ♀ ☍ ♅ 7:12
- 30 ☽ ☍ ♆ 2: 6
- ☿ □ ♄ 12: 9
- ☽ □ ♂ 19:51

SIDEREAL GEOCENTRIC LONGITUDES : FEBRUARY 2024 Gregorian at 0 hours UT

DAY	☉	☽	☊	☿	♀	♂	♃	♄	⛢	♆	♇
1 TH	16 ♑ 31	24 ♍ 38	22 ♓ 47	28 ♐ 34	15 ♐ 34	25 ♐ 33	12 ♈ 12	11 ♒ 22	24 ♈ 1	0 ♓ 42	5 ♑ 17
2 FR	17 32	6 ♎ 38	22 47	0 ♑ 3	16 48	26 19	12 19	11 29	24 2	0 44	5 18
3 SA	18 33	18 54	22 48R	1 33	18 2	27 4	12 25	11 36	24 2	0 45	5 20
4 SU	19 34	1 ♏ 29	22 47	3 4	19 16	27 50	12 32	11 43	24 2	0 47	5 22
5 MO	20 35	14 28	22 44	4 36	20 30	28 36	12 38	11 50	24 3	0 49	5 24
6 TU	21 36	27 56	22 39	6 8	21 44	29 22	12 45	11 57	24 3	0 51	5 26
7 WE	22 37	11 ♐ 54	22 32	7 41	22 58	0 ♑ 8	12 52	12 4	24 4	0 53	5 28
8 TH	23 37	26 20	22 23	9 15	24 12	0 54	12 59	12 11	24 4	0 55	5 30
9 FR	24 38	11 ♑ 10	22 13	10 50	25 26	1 40	13 7	12 18	24 5	0 57	5 32
10 SA	25 39	26 16	22 4	12 25	26 41	2 26	13 14	12 25	24 6	0 59	5 34
11 SU	26 40	11 ♒ 27	21 57	14 1	27 55	3 12	13 22	12 32	24 6	1 0	5 35
12 MO	27 40	26 34	21 52	15 38	29 9	3 58	13 30	12 39	24 7	1 2	5 37
13 TU	28 41	11 ♓ 27	21 49	17 16	0 ♑ 23	4 44	13 38	12 46	24 8	1 4	5 39
14 WE	29 42	26 1	21 49D	18 55	1 37	5 30	13 46	12 54	24 9	1 6	5 41
15 TH	0 ♒ 42	10 ♈ 11	21 50	20 34	2 52	6 16	13 54	13 1	24 10	1 8	5 43
16 FR	1 43	23 57	21 51	22 15	4 6	7 2	14 3	13 8	24 11	1 10	5 44
17 SA	2 44	7 ♉ 20	21 51R	23 56	5 20	7 48	14 11	13 15	24 12	1 12	5 46
18 SU	3 44	20 23	21 50	25 38	6 34	8 34	14 20	13 23	24 13	1 15	5 48
19 MO	4 45	3 ♊ 8	21 46	27 21	7 48	9 21	14 29	13 30	24 14	1 17	5 50
20 TU	5 45	15 40	21 40	29 5	9 3	10 7	14 38	13 37	24 15	1 19	5 52
21 WE	6 46	27 59	21 33	0 ♒ 50	10 17	10 53	14 47	13 44	24 17	1 21	5 53
22 TH	7 46	10 ♋ 9	21 24	2 35	11 31	11 39	14 56	13 52	24 18	1 23	5 55
23 FR	8 47	22 11	21 16	4 22	12 45	12 26	15 5	13 59	24 19	1 25	5 57
24 SA	9 47	4 ♌ 8	21 8	6 10	13 59	13 12	15 15	14 6	24 21	1 27	5 58
25 SU	10 47	15 59	21 1	7 58	15 14	13 58	15 24	14 14	24 22	1 29	6 0
26 MO	11 48	27 48	20 56	9 48	16 28	14 45	15 34	14 21	24 24	1 31	6 2
27 TU	12 48	9 ♍ 37	20 53	11 38	17 42	15 31	15 44	14 28	24 25	1 34	6 3
28 WE	13 48	21 27	20 53	13 30	18 56	16 18	15 54	14 36	24 27	1 36	6 5
29 TH	14 49	3 ♎ 21	20 53D	15 22	20 11	17 4	16 4	14 43	24 28	1 38	6 7

INGRESSES :

1 ☽ → ♎ 10:46	16 ☽ → ♉ 10:46		
☿ → ♑ 23: 6	18 ☽ → ♊ 18: 3		
3 ☽ → ♏ 21:13	20 ☿ → ♒ 12:40		
6 ☽ → ♐ 3:36	21 ☽ → ♋ 3:57		
♂ → ♑ 19:55	23 ☽ → ♌ 15:41		
8 ☽ → ♑ 5:59	26 ☽ → ♍ 4:27		
10 ☽ → ♒ 5:54	28 ☽ → ♎ 17:15		
12 ☽ → ♓ 5:29			
♀ → ♑ 16:31			
14 ☽ → ♈ 6:41			
☉ → ♒ 7:11			

ASPECTS & ECLIPSES :

2 ☽ ☍ ♃ 11:16	9 ☉ ☌ ☽ 22:58	♀ ☌ ♇ 8:43	26 ☽ ☍ ♆ 7:34
☉ □ ☽ 23:16	10 ☿ □ ♃ 13:23	20 ☽ N ☊ 11:33	27 ♂ □ ♃ 8:28
3 ☽ ☍ ⛢ 9:53	☽ ☌ P 18:46	21 ☽ ☍ ♇ 15:35	☽ ☌ ☋ 22:51
5 ☿ ☌ ♇ 12:53	11 ☽ ☌ ♄ 1:43	22 ☽ ☍ ♀ 3: 1	28 ☉ S☋ ☿ 8:41
6 ♀ □ ☊ 16:16	12 ☽ ☌ ♆ 7:10	☽ ☍ ♂ 3:11	☿ ☌ ♄ 15: 6
7 ☽ S ☊ 17:34	13 ☽ ☌ ☊ 17: 0	♀ ☌ ♂ 7:13	☉ ☌ ♄ 21:24
☽ ☌ ♀ 20:11	14 ♂ ☌ ♇ 5:57	24 ☽ ☍ ☿ 4:50	
8 ☽ ☌ ♂ 7:51	15 ☽ ☌ ♃ 6:29	☉ ☍ ☽ 12:29	
☉ □ ⛢ 10:43	16 ☽ ☌ ⛢ 0:25	☽ ☍ ♄ 20:23	
☽ ☌ ♇ 14:55	☉ □ ☽ 14:59	25 ♀ □ ♃ 3:59	
☽ ☌ ☿ 23:24	17 ☿ □ ⛢ 3:50	☽ ☌ A 14:46	

SIDEREAL HELIOCENTRIC LONGITUDES : FEBRUARY 2024 Gregorian at 0 hours UT

DAY	Sid. Time	☿	♀	⊕	♂	♃	♄	⛢	♆	♇	Vernal Point
1 TH	8:42:50	17 ♏ 52	1 ♏ 9	16 ♋ 32	11 ♐ 24	23 ♈ 34	13 ♒ 49	26 ♈ 53	2 ♓ 1	4 ♑ 58	4 ♓ 55'26"
2 FR	8:46:46	20 37	2 45	17 33	11 59	23 39	13 51	26 53	2 2	4 58	4 ♓ 55'26"
3 SA	8:50:43	23 21	4 21	18 34	12 34	23 44	13 52	26 54	2 2	4 59	4 ♓ 55'26"
4 SU	8:54:40	26 6	5 56	19 34	13 9	23 50	13 54	26 55	2 2	4 59	4 ♓ 55'26"
5 MO	8:58:36	28 51	7 32	20 35	13 44	23 55	13 56	26 55	2 3	4 59	4 ♓ 55'26"
6 TU	9: 2:33	1 ♐ 37	9 7	21 36	14 20	24 1	13 58	26 56	2 3	4 59	4 ♓ 55'25"
7 WE	9: 6:29	4 24	10 43	22 37	14 55	24 6	14 0	26 57	2 3	5 0	4 ♓ 55'25"
8 TH	9:10:26	7 11	12 18	23 38	15 30	24 11	14 2	26 57	2 4	5 0	4 ♓ 55'25"
9 FR	9:14:22	10 0	13 54	24 39	16 5	24 17	14 4	26 58	2 4	5 0	4 ♓ 55'25"
10 SA	9:18:19	12 50	15 29	25 39	16 41	24 22	14 6	26 59	2 4	5 1	4 ♓ 55'25"
11 SU	9:22:15	15 42	17 4	26 40	17 16	24 28	14 8	26 59	2 5	5 1	4 ♓ 55'25"
12 MO	9:26:12	18 35	18 40	27 41	17 52	24 33	14 10	27 0	2 5	5 1	4 ♓ 55'25"
13 TU	9:30: 9	21 31	20 15	28 42	18 27	24 39	14 12	27 1	2 6	5 1	4 ♓ 55'24"
14 WE	9:34: 5	24 29	21 50	29 42	19 3	24 44	14 14	27 1	2 6	5 2	4 ♓ 55'24"
15 TH	9:38: 2	27 29	23 25	0 ♌ 43	19 38	24 49	14 16	27 2	2 6	5 2	4 ♓ 55'24"
16 FR	9:41:58	0 ♑ 33	25 1	1 44	20 14	24 55	14 18	27 3	2 7	5 2	4 ♓ 55'24"
17 SA	9:45:55	3 39	26 36	2 44	20 50	25 0	14 19	27 3	2 7	5 3	4 ♓ 55'24"
18 SU	9:49:51	6 49	28 11	3 45	21 25	25 6	14 21	27 4	2 7	5 3	4 ♓ 55'24"
19 MO	9:53:48	10 2	29 46	4 45	22 1	25 11	14 23	27 5	2 8	5 3	4 ♓ 55'24"
20 TU	9:57:44	13 20	1 ♐ 21	5 46	22 37	25 16	14 25	27 5	2 8	5 3	4 ♓ 55'23"
21 WE	10: 1:41	16 42	2 56	6 46	23 13	25 22	14 27	27 6	2 8	5 4	4 ♓ 55'23"
22 TH	10: 5:38	20 8	4 31	7 47	23 49	25 27	14 29	27 7	2 9	5 4	4 ♓ 55'23"
23 FR	10: 9:34	23 39	6 6	8 47	24 25	25 33	14 31	27 7	2 9	5 4	4 ♓ 55'23"
24 SA	10:13:31	27 16	7 41	9 47	25 1	25 38	14 33	27 8	2 10	5 4	4 ♓ 55'23"
25 SU	10:17:27	0 ♒ 58	9 16	10 48	25 37	25 43	14 35	27 9	2 10	5 5	4 ♓ 55'23"
26 MO	10:21:24	4 46	10 51	11 48	26 13	25 49	14 37	27 10	2 10	5 5	4 ♓ 55'23"
27 TU	10:25:20	8 40	12 26	12 48	26 50	25 54	14 39	27 10	2 11	5 5	4 ♓ 55'22"
28 WE	10:29:17	12 41	14 1	13 49	27 26	26 0	14 41	27 11	2 11	5 6	4 ♓ 55'22"
29 TH	10:33:13	16 50	15 36	14 49	28 2	26 5	14 43	27 12	2 11	5 6	4 ♓ 55'22"

INGRESSES :

5 ☿ → ♐ 9:56
14 ⊕ → ♌ 7: 1
15 ☿ → ♑ 19:45
19 ♀ → ♐ 3:33
24 ☿ → ♒ 17:49

ASPECTS (HELIOCENTRIC +MOON(TYCHONIC)) :

1 ☽ □ ♇ 20:41	⊕ □ ♃ 14:35	♀ ☌ ☋ 23:46	22 ☿ S ☊ 23:15	☽ □ ♂ 12:44
2 ☿ ☌ A 18:43	9 ♀ □ ♄ 2:40	14 ☽ □ ♇ 15:12	23 ☽ ☍ ☿ 4:10	⊕ ☍ ♄ 21:24
3 ☽ ☍ ♃ 9:23	☽ □ ♃ 20:59	16 ☽ ☌ ♃ 1:43	☽ □ ♃ 6:46	29 ☽ □ ♇ 3:29
☽ ☍ ⛢ 15:22	10 ☽ □ ⛢ 1: 8	☽ ☌ ⛢ 5:30	☽ □ ⛢ 9:54	
4 ☽ ☌ ♀ 9:30	11 ☽ ☌ ♄ 4:14	17 ☿ ☌ ♇ 10:36	☿ □ ♃ 12:58	
☽ □ ♄ 23: 2	⊕ □ ⛢ 7:41	☽ □ ♄ 12:49	☿ □ ⛢ 23:11	
6 ☿ □ ♆ 3:44	☽ □ ♀ 9:56	18 ☽ ☍ ♀ 16:41	24 ☽ ☍ ♄ 21: 8	
☽ □ ♆ 7:10	☿ ☌ ♂ 16:27	☽ □ ♆ 22: 4	26 ☽ ☍ ♆ 8:52	
☽ ☌ ☿ 8: 1	12 ☽ ☌ ♆ 8:50	20 ♀ □ ♆ 11:55	27 ☽ □ ♀ 6:37	
7 ☽ ☌ ♂ 5:17	13 ☽ □ ♂ 11:56	☽ ☍ ♂ 14:12	28 ☿ ☍ ⊕ 8:41	
8 ☽ ☌ ♇ 14: 5	☽ □ ☿ 20:46	21 ☽ ☍ ♇ 13:55	☿ ☌ ♄ 11:42	

SIDEREAL GEOCENTRIC LONGITUDES : MARCH 2024 Gregorian at 0 hours UT

DAY	☉	☽	☊	☿	♀	♂	♃	♄	♅	♆	♇
1 FR	15 ♒ 49	15 ♎ 25	20 ♓ 55	17 ♒ 15	21 ♑ 25	17 ♑ 50	16 ♈ 14	14 ♒ 50	24 ♈ 30	1 ♓ 40	6 ♑ 8
2 SA	16 49	27 41	20 57	19 9	22 39	18 37	16 25	14 57	24 32	1 42	6 10
3 SU	17 49	10 ♏ 14	20 58	21 3	23 54	19 23	16 35	15 5	24 34	1 45	6 11
4 MO	18 49	23 9	20 58R	22 59	25 8	20 10	16 45	15 12	24 35	1 47	6 13
5 TU	19 49	6 ♐ 29	20 57	24 55	26 22	20 56	16 56	15 19	24 37	1 49	6 14
6 WE	20 50	20 17	20 55	26 51	27 36	21 43	17 7	15 27	24 39	1 51	6 16
7 TH	21 50	4 ♑ 33	20 51	28 47	28 51	22 30	17 18	15 34	24 41	1 54	6 17
8 FR	22 50	19 14	20 47	0 ♓ 44	0 ♒ 5	23 16	17 29	15 41	24 43	1 56	6 19
9 SA	23 50	4 ♒ 16	20 43	2 40	1 19	24 3	17 40	15 49	24 45	1 58	6 20
10 SU	24 50	19 29	20 40	4 36	2 34	24 49	17 51	15 56	24 47	2 0	6 22
11 MO	25 50	4 ♓ 44	20 38	6 31	3 48	25 36	18 2	16 3	24 49	2 3	6 23
12 TU	26 50	19 50	20 38	8 25	5 2	26 23	18 13	16 10	24 51	2 5	6 24
13 WE	27 49	4 ♈ 39	20 38D	10 18	6 16	27 9	18 25	16 18	24 54	2 7	6 26
14 TH	28 49	19 4	20 39	12 9	7 31	27 56	18 36	16 25	24 56	2 9	6 27
15 FR	29 49	3 ♉ 4	20 41	13 58	8 45	28 42	18 48	16 32	24 58	2 12	6 28
16 SA	0 ♓ 49	16 37	20 42	15 43	9 59	29 29	18 59	16 39	25 1	2 14	6 30
17 SU	1 49	29 45	20 43	17 26	11 13	0 ♒ 16	19 11	16 47	25 3	2 16	6 31
18 MO	2 48	12 ♊ 31	20 42R	19 5	12 28	1 2	19 23	16 54	25 5	2 18	6 32
19 TU	3 48	24 58	20 41	20 40	13 42	1 49	19 35	17 1	25 8	2 21	6 33
20 WE	4 48	7 ♋ 11	20 39	22 11	14 56	2 36	19 47	17 8	25 10	2 23	6 35
21 TH	5 47	19 13	20 37	23 36	16 10	3 22	19 59	17 15	25 13	2 25	6 36
22 FR	6 47	1 ♌ 8	20 35	24 56	17 25	4 9	20 11	17 22	25 15	2 28	6 37
23 SA	7 46	12 58	20 32	26 9	18 39	4 56	20 23	17 29	25 18	2 30	6 38
24 SU	8 46	24 47	20 31	27 17	19 53	5 42	20 36	17 36	25 20	2 32	6 39
25 MO	9 45	6 ♍ 36	20 30	28 18	21 7	6 29	20 48	17 43	25 23	2 34	6 40
26 TU	10 45	18 28	20 30	29 12	22 21	7 16	21 0	17 50	25 26	2 37	6 41
27 WE	11 44	0 ♎ 24	20 30D	0 ♈ 0	23 35	8 3	21 13	17 57	25 28	2 39	6 42
28 TH	12 43	12 28	20 30	0 40	24 50	8 49	21 26	18 4	25 31	2 41	6 43
29 FR	13 43	24 41	20 31	1 12	26 4	9 36	21 38	18 11	25 34	2 43	6 44
30 SA	14 42	7 ♏ 5	20 32	1 37	27 18	10 23	21 51	18 18	25 37	2 46	6 45
31 SU	15 41	19 45	20 32	1 55	28 32	11 9	22 4	18 24	25 40	2 48	6 46

INGRESSES :		ASPECTS & ECLIPSES :			
2 ☽ → ♏ 4:28	17 ☽ → ♊ 0:28	1 ☽ ☍ ♃ 1:38	10 ☽ ☌ P 7: 4	☽ ☍ ♇ 22:47	28 ☽ ☍ ♃ 17:57
4 ☽ → ♐ 12:25	19 ☽ → ♋ 9:50	☽ ☍ ♅ 17:51	☉ ☌ ☽ 8:59	21 ♀ ☌ ♄ 23: 8	29 ☽ ☍ ♅ 1:44
6 ☽ → ♑ 16:25	21 ☽ → ♌ 21:42	3 ♀ □ ♅ 13:15	☽ ☌ ♆ 19:44	22 ☽ ☍ ♂ 6:32	
7 ☿ → ♓ 14:59	24 ☽ → ♍ 10:36	☉ □ ☽ 15:22	11 ☽ ☌ ☿ 3:13	23 ☽ ☍ ♄ 9:16	
♀ → ♒ 22:23	26 ☽ → ♎ 23:11	6 ☽ S ☊ 1: 4	12 ☽ ☌ ☊ 1:16	☽ ☍ ♀ 12:53	
8 ☽ → ♒ 17:13	27 ☿ → ♈ 0:12	7 ☽ ☌ ♇ 2:52	13 ☽ ☌ ♃ 23:11	☽ ☌ A 15:16	
10 ☽ → ♓ 16:32	29 ☽ → ♏ 10:20	8 ☽ ☌ ♂ 6:49	14 ☽ ☌ ♅ 9:58	24 ☽ ☍ ♆ 15:48	
12 ☽ → ♈ 16:24	31 ☽ → ♐ 19: 3	☿ ☌ ♆ 15: 9	17 ☉ □ ☽ 4: 9	25 ☉ ☍ ☽ 6:59	
14 ☽ → ♉ 18:40		☽ ☌ ♀ 18:54	☉ ☌ ♆ 11:31	☽ ☍ PN 7:11	
15 ☉ → ♓ 4:22		9 ☽ ☌ ♄ 18:21	18 ☽ N ☊ 15:42	26 ☽ ☌ ☋ 4: 5	
16 ♂ → ♒ 15:54		♂ □ ♅ 22:52	19 ☿ ☌ ☊ 0:12	☽ ☍ ☿ 23: 7	

SIDEREAL HELIOCENTRIC LONGITUDES : MARCH 2024 Gregorian at 0 hours UT

DAY	Sid. Time	☿	♀	⊕	♂	♃	♄	♅	♆	♇	Vernal Point
1 FR	10:37:10	21 ♒ 6	17 ♐ 11	15 ♌ 49	28 ♐ 39	26 ♈ 10	14 ♒ 45	27 ♈ 12	2 ♓ 12	5 ♑ 6	4 ♓ 55'22"
2 SA	10:41: 7	25 29	18 46	16 49	29 15	26 16	14 47	27 13	2 12	5 6	4 ♓ 55'22"
3 SU	10:45: 3	0 ♓ 1	20 21	17 50	29 51	26 21	14 48	27 14	2 12	5 7	4 ♓ 55'22"
4 MO	10:49: 0	4 41	21 55	18 50	0 ♑ 28	26 27	14 50	27 14	2 13	5 7	4 ♓ 55'22"
5 TU	10:52:56	9 30	23 30	19 50	1 5	26 32	14 52	27 15	2 13	5 7	4 ♓ 55'22"
6 WE	10:56:53	14 28	25 5	20 50	1 41	26 37	14 54	27 16	2 14	5 8	4 ♓ 55'21"
7 TH	11: 0:49	19 35	26 40	21 50	2 18	26 43	14 56	27 16	2 14	5 8	4 ♓ 55'21"
8 FR	11: 4:46	24 52	28 15	22 50	2 54	26 48	14 58	27 17	2 14	5 8	4 ♓ 55'21"
9 SA	11: 8:42	0 ♈ 17	29 50	23 50	3 31	26 53	15 0	27 18	2 15	5 8	4 ♓ 55'21"
10 SU	11:12:39	5 51	1 ♑ 25	24 50	4 8	26 59	15 2	27 18	2 15	5 9	4 ♓ 55'21"
11 MO	11:16:36	11 34	3 0	25 50	4 45	27 4	15 4	27 19	2 15	5 9	4 ♓ 55'21"
12 TU	11:20:32	17 25	4 34	26 50	5 22	27 10	15 6	27 20	2 16	5 9	4 ♓ 55'21"
13 WE	11:24:29	23 23	6 9	27 50	5 58	27 15	15 8	27 20	2 16	5 10	4 ♓ 55'20"
14 TH	11:28:25	29 28	7 44	28 50	6 35	27 20	15 10	27 21	2 16	5 10	4 ♓ 55'20"
15 FR	11:32:22	5 ♉ 38	9 19	29 50	7 12	27 26	15 12	27 22	2 17	5 10	4 ♓ 55'20"
16 SA	11:36:18	11 53	10 54	0 ♍ 49	7 49	27 31	15 14	27 22	2 17	5 10	4 ♓ 55'20"
17 SU	11:40:15	18 10	12 29	1 49	8 26	27 37	15 16	27 23	2 18	5 11	4 ♓ 55'20"
18 MO	11:44:11	24 29	14 4	2 49	9 3	27 42	15 17	27 24	2 18	5 11	4 ♓ 55'20"
19 TU	11:48: 8	0 ♊ 49	15 38	3 48	9 41	27 47	15 19	27 24	2 18	5 11	4 ♓ 55'20"
20 WE	11:52: 5	7 6	17 13	4 48	10 18	27 53	15 21	27 25	2 19	5 12	4 ♓ 55'19"
21 TH	11:56: 1	13 21	18 48	5 48	10 55	27 58	15 23	27 26	2 19	5 12	4 ♓ 55'19"
22 FR	11:59:58	19 32	20 23	6 47	11 32	28 4	15 25	27 26	2 19	5 12	4 ♓ 55'19"
23 SA	12: 3:54	25 37	21 58	7 47	12 9	28 9	15 27	27 27	2 20	5 12	4 ♓ 55'19"
24 SU	12: 7:51	1 ♋ 35	23 33	8 46	12 47	28 14	15 29	27 28	2 20	5 13	4 ♓ 55'19"
25 MO	12:11:47	7 25	25 8	9 46	13 24	28 20	15 31	27 28	2 20	5 13	4 ♓ 55'19"
26 TU	12:15:44	13 7	26 43	10 45	14 1	28 25	15 33	27 29	2 21	5 13	4 ♓ 55'19"
27 WE	12:19:40	18 40	28 18	11 44	14 39	28 30	15 35	27 30	2 21	5 14	4 ♓ 55'19"
28 TH	12:23:37	24 3	29 53	12 44	15 16	28 36	15 37	27 30	2 22	5 14	4 ♓ 55'18"
29 FR	12:27:34	29 17	1 ♒ 28	13 43	15 54	28 41	15 39	27 31	2 22	5 14	4 ♓ 55'18"
30 SA	12:31:30	4 ♌ 22	3 3	14 42	16 31	28 47	15 41	27 32	2 22	5 14	4 ♓ 55'18"
31 SU	12:35:27	9 16	4 38	15 42	17 9	28 52	15 43	27 32	2 23	5 15	4 ♓ 55'18"

INGRESSES :	ASPECTS (HELIOCENTRIC +MOON(TYCHONIC)) :					
2 ☿ → ♓ 23:54	1 ☽ ☍ ♃ 21:13	☿ □ ♀ 21:12	☽ □ ♀ 2:46	☿ ☌ P 17:25	☽ ☍ ♆ 15:21	☿ ☍ ♀ 14:50
3 ♂ → ♑ 5:35	☽ ☍ ♅ 23: 5	9 ☿ □ ♂ 15:44	☿ ☌ ♃ 15:32	19 ☿ □ ♆ 5:41	26 ☿ ☍ ♂ 4:20	☽ □ ♀ 15: 6
8 ☿ → ♈ 22:45	3 ☽ □ ♄ 8:36	☽ ☌ ♄ 16:58	☿ ☌ ♅ 15:41	☿ □ ⊕ 13:33	♀ □ ♅ 11:44	☽ □ ☿ 15:13
9 ♀ → ♑ 2:34	☿ ☌ ♆ 11:21	☿ □ ♇ 20:58	14 ♃ ☌ ♅ 2:44	♀ ☌ A 17:57	27 ♀ □ ♃ 3:22	30 ☽ □ ♄ 16:23
14 ☿ → ♉ 2: 6	4 ☽ □ ♆ 16:24	10 ☽ ☌ ♆ 20: 5	☽ ☌ ♅ 14: 6	☽ ☍ ♇ 20: 3	☽ □ ♇ 9:38	31 ☽ □ ♆ 23:25
15 ⊕ → ♍ 4:11	5 ☽ □ ☿ 8:18	11 ♂ ☌ ♇ 15:57	☽ ☌ ♃ 14:10	20 ☽ ☍ ♂ 6:30	☿ N ☊ 21:39	
18 ☿ → ♊ 20:55	6 ☽ ☌ ♀ 9:11	12 ♀ ☌ ♇ 8:51	15 ☽ ☌ ☿ 8:14	☽ ☍ ♀ 23: 2	28 ☽ □ ♂ 5:50	
23 ☿ → ♋ 17:36	☽ ☌ ♂ 20: 5	♀ ☌ ♂ 19:31	☽ □ ♄ 21:30	21 ☽ □ ♅ 16:32	☿ □ ♅ 15:46	
28 ♀ → ♒ 1:47	7 ☽ ☌ ♇ 0:58	13 ☿ ☌ ☊ 0:37	16 ☿ □ ♄ 12:51	☽ □ ♃ 17:44	☿ □ ♃ 21: 9	
29 ☿ → ♌ 3:19	8 ☽ □ ♃ 12:12	☽ □ ♇ 0:50	17 ☽ □ ♆ 4:44	23 ☽ ☍ ♄ 5: 3	29 ☽ ☍ ♅ 5:32	
	☽ □ ♅ 12:54	☽ □ ♂ 2:16	⊕ ☍ ♆ 11:31	24 ☿ ☍ ♇ 14:52	☽ ☍ ♃ 7:51	

SIDEREAL GEOCENTRIC LONGITUDES : APRIL 2024 Gregorian at 0 hours UT

DAY	☉	☽	☊	☿	♀	♂	♃	♄	⛢	♆	♇
1 MO	16 ♓ 40	2 ♐ 42	20 ♓ 33	2 ♈ 5	29 ♒ 46	11 ♒ 56	22 ♈ 16	18 ♒ 31	25 ♈ 42	2 ♓ 50	6 ♑ 47
2 TU	17 40	15 59	20 33	2 8R	1 ♓ 1	12 43	22 29	18 38	25 45	2 52	6 48
3 WE	18 39	29 38	20 33R	2 4	2 15	13 29	22 42	18 45	25 48	2 55	6 49
4 TH	19 38	13 ♑ 41	20 33	1 54	3 29	14 16	22 55	18 51	25 51	2 57	6 50
5 FR	20 37	28 5	20 32	1 36	4 43	15 3	23 8	18 58	25 54	2 59	6 50
6 SA	21 36	12 ♒ 49	20 32D	1 13	5 57	15 49	23 22	19 5	25 57	3 1	6 51
7 SU	22 35	27 46	20 33	0 45	7 11	16 36	23 35	19 11	26 0	3 3	6 52
8 MO	23 34	12 ♓ 50	20 33	0 11	8 25	17 23	23 48	19 18	26 3	3 5	6 53
9 TU	24 33	27 52	20 33R	29 ♓ 34	9 39	18 9	24 1	19 24	26 6	3 8	6 53
10 WE	25 32	12 ♈ 42	20 33	28 53	10 54	18 56	24 14	19 31	26 9	3 10	6 54
11 TH	26 31	27 14	20 32	28 10	12 8	19 43	24 28	19 37	26 12	3 12	6 55
12 FR	27 30	11 ♉ 23	20 31	27 26	13 22	20 29	24 41	19 43	26 16	3 14	6 55
13 SA	28 29	25 5	20 31	26 41	14 36	21 16	24 55	19 50	26 19	3 16	6 56
14 SU	29 28	8 ♊ 21	20 30	25 55	15 50	22 2	25 8	19 56	26 22	3 18	6 56
15 MO	0 ♈ 26	21 12	20 29	25 11	17 4	22 49	25 22	20 2	26 25	3 20	6 57
16 TU	1 25	3 ♋ 42	20 29D	24 29	18 18	23 36	25 35	20 8	26 28	3 22	6 57
17 WE	2 24	15 55	20 29	23 49	19 32	24 22	25 49	20 14	26 32	3 24	6 58
18 TH	3 23	27 55	20 30	23 12	20 46	25 9	26 3	20 20	26 35	3 26	6 58
19 FR	4 21	9 ♌ 47	20 31	22 39	22 0	25 55	26 16	20 26	26 38	3 28	6 59
20 SA	5 20	21 35	20 33	22 10	23 14	26 42	26 30	20 32	26 41	3 30	6 59
21 SU	6 18	3 ♍ 23	20 34	21 45	24 28	27 28	26 44	20 38	26 45	3 32	6 59
22 MO	7 17	15 15	20 35	21 25	25 42	28 14	26 57	20 44	26 48	3 34	7 0
23 TU	8 15	27 13	20 35R	21 10	26 56	29 1	27 11	20 50	26 51	3 36	7 0
24 WE	9 14	9 ♎ 19	20 34	21 0	28 10	29 47	27 25	20 55	26 55	3 38	7 0
25 TH	10 12	21 36	20 32	20 55	29 24	0 ♓ 34	27 39	21 1	26 58	3 40	7 0
26 FR	11 11	4 ♏ 5	20 29	20 55D	0 ♈ 38	1 20	27 53	21 6	27 1	3 42	7 1
27 SA	12 9	16 46	20 26	20 59	1 52	2 6	28 7	21 12	27 5	3 44	7 1
28 SU	13 7	29 41	20 23	21 9	3 6	2 53	28 21	21 17	27 8	3 46	7 1
29 MO	14 6	12 ♐ 50	20 20	21 23	4 20	3 39	28 35	21 23	27 12	3 48	7 1
30 TU	15 4	26 14	20 17	21 42	5 34	4 25	28 49	21 28	27 15	3 50	7 1

INGRESSES :

1	♀ → ♓	4:24	20	☽ → ♍	17: 7
3	☽ → ♑	0:37	23	☽ → ♎	5:33
5	☽ → ♒	3: 8	24	♂ → ♓	6:33
7	☽ → ♓	3:33	25	♀ → ♈	11:40
8	☿ → ♓	7:33		☽ → ♏	16:11
9	☽ → ♈	3:26	28	☽ → ♐	0:34
11	☽ → ♉	4:38	30	☽ → ♑	6:39
13	☽ → ♊	8:48			
14	☉ → ♈	13:12			
15	☽ → ♋	16:50			
18	☽ → ♌	4:12			

ASPECTS & ECLIPSES :

2	☉ □ ☽	3:13		☉ ● T	18:16	19	☿ ☌ ♀	8:58	25	☽ ☍ ⛢	10:24
	☽ S□ ☊	8: 5		☉ ☌ ☽	18:19		☽ ☍ ♄	21:51		☽ ☍ ♃	11:53
3	☽ ☌ ♇	12:21	9	☽ ☌ ☿	2:37	20	☽ ☌ A	2: 0	29	♂ ☌ ♆	4:42
	♀ ☌ ♆	13:17	10	☽ ☌ ♃	19:18		☽ ☍ ♂	11: 8		☽ S□ ☊	13:25
4	☉ ☌ ☊	22: 7		♂ ☌ ♄	20:35	21	☽ ☍ ♆	0:19	30	☽ ☌ ♇	18:58
6	☽ ☌ ♂	5: 6		☽ ☌ ⛢	22:16		♃ ☌ ⛢	2:21			
	☽ ☌ ♄	10: 9	11	☉ i☌ ☿	23: 1		☉ □ ♇	16:55			
7	☽ ☌ ♆	8:26	14	☽ N□ ☊	22:39	22	☽ ☌ ☋	10:43			
	☽ ☌ ♀	16:20	15	☉ □ ☽	19:12		☽ ☍ ☿	12: 8			
	☽ ☌ P	17:55	16	☽ ☍ ♇	6:21		☽ ☍ ♀	23:22			
8	☽ ☌ ☊	12:17	17	♀ ☌ ☊	18:46	23	☉ ☍ ☽	23:47			

SIDEREAL HELIOCENTRIC LONGITUDES : APRIL 2024 Gregorian at 0 hours UT

DAY	Sid. Time	☿	♀	⊕	♂	♃	♄	⛢	♆	♇	Vernal Point
1 MO	12:39:23	14 ♌ 1	6 ♒ 13	16 ♍ 41	17 ♑ 46	28 ♈ 57	15 ♒ 45	27 ♈ 33	2 ♓ 23	5 ♑ 15	4 ♓ 55'18"
2 TU	12:43:20	18 37	7 48	17 40	18 24	29 3	15 47	27 34	2 23	5 15	4 ♓ 55'18"
3 WE	12:47:16	23 4	9 23	18 39	19 1	29 8	15 48	27 34	2 24	5 15	4 ♓ 55'18"
4 TH	12:51:13	27 23	10 58	19 38	19 39	29 14	15 50	27 35	2 24	5 16	4 ♓ 55'17"
5 FR	12:55: 9	1 ♍ 33	12 33	20 38	20 17	29 19	15 52	27 36	2 24	5 16	4 ♓ 55'17"
6 SA	12:59: 6	5 36	14 8	21 37	20 54	29 24	15 54	27 37	2 25	5 16	4 ♓ 55'17"
7 SU	13: 3: 3	9 32	15 44	22 36	21 32	29 30	15 56	27 37	2 25	5 17	4 ♓ 55'17"
8 MO	13: 6:59	13 21	17 19	23 35	22 10	29 35	15 58	27 38	2 26	5 17	4 ♓ 55'17"
9 TU	13:10:56	17 3	18 54	24 34	22 47	29 40	16 0	27 39	2 26	5 17	4 ♓ 55'17"
10 WE	13:14:52	20 40	20 29	25 33	23 25	29 46	16 2	27 39	2 26	5 17	4 ♓ 55'17"
11 TH	13:18:49	24 10	22 4	26 32	24 3	29 51	16 4	27 40	2 27	5 18	4 ♓ 55'16"
12 FR	13:22:45	27 36	23 40	27 30	24 41	29 57	16 6	27 41	2 27	5 18	4 ♓ 55'16"
13 SA	13:26:42	0 ♎ 57	25 15	28 29	25 19	0 ♉ 2	16 8	27 41	2 27	5 18	4 ♓ 55'16"
14 SU	13:30:38	4 14	26 50	29 28	25 56	0 7	16 10	27 42	2 28	5 19	4 ♓ 55'16"
15 MO	13:34:35	7 26	28 26	0 ♎ 27	26 34	0 13	16 12	27 43	2 28	5 19	4 ♓ 55'16"
16 TU	13:38:32	10 35	0 ♓ 1	1 26	27 12	0 18	16 14	27 43	2 28	5 19	4 ♓ 55'16"
17 WE	13:42:28	13 41	1 36	2 24	27 50	0 23	16 16	27 44	2 29	5 19	4 ♓ 55'16"
18 TH	13:46:25	16 43	3 12	3 23	28 28	0 29	16 18	27 45	2 29	5 20	4 ♓ 55'15"
19 FR	13:50:21	19 42	4 47	4 22	29 6	0 34	16 19	27 45	2 30	5 20	4 ♓ 55'15"
20 SA	13:54:18	22 39	6 22	5 20	29 44	0 40	16 21	27 46	2 30	5 20	4 ♓ 55'15"
21 SU	13:58:14	25 34	7 58	6 19	0 ♒ 22	0 45	16 23	27 47	2 30	5 21	4 ♓ 55'15"
22 MO	14: 2:11	28 26	9 33	7 17	1 0	0 50	16 25	27 47	2 31	5 21	4 ♓ 55'15"
23 TU	14: 6: 7	1 ♏ 17	11 9	8 16	1 38	0 56	16 27	27 48	2 31	5 21	4 ♓ 55'15"
24 WE	14:10: 4	4 7	12 44	9 14	2 16	1 1	16 29	27 49	2 31	5 21	4 ♓ 55'15"
25 TH	14:14: 0	6 55	14 20	10 13	2 54	1 6	16 31	27 49	2 32	5 22	4 ♓ 55'15"
26 FR	14:17:57	9 42	15 55	11 11	3 32	1 12	16 33	27 50	2 32	5 22	4 ♓ 55'14"
27 SA	14:21:54	12 28	17 31	12 9	4 10	1 17	16 35	27 51	2 32	5 22	4 ♓ 55'14"
28 SU	14:25:50	15 13	19 7	13 8	4 48	1 23	16 37	27 51	2 33	5 23	4 ♓ 55'14"
29 MO	14:29:47	17 58	20 42	14 6	5 26	1 28	16 39	27 52	2 33	5 23	4 ♓ 55'14"
30 TU	14:33:43	20 43	22 18	15 4	6 4	1 33	16 41	27 53	2 34	5 23	4 ♓ 55'14"

INGRESSES :

4	☿ → ♍	14:57
12	♃ → ♉	15:14
	☿ → ♎	17: 6
14	⊕ → ♎	13: 2
15	♀ → ♓	23:46
20	♂ → ♒	10: 8
22	☿ → ♏	13: 6

ASPECTS (HELIOCENTRIC +MOON(TYCHONIC)) :

1	☿ ☍ ♄	8:57	9	☽ □ ♇	11:57	16	☽ ☍ ♇	3: 9	21	☽ ☍ ♀	10:43	28	☽ □ ♆	5:15
3	☽ ☌ ♇	9:41	10	☽ □ ♂	18:26		☽ □ ☿	18: 4		♂ □ ♃	16:56		☿ □ ♄	12:21
4	☽ ☌ ♂	10:28		♀ S□ ☊	20: 9		♂ □ ⛢	20: 1		☿ ☍ ⛢	18:30	29	☽ □ ♀	16: 2
	☽ □ ⛢	23:11	11	☽ ☌ ⛢	0:43	17	♀ ☌ ♆	13:16	22	☿ ☍ ♃	20:50	30	☽ ☌ ♇	16: 7
5	☽ □ ♃	2: 1		☽ ☌ ♃	4:25		☽ □ ⛢	23:39	23	☿ □ ♂	3:44		☿ ☌ A	17:54
	☿ ☍ ♆	4:59		☿ ☌ ⊕	23: 1	18	☽ ☍ ♂	1:11		☽ □ ♇	16:10			
6	☽ ☌ ♀	2:23		♂ S□ ☊	23:30		☽ □ ♃	5:13	25	☽ ☍ ⛢	12: 1			
	☽ ☌ ♄	4:59	12	☽ □ ♄	8:12	19	☽ ☍ ♄	13:20		☽ ☍ ♃	18:26			
7	♀ ☌ ♄	3:14	13	☽ □ ♀	0:20	20	⊕ □ ♇	0: 3		☽ □ ♂	22:53			
	☽ ☌ ♆	7:24		☽ □ ♆	13:15		☿ ☌ ☋	7:16	26	☽ ☌ ☿	13:38			
8	☽ ☍ ☿	1: 4	14	☿ □ ♇	8: 1		☽ ☍ ♆	22:12		☽ □ ♄	23:38			

SIDEREAL GEOCENTRIC LONGITUDES : MAY 2024 Gregorian at 0 hours UT

DAY	☉	☽	☊	☿	♀	♂	♃	♄	⛢	♆	♇
1 WE	16 ♈ 2	9 ♑ 54	20 ♓ 16R	22 ♓ 6	6 ♈ 48	5 ♓ 12	29 ♈ 3	21 ♒ 33	27 ♈ 18	3 ♓ 51	7 ♑ 1
2 TH	17 0	23 49	20 16D	22 34	8 2	5 58	29 17	21 39	27 22	3 53	7 1
3 FR	17 59	7 ♒ 59	20 17	23 6	9 15	6 44	29 31	21 44	27 25	3 55	7 1R
4 SA	18 57	22 23	20 18	23 42	10 29	7 30	29 45	21 49	27 29	3 57	7 1
5 SU	19 55	6 ♓ 57	20 19	24 22	11 43	8 16	29 59	21 54	27 32	3 58	7 1
6 MO	20 53	21 38	20 20R	25 5	12 57	9 2	0 ♉ 13	21 59	27 36	4 0	7 1
7 TU	21 51	6 ♈ 20	20 19	25 52	14 11	9 48	0 27	22 4	27 39	4 2	7 1
8 WE	22 49	20 56	20 16	26 43	15 25	10 35	0 41	22 9	27 43	4 3	7 1
9 TH	23 47	5 ♉ 19	20 12	27 37	16 39	11 21	0 55	22 13	27 46	4 5	7 1
10 FR	24 45	19 24	20 7	28 34	17 53	12 7	1 9	22 18	27 50	4 7	7 0
11 SA	25 43	3 ♊ 7	20 2	29 34	19 7	12 52	1 23	22 22	27 53	4 8	7 0
12 SU	26 41	16 26	19 57	0 ♈ 37	20 20	13 38	1 38	22 27	27 57	4 10	7 0
13 MO	27 39	29 21	19 52	1 43	21 34	14 24	1 52	22 31	28 0	4 11	7 0
14 TU	28 37	11 ♋ 54	19 49	2 52	22 48	15 10	2 6	22 36	28 4	4 13	6 59
15 WE	29 35	24 8	19 48	4 3	24 2	15 56	2 20	22 40	28 7	4 14	6 59
16 TH	0 ♉ 33	6 ♌ 9	19 48D	5 17	25 16	16 42	2 34	22 44	28 10	4 16	6 59
17 FR	1 31	18 1	19 49	6 33	26 30	17 27	2 48	22 48	28 14	4 17	6 58
18 SA	2 28	29 49	19 50	7 52	27 43	18 13	3 3	22 52	28 17	4 19	6 58
19 SU	3 26	11 ♍ 39	19 52	9 14	28 57	18 59	3 17	22 56	28 21	4 20	6 58
20 MO	4 24	23 34	19 52R	10 38	0 ♉ 11	19 44	3 31	23 0	28 24	4 21	6 57
21 TU	5 22	5 ♎ 39	19 50	12 4	1 25	20 30	3 45	23 4	28 28	4 23	6 57
22 WE	6 19	17 57	19 47	13 33	2 38	21 15	3 59	23 8	28 31	4 24	6 56
23 TH	7 17	0 ♏ 29	19 42	15 4	3 52	22 1	4 13	23 11	28 35	4 25	6 56
24 FR	8 15	13 16	19 35	16 37	5 6	22 46	4 27	23 15	28 38	4 27	6 55
25 SA	9 12	26 19	19 26	18 13	6 20	23 32	4 42	23 18	28 42	4 28	6 54
26 SU	10 10	9 ♐ 36	19 18	19 51	7 33	24 17	4 56	23 22	28 45	4 29	6 54
27 MO	11 8	23 7	19 10	21 31	8 47	25 2	5 10	23 25	28 49	4 30	6 53
28 TU	12 5	6 ♑ 48	19 4	23 14	10 1	25 47	5 24	23 28	28 52	4 31	6 52
29 WE	13 3	20 38	19 0	24 59	11 15	26 33	5 38	23 31	28 55	4 32	6 52
30 TH	14 0	4 ♒ 37	18 57	26 46	12 28	27 18	5 52	23 34	28 59	4 33	6 51
31 FR	14 58	18 42	18 57D	28 36	13 42	28 3	6 6	23 37	29 2	4 34	6 50

INGRESSES :

2 ☽ → ♒ 10:31	19 ♀ → ♉ 20:27
4 ☽ → ♓ 12:34	20 ☽ → ♎ 12:48
5 ♃ → ♉ 2: 6	22 ☽ → ♏ 23: 5
6 ☽ → ♈ 13:38	25 ☽ → ♐ 6:41
8 ☽ → ♉ 15: 4	27 ☽ → ♑ 12: 7
10 ☽ → ♊ 18:28	29 ☽ → ♒ 16: 6
11 ☿ → ♈ 10: 2	31 ☿ → ♉ 18: 6
13 ☽ → ♋ 1:14	☽ → ♓ 19: 8
15 ☉ → ♉ 10:22	
☽ → ♌ 11:40	
18 ☽ → ♍ 0:21	

ASPECTS & ECLIPSES :

1 ♀ ☐ ♇ 4:24	☽ ☌ ♃ 16:29	19 ☽ ☍ ♂ 15:47	30 ☉ ☐ ☽ 17:11
☉ ☐ ☽ 11:26	12 ☽ [N] ☊ 6:25	☽ ☌ ☋ 16:33	31 ☿ ☌ ⛢ 5:52
3 ☽ ☌ ♄ 23: 3	13 ☉ ☌ ⛢ 9:11	20 ♂ ☌ ☊ 3:54	☽ ☌ ♄ 8:22
4 ☽ ☌ ♆ 19: 5	☽ ☍ ♇ 14:33	21 ☽ ☍ ☿ 14:17	
5 ☽ ☌ ♂ 2:16	15 ☉ ☐ ☽ 11:46	22 ☽ ☍ ⛢ 20:22	
☽ ☌ ☊ 21:51	17 ☿ ☐ ♇ 7:38	23 ☽ ☍ ♀ 7: 5	
☽ ☌ P 22: 9	☽ ☍ ♄ 9:47	☽ ☍ ♃ 7:12	
6 ☽ ☌ ☿ 5:56	☽ ☌ A 18:37	♀ ☌ ♃ 8:27	
7 ☽ ☌ ♀ 14: 3	18 ☽ ☍ ♆ 9: 8	☉ ☍ ☽ 13:52	
8 ☉ ☌ ☽ 3:20	♀ ☌ ⛢ 11:38	26 ☽ [S] ☊ 17: 5	
☽ ☌ ⛢ 11:17	☉ ☌ ♃ 18:44	28 ☽ ☌ ♇ 0: 8	

SIDEREAL HELIOCENTRIC LONGITUDES : MAY 2024 Gregorian at 0 hours UT

DAY	Sid. Time	☿	♀	⊕	♂	♃	♄	⛢	♆	♇	Vernal Point
1 WE	14:37:40	23 ♏ 27	23 ♓ 54	16 ♎ 2	6 ♒ 42	1 ♉ 39	16 ♒ 43	27 ♈ 53	2 ♓ 34	5 ♑ 23	4 ♓ 55'14"
2 TH	14:41:36	26 12	25 29	17 1	7 20	1 44	16 45	27 54	2 34	5 24	4 ♓ 55'14"
3 FR	14:45:33	28 57	27 5	17 59	7 58	1 49	16 47	27 55	2 35	5 24	4 ♓ 55'13"
4 SA	14:49:29	1 ♐ 43	28 41	18 57	8 37	1 55	16 49	27 55	2 35	5 24	4 ♓ 55'13"
5 SU	14:53:26	4 29	0 ♈ 17	19 55	9 15	2 0	16 51	27 56	2 35	5 25	4 ♓ 55'13"
6 MO	14:57:23	7 17	1 52	20 53	9 53	2 5	16 52	27 57	2 36	5 25	4 ♓ 55'13"
7 TU	15: 1:19	10 6	3 28	21 52	10 31	2 11	16 54	27 57	2 36	5 25	4 ♓ 55'13"
8 WE	15: 5:16	12 56	5 4	22 50	11 9	2 16	16 56	27 58	2 36	5 25	4 ♓ 55'13"
9 TH	15: 9:12	15 48	6 40	23 48	11 47	2 22	16 58	27 59	2 37	5 26	4 ♓ 55'13"
10 FR	15:13: 9	18 41	8 16	24 46	12 25	2 27	17 0	28 0	2 37	5 26	4 ♓ 55'12"
11 SA	15:17: 5	21 37	9 52	25 44	13 3	2 32	17 2	28 0	2 38	5 26	4 ♓ 55'12"
12 SU	15:21: 2	24 35	11 28	26 42	13 41	2 38	17 4	28 1	2 38	5 26	4 ♓ 55'12"
13 MO	15:24:58	27 35	13 4	27 40	14 19	2 43	17 6	28 2	2 38	5 27	4 ♓ 55'12"
14 TU	15:28:55	0 ♑ 39	14 40	28 38	14 57	2 48	17 8	28 2	2 39	5 27	4 ♓ 55'12"
15 WE	15:32:52	3 45	16 16	29 35	15 36	2 54	17 10	28 3	2 39	5 27	4 ♓ 55'12"
16 TH	15:36:48	6 55	17 52	0 ♏ 33	16 14	2 59	17 12	28 4	2 39	5 28	4 ♓ 55'12"
17 FR	15:40:45	10 9	19 28	1 31	16 52	3 4	17 14	28 4	2 40	5 28	4 ♓ 55'11"
18 SA	15:44:41	13 26	21 4	2 29	17 30	3 10	17 16	28 5	2 40	5 28	4 ♓ 55'11"
19 SU	15:48:38	16 48	22 40	3 27	18 8	3 15	17 18	28 6	2 40	5 28	4 ♓ 55'11"
20 MO	15:52:34	20 15	24 17	4 24	18 46	3 21	17 20	28 6	2 41	5 29	4 ♓ 55'11"
21 TU	15:56:31	23 46	25 53	5 22	19 24	3 26	17 22	28 7	2 41	5 29	4 ♓ 55'11"
22 WE	16: 0:27	27 23	27 29	6 20	20 2	3 31	17 24	28 8	2 42	5 29	4 ♓ 55'11"
23 TH	16: 4:24	1 ♒ 5	29 5	7 17	20 40	3 37	17 25	28 8	2 42	5 30	4 ♓ 55'11"
24 FR	16: 8:21	4 53	0 ♉ 42	8 15	21 18	3 42	17 27	28 9	2 42	5 30	4 ♓ 55'11"
25 SA	16:12:17	8 48	2 18	9 13	21 56	3 47	17 29	28 10	2 43	5 30	4 ♓ 55'10"
26 SU	16:16:14	12 49	3 54	10 10	22 34	3 53	17 31	28 10	2 43	5 30	4 ♓ 55'10"
27 MO	16:20:10	16 58	5 31	11 8	23 12	3 58	17 33	28 11	2 43	5 31	4 ♓ 55'10"
28 TU	16:24: 7	21 14	7 7	12 6	23 50	4 3	17 35	28 12	2 44	5 31	4 ♓ 55'10"
29 WE	16:28: 3	25 38	8 43	13 3	24 28	4 9	17 37	28 12	2 44	5 31	4 ♓ 55'10"
30 TH	16:32: 0	0 ♓ 10	10 20	14 1	25 6	4 14	17 39	28 13	2 44	5 32	4 ♓ 55'10"
31 FR	16:35:56	4 50	11 56	14 58	25 44	4 19	17 41	28 14	2 45	5 32	4 ♓ 55'10"

INGRESSES :

3 ☿ → ♐ 9: 6
4 ♀ → ♈ 19:49
13 ☿ → ♑ 18:56
15 ⊕ → ♏ 10:11
22 ☿ → ♒ 17: 2
23 ♀ → ♉ 13:38
29 ☿ → ♓ 23: 9

ASPECTS (HELIOCENTRIC +MOON(TYCHONIC)) :

2 ☽ ☐ ⛢ 6:58	☽ ☌ ⛢ 11:41	☽ ☐ ♃ 17:35	☽ ☍ ⛢ 19:32	☽ ☌ ♇ 21:45
☽ ☐ ♃ 13:32	☽ ☌ ♃ 18:59	16 ☽ ☍ ♂ 21:31	☽ ☍ ♀ 20:58	28 ☿ ☌ ♂ 16:39
☽ ☌ ♂ 23:58	9 ☽ ☐ ♂ 11:27	☽ ☍ ♄ 22:23	23 ☽ ☐ ☿ 1:37	29 ☽ ☐ ⛢ 13: 2
3 ☽ ☌ ♄ 14:43	☽ ☐ ♄ 19:51	17 ♂ ☌ ♄ 14:42	☽ ☍ ♃ 5:57	☽ ☐ ♃ 23:21
4 ☿ ☐ ♆ 7:32	10 ☽ ☐ ♆ 23: 7	18 ☽ ☍ ♆ 5:47	☿ ☐ ♃ 16:23	30 ☽ ☐ ♀ 11: 1
☽ ☌ ♆ 16:49	12 ☽ ☍ ☿ 19:40	⊕ ☍ ♃ 18:44	24 ☽ ☐ ♄ 7:46	☿ ☌ ♆ 13:20
☽ ☐ ☿ 19: 0	13 ⊕ ☍ ⛢ 9:11	20 ☿ [S] ☊ 22:27	☽ ☐ ♂ 15:34	☽ ☌ ♄ 22:16
6 ☽ ☌ ♀ 18:44	☽ ☍ ♇ 11:35	☽ ☐ ♇ 23:39	25 ☿ ☐ ⊕ 3:17	31 ☽ ☌ ♂ 12:28
☽ ☐ ♇ 22:29	14 ☽ ☐ ♀ 6:11	22 ☿ ☐ ♀ 1:13	☽ ☐ ♆ 11:35	☽ ☌ ♆ 23:47
8 ♀ ☐ ♇ 5:19	15 ☽ ☐ ⛢ 7:46	☿ ☐ ⛢ 4:54	♀ ☌ ♃ 23:34	
♂ ☌ P 10:35	☿ ☌ ♇ 12:56	♀ ☌ ⛢ 9:41	27 ☿ ☌ ♄ 3:23	

SIDEREAL GEOCENTRIC LONGITUDES : JUNE 2024 Gregorian at 0 hours UT

DAY	☉	☽	☊	☿	♀	♂	♃	♄	⛢	♆	♇
1 SA	15 ♉ 55	2 ♓ 52	18 ♓ 58	0 ♉ 28	14 ♉ 56	28 ♓ 48	6 ♉ 20	23 ♒ 40	29 ♈ 6	4 ♓ 36	6 ♑ 50R
2 SU	16 53	17 7	18 58R	2 22	16 10	29 33	6 34	23 43	29 9	4 36	6 49
3 MO	17 50	1 ♈ 24	18 58	4 18	17 23	0 ♈ 18	6 48	23 45	29 12	4 37	6 48
4 TU	18 48	15 41	18 55	6 16	18 37	1 3	7 2	23 48	29 16	4 38	6 47
5 WE	19 45	29 52	18 50	8 17	19 51	1 48	7 16	23 50	29 19	4 39	6 46
6 TH	20 43	13 ♉ 55	18 42	10 19	21 5	2 33	7 30	23 53	29 22	4 40	6 45
7 FR	21 40	27 44	18 33	12 23	22 18	3 17	7 44	23 55	29 25	4 41	6 45
8 SA	22 38	11 ♊ 16	18 22	14 29	23 32	4 2	7 58	23 57	29 29	4 42	6 44
9 SU	23 35	24 28	18 12	16 37	24 46	4 47	8 12	23 59	29 32	4 43	6 43
10 MO	24 32	7 ♋ 19	18 3	18 46	26 0	5 31	8 26	24 1	29 35	4 43	6 42
11 TU	25 30	19 51	17 56	20 56	27 13	6 16	8 39	24 3	29 39	4 44	6 41
12 WE	26 27	2 ♌ 5	17 51	23 7	28 27	7 0	8 53	24 5	29 42	4 45	6 40
13 TH	27 24	14 6	17 48	25 18	29 41	7 45	9 7	24 7	29 45	4 45	6 39
14 FR	28 22	25 58	17 47	27 30	0 ♊ 55	8 29	9 21	24 8	29 48	4 46	6 38
15 SA	29 19	7 ♍ 47	17 47D	29 42	2 8	9 13	9 34	24 10	29 51	4 47	6 37
16 SU	0 ♊ 16	19 37	17 47R	1 ♊ 54	3 22	9 57	9 48	24 11	29 54	4 47	6 36
17 MO	1 14	1 ♎ 35	17 46	4 6	4 36	10 42	10 2	24 13	29 57	4 48	6 35
18 TU	2 11	13 45	17 43	6 16	5 49	11 26	10 15	24 14	0 ♉ 1	4 48	6 33
19 WE	3 8	26 11	17 38	8 26	7 3	12 10	10 29	24 15	0 4	4 48	6 32
20 TH	4 5	8 ♏ 56	17 31	10 34	8 17	12 54	10 42	24 16	0 7	4 49	6 31
21 FR	5 3	22 1	17 21	12 42	9 31	13 37	10 56	24 17	0 10	4 49	6 30
22 SA	6 0	5 ♐ 25	17 10	14 47	10 44	14 21	11 9	24 18	0 13	4 50	6 29
23 SU	6 57	19 7	16 58	16 51	11 58	15 5	11 23	24 18	0 16	4 50	6 28
24 MO	7 54	3 ♑ 2	16 47	18 53	13 12	15 49	11 36	24 19	0 18	4 50	6 26
25 TU	8 52	17 7	16 38	20 54	14 25	16 32	11 49	24 20	0 21	4 51	6 25
26 WE	9 49	1 ♒ 18	16 31	22 52	15 39	17 16	12 2	24 20	0 24	4 51	6 24
27 TH	10 46	15 31	16 27	24 49	16 53	17 59	12 16	24 20	0 27	4 51	6 23
28 FR	11 43	29 42	16 26	26 43	18 6	18 43	12 29	24 21	0 30	4 51	6 22
29 SA	12 40	13 ♓ 50	16 26	28 35	19 20	19 26	12 42	24 21	0 33	4 51	6 20
30 SU	13 38	27 55	16 26	0 ♋ 25	20 34	20 10	12 55	24 21R	0 36	4 51	6 19

INGRESSES :

Day	Ingress	Time
2	♂ → ♈	14:23
	☽ → ♈	21:38
5	☽ → ♉	0:12
7	☽ → ♊	3:58
9	☽ → ♋	10:14
11	☽ → ♌	19:52
13	♀ → ♊	6:14
14	☽ → ♍	8:11
15	☿ → ♊	3:12
	☉ → ♊	17: 8
16	☽ → ♎	20:49
17	⛢ → ♉	20: 1
19	☽ → ♏	7:14
21	☽ → ♐	14:22
23	☽ → ♑	18:47
25	☽ → ♒	21:47
28	☽ → ♓	0:30
29	☿ → ♋	18:26
30	☽ → ♈	3:33

ASPECTS & ECLIPSES :

Day	Aspect	Time
1	☽ ☌ ♆	2:54
2	☽ ☌ ☊	3: 6
	☽ ☌ P	7:18
	☽ ☌ ♂	22: 2
4	☿ ☌ ♃	10:22
	☉ s☌ ♀	15:32
	☽ ☌ ⛢	23: 2
5	☽ ☌ ♃	12:48
	☽ ☌ ☿	16:45
6	☉ ☌ ☽	12:36
	☽ ☌ ♀	13:34
8	♀ □ ♄	8:24
	☽ N□ ☊	12:39
9	☉ □ ♄	10:34
	☽ ☍ ♇	22:48
11	♂ □ ♇	13:13
12	☿ □ ♄	10:46
13	☽ ☍ ♄	20:16
14	☉ □ ☽	5:17
	☽ ☌ A	13:29
	☉ s☌ ☿	16:31
	☽ ☍ ♆	17:53
15	☽ ☌ ☋	20:16
16	☉ □ Π	4:30
17	♀ □ ♆	3:53
	☿ □ ♆	7:44
	☿ ☌ ♀	12:41
	☽ ☍ ♂	19: 9
19	☽ ☍ ⛢	7:23
20	☽ ☍ ♃	3:20
	☉ □ ♆	18:21
22	☉ ☍ ☽	1: 6
	☽ ☍ ♀	10:18
	☽ ☍ ☿	19:23
	☽ □S ☊	20:19
23	☿ □ ☊	1:10
24	☽ ☌ ♇	5:48
26	♀ □ ☊	16: 1
27	☽ ☌ P	11:49
	☽ ☌ ♄	14:55
28	☽ ☌ ♆	8:44
	☉ □ ☽	21:52
29	☽ ☌ ☊	4:24

SIDEREAL HELIOCENTRIC LONGITUDES : JUNE 2024 Gregorian at 0 hours UT

DAY	Sid. Time	☿	♀	⊕	♂	♃	♄	⛢	♆	♇	Vernal Point
1 SA	16:39:53	9 ♓ 40	13 ♉ 33	15 ♏ 56	26 ♒ 21	4 ♉ 25	17 ♒ 43	28 ♈ 14	2 ♓ 45	5 ♑ 32	4♓55' 9"
2 SU	16:43:50	14 38	15 10	16 53	26 59	4 30	17 45	28 15	2 46	5 32	4♓55' 9"
3 MO	16:47:46	19 45	16 46	17 51	27 37	4 35	17 47	28 16	2 46	5 33	4♓55' 9"
4 TU	16:51:43	25 2	18 23	18 48	28 15	4 41	17 49	28 16	2 46	5 33	4♓55' 9"
5 WE	16:55:39	0 ♈ 27	19 59	19 46	28 53	4 46	17 51	28 17	2 47	5 33	4♓55' 9"
6 TH	16:59:36	6 2	21 36	20 43	29 31	4 52	17 53	28 18	2 47	5 34	4♓55' 9"
7 FR	17: 3:32	11 45	23 13	21 41	0 ♓ 8	4 57	17 55	28 18	2 47	5 34	4♓55' 9"
8 SA	17: 7:29	17 36	24 50	22 38	0 46	5 2	17 57	28 19	2 48	5 34	4♓55' 8"
9 SU	17:11:25	23 34	26 26	23 35	1 24	5 8	17 59	28 20	2 48	5 34	4♓55' 8"
10 MO	17:15:22	29 39	28 3	24 33	2 1	5 13	18 0	28 20	2 48	5 35	4♓55' 8"
11 TU	17:19:19	5 ♉ 49	29 40	25 30	2 39	5 18	18 2	28 21	2 49	5 35	4♓55' 8"
12 WE	17:23:15	12 4	1 ♊ 17	26 27	3 17	5 24	18 4	28 22	2 49	5 35	4♓55' 8"
13 TH	17:27:12	18 21	2 54	27 25	3 54	5 29	18 6	28 23	2 50	5 35	4♓55' 8"
14 FR	17:31: 8	24 40	4 31	28 22	4 32	5 34	18 8	28 23	2 50	5 36	4♓55' 8"
15 SA	17:35: 5	1 ♊ 0	6 8	29 19	5 9	5 40	18 10	28 24	2 50	5 36	4♓55' 7"
16 SU	17:39: 1	7 17	7 45	0 ♐ 17	5 47	5 45	18 12	28 25	2 51	5 36	4♓55' 7"
17 MO	17:42:58	13 32	9 22	1 14	6 24	5 50	18 14	28 25	2 51	5 37	4♓55' 7"
18 TU	17:46:54	19 42	10 59	2 11	7 2	5 56	18 16	28 26	2 51	5 37	4♓55' 7"
19 WE	17:50:51	25 47	12 36	3 9	7 39	6 1	18 18	28 27	2 52	5 37	4♓55' 7"
20 TH	17:54:48	1 ♋ 45	14 13	4 6	8 17	6 6	18 20	28 27	2 52	5 37	4♓55' 7"
21 FR	17:58:44	7 35	15 50	5 3	8 54	6 12	18 22	28 28	2 52	5 38	4♓55' 7"
22 SA	18: 2:41	13 17	17 27	6 0	9 31	6 17	18 24	28 29	2 53	5 38	4♓55' 7"
23 SU	18: 6:37	18 49	19 4	6 58	10 9	6 22	18 26	28 29	2 53	5 38	4♓55' 6"
24 MO	18:10:34	24 13	20 41	7 55	10 46	6 28	18 28	28 30	2 54	5 39	4♓55' 6"
25 TU	18:14:30	29 26	22 19	8 52	11 23	6 33	18 30	28 31	2 54	5 39	4♓55' 6"
26 WE	18:18:27	4 ♌ 30	23 56	9 49	12 0	6 38	18 32	28 31	2 54	5 39	4♓55' 6"
27 TH	18:22:23	9 24	25 33	10 46	12 38	6 44	18 34	28 32	2 55	5 39	4♓55' 6"
28 FR	18:26:20	14 9	27 10	11 44	13 15	6 49	18 35	28 33	2 55	5 40	4♓55' 6"
29 SA	18:30:17	18 45	28 48	12 41	13 52	6 54	18 37	28 33	2 55	5 40	4♓55' 6"
30 SU	18:34:13	23 12	0 ♋ 25	13 38	14 29	7 0	18 39	28 34	2 56	5 40	4♓55' 5"

INGRESSES :

Day	Ingress	Time
4	☿ → ♈	22: 1
6	♂ → ♓	18:44
10	☿ → ♉	1:23
11	♀ → ♊	4:57
14	☿ → ♊	20:13
15	⊕ → ♐	16:58
19	☿ → ♋	16:54
25	☿ → ♌	2:38
29	♀ → ♋	17:48

ASPECTS (HELIOCENTRIC +MOON(TYCHONIC)) :

Day	Aspect	Time
1	☽ ☌ ☿	17:31
2	⊕ □ ♄	22:20
3	☽ □ ♇	6:57
	♀ □ ♄	15:22
4	♀ ☍ ⊕	15:32
	☽ ☌ ⛢	21:18
5	☽ ☌ ♃	8:22
	☿ □ ♇	22: 0
6	♀ ☌ ☊	3:13
	☽ □ ♄	6:50
	☽ ☌ ♀	15: 2
7	☽ □ ♂	4:25
	☽ □ ♆	8:53
8	☿ ☌ ☊	23:54
9	☿ ☌ ⛢	18:52
	☽ ☍ ♇	20:42
10	☿ ☌ ♃	21:58
11	♂ ☌ ♆	6:17
	☽ □ ⛢	16:38
12	☽ □ ♃	6:37
	♀ □ ♆	22:57
	☿ □ ♄	23: 2
13	☽ ☍ ♄	8: 5
	☿ ☌ P	16:42
	☽ □ ☿	18:21
14	♀ □ ♂	0:28
	☽ ☍ ♆	13:57
	☿ ☍ ⊕	16:31
	☽ ☍ ♂	18:22
	☽ □ ♀	20: 6
15	☿ □ ♆	7: 1
	☿ □ ♂	17:36
16	☿ ☌ ♀	2:20
17	☽ □ ♇	7:59
18	⊕ □ ♆	16:53
19	☽ ☍ ⛢	4:17
	☽ ☍ ♃	18:41
20	☿ ☍ ♇	15:53
	☽ □ ♄	17:21
21	☽ □ ♆	19:30
22	☽ □ ♂	7:35
	☽ ☍ ♀	23:55
23	☿ N□ ☊	20:58
24	☽ ☌ ♇	4:27
	☿ □ ⛢	19:41
25	☽ □ ⛢	19:17
26	☽ ☍ ☿	8:17
	☽ □ ♃	9: 4
	☿ □ ♃	10:33
27	☽ ☌ ♄	5: 9
28	☽ ☌ ♆	5:27
	☿ ☍ ♄	23:20
29	☽ ☌ ♂	0: 2
30	☽ □ ♀	4:50
	☽ □ ♇	13:16

SIDEREAL GEOCENTRIC LONGITUDES : JULY 2024 Gregorian at 0 hours UT

DAY	☉	☽	☊	☿	♀	♂	♃	♄	♅	♆	♇
1 MO	14 ♊ 35	11 ♈ 55	16 ♓ 24R	2 ♋ 13	21 ♊ 48	20 ♈ 53	13 ♉ 8	24 ♒ 21R	0 ♉ 38	4 ♓ 51	6 ♑ 18R
2 TU	15 32	25 49	16 21	3 59	23 1	21 36	13 21	24 21	0 41	4 51	6 16
3 WE	16 29	9 ♉ 36	16 14	5 43	24 15	22 19	13 34	24 20	0 44	4 51R	6 15
4 TH	17 26	23 14	16 5	7 25	25 29	23 2	13 47	24 20	0 46	4 51	6 14
5 FR	18 24	6 ♊ 41	15 54	9 4	26 43	23 45	14 0	24 19	0 49	4 51	6 12
6 SA	19 21	19 53	15 41	10 42	27 56	24 28	14 12	24 19	0 52	4 51	6 11
7 SU	20 18	2 ♋ 50	15 29	12 17	29 10	25 11	14 25	24 18	0 54	4 51	6 10
8 MO	21 15	15 30	15 18	13 50	0 ♋ 24	25 53	14 38	24 17	0 57	4 51	6 8
9 TU	22 13	27 55	15 9	15 21	1 38	26 36	14 50	24 17	0 59	4 51	6 7
10 WE	23 10	10 ♌ 4	15 2	16 50	2 51	27 18	15 3	24 16	1 1	4 50	6 6
11 TH	24 7	22 3	14 58	18 17	4 5	28 1	15 15	24 15	1 4	4 50	6 4
12 FR	25 4	3 ♍ 53	14 56	19 41	5 19	28 43	15 28	24 13	1 6	4 50	6 3
13 SA	26 2	15 41	14 55	21 3	6 32	29 26	15 40	24 12	1 9	4 50	6 2
14 SU	26 59	27 32	14 55	22 23	7 46	0 ♉ 8	15 52	24 11	1 11	4 49	6 0
15 MO	27 56	9 ♎ 30	14 55	23 41	9 0	0 50	16 4	24 9	1 13	4 49	5 59
16 TU	28 53	21 41	14 53	24 56	10 14	1 32	16 16	24 8	1 15	4 48	5 57
17 WE	29 50	4 ♏ 11	14 48	26 8	11 27	2 14	16 28	24 6	1 18	4 48	5 56
18 TH	0 ♋ 48	17 2	14 42	27 18	12 41	2 56	16 40	24 4	1 20	4 47	5 54
19 FR	1 45	0 ♐ 17	14 33	28 26	13 55	3 37	16 52	24 3	1 22	4 47	5 53
20 SA	2 42	13 57	14 23	29 31	15 9	4 19	17 4	24 1	1 24	4 46	5 52
21 SU	3 39	27 58	14 12	0 ♌ 33	16 22	5 1	17 16	23 59	1 26	4 46	5 50
22 MO	4 37	12 ♑ 17	14 2	1 32	17 36	5 42	17 27	23 57	1 28	4 45	5 49
23 TU	5 34	26 48	13 53	2 28	18 50	6 24	17 39	23 54	1 30	4 45	5 47
24 WE	6 31	11 ♒ 23	13 47	3 21	20 3	7 5	17 50	23 52	1 32	4 44	5 46
25 TH	7 28	25 57	13 44	4 11	21 17	7 46	18 2	23 50	1 34	4 43	5 45
26 FR	8 26	10 ♓ 25	13 43	4 58	22 31	8 27	18 13	23 47	1 35	4 43	5 43
27 SA	9 23	24 42	13 43D	5 41	23 44	9 9	18 24	23 45	1 37	4 42	5 42
28 SU	10 20	8 ♈ 48	13 43	6 20	24 58	9 49	18 35	23 42	1 39	4 41	5 40
29 MO	11 18	22 41	13 43R	6 55	26 12	10 30	18 46	23 39	1 41	4 40	5 39
30 TU	12 15	6 ♉ 22	13 41	7 27	27 26	11 11	18 57	23 37	1 42	4 39	5 37
31 WE	13 12	19 50	13 36	7 54	28 39	11 52	19 8	23 34	1 44	4 38	5 36

INGRESSES :

2	☽ → ♉	7:15	20	☿ → ♌	11:13
4	☽ → ♊	12: 1	21	☽ → ♑	3:25
6	☽ → ♋	18:42	23	☽ → ♒	5:16
7	♀ → ♋	16:15	25	☽ → ♓	6:41
9	☽ → ♌	4: 5	27	☽ → ♈	8:58
11	☽ → ♍	16: 5	29	☽ → ♉	12:47
13	♂ → ♉	19:34	31	☽ → ♊	18:20
14	☽ → ♎	4:59			
16	☽ → ♏	16: 2			
17	☉ → ♋	4: 1			
18	☽ → ♐	23:28			

ASPECTS & ECLIPSES :

1	☽ ☌ ♂	16:17	12	☽ ☍ ♆	1:54		☽ ☌ ♇	13:13	30	☽ ☌ ♂	8:59
2	☽ ☌ ♅	8:28		☽ ☌ A	8: 9		☿ □ ♅	22:18		☽ ☌ ♃	22:43
	☉ □ ☊	18:28		♀ ☍ ♇	14: 6	22	☽ ☍ ♀	9:37			
3	☽ ☌ ♃	7: 3		☽ ☌ ☋	22:26	23	☉ ☍ ♇	5:31			
	☿ ☍ ♇	7:22	13	☉ □ ☽	22:47		☽ ☍ ☿	9:56			
5	☽ ⌂N ☊	16:27	15	♂ ☌ ♅	14: 2	24	☽ ☌ P	5:26			
	☉ ☌ ☽	22:56	16	☽ ☍ ♅	18:29		☽ ☌ ♄	20:30			
6	☽ ☌ ♀	16:25		☽ ☍ ♂	20: 4	25	☽ ☌ ♆	14:30			
7	☽ ☍ ♇	6:14	17	☽ ☍ ♃	23:19	26	☽ ☌ ☊	5:30			
	☽ ☌ ☿	20:22	20	☽ ⌂S ☊	0:44	28	☉ □ ☽	2:50			
11	☽ ☍ ♄	4:25	21	☉ ☍ ☽	10:16	29	☽ ☌ ♅	15:46			

SIDEREAL HELIOCENTRIC LONGITUDES : JULY 2024 Gregorian at 0 hours UT

DAY	Sid. Time	☿	♀	⊕	♂	♃	♄	♅	♆	♇	Vernal Point
1 MO	18:38:10	27 ♌ 30	2 ♋ 2	14 ♐ 35	15 ♓ 6	7 ♉ 5	18 ♒ 41	28 ♈ 35	2 ♓ 56	5 ♑ 41	4 ♓ 55' 5"
2 TU	18:42: 6	1 ♍ 40	3 40	15 32	15 43	7 10	18 43	28 35	2 56	5 41	4 ♓ 55' 5"
3 WE	18:46: 3	5 43	5 17	16 30	16 20	7 16	18 45	28 36	2 57	5 41	4 ♓ 55' 5"
4 TH	18:49:59	9 38	6 55	17 27	16 57	7 21	18 47	28 37	2 57	5 41	4 ♓ 55' 5"
5 FR	18:53:56	13 27	8 32	18 24	17 34	7 26	18 49	28 37	2 58	5 42	4 ♓ 55' 5"
6 SA	18:57:52	17 9	10 10	19 21	18 10	7 32	18 51	28 38	2 58	5 42	4 ♓ 55' 5"
7 SU	19: 1:49	20 46	11 47	20 19	18 47	7 37	18 53	28 39	2 58	5 42	4 ♓ 55' 4"
8 MO	19: 5:46	24 16	13 24	21 16	19 24	7 42	18 55	28 39	2 59	5 42	4 ♓ 55' 4"
9 TU	19: 9:42	27 42	15 2	22 13	20 1	7 48	18 57	28 40	2 59	5 43	4 ♓ 55' 4"
10 WE	19:13:39	1 ♎ 3	16 39	23 10	20 37	7 53	18 59	28 41	2 59	5 43	4 ♓ 55' 4"
11 TH	19:17:35	4 19	18 17	24 7	21 14	7 58	19 1	28 41	3 0	5 43	4 ♓ 55' 4"
12 FR	19:21:32	7 32	19 54	25 5	21 50	8 4	19 3	28 42	3 0	5 44	4 ♓ 55' 4"
13 SA	19:25:28	10 41	21 32	26 2	22 27	8 9	19 5	28 43	3 0	5 44	4 ♓ 55' 4"
14 SU	19:29:25	13 46	23 9	26 59	23 3	8 14	19 7	28 43	3 1	5 44	4 ♓ 55' 4"
15 MO	19:33:21	16 48	24 47	27 56	23 40	8 20	19 9	28 44	3 1	5 44	4 ♓ 55' 3"
16 TU	19:37:18	19 47	26 24	28 54	24 16	8 25	19 11	28 45	3 2	5 45	4 ♓ 55' 3"
17 WE	19:41:15	22 44	28 2	29 51	24 53	8 30	19 13	28 46	3 2	5 45	4 ♓ 55' 3"
18 TH	19:45:11	25 39	29 40	0 ♑ 48	25 29	8 36	19 14	28 46	3 2	5 45	4 ♓ 55' 3"
19 FR	19:49: 8	28 32	1 ♌ 17	1 45	26 5	8 41	19 16	28 47	3 3	5 46	4 ♓ 55' 3"
20 SA	19:53: 4	1 ♏ 22	2 55	2 42	26 41	8 46	19 18	28 48	3 3	5 46	4 ♓ 55' 3"
21 SU	19:57: 1	4 12	4 32	3 40	27 17	8 52	19 20	28 48	3 3	5 46	4 ♓ 55' 3"
22 MO	20: 0:57	7 0	6 10	4 37	27 54	8 57	19 22	28 49	3 4	5 46	4 ♓ 55' 2"
23 TU	20: 4:54	9 46	7 47	5 34	28 30	9 2	19 24	28 50	3 4	5 47	4 ♓ 55' 2"
24 WE	20: 8:50	12 33	9 25	6 32	29 6	9 8	19 26	28 50	3 4	5 47	4 ♓ 55' 2"
25 TH	20:12:47	15 18	11 2	7 29	29 42	9 13	19 28	28 51	3 5	5 47	4 ♓ 55' 2"
26 FR	20:16:44	18 3	12 40	8 26	0 ♈ 17	9 18	19 30	28 52	3 5	5 48	4 ♓ 55' 2"
27 SA	20:20:40	20 48	14 17	9 23	0 53	9 23	19 32	28 52	3 6	5 48	4 ♓ 55' 2"
28 SU	20:24:37	23 32	15 54	10 21	1 29	9 29	19 34	28 53	3 6	5 48	4 ♓ 55' 2"
29 MO	20:28:33	26 17	17 32	11 18	2 5	9 34	19 36	28 54	3 6	5 48	4 ♓ 55' 1"
30 TU	20:32:30	29 2	19 9	12 15	2 41	9 39	19 38	28 54	3 7	5 49	4 ♓ 55' 1"
31 WE	20:36:26	1 ♐ 48	20 47	13 13	3 16	9 45	19 40	28 55	3 7	5 49	4 ♓ 55' 1"

INGRESSES :

1	☿ → ♍	14:17
9	☿ → ♎	16:25
17	⊕ → ♑	3:51
18	♀ → ♌	5: 2
19	☿ → ♏	12:24
25	♂ → ♈	12:19
30	☿ → ♐	8:22

ASPECTS (HELIOCENTRIC +MOON(TYCHONIC)) :

2	☽ ☌ ♅	4:48		☿ □ ⊕	19:51	15	☽ ☌ ☿	19: 6		☽ ☌ ♇	13: 7	27	☽ ☌ ♂	10:57
	☿ ☍ ♆	7:27	7	☽ ☍ ♇	5:23	16	☽ □ ♀	10:30	22	☿ ☍ ♃	17:24		☿ ☌ A	17:10
	⊕ □ ♂	12:23		☽ ☌ ♀	19:23		☽ ☍ ♅	13:39	23	☽ □ ♅	3:20		☽ □ ♇	18:51
	☽ ☌ ♃	19:52	9	☽ □ ♅	1:28	17	☿ ☌ ☋	6:34		⊕ ☌ ♇	5:14	29	☽ ☌ ♅	10:51
3	♀ ☍ ♇	5:53		☽ □ ♃	19:36		☽ ☍ ♃	8:12		♀ □ ♃	19:33	30	☽ ☌ ♃	5:52
	☽ □ ♄	16: 6	10	♀ ☌ P	2:29		♀ □ ♅	10:46		☽ □ ♃	20:15		♀ ☍ ♄	7:10
4	☽ □ ♆	17:19		☽ ☍ ♄	17:52	18	☽ □ ♄	4: 3		☽ ☍ ♀	20:20		☽ □ ♄	23:41
	⊕ ☌ A	20:51	11	☿ □ ♇	10:25	19	☿ ☍ ♅	2: 9	24	☽ □ ☿	2:20	31	☽ □ ♀	1:55
5	☽ □ ☿	17: 3		☽ ☍ ♆	22:11		☽ □ ♆	4:53		☽ ☌ ♄	13:16		☿ □ ♆	11:24
	☽ □ ♂	20:42	13	☽ ☍ ♂	14:28	20	☽ □ ♂	22:47	25	☽ ☌ ♆	11:48		♀ ⌂N ☊	15:22
6	☿ ☍ ♂	8: 5	14	☽ □ ♇	16:30	21	☿ □ ♀	6:55	26	☿ □ ♄	12:51			

SIDEREAL GEOCENTRIC LONGITUDES : AUGUST 2024 Gregorian at 0 hours UT

DAY	☉	☽	☊	☿	♀	♂	♃	♄	♅	♆	♇
1 TH	14 ♋ 10	3 ♊ 7	13 ♓ 29R	8 ♌ 17	29 ♋ 53	12 ♉ 32	19 ♉ 19	23 ♒ 31R	1 ♉ 46	4 ♓ 38R	5 ♑ 35R
2 FR	15 7	16 10	13 20	8 35	1 ♌ 7	13 13	19 30	23 28	1 47	4 37	5 33
3 SA	16 5	29 1	13 10	8 49	2 20	13 53	19 40	23 25	1 48	4 36	5 32
4 SU	17 2	11 ♋ 40	13 0	8 58	3 34	14 34	19 51	23 22	1 50	4 35	5 30
5 MO	18 0	24 5	12 51	9 1	4 48	15 14	20 1	23 18	1 51	4 34	5 29
6 TU	18 57	6 ♌ 18	12 44	9 0R	6 1	15 54	20 11	23 15	1 53	4 33	5 28
7 WE	19 55	18 20	12 39	8 53	7 15	16 34	20 22	23 12	1 54	4 32	5 26
8 TH	20 52	0 ♍ 14	12 36	8 41	8 29	17 14	20 32	23 8	1 55	4 31	5 25
9 FR	21 50	12 2	12 35	8 23	9 42	17 53	20 42	23 5	1 56	4 30	5 24
10 SA	22 47	23 49	12 35D	8 0	10 56	18 33	20 51	23 1	1 57	4 28	5 22
11 SU	23 45	5 ♎ 38	12 36	7 32	12 10	19 13	21 1	22 57	1 59	4 27	5 21
12 MO	24 42	17 35	12 37	6 59	13 23	19 52	21 11	22 54	2 0	4 26	5 20
13 TU	25 40	29 46	12 38R	6 22	14 37	20 31	21 20	22 50	2 1	4 25	5 18
14 WE	26 38	12 ♏ 14	12 36	5 41	15 51	21 10	21 30	22 46	2 2	4 24	5 17
15 TH	27 35	25 5	12 33	4 55	17 4	21 50	21 39	22 42	2 3	4 22	5 16
16 FR	28 33	8 ♐ 22	12 28	4 8	18 18	22 29	21 48	22 38	2 3	4 21	5 14
17 SA	29 31	22 6	12 22	3 17	19 32	23 7	21 57	22 34	2 4	4 20	5 13
18 SU	0 ♌ 28	6 ♑ 17	12 16	2 26	20 45	23 46	22 6	22 30	2 5	4 19	5 12
19 MO	1 26	20 49	12 10	1 35	21 59	24 25	22 15	22 26	2 6	4 17	5 11
20 TU	2 24	5 ♒ 38	12 5	0 44	23 12	25 3	22 23	22 22	2 6	4 16	5 9
21 WE	3 21	20 35	12 1	29 ♋ 55	24 26	25 42	22 32	22 18	2 7	4 15	5 8
22 TH	4 19	5 ♓ 32	12 0	29 9	25 39	26 20	22 40	22 14	2 7	4 13	5 7
23 FR	5 17	20 21	12 0D	28 27	26 53	26 58	22 48	22 9	2 8	4 12	5 6
24 SA	6 15	4 ♈ 55	12 1	27 49	28 6	27 36	22 56	22 5	2 8	4 10	5 5
25 SU	7 13	19 13	12 2	27 18	29 20	28 14	23 4	22 1	2 9	4 9	5 3
26 MO	8 10	3 ♉ 10	12 3	26 52	0 ♍ 34	28 51	23 12	21 56	2 9	4 8	5 2
27 TU	9 8	16 48	12 3R	26 34	1 47	29 29	23 20	21 52	2 10	4 6	5 1
28 WE	10 6	0 ♊ 7	12 1	26 23	3 1	0 ♊ 7	23 28	21 48	2 10	4 5	5 0
29 TH	11 4	13 9	11 58	26 20D	4 14	0 44	23 35	21 43	2 10	4 3	4 59
30 FR	12 2	25 56	11 54	26 25	5 28	1 21	23 42	21 39	2 10	4 2	4 58
31 SA	13 0	8 ♋ 29	11 49	26 38	6 41	1 58	23 49	21 34	2 10	4 0	4 57

INGRESSES :

1 ♀ → ♌ 2:17
3 ☽ → ♋ 1:50
5 ☽ → ♌ 11:34
7 ☽ → ♍ 23:31
10 ☽ → ♎ 12:34
13 ☽ → ♏ 0:27
15 ☽ → ♐ 8:58
17 ☉ → ♌ 12:16
☽ → ♑ 13:27
19 ☽ → ♒ 14:54
20 ☿ → ♋ 21:33
21 ☽ → ♓ 15: 6
23 ☽ → ♈ 15:50
25 ♀ → ♍ 13: 3
☽ → ♉ 18:30
27 ♂ → ♊ 19:46
☽ → ♊ 23:46
30 ☽ → ♋ 7:43

ASPECTS & ECLIPSES :

1 ☽ N ☊ 18:48
2 ♀ □ ♅ 13:24
3 ☽ ☍ ♇ 12:16
4 ☉ ☌ ☽ 11:11
5 ☽ ☌ ♀ 23:23
6 ☽ ☌ ☿ 5:18
7 ☽ ☍ ♄ 9:43
8 ☿ ☌ ♀ 3:11
☽ ☍ ♆ 8:39
9 ☽ ☌ ☋ 1: 6
☽ ☌ A 1:27
12 ☉ □ ☽ 15:17
13 ☽ ☍ ♅ 4:22
14 ♂ ☌ ♃ 15:20
☽ ☍ ♃ 17:34
☽ ☍ ♂ 17:39
16 ♂ □ ♄ 5:29
☽ S ☊ 7:12
17 ☽ ☌ ♇ 22:11
18 ☿ □ ♅ 9:46
19 ☉ i☌ ☿ 1:57
♀ □ ♃ 5:51
♀ ☍ ♄ 8:28
☽ ☍ ☿ 16:30
☉ □ ♅ 16:43
☉ ☍ ☽ 18:24
♃ □ ♄ 21:46
21 ☽ ☌ ♄ 2:43
☽ ☌ P 4:48
☽ ☍ ♀ 6:42
☽ ☌ ♆ 21:53
22 ☽ ☌ ☊ 10:25
23 ♀ □ ♂ 3:19
25 ☽ ☌ ♅ 22:14
26 ☉ □ ☽ 9:24
27 ☽ ☌ ♃ 11:49
☽ ☌ ♂ 23:58
28 ♀ ☍ ♆ 20:31
☽ N ☊ 21:48
30 ☽ ☍ ♇ 17:12

SIDEREAL HELIOCENTRIC LONGITUDES : AUGUST 2024 Gregorian at 0 hours UT

DAY	Sid. Time	☿	♀	⊕	♂	♃	♄	♅	♆	♇	Vernal Point
1 TH	20:40:23	4 ♐ 35	22 ♌ 24	14 ♑ 10	3 ♈ 52	9 ♉ 50	19 ♒ 42	28 ♈ 56	3 ♓ 7	5 ♑ 49	4 ♓ 55' 1"
2 FR	20:44:19	7 22	24 1	15 8	4 27	9 55	19 44	28 56	3 8	5 50	4 ♓ 55' 1"
3 SA	20:48:16	10 11	25 39	16 5	5 3	10 1	19 46	28 57	3 8	5 50	4 ♓ 55' 1"
4 SU	20:52:13	13 1	27 16	17 3	5 38	10 6	19 48	28 58	3 8	5 50	4 ♓ 55' 1"
5 MO	20:56: 9	15 53	28 53	18 0	6 14	10 11	19 50	28 58	3 9	5 50	4 ♓ 55' 0"
6 TU	21: 0: 6	18 47	0 ♍ 31	18 58	6 49	10 17	19 52	28 59	3 9	5 51	4 ♓ 55' 0"
7 WE	21: 4: 2	21 43	2 8	19 55	7 24	10 22	19 53	29 0	3 10	5 51	4 ♓ 55' 0"
8 TH	21: 7:59	24 41	3 45	20 53	8 0	10 27	19 55	29 0	3 10	5 51	4 ♓ 55' 0"
9 FR	21:11:55	27 41	5 22	21 50	8 35	10 33	19 57	29 1	3 10	5 51	4 ♓ 55' 0"
10 SA	21:15:52	0 ♑ 45	6 59	22 48	9 10	10 38	19 59	29 2	3 11	5 52	4 ♓ 55' 0"
11 SU	21:19:48	3 52	8 36	23 45	9 45	10 43	20 1	29 2	3 11	5 52	4 ♓ 55' 0"
12 MO	21:23:45	7 2	10 14	24 43	10 20	10 49	20 3	29 3	3 11	5 52	4 ♓ 55' 0"
13 TU	21:27:42	10 15	11 51	25 40	10 55	10 54	20 5	29 4	3 12	5 53	4 ♓ 54'59"
14 WE	21:31:38	13 33	13 28	26 38	11 30	10 59	20 7	29 4	3 12	5 53	4 ♓ 54'59"
15 TH	21:35:35	16 55	15 5	27 36	12 5	11 4	20 9	29 5	3 12	5 53	4 ♓ 54'59"
16 FR	21:39:31	20 22	16 41	28 33	12 39	11 10	20 11	29 6	3 13	5 53	4 ♓ 54'59"
17 SA	21:43:28	23 53	18 18	29 31	13 14	11 15	20 13	29 7	3 13	5 54	4 ♓ 54'59"
18 SU	21:47:24	27 30	19 55	0 ♒ 29	13 49	11 20	20 15	29 7	3 14	5 54	4 ♓ 54'59"
19 MO	21:51:21	1 ♒ 13	21 32	1 26	14 24	11 26	20 17	29 8	3 14	5 54	4 ♓ 54'59"
20 TU	21:55:17	5 1	23 9	2 24	14 58	11 31	20 19	29 9	3 14	5 55	4 ♓ 54'58"
21 WE	21:59:14	8 56	24 45	3 22	15 33	11 36	20 21	29 9	3 15	5 55	4 ♓ 54'58"
22 TH	22: 3:11	12 58	26 22	4 19	16 7	11 42	20 23	29 10	3 15	5 55	4 ♓ 54'58"
23 FR	22: 7: 7	17 6	27 59	5 17	16 42	11 47	20 25	29 11	3 15	5 55	4 ♓ 54'58"
24 SA	22:11: 4	21 23	29 35	6 15	17 16	11 52	20 27	29 11	3 16	5 56	4 ♓ 54'58"
25 SU	22:15: 0	25 47	1 ♎ 12	7 13	17 50	11 57	20 29	29 12	3 16	5 56	4 ♓ 54'58"
26 MO	22:18:57	0 ♓ 19	2 48	8 11	18 24	12 3	20 31	29 13	3 16	5 56	4 ♓ 54'58"
27 TU	22:22:53	5 0	4 25	9 9	18 59	12 8	20 33	29 13	3 17	5 57	4 ♓ 54'57"
28 WE	22:26:50	9 50	6 1	10 7	19 33	12 13	20 34	29 14	3 17	5 57	4 ♓ 54'57"
29 TH	22:30:46	14 48	7 38	11 5	20 7	12 19	20 36	29 15	3 18	5 57	4 ♓ 54'57"
30 FR	22:34:43	19 56	9 14	12 3	20 41	12 24	20 38	29 15	3 18	5 57	4 ♓ 54'57"
31 SA	22:38:40	25 12	10 50	13 1	21 15	12 29	20 40	29 16	3 18	5 58	4 ♓ 54'57"

INGRESSES :

5 ♀ → ♍ 16:26
9 ☿ → ♑ 18: 9
17 ⊕ → ♒ 12: 7
18 ☿ → ♒ 16:14
24 ♀ → ♎ 6: 6
25 ☿ → ♓ 22:20
31 ☿ → ♈ 21:12

ASPECTS (HELIOCENTRIC +MOON(TYCHONIC)) :

1 ☽ □ ♆ 0: 1
☽ ☍ ☿ 3:23
3 ☽ □ ♂ 11:56
☽ ☍ ♇ 12:52
4 ♂ □ ♇ 8: 1
5 ☽ □ ♅ 9:34
6 ☽ □ ♃ 7:56
7 ☽ ☍ ♄ 3: 7
♀ ☍ ♆ 15:17
8 ☽ ☍ ♆ 5:56
☽ ☌ ♀ 8:16
10 ☽ □ ☿ 19: 6
11 ☽ □ ♇ 0:27
☽ ☍ ♂ 8:43
☿ ☌ ♇ 15:16
12 ☽ ☍ ♅ 22:37
13 ☿ □ ♂ 5:52
☽ ☍ ♃ 21:36
14 ☽ □ ♄ 14:50
15 ☽ □ ♆ 14:46
16 ⊕ □ ♅ 13:44
☽ □ ♀ 16:34
☿ S ☊ 21:39
17 ☽ ☌ ♇ 23:22
18 ☿ □ ♅ 10:34
☽ □ ♂ 13: 1
19 ☿ ☌ ⊕ 1:57
☽ □ ♅ 13:30
☽ ☌ ☿ 22:39
20 ☽ □ ♃ 9:30
☽ ☌ ♄ 23:36
21 ☿ □ ♃ 16:21
☽ ☌ ♆ 20:19
23 ☽ ☍ ♀ 14: 4
☿ ☌ ♄ 18:46
24 ☽ □ ♇ 1:40
☽ ☌ ♂ 21:34
25 ☽ ☌ ♅ 17: 7
26 ☿ ☌ ♆ 15:15
☽ ☌ ♃ 15:40
27 ☽ □ ♄ 6:42
♀ □ ♇ 22:51
28 ☽ □ ♆ 5:47
29 ☽ □ ☿ 5: 3
30 ⊕ □ ♃ 9:43
☽ ☍ ♇ 19: 8
31 ☽ □ ♀ 5:13

SIDEREAL GEOCENTRIC LONGITUDES : SEPTEMBER 2024 Gregorian at 0 hours UT

DAY	☉	☽	☊	☿	♀	♂	♃	♄	♅	♆	♇
1 SU	13 ♌ 58	20 ♋ 50	11 ♓ 44R	27 ♋ 0	7 ♍ 54	2 ♊ 35	23 ♉ 56	21 ♒ 30R	2 ♉ 10	3 ♓ 59R	4 ♑ 56R
2 MO	14 56	3 ♌ 1	11 40	27 30	9 8	3 12	24 3	21 25	2 10R	3 57	4 55
3 TU	15 55	15 2	11 37	28 8	10 21	3 49	24 10	21 20	2 10	3 56	4 54
4 WE	16 53	26 57	11 35	28 54	11 35	4 25	24 16	21 16	2 10	3 54	4 53
5 TH	17 51	8 ♍ 46	11 34	29 48	12 48	5 1	24 23	21 11	2 10	3 52	4 52
6 FR	18 49	20 32	11 34D	0 ♌ 49	14 2	5 38	24 29	21 7	2 10	3 51	4 51
7 SA	19 47	2 ♎ 19	11 35	1 57	15 15	6 14	24 35	21 2	2 10	3 49	4 50
8 SU	20 45	14 9	11 37	3 11	16 28	6 49	24 41	20 57	2 9	3 48	4 49
9 MO	21 44	26 7	11 39	4 31	17 42	7 25	24 47	20 53	2 9	3 46	4 48
10 TU	22 42	8 ♏ 17	11 40	5 57	18 55	8 1	24 52	20 48	2 9	3 44	4 47
11 WE	23 40	20 43	11 40	7 27	20 8	8 36	24 58	20 44	2 8	3 43	4 46
12 TH	24 39	3 ♐ 30	11 40R	9 2	21 22	9 11	25 3	20 39	2 8	3 41	4 46
13 FR	25 37	16 42	11 39	10 40	22 35	9 46	25 8	20 35	2 7	3 39	4 45
14 SA	26 36	0 ♑ 20	11 38	12 22	23 48	10 21	25 13	20 30	2 6	3 38	4 44
15 SU	27 34	14 27	11 36	14 6	25 2	10 56	25 18	20 25	2 6	3 36	4 43
16 MO	28 32	28 59	11 34	15 52	26 15	11 30	25 22	20 21	2 5	3 35	4 43
17 TU	29 31	13 ♒ 52	11 33	17 40	27 28	12 5	25 26	20 16	2 4	3 33	4 42
18 WE	0 ♍ 29	28 59	11 32	19 30	28 41	12 39	25 31	20 12	2 4	3 31	4 41
19 TH	1 28	14 ♓ 10	11 32D	21 20	29 54	13 13	25 35	20 7	2 3	3 30	4 41
20 FR	2 27	29 17	11 32	23 11	1 ♎ 8	13 47	25 38	20 3	2 2	3 28	4 40
21 SA	3 25	14 ♈ 10	11 33	25 2	2 21	14 20	25 42	19 59	2 1	3 26	4 39
22 SU	4 24	28 44	11 33	26 54	3 34	14 54	25 46	19 54	2 0	3 25	4 39
23 MO	5 23	12 ♉ 54	11 34	28 45	4 47	15 27	25 49	19 50	1 59	3 23	4 38
24 TU	6 21	26 38	11 34	0 ♍ 37	6 0	16 0	25 52	19 45	1 58	3 21	4 38
25 WE	7 20	9 ♊ 58	11 34R	2 27	7 13	16 33	25 55	19 41	1 57	3 20	4 37
26 TH	8 19	22 56	11 34	4 18	8 26	17 6	25 58	19 37	1 56	3 18	4 37
27 FR	9 18	5 ♋ 33	11 34	6 7	9 39	17 38	26 0	19 33	1 54	3 16	4 36
28 SA	10 17	17 55	11 34	7 56	10 52	18 10	26 2	19 29	1 53	3 15	4 36
29 SU	11 15	0 ♌ 4	11 34D	9 45	12 5	18 42	26 5	19 24	1 52	3 13	4 36
30 MO	12 14	12 3	11 34	11 32	13 18	19 14	26 7	19 20	1 51	3 11	4 35

INGRESSES :

1 ☽ → ♌ 18: 2	20 ☽ → ♈ 1: 8
4 ☽ → ♍ 6:11	22 ☽ → ♉ 2: 6
5 ☿ → ♌ 5: 5	23 ☿ → ♍ 16: 5
6 ☽ → ♎ 19:17	24 ☽ → ♊ 5:59
9 ☽ → ♏ 7:42	26 ☽ → ♋ 13:22
11 ☽ → ♐ 17:29	28 ☽ → ♌ 23:52
13 ☽ → ♑ 23:24	
16 ☽ → ♒ 1:39	
17 ☉ → ♍ 11:56	
18 ☽ → ♓ 1:36	
19 ♀ → ♎ 1:48	

ASPECTS & ECLIPSES :

1 ☽ ☌ ☿ 12:35	9 ☽ ☍ ♅ 11:57	☽ ●-● P 2:44	24 ☉ □ ☽ 18:48
3 ☉ ☌ ☽ 1:54	11 ☉ □ ☽ 6: 4	☽ ☌ ♆ 7: 9	25 ☽ □N ☊ 2:55
♂ □ ♆ 4:24	☽ ☍ ♃ 8: 5	☿ ☍ ♄ 8:49	☿ ☍ ♆ 11:11
☽ ☍ ♄ 12:36	12 ☉ □ ♃ 10:51	☽ ☌ P 13:11	☽ ☌ ♂ 12:38
4 ♀ ☍ ☊ 0: 0	☽ ☍ ♂ 10:55	☽ ☌ ☊ 19:49	26 ☽ ☍ ♇ 22:10
☽ ☍ ♆ 14: 4	☽ □S ☊ 14:55	20 ☽ ☍ ♀ 3:12	29 ☉ ☍ ☊ 7:22
5 ☽ ☌ ☋ 5:42	14 ☽ ☌ ♇ 7:33	21 ☉ ☍ ♆ 0:25	30 ☿ ☍ ☊ 0:18
☽ ☌ ♀ 9:11	16 ♂ □ ☊ 2:32	☿ □ ♃ 8:48	☽ ☍ ♄ 14:36
☽ ☌ A 14:58	17 ☽ ☍ ☿ 6:54	22 ☽ ☌ ♅ 5:27	☉ ☋S ☿ 21: 8
7 ☿ □ ♅ 4:19	☽ ☌ ♄ 10: 9	♀ □ ♇ 21: 9	
8 ☉ ☍ ♄ 4:34	18 ☉ ☍ ☽ 2:33	23 ☽ ☌ ♃ 22:37	

SIDEREAL HELIOCENTRIC LONGITUDES : SEPTEMBER 2024 Gregorian at 0 hours UT

DAY	Sid. Time	☿	♀	⊕	♂	♃	♄	♅	♆	♇	Vernal Point
1 SU	22:42:36	0 ♈ 38	12 ♎ 27	13 ♒ 59	21 ♈ 49	12 ♉ 35	20 ♒ 42	29 ♈ 17	3 ♓ 19	5 ♑ 58	4 ♓ 54'57"
2 MO	22:46:33	6 13	14 3	14 57	22 22	12 40	20 44	29 17	3 19	5 58	4 ♓ 54'57"
3 TU	22:50:29	11 56	15 39	15 55	22 56	12 45	20 46	29 18	3 19	5 58	4 ♓ 54'56"
4 WE	22:54:26	17 47	17 15	16 53	23 30	12 50	20 48	29 19	3 20	5 59	4 ♓ 54'56"
5 TH	22:58:22	23 46	18 51	17 51	24 4	12 56	20 50	29 19	3 20	5 59	4 ♓ 54'56"
6 FR	23: 2:19	29 51	20 27	18 49	24 37	13 1	20 52	29 20	3 20	5 59	4 ♓ 54'56"
7 SA	23: 6:15	6 ♉ 1	22 3	19 48	25 11	13 6	20 54	29 21	3 21	6 0	4 ♓ 54'56"
8 SU	23:10:12	12 16	23 39	20 46	25 44	13 12	20 56	29 21	3 21	6 0	4 ♓ 54'56"
9 MO	23:14: 9	18 34	25 15	21 44	26 18	13 17	20 58	29 22	3 22	6 0	4 ♓ 54'56"
10 TU	23:18: 5	24 53	26 51	22 42	26 51	13 22	21 0	29 23	3 22	6 0	4 ♓ 54'56"
11 WE	23:22: 2	1 ♊ 12	28 26	23 41	27 24	13 27	21 2	29 23	3 22	6 1	4 ♓ 54'55"
12 TH	23:25:58	7 29	0 ♏ 2	24 39	27 58	13 33	21 4	29 24	3 23	6 1	4 ♓ 54'55"
13 FR	23:29:55	13 44	1 38	25 37	28 31	13 38	21 6	29 25	3 23	6 1	4 ♓ 54'55"
14 SA	23:33:51	19 54	3 14	26 36	29 4	13 43	21 8	29 25	3 23	6 2	4 ♓ 54'55"
15 SU	23:37:48	25 59	4 49	27 34	29 37	13 49	21 10	29 26	3 24	6 2	4 ♓ 54'55"
16 MO	23:41:44	1 ♋ 56	6 25	28 33	0 ♉ 10	13 54	21 12	29 27	3 24	6 2	4 ♓ 54'55"
17 TU	23:45:41	7 46	8 0	29 31	0 43	13 59	21 14	29 28	3 24	6 2	4 ♓ 54'55"
18 WE	23:49:38	13 27	9 36	0 ♓ 30	1 16	14 5	21 16	29 28	3 25	6 3	4 ♓ 54'54"
19 TH	23:53:34	19 0	11 11	1 28	1 49	14 10	21 17	29 29	3 25	6 3	4 ♓ 54'54"
20 FR	23:57:31	24 22	12 47	2 27	2 22	14 15	21 19	29 30	3 26	6 3	4 ♓ 54'54"
21 SA	0: 1:27	29 36	14 22	3 26	2 55	14 20	21 21	29 30	3 26	6 4	4 ♓ 54'54"
22 SU	0: 5:24	4 ♌ 39	15 57	4 24	3 27	14 26	21 23	29 31	3 26	6 4	4 ♓ 54'54"
23 MO	0: 9:20	9 33	17 33	5 23	4 0	14 31	21 25	29 32	3 27	6 4	4 ♓ 54'54"
24 TU	0:13:17	14 18	19 8	6 22	4 33	14 36	21 27	29 32	3 27	6 4	4 ♓ 54'54"
25 WE	0:17:13	18 53	20 43	7 20	5 5	14 42	21 29	29 33	3 27	6 5	4 ♓ 54'53"
26 TH	0:21:10	23 20	22 19	8 19	5 38	14 47	21 31	29 34	3 28	6 5	4 ♓ 54'53"
27 FR	0:25: 7	27 38	23 54	9 18	6 10	14 52	21 33	29 34	3 28	6 5	4 ♓ 54'53"
28 SA	0:29: 3	1 ♍ 48	25 29	10 17	6 42	14 57	21 35	29 35	3 28	6 5	4 ♓ 54'53"
29 SU	0:33: 0	5 50	27 4	11 16	7 15	15 3	21 37	29 36	3 29	6 6	4 ♓ 54'53"
30 MO	0:36:56	9 45	28 39	12 15	7 47	15 8	21 39	29 36	3 29	6 6	4 ♓ 54'53"

INGRESSES :

6 ☿ → ♉ 0:35
10 ☿ → ♊ 19:26
11 ♀ → ♏ 23:27
15 ☿ → ♋ 16: 9
♂ → ♉ 16:32
17 ⊕ → ♓ 11:46
21 ☿ → ♌ 1:53
27 ☿ → ♍ 13:34
30 ♀ → ♐ 20:21

ASPECTS (HELIOCENTRIC +MOON(TYCHONIC)) :

1 ☽ □ ♂ 2: 0	7 ☽ □ ♇ 7:28	11 ☽ □ ♄ 0:35	17 ☽ □ ♃ 0:11	☽ □ ☿ 15:15	28 ☿ ☍ ♆ 9:54
☽ □ ♅ 16:37	8 ☿ ☌ ♃ 3:35	☿ □ ♆ 8:16	☽ ☌ ♄ 11:44	23 ☽ ☌ ♃ 2:48	☽ □ ♅ 23: 3
☿ □ ♇ 22:57	⊕ ☌ ♄ 4:18	♀ ☍ ♅ 14:23	18 ☽ ☌ ♆ 7: 0	☽ ☍ ♀ 9: 4	29 ☽ □ ♂ 15: 0
2 ☽ □ ♃ 19:23	☽ ☌ ♀ 21:59	☽ □ ♆ 23:46	19 ☿ □N ☊ 20:13	☽ □ ♄ 14:50	30 ☽ □ ♃ 6:14
3 ☽ ☍ ♄ 11:33	9 ☽ ☍ ♂ 0:22	12 ☽ ☍ ☿ 13:58	20 ☽ □ ♇ 10:51	24 ☿ □ ♃ 1:37	☽ ☍ ♄ 19:25
☿ ☍ ♀ 20:59	☽ ☍ ♅ 6:27	14 ☽ ☌ ♇ 9:46	♀ ☍ ♃ 23:32	☽ □ ♆ 12:10	☿ ☍ ⊕ 21: 8
4 ☽ ☍ ♆ 12:57	☿ □ ♄ 9:10	♂ ☌ ♅ 15:47	☿ □ ♅ 23:34	25 ♀ □ ♄ 11:47	
☿ ☌ ☊ 23: 6	☿ □ ⊕ 14:15	16 ☽ □ ♅ 0:45	21 ⊕ ☌ ♆ 0: 9	☿ ☍ ♄ 14: 4	
5 ☿ ☌ ♂ 1:17	☿ ☌ P 15:56	☽ □ ♂ 2: 1	☿ □ ♂ 17:32	☿ □ ♀ 15:19	
☿ ☌ ♅ 21:58	10 ♀ ☍ ♂ 0:12	☽ □ ♀ 13:29	22 ☽ ☌ ♅ 1:18	♀ ☌ ☋ 16:32	
6 ♂ ☌ ☊ 1:50	☽ ☍ ♃ 9:57	☿ ☍ ♇ 16:49	☽ ☌ ♂ 8:14	27 ☽ ☍ ♇ 1: 1	

SIDEREAL GEOCENTRIC LONGITUDES : OCTOBER 2024 Gregorian at 0 hours UT

DAY	☉	☽	☊	☿	♀	♂	♃	♄	♅	♆	♇
1 TU	13 ♍ 13	23 ♌ 56	11 ♓ 34	13 ♍ 19	14 ♎ 31	19 ♊ 46	26 ♉ 8	19 ♒ 16R	1 ♉ 49R	3 ♓ 10R	4 ♑ 35R
2 WE	14 12	5 ♍ 45	11 34	15 5	15 44	20 17	26 10	19 12	1 48	3 8	4 35
3 TH	15 11	17 32	11 34R	16 50	16 57	20 48	26 11	19 9	1 46	3 6	4 34
4 FR	16 11	29 19	11 34	18 34	18 10	21 19	26 12	19 5	1 45	3 5	4 34
5 SA	17 10	11 ♎ 10	11 33	20 18	19 23	21 50	26 13	19 1	1 43	3 3	4 34
6 SU	18 9	23 5	11 32	22 1	20 36	22 20	26 14	18 57	1 42	3 2	4 34
7 MO	19 8	5 ♏ 8	11 31	23 42	21 49	22 50	26 15	18 54	1 40	3 0	4 34
8 TU	20 7	17 22	11 30	25 23	23 2	23 20	26 15	18 50	1 38	2 58	4 33
9 WE	21 7	29 50	11 29	27 4	24 15	23 50	26 15	18 46	1 37	2 57	4 33
10 TH	22 6	12 ♐ 36	11 29	28 43	25 27	24 19	26 15R	18 43	1 35	2 55	4 33
11 FR	23 5	25 41	11 28D	0 ♎ 22	26 40	24 48	26 15	18 40	1 33	2 54	4 33
12 SA	24 4	9 ♑ 10	11 29	2 0	27 53	25 17	26 14	18 36	1 31	2 52	4 33
13 SU	25 4	23 4	11 29	3 37	29 6	25 46	26 14	18 33	1 29	2 51	4 33D
14 MO	26 3	7 ♒ 23	11 31	5 13	0 ♏ 18	26 14	26 13	18 30	1 28	2 49	4 33
15 TU	27 3	22 5	11 32	6 49	1 31	26 42	26 12	18 27	1 26	2 48	4 33
16 WE	28 2	7 ♓ 5	11 32	8 24	2 43	27 10	26 11	18 24	1 24	2 46	4 33
17 TH	29 2	22 15	11 32R	9 59	3 56	27 37	26 9	18 21	1 22	2 45	4 33
18 FR	0 ♎ 1	7 ♈ 27	11 31	11 33	5 9	28 4	26 7	18 18	1 20	2 43	4 34
19 SA	1 1	22 31	11 29	13 6	6 21	28 31	26 6	18 15	1 18	2 42	4 34
20 SU	2 0	7 ♉ 17	11 27	14 39	7 34	28 57	26 4	18 13	1 16	2 41	4 34
21 MO	3 0	21 40	11 24	16 11	8 46	29 23	26 1	18 10	1 14	2 39	4 34
22 TU	4 0	5 ♊ 36	11 21	17 42	9 59	29 49	25 59	18 7	1 11	2 38	4 35
23 WE	4 59	19 3	11 19	19 13	11 11	0 ♋ 15	25 56	18 5	1 9	2 37	4 35
24 TH	5 59	2 ♋ 3	11 18	20 43	12 23	0 40	25 53	18 3	1 7	2 35	4 35
25 FR	6 59	14 40	11 18D	22 13	13 36	1 5	25 50	18 1	1 5	2 34	4 36
26 SA	7 59	26 58	11 20	23 42	14 48	1 29	25 47	17 58	1 3	2 33	4 36
27 SU	8 58	9 ♌ 2	11 21	25 10	16 0	1 53	25 44	17 56	1 0	2 31	4 36
28 MO	9 58	20 55	11 23	26 38	17 12	2 17	25 40	17 54	0 58	2 30	4 37
29 TU	10 58	2 ♍ 43	11 25	28 5	18 25	2 40	25 36	17 53	0 56	2 29	4 37
30 WE	11 58	14 29	11 25R	29 32	19 37	3 3	25 32	17 51	0 53	2 28	4 38
31 TH	12 58	26 17	11 24	0 ♏ 58	20 49	3 25	25 28	17 49	0 51	2 26	4 38

INGRESSES :

1 ☽ → ♍ 12:18	19 ☽ → ♉ 12: 5
4 ☽ → ♎ 1:22	21 ☽ → ♊ 14:15
6 ☽ → ♏ 13:48	22 ♂ → ♋ 10: 4
9 ☽ → ♐ 0:18	23 ☽ → ♋ 20: 9
10 ☿ → ♎ 18:42	26 ☽ → ♌ 5:59
11 ☽ → ♑ 7:45	28 ☽ → ♍ 18:27
13 ☽ → ♒ 11:42	30 ☿ → ♏ 7:51
♀ → ♏ 17:59	31 ☽ → ♎ 7:31
15 ☽ → ♓ 12:42	
17 ☽ → ♈ 12:12	
☉ → ♎ 23:33	

ASPECTS & ECLIPSES :

1 ☽ ☍ ♆ 18:41	10 ☉ □ ☽ 18:54	18 ☽ ☍ ☿ 7:13	☽ ☍ ♆ 23:31
2 ☽ ☌ ☋ 11:51	☽ ☍ ♂ 22:20	19 ☽ ☌ ♅ 14: 9	29 ☽ ☌ ☋ 17:43
☉ ● A 18:44	11 ☽ ☌ ♇ 15:51	20 ☽ ☍ ♀ 0:28	☽ ☌ A 22:45
☉ ☌ ☽ 18:48	13 ☿ □ ♇ 13:58	21 ☽ ☌ ♃ 7:23	30 ☿ ☍ ♅ 22:12
☽ ☌ A 19:46	14 ☉ □ ♂ 8:13	22 ☽ ⚺ ☊ 10: 8	
☽ ☌ ☿ 22:20	☽ ☌ ♄ 18: 7	☉ □ ♇ 14: 9	
5 ☽ ☌ ♀ 18:27	♀ ☍ ♅ 22:20	23 ☽ ☌ ♂ 21:18	
6 ☿ □ ♂ 6:35	15 ☽ ☌ ♆ 17: 9	24 ☽ ☍ ♇ 4:45	
☽ ☍ ♅ 17: 7	16 ☽ ☌ ☊ 7: 3	☉ □ ☽ 8: 1	
8 ☽ ☍ ♃ 17: 8	17 ☽ ☌ P 0:42	27 ☽ ☍ ♄ 17:54	
9 ☽ ⚼ ☊ 21:55	☉ ☍ ☽ 11:25	28 ♀ □ ♄ 13:33	

SIDEREAL HELIOCENTRIC LONGITUDES : OCTOBER 2024 Gregorian at 0 hours UT

DAY	Sid. Time	☿	♀	⊕	♂	♃	♄	♅	♆	♇	Vernal Point
1 TU	0:40:53	13 ♍ 34	0 ♐ 14	13 ♓ 14	8 ♉ 19	15 ♉ 13	21 ♒ 41	29 ♈ 37	3 ♓ 30	6 ♑ 6	4 ♓ 54'53"
2 WE	0:44:49	17 16	1 49	14 13	8 51	15 18	21 43	29 38	3 30	6 7	4 ♓ 54'52"
3 TH	0:48:46	20 52	3 25	15 12	9 23	15 24	21 45	29 38	3 30	6 7	4 ♓ 54'52"
4 FR	0:52:42	24 22	5 0	16 11	9 55	15 29	21 47	29 39	3 31	6 7	4 ♓ 54'52"
5 SA	0:56:39	27 48	6 35	17 10	10 27	15 34	21 49	29 40	3 31	6 7	4 ♓ 54'52"
6 SU	1: 0:36	1 ♎ 9	8 10	18 9	10 59	15 40	21 51	29 40	3 31	6 8	4 ♓ 54'52"
7 MO	1: 4:32	4 25	9 45	19 8	11 31	15 45	21 53	29 41	3 32	6 8	4 ♓ 54'52"
8 TU	1: 8:29	7 37	11 20	20 8	12 3	15 50	21 55	29 42	3 32	6 8	4 ♓ 54'52"
9 WE	1:12:25	10 46	12 55	21 7	12 35	15 55	21 57	29 42	3 32	6 9	4 ♓ 54'52"
10 TH	1:16:22	13 51	14 29	22 6	13 6	16 1	21 59	29 43	3 33	6 9	4 ♓ 54'51"
11 FR	1:20:18	16 53	16 4	23 5	13 38	16 6	22 1	29 44	3 33	6 9	4 ♓ 54'51"
12 SA	1:24:15	19 53	17 39	24 5	14 10	16 11	22 3	29 44	3 34	6 9	4 ♓ 54'51"
13 SU	1:28:11	22 49	19 14	25 4	14 41	16 16	22 4	29 45	3 34	6 10	4 ♓ 54'51"
14 MO	1:32: 8	25 44	20 49	26 4	15 13	16 22	22 6	29 46	3 34	6 10	4 ♓ 54'51"
15 TU	1:36: 5	28 36	22 24	27 3	15 44	16 27	22 8	29 46	3 35	6 10	4 ♓ 54'51"
16 WE	1:40: 1	1 ♏ 27	23 59	28 2	16 15	16 32	22 10	29 47	3 35	6 11	4 ♓ 54'51"
17 TH	1:43:58	4 16	25 34	29 2	16 47	16 38	22 12	29 48	3 35	6 11	4 ♓ 54'50"
18 FR	1:47:54	7 4	27 9	0 ♈ 1	17 18	16 43	22 14	29 49	3 36	6 11	4 ♓ 54'50"
19 SA	1:51:51	9 51	28 43	1 1	17 49	16 48	22 16	29 49	3 36	6 11	4 ♓ 54'50"
20 SU	1:55:47	12 37	0 ♑ 18	2 1	18 20	16 53	22 18	29 50	3 36	6 12	4 ♓ 54'50"
21 MO	1:59:44	15 22	1 53	3 0	18 52	16 59	22 20	29 51	3 37	6 12	4 ♓ 54'50"
22 TU	2: 3:40	18 7	3 28	4 0	19 23	17 4	22 22	29 51	3 37	6 12	4 ♓ 54'50"
23 WE	2: 7:37	20 52	5 3	5 0	19 54	17 9	22 24	29 52	3 38	6 12	4 ♓ 54'50"
24 TH	2:11:34	23 37	6 38	5 59	20 25	17 14	22 26	29 53	3 38	6 13	4 ♓ 54'49"
25 FR	2:15:30	26 22	8 13	6 59	20 55	17 20	22 28	29 53	3 38	6 13	4 ♓ 54'49"
26 SA	2:19:27	29 7	9 48	7 59	21 26	17 25	22 30	29 54	3 39	6 13	4 ♓ 54'49"
27 SU	2:23:23	1 ♐ 53	11 22	8 59	21 57	17 30	22 32	29 55	3 39	6 14	4 ♓ 54'49"
28 MO	2:27:20	4 39	12 57	9 59	22 28	17 35	22 34	29 55	3 39	6 14	4 ♓ 54'49"
29 TU	2:31:16	7 27	14 32	10 59	22 59	17 41	22 36	29 56	3 40	6 14	4 ♓ 54'49"
30 WE	2:35:13	10 16	16 7	11 59	23 29	17 46	22 38	29 57	3 40	6 14	4 ♓ 54'49"
31 TH	2:39: 9	13 6	17 42	12 59	24 0	17 51	22 40	29 57	3 40	6 15	4 ♓ 54'49"

INGRESSES :

5 ☿ → ♎ 15:43
15 ☿ → ♏ 11:43
17 ⊕ → ♈ 23:24
19 ♀ → ♑ 19:21
26 ☿ → ♐ 7:42

ASPECTS (HELIOCENTRIC +MOON(TYCHONIC)) :

1 ☽ □ ♀ 14:47	10 ☽ ☌ ♀ 4: 0	17 ☽ □ ♀ 5:49	23 ☿ □ ♄ 13:34	♂ □ ♄ 5: 2
☽ ☍ ♆ 19:25	11 ☽ ☌ ♇ 18:41	☽ □ ♇ 21:59	☿ ☌ A 16:30	29 ☽ ☍ ♆ 1:55
3 ♀ □ ♆ 1:27	12 ☽ □ ☿ 23:27	19 ☽ ☌ ♅ 11:48	♀ ☌ ♇ 17:38	☽ □ ☿ 12:39
☽ ☌ ☿ 9:42	13 ☿ ☌ ☋ 5:53	20 ☽ ☍ ☿ 10:53	24 ⊕ □ ♇ 5:23	30 ♀ ☌ A 10:43
4 ☽ □ ♇ 13:48	☽ □ ♅ 11:17	☽ ☌ ♃ 16: 2	☽ ☍ ♇ 7:50	31 ☽ □ ♇ 20: 9
6 ☽ ☍ ♅ 13: 9	14 ☽ □ ♂ 13:19	☽ ☌ ♂ 19: 4	☽ ☍ ♀ 9:51	
7 ☿ □ ♇ 12:48	☽ □ ♃ 14:48	21 ☽ □ ♄ 1: 7	26 ☽ □ ♅ 5:48	
☽ ☍ ♂ 13: 7	15 ☽ ☌ ♄ 0: 5	☿ ☍ ♃ 14:26	27 ☿ □ ♆ 15:22	
☽ ☍ ♃ 20:58	☿ ☍ ♅ 9:51	☽ □ ♆ 20:32	☽ □ ♃ 17:12	
8 ☽ □ ♄ 8:48	☽ ☌ ♆ 18:25	22 ☿ ☍ ♂ 13:29	28 ☽ □ ♂ 3:16	
9 ☽ □ ♆ 7: 1	16 ♂ ☌ ♃ 15:28	♀ □ ⊕ 21:44	☽ ☍ ♄ 3:21	

SIDEREAL GEOCENTRIC LONGITUDES : NOVEMBER 2024 Gregorian at 0 hours UT

DAY	☉	☽	☊	☿	♀	♂	♃	♄	♅	♆	♇
1 FR	13 ♎ 58	8 ♎ 9	11 ♓ 21R	2 ♏ 23	22 ♏ 1	3 ♋ 48	25 ♉ 24R	17 ♒ 48R	0 ♉ 49R	2 ♓ 25R	4 ♑ 39
2 SA	14 58	20 7	11 16	3 47	23 13	4 9	25 19	17 46	0 46	2 24	4 39
3 SU	15 58	2 ♏ 13	11 11	5 11	24 25	4 30	25 15	17 45	0 44	2 23	4 40
4 MO	16 58	14 28	11 4	6 34	25 37	4 51	25 10	17 43	0 42	2 22	4 41
5 TU	17 59	26 54	10 57	7 56	26 49	5 12	25 5	17 42	0 39	2 21	4 41
6 WE	18 59	9 ♐ 32	10 51	9 17	28 1	5 31	24 59	17 41	0 37	2 20	4 42
7 TH	19 59	22 23	10 46	10 37	29 13	5 51	24 54	17 40	0 34	2 19	4 43
8 FR	20 59	5 ♑ 30	10 43	11 56	0 ♐ 25	6 10	24 48	17 39	0 32	2 18	4 44
9 SA	22 0	18 54	10 42	13 14	1 37	6 28	24 43	17 39	0 29	2 17	4 44
10 SU	23 0	2 ♒ 36	10 42D	14 30	2 48	6 46	24 37	17 38	0 27	2 16	4 45
11 MO	24 0	16 39	10 44	15 44	4 0	7 4	24 31	17 37	0 24	2 15	4 46
12 TU	25 0	1 ♓ 1	10 45	16 57	5 11	7 21	24 25	17 37	0 22	2 14	4 47
13 WE	26 1	15 41	10 45R	18 8	6 23	7 37	24 18	17 37	0 19	2 13	4 48
14 TH	27 1	0 ♈ 34	10 43	19 17	7 34	7 53	24 12	17 36	0 17	2 13	4 49
15 FR	28 2	15 33	10 39	20 23	8 46	8 8	24 5	17 36	0 14	2 12	4 50
16 SA	29 2	0 ♉ 30	10 33	21 26	9 57	8 23	23 59	17 36D	0 12	2 11	4 51
17 SU	0 ♏ 2	15 16	10 26	22 26	11 8	8 38	23 52	17 36	0 9	2 10	4 52
18 MO	1 3	29 43	10 17	23 22	12 20	8 51	23 45	17 37	0 7	2 10	4 53
19 TU	2 3	13 ♊ 44	10 9	24 15	13 31	9 4	23 38	17 37	0 4	2 9	4 54
20 WE	3 4	27 18	10 2	25 2	14 42	9 17	23 31	17 37	0 2	2 9	4 55
21 TH	4 4	10 ♋ 25	9 57	25 45	15 53	9 29	23 23	17 38	29 ♈ 59	2 8	4 56
22 FR	5 5	23 6	9 54	26 22	17 4	9 40	23 16	17 38	29 57	2 7	4 57
23 SA	6 6	5 ♌ 25	9 53	26 52	18 15	9 51	23 9	17 39	29 55	2 7	4 58
24 SU	7 6	17 29	9 54D	27 15	19 25	10 1	23 1	17 40	29 52	2 6	4 59
25 MO	8 7	29 21	9 55	27 29	20 36	10 10	22 53	17 41	29 50	2 6	5 0
26 TU	9 8	11 ♍ 8	9 55R	27 35	21 47	10 18	22 46	17 42	29 47	2 5	5 2
27 WE	10 8	22 55	9 54	27 31R	22 57	10 26	22 38	17 43	29 45	2 5	5 3
28 TH	11 9	4 ♎ 45	9 51	27 17	24 8	10 34	22 30	17 44	29 42	2 5	5 4
29 FR	12 10	16 43	9 45	26 52	25 18	10 40	22 22	17 46	29 40	2 4	5 5
30 SA	13 11	28 51	9 36	26 16	26 28	10 46	22 14	17 47	29 37	2 4	5 7

INGRESSES :

2 ☽ → ♏ 19:37
5 ☽ → ♐ 5:55
7 ☽ → ♑ 13:59
♀ → ♐ 15:43
9 ☽ → ♒ 19:28
11 ☽ → ♓ 22:18
13 ☽ → ♈ 23: 5
15 ☽ → ♉ 23:11
16 ☉ → ♏ 23: 3
18 ☽ → ♊ 0:29
20 ☽ → ♋ 4:51
♅ → ♈ 19: 9
22 ☽ → ♌ 13:22
25 ☽ → ♍ 1:18
27 ☽ → ♎ 14:23
30 ☽ → ♏ 2:15

ASPECTS & ECLIPSES :

1 ☉ ☌ ☽ 12:46
2 ☽ ☍ ♅ 21: 4
3 ☽ ☌ ☿ 6:35
♂ ☍ ♇ 11:21
♀ ☍ ♃ 15:23
4 ☽ ☍ ♃ 20:31
☽ ☌ ♀ 23:49
6 ☽ S ☊ 2:27
7 ☽ ☌ ♇ 22:36
8 ☽ ☍ ♂ 1:14
9 ☉ □ ☽ 5:54
♀ □ ♆ 13:22
11 ☽ ☌ ♄ 1:38
12 ☽ ☌ ♆ 2: 0
☿ □ ♄ 13:20
☽ ☌ ☊ 15:57
14 ☽ ☌ P 11:27
15 ☉ ☍ ☽ 21:27
☽ ☌ ♅ 23:30
16 ♀ □ ☊ 11: 0
17 ☉ ☍ ♅ 2:42
☽ ☍ ☿ 12:40
☽ ☌ ♃ 14: 5
18 ☿ ☍ ♃ 8:54
☽ N ☊ 17:50
☽ ☍ ♀ 23:34
20 ☽ ☍ ♇ 13:50
☽ ☌ ♂ 22:14
23 ☉ □ ☽ 1:26
24 ☽ ☍ ♄ 0:22
25 ☽ ☍ ♆ 5:34
☽ ☌ ☋ 21:30
26 ☽ ☌ A 12:10
30 ☽ ☍ ♅ 1:31

SIDEREAL HELIOCENTRIC LONGITUDES : NOVEMBER 2024 Gregorian at 0 hours UT

DAY	Sid. Time	☿	♀	⊕	♂	♃	♄	♅	♆	♇	Vernal Point
1 FR	2:43: 6	15 ♐ 58	19 ♑ 17	13 ♈ 59	24 ♉ 30	17 ♉ 56	22 ♒ 42	29 ♈ 58	3 ♓ 41	6 ♑ 15	4 ♓ 54'48"
2 SA	2:47: 3	18 52	20 52	14 59	25 1	18 2	22 44	29 59	3 41	6 15	4 ♓ 54'48"
3 SU	2:50:59	21 47	22 27	15 59	25 31	18 7	22 46	29 59	3 42	6 16	4 ♓ 54'48"
4 MO	2:54:56	24 46	24 2	16 59	26 2	18 12	22 48	0 ♉ 0	3 42	6 16	4 ♓ 54'48"
5 TU	2:58:52	27 46	25 37	17 59	26 32	18 18	22 50	0 1	3 42	6 16	4 ♓ 54'48"
6 WE	3: 2:49	0 ♑ 50	27 12	18 59	27 2	18 23	22 52	0 1	3 43	6 16	4 ♓ 54'48"
7 TH	3: 6:45	3 57	28 47	19 59	27 33	18 28	22 54	0 2	3 43	6 17	4 ♓ 54'48"
8 FR	3:10:42	7 7	0 ♒ 22	21 0	28 3	18 33	22 55	0 3	3 43	6 17	4 ♓ 54'47"
9 SA	3:14:38	10 21	1 57	22 0	28 33	18 39	22 57	0 3	3 44	6 17	4 ♓ 54'47"
10 SU	3:18:35	13 39	3 32	23 0	29 3	18 44	22 59	0 4	3 44	6 17	4 ♓ 54'47"
11 MO	3:22:32	17 1	5 7	24 0	29 33	18 49	23 1	0 5	3 44	6 18	4 ♓ 54'47"
12 TU	3:26:28	20 28	6 42	25 1	0 ♊ 3	18 54	23 3	0 5	3 45	6 18	4 ♓ 54'47"
13 WE	3:30:25	23 59	8 17	26 1	0 33	19 0	23 5	0 6	3 45	6 18	4 ♓ 54'47"
14 TH	3:34:21	27 36	9 52	27 2	1 3	19 5	23 7	0 7	3 46	6 19	4 ♓ 54'47"
15 FR	3:38:18	1 ♒ 19	11 27	28 2	1 33	19 10	23 9	0 8	3 46	6 19	4 ♓ 54'46"
16 SA	3:42:14	5 8	13 2	29 2	2 3	19 15	23 11	0 8	3 46	6 19	4 ♓ 54'46"
17 SU	3:46:11	9 3	14 37	0 ♉ 3	2 32	19 21	23 13	0 9	3 47	6 19	4 ♓ 54'46"
18 MO	3:50: 7	13 5	16 12	1 3	3 2	19 26	23 15	0 10	3 47	6 20	4 ♓ 54'46"
19 TU	3:54: 4	17 14	17 48	2 4	3 32	19 31	23 17	0 10	3 47	6 20	4 ♓ 54'46"
20 WE	3:58: 1	21 30	19 23	3 4	4 1	19 36	23 19	0 11	3 48	6 20	4 ♓ 54'46"
21 TH	4: 1:57	25 55	20 58	4 5	4 31	19 41	23 21	0 12	3 48	6 21	4 ♓ 54'46"
22 FR	4: 5:54	0 ♓ 27	22 33	5 5	5 1	19 47	23 23	0 12	3 48	6 21	4 ♓ 54'45"
23 SA	4: 9:50	5 9	24 9	6 6	5 30	19 52	23 25	0 13	3 49	6 21	4 ♓ 54'45"
24 SU	4:13:47	9 58	25 44	7 7	6 0	19 57	23 27	0 14	3 49	6 21	4 ♓ 54'45"
25 MO	4:17:43	14 57	27 19	8 7	6 29	20 2	23 29	0 14	3 50	6 22	4 ♓ 54'45"
26 TU	4:21:40	20 5	28 55	9 8	6 58	20 8	23 31	0 15	3 50	6 22	4 ♓ 54'45"
27 WE	4:25:36	25 22	0 ♓ 30	10 9	7 28	20 13	23 33	0 16	3 50	6 22	4 ♓ 54'45"
28 TH	4:29:33	0 ♈ 49	2 5	11 10	7 57	20 18	23 35	0 16	3 51	6 23	4 ♓ 54'45"
29 FR	4:33:30	6 24	3 41	12 10	8 26	20 23	23 37	0 17	3 51	6 23	4 ♓ 54'45"
30 SA	4:37:26	12 7	5 16	13 11	8 55	20 29	23 39	0 18	3 51	6 23	4 ♓ 54'44"

INGRESSES :

3 ♅ → ♉ 22:16
5 ☿ → ♑ 17:29
7 ♀ → ♒ 18:32
11 ♂ → ♊ 21:32
14 ☿ → ♒ 15:33
16 ⊕ → ♉ 22:54
21 ☿ → ♓ 21:37
26 ♀ → ♓ 16:29
27 ☿ → ♈ 20:27

ASPECTS (HELIOCENTRIC +MOON(TYCHONIC)) :

2 ☽ □ ♀ 1:42
☽ ☍ ♅ 19:35
4 ☽ ☍ ♃ 7:17
☽ □ ♄ 16: 8
☽ ☍ ♂ 23:15
5 ☽ □ ♆ 12:58
7 ☿ ☌ ♇ 17:42
♀ □ ♅ 19:12
8 ☽ ☌ ♇ 1:25
☽ ☌ ☿ 3:51
9 ☽ □ ♅ 19:35
10 ☽ ☌ ♀ 1:47
11 ☽ □ ♃ 3:40
☽ ☌ ♄ 10:43
☽ □ ♂ 22:20
12 ☽ ☌ ♆ 4:29
☿ S ☊ 20:58
13 ☿ □ ⊕ 18:43
14 ☽ □ ♇ 9:12
☿ □ ♅ 16:20
15 ☽ ☌ ♅ 23:24
16 ☽ □ ☿ 10: 8
☽ □ ♀ 22:48
17 ⊕ ☌ ♅ 2:26
☽ ☌ ♃ 6:45
☽ □ ♄ 13:10
18 ☽ ☌ ♂ 5:49
☽ □ ♆ 6:53
19 ☿ ☌ ♀ 5: 8
♂ □ ♆ 12:46
☿ □ ♃ 13:11
20 ♀ □ ♃ 3:34
☿ ☌ ♄ 10: 1
☽ ☍ ♇ 16:27
21 ♀ S ☊ 12:50
22 ♀ ☌ ♄ 12:46
☽ □ ♅ 13:46
☿ ☌ ♆ 17:15
23 ☿ □ ♂ 2: 0
24 ☽ □ ♃ 5: 0
☽ ☍ ♄ 12: 3
☽ ☍ ♀ 19:13
25 ☽ ☍ ♆ 9: 6
☽ □ ♂ 15: 8
27 ☽ ☍ ☿ 9:12
28 ☽ □ ♇ 3:16
☿ □ ♇ 23:56
29 ♀ ☌ ♆ 2:37
30 ☽ ☍ ♅ 2:50

SIDEREAL GEOCENTRIC LONGITUDES : DECEMBER 2024 Gregorian at 0 hours UT

DAY	☉	☽	☊	☿	♀	♂	♃	♄	♅	♆	♇
1 SU	14 ♏ 12	11 ♏ 10	9 ♓ 25R	25 ♏ 29R	27 ♐ 38	10 ♋ 51	22 ♉ 6R	17 ♒ 49	29 ♈ 35R	2 ♓ 4R	5 ♑ 8
2 MO	15 12	23 42	9 13	24 32	28 48	10 55	21 58	17 50	29 33	2 4	5 9
3 TU	16 13	6 ♐ 27	9 0	23 26	29 58	10 59	21 50	17 52	29 30	2 3	5 11
4 WE	17 14	19 23	8 49	22 12	1 ♑ 8	11 1	21 42	17 54	29 28	2 3	5 12
5 TH	18 15	2 ♑ 31	8 39	20 52	2 18	11 3	21 34	17 56	29 25	2 3	5 14
6 FR	19 16	15 50	8 32	19 30	3 27	11 5	21 25	17 58	29 23	2 3	5 15
7 SA	20 17	29 21	8 28	18 7	4 37	11 5R	21 17	18 0	29 21	2 3	5 17
8 SU	21 18	13 ♒ 2	8 26	16 47	5 46	11 5	21 9	18 3	29 19	2 3	5 18
9 MO	22 19	26 56	8 26D	15 32	6 55	11 3	21 1	18 5	29 16	2 3D	5 19
10 TU	23 20	11 ♓ 3	8 27R	14 25	8 4	11 1	20 53	18 8	29 14	2 3	5 21
11 WE	24 21	25 21	8 26	13 27	9 13	10 58	20 45	18 10	29 12	2 3	5 23
12 TH	25 22	9 ♈ 49	8 22	12 39	10 22	10 55	20 36	18 13	29 10	2 3	5 24
13 FR	26 23	24 23	8 16	12 2	11 31	10 50	20 28	18 16	29 8	2 3	5 26
14 SA	27 24	8 ♉ 57	8 7	11 37	12 39	10 45	20 20	18 19	29 5	2 4	5 27
15 SU	28 25	23 25	7 56	11 22	13 47	10 39	20 12	18 22	29 3	2 4	5 29
16 MO	29 26	7 ♊ 39	7 43	11 19D	14 56	10 32	20 4	18 25	29 1	2 4	5 30
17 TU	0 ♐ 27	21 35	7 31	11 25	16 3	10 24	19 56	18 28	28 59	2 4	5 32
18 WE	1 28	5 ♋ 7	7 19	11 40	17 11	10 15	19 48	18 31	28 57	2 5	5 34
19 TH	2 29	18 14	7 11	12 4	18 19	10 6	19 41	18 34	28 55	2 5	5 35
20 FR	3 30	0 ♌ 58	7 5	12 35	19 26	9 55	19 33	18 38	28 53	2 5	5 37
21 SA	4 31	13 20	7 1	13 13	20 33	9 44	19 25	18 41	28 51	2 6	5 39
22 SU	5 32	25 26	7 0	13 57	21 40	9 32	19 18	18 45	28 49	2 6	5 41
23 MO	6 33	7 ♍ 20	7 0	14 46	22 47	9 19	19 10	18 49	28 48	2 7	5 42
24 TU	7 34	19 8	6 59	15 40	23 54	9 6	19 3	18 53	28 46	2 7	5 44
25 WE	8 35	0 ♎ 55	6 58	16 38	25 0	8 51	18 55	18 56	28 44	2 8	5 46
26 TH	9 37	12 48	6 54	17 40	26 6	8 36	18 48	19 0	28 42	2 9	5 48
27 FR	10 38	24 50	6 48	18 45	27 12	8 20	18 41	19 4	28 41	2 9	5 49
28 SA	11 39	7 ♏ 6	6 39	19 53	28 18	8 3	18 34	19 9	28 39	2 10	5 51
29 SU	12 40	19 37	6 27	21 3	29 23	7 46	18 27	19 13	28 37	2 11	5 53
30 MO	13 41	2 ♐ 25	6 14	22 16	0 ♒ 28	7 28	18 21	19 17	28 36	2 11	5 55
31 TU	14 42	15 30	6 0	23 31	1 33	7 9	18 14	19 22	28 34	2 12	5 57

INGRESSES :

2 ☽ → ♐ 11:54
3 ♀ → ♑ 0:37
4 ☽ → ♑ 19:25
7 ☽ → ♒ 1: 9
9 ☽ → ♓ 5:14
11 ☽ → ♈ 7:44
13 ☽ → ♉ 9:15
15 ☽ → ♊ 11: 2
16 ☉ → ♐ 13:29
17 ☽ → ♋ 14:50
19 ☽ → ♌ 22: 9
22 ☽ → ♍ 9:11
24 ☽ → ♎ 22: 7
27 ☽ → ♏ 10: 9
29 ♀ → ♒ 13:38
☽ → ♐ 19:29

ASPECTS & ECLIPSES :

1 ☉ ☌ ☽ 6:20
☽ ☍ ♃ 20:43
2 ☽ ☌ ☿ 1:27
3 ☽ S ☊ 4:42
4 ☿ ☍ ♃ 10:14
☉ □ ♄ 16:17
☽ ☌ ♀ 23:33
5 ☽ ☌ ♇ 4:54
☽ ☍ ♂ 15:26
6 ☉ ☌ ☿ 2:16
7 ☿ □ ♄ 1:52
♀ ☌ ♇ 14: 2
☉ ☍ ♃ 20:56
8 ☽ ☌ ♄ 8:42
☉ □ ☽ 15:25
9 ☽ ☌ ♆ 8:44
☽ ☌ ☊ 19:35
12 ♀ ☍ ♂ 10:44
☽ ☌ P 13:34
13 ☽ ☌ ♅ 7:47
14 ☽ ☍ ☿ 4:18
☽ ☌ ♃ 18:41
15 ☉ ☍ ☽ 9: 0
16 ☽ N ☊ 0: 6
18 ☽ ☍ ♇ 0:48
☽ ☌ ♂ 9:11
☉ □ ♆ 14:37
19 ☽ ☍ ♀ 0: 9
21 ☽ ☍ ♄ 10:37
22 ☽ ☍ ♆ 13:26
☉ □ ☽ 22:17
☽ ☌ ☋ 23:19
23 ☉ □ ☊ 10:24
24 ☽ ☌ A 7:33
♃ □ ♄ 21:56
26 ☿ ☍ ♃ 22:46
27 ☿ □ ♄ 7:27
☽ ☍ ♅ 7:32
28 ♀ □ ♅ 7:39
☽ ☍ ♃ 21:48
29 ☽ ☌ ☿ 2:59
☉ □ π 14: 7
30 ☽ S ☊ 6:55
☉ ☌ ☽ 22:25

SIDEREAL HELIOCENTRIC LONGITUDES : DECEMBER 2024 Gregorian at 0 hours UT

DAY	Sid. Time	☿	♀	⊕	♂	♃	♄	♅	♆	♇	Vernal Point
1 SU	4:41:23	17 ♈ 59	6 ♓ 51	14 ♉ 12	9 ♊ 24	20 ♉ 34	23 ♒ 41	0 ♉ 18	3 ♓ 52	6 ♑ 23	4 ♓ 54'44"
2 MO	4:45:19	23 58	8 27	15 13	9 54	20 39	23 43	0 19	3 52	6 24	4 ♓ 54'44"
3 TU	4:49:16	0 ♉ 3	10 2	16 14	10 23	20 44	23 45	0 20	3 52	6 24	4 ♓ 54'44"
4 WE	4:53:12	6 14	11 38	17 15	10 52	20 50	23 47	0 20	3 53	6 24	4 ♓ 54'44"
5 TH	4:57: 9	12 28	13 13	18 15	11 21	20 55	23 48	0 21	3 53	6 24	4 ♓ 54'44"
6 FR	5: 1: 5	18 46	14 49	19 16	11 50	21 0	23 50	0 22	3 54	6 25	4 ♓ 54'44"
7 SA	5: 5: 2	25 5	16 25	20 17	12 18	21 5	23 52	0 22	3 54	6 25	4 ♓ 54'43"
8 SU	5: 8:59	1 ♊ 24	18 0	21 18	12 47	21 11	23 54	0 23	3 54	6 25	4 ♓ 54'43"
9 MO	5:12:55	7 42	19 36	22 19	13 16	21 16	23 56	0 24	3 55	6 26	4 ♓ 54'43"
10 TU	5:16:52	13 56	21 11	23 20	13 45	21 21	23 58	0 24	3 55	6 26	4 ♓ 54'43"
11 WE	5:20:48	20 6	22 47	24 21	14 14	21 26	24 0	0 25	3 55	6 26	4 ♓ 54'43"
12 TH	5:24:45	26 11	24 23	25 22	14 42	21 31	24 2	0 26	3 56	6 26	4 ♓ 54'43"
13 FR	5:28:41	2 ♋ 8	25 59	26 23	15 11	21 37	24 4	0 27	3 56	6 27	4 ♓ 54'43"
14 SA	5:32:38	7 57	27 34	27 24	15 40	21 42	24 6	0 27	3 56	6 27	4 ♓ 54'42"
15 SU	5:36:34	13 39	29 10	28 25	16 8	21 47	24 8	0 28	3 57	6 27	4 ♓ 54'42"
16 MO	5:40:31	19 10	0 ♈ 46	29 26	16 37	21 52	24 10	0 29	3 57	6 28	4 ♓ 54'42"
17 TU	5:44:28	24 33	2 22	0 ♊ 27	17 5	21 58	24 12	0 29	3 58	6 28	4 ♓ 54'42"
18 WE	5:48:24	29 46	3 58	1 28	17 34	22 3	24 14	0 30	3 58	6 28	4 ♓ 54'42"
19 TH	5:52:21	4 ♌ 49	5 33	2 29	18 2	22 8	24 16	0 31	3 58	6 28	4 ♓ 54'42"
20 FR	5:56:17	9 43	7 9	3 30	18 31	22 13	24 18	0 31	3 59	6 29	4 ♓ 54'42"
21 SA	6: 0:14	14 27	8 45	4 31	18 59	22 19	24 20	0 32	3 59	6 29	4 ♓ 54'41"
22 SU	6: 4:10	19 2	10 21	5 32	19 27	22 24	24 22	0 33	3 59	6 29	4 ♓ 54'41"
23 MO	6: 8: 7	23 28	11 57	6 34	19 56	22 29	24 24	0 33	4 0	6 29	4 ♓ 54'41"
24 TU	6:12: 3	27 46	13 33	7 35	20 24	22 34	24 26	0 34	4 0	6 30	4 ♓ 54'41"
25 WE	6:16: 0	1 ♍ 56	15 9	8 36	20 52	22 39	24 28	0 35	4 0	6 30	4 ♓ 54'41"
26 TH	6:19:57	5 58	16 45	9 37	21 20	22 45	24 30	0 35	4 1	6 30	4 ♓ 54'41"
27 FR	6:23:53	9 53	18 21	10 38	21 48	22 50	24 32	0 36	4 1	6 31	4 ♓ 54'41"
28 SA	6:27:50	13 41	19 57	11 39	22 16	22 55	24 34	0 37	4 2	6 31	4 ♓ 54'41"
29 SU	6:31:46	17 23	21 34	12 40	22 44	23 0	24 36	0 37	4 2	6 31	4 ♓ 54'40"
30 MO	6:35:43	20 59	23 10	13 42	23 13	23 6	24 38	0 38	4 2	6 31	4 ♓ 54'40"
31 TU	6:39:39	24 29	24 46	14 43	23 41	23 11	24 40	0 39	4 3	6 32	4 ♓ 54'40"

INGRESSES :

2 ☿ → ♉ 23:48
7 ☿ → ♊ 18:38
12 ☿ → ♋ 15:21
15 ♀ → ♈ 12:30
16 ⊕ → ♊ 13:21
18 ☿ → ♌ 1: 6
24 ☿ → ♍ 12:47

ASPECTS (HELIOCENTRIC +MOON(TYCHONIC)) :

1 ☽ ☍ ♃ 18: 9
☿ ☌ ☊ 22:19
2 ☽ □ ♄ 0: 0
☽ □ ♆ 19:11
3 ☿ ☌ ♅ 1: 6
♀ □ ♂ 7:17
☽ ☍ ♂ 7:36
☽ □ ♀ 7:38
5 ☽ ☌ ♇ 7: 2
6 ☿ ☌ ⊕ 2:16
☿ ☌ ♃ 8:35
☿ ☌ P 15: 8
☿ □ ♄ 19:21
7 ☽ □ ♅ 1:48
⊕ ☌ ♃ 20:42
8 ☿ □ ♆ 9:31
☽ □ ♃ 14:10
☽ ☌ ♄ 18:50
9 ☽ ☌ ♆ 11:54
☿ ☌ ♂ 23:11
10 ☽ □ ♂ 4:43
☽ □ ☿ 8:38
⊕ □ ♄ 15:33
☽ ☌ ♀ 19:11
11 ☿ □ ♀ 14:18
☽ □ ♇ 18:25
13 ☽ ☌ ♅ 9:59
☿ ☍ ♇ 17:43
14 ☽ ☌ ♃ 21:16
15 ☽ □ ♄ 1:12
☽ □ ♆ 17:42
16 ☽ ☌ ♂ 15:54
☿ N ☊ 19:25
17 ☽ □ ♀ 21:38
18 ☽ ☍ ♇ 2:26
☿ □ ♅ 3:26
19 ♀ □ ♇ 13:47
☽ □ ♅ 23: 9
20 ⊕ □ ♆ 11:14
21 ☽ ☌ ☿ 3:32
☽ □ ♃ 17:53
☽ ☍ ♄ 21:52
22 ☽ ☍ ♆ 17:15
☿ □ ♃ 18:29
23 ☿ ☍ ♄ 5: 9
24 ☽ □ ♂ 2:41
25 ☽ □ ♇ 11:18
☿ ☍ ♆ 12:17
26 ☽ ☍ ♀ 9: 8
27 ☿ □ ⊕ 6:24
☽ ☍ ♅ 11:20
29 ☽ ☍ ♃ 6:26
☽ □ ♄ 9:24
30 ☽ □ ♆ 2:59
☿ □ ♂ 17:32
31 ☽ ☍ ♂ 15:17
☽ □ ☿ 21:46

EPHEMERIDES FOR THE MINISTRY OF CHRIST

SIDEREAL GEOCENTRIC LONGITUDES : APRIL 29 Julian at 0 hours UT

DAY	☉	☽	☊	☿	♀	♂	♃	♄	♅	♆	♇
1 FR	11 ♈ 41	22 ♓ 45	24 ♊ 0R	24 ♈ 40	13 ♈ 24	10 ♉ 57	26 ♒ 21	26 ♉ 7	1 ♌ 1R	24 ♑ 31	9 ♐ 4R
2 SA	12 39	4 ♈ 38	23 46	26 36	14 38	11 37	26 33	26 14	1 1	24 31	9 4
3 SU	13 37	16 33	23 33	28 30	15 52	12 17	26 45	26 20	1 0	24 32	9 3
4 MO	14 35	28 33	23 22	0 ♉ 21	17 6	12 58	26 57	26 27	1 0	24 33	9 2
5 TU	15 33	10 ♉ 39	23 13	2 8	18 20	13 38	27 9	26 33	1 0	24 34	9 2
6 WE	16 31	22 52	23 6	3 53	19 34	14 18	27 21	26 40	1 0	24 34	9 1
7 TH	17 29	5 ♊ 14	23 2	5 34	20 47	14 58	27 32	26 47	1 0	24 35	9 0
8 FR	18 27	17 49	23 1	7 11	22 1	15 38	27 44	26 53	1 0D	24 36	8 59
9 SA	19 25	0 ♋ 39	23 1D	8 45	23 15	16 18	27 56	27 0	1 0	24 36	8 58
10 SU	20 23	13 47	23 2	10 15	24 29	16 58	28 7	27 7	1 0	24 37	8 58
11 MO	21 21	27 18	23 2R	11 41	25 43	17 38	28 18	27 14	1 0	24 37	8 57
12 TU	22 19	11 ♌ 12	23 0	13 3	26 57	18 18	28 30	27 21	1 0	24 38	8 56
13 WE	23 16	25 31	22 56	14 21	28 11	18 58	28 41	27 28	1 1	24 38	8 55
14 TH	24 14	10 ♍ 13	22 51	15 36	29 24	19 38	28 52	27 35	1 1	24 39	8 54
15 FR	25 12	25 12	22 43	16 46	0 ♉ 38	20 18	29 3	27 42	1 1	24 39	8 53
16 SA	26 10	10 ♎ 20	22 35	17 52	1 52	20 57	29 14	27 49	1 2	24 39	8 52
17 SU	27 7	25 27	22 27	18 54	3 6	21 37	29 24	27 56	1 2	24 40	8 51
18 MO	28 5	10 ♏ 23	22 20	19 51	4 19	22 17	29 35	28 3	1 3	24 40	8 50
19 TU	29 3	25 0	22 15	20 44	5 33	22 57	29 46	28 10	1 3	24 40	8 49
20 WE	0 ♉ 0	9 ♐ 12	22 12	21 33	6 47	23 36	29 56	28 18	1 4	24 40	8 48
21 TH	0 58	22 56	22 12	22 18	8 1	24 16	0 ♓ 6	28 25	1 5	24 41	8 46
22 FR	1 55	6 ♑ 12	22 12D	22 58	9 14	24 56	0 17	28 32	1 5	24 41	8 45
23 SA	2 53	19 3	22 13	23 33	10 28	25 35	0 27	28 40	1 6	24 41	8 44
24 SU	3 51	1 ♒ 33	22 14	24 4	11 42	26 15	0 37	28 47	1 7	24 41	8 43
25 MO	4 48	13 46	22 13R	24 29	12 55	26 55	0 47	28 54	1 8	24 41	8 42
26 TU	5 46	25 48	22 11	24 51	14 9	27 34	0 57	29 2	1 9	24 41	8 41
27 WE	6 43	7 ♓ 42	22 7	25 7	15 23	28 14	1 6	29 9	1 10	24 41R	8 39
28 TH	7 41	19 34	22 1	25 19	16 36	28 53	1 16	29 17	1 11	24 41	8 38
29 FR	8 38	1 ♈ 26	21 54	25 26	17 50	29 32	1 25	29 24	1 12	24 41	8 37
30 SA	9 35	13 21	21 46	25 29	19 4	0 ♊ 12	1 35	29 32	1 13	24 41	8 35

INGRESSES :

1 ☽ → ♈ 14:39
3 ☿ → ♉ 19:28
4 ☽ → ♉ 2:52
6 ☽ → ♊ 13:53
8 ☽ → ♋ 22:48
11 ☽ → ♌ 4:43
13 ☽ → ♍ 7:22
14 ♀ → ♉ 11:35
15 ☽ → ♎ 7:38
17 ☽ → ♏ 7:15
19 ☽ → ♐ 8:21
☉ → ♉ 23:54
20 ♃ → ♓ 8:59
21 ☽ → ♑ 12:41
23 ☽ → ♒ 20:59
26 ☽ → ♓ 8:26
28 ☽ → ♈ 21: 6
29 ♂ → ♊ 16:44

ASPECTS & ECLIPSES :

1 ☽ ⊓S ☊ 2:28
2 ☉ ☌ ☽ 17:34
☽ ☌ ♀ 22:27
4 ☽ ☌ ☿ 4:11
☿ □ ♅ 8:43
5 ☽ ☌ ♂ 6:13
6 ☽ ☌ ♄ 7:28
7 ☽ ☍ ♇ 7:13
8 ☽ ☌ ☊ 9:47
10 ♀ □ ♆ 2:30
☉ □ ☽ 12:42
☽ ☍ ♆ 19:17
11 ☽ ☌ ♅ 6:27
13 ☽ ☍ ♃ 5:16
14 ☉ □ ♆ 10:13
☽ ⊓N ☊ 20: 5
15 ♀ □ ♅ 7:34
☽ ☌ P 22:51
17 ☉ ☍ ☽ 2:50
☽ ☍ ♀ 13:19
18 ☽ ☍ ☿ 16:29
☽ ☍ ♂ 20:24
19 ☽ ☍ ♄ 5:20
☽ ☌ ♇ 23:18
20 ☽ ☌ ☋ 22:41
21 ☉ □ ♅ 2:52
23 ☽ ☌ ♆ 10:44
☽ ☍ ♅ 23: 9
24 ☉ □ ☽ 4:50
26 ☽ ☌ ♃ 10:29
28 ☽ ⊓S ☊ 4:54
☽ ☌ A 6:28
♂ ☌ ♄ 17:46

SIDEREAL HELIOCENTRIC LONGITUDES : APRIL 29 Julian at 0 hours UT

DAY	Sid. Time	☿	♀	⊕	♂	♃	♄	♅	♆	♇	Vernal Point
1 FR	12:28:48	11 ♊ 34	15 ♈ 48	11 ♎ 41	29 ♉ 11	18 ♒ 6	0 ♊ 39	3 ♌ 59	22 ♑ 39	7 ♐ 32	2♈39' 6"
2 SA	12:32:45	17 42	17 25	12 39	29 41	18 11	0 42	4 0	22 39	7 32	2♈39' 6"
3 SU	12:36:42	23 44	19 1	13 38	0 ♊ 10	18 17	0 44	4 1	22 39	7 32	2♈39' 6"
4 MO	12:40:38	29 40	20 37	14 36	0 39	18 22	0 46	4 1	22 40	7 33	2♈39' 5"
5 TU	12:44:35	5 ♋ 28	22 13	15 34	1 8	18 27	0 48	4 2	22 40	7 33	2♈39' 5"
6 WE	12:48:31	11 7	23 49	16 32	1 37	18 33	0 51	4 3	22 40	7 34	2♈39' 5"
7 TH	12:52:28	16 37	25 26	17 30	2 6	18 38	0 53	4 4	22 41	7 34	2♈39' 5"
8 FR	12:56:24	21 58	27 2	18 28	2 35	18 44	0 55	4 5	22 41	7 34	2♈39' 5"
9 SA	13: 0:21	27 10	28 38	19 26	3 4	18 49	0 58	4 5	22 41	7 35	2♈39' 5"
10 SU	13: 4:17	2 ♌ 12	0 ♉ 15	20 23	3 33	18 55	1 0	4 6	22 42	7 35	2♈39' 5"
11 MO	13: 8:14	7 4	1 51	21 21	4 2	19 0	1 2	4 7	22 42	7 35	2♈39' 4"
12 TU	13:12:11	11 48	3 28	22 19	4 31	19 5	1 4	4 8	22 43	7 36	2♈39' 4"
13 WE	13:16: 7	16 22	5 4	23 17	5 0	19 11	1 7	4 8	22 43	7 36	2♈39' 4"
14 TH	13:20: 4	20 47	6 41	24 15	5 28	19 16	1 9	4 9	22 43	7 36	2♈39' 4"
15 FR	13:24: 0	25 4	8 17	25 13	5 57	19 22	1 11	4 10	22 44	7 37	2♈39' 4"
16 SA	13:27:57	29 14	9 54	26 10	6 26	19 27	1 13	4 11	22 44	7 37	2♈39' 4"
17 SU	13:31:53	3 ♍ 15	11 30	27 8	6 54	19 32	1 16	4 11	22 44	7 37	2♈39' 4"
18 MO	13:35:50	7 10	13 7	28 6	7 23	19 38	1 18	4 12	22 45	7 38	2♈39' 3"
19 TU	13:39:46	10 58	14 44	29 3	7 52	19 43	1 20	4 13	22 45	7 38	2♈39' 3"
20 WE	13:43:43	14 39	16 21	0 ♏ 1	8 20	19 49	1 23	4 14	22 45	7 38	2♈39' 3"
21 TH	13:47:40	18 15	17 57	0 58	8 49	19 54	1 25	4 14	22 46	7 39	2♈39' 3"
22 FR	13:51:36	21 45	19 34	1 56	9 17	19 59	1 27	4 15	22 46	7 39	2♈39' 3"
23 SA	13:55:33	25 10	21 11	2 54	9 45	20 5	1 29	4 16	22 46	7 39	2♈39' 3"
24 SU	13:59:29	28 30	22 48	3 51	10 14	20 10	1 32	4 17	22 47	7 40	2♈39' 3"
25 MO	14: 3:26	1 ♎ 46	24 25	4 49	10 42	20 16	1 34	4 18	22 47	7 40	2♈39' 3"
26 TU	14: 7:22	4 59	26 2	5 46	11 10	20 21	1 36	4 18	22 48	7 40	2♈39' 2"
27 WE	14:11:19	8 7	27 38	6 44	11 39	20 27	1 38	4 19	22 48	7 41	2♈39' 2"
28 TH	14:15:15	11 12	29 15	7 41	12 7	20 32	1 41	4 20	22 48	7 41	2♈39' 2"
29 FR	14:19:12	14 14	0 ♊ 52	8 39	12 35	20 37	1 43	4 21	22 49	7 41	2♈39' 2"
30 SA	14:23: 9	17 13	2 29	9 36	13 3	20 43	1 45	4 21	22 49	7 42	2♈39' 2"

INGRESSES :

2 ♂ → ♊ 15:51
4 ☿ → ♋ 1:22
9 ☿ → ♌ 13:25
♀ → ♉ 20:18
16 ☿ → ♍ 4:33
19 ⊕ → ♏ 23:39
24 ☿ → ♎ 10:54
28 ♀ → ♊ 11: 1

ASPECTS (HELIOCENTRIC +MOON(TYCHONIC)) :

3 ☽ ☌ ♀ 5:41
☽ □ ♆ 12:13
4 ♂ ☌ ♄ 6:21
☽ □ ♅ 10:53
5 ♀ □ ♆ 6:43
☽ □ ♃ 15:29
6 ☽ ☌ ♄ 15:34
☽ ☌ ♂ 17:42
7 ☽ ☍ ♇ 4:28
☿ □ ⊕ 4:42
8 ☿ ☍ ♆ 3:14
9 ☿ ⊓N ☊ 2:23
☿ □ ♀ 10:11
10 ☿ ☌ ♅ 9:18
☽ ☍ ♆ 15:54
11 ☽ □ ♀ 8:59
☽ ☌ ♅ 11:51
12 ☽ ☌ ☿ 1:29
⊕ □ ♆ 9:44
♀ □ ♅ 10: 0
☽ ☍ ♃ 13:22
13 ☽ □ ♄ 9:12
☿ ☍ ♃ 15:30
☽ □ ♂ 16: 3
☽ □ ♇ 19:46
16 ☿ □ ♄ 11:55
☽ □ ♆ 19:40
17 ☽ □ ♅ 14: 0
18 ☿ □ ♂ 1:34
☿ □ ♇ 2:54
☽ ☍ ♀ 4:58
♂ ☍ ♇ 12:30
☽ □ ♃ 15:11
19 ☽ ☍ ♄ 10:38
☽ ☌ ♇ 21:19
☽ ☍ ♂ 22:27
20 ☽ □ ☿ 12:47
22 ♀ □ ♃ 6:39
23 ☽ ☌ ♆ 7: 5
24 ☽ ☍ ♅ 5:19
⊕ □ ♅ 10:50
25 ☽ ☌ ♃ 13: 0
26 ☽ □ ♀ 0:31
☽ □ ♄ 11:42
☽ □ ♇ 23:56
27 ☽ □ ♂ 8:17
29 ♀ ☌ ☊ 12:43
♀ ☌ ♄ 12:48
30 ☽ ☍ ☿ 10:15
♆ ☌ ☋ 14: 1
☽ □ ♆ 18:55

SIDEREAL GEOCENTRIC LONGITUDES : MAY 29 Julian at 0 hours UT

DAY	☉	☽	☊	☿	♀	♂	♃	♄	♅	♆	♇
1 SU	10 ♉ 33	25 ♈ 22	21 ♊ 38R	25 ♉ 26R	20 ♉ 17	0 ♊ 51	1 ♓ 44	29 ♉ 39	1 ♌ 14	24 ♑ 41R	8 ♐ 34R
2 MO	11 30	7 ♉ 31	21 31	25 20	21 31	1 31	1 53	29 47	1 16	24 41	8 33
3 TU	12 28	19 48	21 26	25 9	22 44	2 10	2 2	29 55	1 17	24 40	8 31
4 WE	13 25	2 ♊ 15	21 23	24 54	23 58	2 49	2 11	0 ♊ 2	1 18	24 40	8 30
5 TH	14 22	14 52	21 21	24 35	25 12	3 29	2 20	0 10	1 20	24 40	8 29
6 FR	15 20	27 42	21 21D	24 13	26 25	4 8	2 28	0 18	1 21	24 40	8 27
7 SA	16 17	10 ♋ 45	21 22	23 48	27 39	4 47	2 37	0 25	1 23	24 39	8 26
8 SU	17 14	24 4	21 24	23 20	28 52	5 27	2 45	0 33	1 24	24 39	8 25
9 MO	18 12	7 ♌ 38	21 25	22 50	0 ♊ 6	6 6	2 53	0 41	1 26	24 39	8 23
10 TU	19 9	21 31	21 25R	22 18	1 19	6 45	3 1	0 49	1 27	24 38	8 22
11 WE	20 6	5 ♍ 40	21 24	21 45	2 33	7 24	3 9	0 56	1 29	24 38	8 20
12 TH	21 4	20 6	21 22	21 11	3 46	8 3	3 17	1 4	1 31	24 37	8 19
13 FR	22 1	4 ♎ 43	21 19	20 37	5 0	8 42	3 24	1 12	1 33	24 37	8 17
14 SA	22 58	19 28	21 15	20 4	6 13	9 21	3 32	1 20	1 35	24 36	8 16
15 SU	23 55	4 ♏ 13	21 11	19 32	7 27	10 0	3 39	1 28	1 36	24 36	8 14
16 MO	24 52	18 50	21 8	19 2	8 40	10 39	3 46	1 35	1 38	24 35	8 13
17 TU	25 49	3 ♐ 13	21 6	18 34	9 54	11 18	3 54	1 43	1 40	24 34	8 11
18 WE	26 47	17 17	21 6	18 9	11 7	11 57	4 0	1 51	1 42	24 34	8 10
19 TH	27 44	0 ♑ 57	21 6D	17 47	12 21	12 36	4 7	1 59	1 44	24 33	8 8
20 FR	28 41	14 14	21 7	17 28	13 34	13 15	4 14	2 7	1 47	24 32	8 7
21 SA	29 38	27 8	21 8	17 13	14 47	13 54	4 20	2 15	1 49	24 32	8 5
22 SU	0 ♊ 35	9 ♒ 41	21 10	17 2	16 1	14 33	4 26	2 22	1 51	24 31	8 4
23 MO	1 32	21 58	21 11	16 55	17 14	15 12	4 33	2 30	1 53	24 30	8 2
24 TU	2 30	4 ♓ 2	21 11R	16 53D	18 28	15 51	4 39	2 38	1 55	24 29	8 1
25 WE	3 27	15 58	21 10	16 55	19 41	16 30	4 44	2 46	1 58	24 28	7 59
26 TH	4 24	27 51	21 9	17 3	20 54	17 9	4 50	2 54	2 0	24 27	7 58
27 FR	5 21	9 ♈ 45	21 7	17 14	22 8	17 48	4 55	3 2	2 2	24 26	7 56
28 SA	6 18	21 43	21 5	17 31	23 21	18 26	5 1	3 10	2 5	24 26	7 55
29 SU	7 15	3 ♉ 50	21 3	17 52	24 34	19 5	5 6	3 18	2 7	24 25	7 53
30 MO	8 12	16 7	21 1	18 18	25 48	19 44	5 11	3 25	2 10	24 24	7 52
31 TU	9 9	28 37	21 0	18 49	27 1	20 23	5 16	3 33	2 12	24 23	7 50

INGRESSES :

1 ☽ → ♉ 9:10	21 ☽ → ♒ 5:25
3 ♄ → ♊ 17: 0	☉ → ♊ 9:12
☽ → ♊ 19:41	23 ☽ → ♓ 15:56
6 ☽ → ♋ 4:15	26 ☽ → ♈ 4:21
8 ☽ → ♌ 10:33	28 ☽ → ♉ 16:26
♀ → ♊ 22: 5	31 ☽ → ♊ 2:38
10 ☽ → ♍ 14:26	
12 ☽ → ♎ 16:16	
14 ☽ → ♏ 17: 7	
16 ☽ → ♐ 18:35	
18 ☽ → ♑ 22:18	

ASPECTS & ECLIPSES :

2 ☉ ☌ ☽ 8:29	9 ♀ ☌ ♄ 12:44	☽ ☍ ♄ 21:27	25 ☽ S ☊ 10:29
♂ □ ♃ 17:38	☉ □ ☽ 19:39	17 ☽ ☌ ♇ 8:24	☽ ☌ A 22:40
3 ☽ ☌ ♀ 6:19	10 ☽ ☍ ♃ 19:43	☽ ☍ ♀ 12:23	26 ♀ ☌ ☊ 4:39
☽ ☌ ☿ 10:10	11 ♀ □ ♃ 13:12	☽ ☍ ♂ 14:24	☉ □ ♃ 12:11
☽ ☌ ♄ 19:43	12 ☉ i☌ ☿ 1:58	18 ☽ ☌ ☋ 6:37	29 ☉ ☍ ♇ 15:30
4 ☽ ☌ ♂ 1:10	☽ N ☊ 2: 5	19 ♀ ☌ ♂ 11: 4	30 ☽ ☌ ☿ 4:24
☽ ☍ ♇ 11:54	♂ ☍ ♇ 9:15	20 ☽ ☌ ♆ 19: 6	31 ☽ ☌ ♄ 9:28
☿ ☌ ♀ 14:38	14 ☽ ☌ P 1: 9	21 ☽ ☍ ♅ 8:54	☽ ☍ ♇ 17:24
5 ☽ ☌ ☊ 12: 9	15 ♀ ☍ ♇ 15:14	23 ☉ □ ☽ 20:39	☉ ☌ ☽ 21:31
8 ☽ ☍ ♆ 1: 3	16 ☽ ☍ ☿ 0:19	24 ☽ ☌ ♃ 1:14	☉ ● P 21:40
☽ ☌ ♅ 13: 4	☉ ☍ ☽ 10:43	☉ ☌ ♄ 4:13	♂ ☌ ☊ 22:31

SIDEREAL HELIOCENTRIC LONGITUDES : MAY 29 Julian at 0 hours UT

DAY	Sid. Time	☿	♀	⊕	♂	♃	♄	♅	♆	♇	Vernal Point
1 SU	14:27: 5	20 ♎ 9	4 ♐ 7	10 ♏ 34	13 ♊ 31	20 ♒ 48	1 ♊ 48	4 ♌ 22	22 ♑ 49	7 ♐ 42	2♈39' 2"
2 MO	14:31: 2	23 4	5 44	11 31	14 0	20 54	1 50	4 23	22 50	7 43	2♈39' 2"
3 TU	14:34:58	25 56	7 21	12 28	14 28	20 59	1 52	4 24	22 50	7 43	2♈39' 1"
4 WE	14:38:55	28 47	8 58	13 26	14 56	21 4	1 54	4 24	22 50	7 43	2♈39' 1"
5 TH	14:42:51	1 ♏ 36	10 35	14 23	15 24	21 10	1 57	4 25	22 51	7 44	2♈39' 1"
6 FR	14:46:48	4 23	12 12	15 20	15 52	21 15	1 59	4 26	22 51	7 44	2♈39' 1"
7 SA	14:50:44	7 10	13 50	16 18	16 20	21 21	2 1	4 27	22 52	7 44	2♈39' 1"
8 SU	14:54:41	9 56	15 27	17 15	16 47	21 26	2 3	4 27	22 52	7 45	2♈39' 1"
9 MO	14:58:38	12 41	17 4	18 12	17 15	21 32	2 6	4 28	22 52	7 45	2♈39' 1"
10 TU	15: 2:34	15 26	18 41	19 10	17 43	21 37	2 8	4 29	22 53	7 45	2♈39' 0"
11 WE	15: 6:31	18 11	20 19	20 7	18 11	21 42	2 10	4 30	22 53	7 46	2♈39' 0"
12 TH	15:10:27	20 55	21 56	21 4	18 39	21 48	2 13	4 31	22 53	7 46	2♈39' 0"
13 FR	15:14:24	23 40	23 33	22 1	19 6	21 53	2 15	4 31	22 54	7 46	2♈39' 0"
14 SA	15:18:20	26 25	25 11	22 59	19 34	21 59	2 17	4 32	22 54	7 47	2♈39' 0"
15 SU	15:22:17	29 11	26 48	23 56	20 2	22 4	2 19	4 33	22 54	7 47	2♈39' 0"
16 MO	15:26:13	1 ♐ 58	28 26	24 53	20 30	22 9	2 22	4 34	22 55	7 47	2♈39' 0"
17 TU	15:30:10	4 45	0 ♋ 3	25 50	20 57	22 15	2 24	4 34	22 55	7 48	2♈39' 0"
18 WE	15:34: 7	7 34	1 41	26 47	21 25	22 20	2 26	4 35	22 55	7 48	2♈38'59"
19 TH	15:38: 3	10 24	3 18	27 44	21 52	22 26	2 28	4 36	22 56	7 48	2♈38'59"
20 FR	15:42: 0	13 16	4 56	28 42	22 20	22 31	2 31	4 37	22 56	7 49	2♈38'59"
21 SA	15:45:56	16 10	6 33	29 39	22 47	22 37	2 33	4 37	22 57	7 49	2♈38'59"
22 SU	15:49:53	19 6	8 11	0 ♐ 36	23 15	22 42	2 35	4 38	22 57	7 49	2♈38'59"
23 MO	15:53:49	22 5	9 48	1 33	23 42	22 47	2 38	4 39	22 57	7 50	2♈38'59"
24 TU	15:57:46	25 6	11 26	2 30	24 10	22 53	2 40	4 40	22 58	7 50	2♈38'59"
25 WE	16: 1:42	28 10	13 4	3 27	24 37	22 58	2 42	4 40	22 58	7 50	2♈38'58"
26 TH	16: 5:39	1 ♑ 17	14 41	4 24	25 5	23 4	2 44	4 41	22 58	7 51	2♈38'58"
27 FR	16: 9:36	4 28	16 19	5 22	25 32	23 9	2 47	4 42	22 59	7 51	2♈38'58"
28 SA	16:13:32	7 42	17 56	6 19	25 59	23 15	2 49	4 43	22 59	7 52	2♈38'58"
29 SU	16:17:29	11 0	19 34	7 16	26 27	23 20	2 51	4 44	22 59	7 52	2♈38'58"
30 MO	16:21:25	14 23	21 12	8 13	26 54	23 25	2 53	4 44	23 0	7 52	2♈38'58"
31 TU	16:25:22	17 51	22 49	9 10	27 21	23 31	2 56	4 45	23 0	7 53	2♈38'58"

INGRESSES :

4 ☿ → ♏ 10:23
15 ☿ → ♐ 7: 4
16 ♀ → ♋ 23:12
21 ⊕ → ♐ 8:56
25 ☿ → ♑ 14:11

ASPECTS (HELIOCENTRIC +MOON(TYCHONIC)) :

1 ☽ □ ♅ 17:49	8 ☽ ☌ ♅ 18:26	⊕ □ ♃ 20:13	20 ☽ ☌ ♆ 16: 7	28 ☽ □ ♆ 2:31
☿ □ ♆ 22: 3	9 ♀ ☌ ♂ 3:53	14 ☽ □ ♆ 5:34	21 ☽ ☍ ♅ 14:15	29 ☽ □ ♅ 1:46
3 ☽ □ ♃ 2:19	☽ □ ☿ 10:58	15 ☽ □ ♅ 0:32	23 ☽ ☌ ♃ 1:38	⊕ ☌ ♇ 15:13
♀ ☍ ♇ 5:28	10 ☽ ☍ ♃ 0:11	16 ☿ ☍ ♄ 3:30	☿ ☍ ♂ 15:19	30 ☽ □ ♃ 14:11
☿ ☌ ☋ 14:38	☽ □ ♄ 18: 5	☽ □ ♃ 5:32	☽ □ ♄ 21:15	31 ♀ ☍ ♆ 2:37
☽ ☌ ♄ 23:20	11 ☽ □ ♇ 3:30	☽ ☍ ♄ 22:36	24 ⊕ ☍ ♄ 4:13	☽ ☌ ♄ 8:13
4 ☽ ☍ ♇ 10:27	☿ ☌ A 11:59	17 ☽ ☌ ☿ 3:13	☽ □ ♇ 7:37	☽ ☍ ♇ 17:31
☽ ☌ ♀ 14:41	☽ □ ♂ 21:31	☽ ☌ ♇ 7:44	25 ☽ □ ♂ 18:10	
5 ☽ ☌ ♂ 1: 1	12 ☿ ☌ ⊕ 1:58	18 ☿ ☌ ♇ 1:59	26 ☽ □ ☿ 9:27	
6 ☿ □ ♅ 0:21	☽ □ ♀ 3:24	☽ ☍ ♂ 7:25	♀ ☌ P 22:23	
7 ☽ ☍ ♆ 21:51	☿ □ ♃ 7:55	19 ☽ ☍ ♀ 4:46	27 ☽ □ ♀ 15:16	

SIDEREAL GEOCENTRIC LONGITUDES : JUNE 29 Julian at 0 hours UT

DAY	☉	☽	☊	☿	♀	♂	♃	♄	♅	♆	♇
1 WE	10 ♊ 7	11 ♊ 20	20 ♊ 59R	19 ♉ 24	28 ♊ 14	21 ♊ 1	5 ♓ 20	3 ♊ 41	2 ♌ 15	24 ♑ 22R	7 ♐ 48R
2 TH	11 4	24 18	20 59D	20 5	29 28	21 40	5 25	3 49	2 18	24 21	7 47
3 FR	12 1	7 ♋ 29	20 59	20 49	0 ♋ 41	22 19	5 29	3 57	2 20	24 19	7 45
4 SA	12 58	20 54	21 0	21 38	1 54	22 58	5 33	4 5	2 23	24 18	7 44
5 SU	13 55	4 ♌ 32	21 1	22 32	3 7	23 36	5 37	4 12	2 26	24 17	7 42
6 MO	14 52	18 22	21 1	23 30	4 21	24 15	5 41	4 20	2 29	24 16	7 41
7 TU	15 49	2 ♍ 22	21 1	24 32	5 34	24 54	5 44	4 28	2 31	24 15	7 39
8 WE	16 46	16 31	21 1R	25 39	6 47	25 32	5 48	4 36	2 34	24 14	7 38
9 TH	17 44	0 ♎ 47	21 1	26 49	8 0	26 11	5 51	4 43	2 37	24 12	7 36
10 FR	18 41	15 7	21 1	28 4	9 14	26 49	5 54	4 51	2 40	24 11	7 35
11 SA	19 38	29 27	21 1	29 23	10 27	27 28	5 57	4 59	2 43	24 10	7 33
12 SU	20 35	13 ♏ 45	21 1	0 ♊ 46	11 40	28 6	6 0	5 7	2 46	24 9	7 32
13 MO	21 32	27 55	21 1D	2 13	12 53	28 45	6 2	5 14	2 49	24 7	7 30
14 TU	22 29	11 ♐ 54	21 1	3 44	14 6	29 24	6 4	5 22	2 52	24 6	7 29
15 WE	23 26	25 39	21 1R	5 19	15 19	0 ♋ 2	6 6	5 30	2 55	24 5	7 27
16 TH	24 23	9 ♑ 6	21 1	6 57	16 32	0 41	6 8	5 37	2 58	24 3	7 26
17 FR	25 21	22 15	21 1	8 39	17 46	1 19	6 10	5 45	3 1	24 2	7 24
18 SA	26 18	5 ♒ 5	21 0	10 24	18 59	1 58	6 11	5 52	3 4	24 1	7 23
19 SU	27 15	17 37	20 59	12 13	20 12	2 36	6 13	6 0	3 8	23 59	7 21
20 MO	28 12	29 54	20 59	14 5	21 25	3 14	6 14	6 7	3 11	23 58	7 20
21 TU	29 9	11 ♓ 59	20 58	15 59	22 38	3 53	6 15	6 15	3 14	23 56	7 19
22 WE	0 ♋ 6	23 57	20 57	17 56	23 51	4 31	6 16	6 22	3 17	23 55	7 17
23 TH	1 4	5 ♈ 50	20 57D	19 56	25 4	5 10	6 16	6 30	3 21	23 53	7 16
24 FR	2 1	17 44	20 58	21 57	26 17	5 48	6 16	6 37	3 24	23 52	7 14
25 SA	2 58	29 44	20 58	24 0	27 30	6 27	6 17	6 44	3 27	23 50	7 13
26 SU	3 55	11 ♉ 54	20 59	26 4	28 43	7 5	6 17R	6 52	3 31	23 49	7 12
27 MO	4 53	24 17	21 1	28 10	29 56	7 43	6 16	6 59	3 34	23 47	7 10
28 TU	5 50	6 ♊ 57	21 2	0 ♋ 16	1 ♌ 9	8 22	6 16	7 6	3 37	23 46	7 9
29 WE	6 47	19 55	21 2	2 22	2 22	9 0	6 15	7 14	3 41	23 44	7 8
30 TH	7 45	3 ♋ 12	21 2R	4 29	3 35	9 38	6 14	7 21	3 44	23 43	7 7

INGRESSES :

2	☽ → ♋	10:26	20	☽ → ♓	0:11
	♀ → ♋	10:36	21	☉ → ♋	21:17
4	☽ → ♌	16: 2	22	☽ → ♈	12:13
6	☽ → ♍	19:57	25	☽ → ♉	0:31
8	☽ → ♎	22:41	27	♀ → ♌	1:24
11	☽ → ♏	0:54		☽ → ♊	10:54
	☿ → ♊	10:47		☿ → ♋	21: 2
13	☽ → ♐	3:33	29	☽ → ♋	18:16
14	♂ → ♋	22:42			
15	☽ → ♑	7:42			
17	☽ → ♒	14:26			

ASPECTS & ECLIPSES :

1	☽ ☌ ☊	17:54		☽ ☍ ♄	12:37		☽ ☍ ♅	20:11		♄ ☍ ♇	7:50
	☽ ☌ ♂	18:55		☽ ☌ ♇	16:22	20	☽ ☌ ♃	12:32	29	☽ ☌ ☊	2: 2
2	☽ ☌ ♀	10:24	14	☽ ☌ ☋	15:51	21	♃ □ ♄	0:11	30	☽ ☌ ☿	2:41
4	☽ ☍ ♆	6: 0		☽ •–• T	19:42		☽ □S ☊	17:59		♀ ☌ ♅	3:20
	☽ ☌ ♅	20:17		☉ ☍ ☽	19:49	22	♀ ☍ ♆	1:19		☉ ☌ ☽	8:41
7	☽ ☍ ♃	5:45	15	☿ ☌ ♄	2:53		☉ □ ☽	13:31		☽ ☌ ♂	11:59
8	☉ □ ☽	0:27		☽ ☍ ♂	8: 9		☽ ☌ A	16:59			
	☽ □N ☊	7:35		☿ □ ♃	11:56	23	☉ □ Π	10:41			
10	☽ ☌ P	6:43	16	☿ ☍ ♇	6:43		☿ ☌ ☊	12:16			
12	☉ ☌ ☊	10:53		☽ ☍ ♀	14:54	28	☽ ☌ ♄	0:18			
13	☽ ☍ ☿	8:13	17	☽ ☌ ♆	3:18		☽ ☍ ♇	0:23			

SIDEREAL HELIOCENTRIC LONGITUDES : JUNE 29 Julian at 0 hours UT

DAY	Sid. Time	☿	♀	⊕	♂	♃	♄	♅	♆	♇	Vernal Point
1 WE	16:29:18	21 ♑ 23	24 ♋ 27	10 ♐ 7	27 ♊ 48	23 ♒ 36	2 ♊ 58	4 ♌ 46	23 ♑ 0	7 ♐ 53	2 ♈ 38'57"
2 TH	16:33:15	25 1	26 5	11 4	28 16	23 42	3 0	4 47	23 1	7 53	2 ♈ 38'57"
3 FR	16:37:11	28 45	27 42	12 1	28 43	23 47	3 3	4 47	23 1	7 54	2 ♈ 38'57"
4 SA	16:41: 8	2 ♒ 35	29 20	12 59	29 10	23 53	3 5	4 48	23 2	7 54	2 ♈ 38'57"
5 SU	16:45: 5	6 31	0 ♌ 58	13 56	29 37	23 58	3 7	4 49	23 2	7 54	2 ♈ 38'57"
6 MO	16:49: 1	10 35	2 35	14 53	0 ♋ 4	24 3	3 9	4 50	23 2	7 55	2 ♈ 38'57"
7 TU	16:52:58	14 45	4 13	15 50	0 31	24 9	3 12	4 50	23 3	7 55	2 ♈ 38'57"
8 WE	16:56:54	19 3	5 51	16 47	0 58	24 14	3 14	4 51	23 3	7 55	2 ♈ 38'57"
9 TH	17: 0:51	23 30	7 28	17 44	1 25	24 20	3 16	4 52	23 3	7 56	2 ♈ 38'56"
10 FR	17: 4:47	28 4	9 6	18 41	1 53	24 25	3 18	4 53	23 4	7 56	2 ♈ 38'56"
11 SA	17: 8:44	2 ♓ 47	10 44	19 38	2 20	24 31	3 21	4 54	23 4	7 56	2 ♈ 38'56"
12 SU	17:12:40	7 39	12 21	20 36	2 47	24 36	3 23	4 54	23 4	7 57	2 ♈ 38'56"
13 MO	17:16:37	12 40	13 59	21 33	3 13	24 41	3 25	4 55	23 5	7 57	2 ♈ 38'56"
14 TU	17:20:34	17 50	15 37	22 30	3 40	24 47	3 28	4 56	23 5	7 57	2 ♈ 38'56"
15 WE	17:24:30	23 9	17 14	23 27	4 7	24 52	3 30	4 57	23 6	7 58	2 ♈ 38'56"
16 TH	17:28:27	28 37	18 52	24 24	4 34	24 58	3 32	4 57	23 6	7 58	2 ♈ 38'55"
17 FR	17:32:23	4 ♈ 13	20 29	25 21	5 1	25 3	3 34	4 58	23 6	7 58	2 ♈ 38'55"
18 SA	17:36:20	9 58	22 7	26 18	5 28	25 9	3 37	4 59	23 7	7 59	2 ♈ 38'55"
19 SU	17:40:16	15 51	23 44	27 15	5 55	25 14	3 39	5 0	23 7	7 59	2 ♈ 38'55"
20 MO	17:44:13	21 51	25 22	28 13	6 22	25 19	3 41	5 0	23 7	7 59	2 ♈ 38'55"
21 TU	17:48: 9	27 57	26 59	29 10	6 49	25 25	3 43	5 1	23 8	8 0	2 ♈ 38'55"
22 WE	17:52: 6	4 ♉ 8	28 37	0 ♑ 7	7 15	25 30	3 46	5 2	23 8	8 0	2 ♈ 38'55"
23 TH	17:56: 3	10 22	0 ♍ 14	1 4	7 42	25 36	3 48	5 3	23 8	8 0	2 ♈ 38'54"
24 FR	17:59:59	16 40	1 51	2 2	8 9	25 41	3 50	5 3	23 9	8 1	2 ♈ 38'54"
25 SA	18: 3:56	22 58	3 29	2 59	8 36	25 47	3 53	5 4	23 9	8 1	2 ♈ 38'54"
26 SU	18: 7:52	29 16	5 6	3 56	9 2	25 52	3 55	5 5	23 9	8 2	2 ♈ 38'54"
27 MO	18:11:49	5 ♊ 32	6 43	4 53	9 29	25 57	3 57	5 6	23 10	8 2	2 ♈ 38'54"
28 TU	18:15:45	11 45	8 21	5 51	9 56	26 3	3 59	5 7	23 10	8 2	2 ♈ 38'54"
29 WE	18:19:42	17 53	9 58	6 48	10 22	26 8	4 2	5 7	23 11	8 3	2 ♈ 38'54"
30 TH	18:23:38	23 55	11 35	7 45	10 49	26 14	4 4	5 8	23 11	8 3	2 ♈ 38'54"

INGRESSES :

3	☿ → ♒	7:53
4	♀ → ♌	9:47
5	♂ → ♋	20:13
10	☿ → ♓	9:55
16	☿ → ♈	6: 0
21	☿ → ♉	8: 0
	⊕ → ♑	21: 2
22	♀ → ♍	20:31
26	☿ → ♊	2:48

ASPECTS (HELIOCENTRIC +MOON(TYCHONIC)) :

1	☿ ☌ ♆	10:47	7	☽ □ ♄	1:24	13	☽ ☍ ♄	9:25	20	☿ □ ♆	5: 3		☿ □ ♃	10:51
2	☽ ☌ ♂	7:31		♀ ☌ ♅	9:14		☽ ☌ ♇	17:11		☽ □ ♄	7:29	26	☿ ☌ ♄	17:53
	☿ ☍ ♀	12:13		☽ □ ♇	9:26	14	☽ □ ☿	16:44		☽ □ ♇	16: 1	27	☽ □ ♃	3:13
	☿ □S ☊	17: 7	9	☽ □ ♂	1: 6	15	☿ □ ⊕	1:38		☿ ☌ ☊	22:56		☿ □ ♀	6:11
	⊕ ☌ A	20:17		☿ ☌ ♃	4:32		☽ ☍ ♂	15:34	22	☿ □ ♅	3:29		☿ ☍ ♇	9:37
4	☽ ☍ ♆	3:45	10	☽ □ ♆	13:18	17	☽ ☌ ♆	1:35	23	☽ □ ♂	3:55		☽ ☌ ♄	18:25
	☿ ☍ ♅	13:39	11	☿ □ ♄	2:49		☿ □ ♂	3:39		♀ □N ☊	22: 7		♀ □ ♇	19:26
	☽ ☌ ♀	16:53		☽ □ ♅	9: 7		☽ ☍ ♅	23:49	24	☽ □ ♆	10:51	28	☽ ☍ ♇	2: 2
5	☽ ☌ ♅	0:29		☽ □ ♀	21:21	19	☽ ☍ ♀	13:42		☿ ☌ P	10:59		☽ □ ♀	2:59
	☽ ☍ ☿	4:53	12	☿ □ ♇	1:26		☽ ☌ ♃	14:56	25	♀ □ ♄	5:59		☽ ☌ ☿	17: 0
6	☽ ☍ ♃	9:50		☽ □ ♃	18:28		♀ ☍ ♃	23:23		☽ □ ♅	10:35	30	☽ ☌ ♂	13:58

SIDEREAL GEOCENTRIC LONGITUDES : JULY 29 Julian at 0 hours UT											
DAY	☉	☽	☊	☿	♀	♂	♃	♄	⛢	♆	♇
1 FR	8 ♋ 42	16 ♋ 48	21 ♊ 1R	6 ♋ 35	4 ♌ 47	10 ♋ 17	6 ♓ 13R	7 ♊ 28	3 ♌ 48	23 ♑ 41R	7 ♐ 5R
2 SA	9 39	0 ♌ 39	20 59	8 41	6 0	10 55	6 12	7 35	3 51	23 40	7 4
3 SU	10 37	14 44	20 57	10 46	7 13	11 34	6 11	7 42	3 55	23 38	7 3
4 MO	11 34	28 58	20 54	12 51	8 26	12 12	6 9	7 49	3 58	23 37	7 2
5 TU	12 32	13 ♍ 16	20 52	14 54	9 39	12 50	6 7	7 56	4 2	23 35	7 0
6 WE	13 29	27 35	20 50	16 57	10 52	13 28	6 5	8 3	4 5	23 33	6 59
7 TH	14 26	11 ♎ 51	20 49	18 58	12 4	14 7	6 3	8 10	4 9	23 32	6 58
8 FR	15 24	26 1	20 49D	20 58	13 17	14 45	6 1	8 17	4 12	23 30	6 57
9 SA	16 21	10 ♏ 4	20 51	22 57	14 30	15 23	5 58	8 23	4 16	23 29	6 56
10 SU	17 19	23 58	20 52	24 54	15 43	16 2	5 55	8 30	4 20	23 27	6 55
11 MO	18 16	7 ♐ 42	20 53	26 50	16 55	16 40	5 52	8 37	4 23	23 25	6 54
12 TU	19 14	21 14	20 54R	28 44	18 8	17 18	5 49	8 44	4 27	23 24	6 53
13 WE	20 11	4 ♑ 35	20 53	0 ♌ 37	19 21	17 56	5 46	8 50	4 31	23 22	6 52
14 TH	21 9	17 42	20 51	2 28	20 33	18 35	5 42	8 57	4 34	23 20	6 51
15 FR	22 6	0 ♒ 36	20 47	4 18	21 46	19 13	5 39	9 3	4 38	23 19	6 50
16 SA	23 4	13 15	20 42	6 6	22 58	19 51	5 35	9 10	4 42	23 17	6 49
17 SU	24 2	25 41	20 37	7 53	24 11	20 29	5 31	9 16	4 45	23 16	6 48
18 MO	24 59	7 ♓ 55	20 31	9 39	25 23	21 8	5 27	9 22	4 49	23 14	6 47
19 TU	25 57	19 58	20 26	11 23	26 36	21 46	5 22	9 29	4 53	23 12	6 46
20 WE	26 54	1 ♈ 54	20 21	13 5	27 48	22 24	5 18	9 35	4 56	23 11	6 45
21 TH	27 52	13 47	20 19	14 46	29 1	23 2	5 13	9 41	5 0	23 9	6 44
22 FR	28 50	25 40	20 17	16 26	0 ♍ 13	23 41	5 8	9 47	5 4	23 7	6 43
23 SA	29 48	7 ♉ 38	20 17D	18 4	1 25	24 19	5 3	9 53	5 7	23 6	6 43
24 SU	0 ♌ 46	19 47	20 19	19 41	2 38	24 57	4 58	9 59	5 11	23 4	6 42
25 MO	1 43	2 ♊ 11	20 20	21 16	3 50	25 35	4 52	10 5	5 15	23 2	6 41
26 TU	2 41	14 55	20 21	22 50	5 2	26 13	4 47	10 11	5 19	23 1	6 40
27 WE	3 39	28 1	20 21R	24 23	6 14	26 52	4 41	10 16	5 22	22 59	6 40
28 TH	4 37	11 ♋ 32	20 19	25 54	7 27	27 30	4 35	10 22	5 26	22 58	6 39
29 FR	5 35	25 27	20 15	27 24	8 39	28 8	4 29	10 28	5 30	22 56	6 39
30 SA	6 33	9 ♌ 43	20 10	28 52	9 51	28 46	4 23	10 33	5 34	22 54	6 38
31 SU	7 31	24 15	20 3	0 ♍ 19	11 3	29 24	4 17	10 39	5 37	22 53	6 37

INGRESSES :			ASPECTS & ECLIPSES :			
1 ☽ → ♌ 22:52	22 ☽ → ♉ 8:43		1 ☽ ☍ ♆ 11:57	10 ☽ ☌ ♇ 22:35	17 ☽ ☌ ♃ 19: 8	☉ ☌ ⛢ 21:45
4 ☽ → ♍ 1:44	23 ☉ → ♌ 5: 6		2 ☽ ☌ ⛢ 5:29	11 ☽ ☍ ♄ 1:38	19 ☽ ⌂S ☊ 0:54	29 ☽ ☌ ♂ 4:47
6 ☽ → ♎ 4: 3	24 ☽ → ♊ 19:48		☽ ☌ ♀ 10: 1	☽ ☌ ☋ 23:23	20 ☽ ☌ A 11:39	☽ ☌ ⛢ 17: 2
8 ☽ → ♏ 6:46	27 ☽ → ♋ 3:33		☉ S☋ ☿ 20:35	14 ☽ ☍ ♂ 1:42	21 ♂ ☍ ♆ 4: 1	☉ ☌ ☽ 18:20
10 ☽ → ♐ 10:30	29 ☽ → ♌ 7:43		3 ☿ ☌ ♂ 13: 6	☉ ☍ ☽ 6:52	22 ☉ □ ☽ 6:56	30 ♀ □ ♄ 15:16
12 ☽ → ♑ 15:43	30 ☿ → ♍ 18:37		4 ☽ ☍ ♃ 12: 2	☽ ☌ ♆ 10:25	25 ☽ ☍ ♇ 8:33	31 ☽ ☌ ☿ 11: 1
☿ → ♌ 16: 6	31 ☽ → ♍ 9:25		5 ☽ ☌ P 9:29	15 ☿ ☌ ⛢ 4:30	☽ ☌ ♄ 15: 4	☽ ☍ ♃ 16:17
14 ☽ → ♒ 22:52	♂ → ♌ 22:19		☽ ⌂N ☊ 12:41	☽ ☍ ⛢ 7:38	♀ ☍ ♃ 19:14	
17 ☽ → ♓ 8:25			☉ ☌ ♂ 23:27	☽ ☍ ☿ 8: 8	26 ☽ ☌ ☊ 10: 2	
19 ☽ → ♈ 20: 9			7 ☉ □ ☽ 4:41	16 ☉ ☍ ♆ 5:21	27 ♀ □ ♇ 8:22	
21 ♀ → ♍ 19:43			9 ☿ ☍ ♆ 6:22	☽ ☍ ♀ 20:44	28 ☽ ☍ ♆ 19:43	

SIDEREAL HELIOCENTRIC LONGITUDES : JULY 29 Julian at 0 hours UT											
DAY	Sid. Time	☿	♀	⊕	♂	♃	♄	⛢	♆	♇	Vernal Point
1 FR	18:27:35	29 ♊ 50	13 ♍ 12	8 ♑ 43	11 ♋ 16	26 ♒ 19	4 ♊ 6	5 ♌ 9	23 ♑ 11	8 ♐ 3	2♈38'53"
2 SA	18:31:32	5 ♋ 38	14 49	9 40	11 42	26 25	4 8	5 10	23 12	8 4	2♈38'53"
3 SU	18:35:28	11 17	16 26	10 37	12 9	26 30	4 11	5 10	23 12	8 4	2♈38'53"
4 MO	18:39:25	16 47	18 3	11 35	12 36	26 35	4 13	5 11	23 12	8 4	2♈38'53"
5 TU	18:43:21	22 7	19 40	12 32	13 2	26 41	4 15	5 12	23 13	8 5	2♈38'53"
6 WE	18:47:18	27 19	21 17	13 30	13 29	26 46	4 18	5 13	23 13	8 5	2♈38'53"
7 TH	18:51:14	2 ♌ 20	22 54	14 27	13 55	26 52	4 20	5 13	23 13	8 5	2♈38'53"
8 FR	18:55:11	7 12	24 31	15 24	14 22	26 57	4 22	5 14	23 14	8 6	2♈38'52"
9 SA	18:59: 7	11 55	26 8	16 22	14 48	27 3	4 24	5 15	23 14	8 6	2♈38'52"
10 SU	19: 3: 4	16 29	27 44	17 19	15 15	27 8	4 27	5 16	23 14	8 6	2♈38'52"
11 MO	19: 7: 1	20 55	29 21	18 17	15 42	27 14	4 29	5 16	23 15	8 7	2♈38'52"
12 TU	19:10:57	25 11	0 ♎ 58	19 14	16 8	27 19	4 31	5 17	23 15	8 7	2♈38'52"
13 WE	19:14:54	29 20	2 34	20 12	16 35	27 24	4 33	5 18	23 16	8 7	2♈38'52"
14 TH	19:18:50	3 ♍ 22	4 11	21 9	17 1	27 30	4 36	5 19	23 16	8 8	2♈38'52"
15 FR	19:22:47	7 16	5 48	22 7	17 27	27 35	4 38	5 20	23 16	8 8	2♈38'51"
16 SA	19:26:43	11 4	7 24	23 4	17 54	27 41	4 40	5 20	23 17	8 8	2♈38'51"
17 SU	19:30:40	14 45	9 0	24 2	18 20	27 46	4 42	5 21	23 17	8 9	2♈38'51"
18 MO	19:34:36	18 21	10 37	25 0	18 47	27 52	4 45	5 22	23 17	8 9	2♈38'51"
19 TU	19:38:33	21 51	12 13	25 57	19 13	27 57	4 47	5 23	23 18	8 9	2♈38'51"
20 WE	19:42:30	25 16	13 49	26 55	19 40	28 2	4 49	5 23	23 18	8 10	2♈38'51"
21 TH	19:46:26	28 36	15 25	27 53	20 6	28 8	4 52	5 24	23 18	8 10	2♈38'51"
22 FR	19:50:23	1 ♎ 52	17 2	28 51	20 33	28 13	4 54	5 25	23 19	8 10	2♈38'51"
23 SA	19:54:19	5 4	18 38	29 48	20 59	28 19	4 56	5 26	23 19	8 11	2♈38'50"
24 SU	19:58:16	8 12	20 14	0 ♒ 46	21 25	28 24	4 58	5 26	23 20	8 11	2♈38'50"
25 MO	20: 2:12	11 17	21 50	1 44	21 52	28 30	5 1	5 27	23 20	8 12	2♈38'50"
26 TU	20: 6: 9	14 19	23 26	2 42	22 18	28 35	5 3	5 28	23 20	8 12	2♈38'50"
27 WE	20:10: 5	17 18	25 2	3 40	22 44	28 41	5 5	5 29	23 21	8 12	2♈38'50"
28 TH	20:14: 2	20 14	26 37	4 38	23 11	28 46	5 7	5 29	23 21	8 13	2♈38'50"
29 FR	20:17:59	23 8	28 13	5 36	23 37	28 51	5 10	5 30	23 21	8 13	2♈38'50"
30 SA	20:21:55	26 1	29 49	6 34	24 4	28 57	5 12	5 31	23 22	8 13	2♈38'49"
31 SU	20:25:52	28 51	1 ♏ 25	7 32	24 30	29 2	5 14	5 32	23 22	8 14	2♈38'49"

INGRESSES :	ASPECTS (HELIOCENTRIC +MOON(TYCHONIC)) :				
1 ☿ → ♋ 0:40	1 ☽ ☍ ♆ 11: 7	7 ☽ □ ♂ 3:37	14 ☿ □ ♄ 7:34	☽ □ ♆ 19:15	⊕ ☍ ⛢ 21:45
6 ☿ → ♌ 12:44	2 ☽ ☌ ⛢ 7:43	☿ ☌ ⛢ 14: 9	☽ ☌ ♆ 10:18	22 ☽ □ ⛢ 19:35	29 ☿ □ ♆ 1:47
11 ♀ → ♎ 9:38	☿ ☍ ⊕ 20:35	☽ □ ♆ 19:15	15 ☿ □ ♇ 5:25	24 ☽ □ ♃ 16:51	☿ □ ♂ 4:42
13 ☿ → ♍ 3:53	3 ☿ ☌ ♂ 4: 5	8 ☽ □ ⛢ 15:44	☽ ☍ ⛢ 8:55	25 ♀ □ ♂ 0:39	☽ □ ♀ 5:18
21 ☿ → ♎ 10:14	☽ ☍ ♃ 19:59	9 ☽ □ ☿ 4:46	16 ⊕ ☌ ♆ 5: 5	☽ ☌ ♄ 5:23	☽ ☌ ⛢ 16:59
23 ⊕ → ♒ 4:51	4 ☽ □ ♄ 8:50	10 ☽ □ ♃ 5:33	17 ☽ ☌ ♃ 4: 5	☽ ☍ ♇ 11:24	30 ☿ ☌ ☋ 13:59
30 ♀ → ♏ 2:45	☽ □ ♇ 15:17	☽ ☍ ♄ 18:20	☽ □ ♄ 17:43	♀ □ ♆ 22:37	31 ☽ ☍ ♃ 7:53
31 ☿ → ♏ 9:44	5 ☿ ☍ ♆ 4:58	11 ☽ ☌ ♇ 0:44	18 ☽ □ ♇ 0:28	28 ♂ ☍ ♆ 9:21	☽ □ ♄ 18: 1
	☽ ☌ ♀ 12: 5	12 ☿ ☍ ♃ 12:28	19 ☽ ☍ ☿ 5:16	☽ □ ☿ 19: 3	☽ □ ♇ 22:51
	⊕ ☍ ♂ 23:27	☽ □ ♀ 19:52	21 ☽ ☍ ♀ 3:51	☽ ☍ ♆ 20:26	
	6 ☿ ⌂N ☊ 1:42	13 ☽ ☍ ♂ 22:41	☽ □ ♂ 13:16	☽ ☌ ♂ 20:47	

SIDEREAL GEOCENTRIC LONGITUDES : AUGUST 29 Julian at 0 hours UT

DAY	☉	☽	☊	☿	♀	♂	♃	♄	♅	♆	♇
1 MO	8 ♌ 29	8 ♍ 56	19 ♊ 56R	1 ♍ 45	12 ♍ 15	0 ♌ 3	4 ♓ 10R	10 ♊ 44	5 ♌ 41	22 ♑ 51R	6 ♐ 37R
2 TU	9 27	23 39	19 49	3 9	13 27	0 41	4 4	10 50	5 45	22 50	6 36
3 WE	10 25	8 ♎ 17	19 43	4 32	14 39	1 19	3 57	10 55	5 49	22 48	6 36
4 TH	11 23	22 43	19 40	5 53	15 51	1 57	3 50	11 0	5 52	22 47	6 35
5 FR	12 21	6 ♏ 55	19 38	7 12	17 3	2 35	3 43	11 5	5 56	22 45	6 35
6 SA	13 20	20 51	19 38D	8 30	18 15	3 14	3 37	11 10	6 0	22 44	6 35
7 SU	14 18	4 ♐ 30	19 39	9 47	19 27	3 52	3 29	11 15	6 4	22 42	6 34
8 MO	15 16	17 55	19 40	11 1	20 39	4 30	3 22	11 20	6 7	22 41	6 34
9 TU	16 14	1 ♑ 5	19 39R	12 14	21 51	5 8	3 15	11 25	6 11	22 39	6 34
10 WE	17 13	14 3	19 37	13 25	23 2	5 46	3 8	11 29	6 15	22 38	6 33
11 TH	18 11	26 50	19 31	14 34	24 14	6 25	3 0	11 34	6 18	22 36	6 33
12 FR	19 9	9 ♒ 26	19 24	15 41	25 26	7 3	2 53	11 39	6 22	22 35	6 33
13 SA	20 8	21 52	19 13	16 45	26 37	7 41	2 45	11 43	6 26	22 33	6 33
14 SU	21 6	4 ♓ 8	19 2	17 48	27 49	8 19	2 37	11 47	6 29	22 32	6 33
15 MO	22 4	16 15	18 50	18 48	29 0	8 57	2 30	11 52	6 33	22 31	6 33
16 TU	23 3	28 14	18 39	19 45	0 ♎ 12	9 36	2 22	11 56	6 37	22 29	6 32
17 WE	24 1	10 ♈ 7	18 29	20 40	1 23	10 14	2 14	12 0	6 40	22 28	6 32
18 TH	25 0	21 58	18 22	21 31	2 34	10 52	2 6	12 4	6 44	22 27	6 32
19 FR	25 58	3 ♉ 49	18 17	22 20	3 46	11 30	1 58	12 8	6 48	22 25	6 32D
20 SA	26 57	15 45	18 15	23 4	4 57	12 8	1 50	12 12	6 51	22 24	6 32
21 SU	27 56	27 50	18 14	23 46	6 8	12 47	1 42	12 16	6 55	22 23	6 33
22 MO	28 54	10 ♊ 11	18 14D	24 23	7 19	13 25	1 34	12 19	6 58	22 22	6 33
23 TU	29 53	22 52	18 14R	24 56	8 30	14 3	1 26	12 23	7 2	22 20	6 33
24 WE	0 ♍ 52	5 ♋ 58	18 13	25 24	9 42	14 41	1 18	12 26	7 5	22 19	6 33
25 TH	1 51	19 32	18 10	25 48	10 53	15 20	1 10	12 30	7 9	22 18	6 33
26 FR	2 50	3 ♌ 35	18 4	26 5	12 4	15 58	1 2	12 33	7 12	22 17	6 33
27 SA	3 48	18 4	17 55	26 18	13 14	16 36	0 54	12 36	7 16	22 16	6 34
28 SU	4 47	2 ♍ 55	17 45	26 24	14 25	17 14	0 46	12 39	7 19	22 15	6 34
29 MO	5 46	17 59	17 34	26 23R	15 36	17 53	0 38	12 42	7 23	22 14	6 34
30 TU	6 45	3 ♎ 6	17 23	26 16	16 47	18 31	0 30	12 45	7 26	22 12	6 35
31 WE	7 44	18 6	17 14	26 1	17 58	19 9	0 22	12 48	7 29	22 11	6 35

INGRESSES :

2	☽ → ♎ 10:23		☽ → ♋ 13: 9
4	☽ → ♏ 12:15	25	☽ → ♌ 17:57
6	☽ → ♐ 16: 2	27	☽ → ♍ 19:19
8	☽ → ♑ 22: 0	29	☽ → ♎ 19: 4
11	☽ → ♒ 5:59	31	☽ → ♏ 19:20
13	☽ → ♓ 15:53		
15	♀ → ♎ 20: 4		
16	☽ → ♈ 3:33		
18	☽ → ♉ 16:17		
21	☽ → ♊ 4:14		
23	☉ → ♍ 2:49		

ASPECTS & ECLIPSES :

1	☽ ☌ ♀	5:53	10	☽ ☌ ♆	16: 1	21	☉ □ ☽	0:11	29	☽ ☌ P	9:37
	☽ ☌ P	8:29		♂ ☌ ♅	19:40		☽ ☍ ♇	16:58		☽ ☌ ☿	13:14
	☽ N☐ ☊	17:46	11	☽ ☍ ♅	18: 5	22	☽ ☌ ♄	4: 6		☉ □ ♇	19:40
2	☿ ☍ ♃	14:40		☽ ☍ ♂	19:10		☽ ☌ ☊	15:18	30	☽ ☌ ♀	23:45
4	☿ □ ♇	12:44	12	☉ ☍ ☽	20:20	24	☉ ☍ ♃	9:28			
5	☉ □ ☽	10: 1	13	☽ ☌ ♃	21: 3	25	☽ ☍ ♆	4:46			
7	☽ ☌ ♇	3:40	15	☿ □ ☊	0:49	26	☽ ☌ ♅	6: 5			
	♀ □ ☊	4: 7		☽ S☐ ☊	5: 5		☽ ☌ ♂	21:29			
	☽ ☍ ♄	12: 5		☽ ☍ ☿	5:32	27	☽ ☍ ♃	20:35			
8	☽ ☌ ☋	3:10	16	☽ ☍ ♀	4:23	28	☉ ☌ ☽	3:12			
	☿ □ ♄	6:35	17	☽ ☌ A	4:54		☽ N☐ ☊	23:20			

SIDEREAL HELIOCENTRIC LONGITUDES : AUGUST 29 Julian at 0 hours UT

DAY	Sid. Time	☿	♀	⊕	♂	♃	♄	♅	♆	♇	Vernal Point
1 MO	20:29:48	1 ♏ 40	3 ♏ 0	8 ♒ 30	24 ♋ 56	29 ♒ 8	5 ♊ 17	5 ♌ 33	23 ♑ 22	8 ♐ 14	2 ♈ 38'49"
2 TU	20:33:45	4 28	4 36	9 28	25 23	29 13	5 19	5 33	23 23	8 14	2 ♈ 38'49"
3 WE	20:37:41	7 15	6 12	10 26	25 49	29 19	5 21	5 34	23 23	8 15	2 ♈ 38'49"
4 TH	20:41:38	10 1	7 47	11 24	26 15	29 24	5 23	5 35	23 23	8 15	2 ♈ 38'49"
5 FR	20:45:34	12 46	9 23	12 22	26 41	29 30	5 26	5 36	23 24	8 15	2 ♈ 38'49"
6 SA	20:49:31	15 31	10 58	13 20	27 8	29 35	5 28	5 36	23 24	8 16	2 ♈ 38'48"
7 SU	20:53:28	18 15	12 33	14 18	27 34	29 40	5 30	5 37	23 25	8 16	2 ♈ 38'48"
8 MO	20:57:24	21 0	14 9	15 17	28 0	29 46	5 32	5 38	23 25	8 16	2 ♈ 38'48"
9 TU	21: 1:21	23 45	15 44	16 15	28 27	29 51	5 35	5 39	23 25	8 17	2 ♈ 38'48"
10 WE	21: 5:17	26 30	17 19	17 13	28 53	29 57	5 37	5 39	23 26	8 17	2 ♈ 38'48"
11 TH	21: 9:14	29 16	18 54	18 11	29 19	0 ♓ 2	5 39	5 40	23 26	8 17	2 ♈ 38'48"
12 FR	21:13:10	2 ♐ 2	20 30	19 10	29 46	0 8	5 42	5 41	23 26	8 18	2 ♈ 38'48"
13 SA	21:17: 7	4 50	22 5	20 8	0 ♌ 12	0 13	5 44	5 42	23 27	8 18	2 ♈ 38'48"
14 SU	21:21: 3	7 39	23 40	21 7	0 38	0 19	5 46	5 43	23 27	8 18	2 ♈ 38'47"
15 MO	21:25: 0	10 29	25 15	22 5	1 5	0 24	5 48	5 43	23 27	8 19	2 ♈ 38'47"
16 TU	21:28:57	13 21	26 50	23 3	1 31	0 29	5 51	5 44	23 28	8 19	2 ♈ 38'47"
17 WE	21:32:53	16 15	28 25	24 2	1 57	0 35	5 53	5 45	23 28	8 19	2 ♈ 38'47"
18 TH	21:36:50	19 11	0 ♐ 0	25 0	2 23	0 40	5 55	5 46	23 28	8 20	2 ♈ 38'47"
19 FR	21:40:46	22 10	1 35	25 59	2 50	0 46	5 57	5 46	23 29	8 20	2 ♈ 38'47"
20 SA	21:44:43	25 11	3 10	26 58	3 16	0 51	6 0	5 47	23 29	8 20	2 ♈ 38'47"
21 SU	21:48:39	28 15	4 45	27 56	3 42	0 57	6 2	5 48	23 30	8 21	2 ♈ 38'46"
22 MO	21:52:36	1 ♑ 22	6 19	28 55	4 9	1 2	6 4	5 49	23 30	8 21	2 ♈ 38'46"
23 TU	21:56:32	4 33	7 54	29 54	4 35	1 8	6 7	5 49	23 30	8 22	2 ♈ 38'46"
24 WE	22: 0:29	7 48	9 29	0 ♓ 52	5 1	1 13	6 9	5 50	23 31	8 22	2 ♈ 38'46"
25 TH	22: 4:26	11 6	11 4	1 51	5 27	1 18	6 11	5 51	23 31	8 22	2 ♈ 38'46"
26 FR	22: 8:22	14 29	12 39	2 50	5 54	1 24	6 13	5 52	23 31	8 23	2 ♈ 38'46"
27 SA	22:12:19	17 57	14 13	3 49	6 20	1 29	6 16	5 52	23 32	8 23	2 ♈ 38'46"
28 SU	22:16:15	21 30	15 48	4 48	6 46	1 35	6 18	5 53	23 32	8 23	2 ♈ 38'45"
29 MO	22:20:12	25 8	17 23	5 47	7 13	1 40	6 20	5 54	23 32	8 24	2 ♈ 38'45"
30 TU	22:24: 8	28 52	18 58	6 46	7 39	1 46	6 22	5 55	23 33	8 24	2 ♈ 38'45"
31 WE	22:28: 5	2 ♒ 42	20 32	7 45	8 5	1 51	6 25	5 56	23 33	8 24	2 ♈ 38'45"

INGRESSES :

10	♃ → ♓ 14:24
11	☿ → ♐ 6:24
12	♂ → ♌ 13: 6
18	♀ → ♐ 0: 1
21	☿ → ♑ 13:29
23	⊕ → ♓ 2:34
30	☿ → ♒ 7: 9

ASPECTS (HELIOCENTRIC +MOON(TYCHONIC)) :

2	☿ ☌ ♀	2:39		☽ ☌ ♇	6:41		☿ ☌ ♇	5:36		☽ ☌ ♄	16: 2	28	☽ □ ♄	5:25
	☿ □ ♅	9:25		☿ ☌ A	11:20		☽ □ ♇	8:14		♀ ☍ ♄	20: 3		☽ □ ♇	8:44
	♀ □ ♅	14:30	9	♀ □ ⊕	20: 3		☽ □ ☿	9: 2		☽ ☍ ♇	20:28		♂ N☐ ☊	11:20
4	☽ □ ♆	1: 7	10	☽ ☌ ♆	17:34	18	☽ □ ♆	3: 4	23	♀ ☌ ♇	6:55		☿ ☌ ♆	13:32
	☽ □ ♂	6: 7	11	☽ ☍ ♂	4:52		♂ ☌ A	5: 2	24	☽ ☍ ☿	4:20		☽ □ ♀	22:55
	☿ □ ⊕	18:39		☿ □ ♃	6:56		♀ □ ♃	10:50		⊕ ☌ ♃	9:13	29	⊕ □ ♄	14: 5
	☽ □ ♅	21:44		☽ ☍ ♅	16:48		☽ □ ♂	21:56	25	☽ ☍ ♆	6:53		☿ S☐ ☊	16:23
5	☽ ☌ ♀	4:44	13	☽ □ ♀	0:28	19	♀ ☌ ☋	2:15		♂ ☌ ♅	22: 3	31	☽ □ ♆	8:49
	☽ ☌ ☿	12:28		☿ ☍ ♄	7:47		☽ □ ♅	3:58	26	☽ ☌ ♅	3:49		⊕ □ ♇	16: 7
6	☽ □ ♃	15:24		☽ ☌ ♃	16:26	21	☽ □ ♃	6: 7		☽ ☌ ♂	4: 0		☿ ☍ ♅	19:43
7	☽ ☍ ♄	1:46	14	☽ □ ♄	3:14		☽ ☍ ♀	15:27	27	☽ ☍ ♃	21:50			

SIDEREAL GEOCENTRIC LONGITUDES : SEPTEMBER 29 Julian at 0 hours UT

DAY	☉	☽	☊	☿	♀	♂	♃	♄	♅	♆	♇
1 TH	8 ♍ 43	2 ♏ 50	17 ♊ 8R	25 ♍ 39R	19 ♎ 8	19 ♌ 47	0 ♓ 14R	12 ♊ 50	7 ♌ 33	22 ♑ 10R	6 ♐ 36
2 FR	9 42	17 14	17 4	25 9	20 19	20 26	0 7	12 53	7 36	22 9	6 36
3 SA	10 41	1 ♐ 14	17 3	24 31	21 29	21 4	29 ♒ 59	12 55	7 39	22 8	6 36
4 SU	11 41	14 51	17 3	23 47	22 40	21 42	29 51	12 58	7 43	22 8	6 37
5 MO	12 40	28 7	17 2	22 55	23 50	22 20	29 44	13 0	7 46	22 7	6 38
6 TU	13 39	11 ♑ 5	17 1	21 57	25 0	22 59	29 36	13 2	7 49	22 6	6 38
7 WE	14 38	23 48	16 58	20 53	26 10	23 37	29 28	13 4	7 52	22 5	6 39
8 TH	15 38	6 ♒ 18	16 51	19 45	27 21	24 15	29 21	13 6	7 55	22 4	6 39
9 FR	16 37	18 39	16 41	18 35	28 31	24 53	29 14	13 8	7 59	22 3	6 40
10 SA	17 36	0 ♓ 51	16 29	17 24	29 41	25 32	29 7	13 10	8 2	22 3	6 41
11 SU	18 36	12 57	16 15	16 15	0 ♏ 50	26 10	28 59	13 11	8 5	22 2	6 41
12 MO	19 35	24 56	16 0	15 8	2 0	26 48	28 52	13 13	8 8	22 1	6 42
13 TU	20 34	6 ♈ 51	15 46	14 7	3 10	27 27	28 45	13 14	8 11	22 0	6 43
14 WE	21 34	18 42	15 34	13 12	4 19	28 5	28 39	13 15	8 14	22 0	6 44
15 TH	22 33	0 ♉ 32	15 24	12 26	5 29	28 43	28 32	13 17	8 17	21 59	6 45
16 FR	23 33	12 23	15 17	11 49	6 38	29 22	28 25	13 18	8 20	21 59	6 46
17 SA	24 32	24 18	15 14	11 23	7 48	0 ♍ 0	28 19	13 19	8 23	21 58	6 47
18 SU	25 32	6 ♊ 23	15 12	11 7	8 57	0 38	28 13	13 19	8 25	21 58	6 48
19 MO	26 32	18 41	15 12	11 3D	10 6	1 17	28 7	13 20	8 28	21 57	6 48
20 TU	27 31	1 ♋ 17	15 12	11 10	11 15	1 55	28 1	13 21	8 31	21 57	6 49
21 WE	28 31	14 17	15 11	11 28	12 24	2 33	27 55	13 21	8 34	21 56	6 51
22 TH	29 31	27 45	15 8	11 55	13 33	3 12	27 49	13 22	8 36	21 56	6 52
23 FR	0 ♎ 31	11 ♌ 43	15 3	12 33	14 42	3 50	27 43	13 22	8 39	21 55	6 53
24 SA	1 31	26 10	14 55	13 18	15 50	4 28	27 38	13 22	8 42	21 55	6 54
25 SU	2 31	11 ♍ 4	14 45	14 12	16 59	5 7	27 33	13 22R	8 44	21 55	6 55
26 MO	3 31	26 15	14 35	15 13	18 7	5 45	27 28	13 22	8 47	21 55	6 56
27 TU	4 31	11 ♎ 35	14 24	16 19	19 15	6 24	27 23	13 22	8 49	21 54	6 57
28 WE	5 31	26 51	14 16	17 32	20 24	7 2	27 18	13 21	8 52	21 54	6 59
29 TH	6 31	11 ♏ 52	14 9	18 48	21 32	7 40	27 13	13 21	8 54	21 54	7 0
30 FR	7 31	26 31	14 5	20 9	22 39	8 19	27 9	13 20	8 57	21 54	7 1

INGRESSES :

2 ♃ → ♒ 20:31
☽ → ♐ 21:52
5 ☽ → ♑ 3:27
7 ☽ → ♒ 11:51
9 ☽ → ♓ 22:18
10 ♀ → ♏ 6:41
12 ☽ → ♈ 10:11
14 ☽ → ♉ 22:55
17 ♂ → ♍ 0: 6
☽ → ♊ 11:21
19 ☽ → ♋ 21:35
22 ☽ → ♌ 3:55
☉ → ♎ 11:37
24 ☽ → ♍ 6:13
26 ☽ → ♎ 5:52
28 ☽ → ♏ 5: 0
30 ☽ → ♐ 5:48

ASPECTS & ECLIPSES :

3 ☽ ☌ ♇ 9:24
♀ □ ♆ 13:12
☉ □ ☽ 17:54
☽ ☍ ♄ 20:37
4 ☽ ☌ ☋ 3:55
5 ☉ □ ♄ 8:30
6 ☽ ☌ ♆ 20:44
8 ☽ ☍ ♅ 3: 8
9 ☉ □ ☊ 1:28
☽ ☍ ♂ 12:55
☽ ☌ ♃ 20:35
☉ ☌ ☿ 21:50
10 ☿ □ ☊ 23:59
11 ☽ ☍ ☿ 6: 1
☽ S ☊ 6:27
☉ ☍ ☽ 12:17
13 ☽ ☌ A 17:41
☿ □ ♄ 22:26
14 ♂ ☍ ♃ 18: 1
15 ☽ ☍ ♀ 11: 7
17 ♀ □ ♅ 12:34
18 ☽ ☍ ♇ 0:48
☽ ☌ ♄ 13:37
☽ ☌ ☊ 17:15
19 ☉ □ ☽ 16:18
21 ☽ ☍ ♆ 13:44
22 ☽ ☌ ♅ 18:47
24 ☿ □ ♄ 1:44
☽ ☍ ♃ 2:21
☽ ☌ ♂ 14: 3
25 ☽ ☌ ☿ 5:19
☽ N ☊ 5:47
☿ □ ☊ 11:31
26 ☉ ☌ ☽ 12: 9
☽ ☌ P 19:16
27 ♂ □ ♇ 21:50
29 ☽ ☌ ♀ 17: 4
30 ☽ ☌ ♇ 17:41

SIDEREAL HELIOCENTRIC LONGITUDES : SEPTEMBER 29 Julian at 0 hours UT

DAY	Sid. Time	☿	♀	⊕	♂	♃	♄	♅	♆	♇	Vernal Point
1 TH	22:32: 1	6 ♒ 39	22 ♐ 7	8 ♓ 44	8 ♌ 32	1 ♓ 57	6 ♊ 27	5 ♌ 56	23 ♑ 34	8 ♐ 25	2♈38'45"
2 FR	22:35:58	10 42	23 42	9 43	8 58	2 2	6 29	5 57	23 34	8 25	2♈38'45"
3 SA	22:39:55	14 53	25 16	10 42	9 24	2 7	6 32	5 58	23 34	8 25	2♈38'45"
4 SU	22:43:51	19 12	26 51	11 41	9 51	2 13	6 34	5 59	23 35	8 26	2♈38'45"
5 MO	22:47:48	23 38	28 25	12 40	10 17	2 18	6 36	5 59	23 35	8 26	2♈38'44"
6 TU	22:51:44	28 13	0 ♑ 0	13 40	10 43	2 24	6 38	6 0	23 35	8 26	2♈38'44"
7 WE	22:55:41	2 ♓ 56	1 35	14 39	11 10	2 29	6 41	6 1	23 36	8 27	2♈38'44"
8 TH	22:59:37	7 48	3 9	15 38	11 36	2 35	6 43	6 2	23 36	8 27	2♈38'44"
9 FR	23: 3:34	12 49	4 44	16 37	12 2	2 40	6 45	6 2	23 36	8 27	2♈38'44"
10 SA	23: 7:30	18 0	6 19	17 37	12 29	2 46	6 47	6 3	23 37	8 28	2♈38'44"
11 SU	23:11:27	23 19	7 53	18 36	12 55	2 51	6 50	6 4	23 37	8 28	2♈38'44"
12 MO	23:15:23	28 47	9 28	19 36	13 21	2 56	6 52	6 5	23 37	8 28	2♈38'43"
13 TU	23:19:20	4 ♈ 24	11 2	20 35	13 48	3 2	6 54	6 5	23 38	8 29	2♈38'43"
14 WE	23:23:17	10 10	12 37	21 34	14 14	3 7	6 56	6 6	23 38	8 29	2♈38'43"
15 TH	23:27:13	16 3	14 12	22 34	14 41	3 13	6 59	6 7	23 39	8 29	2♈38'43"
16 FR	23:31:10	22 3	15 46	23 33	15 7	3 18	7 1	6 8	23 39	8 30	2♈38'43"
17 SA	23:35: 6	28 9	17 21	24 33	15 34	3 24	7 3	6 9	23 39	8 30	2♈38'43"
18 SU	23:39: 3	4 ♉ 20	18 56	25 33	16 0	3 29	7 6	6 9	23 40	8 30	2♈38'43"
19 MO	23:42:59	10 35	20 30	26 32	16 26	3 35	7 8	6 10	23 40	8 31	2♈38'42"
20 TU	23:46:56	16 52	22 5	27 32	16 53	3 40	7 10	6 11	23 40	8 31	2♈38'42"
21 WE	23:50:52	23 10	23 40	28 32	17 19	3 45	7 12	6 12	23 41	8 32	2♈38'42"
22 TH	23:54:49	29 28	25 14	29 32	17 46	3 51	7 15	6 12	23 41	8 32	2♈38'42"
23 FR	23:58:46	5 ♊ 44	26 49	0 ♈ 31	18 12	3 56	7 17	6 13	23 41	8 32	2♈38'42"
24 SA	0: 2:42	11 57	28 24	1 31	18 39	4 2	7 19	6 14	23 42	8 33	2♈38'42"
25 SU	0: 6:39	18 4	29 59	2 31	19 5	4 7	7 21	6 15	23 42	8 33	2♈38'42"
26 MO	0:10:35	24 6	1 ♒ 33	3 31	19 32	4 13	7 24	6 15	23 42	8 33	2♈38'42"
27 TU	0:14:32	0 ♋ 1	3 8	4 31	19 58	4 18	7 26	6 16	23 43	8 34	2♈38'41"
28 WE	0:18:28	5 49	4 43	5 31	20 25	4 24	7 28	6 17	23 43	8 34	2♈38'41"
29 TH	0:22:25	11 27	6 18	6 31	20 51	4 29	7 31	6 18	23 44	8 34	2♈38'41"
30 FR	0:26:21	16 57	7 53	7 31	21 18	4 35	7 33	6 19	23 44	8 35	2♈38'41"

INGRESSES :

5 ♀ → ♑ 23:59
6 ☿ → ♓ 9:10
12 ☿ → ♈ 5:13
17 ☿ → ♉ 7:13
22 ☿ → ♊ 2: 1
⊕ → ♈ 11:23
25 ♀ → ♒ 0:20
26 ☿ → ♋ 23:54

ASPECTS (HELIOCENTRIC +MOON(TYCHONIC)) :

1 ☽ □ ♅ 5: 7
☽ □ ☿ 8:43
☽ □ ♂ 9:42
☿ ☍ ♂ 12:34
3 ☽ □ ♃ 1:34
☽ ☍ ♄ 9:17
☽ ☌ ♇ 12:36
5 ☽ ☌ ♀ 0:38
6 ☿ ☌ ♃ 21:42
☽ ☌ ♆ 23:37
7 ☿ □ ♄ 18:38
☽ ☍ ♅ 23:27
8 ☿ □ ♇ 3: 7
☽ ☍ ♂ 10:38
9 ☿ ☌ ⊕ 21:50
10 ☽ ☌ ♃ 3:47
☽ □ ♄ 11:47
☽ □ ♇ 15: 5
12 ☽ ☌ ☿ 14:35
13 ☽ □ ♀ 9:46
14 ☽ □ ♆ 10: 0
☿ □ ♀ 13:46
15 ☽ □ ♅ 11:20
16 ☽ □ ♂ 5:44
☿ □ ♆ 6:21
♀ ☌ A 6:35
☿ ☌ ☊ 22: 8
17 ☽ □ ♃ 18:14
18 ☽ ☌ ♄ 1:24
☽ ☍ ♇ 4:11
☿ □ ♅ 7: 2
20 ☿ □ ♂ 0: 3
☿ ☌ P 10:12
21 ♀ ☌ ♆ 0:14
☽ ☍ ♆ 16:50
☽ ☍ ♀ 19: 0
22 ☽ ☌ ♅ 14:39
☿ □ ♃ 17: 0
23 ☿ ☌ ♄ 5:59
☿ ☍ ♇ 10:48
☽ ☌ ♂ 11:12
24 ☽ ☍ ♃ 12:49
☽ □ ♄ 18: 3
☽ □ ♇ 19:59
25 ☽ □ ☿ 18:26
27 ☽ □ ♆ 19: 3
☿ □ ⊕ 22:30
28 ☽ □ ♀ 13:59
☽ □ ♅ 15: 2
♀ ☍ ♅ 23:57
29 ☽ □ ♂ 15: 6
30 ☽ □ ♃ 13:36
☽ ☍ ♄ 18:36
☽ ☌ ♇ 20:19

SIDEREAL GEOCENTRIC LONGITUDES : OCTOBER 29 Julian at 0 hours UT

DAY	☉	☽	☊	☿	♀	♂	♃	♄	♅	♆	♇
1 SA	8 ♎ 31	10 ♐ 44	14 ♊ 4R	21 ♍ 33	23 ♏ 47	8 ♍ 57	27 ♒ 5R	13 ♊ 20R	8 ♌ 59	21 ♑ 54R	7 ♐ 2
2 SU	9 31	24 29	14 4D	23 0	24 55	9 36	27 1	13 19	9 1	21 54	7 4
3 MO	10 31	7 ♑ 48	14 5	24 30	26 2	10 14	26 57	13 18	9 3	21 54	7 5
4 TU	11 31	20 44	14 5R	26 1	27 10	10 52	26 53	13 17	9 6	21 54D	7 7
5 WE	12 31	3 ♒ 21	14 2	27 34	28 17	11 31	26 50	13 16	9 8	21 54	7 8
6 TH	13 32	15 43	13 58	29 8	29 24	12 9	26 46	13 15	9 10	21 54	7 9
7 FR	14 32	27 54	13 51	0 ♎ 43	0 ♐ 31	12 48	26 43	13 14	9 12	21 54	7 11
8 SA	15 32	9 ♓ 57	13 42	2 19	1 37	13 26	26 40	13 12	9 14	21 54	7 12
9 SU	16 32	21 55	13 31	3 55	2 44	14 5	26 38	13 11	9 16	21 54	7 14
10 MO	17 33	3 ♈ 49	13 19	5 32	3 50	14 43	26 35	13 9	9 18	21 54	7 15
11 TU	18 33	15 40	13 8	7 9	4 56	15 22	26 33	13 7	9 20	21 55	7 17
12 WE	19 34	27 32	12 59	8 47	6 2	16 0	26 31	13 5	9 22	21 55	7 19
13 TH	20 34	9 ♉ 24	12 51	10 24	7 7	16 39	26 29	13 3	9 23	21 55	7 20
14 FR	21 34	21 20	12 46	12 1	8 13	17 17	26 27	13 1	9 25	21 56	7 22
15 SA	22 35	3 ♊ 20	12 44	13 39	9 18	17 56	26 26	12 59	9 27	21 56	7 23
16 SU	23 35	15 29	12 43D	15 16	10 23	18 34	26 25	12 57	9 28	21 56	7 25
17 MO	24 36	27 50	12 44	16 53	11 28	19 13	26 24	12 55	9 30	21 57	7 27
18 TU	25 37	10 ♋ 27	12 45	18 30	12 32	19 51	26 23	12 52	9 31	21 57	7 29
19 WE	26 37	23 23	12 46	20 6	13 36	20 30	26 22	12 49	9 33	21 58	7 30
20 TH	27 38	6 ♌ 43	12 46R	21 43	14 40	21 8	26 22	12 47	9 34	21 58	7 32
21 FR	28 39	20 30	12 44	23 19	15 44	21 47	26 21	12 44	9 36	21 59	7 34
22 SA	29 39	4 ♍ 44	12 40	24 55	16 47	22 25	26 21D	12 41	9 37	22 0	7 36
23 SU	0 ♏ 40	19 24	12 34	26 31	17 51	23 4	26 21	12 38	9 38	22 0	7 37
24 MO	1 41	4 ♎ 25	12 28	28 7	18 54	23 42	26 22	12 35	9 39	22 1	7 39
25 TU	2 41	19 37	12 22	29 42	19 56	24 21	26 22	12 32	9 41	22 2	7 41
26 WE	3 42	4 ♏ 52	12 17	1 ♏ 18	20 58	25 0	26 23	12 29	9 42	22 2	7 43
27 TH	4 43	19 58	12 13	2 53	22 0	25 38	26 24	12 25	9 43	22 3	7 45
28 FR	5 44	4 ♐ 47	12 11	4 28	23 2	26 17	26 25	12 22	9 44	22 4	7 47
29 SA	6 45	19 11	12 11D	6 3	24 3	26 55	26 27	12 19	9 45	22 5	7 49
30 SU	7 46	3 ♑ 7	12 12	7 37	25 4	27 34	26 29	12 15	9 46	22 6	7 51
31 MO	8 47	16 36	12 14	9 12	26 4	28 12	26 30	12 11	9 46	22 7	7 53

INGRESSES :

2	☽ → ♑	9:51	22	☉ → ♏	8:13
4	☽ → ♒	17:34	23	☽ → ♎	16:59
6	♀ → ♐	13: 1	25	☿ → ♏	4:26
	☿ → ♎	13: 9		☽ → ♏	16:19
7	☽ → ♓	4: 9	27	☽ → ♐	16:11
9	☽ → ♈	16:18	29	☽ → ♑	18:33
12	☽ → ♉	4:59			
14	☽ → ♊	17:21			
17	☽ → ♋	4: 9			
19	☽ → ♌	11:59			
21	☽ → ♍	16: 5			

ASPECTS & ECLIPSES :

1	☽ ☍ ♄	4:28	10	☽ ☍ ☿	4: 2		♀ ☍ ♄	7: 9	28	☽ ☌ ♇	4:57
	☽ ☌ ☋	5:45		☽ ☌ A	19:26		☽ ☍ ♆	21:23		☽ ☌ ☋	12:14
3	☉ □ ☽	5:24	11	♄ ☌ ☊	3: 5	19	☉ □ ☽	6:22		☽ ☍ ♄	12:30
	♀ □ ♃	18:25		☉ ☍ ☽	6:22	20	☿ □ ♆	3:53	29	☽ ☌ ♀	8:56
4	☽ ☌ ♆	2:11	13	♀ ☌ ♇	4:50		☽ ☌ ♅	5: 2	30	☉ ☌S ☿	6: 7
5	☽ ☍ ♅	11:11	14	☉ □ ♆	8:28	21	☽ ☍ ♃	9:57		♄ ☌ ☊	13:40
6	☽ ☌ ♃	21:39	15	☽ ☍ ♇	8: 3	22	☽ N ☊	12:57	31	☿ □ ♅	8:53
7	♂ □ ♄	15:33		☽ ☍ ♀	12:58	23	☽ ☌ ♂	6: 9		☽ ☌ ♆	10: 3
8	☽ ☍ ♂	7:21		☽ ☌ ☊	18:33	25	☽ ☌ P	7:41		☉ □ ♅	23:50
	☽ S ☊	7:22		☽ ☌ ♄	19: 1		☽ ☌ ☿	17:42			
	♂ □ ☊	7:35	18	♀ ☍ ☊	5: 1		☉ ☌ ☽	22: 1			

SIDEREAL HELIOCENTRIC LONGITUDES : OCTOBER 29 Julian at 0 hours UT

DAY	Sid. Time	☿	♀	⊕	♂	♃	♄	♅	♆	♇	Vernal Point
1 SA	0:30:18	22 ♋ 17	9 ♒ 28	8 ♈ 31	21 ♌ 45	4 ♓ 40	7 ♊ 35	6 ♌ 19	23 ♑ 44	8 ♐ 35	2 ♈ 38'41"
2 SU	0:34:15	27 28	11 3	9 31	22 11	4 45	7 37	6 20	23 45	8 35	2 ♈ 38'41"
3 MO	0:38:11	2 ♌ 30	12 37	10 32	22 38	4 51	7 40	6 21	23 45	8 36	2 ♈ 38'41"
4 TU	0:42: 8	7 21	14 12	11 32	23 4	4 56	7 42	6 22	23 45	8 36	2 ♈ 38'40"
5 WE	0:46: 4	12 4	15 47	12 32	23 31	5 2	7 44	6 22	23 46	8 36	2 ♈ 38'40"
6 TH	0:50: 1	16 38	17 22	13 32	23 58	5 7	7 46	6 23	23 46	8 37	2 ♈ 38'40"
7 FR	0:53:57	21 3	18 57	14 32	24 24	5 13	7 49	6 24	23 46	8 37	2 ♈ 38'40"
8 SA	0:57:54	25 19	20 32	15 33	24 51	5 18	7 51	6 25	23 47	8 37	2 ♈ 38'40"
9 SU	1: 1:50	29 28	22 8	16 33	25 18	5 24	7 53	6 25	23 47	8 38	2 ♈ 38'40"
10 MO	1: 5:47	3 ♍ 29	23 43	17 33	25 44	5 29	7 55	6 26	23 48	8 38	2 ♈ 38'40"
11 TU	1: 9:44	7 23	25 18	18 34	26 11	5 35	7 58	6 27	23 48	8 38	2 ♈ 38'39"
12 WE	1:13:40	11 11	26 53	19 34	26 38	5 40	8 0	6 28	23 48	8 39	2 ♈ 38'39"
13 TH	1:17:37	14 52	28 28	20 35	27 5	5 45	8 2	6 28	23 49	8 39	2 ♈ 38'39"
14 FR	1:21:33	18 27	0 ♓ 3	21 35	27 31	5 51	8 5	6 29	23 49	8 39	2 ♈ 38'39"
15 SA	1:25:30	21 57	1 39	22 36	27 58	5 56	8 7	6 30	23 49	8 40	2 ♈ 38'39"
16 SU	1:29:26	25 22	3 14	23 36	28 25	6 2	8 9	6 31	23 50	8 40	2 ♈ 38'39"
17 MO	1:33:23	28 42	4 49	24 37	28 52	6 7	8 11	6 32	23 50	8 40	2 ♈ 38'39"
18 TU	1:37:19	1 ♎ 58	6 25	25 37	29 19	6 13	8 14	6 32	23 50	8 41	2 ♈ 38'39"
19 WE	1:41:16	5 9	8 0	26 38	29 46	6 18	8 16	6 33	23 51	8 41	2 ♈ 38'38"
20 TH	1:45:13	8 17	9 35	27 38	0 ♍ 13	6 24	8 18	6 34	23 51	8 41	2 ♈ 38'38"
21 FR	1:49: 9	11 22	11 11	28 39	0 39	6 29	8 20	6 35	23 51	8 42	2 ♈ 38'38"
22 SA	1:53: 6	14 24	12 46	29 40	1 6	6 35	8 23	6 35	23 52	8 42	2 ♈ 38'38"
23 SU	1:57: 2	17 23	14 22	0 ♉ 41	1 33	6 40	8 25	6 36	23 52	8 43	2 ♈ 38'38"
24 MO	2: 0:59	20 19	15 57	1 41	2 0	6 45	8 27	6 37	23 53	8 43	2 ♈ 38'38"
25 TU	2: 4:55	23 13	17 33	2 42	2 27	6 51	8 30	6 38	23 53	8 43	2 ♈ 38'38"
26 WE	2: 8:52	26 6	19 8	3 43	2 54	6 56	8 32	6 38	23 53	8 44	2 ♈ 38'37"
27 TH	2:12:48	28 56	20 44	4 44	3 21	7 2	8 34	6 39	23 54	8 44	2 ♈ 38'37"
28 FR	2:16:45	1 ♏ 45	22 20	5 45	3 48	7 7	8 36	6 40	23 54	8 44	2 ♈ 38'37"
29 SA	2:20:42	4 33	23 55	6 46	4 16	7 13	8 39	6 41	23 54	8 45	2 ♈ 38'37"
30 SU	2:24:38	7 20	25 31	7 46	4 43	7 18	8 41	6 41	23 55	8 45	2 ♈ 38'37"
31 MO	2:28:35	10 5	27 7	8 47	5 10	7 24	8 43	6 42	23 55	8 45	2 ♈ 38'37"

INGRESSES :

2	☿ → ♌	11:59
9	☿ → ♍	3: 9
13	♀ → ♓	23: 9
17	☿ → ♎	9:31
19	♂ → ♍	12:47
22	⊕ → ♉	7:58
27	☿ → ♏	9: 2

ASPECTS (HELIOCENTRIC +MOON(TYCHONIC)) :

1	☿ ☍ ♆	6:38		☿ ☌ ♂	21: 1		☽ □ ♃	5:12	22	☽ ☍ ♃	3: 3		☽ ☍ ♄	6:19
2	☿ N ☊	0:56		☽ □ ♇	21:19		☽ ☌ ♄	9:30		☽ □ ♄	6: 1		☽ ☌ ♇	6:31
3	☿ ☌ ♅	18:59	10	☿ ☍ ♃	12:30		☽ ☍ ♇	10:33		☽ □ ♇	6:33		⊕ □ ♅	22: 5
4	☽ ☌ ♆	5:42	11	☿ □ ♄	3:38	16	⊕ □ ♆	5:25		☽ ☍ ♀	14:49	29	☽ □ ♀	9: 6
5	☽ ☍ ♅	5:49		☿ □ ♇	7:52	17	☽ □ ☿	2:15	25	☿ □ ♆	5:28		☿ □ ♅	18:29
6	☽ ☍ ☿	2:47		☽ □ ♆	16:27		♀ ☌ ♃	20:50		☽ □ ♆	6:41	30	☿ ☍ ⊕	6: 7
	☽ ☌ ♀	3:42		♀ ☍ ♂	18:44	19	☽ ☍ ♆	0:50		☽ ☌ ☿	6:58	31	☽ ☌ ♆	13:22
	☿ ☍ ♀	6:12	12	☽ □ ♅	18: 4		♀ □ ♄	4: 8	26	☽ □ ♅	2:48			
	☽ ☍ ♂	16:48	14	☽ □ ♂	12:53		♀ □ ♇	10:25		☿ ☌ ☋	13:17			
7	☽ ☌ ♃	14:37		☽ □ ♀	20: 6		☽ ☌ ♅	23:43	27	☽ □ ♂	22:21			
	☽ □ ♄	19:46	15	♀ S ☊	1:17	21	☽ ☌ ♂	17:45	28	☽ □ ♃	3:53			

SIDEREAL GEOCENTRIC LONGITUDES : NOVEMBER 29 Julian at 0 hours UT

DAY	☉	☽	☊	☿	♀	♂	♃	♄	♅	♆	♇
1 TU	9 ♏ 48	29 ♑ 39	12 ♊ 15	10 ♏ 46	27 ♐ 4	28 ♍ 51	26 ♒ 32	12 ♊ 8R	9 ♌ 47	22 ♑ 8	7 ♐ 55
2 WE	10 49	12 ♒ 19	12 15R	12 20	28 4	29 30	26 35	12 4	9 48	22 9	7 57
3 TH	11 50	24 41	12 15	13 55	29 3	0 ♎ 8	26 37	12 0	9 49	22 10	7 59
4 FR	12 50	6 ♓ 50	12 12	15 29	0 ♑ 2	0 47	26 40	11 56	9 49	22 11	8 1
5 SA	13 51	18 49	12 9	17 3	1 0	1 25	26 43	11 52	9 50	22 12	8 3
6 SU	14 52	0 ♈ 42	12 4	18 37	1 58	2 4	26 46	11 48	9 50	22 13	8 5
7 MO	15 53	12 33	11 59	20 11	2 55	2 43	26 49	11 43	9 51	22 14	8 7
8 TU	16 54	24 24	11 55	21 45	3 52	3 21	26 52	11 39	9 51	22 15	8 9
9 WE	17 56	6 ♉ 18	11 51	23 19	4 48	4 0	26 56	11 35	9 51	22 16	8 11
10 TH	18 57	18 16	11 48	24 53	5 44	4 39	27 0	11 31	9 52	22 18	8 13
11 FR	19 58	0 ♊ 21	11 46	26 27	6 38	5 17	27 4	11 26	9 52	22 19	8 15
12 SA	20 59	12 33	11 45	28 2	7 33	5 56	27 8	11 22	9 52	22 20	8 17
13 SU	22 0	24 55	11 46D	29 36	8 27	6 35	27 12	11 17	9 52	22 22	8 19
14 MO	23 1	7 ♋ 28	11 47	1 ♐ 10	9 20	7 13	27 17	11 13	9 52	22 23	8 21
15 TU	24 2	20 15	11 48	2 44	10 12	7 52	27 22	11 8	9 52R	22 24	8 23
16 WE	25 3	3 ♌ 18	11 50	4 19	11 3	8 30	27 27	11 3	9 52	22 26	8 25
17 TH	26 4	16 38	11 51	5 53	11 54	9 9	27 32	10 59	9 52	22 27	8 28
18 FR	27 6	0 ♍ 19	11 51R	7 27	12 44	9 48	27 37	10 54	9 52	22 29	8 30
19 SA	28 7	14 19	11 50	9 2	13 34	10 27	27 42	10 49	9 51	22 30	8 32
20 SU	29 8	28 40	11 49	10 36	14 22	11 5	27 48	10 44	9 51	22 32	8 34
21 MO	0 ♐ 9	13 ♎ 17	11 48	12 10	15 10	11 44	27 54	10 39	9 51	22 33	8 36
22 TU	1 10	28 7	11 46	13 44	15 56	12 23	28 0	10 35	9 50	22 35	8 38
23 WE	2 12	13 ♏ 2	11 45	15 18	16 42	13 1	28 6	10 30	9 50	22 36	8 40
24 TH	3 13	27 54	11 44	16 52	17 27	13 40	28 12	10 25	9 49	22 38	8 43
25 FR	4 14	12 ♐ 35	11 44D	18 25	18 10	14 19	28 19	10 20	9 49	22 39	8 45
26 SA	5 15	26 58	11 45	19 58	18 53	14 57	28 26	10 15	9 48	22 41	8 47
27 SU	6 17	10 ♑ 59	11 45	21 31	19 34	15 36	28 33	10 10	9 47	22 43	8 49
28 MO	7 18	24 35	11 46	23 2	20 14	16 15	28 40	10 5	9 47	22 45	8 51
29 TU	8 19	7 ♒ 46	11 46	24 33	20 54	16 53	28 47	10 0	9 46	22 46	8 54
30 WE	9 20	20 33	11 46	26 3	21 31	17 32	28 54	9 55	9 45	22 48	8 56

INGRESSES :

1	☽ → ♒	0:39	20	☽ → ♎	2:12
2	♂ → ♎	18:51		☉ → ♐	20:24
3	☽ → ♓	10:27	22	☽ → ♏	3: 2
	♀ → ♑	23:13	24	☽ → ♐	3:25
5	☽ → ♈	22:35	26	☽ → ♑	5: 7
8	☽ → ♉	11:18	28	☽ → ♒	9:45
10	☽ → ♊	23:18	30	☽ → ♓	18: 9
13	☿ → ♐	6:10			
	☽ → ♋	9:45			
15	☽ → ♌	17:59			
17	☽ → ♍	23:27			

ASPECTS & ECLIPSES :

1	☽ ☍ ♅	19:10		☽ ☌ ♄	21:40		☿ ☍ ☊	18:19	29	☽ ☍ ♅	3:41
	☉ □ ☽	20:51		☽ ☌ ☊	22:26		☽ ☌ ♂	21:20		☉ ☌ ♇	13:57
3	☽ ☌ ♃	3:47	14	☽ ☍ ♀	3:45	22	☽ ☌ P	17:48	30	☉ ☍ ♄	12:30
4	☽ S ☊	10:41	15	☽ ☍ ♆	4: 0	24	☉ ☌ ☽	9:17		☽ ☌ ♃	16:11
6	☽ ☍ ♂	2:55	16	☽ ☌ ♅	11:53		☉ ● T	9:23			
	♀ □ ♂	7:56	17	☉ □ ☽	17:57		☽ ☌ ♇	17:40			
	☽ ☌ A	23:15		☽ ☍ ♃	19:17		☽ ☍ ♄	20:18			
10	☉ ☍ ☽	1:28	18	☉ □ ♃	13:30		☽ ☌ ☋	22:36			
	☽ ☍ ☿	15: 8		☿ ☌ ♇	16:14	25	☽ ☌ ☿	10:50			
11	☿ □ ♃	9:39		☽ N ☊	19:47	27	☽ ☌ ♀	15:50			
	☽ ☍ ♇	15:36	20	☿ ☍ ♄	2: 1		☽ ☌ ♆	20:41			

SIDEREAL HELIOCENTRIC LONGITUDES : NOVEMBER 29 Julian at 0 hours UT

DAY	Sid. Time	☿	♀	⊕	♂	♃	♄	♅	♆	♇	Vernal Point
1 TU	2:32:31	12 ♏ 51	28 ♓ 42	9 ♉ 48	5 ♍ 37	7 ♓ 29	8 ♊ 45	6 ♌ 43	23 ♑ 55	8 ♐ 46	2 ♈ 38'37"
2 WE	2:36:28	15 35	0 ♈ 18	10 49	6 4	7 35	8 48	6 44	23 56	8 46	2 ♈ 38'36"
3 TH	2:40:24	18 20	1 54	11 50	6 31	7 40	8 50	6 45	23 56	8 46	2 ♈ 38'36"
4 FR	2:44:21	21 4	3 30	12 51	6 58	7 45	8 52	6 45	23 56	8 47	2 ♈ 38'36"
5 SA	2:48:17	23 49	5 6	13 52	7 26	7 51	8 54	6 46	23 57	8 47	2 ♈ 38'36"
6 SU	2:52:14	26 34	6 42	14 53	7 53	7 56	8 57	6 47	23 57	8 47	2 ♈ 38'36"
7 MO	2:56:11	29 20	8 18	15 54	8 20	8 2	8 59	6 48	23 58	8 48	2 ♈ 38'36"
8 TU	3: 0: 7	2 ♐ 7	9 54	16 55	8 48	8 7	9 1	6 48	23 58	8 48	2 ♈ 38'36"
9 WE	3: 4: 4	4 55	11 30	17 56	9 15	8 13	9 4	6 49	23 58	8 48	2 ♈ 38'36"
10 TH	3: 8: 0	7 44	13 6	18 57	9 42	8 18	9 6	6 50	23 59	8 49	2 ♈ 38'35"
11 FR	3:11:57	10 34	14 42	19 58	10 10	8 24	9 8	6 51	23 59	8 49	2 ♈ 38'35"
12 SA	3:15:53	13 26	16 18	20 59	10 37	8 29	9 10	6 51	23 59	8 49	2 ♈ 38'35"
13 SU	3:19:50	16 20	17 54	22 0	11 4	8 35	9 13	6 52	24 0	8 50	2 ♈ 38'35"
14 MO	3:23:46	19 16	19 30	23 2	11 32	8 40	9 15	6 53	24 0	8 50	2 ♈ 38'35"
15 TU	3:27:43	22 15	21 7	24 3	11 59	8 45	9 17	6 54	24 0	8 50	2 ♈ 38'35"
16 WE	3:31:40	25 16	22 43	25 4	12 27	8 51	9 19	6 55	24 1	8 51	2 ♈ 38'35"
17 TH	3:35:36	28 20	24 19	26 5	12 55	8 56	9 22	6 55	24 1	8 51	2 ♈ 38'34"
18 FR	3:39:33	1 ♑ 28	25 55	27 6	13 22	9 2	9 24	6 56	24 2	8 51	2 ♈ 38'34"
19 SA	3:43:29	4 38	27 32	28 7	13 50	9 7	9 26	6 57	24 2	8 52	2 ♈ 38'34"
20 SU	3:47:26	7 53	29 8	29 9	14 17	9 13	9 28	6 58	24 2	8 52	2 ♈ 38'34"
21 MO	3:51:22	11 12	0 ♉ 45	0 ♊ 10	14 45	9 18	9 31	6 58	24 3	8 52	2 ♈ 38'34"
22 TU	3:55:19	14 35	2 21	1 11	15 13	9 24	9 33	6 59	24 3	8 53	2 ♈ 38'34"
23 WE	3:59:15	18 3	3 57	2 12	15 40	9 29	9 35	7 0	24 3	8 53	2 ♈ 38'34"
24 TH	4: 3:12	21 36	5 34	3 14	16 8	9 35	9 38	7 1	24 4	8 54	2 ♈ 38'33"
25 FR	4: 7: 9	25 14	7 11	4 15	16 36	9 40	9 40	7 1	24 4	8 54	2 ♈ 38'33"
26 SA	4:11: 5	28 58	8 47	5 16	17 4	9 45	9 42	7 2	24 4	8 54	2 ♈ 38'33"
27 SU	4:15: 2	2 ♒ 49	10 24	6 17	17 32	9 51	9 44	7 3	24 5	8 55	2 ♈ 38'33"
28 MO	4:18:58	6 45	12 0	7 19	17 59	9 56	9 47	7 4	24 5	8 55	2 ♈ 38'33"
29 TU	4:22:55	10 49	13 37	8 20	18 27	10 2	9 49	7 4	24 5	8 55	2 ♈ 38'33"
30 WE	4:26:51	15 0	15 14	9 21	18 55	10 7	9 51	7 5	24 6	8 56	2 ♈ 38'33"

INGRESSES :

1	♀ → ♈	19:26
7	☿ → ♐	5:43
17	☿ → ♑	12:49
20	♀ → ♉	12:54
	⊕ → ♊	20: 9
26	☿ → ♒	6:30

ASPECTS (HELIOCENTRIC +MOON(TYCHONIC)) :

1	♄ ☍ ♇	2:30	8	♂ □ ♇	0:24	12	☽ ☍ ☿	2:14	21	☽ □ ♆	17:26	27	☽ ☌ ♆	23: 5
	☽ ☍ ♅	13:19		♂ □ ♄	13: 9	15	☽ □ ♀	1:48	22	☽ ☍ ♀	7:38	28	☿ ☍ ♅	1:50
2	☽ □ ☿	8: 4	9	☽ □ ♅	1: 3		☽ ☍ ♆	6:57		☽ □ ♅	14:17		☽ ☍ ♅	22:43
3	☿ ☌ A	10:39	10	☿ □ ♃	5: 3		♃ □ ♇	23:14	24	☿ ☌ ♆	16:21	29	☽ ☌ ☿	8:21
4	☽ ☍ ♂	0:17		☿ ☌ ♇	9:13	16	☽ ☌ ♅	6:33		☽ ☌ ♇	17:56		☽ □ ♀	12:27
	☽ ☌ ♃	1:51		☿ ☍ ♄	11:46		♀ □ ♆	19:30		☽ □ ♃	19:10		⊕ ☍ ♇	13:57
	☽ □ ♇	3:53		☿ □ ♂	19:56	18	☽ □ ♇	14:42		☽ ☍ ♄	19:11	30	☿ □ ♀	2: 3
	☽ □ ♄	4: 4	11	☽ □ ♃	15:58		☽ ☍ ♃	15: 6		♀ □ ♅	21:43		⊕ ☌ ♄	12:15
6	♂ ☍ ♃	3:44		☽ ☍ ♇	16:41		☽ □ ♄	15:40		♃ □ ♄	22:30		⊕ □ ♃	19:54
	☽ ☌ ♀	14: 2		☽ ☌ ♄	17:21		☽ ☌ ♂	23: 8	25	☽ □ ♂	6:51			
7	☽ □ ♆	23: 7		☽ □ ♂	20: 3	20	☽ □ ☿	19:35		☿ S ☊	15:43			

SIDEREAL GEOCENTRIC LONGITUDES : DECEMBER 29 Julian at 0 hours UT

DAY	☉	☽	☊	☿	♀	♂	♃	♄	♅	♆	♇
1 TH	10 ♐ 22	3 ♓ 0	11 ♊ 46	27 ♐ 31	22 ♑ 8	18 ♎ 11	29 ♒ 2	9 ♊ 50R	9 ♌ 44R	22 ♑ 50	8 ♐ 58
2 FR	11 23	15 11	11 46	28 58	22 43	18 49	29 9	9 45	9 43	22 52	9 0
3 SA	12 24	27 10	11 46	0 ♑ 23	23 16	19 28	29 17	9 40	9 42	22 53	9 2
4 SU	13 25	9 ♈ 3	11 47	1 45	23 48	20 7	29 25	9 35	9 41	22 55	9 4
5 MO	14 27	20 53	11 47	3 5	24 19	20 45	29 33	9 30	9 40	22 57	9 7
6 TU	15 28	2 ♉ 45	11 47	4 22	24 48	21 24	29 41	9 25	9 39	22 59	9 9
7 WE	16 29	14 42	11 48	5 34	25 15	22 3	29 50	9 20	9 38	23 1	9 11
8 TH	17 30	26 47	11 48	6 43	25 40	22 41	29 58	9 15	9 36	23 3	9 13
9 FR	18 32	9 ♊ 3	11 48	7 46	26 4	23 20	0 ♓ 7	9 10	9 35	23 5	9 15
10 SA	19 33	21 31	11 48R	8 43	26 25	23 59	0 16	9 5	9 34	23 7	9 17
11 SU	20 34	4 ♋ 12	11 48	9 33	26 45	24 38	0 25	9 1	9 32	23 9	9 20
12 MO	21 35	17 7	11 47	10 16	27 3	25 16	0 34	8 56	9 31	23 11	9 22
13 TU	22 36	0 ♌ 15	11 45	10 50	27 18	25 55	0 43	8 51	9 29	23 13	9 24
14 WE	23 38	13 36	11 44	11 15	27 32	26 34	0 53	8 46	9 28	23 15	9 26
15 TH	24 39	27 10	11 42	11 29	27 43	27 12	1 2	8 42	9 26	23 17	9 28
16 FR	25 40	10 ♍ 56	11 41	11 33R	27 52	27 51	1 12	8 37	9 25	23 19	9 30
17 SA	26 41	24 53	11 40	11 25	27 59	28 30	1 22	8 32	9 23	23 21	9 32
18 SU	27 42	9 ♎ 1	11 41D	11 5	28 3	29 8	1 31	8 28	9 21	23 23	9 34
19 MO	28 43	23 18	11 42	10 33	28 5	29 47	1 41	8 23	9 20	23 25	9 36
20 TU	29 45	7 ♏ 41	11 43	9 51	28 4R	0 ♏ 26	1 52	8 19	9 18	23 27	9 39
21 WE	0 ♑ 46	22 7	11 44	8 58	28 1	1 4	2 2	8 14	9 16	23 29	9 41
22 TH	1 47	6 ♐ 31	11 45	7 56	27 56	1 43	2 12	8 10	9 14	23 31	9 43
23 FR	2 48	20 49	11 44R	6 47	27 48	2 22	2 23	8 6	9 12	23 34	9 45
24 SA	3 49	4 ♑ 56	11 43	5 33	27 37	3 0	2 33	8 1	9 10	23 36	9 47
25 SU	4 50	18 47	11 40	4 17	27 24	3 39	2 44	7 57	9 8	23 38	9 49
26 MO	5 51	2 ♒ 19	11 37	3 0	27 9	4 17	2 55	7 53	9 6	23 40	9 51
27 TU	6 53	15 30	11 33	1 45	26 51	4 56	3 6	7 49	9 4	23 42	9 53
28 WE	7 54	28 20	11 29	0 34	26 30	5 35	3 17	7 45	9 2	23 45	9 55
29 TH	8 55	10 ♓ 51	11 25	29 ♐ 29	26 8	6 13	3 28	7 41	9 0	23 47	9 57
30 FR	9 56	23 4	11 23	28 30	25 43	6 52	3 39	7 37	8 58	23 49	9 59
31 SA	10 57	5 ♈ 5	11 22	27 40	25 16	7 30	3 50	7 34	8 56	23 51	10 1

INGRESSES :

2 ☿ → ♑ 17:28	20 ☉ → ♑ 6: 1
3 ☽ → ♈ 5:41	21 ☽ → ♐ 13: 7
5 ☽ → ♉ 18:27	23 ☽ → ♑ 15:34
8 ♃ → ♓ 4:19	25 ☽ → ♒ 19:50
☽ → ♊ 6:19	28 ☽ → ♓ 3: 9
10 ☽ → ♋ 16: 5	☿ → ♐ 12:12
12 ☽ → ♌ 23:33	30 ☽ → ♈ 13:47
15 ☽ → ♍ 4:58	
17 ☽ → ♎ 8:42	
19 ♂ → ♏ 8: 7	
☽ → ♏ 11:11	

ASPECTS & ECLIPSES :

1 ☉ □ ☽ 15:45	☽ ●-● P 19:43	20 ☽ ☌ P 15:33	29 ☽ ☐S ☊ 1: 7
☽ ☐S ☊ 17:13	☉ ☍ ☽ 19:54	22 ☽ ☍ ♄ 2:44	31 ☉ □ ☽ 12:54
2 ♀ ☌ ♆ 6:37	11 ☽ ☍ ☿ 10:37	☽ ☌ ♇ 5:21	
☉ ☍ ☊ 9:12	12 ☽ ☍ ♆ 11:10	☽ ☌ ☋ 8:44	
4 ☽ ☌ A 14:43	☽ ☍ ♀ 18:34	23 ☉ ☌ ☽ 21:56	
☽ ☍ ♂ 23:44	13 ☽ ☌ ♅ 16:38	24 ☽ ☌ ☿ 0:58	
8 ♄ ☍ ♇ 7:22	15 ☽ ☍ ♃ 6:52	☉ ☌' ☿ 18: 8	
♂ □ ♆ 13:56	16 ♀ □ ♂ 0:55	25 ☽ ☌ ♆ 8:33	
9 ☽ ☌ ♄ 0:14	☽ ☐N ☊ 1:17	☽ ☌ ♀ 14:56	
☽ ☍ ♇ 0:23	17 ☉ □ ☽ 3:18	26 ☽ ☍ ♅ 12:14	
☽ ☌ ☊ 5:20	19 ☽ ☌ ♂ 11:20	28 ☽ ☌ ♃ 9:33	

SIDEREAL HELIOCENTRIC LONGITUDES : DECEMBER 29 Julian at 0 hours UT

DAY	Sid. Time	☿	♀	⊕	♂	♃	♄	♅	♆	♇	Vernal Point
1 TH	4:30:48	19 ♒ 19	16 ♉ 50	10 ♊ 22	19 ♍ 23	10 ♓ 13	9 ♊ 53	7 ♌ 6	24 ♑ 6	8 ♐ 56	2♈38'33"
2 FR	4:34:44	23 46	18 27	11 24	19 51	10 18	9 56	7 7	24 7	8 56	2♈38'32"
3 SA	4:38:41	28 21	20 4	12 25	20 19	10 24	9 58	7 8	24 7	8 57	2♈38'32"
4 SU	4:42:38	3 ♓ 4	21 41	13 26	20 47	10 29	10 0	7 8	24 7	8 57	2♈38'32"
5 MO	4:46:34	7 57	23 18	14 27	21 16	10 35	10 3	7 9	24 8	8 57	2♈38'32"
6 TU	4:50:31	12 58	24 55	15 29	21 44	10 40	10 5	7 10	24 8	8 58	2♈38'32"
7 WE	4:54:27	18 9	26 32	16 30	22 12	10 46	10 7	7 11	24 8	8 58	2♈38'32"
8 TH	4:58:24	23 28	28 8	17 31	22 40	10 51	10 9	7 11	24 9	8 58	2♈38'32"
9 FR	5: 2:20	28 57	29 45	18 32	23 8	10 56	10 12	7 12	24 9	8 59	2♈38'32"
10 SA	5: 6:17	4 ♈ 34	1 ♊ 22	19 33	23 37	11 2	10 14	7 13	24 9	8 59	2♈38'31"
11 SU	5:10:13	10 20	3 0	20 35	24 5	11 7	10 16	7 14	24 10	8 59	2♈38'31"
12 MO	5:14:10	16 13	4 37	21 36	24 33	11 13	10 18	7 14	24 10	9 0	2♈38'31"
13 TU	5:18: 7	22 13	6 14	22 37	25 2	11 18	10 21	7 15	24 10	9 0	2♈38'31"
14 WE	5:22: 3	28 20	7 51	23 38	25 30	11 24	10 23	7 16	24 11	9 0	2♈38'31"
15 TH	5:26: 0	4 ♉ 31	9 28	24 39	25 58	11 29	10 25	7 17	24 11	9 1	2♈38'31"
16 FR	5:29:56	10 46	11 5	25 41	26 27	11 35	10 27	7 18	24 12	9 1	2♈38'30"
17 SA	5:33:53	17 4	12 42	26 42	26 55	11 40	10 30	7 18	24 12	9 1	2♈38'30"
18 SU	5:37:49	23 22	14 20	27 43	27 24	11 46	10 32	7 19	24 12	9 2	2♈38'30"
19 MO	5:41:46	29 40	15 57	28 44	27 53	11 51	10 34	7 20	24 13	9 2	2♈38'30"
20 TU	5:45:42	5 ♊ 56	17 34	29 45	28 21	11 57	10 37	7 21	24 13	9 2	2♈38'30"
21 WE	5:49:39	12 8	19 12	0 ♋ 46	28 50	12 2	10 39	7 21	24 13	9 3	2♈38'30"
22 TH	5:53:36	18 16	20 49	1 48	29 19	12 7	10 41	7 22	24 14	9 3	2♈38'30"
23 FR	5:57:32	24 18	22 26	2 49	29 47	12 13	10 43	7 23	24 14	9 3	2♈38'30"
24 SA	6: 1:29	0 ♋ 13	24 4	3 50	0 ♎ 16	12 18	10 46	7 24	24 14	9 4	2♈38'29"
25 SU	6: 5:25	6 0	25 41	4 51	0 45	12 24	10 48	7 24	24 15	9 4	2♈38'29"
26 MO	6: 9:22	11 38	27 18	5 52	1 14	12 29	10 50	7 25	24 15	9 4	2♈38'29"
27 TU	6:13:18	17 8	28 56	6 53	1 43	12 35	10 52	7 26	24 16	9 5	2♈38'29"
28 WE	6:17:15	22 28	0 ♋ 33	7 54	2 12	12 40	10 55	7 27	24 16	9 5	2♈38'29"
29 TH	6:21:11	27 39	2 11	8 55	2 41	12 46	10 57	7 27	24 16	9 6	2♈38'29"
30 FR	6:25: 8	2 ♌ 40	3 48	9 56	3 10	12 51	10 59	7 28	24 17	9 6	2♈38'29"
31 SA	6:29: 5	7 31	5 26	10 57	3 39	12 57	11 1	7 29	24 17	9 6	2♈38'28"

INGRESSES :

3 ☿ → ♓ 8:29
9 ♀ → ♊ 3:35
☿ → ♈ 4:31
14 ☿ → ♉ 6:30
19 ☿ → ♊ 1:16
20 ⊕ → ♋ 5:47
23 ♂ → ♎ 10:33
☿ → ♋ 23: 6
27 ♀ → ♋ 15:46
29 ☿ → ♌ 11:11

ASPECTS (HELIOCENTRIC +MOON(TYCHONIC)) :

1 ☽ □ ♇ 11:37	7 ☿ ☍ ♂ 20: 4	☿ ☌ ☊ 21:25	⊕ □ ♂ 10: 4	☽ ☍ ☿ 10: 9	♀ □ ♂ 10:26
☽ □ ♄ 13:33	8 ☽ ☌ ♀ 3: 4	14 ♀ ☍ ♇ 17:14	19 ☽ □ ♆ 1:31	☽ □ ♂ 15:44	30 ☽ ☍ ♂ 20:58
☽ ☌ ♃ 14:15	☽ ☍ ♇ 23:51	15 ☿ □ ♅ 10:38	☽ □ ♅ 23:26	24 ☿ □ ♂ 0:14	☿ ☌ ♅ 23:49
2 ☽ ☍ ♂ 9:41	9 ☽ ☌ ♄ 2:13	♀ ☌ ♄ 14:27	20 ☿ ☍ ♇ 11:59	☿ ☌ ⊕ 18: 8	31 ☽ □ ♀ 0:47
⊕ ☌ P 11:25	☽ □ ♃ 3:41	☽ □ ♇ 20:41	☿ ☌ ♄ 18: 9	25 ☽ ☌ ♆ 9:37	
5 ☿ □ ♇ 4:53	10 ☽ □ ♂ 4: 8	☽ □ ♄ 23:10	☿ □ ♃ 23:34	26 ☽ ☍ ♅ 9:13	
☽ □ ♆ 6:34	♀ ☌ ☊ 5:14	16 ☽ □ ♀ 0:18	22 ☽ ☌ ♇ 4:14	28 ☿ ☍ ♆ 8:15	
☿ □ ♄ 10:11	11 ☽ □ ☿ 20:58	☽ ☍ ♃ 1: 7	☽ ☍ ♄ 6:59	☽ □ ♇ 20:36	
☿ ☌ ♃ 12:53	12 ☽ ☍ ♆ 12:57	♀ □ ♃ 7:42	☽ □ ♃ 9:26	29 ☿ ☐N ☊ 0: 8	
6 ☽ □ ♅ 8:54	13 ☿ □ ♆ 7:42	17 ☽ ☌ ♂ 3:35	☿ ☌ ♀ 13:46	☽ □ ♄ 0:12	
☿ □ ⊕ 14:34	☽ ☌ ♅ 12:39	☿ ☌ P 9:28	23 ☽ ☍ ♀ 3: 5	☽ ☌ ♃ 3:45	

SIDEREAL GEOCENTRIC LONGITUDES : JANUARY 30 Julian at 0 hours UT

DAY	☉	☽	☊	☿	♀	♂	♃	♄	♅	♆	♇
1 SU	11 ♑ 58	16 ♈ 58	11 ♊ 22	26 ♐ 58R	24 ♑ 47R	8 ♏ 9	4 ♓ 2	7 ♊ 30R	8 ♌ 53R	23 ♑ 53	10 ♐ 3
2 MO	12 59	28 48	11 23	26 25	24 16	8 47	4 13	7 26	8 51	23 56	10 4
3 TU	13 59	10 ♉ 40	11 24	26 1	23 43	9 26	4 25	7 23	8 49	23 58	10 6
4 WE	15 0	22 39	11 26	25 45	23 9	10 5	4 37	7 19	8 46	24 0	10 8
5 TH	16 1	4 ♊ 49	11 27	25 37	22 34	10 43	4 49	7 16	8 44	24 2	10 10
6 FR	17 2	17 14	11 27R	25 38D	21 58	11 22	5 0	7 13	8 42	24 5	10 12
7 SA	18 3	29 55	11 26	25 45	21 22	12 0	5 12	7 10	8 39	24 7	10 14
8 SU	19 4	12 ♋ 56	11 22	25 59	20 44	12 39	5 24	7 7	8 37	24 9	10 15
9 MO	20 5	26 14	11 17	26 20	20 7	13 17	5 37	7 4	8 35	24 11	10 17
10 TU	21 5	9 ♌ 49	11 11	26 47	19 29	13 56	5 49	7 1	8 32	24 14	10 19
11 WE	22 6	23 38	11 4	27 19	18 52	14 34	6 1	6 58	8 30	24 16	10 21
12 TH	23 7	7 ♍ 37	10 57	27 55	18 16	15 13	6 14	6 55	8 27	24 18	10 23
13 FR	24 8	21 43	10 52	28 36	17 40	15 51	6 26	6 53	8 25	24 21	10 24
14 SA	25 8	5 ♎ 51	10 48	29 22	17 6	16 29	6 39	6 50	8 22	24 23	10 26
15 SU	26 9	20 1	10 46	0 ♑ 11	16 32	17 8	6 51	6 48	8 20	24 25	10 28
16 MO	27 10	4 ♏ 9	10 46D	1 4	16 0	17 46	7 4	6 46	8 17	24 27	10 29
17 TU	28 10	18 14	10 47	1 59	15 30	18 25	7 17	6 44	8 14	24 30	10 31
18 WE	29 11	2 ♐ 16	10 48	2 58	15 2	19 3	7 29	6 41	8 12	24 32	10 32
19 TH	0 ♒ 11	16 12	10 48R	3 59	14 36	19 41	7 42	6 39	8 9	24 34	10 34
20 FR	1 12	0 ♑ 1	10 46	5 3	14 12	20 20	7 55	6 38	8 7	24 37	10 36
21 SA	2 12	13 42	10 42	6 9	13 50	20 58	8 8	6 36	8 4	24 39	10 37
22 SU	3 13	27 12	10 36	7 18	13 30	21 36	8 21	6 34	8 1	24 41	10 39
23 MO	4 13	10 ♒ 27	10 27	8 28	13 13	22 15	8 35	6 33	7 59	24 43	10 40
24 TU	5 14	23 28	10 17	9 40	12 58	22 53	8 48	6 31	7 56	24 46	10 41
25 WE	6 14	6 ♓ 12	10 6	10 54	12 46	23 31	9 1	6 30	7 54	24 48	10 43
26 TH	7 15	18 39	9 57	12 10	12 36	24 9	9 14	6 29	7 51	24 50	10 44
27 FR	8 15	0 ♈ 52	9 49	13 27	12 28	24 48	9 28	6 28	7 48	24 52	10 46
28 SA	9 15	12 53	9 43	14 46	12 23	25 26	9 41	6 27	7 46	24 54	10 47
29 SU	10 16	24 46	9 39	16 7	12 21	26 4	9 55	6 26	7 43	24 57	10 48
30 MO	11 16	6 ♉ 35	9 38	17 28	12 21D	26 42	10 8	6 25	7 40	24 59	10 50
31 TU	12 16	18 26	9 38D	18 51	12 23	27 20	10 22	6 24	7 38	25 1	10 51

INGRESSES :

2 ☽ → ♉	2:25	22 ☽ → ♒ 5: 2
4 ☽ → ♊	14:32	24 ☽ → ♓ 12:15
7 ☽ → ♋	0: 8	26 ☽ → ♈ 22:16
9 ☽ → ♌	6:42	29 ☽ → ♉ 10:37
11 ☽ → ♍	10:57	31 ☽ → ♊ 23:12
13 ☽ → ♎	14: 4	
14 ☿ → ♑	18:47	
15 ☽ → ♏	16:56	
17 ☽ → ♐	20: 7	
18 ☉ → ♒	19:30	
19 ☽ → ♑	23:57	

ASPECTS & ECLIPSES :

1 ☽ ☌ A 11:15	☽ ☍ ♆ 20:20	18 ☽ ☍ ♄ 7:35	☽ ☿ ☊ 7:23
2 ♂ □ ♅ 2: 5	9 ☉ ☌ ♀ 0:32	☽ ☌ ♇ 14:15	26 ☿ ☌ ♀ 7:15
♀ ☌ ♆ 14: 0	☽ ☌ ♅ 21:45	☽ ☌ ☋ 14:41	☉ ☍ ♅ 13:51
☽ ☍ ♂ 21:21	11 ☽ ☍ ♃ 21:35	20 ☽ ☌ ☿ 9:33	28 ♃ □ ☊ 2:14
5 ☉ □ Π 1:10	12 ☽ ☌N ☊ 5:39	21 ☽ ☌ ♀ 0:13	29 ☽ ☌ A 8:17
☽ ☌ ♄ 4:45	13 ☉ ☌ ♆ 5:21	♇ ☍ ☊ 15:56	30 ☉ □ ☽ 10:22
☽ ☍ ♇ 10:26	14 ♃ □ ♄ 18:56	☽ ☌ ♆ 19:29	31 ☽ ☍ ♂ 18:52
☽ ☌ ☊ 12:54	15 ☽ ☌ P 6:55	22 ☉ ☌ ☽ 11:44	
6 ☽ ☍ ☿ 16: 4	☉ □ ☽ 11:12	☽ ☍ ♅ 19:30	
8 ☉ ☍ ☽ 12: 3	16 ☉ □ Π 12:25	25 ☉ □ Π 4:24	
☽ ☍ ♀ 13:31	17 ☽ ☌ ♂ 0:18	☽ ☌ ♃ 5:29	

SIDEREAL HELIOCENTRIC LONGITUDES : JANUARY 30 Julian at 0 hours UT

DAY	Sid. Time	☿	♀	⊕	♂	♃	♄	♅	♆	♇	Vernal Point
1 SU	6:33: 1	12 ♌ 13	7 ♋ 3	11 ♋ 58	4 ♎ 8	13 ♓ 2	11 ♊ 4	7 ♌ 30	24 ♑ 17	9 ♐ 7	2♈38'28"
2 MO	6:36:58	16 47	8 41	12 59	4 37	13 7	11 6	7 31	24 18	9 7	2♈38'28"
3 TU	6:40:54	21 11	10 19	14 0	5 6	13 13	11 8	7 31	24 18	9 7	2♈38'28"
4 WE	6:44:51	25 28	11 56	15 1	5 35	13 18	11 10	7 32	24 18	9 8	2♈38'28"
5 TH	6:48:47	29 36	13 34	16 2	6 5	13 24	11 13	7 33	24 19	9 8	2♈38'28"
6 FR	6:52:44	3 ♍ 37	15 11	17 3	6 34	13 29	11 15	7 34	24 19	9 8	2♈38'28"
7 SA	6:56:40	7 31	16 49	18 4	7 3	13 35	11 17	7 34	24 19	9 9	2♈38'27"
8 SU	7: 0:37	11 18	18 27	19 4	7 33	13 40	11 20	7 35	24 20	9 9	2♈38'27"
9 MO	7: 4:34	14 59	20 4	20 5	8 2	13 46	11 22	7 36	24 20	9 9	2♈38'27"
10 TU	7: 8:30	18 34	21 42	21 6	8 32	13 51	11 24	7 37	24 21	9 10	2♈38'27"
11 WE	7:12:27	22 4	23 20	22 7	9 1	13 57	11 26	7 37	24 21	9 10	2♈38'27"
12 TH	7:16:23	25 28	24 57	23 7	9 31	14 2	11 29	7 38	24 21	9 10	2♈38'27"
13 FR	7:20:20	28 48	26 35	24 8	10 0	14 8	11 31	7 39	24 22	9 11	2♈38'27"
14 SA	7:24:16	2 ♎ 4	28 13	25 9	10 30	14 13	11 33	7 40	24 22	9 11	2♈38'27"
15 SU	7:28:13	5 16	29 50	26 9	11 0	14 18	11 35	7 41	24 22	9 11	2♈38'26"
16 MO	7:32: 9	8 24	1 ♌ 28	27 10	11 30	14 24	11 38	7 41	24 23	9 12	2♈38'26"
17 TU	7:36: 6	11 28	3 6	28 11	11 59	14 29	11 40	7 42	24 23	9 12	2♈38'26"
18 WE	7:40: 3	14 30	4 43	29 11	12 29	14 35	11 42	7 43	24 23	9 12	2♈38'26"
19 TH	7:43:59	17 29	6 21	0 ♌ 12	12 59	14 40	11 44	7 44	24 24	9 13	2♈38'26"
20 FR	7:47:56	20 25	7 59	1 12	13 29	14 46	11 47	7 44	24 24	9 13	2♈38'26"
21 SA	7:51:52	23 19	9 36	2 13	13 59	14 51	11 49	7 45	24 24	9 13	2♈38'26"
22 SU	7:55:49	26 11	11 14	3 13	14 29	14 57	11 51	7 46	24 25	9 14	2♈38'25"
23 MO	7:59:45	29 2	12 51	4 14	14 59	15 2	11 54	7 47	24 25	9 14	2♈38'25"
24 TU	8: 3:42	1 ♏ 51	14 29	5 14	15 29	15 8	11 56	7 47	24 26	9 14	2♈38'25"
25 WE	8: 7:38	4 38	16 7	6 15	15 59	15 13	11 58	7 48	24 26	9 15	2♈38'25"
26 TH	8:11:35	7 25	17 44	7 15	16 30	15 19	12 0	7 49	24 26	9 15	2♈38'25"
27 FR	8:15:32	10 11	19 22	8 16	17 0	15 24	12 3	7 50	24 27	9 15	2♈38'25"
28 SA	8:19:28	12 56	20 59	9 16	17 30	15 29	12 5	7 50	24 27	9 16	2♈38'25"
29 SU	8:23:25	15 41	22 37	10 16	18 1	15 35	12 7	7 51	24 27	9 16	2♈38'24"
30 MO	8:27:21	18 25	24 14	11 16	18 31	15 40	12 9	7 52	24 28	9 16	2♈38'24"
31 TU	8:31:18	21 10	25 52	12 17	19 2	15 46	12 12	7 53	24 28	9 17	2♈38'24"

INGRESSES :

5 ☿ → ♍	2:20
13 ☿ → ♎	8:43
15 ♀ → ♌	2:22
18 ⊕ → ♌	19:17
23 ☿ → ♏	8:14

ASPECTS (HELIOCENTRIC +MOON(TYCHONIC)) :

1 ☽ □ ♆ 14:50	☿ ☍ ♃ 15:45	15 ☽ □ ♆ 7:23	☽ □ ☿ 21:43	☽ □ ♆ 23:22
2 ☽ □ ♅ 17:38	☽ ☍ ♆ 20:36	☽ □ ♀ 18:50	22 ☿ ☌ ☋ 12:29	29 ♃ ☌ P 15: 0
4 ☽ □ ☿ 8:31	9 ♀ ☌ ⊕ 0:32	16 ☽ □ ♅ 6: 1	☽ ☍ ♅ 19: 6	30 ☽ □ ♅ 2:36
5 ☽ ☍ ♇ 8:24	☽ ☌ ♅ 20: 7	17 ☿ ☌ ♂ 4:52	23 ☽ ☍ ♀ 5: 1	☿ ☌ A 9:52
☽ ☌ ♄ 12:28	11 ♀ ☍ ♆ 15: 6	18 ☽ ☌ ♇ 11:56	25 ☽ □ ♇ 5:50	31 ☽ ☍ ☿ 7: 9
☽ □ ♃ 16:46	12 ☽ □ ♇ 2:39	☽ ☍ ♄ 16:17	☽ □ ♄ 11: 5	☽ □ ♀ 17:16
6 ♀ ☌ P 14:58	☽ □ ♄ 6:36	☽ □ ♃ 21:20	☽ ☌ ♃ 17:27	
7 ☿ □ ♇ 10:14	☽ ☍ ♃ 11: 1	19 ♀ ☌ ♅ 20:28	☿ □ ⊕ 21:46	
☽ □ ♂ 13:45	13 ⊕ ☍ ♆ 5:21	21 ☽ □ ♂ 0:31	26 ☿ □ ♅ 3:28	
8 ☿ □ ♄ 0: 9	☽ ☌ ☿ 15:40	☿ □ ♆ 9: 5	⊕ ☌ ♅ 13:36	
☽ ☌ ♀ 11:24	14 ☽ ☌ ♂ 8: 9	☽ ☌ ♆ 19: 1	28 ☽ ☍ ♂ 9:43	

SIDEREAL GEOCENTRIC LONGITUDES : FEBRUARY 30 Julian at 0 hours UT

DAY	☉	☽	☊	☿	♀	♂	♃	♄	♅	♆	♇
1 WE	13 ♒ 16	0 ♊ 24	9 ♊ 39	20 ♑ 16	12 ♑ 28	27 ♏ 58	10 ♓ 35	6 ♊ 24R	7 ♌ 35R	25 ♑ 3	10 ♐ 52
2 TH	14 16	12 34	9 39R	21 41	12 35	28 36	10 49	6 23	7 33	25 5	10 53
3 FR	15 16	25 2	9 37	23 8	12 44	29 14	11 3	6 23	7 30	25 8	10 54
4 SA	16 16	7 ♋ 51	9 34	24 36	12 55	29 52	11 17	6 23	7 27	25 10	10 56
5 SU	17 16	21 3	9 28	26 5	13 9	0 ♐ 30	11 30	6 23	7 25	25 12	10 57
6 MO	18 16	4 ♌ 40	9 19	27 36	13 24	1 8	11 44	6 23D	7 22	25 14	10 58
7 TU	19 16	18 38	9 9	29 7	13 42	1 46	11 58	6 23	7 20	25 16	10 59
8 WE	20 16	2 ♍ 54	8 57	0 ♒ 40	14 1	2 24	12 12	6 23	7 17	25 18	11 0
9 TH	21 16	17 23	8 46	2 14	14 23	3 2	12 26	6 24	7 15	25 20	11 1
10 FR	22 16	1 ♎ 56	8 37	3 49	14 46	3 39	12 40	6 24	7 12	25 23	11 2
11 SA	23 16	16 27	8 30	5 26	15 11	4 17	12 54	6 25	7 10	25 25	11 3
12 SU	24 16	0 ♏ 52	8 26	7 3	15 38	4 55	13 8	6 26	7 7	25 27	11 4
13 MO	25 16	15 6	8 24	8 42	16 6	5 33	13 22	6 26	7 5	25 29	11 5
14 TU	26 15	29 8	8 24	10 22	16 36	6 10	13 36	6 27	7 2	25 31	11 6
15 WE	27 15	12 ♐ 58	8 24	12 3	17 7	6 48	13 50	6 28	7 0	25 33	11 6
16 TH	28 15	26 36	8 23	13 45	17 40	7 26	14 5	6 30	6 57	25 35	11 7
17 FR	29 14	10 ♑ 3	8 20	15 28	18 14	8 3	14 19	6 31	6 55	25 37	11 8
18 SA	0 ♓ 14	23 20	8 14	17 13	18 50	8 41	14 33	6 32	6 53	25 39	11 9
19 SU	1 14	6 ♒ 25	8 5	18 59	19 27	9 18	14 47	6 34	6 50	25 41	11 10
20 MO	2 13	19 19	7 53	20 46	20 5	9 56	15 2	6 35	6 48	25 43	11 10
21 TU	3 13	2 ♓ 2	7 40	22 35	20 44	10 33	15 16	6 37	6 46	25 44	11 11
22 WE	4 12	14 33	7 26	24 24	21 24	11 11	15 30	6 39	6 44	25 46	11 11
23 TH	5 12	26 51	7 12	26 15	22 6	11 48	15 44	6 41	6 41	25 48	11 12
24 FR	6 11	8 ♈ 58	7 1	28 8	22 48	12 25	15 59	6 43	6 39	25 50	11 13
25 SA	7 10	20 55	6 52	0 ♓ 1	23 32	13 2	16 13	6 45	6 37	25 52	11 13
26 SU	8 10	2 ♉ 46	6 46	1 56	24 16	13 40	16 28	6 47	6 35	25 54	11 14
27 MO	9 9	14 34	6 42	3 52	25 1	14 17	16 42	6 49	6 33	25 55	11 14
28 TU	10 8	26 23	6 41	5 49	25 47	14 54	16 56	6 52	6 31	25 57	11 14

INGRESSES :

3 ☽ → ♋ 9:22	20 ☽ → ♓ 20: 7
4 ♂ → ♐ 4:58	23 ☽ → ♈ 6:12
5 ☽ → ♌ 15:51	24 ☿ → ♓ 23:44
7 ☿ → ♒ 13:36	25 ☽ → ♉ 18:22
☽ → ♍ 19: 8	28 ☽ → ♊ 7:17
9 ☽ → ♎ 20:49	
11 ☽ → ♏ 22:33	
14 ☽ → ♐ 1:29	
16 ☽ → ♑ 6: 1	
17 ☉ → ♓ 18:23	
18 ☽ → ♒ 12:11	

ASPECTS & ECLIPSES :

1 ☽ ☌ ♄ 11:52	☽ ☍ ♃ 15:41	18 ☽ ☌ ♆ 4:14	28 ♀ ☌ ♆ 5:15
☽ ☌ ☊ 18:16	10 ☽ ☌ P 4:19	19 ☽ ☍ ♅ 0:46	☿ □ ☊ 10:23
☽ ☍ ♇ 20:42	12 ☿ ☍ ♅ 0:56	20 ☽ ☌ ☿ 3: 9	☿ □ ♄ 12:58
2 ♃ □ ♇ 8: 2	13 ☉ □ ☽ 18:39	21 ☉ ☌ ☽ 2:25	☽ ☌ ☊ 20:42
4 ☿ ☌ ♆ 9:19	14 ♂ ☍ ♄ 11: 1	☽ □S ☊ 10:33	☽ ☌ ♄ 21: 9
☽ ☍ ♀ 9:27	☽ ☍ ♄ 12:40	22 ♂ ☌ ♇ 0:33	
5 ☽ ☍ ♆ 7:23	☽ ☌ ♂ 12:44	☽ ☌ ♃ 1:53	
☽ ☍ ☿ 10: 4	☽ ☌ ☋ 16: 1	24 ☉ □ ♄ 13:20	
6 ☽ ☌ ♅ 4:41	☽ ☌ ♇ 20:44	☉ □ ☊ 17:25	
7 ☉ ☍ ☽ 1: 9	17 ♂ ☍ ☊ 9:18	25 ♄ ☌ ☊ 19:12	
8 ☽ □N ☊ 9:56	☽ ☌ ♀ 15:27	26 ☽ ☌ A 3: 3	

SIDEREAL HELIOCENTRIC LONGITUDES : FEBRUARY 30 Julian at 0 hours UT

DAY	Sid. Time	☿	♀	⊕	♂	♃	♄	♅	♆	♇	Vernal Point
1 WE	8:35:14	23 ♏ 55	27 ♌ 29	13 ♌ 17	19 ♎ 32	15 ♓ 51	12 ♊ 14	7 ♌ 54	24 ♑ 28	9 ♐ 17	2 ♈ 38'24"
2 TH	8:39:11	26 40	29 7	14 17	20 3	15 57	12 16	7 54	24 29	9 17	2 ♈ 38'24"
3 FR	8:43: 7	29 26	0 ♍ 44	15 17	20 33	16 2	12 18	7 55	24 29	9 18	2 ♈ 38'24"
4 SA	8:47: 4	2 ♐ 12	2 21	16 17	21 4	16 8	12 21	7 56	24 30	9 18	2 ♈ 38'24"
5 SU	8:51: 1	5 0	3 59	17 17	21 35	16 13	12 23	7 57	24 30	9 19	2 ♈ 38'24"
6 MO	8:54:57	7 49	5 36	18 17	22 5	16 19	12 25	7 57	24 30	9 19	2 ♈ 38'23"
7 TU	8:58:54	10 39	7 13	19 17	22 36	16 24	12 28	7 58	24 31	9 19	2 ♈ 38'23"
8 WE	9: 2:50	13 32	8 50	20 17	23 7	16 30	12 30	7 59	24 31	9 20	2 ♈ 38'23"
9 TH	9: 6:47	16 26	10 28	21 17	23 38	16 35	12 32	8 0	24 31	9 20	2 ♈ 38'23"
10 FR	9:10:43	19 22	12 5	22 17	24 9	16 40	12 34	8 0	24 32	9 20	2 ♈ 38'23"
11 SA	9:14:40	22 20	13 42	23 17	24 40	16 46	12 37	8 1	24 32	9 21	2 ♈ 38'23"
12 SU	9:18:36	25 22	15 19	24 16	25 11	16 51	12 39	8 2	24 32	9 21	2 ♈ 38'23"
13 MO	9:22:33	28 26	16 56	25 16	25 42	16 57	12 41	8 3	24 33	9 21	2 ♈ 38'22"
14 TU	9:26:30	1 ♑ 34	18 33	26 16	26 13	17 2	12 43	8 4	24 33	9 22	2 ♈ 38'22"
15 WE	9:30:26	4 44	20 10	27 16	26 44	17 8	12 46	8 4	24 33	9 22	2 ♈ 38'22"
16 TH	9:34:23	7 59	21 47	28 15	27 16	17 13	12 48	8 5	24 34	9 22	2 ♈ 38'22"
17 FR	9:38:19	11 18	23 24	29 15	27 47	17 19	12 50	8 6	24 34	9 23	2 ♈ 38'22"
18 SA	9:42:16	14 41	25 0	0 ♍ 14	28 18	17 24	12 52	8 7	24 35	9 23	2 ♈ 38'22"
19 SU	9:46:12	18 9	26 37	1 14	28 50	17 30	12 55	8 7	24 35	9 23	2 ♈ 38'22"
20 MO	9:50: 9	21 42	28 14	2 14	29 21	17 35	12 57	8 8	24 35	9 24	2 ♈ 38'21"
21 TU	9:54: 5	25 21	29 51	3 13	29 53	17 41	12 59	8 9	24 36	9 24	2 ♈ 38'21"
22 WE	9:58: 2	29 5	1 ♎ 27	4 13	0 ♏ 25	17 46	13 1	8 10	24 36	9 24	2 ♈ 38'21"
23 TH	10: 1:59	2 ♒ 56	3 4	5 12	0 56	17 51	13 4	8 10	24 36	9 25	2 ♈ 38'21"
24 FR	10: 5:55	6 53	4 40	6 11	1 28	17 57	13 6	8 11	24 37	9 25	2 ♈ 38'21"
25 SA	10: 9:52	10 57	6 17	7 11	2 0	18 2	13 8	8 12	24 37	9 25	2 ♈ 38'21"
26 SU	10:13:48	15 8	7 53	8 10	2 31	18 8	13 11	8 13	24 37	9 26	2 ♈ 38'21"
27 MO	10:17:45	19 27	9 30	9 9	3 3	18 13	13 13	8 14	24 38	9 26	2 ♈ 38'21"
28 TU	10:21:41	23 54	11 6	10 9	3 35	18 19	13 15	8 14	24 38	9 26	2 ♈ 38'20"

INGRESSES :

2 ♀ → ♍ 13:10
3 ☿ → ♐ 4:57
13 ☿ → ♑ 12: 4
17 ⊕ → ♍ 18: 9
21 ♀ → ♎ 2:20
♂ → ♏ 5:22
22 ☿ → ♒ 5:46

ASPECTS (HELIOCENTRIC +MOON(TYCHONIC)) :

1 ☽ ☍ ♇ 17:34	☽ □ ♇ 10:40	13 ♀ ☍ ♃ 0:14	☿ □S ☊ 14:59
☽ ☌ ♄ 23:24	☽ ☌ ♀ 11: 6	14 ☽ ☌ ♇ 17:42	☽ □ ♄ 21: 3
2 ☽ □ ♃ 6:36	☽ □ ♄ 15:58	☽ ☍ ♄ 23:38	22 ☽ ☌ ♃ 6:17
3 ♀ □N ☊ 14:43	☽ □ ☿ 22: 2	15 ☽ □ ♃ 7:20	☿ □ ♂ 9:40
4 ☿ □ ♀ 3: 5	☽ ☍ ♃ 22:40	☽ □ ♀ 14:19	23 ☽ ☍ ♀ 14: 8
5 ☽ □ ♂ 0:57	9 ☿ □ ♃ 1:19	17 ☽ ☌ ☿ 2:59	24 ☿ ☍ ♅ 7:50
☽ ☍ ♆ 6: 8	10 ♀ □ ♄ 7:29	18 ☽ ☌ ♆ 2:16	25 ☽ □ ♆ 7:28
6 ☽ ☌ ♅ 5:42	♂ □ ♆ 17:48	☽ □ ♂ 9:28	☽ ☍ ♂ 23:29
☿ ☌ ♇ 12:42	11 ☽ □ ♆ 13:26	19 ☽ ☍ ♅ 3: 9	26 ☽ □ ♅ 11: 5
7 ☿ ☍ ♄ 15:18	☽ ☌ ♂ 14: 9	20 ☿ ☌ ♆ 19: 4	27 ⊕ □ ♇ 6:44
8 ♀ □ ♇ 7:13	12 ☽ □ ♅ 12: 3	21 ☽ □ ♇ 14: 5	☽ □ ☿ 15:51

SIDEREAL GEOCENTRIC LONGITUDES : MARCH 30 Julian at 0 hours UT											
DAY	☉	☽	☊	☿	♀	♂	♃	♄	⛢	♆	♇
1 WE	11 ♓ 7	8 ♊ 19	6 ♊ 41R	7 ♓ 48	26 ♑ 34	15 ♐ 31	17 ♓ 11	6 ♊ 54	6 ♌ 29R	25 ♑ 59	11 ♐ 15
2 TH	12 7	20 28	6 40	9 48	27 22	16 8	17 25	6 57	6 27	26 1	11 15
3 FR	13 6	2 ♋ 54	6 39	11 48	28 11	16 44	17 39	7 0	6 25	26 2	11 16
4 SA	14 5	15 43	6 36	13 50	29 0	17 21	17 54	7 3	6 23	26 4	11 16
5 SU	15 4	28 58	6 30	15 53	29 50	17 58	18 8	7 6	6 21	26 6	11 16
6 MO	16 3	12 ♌ 41	6 22	17 56	0 ♒ 41	18 35	18 23	7 9	6 19	26 7	11 16
7 TU	17 2	26 52	6 11	20 0	1 32	19 11	18 37	7 12	6 17	26 9	11 17
8 WE	18 1	11 ♍ 25	6 0	22 4	2 25	19 48	18 52	7 15	6 16	26 11	11 17
9 TH	19 0	26 15	5 49	24 9	3 17	20 24	19 6	7 19	6 14	26 12	11 17
10 FR	19 59	11 ♎ 13	5 39	26 13	4 11	21 1	19 20	7 22	6 12	26 14	11 17
11 SA	20 57	26 9	5 32	28 18	5 4	21 37	19 35	7 26	6 10	26 15	11 17
12 SU	21 56	10 ♏ 55	5 27	0 ♈ 21	5 59	22 14	19 49	7 29	6 9	26 17	11 17
13 MO	22 55	25 26	5 25	2 24	6 54	22 50	20 4	7 33	6 7	26 18	11 17
14 TU	23 54	9 ♐ 38	5 25D	4 25	7 49	23 26	20 18	7 37	6 6	26 20	11 17R
15 WE	24 52	23 30	5 25R	6 25	8 45	24 2	20 33	7 41	6 4	26 21	11 17
16 TH	25 51	7 ♑ 4	5 25	8 23	9 42	24 38	20 47	7 45	6 3	26 22	11 17
17 FR	26 50	20 20	5 23	10 19	10 39	25 14	21 1	7 49	6 2	26 24	11 17
18 SA	27 48	3 ♒ 21	5 18	12 12	11 36	25 50	21 16	7 53	6 0	26 25	11 17
19 SU	28 47	16 8	5 11	14 2	12 34	26 26	21 30	7 57	5 59	26 26	11 17
20 MO	29 46	28 44	5 1	15 49	13 32	27 1	21 44	8 2	5 58	26 28	11 16
21 TU	0 ♈ 44	11 ♓ 9	4 50	17 32	14 31	27 37	21 59	8 6	5 56	26 29	11 16
22 WE	1 43	23 25	4 38	19 12	15 30	28 12	22 13	8 11	5 55	26 30	11 16
23 TH	2 41	5 ♈ 31	4 26	20 47	16 29	28 48	22 27	8 15	5 54	26 31	11 16
24 FR	3 40	17 30	4 16	22 19	17 29	29 23	22 42	8 20	5 53	26 32	11 15
25 SA	4 38	29 22	4 8	23 45	18 29	29 58	22 56	8 25	5 52	26 33	11 15
26 SU	5 36	11 ♉ 11	4 3	25 8	19 30	0 ♑ 33	23 10	8 30	5 51	26 35	11 15
27 MO	6 35	22 58	4 0	26 26	20 30	1 8	23 24	8 35	5 50	26 36	11 14
28 TU	7 33	4 ♊ 47	4 0	27 39	21 31	1 43	23 39	8 40	5 49	26 37	11 14
29 WE	8 31	16 43	4 0D	28 47	22 33	2 18	23 53	8 45	5 49	26 38	11 13
30 TH	9 29	28 50	4 1	29 50	23 34	2 52	24 7	8 50	5 48	26 39	11 13
31 FR	10 28	11 ♋ 14	4 2R	0 ♉ 48	24 36	3 27	24 21	8 55	5 47	26 40	11 12

INGRESSES :					
2	☽ → ♋	18:27		☉ → ♈	5:54
5	☽ → ♌	1:50	22	☽ → ♈	13: 1
	♀ → ♒	4:37	25	♂ → ♑	1:10
7	☽ → ♍	5:13		☽ → ♉	1:16
9	☽ → ♎	6: 1	27	☽ → ♊	14:18
11	☽ → ♏	6:13	30	☽ → ♋	2:16
	☿ → ♈	19:51		☿ → ♉	3:57
13	☽ → ♐	7:39			
15	☽ → ♑	11:25			
17	☽ → ♒	17:47			
20	☽ → ♓	2:25			

ASPECTS & ECLIPSES :											
1	☉ □ ♇	3: 3		☿ □ ♂	10:42	14	☽ ☌ ♇	2:49	27	☿ □ ♆	3:13
	☽ ☍ ♇	5:49	7	☽ N□ ☊	15:14	15	☽ ☌ ♂	0:58		☽ ☌ ☊	22:24
	☉ □ ☽	6: 4	8	☉ ☍ ☽	11:28		☉ □ ☽	2:34	28	☽ ☌ ♄	7:53
	☽ ☍ ♂	15: 1		☽ ☍ ♃	12:16	17	☽ ☌ ♆	11: 8		☽ ☍ ♇	12:59
2	☿ □ ♇	17:30		☽ ☍ ☿	20: 3	18	☽ ☍ ⛢	4:56	30	☽ ☍ ♂	8:15
4	☉ S☋ ☿	5:38	9	☉ ☌ ♃	3:25		☽ ☌ ♀	16:42		☉ □ ☽	22:23
	☽ ☍ ♆	18:51	10	☽ ☌ P	2:44	20	☽ □S ☊	11:55			
5	☽ ☍ ♀	1:39	12	♀ ☍ ⛢	4:13	21	☽ ☌ ♃	21:36			
	♂ □ ♃	11: 4		☉ □ ♂	18:36	22	☉ ☌ ☽	17:51			
	☽ ☌ ⛢	12:59	13	☽ ☌ ☋	16:48	24	☽ ☌ ☿	11: 4			
6	☿ ☌ ♃	5:53		☽ ☍ ♄	20:32	25	☽ ☌ A	16:43			

SIDEREAL HELIOCENTRIC LONGITUDES : MARCH 30 Julian at 0 hours UT											
DAY	Sid. Time	☿	♀	⊕	♂	♃	♄	⛢	♆	♇	Vernal Point
1 WE	10:25:38	28 ♒ 29	12 ♎ 42	11 ♍ 8	4 ♏ 7	18 ♓ 24	13 ♊ 17	8 ♌ 15	24 ♑ 38	9 ♐ 27	2♈38'20"
2 TH	10:29:34	3 ♓ 13	14 18	12 7	4 39	18 30	13 20	8 16	24 39	9 27	2♈38'20"
3 FR	10:33:31	8 5	15 55	13 6	5 11	18 35	13 22	8 17	24 39	9 27	2♈38'20"
4 SA	10:37:28	13 7	17 31	14 5	5 43	18 41	13 24	8 17	24 40	9 28	2♈38'20"
5 SU	10:41:24	18 18	19 7	15 4	6 16	18 46	13 26	8 18	24 40	9 28	2♈38'20"
6 MO	10:45:21	23 38	20 43	16 3	6 48	18 52	13 29	8 19	24 40	9 28	2♈38'20"
7 TU	10:49:17	29 7	22 19	17 2	7 20	18 57	13 31	8 20	24 41	9 29	2♈38'19"
8 WE	10:53:14	4 ♈ 44	23 55	18 1	7 52	19 2	13 33	8 20	24 41	9 29	2♈38'19"
9 TH	10:57:10	10 30	25 30	19 0	8 25	19 8	13 35	8 21	24 41	9 29	2♈38'19"
10 FR	11: 1: 7	16 23	27 6	19 59	8 57	19 13	13 38	8 22	24 42	9 30	2♈38'19"
11 SA	11: 5: 3	22 24	28 42	20 58	9 30	19 19	13 40	8 23	24 42	9 30	2♈38'19"
12 SU	11: 9: 0	28 30	0 ♏ 18	21 57	10 2	19 24	13 42	8 23	24 42	9 30	2♈38'19"
13 MO	11:12:57	4 ♉ 42	1 53	22 56	10 35	19 30	13 44	8 24	24 43	9 31	2♈38'19"
14 TU	11:16:53	10 57	3 29	23 54	11 8	19 35	13 47	8 25	24 43	9 31	2♈38'18"
15 WE	11:20:50	17 14	5 5	24 53	11 40	19 41	13 49	8 26	24 44	9 32	2♈38'18"
16 TH	11:24:46	23 33	6 40	25 52	12 13	19 46	13 51	8 27	24 44	9 32	2♈38'18"
17 FR	11:28:43	29 51	8 16	26 50	12 46	19 52	13 54	8 27	24 44	9 32	2♈38'18"
18 SA	11:32:39	6 ♊ 7	9 51	27 49	13 19	19 57	13 56	8 28	24 45	9 33	2♈38'18"
19 SU	11:36:36	12 19	11 26	28 48	13 52	20 2	13 58	8 29	24 45	9 33	2♈38'18"
20 MO	11:40:32	18 27	13 2	29 46	14 25	20 8	14 0	8 30	24 45	9 33	2♈38'18"
21 TU	11:44:29	24 28	14 37	0 ♎ 45	14 58	20 13	14 3	8 30	24 46	9 34	2♈38'18"
22 WE	11:48:26	0 ♋ 23	16 12	1 43	15 31	20 19	14 5	8 31	24 46	9 34	2♈38'17"
23 TH	11:52:22	6 10	17 48	2 42	16 4	20 24	14 7	8 32	24 46	9 34	2♈38'17"
24 FR	11:56:19	11 48	19 23	3 40	16 38	20 30	14 9	8 33	24 47	9 35	2♈38'17"
25 SA	12: 0:15	17 17	20 58	4 39	17 11	20 35	14 12	8 33	24 47	9 35	2♈38'17"
26 SU	12: 4:12	22 37	22 33	5 37	17 44	20 41	14 14	8 34	24 47	9 35	2♈38'17"
27 MO	12: 8: 8	27 48	24 8	6 35	18 18	20 46	14 16	8 35	24 48	9 36	2♈38'17"
28 TU	12:12: 5	2 ♌ 48	25 43	7 34	18 51	20 52	14 18	8 36	24 48	9 36	2♈38'17"
29 WE	12:16: 1	7 40	27 18	8 32	19 25	20 57	14 21	8 37	24 49	9 36	2♈38'16"
30 TH	12:19:58	12 22	28 53	9 30	19 58	21 3	14 23	8 37	24 49	9 37	2♈38'16"
31 FR	12:23:55	16 55	0 ♐ 28	10 28	20 32	21 8	14 25	8 38	24 49	9 37	2♈38'16"

INGRESSES :		
1	☿ → ♓	7:47
7	☿ → ♈	3:50
11	♀ → ♏	19:32
12	☿ → ♉	5:49
17	☿ → ♊	0:35
20	⊕ → ♎	5:40
21	☿ → ♋	22:25
27	☿ → ♌	10:28
30	♀ → ♐	16:54

ASPECTS (HELIOCENTRIC +MOON(TYCHONIC)) :																	
1	☽ ☍ ♇	2:14		☽ ☌ ⛢	16:26		☿ □ ♆	9: 6	17	♀ □ ⛢	2:57		☽ ☌ ♃	17:51	29	☿ ☌ ⛢	4:47
	☽ ☌ ♄	9:54	6	♂ ☌ ☋	8: 2		☽ □ ⛢	19:51		☽ ☌ ♆	8: 4	22	☿ □ ⊕	6:36		☽ □ ♃	8:30
	☽ □ ♃	20: 6	7	☽ □ ♇	20:50		☿ ☌ ☊	20:44	18	☽ ☍ ⛢	9:34	23	☽ □ ☿	2:26	31	♀ ☌ ☋	19: 6
3	⊕ □ ♄	6:34	8	☽ □ ♄	3:28		☽ ☌ ♂	22:30		☿ ☍ ♇	13:14	24	☽ □ ♆	14:42		☿ □ ♂	22:32
	☿ □ ♇	6:36		♀ □ ♆	11:39	12	☿ ☍ ♀	9:23		☽ □ ♀	13:52	25	☽ □ ⛢	18:41			
4	☿ □ ♄	1:20		☽ ☍ ♃	12:26	13	☿ □ ⛢	14:17		☽ □ ♂	19:30	26	☿ ☍ ♆	9:59			
	☽ □ ♀	3:45		♂ □ ⛢	21:12		☽ ☌ ♇	23:48	19	☿ ☌ ♄	6:28		☽ ☍ ♂	14: 1			
	☿ ☍ ⊕	5:38	9	⊕ ☍ ♃	3:25	14	☿ ☍ ♂	0:45	20	☿ □ ♃	6:46		☿ N□ ☊	23:25			
	☽ ☍ ♆	16:17	10	☽ ☍ ☿	13:50		☽ ☍ ♄	7: 7		☽ □ ♇	20:53	27	☽ ☍ ♀	2:45			
5	☿ ☌ ♃	2:10		☽ □ ♆	21:39		☽ □ ♃	17:16	21	☽ □ ♄	5:38	28	☽ ☍ ♇	9:43			
	☽ □ ♂	13:22	11	☽ ☌ ♀	4:37	15	☿ ☌ P	8:47		♀ ☌ ♂	8: 4		☽ ☌ ♄	19:14			

SIDEREAL GEOCENTRIC LONGITUDES : APRIL 30 Julian at 0 hours UT

DAY	☉	☽	☊	☿	♀	♂	♃	♄	♅	♆	♇
1 SA	11 ♈ 26	24 ♋ 0	4 ♊ 1R	1 ♉ 41	25 ♒ 38	4 ♑ 1	24 ♓ 35	9 ♊ 1	5 ♌ 47R	26 ♑ 41	11 ♐ 12R
2 SU	12 24	7 ♌ 11	3 58	2 29	26 41	4 35	24 49	9 6	5 46	26 41	11 11
3 MO	13 22	20 52	3 53	3 12	27 43	5 10	25 3	9 12	5 46	26 42	11 10
4 TU	14 20	5 ♍ 1	3 47	3 49	28 46	5 44	25 17	9 17	5 45	26 43	11 10
5 WE	15 18	19 37	3 40	4 21	29 49	6 17	25 31	9 23	5 45	26 44	11 9
6 TH	16 16	4 ♎ 34	3 33	4 48	0 ♓ 53	6 51	25 45	9 28	5 44	26 45	11 8
7 FR	17 14	19 44	3 27	5 9	1 56	7 25	25 59	9 34	5 44	26 45	11 8
8 SA	18 12	4 ♏ 56	3 22	5 25	3 0	7 58	26 13	9 40	5 44	26 46	11 7
9 SU	19 10	20 1	3 19	5 36	4 4	8 31	26 27	9 46	5 43	26 47	11 6
10 MO	20 8	4 ♐ 50	3 19D	5 41	5 9	9 4	26 41	9 52	5 43	26 47	11 5
11 TU	21 6	19 17	3 19	5 41R	6 13	9 37	26 54	9 58	5 43	26 48	11 5
12 WE	22 4	3 ♑ 21	3 21	5 37	7 18	10 10	27 8	10 4	5 43	26 48	11 4
13 TH	23 1	17 0	3 22	5 27	8 23	10 43	27 22	10 10	5 43D	26 49	11 3
14 FR	23 59	0 ♒ 16	3 22R	5 13	9 28	11 15	27 35	10 16	5 43	26 50	11 2
15 SA	24 57	13 12	3 20	4 55	10 33	11 48	27 49	10 22	5 43	26 50	11 1
16 SU	25 55	25 51	3 17	4 34	11 38	12 20	28 3	10 29	5 43	26 50	11 0
17 MO	26 52	8 ♓ 15	3 12	4 8	12 44	12 52	28 16	10 35	5 44	26 51	10 59
18 TU	27 50	20 28	3 6	3 40	13 50	13 23	28 30	10 42	5 44	26 51	10 58
19 WE	28 48	2 ♈ 31	3 0	3 9	14 55	13 55	28 43	10 48	5 44	26 52	10 57
20 TH	29 46	14 28	2 54	2 37	16 1	14 26	28 56	10 55	5 44	26 52	10 56
21 FR	0 ♉ 43	26 20	2 49	2 3	17 8	14 57	29 10	11 1	5 45	26 52	10 55
22 SA	1 41	8 ♉ 8	2 45	1 28	18 14	15 28	29 23	11 8	5 45	26 52	10 54
23 SU	2 38	19 56	2 43	0 54	19 20	15 59	29 36	11 14	5 46	26 53	10 53
24 MO	3 36	1 ♊ 45	2 42	0 19	20 27	16 29	29 49	11 21	5 46	26 53	10 52
25 TU	4 34	13 38	2 42D	29 ♈ 46	21 34	16 59	0 ♈ 2	11 28	5 47	26 53	10 50
26 WE	5 31	25 38	2 44	29 15	22 41	17 29	0 15	11 35	5 48	26 53	10 49
27 TH	6 29	7 ♋ 49	2 46	28 45	23 48	17 59	0 28	11 42	5 49	26 53	10 48
28 FR	7 26	20 15	2 47	28 18	24 55	18 28	0 41	11 49	5 49	26 53	10 47
29 SA	8 24	2 ♌ 59	2 48	27 55	26 2	18 57	0 54	11 56	5 50	26 53R	10 46
30 SU	9 21	16 7	2 48R	27 34	27 9	19 26	1 7	12 3	5 51	26 53	10 44

INGRESSES :

1 ☽ → ♌ 11: 1
3 ☽ → ♍ 15:35
5 ♀ → ♓ 4: 0
☽ → ♎ 16:42
7 ☽ → ♏ 16:12
9 ☽ → ♐ 16: 7
11 ☽ → ♑ 18:13
13 ☽ → ♒ 23:30
16 ☽ → ♓ 7:59
18 ☽ → ♈ 18:57
20 ☉ → ♉ 6: 1
21 ☽ → ♉ 7:26
23 ☽ → ♊ 20:27
24 ☿ → ♈ 13:50
♃ → ♈ 19:51
26 ☽ → ♋ 8:39
28 ☽ → ♌ 18:25

ASPECTS & ECLIPSES :

1 ☽ ☍ ♆ 4:56
☽ ☌ ♅ 21:27
3 ☽ ☍ ♀ 12:40
☽ N ☊ 21:57
5 ☽ ☍ ♃ 9:41
6 ☉ ☍ ☽ 19:47
7 ☽ ☌ P 11: 4
8 ☽ ☍ ☿ 0:46
♀ □ ☊ 7:45
9 ☽ ☌ ☋ 21:31
10 ☽ ☍ ♄ 8:20
☽ ☌ ♇ 10:18
12 ☽ ☌ ♂ 12:24
13 ☉ □ ☽ 11:39
☽ ☌ ♆ 17:42
14 ☽ ☍ ♅ 10: 2
♀ □ ♄ 19:46
15 ♀ □ ♇ 10:12
16 ☽ S ☊ 14:14
☉ □ ♆ 23:19
17 ☽ ☌ ♀ 9:37
18 ☽ ☌ ♃ 16:14
20 ♄ ☍ ♇ 4:40
21 ☉ ☌ ☽ 9:41
☽ ☌ ☿ 11: 4
☉ ♭ ☿ 20:44
☽ ☌ A 21:55
24 ☽ ☌ ☊ 1:55
☽ ☍ ♇ 18:23
☽ ☌ ♄ 19:36
26 ☉ □ ♅ 7: 3
27 ☽ ☍ ♂ 20:28
28 ☽ ☍ ♆ 12:35
29 ☽ ☌ ♅ 5:16
☉ □ ☽ 10:45

SIDEREAL HELIOCENTRIC LONGITUDES : APRIL 30 Julian at 0 hours UT

DAY	Sid. Time	☿	♀	⊕	♂	♃	♄	♅	♆	♇	Vernal Point
1 SA	12:27:51	21 ♌ 19	2 ♐ 3	11 ♎ 26	21 ♏ 5	21 ♓ 13	14 ♊ 27	8 ♌ 39	24 ♑ 50	9 ♐ 37	2♈38'16"
2 SU	12:31:48	25 35	3 38	12 25	21 39	21 19	14 30	8 40	24 50	9 38	2♈38'16"
3 MO	12:35:44	29 44	5 13	13 23	22 13	21 24	14 32	8 40	24 50	9 38	2♈38'16"
4 TU	12:39:41	3 ♍ 44	6 48	14 21	22 47	21 30	14 34	8 41	24 51	9 38	2♈38'16"
5 WE	12:43:37	7 38	8 22	15 19	23 21	21 35	14 36	8 42	24 51	9 39	2♈38'15"
6 TH	12:47:34	11 25	9 57	16 17	23 55	21 41	14 39	8 43	24 51	9 39	2♈38'15"
7 FR	12:51:30	15 6	11 32	17 15	24 29	21 46	14 41	8 43	24 52	9 39	2♈38'15"
8 SA	12:55:27	18 41	13 7	18 13	25 3	21 52	14 43	8 44	24 52	9 40	2♈38'15"
9 SU	12:59:24	22 10	14 41	19 11	25 37	21 57	14 46	8 45	24 52	9 40	2♈38'15"
10 MO	13: 3:20	25 35	16 16	20 8	26 11	22 3	14 48	8 46	24 53	9 40	2♈38'15"
11 TU	13: 7:17	28 55	17 51	21 6	26 45	22 8	14 50	8 46	24 53	9 41	2♈38'15"
12 WE	13:11:13	2 ♎ 10	19 25	22 4	27 20	22 14	14 52	8 47	24 54	9 41	2♈38'15"
13 TH	13:15:10	5 22	21 0	23 2	27 54	22 19	14 55	8 48	24 54	9 41	2♈38'14"
14 FR	13:19: 6	8 30	22 35	24 0	28 28	22 24	14 57	8 49	24 54	9 42	2♈38'14"
15 SA	13:23: 3	11 34	24 9	24 58	29 3	22 30	14 59	8 50	24 55	9 42	2♈38'14"
16 SU	13:26:59	14 36	25 44	25 55	29 37	22 35	15 1	8 50	24 55	9 42	2♈38'14"
17 MO	13:30:56	17 35	27 19	26 53	0 ♐ 12	22 41	15 4	8 51	24 55	9 43	2♈38'14"
18 TU	13:34:53	20 31	28 53	27 51	0 47	22 46	15 6	8 52	24 56	9 43	2♈38'14"
19 WE	13:38:49	23 25	0 ♑ 28	28 48	1 21	22 52	15 8	8 53	24 56	9 43	2♈38'14"
20 TH	13:42:46	26 17	2 2	29 46	1 56	22 57	15 10	8 53	24 56	9 44	2♈38'13"
21 FR	13:46:42	29 8	3 37	0 ♏ 44	2 31	23 3	15 13	8 54	24 57	9 44	2♈38'13"
22 SA	13:50:39	1 ♏ 56	5 12	1 41	3 6	23 8	15 15	8 55	24 57	9 44	2♈38'13"
23 SU	13:54:35	4 44	6 46	2 39	3 41	23 14	15 17	8 56	24 58	9 45	2♈38'13"
24 MO	13:58:32	7 31	8 21	3 37	4 16	23 19	15 19	8 56	24 58	9 45	2♈38'13"
25 TU	14: 2:28	10 16	9 56	4 34	4 51	23 24	15 22	8 57	24 58	9 46	2♈38'13"
26 WE	14: 6:25	13 2	11 30	5 32	5 26	23 30	15 24	8 58	24 59	9 46	2♈38'13"
27 TH	14:10:22	15 46	13 5	6 29	6 1	23 35	15 26	8 59	24 59	9 46	2♈38'12"
28 FR	14:14:18	18 31	14 39	7 27	6 36	23 41	15 28	9 0	24 59	9 47	2♈38'12"
29 SA	14:18:15	21 15	16 14	8 24	7 11	23 46	15 31	9 0	25 0	9 47	2♈38'12"
30 SU	14:22:11	24 0	17 49	9 22	7 46	23 52	15 33	9 1	25 0	9 47	2♈38'12"

INGRESSES :

3 ☿ → ♍ 1:36
11 ☿ → ♎ 7:56
16 ♂ → ♐ 15:38
18 ♀ → ♑ 16:56
20 ⊕ → ♏ 5:46
21 ☿ → ♏ 7:26

ASPECTS (HELIOCENTRIC +MOON(TYCHONIC)) :

1 ☽ ☍ ♆ 1:31
2 ☽ ☌ ♅ 2:37
3 ☽ □ ♂ 2:26
☽ ☌ ☿ 21: 3
4 ☽ □ ♀ 3:19
☽ □ ♇ 7:40
☽ □ ♄ 15:49
5 ☽ ☍ ♃ 3:12
☿ □ ♀ 7:53
☿ □ ♇ 12:40
♀ ☌ ♇ 19:24
6 ☿ □ ♄ 21:13
7 ☽ □ ♆ 8: 5
8 ☽ □ ♅ 6: 1
☿ ☍ ♃ 22:24
9 ♀ ☍ ♄ 1: 5
☽ ☌ ♂ 9:22
10 ☽ ☌ ♇ 7:58
☽ ☍ ♄ 16:31
☽ ☌ ♀ 21:16
11 ☽ □ ♃ 4:50
☽ □ ☿ 21:21
13 ☽ ☌ ♆ 14:13
♀ □ ♃ 21:13
14 ☽ ☍ ♅ 15:48
⊕ □ ♆ 22:47
16 ☽ □ ♂ 7:37
17 ☽ □ ♇ 2:51
☽ □ ♄ 13:22
18 ☽ ☌ ♃ 4:36
☽ □ ♀ 19:15
19 ☿ □ ♆ 12:41
20 ☿ ☌ ☋ 11:40
☽ □ ♆ 21:11
21 ☽ ☍ ☿ 7:26
☿ ☌ ⊕ 20:44
22 ☽ □ ♅ 1:34
♃ S ☊ 2:15
24 ☽ ☍ ♂ 5:21
☿ □ ♅ 12:28
☽ ☍ ♇ 16:11
25 ☽ ☌ ♄ 3:29
☽ □ ♃ 19:43
27 ☽ ☍ ♀ 11:43
28 ☽ ☍ ♆ 9: 0
☿ ☌ A 9: 3
♀ ☌ A 23:34
29 ☽ ☌ ♅ 11: 6
⊕ □ ♅ 15:17
30 ☽ □ ☿ 17:37

SIDEREAL GEOCENTRIC LONGITUDES : MAY 30 Julian at 0 hours UT

DAY	☉	☽	☊	☿	♀	♂	♃	♄	♅	♆	♇
1 MO	10 ♉ 18	29 ♌ 40	2 ♊ 47R	27 ♈ 18R	28 ♓ 17	19 ♑ 55	1 ♈ 19	12 ♊ 10	5 ♌ 52	26 ♑ 53R	10 ♐ 43R
2 TU	11 16	13 ♍ 41	2 45	27 5	29 24	20 23	1 32	12 17	5 53	26 53	10 42
3 WE	12 13	28 7	2 43	26 56	0 ♈ 32	20 51	1 45	12 24	5 54	26 53	10 41
4 TH	13 11	12 ♎ 57	2 40	26 52	1 40	21 19	1 57	12 31	5 55	26 53	10 39
5 FR	14 8	28 2	2 38	26 52D	2 48	21 47	2 10	12 38	5 56	26 53	10 38
6 SA	15 5	13 ♏ 15	2 37	26 57	3 56	22 14	2 22	12 45	5 58	26 52	10 37
7 SU	16 3	28 25	2 36	27 6	5 4	22 41	2 34	12 53	5 59	26 52	10 35
8 MO	17 0	13 ♐ 24	2 36D	27 20	6 12	23 7	2 47	13 0	6 0	26 52	10 34
9 TU	17 57	28 4	2 37	27 38	7 20	23 33	2 59	13 7	6 1	26 51	10 33
10 WE	18 54	12 ♑ 19	2 38	28 1	8 29	23 59	3 11	13 15	6 3	26 51	10 31
11 TH	19 52	26 8	2 39	28 27	9 37	24 25	3 23	13 22	6 4	26 51	10 30
12 FR	20 49	9 ♒ 31	2 39	28 59	10 46	24 50	3 35	13 30	6 6	26 50	10 28
13 SA	21 46	22 30	2 40R	29 34	11 54	25 15	3 47	13 37	6 7	26 50	10 27
14 SU	22 43	5 ♓ 8	2 39	0 ♉ 14	13 3	25 39	3 58	13 45	6 9	26 49	10 25
15 MO	23 41	17 28	2 38	0 57	14 12	26 3	4 10	13 52	6 11	26 49	10 24
16 TU	24 38	29 35	2 37	1 45	15 21	26 27	4 22	14 0	6 12	26 48	10 23
17 WE	25 35	11 ♈ 32	2 36	2 37	16 30	26 50	4 33	14 7	6 14	26 48	10 21
18 TH	26 32	23 23	2 35	3 32	17 39	27 13	4 45	14 15	6 16	26 47	10 20
19 FR	27 29	5 ♉ 11	2 35	4 31	18 48	27 35	4 56	14 22	6 18	26 47	10 18
20 SA	28 27	16 59	2 35	5 34	19 58	27 57	5 7	14 30	6 20	26 46	10 17
21 SU	29 24	28 49	2 34D	6 40	21 7	28 18	5 18	14 38	6 21	26 45	10 15
22 MO	0 ♊ 21	10 ♊ 43	2 35	7 50	22 16	28 39	5 29	14 45	6 23	26 45	10 14
23 TU	1 18	22 44	2 35	9 3	23 26	28 59	5 40	14 53	6 25	26 44	10 12
24 WE	2 15	4 ♋ 54	2 35	10 20	24 35	29 19	5 51	15 1	6 28	26 43	10 11
25 TH	3 12	17 15	2 35R	11 40	25 45	29 39	6 2	15 8	6 30	26 42	10 9
26 FR	4 10	29 50	2 35	13 4	26 55	29 58	6 13	15 16	6 32	26 42	10 8
27 SA	5 7	12 ♌ 41	2 35	14 31	28 5	0 ♒ 16	6 23	15 24	6 34	26 41	10 6
28 SU	6 4	25 50	2 34	16 1	29 14	0 34	6 34	15 32	6 36	26 40	10 5
29 MO	7 1	9 ♍ 19	2 34	17 34	0 ♉ 24	0 51	6 44	15 39	6 38	26 39	10 3
30 TU	7 58	23 11	2 34D	19 11	1 34	1 8	6 54	15 47	6 41	26 38	10 1
31 WE	8 55	7 ♎ 24	2 35	20 51	2 44	1 24	7 4	15 55	6 43	26 37	10 0

INGRESSES :

1 ☽ → ♍ 0:34	21 ☽ → ♊ 2:24
2 ♀ → ♈ 12:40	☉ → ♊ 15:11
3 ☽ → ♎ 3: 4	23 ☽ → ♋ 14:21
5 ☽ → ♏ 3: 6	26 ☽ → ♌ 0:19
7 ☽ → ♐ 2:30	♂ → ♒ 2:57
9 ☽ → ♑ 3:12	28 ☽ → ♍ 7:29
11 ☽ → ♒ 6:50	♀ → ♉ 15:39
13 ☽ → ♓ 14:11	30 ☽ → ♎ 11:35
☿ → ♉ 15:53	
16 ☽ → ♈ 0:50	
18 ☽ → ♉ 13:27	

ASPECTS & ECLIPSES :

1 ☽ ⚻ ☊ 5:23	☽ ☍ ♄ 23:20	20 ☿ □ ♅ 17:13	28 ☽ ⚻ ☊ 12: 4
3 ☽ ☍ ♀ 4:15	10 ☽ ☌ ♂ 20:51	21 ☉ ● A 1:16	☉ □ ☽ 19:38
☽ ☍ ♃ 5:59	11 ☽ ☌ ♆ 1:14	☉ ☌ ☽ 1:17	29 ♀ □ ♂ 12: 9
☿ □ ♆ 18:13	☽ ☍ ♅ 17:46	☽ ☌ ☊ 7:36	30 ☽ ☍ ♃ 23:26
4 ♀ ☌ ♃ 7:34	12 ☉ □ ☽ 22:31	☽ ☍ ♇ 23: 0	
☽ ☍ ☿ 22: 9	13 ☽ ⚼ ☊ 19:15	22 ☽ ☌ ♄ 8:10	
5 ☿ □ ♆ 1:51	16 ☽ ☌ ♃ 9:43	24 ☉ ☌ ☊ 8:12	
☽ ☌ P 21: 8	♂ ☌ ♆ 21:58	25 ☽ ☍ ♆ 18: 3	
6 ☉ ☍ ☽ 3: 5	17 ☽ ☌ ♀ 11: 7	♀ □ ♆ 19:30	
7 ☽ ☌ ☋ 6:38	18 ☽ ☌ ☿ 22:31	26 ☽ ☍ ♂ 0:15	
☽ ☌ ♇ 19:25	19 ☽ ☌ A 1:40	☽ ☌ ♅ 12:37	

SIDEREAL HELIOCENTRIC LONGITUDES : MAY 30 Julian at 0 hours UT

DAY	Sid. Time	☿	♀	⊕	♂	♃	♄	♅	♆	♇	Vernal Point
1 MO	14:26: 8	26 ♏ 45	19 ♑ 23	10 ♏ 19	8 ♐ 22	23 ♓ 57	15 ♊ 35	9 ♌ 2	25 ♑ 0	9 ♐ 48	2♈38'12"
2 TU	14:30: 4	29 31	20 58	11 16	8 57	24 3	15 38	9 3	25 1	9 48	2♈38'12"
3 WE	14:34: 1	2 ♐ 18	22 33	12 14	9 32	24 8	15 40	9 3	25 1	9 48	2♈38'12"
4 TH	14:37:57	5 6	24 7	13 11	10 8	24 14	15 42	9 4	25 1	9 49	2♈38'12"
5 FR	14:41:54	7 55	25 42	14 8	10 43	24 19	15 44	9 5	25 2	9 49	2♈38'11"
6 SA	14:45:51	10 45	27 17	15 6	11 19	24 24	15 47	9 6	25 2	9 49	2♈38'11"
7 SU	14:49:47	13 37	28 52	16 3	11 55	24 30	15 49	9 6	25 3	9 50	2♈38'11"
8 MO	14:53:44	16 32	0 ♒ 26	17 0	12 30	24 35	15 51	9 7	25 3	9 50	2♈38'11"
9 TU	14:57:40	19 28	2 1	17 58	13 6	24 41	15 53	9 8	25 3	9 50	2♈38'11"
10 WE	15: 1:37	22 27	3 36	18 55	13 42	24 46	15 56	9 9	25 4	9 51	2♈38'11"
11 TH	15: 5:33	25 28	5 11	19 52	14 18	24 52	15 58	9 10	25 4	9 51	2♈38'11"
12 FR	15: 9:30	28 32	6 46	20 49	14 53	24 57	16 0	9 10	25 4	9 51	2♈38'10"
13 SA	15:13:26	1 ♑ 40	8 20	21 47	15 29	25 3	16 2	9 11	25 5	9 52	2♈38'10"
14 SU	15:17:23	4 51	9 55	22 44	16 5	25 8	16 5	9 12	25 5	9 52	2♈38'10"
15 MO	15:21:20	8 6	11 30	23 41	16 41	25 14	16 7	9 13	25 5	9 52	2♈38'10"
16 TU	15:25:16	11 25	13 5	24 38	17 17	25 19	16 9	9 13	25 6	9 53	2♈38'10"
17 WE	15:29:13	14 48	14 40	25 36	17 54	25 24	16 11	9 14	25 6	9 53	2♈38'10"
18 TH	15:33: 9	18 16	16 15	26 33	18 30	25 30	16 14	9 15	25 6	9 53	2♈38'10"
19 FR	15:37: 6	21 50	17 50	27 30	19 6	25 35	16 16	9 16	25 7	9 54	2♈38' 9"
20 SA	15:41: 2	25 28	19 25	28 27	19 42	25 41	16 18	9 16	25 7	9 54	2♈38' 9"
21 SU	15:44:59	29 13	21 0	29 24	20 18	25 46	16 20	9 17	25 8	9 54	2♈38' 9"
22 MO	15:48:55	3 ♒ 3	22 35	0 ♐ 22	20 55	25 52	16 23	9 18	25 8	9 55	2♈38' 9"
23 TU	15:52:52	7 1	24 10	1 19	21 31	25 57	16 25	9 19	25 8	9 55	2♈38' 9"
24 WE	15:56:49	11 5	25 46	2 16	22 8	26 3	16 27	9 19	25 9	9 55	2♈38' 9"
25 TH	16: 0:45	15 16	27 21	3 13	22 44	26 8	16 30	9 20	25 9	9 56	2♈38' 9"
26 FR	16: 4:42	19 35	28 56	4 10	23 20	26 14	16 32	9 21	25 9	9 56	2♈38' 9"
27 SA	16: 8:38	24 2	0 ♓ 31	5 7	23 57	26 19	16 34	9 22	25 10	9 56	2♈38' 8"
28 SU	16:12:35	28 38	2 6	6 4	24 34	26 24	16 36	9 23	25 10	9 57	2♈38' 8"
29 MO	16:16:31	3 ♓ 22	3 42	7 2	25 10	26 30	16 39	9 23	25 10	9 57	2♈38' 8"
30 TU	16:20:28	8 15	5 17	7 59	25 47	26 35	16 41	9 24	25 11	9 57	2♈38' 8"
31 WE	16:24:24	13 17	6 52	8 56	26 24	26 41	16 43	9 25	25 11	9 58	2♈38' 8"

INGRESSES :

2 ☿ → ♐ 4: 8
7 ♀ → ♒ 17:19
12 ☿ → ♑ 11:15
21 ☿ → ♒ 4:58
⊕ → ♐ 14:56
26 ♀ → ♓ 16: 9
28 ☿ → ♓ 7: 0

ASPECTS (HELIOCENTRIC +MOON(TYCHONIC)) :

1 ☽ □ ♂ 15:38	7 ☽ ☌ ♇ 18:14	♂ ☍ ♄ 23:30	21 ☽ ☍ ♇ 22:22	☿ ☌ ♀ 2:25
☽ □ ♇ 17:25	☿ ☍ ♄ 18:22	14 ☽ □ ♇ 9:10	22 ☽ ☌ ♄ 11:22	☽ □ ♄ 12:47
2 ☽ □ ♄ 3:17	☽ ☌ ♂ 22:29	☽ □ ♄ 21:20	☽ ☍ ♂ 21:26	☿ □ ⊕ 22:22
☽ ☍ ♃ 17:23	8 ☽ ☍ ♄ 3:58	☽ □ ♂ 22:24	23 ☽ □ ♃ 6:25	30 ☽ □ ♂ 4:38
3 ♂ ☌ ♇ 10:46	☽ ☌ ☿ 6:18	15 ☽ ☌ ♃ 15:27	☿ ☍ ♅ 13:42	☽ ☍ ♃ 5:50
4 ♀ ☌ ♆ 13:44	☽ □ ♃ 18:22	17 ☽ □ ☿ 9:19	25 ☽ ☍ ♆ 15: 7	☿ □ ♇ 8:13
☽ □ ♆ 19:14	10 ☿ □ ♃ 19: 5	18 ☽ □ ♆ 3:30	26 ☽ ☌ ♅ 17:51	31 ♂ □ ♃ 13:13
☽ □ ♀ 19:52	☽ ☌ ♆ 22: 6	19 ☽ □ ♅ 8:18	27 ♀ ⚼ ☊ 18:15	☿ □ ♄ 16: 5
5 ☿ ☌ ♇ 16: 7	11 ☽ ☌ ♀ 18:18	☿ ☌ ♆ 21:42	28 ☽ ☍ ☿ 7:44	
☽ □ ♅ 17:26	☽ ☍ ♅ 23:21	20 ☽ □ ♀ 5:43	☽ ☍ ♀ 12:44	
6 ☿ ☌ ♂ 5:57	13 ♀ ☍ ♅ 12:54	☿ ⚼ ☊ 14:11	29 ☽ □ ♇ 1: 6	

SIDEREAL GEOCENTRIC LONGITUDES : JUNE 30 Julian at 0 hours UT

DAY	☉	☽	☊	☿	♀	♂	♃	♄	⛢	♆	♇
1 TH	9 ♊ 52	21 ♎ 57	2 ♊ 35	22 ♉ 34	3 ♉ 54	1 ♒ 40	7 ♈ 14	16 ♊ 3	6 ♌ 46	26 ♑ 36R	9 ♐ 58R
2 FR	10 49	6 ♏ 45	2 36	24 20	5 5	1 55	7 24	16 11	6 48	26 35	9 57
3 SA	11 47	21 44	2 36	26 9	6 15	2 9	7 34	16 18	6 50	26 34	9 55
4 SU	12 44	6 ♐ 45	2 36R	28 0	7 25	2 23	7 44	16 26	6 53	26 33	9 54
5 MO	13 41	21 39	2 36	29 55	8 35	2 36	7 53	16 34	6 56	26 32	9 52
6 TU	14 38	6 ♑ 20	2 35	1 ♊ 52	9 46	2 49	8 3	16 42	6 58	26 31	9 51
7 WE	15 35	20 40	2 33	3 51	10 56	3 0	8 12	16 50	7 1	26 30	9 49
8 TH	16 32	4 ♒ 36	2 32	5 53	12 7	3 12	8 21	16 58	7 3	26 29	9 48
9 FR	17 29	18 5	2 30	7 56	13 18	3 22	8 30	17 5	7 6	26 28	9 46
10 SA	18 26	1 ♓ 8	2 29	10 1	14 28	3 32	8 39	17 13	7 9	26 26	9 45
11 SU	19 23	13 49	2 28	12 8	15 39	3 41	8 48	17 21	7 12	26 25	9 43
12 MO	20 20	26 10	2 28D	14 16	16 50	3 50	8 57	17 29	7 14	26 24	9 42
13 TU	21 18	8 ♈ 15	2 29	16 24	18 1	3 57	9 5	17 37	7 17	26 23	9 40
14 WE	22 15	20 10	2 30	18 33	19 12	4 4	9 14	17 45	7 20	26 21	9 39
15 TH	23 12	2 ♉ 0	2 32	20 42	20 23	4 10	9 22	17 52	7 23	26 20	9 37
16 FR	24 9	13 47	2 33	22 51	21 34	4 16	9 30	18 0	7 26	26 19	9 36
17 SA	25 6	25 37	2 34	25 0	22 45	4 20	9 38	18 8	7 29	26 17	9 34
18 SU	26 3	7 ♊ 32	2 34R	27 8	23 56	4 24	9 46	18 16	7 32	26 16	9 33
19 MO	27 1	19 35	2 33	29 15	25 7	4 27	9 54	18 24	7 35	26 15	9 31
20 TU	27 58	1 ♋ 49	2 31	1 ♋ 22	26 18	4 29	10 2	18 31	7 38	26 13	9 30
21 WE	28 55	14 14	2 28	3 27	27 30	4 31	10 9	18 39	7 41	26 12	9 28
22 TH	29 52	26 52	2 24	5 31	28 41	4 32	10 16	18 47	7 44	26 11	9 27
23 FR	0 ♋ 50	9 ♌ 43	2 19	7 33	29 53	4 31R	10 24	18 55	7 48	26 9	9 26
24 SA	1 47	22 48	2 15	9 35	1 ♊ 4	4 31	10 31	19 2	7 51	26 8	9 24
25 SU	2 44	6 ♍ 7	2 12	11 34	2 16	4 29	10 38	19 10	7 54	26 6	9 23
26 MO	3 41	19 41	2 10	13 32	3 27	4 26	10 44	19 18	7 57	26 5	9 21
27 TU	4 39	3 ♎ 30	2 9	15 29	4 39	4 23	10 51	19 25	8 0	26 3	9 20
28 WE	5 36	17 33	2 9D	17 23	5 51	4 19	10 57	19 33	8 4	26 2	9 19
29 TH	6 33	1 ♏ 50	2 10	19 16	7 2	4 14	11 4	19 41	8 7	26 0	9 17
30 FR	7 30	16 18	2 12	21 8	8 14	4 9	11 10	19 48	8 10	25 59	9 16

INGRESSES :

1	☽ → ♏	13: 5
3	☽ → ♐	13:12
5	☿ → ♊	1: 3
	☽ → ♑	13:35
7	☽ → ♒	16: 0
9	☽ → ♓	21:52
12	☽ → ♈	7:34
14	☽ → ♉	19:56
17	☽ → ♊	8:51
19	☿ → ♋	8:29
	☽ → ♋	20:27
22	☉ → ♋	3:12
	☽ → ♌	5:53
23	♀ → ♊	2:27
24	☽ → ♍	13: 1
26	☽ → ♎	17:57
28	☽ → ♏	20:56
30	☽ → ♐	22:31

ASPECTS & ECLIPSES :

1	☉ ☍ ♇	2:27
	☽ ☍ ♀	21: 3
3	☽ ☌ P	5:37
	☽ ☍ ☿	8: 1
	♀ □ ⛢	12:37
	☽ ☌ ☋	17:21
4	☽ ☌ ♇	5: 2
	☽ ☍ P	10: 0
	☉ ☍ ☽	10:14
	☽ ☍ ♄	15:42
6	☿ ☌ ☊	8:35
7	☽ ☌ ♆	9:56
	☽ ☌ ♂	21:31
8	☽ ☍ ⛢	4:20
	☉ ☌ ♄	12:29
9	☿ ☍ ♇	20:49
10	☽ □S ☊	2:30
11	☉ □ ☽	11:40
13	☽ ☌ ♃	1:41
	☿ ☌ ♄	14:27
15	☽ ☌ A	12:47
16	☽ ☌ ♀	17:32
17	☉ ☌S ☿	2:14
	☽ ☌ ☊	14: 2
18	☽ ☍ ♇	4: 0
	☽ ☌ ♄	21:36
19	☉ ☌ ☽	15:50
	☽ ☌ ☿	22:55
21	☽ ☍ ♆	22:42
22	☽ ☍ ♂	14:21
	☽ ☌ ⛢	20:25
24	☿ □ ♃	11:55
	☽ □N ☊	16:59
	♀ ☌ ☊	22:45
27	☉ □ ☽	2: 6
	☽ ☍ ♃	12:41
30	♀ ☍ ♇	20:15

SIDEREAL HELIOCENTRIC LONGITUDES : JUNE 30 Julian at 0 hours UT

DAY	Sid. Time	☿	♀	⊕	♂	♃	♄	⛢	♆	♇	Vernal Point
1 TH	16:28:21	18 ♓ 28	8 ♓ 28	9 ♐ 53	27 ♐ 0	26 ♓ 46	16 ♊ 45	9 ♌ 26	25 ♑ 12	9 ♐ 58	2♈38' 8"
2 FR	16:32:18	23 48	10 3	10 50	27 37	26 52	16 48	9 26	25 12	9 58	2♈38' 8"
3 SA	16:36:14	29 17	11 38	11 47	28 14	26 57	16 50	9 27	25 12	9 59	2♈38' 7"
4 SU	16:40:11	4 ♈ 55	13 14	12 44	28 51	27 3	16 52	9 28	25 13	9 59	2♈38' 7"
5 MO	16:44: 7	10 41	14 49	13 41	29 28	27 8	16 54	9 29	25 13	9 59	2♈38' 7"
6 TU	16:48: 4	16 35	16 25	14 38	0 ♑ 5	27 14	16 57	9 29	25 13	10 0	2♈38' 7"
7 WE	16:52: 0	22 35	18 1	15 35	0 42	27 19	16 59	9 30	25 14	10 0	2♈38' 7"
8 TH	16:55:57	28 42	19 36	16 33	1 19	27 24	17 1	9 31	25 14	10 0	2♈38' 7"
9 FR	16:59:53	4 ♉ 53	21 12	17 30	1 56	27 30	17 3	9 32	25 14	10 1	2♈38' 7"
10 SA	17: 3:50	11 8	22 47	18 27	2 33	27 35	17 6	9 33	25 15	10 1	2♈38' 6"
11 SU	17: 7:47	17 26	24 23	19 24	3 10	27 41	17 8	9 33	25 15	10 2	2♈38' 6"
12 MO	17:11:43	23 44	25 59	20 21	3 47	27 46	17 10	9 34	25 15	10 2	2♈38' 6"
13 TU	17:15:40	0 ♊ 2	27 35	21 18	4 24	27 52	17 12	9 35	25 16	10 2	2♈38' 6"
14 WE	17:19:36	6 18	29 10	22 15	5 1	27 57	17 15	9 36	25 16	10 3	2♈38' 6"
15 TH	17:23:33	12 30	0 ♈ 46	23 13	5 39	28 3	17 17	9 36	25 17	10 3	2♈38' 6"
16 FR	17:27:29	18 37	2 22	24 10	6 16	28 8	17 19	9 37	25 17	10 3	2♈38' 6"
17 SA	17:31:26	24 39	3 58	25 7	6 53	28 14	17 21	9 38	25 17	10 4	2♈38' 6"
18 SU	17:35:22	0 ♋ 33	5 34	26 4	7 31	28 19	17 24	9 39	25 18	10 4	2♈38' 5"
19 MO	17:39:19	6 20	7 10	27 1	8 8	28 24	17 26	9 39	25 18	10 4	2♈38' 5"
20 TU	17:43:16	11 58	8 46	27 58	8 45	28 30	17 28	9 40	25 18	10 5	2♈38' 5"
21 WE	17:47:12	17 27	10 22	28 56	9 23	28 35	17 30	9 41	25 19	10 5	2♈38' 5"
22 TH	17:51: 9	22 46	11 58	29 53	10 0	28 41	17 33	9 42	25 19	10 5	2♈38' 5"
23 FR	17:55: 5	27 56	13 34	0 ♑ 50	10 38	28 46	17 35	9 43	25 19	10 6	2♈38' 5"
24 SA	17:59: 2	2 ♌ 57	15 10	1 47	11 15	28 52	17 37	9 43	25 20	10 6	2♈38' 5"
25 SU	18: 2:58	7 48	16 46	2 45	11 53	28 57	17 40	9 44	25 20	10 6	2♈38' 4"
26 MO	18: 6:55	12 30	18 22	3 42	12 30	29 3	17 42	9 45	25 20	10 7	2♈38' 4"
27 TU	18:10:51	17 2	19 58	4 39	13 8	29 8	17 44	9 46	25 21	10 7	2♈38' 4"
28 WE	18:14:48	21 27	21 35	5 36	13 46	29 13	17 46	9 46	25 21	10 7	2♈38' 4"
29 TH	18:18:45	25 42	23 11	6 34	14 23	29 19	17 49	9 47	25 22	10 8	2♈38' 4"
30 FR	18:22:41	29 50	24 47	7 31	15 1	29 24	17 51	9 48	25 22	10 8	2♈38' 4"

INGRESSES :

3	☿ → ♈	3: 4
5	♂ → ♑	20:57
8	☿ → ♉	5: 4
12	☿ → ♊	23:52
14	♀ → ♈	12:26
17	☿ → ♋	21:43
22	⊕ → ♑	2:58
23	☿ → ♌	9:47
30	☿ → ♍	0:56

ASPECTS (HELIOCENTRIC +MOON(TYCHONIC)) :

1	⊕ ☌ ♇	2:11
	☽ □ ♆	5:17
	♀ □ ♆	22:50
2	☽ □ ⛢	4:18
	☿ ☌ ♃	13:41
	☿ □ ♂	18:52
3	⊕ ☌ A	2:23
	♀ □ ⊕	5:24
4	☽ ☌ ♇	5:11
	☽ □ ♀	11:38
	☽ ☍ ♄	16:18
5	☽ □ ♃	8:57
	☽ ☌ ♂	13:15
6	♀ □ ♄	8: 8
7	☽ □ ☿	5:44
	☽ ☌ ♆	7:46
	☿ □ ♆	10:25
	☿ ☌ ☊	19:59
8	☽ ☍ ⛢	8:40
	⊕ ☍ ♄	12:29
9	☿ □ ⛢	17:52
10	☽ □ ♇	16:45
11	☽ □ ♄	6:24
	☿ ☌ P	8: 3
	☽ ☌ ♀	23:35
12	☽ ☌ ♃	3:11
	☽ □ ♂	15:53
13	♀ ☌ ♃	4:33
14	☽ □ ♆	10:20
	☿ ☍ ♇	14:28
15	☽ □ ⛢	15:30
	☿ ☌ ♄	18:49
17	☿ ☍ ⊕	2:14
	☿ □ ♃	14:42
18	☽ ☍ ♇	5: 3
	☽ ☌ ♄	19:42
19	☿ □ ♀	4:53
	☿ ☍ ⛢	8:33
	☽ □ ♃	17:28
	♀ □ ♂	23:53
20	☽ ☍ ♂	14:10
	⊕ □ ♃	14:33
	☽ □ ♀	15:27
21	☽ ☌ ☿	10:42
	☽ ☍ ♆	21: 4
22	☿ ☍ ♆	11:45
	☿ □N ☊	22:44
	☽ ☌ ⛢	23:59
25	☽ □ ♇	7: 5
	☿ ☌ ⛢	9:50
	☽ □ ♄	20:29
26	☽ ☍ ♃	16:24
27	☽ □ ♂	17:15
28	☽ ☍ ♀	7:40
	☽ □ ♆	13:10
29	☽ □ ⛢	13:14
30	♀ □ ♆	8:40

SIDEREAL GEOCENTRIC LONGITUDES : JULY 30 Julian at 0 hours UT

DAY	☉	☽	☊	☿	♀	♂	♃	♄	♅	♆	♇
1 SA	8 ♋ 28	0 ♐ 54	2 ♊ 12R	22 ♋ 58	9 ♊ 26	4 ♒ 3R	11 ♈ 16	19 ♊ 56	8 ♌ 14	25 ♑ 57R	9 ♐ 15R
2 SU	9 25	15 33	2 12	24 46	10 38	3 56	11 21	20 4	8 17	25 56	9 13
3 MO	10 22	0 ♑ 10	2 9	26 32	11 50	3 48	11 27	20 11	8 20	25 54	9 12
4 TU	11 20	14 38	2 5	28 17	13 2	3 40	11 33	20 19	8 24	25 53	9 11
5 WE	12 17	28 50	2 0	0 ♌ 0	14 14	3 31	11 38	20 26	8 27	25 51	9 10
6 TH	13 14	12 ♒ 43	1 53	1 41	15 26	3 21	11 43	20 34	8 31	25 49	9 8
7 FR	14 12	26 12	1 47	3 21	16 38	3 11	11 48	20 41	8 34	25 48	9 7
8 SA	15 9	9 ♓ 17	1 41	4 59	17 51	3 0	11 53	20 48	8 38	25 46	9 6
9 SU	16 7	22 0	1 37	6 36	19 3	2 48	11 57	20 56	8 41	25 45	9 5
10 MO	17 4	4 ♈ 22	1 34	8 11	20 15	2 36	12 2	21 3	8 45	25 43	9 4
11 TU	18 2	16 28	1 33	9 44	21 28	2 23	12 6	21 10	8 48	25 41	9 3
12 WE	18 59	28 23	1 33D	11 16	22 40	2 10	12 10	21 18	8 52	25 40	9 2
13 TH	19 57	10 ♉ 13	1 34	12 46	23 53	1 56	12 14	21 25	8 56	25 38	9 1
14 FR	20 54	22 1	1 36	14 14	25 5	1 42	12 18	21 32	8 59	25 37	9 0
15 SA	21 52	3 ♊ 54	1 36R	15 41	26 18	1 28	12 21	21 39	9 3	25 35	8 58
16 SU	22 50	15 54	1 35	17 6	27 31	1 13	12 25	21 46	9 6	25 33	8 57
17 MO	23 47	28 7	1 32	18 29	28 44	0 58	12 28	21 53	9 10	25 32	8 56
18 TU	24 45	10 ♋ 34	1 26	19 51	29 56	0 42	12 31	22 0	9 14	25 30	8 56
19 WE	25 43	23 17	1 19	21 11	1 ♋ 9	0 27	12 34	22 7	9 17	25 28	8 55
20 TH	26 40	6 ♌ 15	1 10	22 29	2 22	0 11	12 36	22 14	9 21	25 27	8 54
21 FR	27 38	19 29	1 0	23 45	3 35	29 ♑ 55	12 39	22 21	9 25	25 25	8 53
22 SA	28 36	2 ♍ 57	0 51	24 59	4 48	29 39	12 41	22 28	9 28	25 23	8 52
23 SU	29 34	16 35	0 43	26 11	6 1	29 23	12 43	22 35	9 32	25 22	8 51
24 MO	0 ♌ 31	0 ♎ 23	0 37	27 21	7 14	29 7	12 45	22 42	9 36	25 20	8 50
25 TU	1 29	14 19	0 34	28 29	8 27	28 51	12 46	22 49	9 40	25 19	8 49
26 WE	2 27	28 21	0 33	29 35	9 40	28 35	12 48	22 55	9 43	25 17	8 49
27 TH	3 25	12 ♏ 29	0 33D	0 ♍ 38	10 54	28 20	12 49	23 2	9 47	25 15	8 48
28 FR	4 23	26 40	0 33	1 39	12 7	28 4	12 50	23 8	9 51	25 14	8 47
29 SA	5 21	10 ♐ 54	0 33R	2 37	13 20	27 49	12 51	23 15	9 55	25 12	8 47
30 SU	6 19	25 9	0 31	3 33	14 34	27 35	12 51	23 21	9 58	25 10	8 46
31 MO	7 17	9 ♑ 21	0 26	4 25	15 47	27 20	12 52	23 28	10 2	25 9	8 45

INGRESSES :

2 ☽ → ♑ 23:43
5 ☿ → ♌ 0: 1
☽ → ♒ 1:58
7 ☽ → ♓ 6:53
9 ☽ → ♈ 15:27
12 ☽ → ♉ 3:15
14 ☽ → ♊ 16: 9
17 ☽ → ♋ 3:39
18 ♀ → ♋ 1:13
19 ☽ → ♌ 12:29
20 ♂ → ♑ 16:37
21 ☽ → ♍ 18:47
23 ☉ → ♌ 10:59
☽ → ♎ 23:19
26 ☽ → ♏ 2:47
☿ → ♍ 9:19
28 ☽ → ♐ 5:37
30 ☽ → ♑ 8:10

ASPECTS & ECLIPSES :

1 ☽ ☌ ☋ 2: 9
☽ ☌ P 8: 8
☽ ☌ ♇ 13:39
☽ ☍ ♀ 15:13
2 ☽ ☍ ♄ 7:26
☿ ☍ ♆ 15:31
3 ☉ ☍ ☽ 18: 5
4 ☉ □ ♃ 5:53
☽ ☌ ♆ 18:54
5 ☽ ☍ ☿ 2:15
☽ ☌ ♂ 7:55
☽ ☍ ♅ 16:37
6 ☿ ☍ ♂ 21:42
7 ☽ ☋(S) ☊ 10: 3
10 ☿ ☌ ♅ 9: 3
☽ ☌ ♃ 15:14
♀ ☌ ♄ 17:33
11 ☉ □ ☽ 3:23
13 ☽ ☌ A 4:56
14 ☽ ☌ ☊ 19:23
15 ☽ ☍ ♇ 10:10
16 ☽ ☌ ♄ 11:41
17 ☽ ☌ ♀ 1:18
18 ☉ ☍ ♆ 18:16
19 ☽ ☍ ♆ 4: 4
☉ ☌ ☽ 4:53
☽ ☍ ♂ 13: 3
20 ☽ ☌ ♅ 5:40
21 ☽ ☌ ☿ 8:25
☽ ☊(N) ☊ 20:19
22 ☉ ☍ ♂ 20:36
24 ☽ ☍ ♃ 21:19
26 ☉ □ ☽ 7:28
☿ □ ☊ 21:48
28 ☽ ☌ ☋ 6:33
♀ □ ♃ 14:15
☽ ☌ P 14:28
☽ ☌ ♇ 20:24
29 ☽ ☍ ♄ 20:57
31 ☽ ☍ ♀ 11:58

SIDEREAL HELIOCENTRIC LONGITUDES : JULY 30 Julian at 0 hours UT

DAY	Sid. Time	☿	♀	⊕	♂	♃	♄	♅	♆	♇	Vernal Point
1 SA	18:26:38	3 ♍ 51	26 ♈ 24	8 ♑ 28	15 ♑ 39	29 ♓ 30	17 ♊ 53	9 ♌ 49	25 ♑ 22	10 ♐ 8	2♈38' 4"
2 SU	18:30:34	7 44	28 0	9 26	16 16	29 35	17 55	9 49	25 23	10 9	2♈38' 3"
3 MO	18:34:31	11 31	29 36	10 23	16 54	29 41	17 58	9 50	25 23	10 9	2♈38' 3"
4 TU	18:38:27	15 12	1 ♉ 13	11 20	17 32	29 46	18 0	9 51	25 23	10 9	2♈38' 3"
5 WE	18:42:24	18 47	2 49	12 18	18 9	29 52	18 2	9 52	25 24	10 10	2♈38' 3"
6 TH	18:46:20	22 16	4 26	13 15	18 47	29 57	18 4	9 52	25 24	10 10	2♈38' 3"
7 FR	18:50:17	25 40	6 2	14 12	19 25	0 ♈ 3	18 7	9 53	25 24	10 10	2♈38' 3"
8 SA	18:54:14	29 0	7 39	15 10	20 3	0 8	18 9	9 54	25 25	10 11	2♈38' 3"
9 SU	18:58:10	2 ♎ 16	9 15	16 7	20 41	0 13	18 11	9 55	25 25	10 11	2♈38' 3"
10 MO	19: 2: 7	5 27	10 52	17 5	21 18	0 19	18 13	9 56	25 25	10 11	2♈38' 2"
11 TU	19: 6: 3	8 35	12 29	18 2	21 56	0 24	18 16	9 56	25 26	10 12	2♈38' 2"
12 WE	19:10: 0	11 39	14 5	19 0	22 34	0 30	18 18	9 57	25 26	10 12	2♈38' 2"
13 TH	19:13:56	14 41	15 42	19 57	23 12	0 35	18 20	9 58	25 27	10 12	2♈38' 2"
14 FR	19:17:53	17 40	17 19	20 55	23 50	0 41	18 22	9 59	25 27	10 13	2♈38' 2"
15 SA	19:21:49	20 36	18 56	21 52	24 28	0 46	18 25	9 59	25 27	10 13	2♈38' 2"
16 SU	19:25:46	23 30	20 32	22 50	25 6	0 52	18 27	10 0	25 28	10 13	2♈38' 2"
17 MO	19:29:43	26 22	22 9	23 48	25 43	0 57	18 29	10 1	25 28	10 14	2♈38' 1"
18 TU	19:33:39	29 12	23 46	24 45	26 21	1 2	18 31	10 2	25 28	10 14	2♈38' 1"
19 WE	19:37:36	2 ♏ 1	25 23	25 43	26 59	1 8	18 34	10 2	25 29	10 14	2♈38' 1"
20 TH	19:41:32	4 49	27 0	26 41	27 37	1 13	18 36	10 3	25 29	10 15	2♈38' 1"
21 FR	19:45:29	7 35	28 37	27 39	28 15	1 19	18 38	10 4	25 29	10 15	2♈38' 1"
22 SA	19:49:25	10 21	0 ♊ 14	28 36	28 53	1 24	18 40	10 5	25 30	10 15	2♈38' 1"
23 SU	19:53:22	13 6	1 51	29 34	29 31	1 30	18 43	10 6	25 30	10 16	2♈38' 1"
24 MO	19:57:18	15 51	3 28	0 ♒ 32	0 ♒ 9	1 35	18 45	10 6	25 31	10 16	2♈38' 0"
25 TU	20: 1:15	18 35	5 5	1 30	0 47	1 41	18 47	10 7	25 31	10 16	2♈38' 0"
26 WE	20: 5:12	21 20	6 42	2 28	1 25	1 46	18 49	10 8	25 31	10 17	2♈38' 0"
27 TH	20: 9: 8	24 5	8 19	3 25	2 3	1 51	18 52	10 9	25 32	10 17	2♈38' 0"
28 FR	20:13: 5	26 50	9 56	4 23	2 41	1 57	18 54	10 9	25 32	10 17	2♈38' 0"
29 SA	20:17: 1	29 36	11 34	5 21	3 19	2 2	18 56	10 10	25 32	10 18	2♈38' 0"
30 SU	20:20:58	2 ♐ 23	13 11	6 19	3 57	2 8	18 58	10 11	25 33	10 18	2♈38' 0"
31 MO	20:24:54	5 11	14 48	7 17	4 35	2 13	19 1	10 12	25 33	10 19	2♈38' 0"

INGRESSES :

3 ♀ → ♉ 5:53
6 ♃ → ♈ 12:54
8 ☿ → ♎ 7:17
18 ☿ → ♏ 6:46
21 ♀ → ♊ 20:34
23 ⊕ → ♒ 10:46
♂ → ♒ 18:17
29 ☿ → ♐ 3:27

ASPECTS (HELIOCENTRIC +MOON(TYCHONIC)) :

1 ☽ □ ☿ 6:36
☽ ☌ ♇ 15: 8
2 ☽ ☍ ♄ 3:53
☿ □ ♇ 15:12
☽ □ ♃ 23:11
4 ☽ ☌ ♂ 5: 4
☽ ☌ ♆ 18: 7
☿ □ ♄ 18:54
5 ☽ □ ♀ 7:42
☽ ☍ ♅ 19: 1
8 ☽ □ ♇ 1:39
☿ ☍ ♃ 8:30
☽ □ ♄ 16:42
9 ♀ □ ♅ 9:52
☽ ☌ ♃ 16: 1
10 ☽ ☍ ☿ 2:52
11 ☽ □ ♂ 11:35
☽ □ ♆ 18: 1
12 ☽ □ ♅ 23:29
13 ☽ ☌ ♀ 12:55
15 ☽ ☍ ♇ 12:41
☿ □ ⊕ 15:46
16 ☽ ☌ ♄ 5: 2
♂ ☌ ♆ 14: 6
☿ □ ♆ 16:27
☿ □ ♂ 17: 6
17 ☽ □ ♃ 5:32
☿ ☌ ☋ 11: 0
18 ⊕ ☌ ♆ 17:59
19 ☽ ☍ ♆ 4: 6
☽ ☍ ♂ 7:15
☽ □ ☿ 20:37
20 ☽ ☌ ♅ 6:56
21 ☽ □ ♀ 18:32
☿ □ ♅ 21:38
22 ☽ □ ♇ 12:54
⊕ ☌ ♂ 20:23
♀ ☌ ☊ 22:10
23 ☽ □ ♄ 3:43
24 ☽ ☍ ♃ 2: 4
25 ☿ ☌ A 8:23
☽ □ ♆ 19: 9
26 ☽ □ ♂ 5:27
☽ □ ♅ 20: 2
27 ♂ ☌ P 16:37
28 ☽ ☌ ☿ 0:20
♀ ☍ ♇ 5:13
☽ ☌ ♇ 22:58
29 ☽ ☍ ♀ 1:14
☽ ☍ ♄ 13:33
30 ☽ □ ♃ 11:51

SIDEREAL GEOCENTRIC LONGITUDES : AUGUST 30 Julian at 0 hours UT											
DAY	☉	☽	☊	☿	♀	♂	♃	♄	♅	♆	♇
1 TU	8 ♌ 15	23 ♑ 26	0 ♊ 18R	5 ♍ 15	17 ♋ 0	27 ♑ 6R	12 ♈ 52	23 ♊ 34	10 ♌ 6	25 ♑ 7R	8 ♐ 45R
2 WE	9 13	7 ♒ 20	0 9	6 1	18 14	26 52	12 52R	23 40	10 10	25 6	8 44
3 TH	10 11	20 58	29 ♉ 57	6 43	19 28	26 39	12 52	23 47	10 13	25 4	8 44
4 FR	11 9	4 ♓ 18	29 46	7 22	20 41	26 26	12 52	23 53	10 17	25 3	8 43
5 SA	12 7	17 18	29 35	7 57	21 55	26 14	12 51	23 59	10 21	25 1	8 43
6 SU	13 5	29 57	29 26	8 28	23 9	26 3	12 51	24 5	10 25	24 59	8 42
7 MO	14 3	12 ♈ 18	29 20	8 54	24 22	25 51	12 50	24 11	10 28	24 58	8 42
8 TU	15 1	24 24	29 16	9 15	25 36	25 41	12 48	24 17	10 32	24 56	8 41
9 WE	16 0	6 ♉ 19	29 14	9 31	26 50	25 31	12 47	24 23	10 36	24 55	8 41
10 TH	16 58	18 8	29 14	9 42	28 4	25 22	12 46	24 29	10 40	24 53	8 41
11 FR	17 56	29 56	29 14	9 47	29 18	25 13	12 44	24 34	10 43	24 52	8 40
12 SA	18 54	11 ♊ 50	29 13	9 46R	0 ♌ 32	25 6	12 42	24 40	10 47	24 50	8 40
13 SU	19 53	23 54	29 11	9 39	1 46	24 58	12 40	24 46	10 51	24 49	8 40
14 MO	20 51	6 ♋ 13	29 6	9 25	3 0	24 52	12 37	24 51	10 54	24 48	8 40
15 TU	21 50	18 51	28 59	9 4	4 14	24 46	12 35	24 57	10 58	24 46	8 39
16 WE	22 48	1 ♌ 48	28 49	8 37	5 28	24 42	12 32	25 2	11 2	24 45	8 39
17 TH	23 47	15 6	28 38	8 3	6 42	24 38	12 29	25 7	11 6	24 43	8 39
18 FR	24 45	28 43	28 25	7 23	7 57	24 34	12 26	25 13	11 9	24 42	8 39
19 SA	25 44	12 ♍ 37	28 13	6 36	9 11	24 32	12 23	25 18	11 13	24 41	8 39
20 SU	26 42	26 41	28 3	5 44	10 25	24 30	12 19	25 23	11 17	24 39	8 39
21 MO	27 41	10 ♎ 52	27 54	4 47	11 39	24 29	12 16	25 28	11 20	24 38	8 39D
22 TU	28 40	25 6	27 49	3 47	12 54	24 29D	12 12	25 33	11 24	24 37	8 39
23 WE	29 39	9 ♏ 19	27 47	2 43	14 8	24 30	12 8	25 38	11 27	24 35	8 39
24 TH	0 ♍ 37	23 29	27 46	1 39	15 23	24 32	12 3	25 42	11 31	24 34	8 39
25 FR	1 36	7 ♐ 34	27 46	0 34	16 37	24 34	11 59	25 47	11 35	24 33	8 39
26 SA	2 35	21 34	27 46	29 ♌ 31	17 52	24 37	11 54	25 52	11 38	24 32	8 39
27 SU	3 34	5 ♑ 29	27 43	28 32	19 6	24 41	11 50	25 56	11 42	24 31	8 40
28 MO	4 33	19 16	27 38	27 38	20 21	24 46	11 45	26 0	11 45	24 29	8 40
29 TU	5 31	2 ♒ 56	27 29	26 50	21 35	24 51	11 40	26 5	11 49	24 28	8 40
30 WE	6 30	16 25	27 18	26 10	22 50	24 58	11 34	26 9	11 52	24 27	8 40
31 TH	7 29	29 42	27 6	25 39	24 5	25 5	11 29	26 13	11 56	24 26	8 41

INGRESSES :	
1 ☽ → ♒ 11:17	22 ☽ → ♏ 8:15
2 ☊ → ♉ 18:40	23 ☉ → ♍ 8:45
3 ☽ → ♓ 16:11	24 ☽ → ♐ 11: 5
6 ☽ → ♈ 0: 5	25 ☿ → ♌ 12:54
8 ☽ → ♉ 11:15	26 ☽ → ♑ 14:31
11 ☽ → ♊ 0: 7	28 ☽ → ♒ 18:49
♀ → ♌ 13:42	31 ☽ → ♓ 0:32
13 ☽ → ♋ 11:56	
15 ☽ → ♌ 20:41	
18 ☽ → ♍ 2:13	
20 ☽ → ♎ 5:37	

ASPECTS & ECLIPSES :				
1 ☽ ☌ ♆ 2:53	9 ☉ □ ☽ 21:25	☽ ☌ ♅ 16:47	♂ ☌ ♆ 18: 8	☿ ☌ ♀ 23:31
☽ ☌ ♂ 6:11	☽ ☌ A 23:43	17 ☉ ☌ ☽ 16:31	25 ☽ ☌ ♇ 1:51	
2 ☉ ☍ ☽ 3:31	10 ☉ □ π 11:19	☽ [N] ☊ 23:28	26 ☽ ☍ ♄ 7:25	
☽ ☍ ♅ 4:57	☽ ☌ ☊ 22:33	18 ☽ ☌ ☿ 14:14	28 ☿ □ ☊ 0:12	
3 ☉ ☌ ♅ 1:11	11 ☽ ☍ ♇ 17:38	20 ♀ ☌ ♅ 17:28	☽ ☌ ♆ 9: 7	
☽ [S] ☊ 15:53	13 ☽ ☌ ♄ 1:41	21 ☽ ☍ ♃ 2:19	☽ ☌ ♂ 9:40	
4 ☽ ☍ ☿ 5:53	15 ♂ ☌ ♆ 1:53	☉ □ ☊ 4:55	29 ☽ ☍ ♅ 15:50	
6 ☿ □ ♇ 12:34	☽ ☍ ♂ 10:59	22 ☽ ☌ P 13:24	30 ☽ ☍ ♀ 12:44	
7 ☽ ☌ ♃ 1: 2	☽ ☍ ♆ 11: 2	24 ☽ ☌ ☋ 7:17	☽ ☍ ☿ 16:53	
♀ ☍ ♆ 11:22	☿ □ ♇ 22:19	☉ ⊻ ☿ 11:53	☽ [S] ☊ 19:20	
8 ♀ ☍ ♂ 1:24	16 ☽ ☌ ♀ 7:21	☉ □ ☽ 13: 3	31 ☉ ☍ ☽ 15:26	

SIDEREAL HELIOCENTRIC LONGITUDES : AUGUST 30 Julian at 0 hours UT											
DAY	Sid. Time	☿	♀	⊕	♂	♃	♄	♅	♆	♇	Vernal Point
1 TU	20:28:51	8 ♐ 0	16 ♊ 25	8 ♒ 15	5 ♒ 13	2 ♈ 19	19 ♊ 3	10 ♌ 12	25 ♑ 33	10 ♐ 19	2♈37'59"
2 WE	20:32:47	10 50	18 3	9 13	5 51	2 24	19 5	10 13	25 34	10 19	2♈37'59"
3 TH	20:36:44	13 43	19 40	10 11	6 29	2 30	19 7	10 14	25 34	10 20	2♈37'59"
4 FR	20:40:41	16 37	21 17	11 9	7 6	2 35	19 10	10 15	25 34	10 20	2♈37'59"
5 SA	20:44:37	19 33	22 55	12 7	7 44	2 40	19 12	10 16	25 35	10 20	2♈37'59"
6 SU	20:48:34	22 32	24 32	13 5	8 22	2 46	19 14	10 16	25 35	10 21	2♈37'59"
7 MO	20:52:30	25 34	26 10	14 4	9 0	2 51	19 17	10 17	25 36	10 21	2♈37'59"
8 TU	20:56:27	28 38	27 47	15 2	9 38	2 57	19 19	10 18	25 36	10 21	2♈37'58"
9 WE	21: 0:23	1 ♑ 46	29 24	16 0	10 16	3 2	19 21	10 19	25 36	10 22	2♈37'58"
10 TH	21: 4:20	4 57	1 ♋ 2	16 58	10 54	3 8	19 23	10 19	25 37	10 22	2♈37'58"
11 FR	21: 8:16	8 12	2 39	17 57	11 32	3 13	19 26	10 20	25 37	10 22	2♈37'58"
12 SA	21:12:13	11 31	4 17	18 55	12 10	3 18	19 28	10 21	25 37	10 23	2♈37'58"
13 SU	21:16:10	14 55	5 54	19 53	12 48	3 24	19 30	10 22	25 38	10 23	2♈37'58"
14 MO	21:20: 6	18 23	7 32	20 52	13 25	3 29	19 32	10 22	25 38	10 23	2♈37'58"
15 TU	21:24: 3	21 56	9 10	21 50	14 3	3 35	19 35	10 23	25 38	10 24	2♈37'57"
16 WE	21:27:59	25 35	10 47	22 49	14 41	3 40	19 37	10 24	25 39	10 24	2♈37'57"
17 TH	21:31:56	29 20	12 25	23 47	15 19	3 46	19 39	10 25	25 39	10 24	2♈37'57"
18 FR	21:35:52	3 ♒ 11	14 2	24 46	15 57	3 51	19 41	10 26	25 39	10 25	2♈37'57"
19 SA	21:39:49	7 8	15 40	25 44	16 34	3 57	19 44	10 26	25 40	10 25	2♈37'57"
20 SU	21:43:45	11 13	17 18	26 43	17 12	4 2	19 46	10 27	25 40	10 25	2♈37'57"
21 MO	21:47:42	15 24	18 55	27 42	17 50	4 7	19 48	10 28	25 41	10 26	2♈37'57"
22 TU	21:51:39	19 44	20 33	28 40	18 28	4 13	19 50	10 29	25 41	10 26	2♈37'57"
23 WE	21:55:35	24 11	22 11	29 39	19 5	4 18	19 53	10 29	25 41	10 26	2♈37'56"
24 TH	21:59:32	28 47	23 48	0 ♓ 38	19 43	4 24	19 55	10 30	25 42	10 27	2♈37'56"
25 FR	22: 3:28	3 ♓ 32	25 26	1 37	20 21	4 29	19 57	10 31	25 42	10 27	2♈37'56"
26 SA	22: 7:25	8 25	27 4	2 35	20 58	4 35	19 59	10 32	25 42	10 27	2♈37'56"
27 SU	22:11:21	13 27	28 41	3 34	21 36	4 40	20 2	10 32	25 43	10 28	2♈37'56"
28 MO	22:15:18	18 38	0 ♌ 19	4 33	22 14	4 45	20 4	10 33	25 43	10 28	2♈37'56"
29 TU	22:19:14	23 59	1 57	5 32	22 51	4 51	20 6	10 34	25 43	10 28	2♈37'56"
30 WE	22:23:11	29 28	3 34	6 31	23 29	4 56	20 8	10 35	25 44	10 29	2♈37'55"
31 TH	22:27: 8	5 ♈ 6	5 12	7 30	24 6	5 2	20 11	10 35	25 44	10 29	2♈37'55"

INGRESSES :
8 ☿ → ♑ 10:32
9 ♀ → ♋ 8:45
17 ☿ → ♒ 4:12
23 ⊕ → ♓ 8:32
24 ☿ → ♓ 6:13
27 ♀ → ♌ 19:21
30 ☿ → ♈ 2:16

ASPECTS (HELIOCENTRIC +MOON(TYCHONIC)) :				
1 ☽ ☌ ♆ 3:38	☽ □ ♀ 12: 8	13 ☽ □ ♃ 18:40	☿ ☍ ♅ 19:33	☽ ☍ ♄ 21:16
☿ ☌ ♇ 19:38	6 ☽ ☌ ♃ 5:27	14 ☽ ☌ ♀ 2:53	20 ☽ ☍ ♃ 12:31	26 ☿ □ ♇ 9:49
☽ ☌ ♂ 21:17	7 ☿ ☍ ♀ 10: 2	15 ☽ ☍ ☿ 8: 3	21 ☽ □ ♀ 15:19	☽ □ ♃ 22:35
2 ☽ ☍ ♅ 5: 3	8 ☽ □ ♆ 2:24	☽ ☍ ♆ 12:40	☿ ☌ ♂ 15:50	28 ☿ □ ♄ 6:30
♀ ☌ ♄ 15:47	9 ♂ ☍ ♅ 1:37	16 ☿ ☌ ♆ 0:22	22 ☽ □ ♆ 0:58	☽ ☌ ♆ 11:17
3 ⊕ ☍ ♅ 1:11	☽ □ ♅ 8: 7	☿ [S] ☊ 13:25	23 ☽ □ ♅ 1:58	☽ ☍ ♀ 22: 0
♂ [S] ☊ 18:54	☽ □ ♂ 8:28	☽ ☌ ♅ 15:35	☽ □ ♂ 17:18	29 ☽ ☍ ♅ 13:33
4 ☽ □ ♇ 11: 4	☿ □ ♃ 9:56	17 ☽ ☍ ♂ 0:23	24 ☿ ☌ ⊕ 11:53	30 ☽ ☌ ♂ 13:19
☿ ☍ ♄ 21: 6	11 ♀ □ ♃ 8:45	18 ☽ □ ♇ 20:14	☽ □ ☿ 13:32	☿ ☌ ♃ 23:40
5 ☽ □ ♄ 3:35	☽ ☍ ♇ 21: 3	19 ♀ ☌ P 7:56	25 ♀ ☍ ♆ 3:58	31 ☽ □ ♇ 19:49
☽ □ ☿ 5:31	12 ☽ ☌ ♄ 15:15	☽ □ ♄ 12:12	☽ ☌ ♇ 4:55	

SIDEREAL GEOCENTRIC LONGITUDES : SEPTEMBER 30 Julian at 0 hours UT

DAY	☉	☽	☊	☿	♀	♂	♃	♄	♅	♆	♇
1 FR	8 ♍ 28	12 ♓ 44	26 ♉ 53R	25 ♌ 18R	25 ♌ 20	25 ♑ 13	11 ♈ 23R	26 ♊ 17	11 ♌ 59	24 ♑ 25R	8 ♐ 41
2 SA	9 27	25 31	26 41	25 6	26 34	25 21	11 18	26 21	12 3	24 24	8 41
3 SU	10 26	8 ♈ 1	26 31	25 5D	27 49	25 30	11 12	26 25	12 6	24 23	8 42
4 MO	11 26	20 16	26 23	25 14	29 4	25 40	11 6	26 29	12 10	24 22	8 42
5 TU	12 25	2 ♉ 19	26 18	25 34	0 ♍ 19	25 51	11 0	26 33	12 13	24 21	8 43
6 WE	13 24	14 12	26 15	26 3	1 34	26 2	10 53	26 36	12 16	24 20	8 43
7 TH	14 23	26 0	26 15	26 42	2 48	26 14	10 47	26 40	12 20	24 19	8 44
8 FR	15 22	7 ♊ 48	26 15D	27 29	4 3	26 27	10 40	26 43	12 23	24 18	8 44
9 SA	16 22	19 41	26 15R	28 24	5 18	26 40	10 33	26 46	12 26	24 17	8 45
10 SU	17 21	1 ♋ 45	26 14	29 27	6 33	26 54	10 27	26 50	12 30	24 16	8 45
11 MO	18 20	14 5	26 11	0 ♍ 36	7 48	27 9	10 20	26 53	12 33	24 16	8 46
12 TU	19 20	26 45	26 5	1 51	9 3	27 24	10 13	26 56	12 36	24 15	8 47
13 WE	20 19	9 ♌ 50	25 58	3 11	10 18	27 40	10 5	26 59	12 39	24 14	8 48
14 TH	21 19	23 19	25 48	4 36	11 34	27 57	9 58	27 2	12 42	24 13	8 48
15 FR	22 18	7 ♍ 13	25 38	6 4	12 49	28 14	9 51	27 4	12 45	24 13	8 49
16 SA	23 18	21 27	25 28	7 35	14 4	28 31	9 43	27 7	12 49	24 12	8 50
17 SU	24 18	5 ♎ 56	25 19	9 9	15 19	28 49	9 36	27 9	12 52	24 11	8 51
18 MO	25 17	20 34	25 12	10 45	16 34	29 8	9 28	27 12	12 55	24 11	8 52
19 TU	26 17	5 ♏ 13	25 7	12 23	17 49	29 28	9 20	27 14	12 58	24 10	8 53
20 WE	27 17	19 47	25 6	14 2	19 5	29 47	9 12	27 16	13 1	24 10	8 53
21 TH	28 16	4 ♐ 12	25 6D	15 42	20 20	0 ♒ 8	9 5	27 18	13 3	24 9	8 54
22 FR	29 16	18 24	25 6	17 23	21 35	0 29	8 57	27 20	13 6	24 9	8 55
23 SA	0 ♎ 16	2 ♑ 23	25 7R	19 4	22 50	0 50	8 49	27 22	13 9	24 8	8 56
24 SU	1 16	16 8	25 6	20 46	24 6	1 12	8 41	27 24	13 12	24 8	8 57
25 MO	2 16	29 39	25 3	22 28	25 21	1 34	8 33	27 26	13 15	24 8	8 59
26 TU	3 15	12 ♒ 58	24 57	24 10	26 36	1 57	8 25	27 27	13 18	24 7	9 0
27 WE	4 15	26 5	24 50	25 52	27 52	2 20	8 16	27 29	13 20	24 7	9 1
28 TH	5 15	8 ♓ 59	24 41	27 33	29 7	2 44	8 8	27 30	13 23	24 7	9 2
29 FR	6 15	21 40	24 32	29 15	0 ♎ 22	3 8	8 0	27 31	13 26	24 6	9 3
30 SA	7 15	4 ♈ 9	24 23	0 ♎ 56	1 38	3 33	7 52	27 32	13 28	24 6	9 4

INGRESSES :

2 ☽ → ♈ 8:33
4 ♀ → ♍ 18: 0
☽ → ♉ 19:21
7 ☽ → ♊ 8: 8
9 ☽ → ♋ 20:33
10 ☿ → ♍ 11:42
12 ☽ → ♌ 6: 1
14 ☽ → ♍ 11:37
16 ☽ → ♎ 14:11
18 ☽ → ♏ 15:26
20 ♂ → ♒ 14:54
☽ → ♐ 16:58
22 ☉ → ♎ 17:37
☽ → ♑ 19:53
25 ☽ → ♒ 0:36
27 ☽ → ♓ 7:15
28 ♀ → ♎ 16:55
29 ☿ → ♎ 10:42
☽ → ♈ 15:57

ASPECTS & ECLIPSES :

1 ☉ □ ♇ 5: 9
2 ♀ □ ☊ 1:50
3 ☽ ☌ ♃ 6: 7
6 ☿ □ ☊ 7:58
☽ ☌ A 19:37
7 ☽ ☌ ☊ 0:29
8 ☽ ☍ ♇ 1:54
☉ □ ☽ 16:43
9 ☽ ☌ ♄ 14:13
11 ♀ □ ♇ 18:39
☽ ☍ ♆ 19:18
12 ☽ ☍ ♂ 1:13
13 ☽ ☌ ♅ 5: 6
14 ☽ ▯N ☊ 4:17
☽ ☌ ☿ 21:48
15 ☽ ☌ ♀ 10:25
16 ☉ ☌ ☽ 3:18
☿ □ ♇ 19:17
17 ☽ ☍ ♃ 5:57
18 ☽ ☌ P 14:40
19 ☉ □ ♄ 23:53
20 ☽ ☌ ☋ 8:48
21 ☽ ☌ ♇ 7:55
22 ☽ ☍ ♄ 15:20
☉ □ ☽ 20: 4
24 ☽ ☌ ♆ 14: 8
25 ☽ ☌ ♂ 3:31
26 ☽ ☍ ♅ 0:35
♀ □ ♄ 16:33
☽ ▯S ☊ 21:43
27 ☿ □ ♄ 23: 9
29 ☽ ☍ ☿ 16:47
☽ ☍ ♀ 18:33
30 ☉ ☍ ☽ 6:32
☽ ☌ ♃ 7: 7
☉ ☍ ♃ 12:55

SIDEREAL HELIOCENTRIC LONGITUDES : SEPTEMBER 30 Julian at 0 hours UT

DAY	Sid. Time	☿	♀	⊕	♂	♃	♄	♅	♆	♇	Vernal Point
1 FR	22:31: 4	10 ♈ 53	6 ♌ 50	8 ♓ 29	24 ♒ 44	5 ♈ 7	20 ♊ 13	10 ♌ 36	25 ♑ 45	10 ♐ 29	2♈37'55"
2 SA	22:35: 1	16 46	8 27	9 28	25 21	5 13	20 15	10 37	25 45	10 30	2♈37'55"
3 SU	22:38:57	22 47	10 5	10 27	25 59	5 18	20 17	10 38	25 45	10 30	2♈37'55"
4 MO	22:42:54	28 54	11 42	11 26	26 36	5 24	20 20	10 39	25 46	10 30	2♈37'55"
5 TU	22:46:50	5 ♉ 6	13 20	12 25	27 13	5 29	20 22	10 39	25 46	10 31	2♈37'55"
6 WE	22:50:47	11 21	14 58	13 24	27 51	5 34	20 24	10 40	25 46	10 31	2♈37'54"
7 TH	22:54:43	17 38	16 35	14 24	28 28	5 40	20 26	10 41	25 47	10 31	2♈37'54"
8 FR	22:58:40	23 57	18 13	15 23	29 5	5 45	20 29	10 42	25 47	10 32	2♈37'54"
9 SA	23: 2:37	0 ♊ 14	19 50	16 22	29 43	5 51	20 31	10 42	25 47	10 32	2♈37'54"
10 SU	23: 6:33	6 30	21 28	17 22	0 ♓ 20	5 56	20 33	10 43	25 48	10 32	2♈37'54"
11 MO	23:10:30	12 42	23 5	18 21	0 57	6 2	20 35	10 44	25 48	10 33	2♈37'54"
12 TU	23:14:26	18 49	24 43	19 20	1 34	6 7	20 38	10 45	25 48	10 33	2♈37'54"
13 WE	23:18:23	24 50	26 20	20 20	2 11	6 12	20 40	10 45	25 49	10 33	2♈37'54"
14 TH	23:22:19	0 ♋ 44	27 58	21 19	2 49	6 18	20 42	10 46	25 49	10 34	2♈37'53"
15 FR	23:26:16	6 31	29 35	22 19	3 26	6 23	20 44	10 47	25 50	10 34	2♈37'53"
16 SA	23:30:12	12 8	1 ♍ 12	23 19	4 3	6 29	20 47	10 48	25 50	10 34	2♈37'53"
17 SU	23:34: 9	17 37	2 50	24 18	4 40	6 34	20 49	10 49	25 50	10 35	2♈37'53"
18 MO	23:38: 6	22 56	4 27	25 18	5 17	6 40	20 51	10 49	25 51	10 35	2♈37'53"
19 TU	23:42: 2	28 6	6 4	26 17	5 54	6 45	20 53	10 50	25 51	10 35	2♈37'53"
20 WE	23:45:59	3 ♌ 6	7 42	27 17	6 30	6 50	20 56	10 51	25 51	10 36	2♈37'53"
21 TH	23:49:55	7 57	9 19	28 17	7 7	6 56	20 58	10 52	25 52	10 36	2♈37'52"
22 FR	23:53:52	12 38	10 56	29 17	7 44	7 1	21 0	10 52	25 52	10 36	2♈37'52"
23 SA	23:57:48	17 11	12 33	0 ♈ 16	8 21	7 7	21 2	10 53	25 52	10 37	2♈37'52"
24 SU	0: 1:45	21 34	14 10	1 16	8 58	7 12	21 5	10 54	25 53	10 37	2♈37'52"
25 MO	0: 5:41	25 50	15 47	2 16	9 34	7 18	21 7	10 55	25 53	10 38	2♈37'52"
26 TU	0: 9:38	29 58	17 24	3 16	10 11	7 23	21 9	10 55	25 53	10 38	2♈37'52"
27 WE	0:13:34	3 ♍ 58	19 1	4 16	10 48	7 28	21 11	10 56	25 54	10 38	2♈37'52"
28 TH	0:17:31	7 51	20 38	5 16	11 24	7 34	21 14	10 57	25 54	10 39	2♈37'51"
29 FR	0:21:28	11 38	22 15	6 16	12 1	7 39	21 16	10 58	25 55	10 39	2♈37'51"
30 SA	0:25:24	15 18	23 52	7 16	12 37	7 45	21 18	10 59	25 55	10 39	2♈37'51"

INGRESSES :

4 ☿ → ♉ 4:17
8 ☿ → ♊ 23: 5
9 ♂ → ♓ 11: 9
13 ☿ → ♋ 20:57
15 ♀ → ♍ 6: 8
19 ☿ → ♌ 9: 2
22 ⊕ → ♈ 17:23
26 ☿ → ♍ 0:12

ASPECTS (HELIOCENTRIC +MOON(TYCHONIC)) :

1 ☽ □ ♄ 14: 1
2 ☽ ☌ ♃ 18:42
3 ⊕ □ ♇ 1:13
♀ ☌ ♅ 8:10
☿ □ ♆ 11:42
☿ ☌ ☊ 19:12
4 ☽ □ ♆ 10:53
5 ☽ ☌ ☿ 11:44
☽ □ ♅ 16:50
☿ □ ♅ 21:24
6 ☽ □ ♀ 1:47
☿ □ ♀ 18:36
7 ☽ □ ♂ 5:18
☿ ☌ P 7:16
8 ☽ ☍ ♇ 5:32
☿ □ ♂ 21:45
9 ☽ ☌ ♄ 1:40
10 ☽ □ ♃ 8:16
☿ ☍ ♇ 15:37
11 ☽ ☍ ♆ 22:13
12 ☿ □ ⊕ 2:27
☿ ☌ ♄ 7:12
13 ☽ ☌ ♅ 1:40
⊕ □ ♄ 8:23
14 ☽ ☌ ♀ 9:10
☽ ☍ ♂ 17:13
☿ □ ♃ 23:28
15 ☽ □ ♇ 5:42
☽ □ ♄ 22:52
16 ♀ ▯N ☊ 7:38
17 ☽ ☍ ♃ 1: 2
18 ☽ □ ☿ 6: 0
☽ □ ♆ 8:38
☿ ☍ ♆ 13:27
♀ ☍ ♂ 19:40
☿ ▯N ☊ 21:59
19 ☽ □ ♅ 9:14
21 ☽ □ ♂ 5: 8
☽ □ ♀ 9:42
☽ ☌ ♇ 10:47
☿ ☌ ♅ 14:52
♀ □ ♇ 19: 9
22 ☽ ☍ ♄ 4:27
23 ☽ □ ♃ 8:16
24 ☽ ☌ ♆ 17:16
25 ☽ ☍ ♅ 20:16
26 ♂ □ ♇ 17:48
27 ☽ ☍ ☿ 20:59
28 ☽ □ ♇ 3: 7
☽ ☌ ♂ 4:46
♀ □ ♄ 8:59
☿ □ ♇ 17:40
☽ □ ♄ 23:13
29 ☽ ☍ ♀ 1:16
☿ ☍ ♂ 2:55
30 ☽ ☌ ♃ 7: 1
⊕ ☌ ♃ 12:40

SIDEREAL GEOCENTRIC LONGITUDES : OCTOBER 30 Julian at 0 hours UT

DAY	☉	☽	☊	☿	♀	♂	♃	♄	♅	♆	♇
1 SU	8 ♎ 15	16 ♈ 27	24 ♉ 16R	2 ♎ 37	2 ♎ 53	3 ♒ 58	7 ♈ 44R	27 ♊ 33	13 ♌ 31	24 ♑ 6R	9 ♐ 6
2 MO	9 15	28 33	24 11	4 17	4 8	4 23	7 36	27 34	13 33	24 6	9 7
3 TU	10 16	10 ♉ 30	24 7	5 57	5 24	4 49	7 28	27 35	13 36	24 6	9 8
4 WE	11 16	22 20	24 6	7 37	6 39	5 15	7 19	27 36	13 38	24 6	9 9
5 TH	12 16	4 ♊ 7	24 7D	9 16	7 54	5 41	7 11	27 36	13 40	24 6	9 11
6 FR	13 16	15 54	24 8	10 55	9 10	6 8	7 3	27 36	13 43	24 6D	9 12
7 SA	14 16	27 46	24 10	12 33	10 25	6 35	6 55	27 37	13 45	24 6	9 14
8 SU	15 17	9 ♋ 48	24 11	14 11	11 41	7 2	6 47	27 37	13 47	24 6	9 15
9 MO	16 17	22 5	24 11R	15 49	12 56	7 30	6 39	27 37	13 50	24 6	9 16
10 TU	17 17	4 ♌ 43	24 9	17 26	14 12	7 58	6 31	27 37R	13 52	24 6	9 18
11 WE	18 18	17 44	24 6	19 2	15 27	8 27	6 24	27 37	13 54	24 6	9 19
12 TH	19 18	1 ♍ 13	24 2	20 39	16 43	8 55	6 16	27 37	13 56	24 6	9 21
13 FR	20 19	15 10	23 57	22 15	17 58	9 24	6 8	27 36	13 58	24 7	9 22
14 SA	21 19	29 32	23 52	23 50	19 14	9 54	6 1	27 36	14 0	24 7	9 24
15 SU	22 20	14 ♎ 15	23 47	25 26	20 29	10 23	5 53	27 35	14 2	24 7	9 26
16 MO	23 20	29 12	23 44	27 1	21 45	10 53	5 46	27 34	14 4	24 7	9 27
17 TU	24 21	14 ♏ 14	23 42	28 35	23 0	11 23	5 38	27 34	14 6	24 8	9 29
18 WE	25 21	29 13	23 42D	0 ♏ 10	24 16	11 53	5 31	27 33	14 7	24 8	9 30
19 TH	26 22	14 ♐ 0	23 43	1 44	25 31	12 24	5 24	27 32	14 9	24 9	9 32
20 FR	27 23	28 30	23 44	3 18	26 47	12 55	5 17	27 30	14 11	24 9	9 34
21 SA	28 23	12 ♑ 40	23 45	4 51	28 2	13 26	5 10	27 29	14 12	24 10	9 36
22 SU	29 24	26 29	23 46	6 25	29 18	13 58	5 3	27 28	14 14	24 10	9 37
23 MO	0 ♏ 25	9 ♒ 57	23 46R	7 58	0 ♏ 33	14 29	4 57	27 26	14 15	24 11	9 39
24 TU	1 25	23 5	23 44	9 31	1 49	15 1	4 50	27 25	14 17	24 11	9 41
25 WE	2 26	5 ♓ 57	23 42	11 4	3 4	15 33	4 44	27 23	14 18	24 12	9 43
26 TH	3 27	18 33	23 39	12 36	4 20	16 5	4 37	27 21	14 20	24 13	9 44
27 FR	4 28	0 ♈ 57	23 36	14 9	5 35	16 38	4 31	27 19	14 21	24 13	9 46
28 SA	5 28	13 10	23 33	15 41	6 51	17 11	4 25	27 17	14 22	24 14	9 48
29 SU	6 29	25 14	23 30	17 13	8 6	17 43	4 20	27 15	14 24	24 15	9 50
30 MO	7 30	7 ♉ 11	23 29	18 45	9 22	18 16	4 14	27 13	14 25	24 16	9 52
31 TU	8 31	19 2	23 28	20 17	10 37	18 50	4 9	27 11	14 26	24 16	9 54

INGRESSES :

2 ☽ → ♉ 2:53
4 ☽ → ♊ 15:36
7 ☽ → ♋ 4:29
9 ☽ → ♌ 15: 7
11 ☽ → ♍ 21:51
14 ☽ → ♎ 0:46
16 ☽ → ♏ 1:16
17 ☿ → ♏ 21:31
18 ☽ → ♐ 1:16
20 ☽ → ♑ 2:30
22 ☽ → ♒ 6:13
♀ → ♏ 13:23
☉ → ♏ 14:14
24 ☽ → ♓ 12:50
26 ☽ → ♈ 22: 8
29 ☽ → ♉ 9:33
31 ☽ → ♊ 22:18

ASPECTS & ECLIPSES :

1 ☿ ☌ ♀ 15:26
3 ☿ ☍ ♃ 20: 8
4 ☽ ☌ ☊ 3:35
♀ ☍ ♃ 11:36
☽ ☌ A 14: 6
5 ☽ ☍ ♇ 10:21
6 ☽ ☌ ♄ 23:41
8 ☉ □ ☽ 11:43
9 ☽ ☍ ♆ 3:52
☉ ☌S ☿ 18:32
10 ☽ ☍ ♂ 6:18
☽ ☌ ♅ 16:59
11 ☽ □N ☊ 11:22
14 ☿ □ ♆ 4: 8
☽ ☍ ♃ 10:32
15 ☽ ☌ ♀ 10:58
☉ ☌ ☽ 13:56
☽ ☌ ☿ 20: 5
16 ☽ ☌ P 18: 8
☉ □ ♆ 18:50
17 ☽ ☌ ☋ 15: 8
♀ □ ♆ 21:34
18 ☽ ☌ ♇ 16:42
19 ☽ ☍ ♄ 22:20
21 ☽ ☌ ♆ 19:56
22 ☉ □ ☽ 5:34
☉ ☌S ♀ 9:51
♂ ☍ ♅ 13: 2
23 ☽ ☍ ♅ 7:49
☽ ☌ ♂ 8:34
24 ☽ □S ☊ 1:12
27 ☿ □ ♅ 3:15
☽ ☌ ♃ 6:55
29 ☿ □ ♂ 12:22
30 ☉ ☍ ☽ 0:43
☽ ☍ ♀ 4:56
31 ☽ ☍ ☿ 2:54
☽ ☌ ☊ 9: 0

SIDEREAL HELIOCENTRIC LONGITUDES : OCTOBER 30 Julian at 0 hours UT

DAY	Sid. Time	☿	♀	⊕	♂	♃	♄	♅	♆	♇	Vernal Point
1 SU	0:29:21	18 ♍ 53	25 ♍ 29	8 ♈ 16	13 ♓ 14	7 ♈ 50	21 ♊ 20	10 ♌ 59	25 ♑ 55	10 ♐ 40	2♈37'51"
2 MO	0:33:17	22 22	27 6	9 16	13 50	7 56	21 23	11 0	25 56	10 40	2♈37'51"
3 TU	0:37:14	25 46	28 42	10 16	14 26	8 1	21 25	11 1	25 56	10 40	2♈37'51"
4 WE	0:41:10	29 6	0 ♎ 19	11 16	15 3	8 6	21 27	11 2	25 56	10 41	2♈37'51"
5 TH	0:45: 7	2 ♎ 21	1 55	12 16	15 39	8 12	21 29	11 2	25 57	10 41	2♈37'51"
6 FR	0:49: 3	5 33	3 32	13 17	16 15	8 17	21 32	11 3	25 57	10 41	2♈37'50"
7 SA	0:53: 0	8 40	5 9	14 17	16 51	8 23	21 34	11 4	25 57	10 42	2♈37'50"
8 SU	0:56:57	11 45	6 45	15 17	17 27	8 28	21 36	11 5	25 58	10 42	2♈37'50"
9 MO	1: 0:53	14 46	8 21	16 18	18 4	8 34	21 38	11 5	25 58	10 42	2♈37'50"
10 TU	1: 4:50	17 45	9 58	17 18	18 40	8 39	21 41	11 6	25 59	10 43	2♈37'50"
11 WE	1: 8:46	20 41	11 34	18 18	19 16	8 44	21 43	11 7	25 59	10 43	2♈37'50"
12 TH	1:12:43	23 35	13 10	19 19	19 51	8 50	21 45	11 8	25 59	10 43	2♈37'50"
13 FR	1:16:39	26 27	14 47	20 19	20 27	8 55	21 47	11 9	26 0	10 44	2♈37'49"
14 SA	1:20:36	29 17	16 23	21 20	21 3	9 1	21 50	11 9	26 0	10 44	2♈37'49"
15 SU	1:24:32	2 ♏ 6	17 59	22 20	21 39	9 6	21 52	11 10	26 0	10 44	2♈37'49"
16 MO	1:28:29	4 53	19 35	23 21	22 15	9 12	21 54	11 11	26 1	10 45	2♈37'49"
17 TU	1:32:26	7 40	21 11	24 21	22 50	9 17	21 56	11 12	26 1	10 45	2♈37'49"
18 WE	1:36:22	10 26	22 47	25 22	23 26	9 22	21 59	11 12	26 1	10 45	2♈37'49"
19 TH	1:40:19	13 11	24 23	26 23	24 2	9 28	22 1	11 13	26 2	10 46	2♈37'49"
20 FR	1:44:15	15 56	25 59	27 23	24 37	9 33	22 3	11 14	26 2	10 46	2♈37'48"
21 SA	1:48:12	18 40	27 34	28 24	25 13	9 39	22 5	11 15	26 2	10 46	2♈37'48"
22 SU	1:52: 8	21 25	29 10	29 25	25 48	9 44	22 8	11 15	26 3	10 47	2♈37'48"
23 MO	1:56: 5	24 9	0 ♏ 46	0 ♉ 25	26 24	9 49	22 10	11 16	26 3	10 47	2♈37'48"
24 TU	2: 0: 1	26 55	2 22	1 26	26 59	9 55	22 12	11 17	26 4	10 47	2♈37'48"
25 WE	2: 3:58	29 41	3 57	2 27	27 34	10 0	22 14	11 18	26 4	10 48	2♈37'48"
26 TH	2: 7:55	2 ♐ 27	5 33	3 27	28 9	10 6	22 17	11 19	26 4	10 48	2♈37'48"
27 FR	2:11:51	5 15	7 8	4 28	28 45	10 11	22 19	11 19	26 5	10 48	2♈37'48"
28 SA	2:15:48	8 4	8 44	5 29	29 20	10 17	22 21	11 20	26 5	10 49	2♈37'47"
29 SU	2:19:44	10 55	10 19	6 30	29 55	10 22	22 23	11 21	26 5	10 49	2♈37'47"
30 MO	2:23:41	13 47	11 54	7 31	0 ♈ 30	10 27	22 26	11 22	26 6	10 49	2♈37'47"
31 TU	2:27:37	16 42	13 30	8 32	1 5	10 33	22 28	11 22	26 6	10 50	2♈37'47"

INGRESSES :

3 ♀ → ♎ 19:18
4 ☿ → ♎ 6:35
14 ☿ → ♏ 6: 5
22 ♀ → ♏ 12:30
⊕ → ♉ 14: 1
25 ☿ → ♐ 2:47
29 ♂ → ♈ 3:31

ASPECTS (HELIOCENTRIC +MOON(TYCHONIC)) :

1 ☿ □ ♄ 17: 2
☽ □ ♆ 18:46
3 ☽ □ ♅ 1: 2
4 ☿ ☌ ♀ 17:38
5 ☽ ☍ ♇ 13:23
6 ☽ □ ♂ 0:45
☽ ☌ ♄ 11:27
☿ ☍ ♃ 21:40
7 ☽ □ ♀ 17: 2
☽ □ ♃ 21:21
8 ☽ □ ☿ 5: 6
9 ♀ ☍ ♃ 3:12
☽ ☍ ♆ 7:27
☿ ☍ ⊕ 18:32
10 ☽ ☌ ♅ 11:53
12 ☽ □ ♇ 16:27
☿ □ ♆ 20:11
13 ☽ ☍ ♂ 9:18
☿ ☌ ☋ 10:19
☽ □ ♄ 11:11
14 ☽ ☍ ♃ 15:36
15 ☽ ☌ ♀ 6:44
♂ □ ♄ 9:15
☽ □ ♆ 18:53
16 ☽ ☌ ☿ 11: 8
☽ □ ♅ 19: 8
18 ☿ □ ♅ 6:49
⊕ □ ♆ 15:43
☽ ☌ ♇ 18:42
19 ☽ ☍ ♄ 13:14
☽ □ ♂ 17:15
20 ♀ □ ♆ 0:52
☽ □ ♃ 18:47
21 ☿ ☌ A 7:43
☽ ☌ ♆ 23:14
22 ☽ □ ♀ 5:22
♀ ☍ ⊕ 9:51
23 ☽ ☍ ♅ 2:23
24 ☽ □ ☿ 9: 0
25 ☽ □ ♇ 9:10
26 ☽ □ ♄ 7:11
☽ ☌ ♂ 19:29
27 ☽ ☌ ♃ 18:14
28 ☿ ☌ ♇ 23:10
29 ☽ □ ♆ 1:42
♀ □ ♅ 15:39
30 ☽ □ ♅ 8:27
☽ ☍ ♀ 11: 2

SIDEREAL GEOCENTRIC LONGITUDES : NOVEMBER 30 Julian at 0 hours UT

DAY	☉	☽	☊	☿	♀	♂	♃	♄	♅	♆	♇
1 WE	9 ♏ 32	0 ♊ 50	23 ♉ 28	21 ♏ 48	11 ♏ 53	19 ♒ 23	4 ♈ 3R	27 ♊ 8R	14 ♌ 27	24 ♑ 17	9 ♐ 56
2 TH	10 33	12 37	23 29	23 19	13 9	19 57	3 58	27 6	14 28	24 18	9 58
3 FR	11 34	24 26	23 30	24 51	14 24	20 30	3 53	27 3	14 29	24 19	10 0
4 SA	12 35	6 ♋ 20	23 31	26 21	15 40	21 4	3 48	27 0	14 30	24 20	10 2
5 SU	13 36	18 23	23 32	27 52	16 55	21 38	3 44	26 57	14 30	24 21	10 3
6 MO	14 37	0 ♌ 39	23 33	29 22	18 11	22 12	3 39	26 54	14 31	24 22	10 5
7 TU	15 38	13 12	23 33	0 ♐ 52	19 26	22 47	3 35	26 51	14 32	24 23	10 7
8 WE	16 39	26 7	23 33R	2 21	20 42	23 21	3 31	26 48	14 33	24 24	10 9
9 TH	17 40	9 ♍ 27	23 33	3 50	21 57	23 56	3 27	26 45	14 33	24 25	10 11
10 FR	18 41	23 14	23 32	5 19	23 13	24 31	3 23	26 42	14 34	24 27	10 14
11 SA	19 42	7 ♎ 28	23 32	6 46	24 28	25 5	3 20	26 38	14 34	24 28	10 16
12 SU	20 43	22 7	23 31	8 13	25 44	25 40	3 17	26 35	14 35	24 29	10 18
13 MO	21 44	7 ♏ 6	23 31	9 39	26 59	26 16	3 14	26 31	14 35	24 30	10 20
14 TU	22 45	22 18	23 31D	11 3	28 15	26 51	3 11	26 28	14 35	24 32	10 22
15 WE	23 47	7 ♐ 31	23 31	12 26	29 30	27 26	3 8	26 24	14 36	24 33	10 24
16 TH	24 48	22 38	23 31R	13 48	0 ♐ 46	28 2	3 6	26 20	14 36	24 34	10 26
17 FR	25 49	7 ♑ 28	23 31	15 7	2 1	28 38	3 3	26 16	14 36	24 36	10 28
18 SA	26 50	21 56	23 31	16 25	3 16	29 13	3 1	26 12	14 36	24 37	10 30
19 SU	27 51	5 ♒ 58	23 30	17 39	4 32	29 49	2 59	26 8	14 36	24 38	10 32
20 MO	28 53	19 34	23 30	18 51	5 47	0 ♓ 25	2 58	26 4	14 36R	24 40	10 34
21 TU	29 54	2 ♓ 44	23 30D	19 59	7 3	1 1	2 56	26 0	14 36	24 41	10 37
22 WE	0 ♐ 55	15 31	23 30	21 2	8 18	1 38	2 55	25 56	14 36	24 43	10 39
23 TH	1 56	27 59	23 31	22 1	9 34	2 14	2 54	25 52	14 36	24 44	10 41
24 FR	2 57	10 ♈ 13	23 32	22 54	10 49	2 50	2 53	25 47	14 35	24 46	10 43
25 SA	3 59	22 14	23 33	23 41	12 5	3 27	2 53	25 43	14 35	24 47	10 45
26 SU	5 0	4 ♉ 9	23 34	24 21	13 20	4 3	2 52	25 39	14 35	24 49	10 47
27 MO	6 1	15 58	23 34	24 53	14 35	4 40	2 52	25 34	14 34	24 51	10 49
28 TU	7 2	27 46	23 34R	25 16	15 51	5 16	2 52D	25 30	14 34	24 52	10 52
29 WE	8 3	9 ♊ 34	23 34	25 29	17 6	5 53	2 52	25 25	14 33	24 54	10 54
30 TH	9 5	21 25	23 32	25 31R	18 21	6 30	2 53	25 20	14 33	24 56	10 56

INGRESSES :

3	☽ → ♋	11:15	
5	☽ → ♌	22:44	
6	☿ → ♐	10: 5	
8	☽ → ♍	7: 4	
10	☽ → ♎	11:30	
12	☽ → ♏	12:40	
14	☽ → ♐	12: 8	
15	♀ → ♐	9:31	
16	☽ → ♑	11:51	
18	☽ → ♒	13:42	
19	♂ → ♓	7:10	
20	☽ → ♓	18:58	
21	☉ → ♐	2:27	
23	☽ → ♈	3:55	
25	☽ → ♉	15:37	
28	☽ → ♊	4:32	
30	☽ → ♋	17:19	

ASPECTS & ECLIPSES :

1	☽ ☌ A	2:44
	☽ ☍ ♇	18:34
2	☿ ☍ ☊	2:28
3	♀ □ ♅	1:31
	☽ ☌ ♄	5:16
5	☽ ☍ ♆	11:45
	☉ □ ♅	21:49
7	☽ ☌ ♅	2:30
	☉ □ ☽	4:57
	☽ ☍ ♂	18:41
	☽ N ☊	19:17
8	♂ □ ☊	8: 2
10	♀ ☍ ☊	6: 8
	☽ ☍ ♃	17: 8
11	♀ □ ♂	22:10
13	☿ ☌ ♇	11:54
14	☉ ● T	0:44
	☉ ☌ ☽	0:46
	☽ ☌ ☋	1:55
	☽ ☌ P	5:54
	☽ ☌ ♀	10:12
	☉ ☍ ☊	17:57
15	☽ ☌ ♇	4:33
	☽ ☌ ☿	8:33
16	☽ ☍ ♄	5:55
18	☽ ☌ ♆	4:32
19	☽ ☍ ♅	15: 9
20	☽ S ☊	7: 6
	☉ □ ☽	18:20
	☽ ☌ ♂	20:41
23	☽ ☌ ♃	9:34
	☉ □ ♂	17: 5
	♀ ☌ ♇	21:58
27	☽ ☌ ☊	15:28
28	☽ ☌ A	2:49
	☿ ☍ ♄	17:32
	☽ ● PN	20:18
	☉ ☍ ☽	20:38
29	☽ ☍ ♇	2:42
	☽ ☍ ♀	17: 5
30	☽ ☌ ♄	7:53
	☽ ☍ ☿	8:13

SIDEREAL HELIOCENTRIC LONGITUDES : NOVEMBER 30 Julian at 0 hours UT

DAY	Sid. Time	☿	♀	⊕	♂	♃	♄	♅	♆	♇	Vernal Point
1 WE	2:31:34	19 ♐ 38	15 ♏ 5	9 ♉ 33	1 ♈ 40	10 ♈ 38	22 ♊ 30	11 ♌ 23	26 ♑ 6	10 ♐ 50	2♈37'47"
2 TH	2:35:30	22 37	16 40	10 33	2 15	10 44	22 32	11 24	26 7	10 50	2♈37'47"
3 FR	2:39:27	25 38	18 16	11 34	2 49	10 49	22 35	11 25	26 7	10 51	2♈37'47"
4 SA	2:43:24	28 43	19 51	12 35	3 24	10 55	22 37	11 25	26 7	10 51	2♈37'46"
5 SU	2:47:20	1 ♑ 51	21 26	13 36	3 59	11 0	22 39	11 26	26 8	10 51	2♈37'46"
6 MO	2:51:17	5 2	23 1	14 37	4 34	11 5	22 41	11 27	26 8	10 52	2♈37'46"
7 TU	2:55:13	8 17	24 36	15 38	5 8	11 11	22 44	11 28	26 9	10 52	2♈37'46"
8 WE	2:59:10	11 36	26 11	16 39	5 43	11 16	22 46	11 29	26 9	10 52	2♈37'46"
9 TH	3: 3: 6	15 0	27 46	17 40	6 17	11 22	22 48	11 29	26 9	10 53	2♈37'46"
10 FR	3: 7: 3	18 29	29 21	18 41	6 52	11 27	22 50	11 30	26 10	10 53	2♈37'46"
11 SA	3:10:59	22 2	0 ♐ 56	19 43	7 26	11 32	22 53	11 31	26 10	10 53	2♈37'45"
12 SU	3:14:56	25 41	2 31	20 44	8 0	11 38	22 55	11 32	26 10	10 54	2♈37'45"
13 MO	3:18:53	29 26	4 6	21 45	8 35	11 43	22 57	11 32	26 11	10 54	2♈37'45"
14 TU	3:22:49	3 ♒ 17	5 41	22 46	9 9	11 49	22 59	11 33	26 11	10 54	2♈37'45"
15 WE	3:26:46	7 15	7 15	23 47	9 43	11 54	23 2	11 34	26 11	10 55	2♈37'45"
16 TH	3:30:42	11 19	8 50	24 48	10 17	11 59	23 4	11 35	26 12	10 55	2♈37'45"
17 FR	3:34:39	15 31	10 25	25 50	10 51	12 5	23 6	11 35	26 12	10 55	2♈37'45"
18 SA	3:38:35	19 51	12 0	26 51	11 25	12 10	23 8	11 36	26 13	10 56	2♈37'45"
19 SU	3:42:32	24 19	13 35	27 52	11 59	12 16	23 11	11 37	26 13	10 56	2♈37'44"
20 MO	3:46:28	28 55	15 9	28 53	12 33	12 21	23 13	11 38	26 13	10 56	2♈37'44"
21 TU	3:50:25	3 ♓ 40	16 44	29 54	13 7	12 27	23 15	11 39	26 14	10 57	2♈37'44"
22 WE	3:54:22	8 33	18 19	0 ♊ 55	13 41	12 32	23 17	11 39	26 14	10 57	2♈37'44"
23 TH	3:58:18	13 36	19 53	1 57	14 14	12 37	23 20	11 40	26 14	10 57	2♈37'44"
24 FR	4: 2:15	18 47	21 28	2 58	14 48	12 43	23 22	11 41	26 15	10 58	2♈37'44"
25 SA	4: 6:11	24 8	23 3	3 59	15 22	12 48	23 24	11 42	26 15	10 58	2♈37'44"
26 SU	4:10: 8	29 38	24 37	5 0	15 55	12 54	23 26	11 42	26 15	10 58	2♈37'43"
27 MO	4:14: 4	5 ♈ 16	26 12	6 2	16 29	12 59	23 29	11 43	26 16	10 59	2♈37'43"
28 TU	4:18: 1	11 3	27 47	7 3	17 2	13 4	23 31	11 44	26 16	10 59	2♈37'43"
29 WE	4:21:57	16 57	29 21	8 4	17 35	13 10	23 33	11 45	26 16	10 59	2♈37'43"
30 TH	4:25:54	22 58	0 ♑ 56	9 5	18 9	13 15	23 35	11 45	26 17	11 0	2♈37'43"

INGRESSES :

4	☿ → ♑	9:53
10	♀ → ♐	9:50
13	☿ → ♒	3:33
20	☿ → ♓	5:33
21	⊕ → ♊	2:14
26	☿ → ♈	1:35
29	♀ → ♑	9:51

ASPECTS (HELIOCENTRIC +MOON(TYCHONIC)) :

1	☽ ☍ ♇	20:22
	☿ ☍ ♄	23:23
2	⊕ □ ♅	20: 8
	☽ ☌ ♄	20:13
3	☽ ☍ ☿	3:18
	☽ □ ♂	17:49
4	☽ □ ♃	9:13
5	☽ ☍ ♆	15:13
	☿ □ ♂	19:40
6	☽ ☌ ♅	20:42
7	☿ □ ♃	21:30
8	☽ □ ♀	0: 8
9	☽ □ ♇	2:32
	☽ □ ♄	23:20
10	☽ ☍ ♂	23:56
11	☽ ☍ ♃	6:46
	♀ ☌ ☋	11:59
12	☿ ☌ ♆	3: 9
	☽ □ ♆	6:32
	☽ □ ☿	7:39
	☿ S ☊	12:46
13	☽ □ ♅	7: 1
14	☽ ☌ ♀	23:32
15	☽ ☌ ♇	5:21
16	☽ ☍ ♄	0:42
	☿ ☍ ♅	1:28
17	☽ □ ♂	5:47
	☽ □ ♃	7:37
	♀ ☌ ♇	7:43
18	☽ ☌ ♆	7:14
19	☽ ☍ ♅	9:53
	♂ ☌ ♃	14: 1
	☿ □ ⊕	23:48
21	☽ ☌ ☿	2:45
	☽ □ ♇	15:21
22	☽ □ ♀	6: 5
	☿ □ ♇	11:31
	☽ □ ♄	14:56
24	☽ ☌ ♃	5: 0
	☽ ☌ ♂	9:33
	☿ □ ♀	17: 8
	☿ □ ♄	20:43
25	♀ ☍ ♄	5:34
	☽ □ ♆	8: 3
26	☽ □ ♅	15:20
28	☿ ☌ ♃	8:25
29	☿ ☌ ♂	2:49
	☽ ☍ ♇	2:53
30	☽ ☌ ♄	4:25
	☿ □ ♆	13: 2
	☿ ☌ ☊	18:28
	☽ ☍ ♀	22: 6

SIDEREAL GEOCENTRIC LONGITUDES : DECEMBER 30 Julian at 0 hours UT

DAY	☉	☽	☊	☿	♀	♂	♃	♄	⛢	♆	♇
1 FR	10 ♐ 6	3 ♋ 20	23 ♉ 30R	25 ♐ 22R	19 ♐ 37	7 ♓ 7	2 ♈ 53	25 ♊ 16R	14 ♌ 32R	24 ♑ 57	10 ♐ 58
2 SA	11 7	15 21	23 27	25 1	20 52	7 44	2 54	25 11	14 32	24 59	11 0
3 SU	12 8	27 31	23 24	24 28	22 7	8 21	2 55	25 6	14 31	25 1	11 2
4 MO	13 10	9 ♌ 53	23 21	23 44	23 23	8 58	2 56	25 1	14 30	25 3	11 4
5 TU	14 11	22 28	23 19	22 49	24 38	9 35	2 58	24 57	14 29	25 5	11 7
6 WE	15 12	5 ♍ 21	23 17	21 44	25 53	10 13	3 0	24 52	14 28	25 6	11 9
7 TH	16 13	18 33	23 17D	20 32	27 9	10 50	3 1	24 47	14 27	25 8	11 11
8 FR	17 14	2 ♎ 7	23 18	19 15	28 24	11 27	3 3	24 42	14 26	25 10	11 13
9 SA	18 16	16 6	23 19	17 55	29 39	12 5	3 6	24 37	14 25	25 12	11 15
10 SU	19 17	0 ♏ 28	23 20	16 34	0 ♑ 55	12 42	3 8	24 32	14 24	25 14	11 17
11 MO	20 18	15 12	23 21	15 16	2 10	13 20	3 11	24 27	14 23	25 16	11 20
12 TU	21 19	0 ♐ 12	23 21R	14 3	3 25	13 57	3 14	24 22	14 22	25 18	11 22
13 WE	22 21	15 22	23 20	12 56	4 40	14 35	3 17	24 17	14 21	25 20	11 24
14 TH	23 22	0 ♑ 31	23 17	11 57	5 56	15 13	3 20	24 12	14 19	25 22	11 26
15 FR	24 23	15 31	23 13	11 7	7 11	15 50	3 24	24 7	14 18	25 24	11 28
16 SA	25 24	0 ♒ 11	23 8	10 27	8 26	16 28	3 27	24 2	14 16	25 26	11 30
17 SU	26 26	14 26	23 3	9 56	9 41	17 6	3 31	23 57	14 15	25 28	11 32
18 MO	27 27	28 13	22 59	9 35	10 57	17 44	3 35	23 52	14 14	25 30	11 34
19 TU	28 28	11 ♓ 31	22 56	9 23	12 12	18 22	3 39	23 48	14 12	25 32	11 36
20 WE	29 29	24 23	22 54	9 21D	13 27	19 0	3 44	23 43	14 10	25 34	11 39
21 TH	0 ♑ 30	6 ♈ 52	22 54D	9 26	14 42	19 38	3 48	23 38	14 9	25 36	11 41
22 FR	1 31	19 3	22 56	9 39	15 57	20 16	3 53	23 33	14 7	25 38	11 43
23 SA	2 33	1 ♉ 1	22 57	9 59	17 12	20 54	3 58	23 28	14 5	25 40	11 45
24 SU	3 34	12 51	22 59	10 26	18 27	21 32	4 3	23 23	14 4	25 42	11 47
25 MO	4 35	24 37	22 59R	10 58	19 42	22 10	4 9	23 18	14 2	25 45	11 49
26 TU	5 36	6 ♊ 24	22 58	11 36	20 58	22 49	4 14	23 13	14 0	25 47	11 51
27 WE	6 37	18 15	22 55	12 19	22 13	23 27	4 20	23 9	13 58	25 49	11 53
28 TH	7 38	0 ♋ 12	22 50	13 6	23 28	24 5	4 26	23 4	13 56	25 51	11 55
29 FR	8 39	12 17	22 42	13 56	24 43	24 43	4 32	22 59	13 54	25 53	11 57
30 SA	9 40	24 31	22 33	14 51	25 58	25 21	4 38	22 55	13 52	25 56	11 59
31 SU	10 41	6 ♌ 56	22 24	15 48	27 13	26 0	4 44	22 50	13 50	25 58	12 1

INGRESSES :

- 3 ☽ → ♌ 4:50
- 5 ☽ → ♍ 14: 6
- 7 ☽ → ♎ 20:17
- 9 ♀ → ♑ 6:34
- ☽ → ♏ 23:13
- 11 ☽ → ♐ 23:40
- 13 ☽ → ♑ 23:10
- 15 ☽ → ♒ 23:41
- 18 ☽ → ♓ 3: 9
- 20 ☽ → ♈ 10:42
- ☉ → ♑ 12: 6
- 22 ☽ → ♉ 21:56
- 25 ☽ → ♊ 10:57
- 27 ☽ → ♋ 23:36
- 30 ☽ → ♌ 10:39

ASPECTS & ECLIPSES :

- 1 ☿ ☍ ♄ 11:12
- ☉ ☌ ♇ 21:11
- 2 ☽ ☍ ♆ 19: 4
- 4 ☿ ☌ ♀ 4: 0
- ☽ ☌ ⛢ 8:51
- 5 ☽ N ☊ 1:34
- ♀ ☍ ♄ 5:32
- 6 ☽ ☍ ♂ 9:21
- ☉ □ ☽ 19:28
- 7 ♂ □ ♇ 14:18
- 8 ☽ ☍ ♃ 1:38
- ☉ ☌ ☿ 20:27
- 11 ☽ ☌ ☋ 13: 5
- ♀ □ ♃ 20:12
- 12 ☿ □ ♂ 1:12
- ☽ ☌ ♇ 17:42
- ☽ ☌ P 19:18
- ☽ ☌ ☿ 20:24
- 13 ☉ ☌ ☽ 11:49
- ☽ ☍ ♄ 14: 2
- 14 ☽ ☌ ♀ 9:24
- ☿ ☌ ♇ 13:47
- ☉ ☍ ♄ 18:16
- 15 ☽ ☌ ♆ 16: 8
- 16 ☽ ☍ ⛢ 23:40
- 17 ☽ S ☊ 14:49
- 19 ☽ ☌ ♂ 13:19
- 20 ☉ □ ☽ 10:35
- ☽ ☌ ♃ 18: 1
- 24 ☉ □ ♃ 12:48
- ☽ ☌ ☊ 20:40
- 25 ☽ ☌ A 8:28
- 26 ☿ ☌ ♇ 9: 4
- ☽ ☍ ♇ 11: 5
- ☽ ☍ ☿ 11:12
- ♂ □ ♄ 13:53
- 27 ☽ ☌ ♄ 9:48
- 28 ☉ ☍ ☽ 16: 9
- 29 ♀ ☌ ♆ 23:19
- 30 ☽ ☍ ♆ 2:45
- ☽ ☍ ♀ 3: 7
- 31 ☽ ☌ ⛢ 13:10

SIDEREAL HELIOCENTRIC LONGITUDES : DECEMBER 30 Julian at 0 hours UT

DAY	Sid. Time	☿	♀	⊕	♂	♃	♄	⛢	♆	♇	Vernal Point
1 FR	4:29:51	29 ♈ 5	2 ♑ 30	10 ♊ 6	18 ♈ 42	13 ♈ 21	23 ♊ 38	11 ♌ 46	26 ♑ 17	11 ♐ 0	2♈37'43"
2 SA	4:33:47	5 ♉ 17	4 5	11 8	19 15	13 26	23 40	11 47	26 18	11 1	2♈37'43"
3 SU	4:37:44	11 32	5 40	12 9	19 48	13 31	23 42	11 48	26 18	11 1	2♈37'42"
4 MO	4:41:40	17 50	7 14	13 10	20 21	13 37	23 44	11 49	26 18	11 1	2♈37'42"
5 TU	4:45:37	24 9	8 49	14 11	20 54	13 42	23 47	11 49	26 19	11 2	2♈37'42"
6 WE	4:49:33	0 ♊ 26	10 23	15 13	21 27	13 48	23 49	11 50	26 19	11 2	2♈37'42"
7 TH	4:53:30	6 42	11 58	16 14	22 0	13 53	23 51	11 51	26 19	11 2	2♈37'42"
8 FR	4:57:26	12 54	13 33	17 15	22 33	13 58	23 53	11 52	26 20	11 3	2♈37'42"
9 SA	5: 1:23	19 1	15 7	18 16	23 6	14 4	23 56	11 52	26 20	11 3	2♈37'42"
10 SU	5: 5:20	25 2	16 42	19 18	23 39	14 9	23 58	11 53	26 20	11 3	2♈37'42"
11 MO	5: 9:16	0 ♋ 56	18 17	20 19	24 11	14 15	24 0	11 54	26 21	11 4	2♈37'41"
12 TU	5:13:13	6 42	19 51	21 20	24 44	14 20	24 2	11 55	26 21	11 4	2♈37'41"
13 WE	5:17: 9	12 19	21 26	22 21	25 17	14 26	24 5	11 55	26 21	11 4	2♈37'41"
14 TH	5:21: 6	17 48	23 1	23 23	25 49	14 31	24 7	11 56	26 22	11 5	2♈37'41"
15 FR	5:25: 2	23 7	24 35	24 24	26 22	14 36	24 9	11 57	26 22	11 5	2♈37'41"
16 SA	5:28:59	28 16	26 10	25 25	26 54	14 42	24 11	11 58	26 23	11 5	2♈37'41"
17 SU	5:32:55	3 ♌ 16	27 45	26 26	27 27	14 47	24 14	11 58	26 23	11 6	2♈37'41"
18 MO	5:36:52	8 6	29 20	27 27	27 59	14 53	24 16	11 59	26 23	11 6	2♈37'40"
19 TU	5:40:49	12 47	0 ♒ 54	28 29	28 31	14 58	24 18	12 0	26 24	11 6	2♈37'40"
20 WE	5:44:45	17 20	2 29	29 30	29 3	15 3	24 20	12 1	26 24	11 7	2♈37'40"
21 TH	5:48:42	21 43	4 4	0 ♋ 31	29 35	15 9	24 23	12 2	26 24	11 7	2♈37'40"
22 FR	5:52:38	25 59	5 39	1 32	0 ♉ 8	15 14	24 25	12 2	26 25	11 7	2♈37'40"
23 SA	5:56:35	0 ♍ 6	7 14	2 33	0 40	15 20	24 27	12 3	26 25	11 8	2♈37'40"
24 SU	6: 0:31	4 6	8 49	3 34	1 12	15 25	24 29	12 4	26 25	11 8	2♈37'40"
25 MO	6: 4:28	7 59	10 23	4 35	1 44	15 30	24 31	12 5	26 26	11 8	2♈37'39"
26 TU	6: 8:24	11 45	11 58	5 36	2 15	15 36	24 34	12 5	26 26	11 9	2♈37'39"
27 WE	6:12:21	15 26	13 33	6 37	2 47	15 41	24 36	12 6	26 27	11 9	2♈37'39"
28 TH	6:16:18	19 0	15 8	7 38	3 19	15 47	24 38	12 7	26 27	11 9	2♈37'39"
29 FR	6:20:14	22 29	16 43	8 39	3 51	15 52	24 40	12 8	26 27	11 10	2♈37'39"
30 SA	6:24:11	25 53	18 18	9 40	4 22	15 57	24 43	12 8	26 28	11 10	2♈37'39"
31 SU	6:28: 7	29 13	19 53	10 41	4 54	16 3	24 45	12 9	26 28	11 10	2♈37'39"

INGRESSES :

- 1 ☿ → ♉ 3:33
- 5 ☿ → ♊ 22:19
- 10 ☿ → ♋ 20:10
- 16 ☿ → ♌ 8:14
- 18 ♀ → ♒ 10:13
- 20 ⊕ → ♋ 11:53
- 21 ♂ → ♉ 18:20
- 22 ☿ → ♍ 23:24
- 31 ☿ → ♎ 5:47

ASPECTS (HELIOCENTRIC +MOON(TYCHONIC)) :

- 1 ☽ □ ♃ 20: 9
- ⊕ ☍ ♇ 21:11
- 2 ☽ □ ♂ 8: 5
- ⊕ ☌ P 17:44
- ☽ ☍ ♆ 21:35
- 3 ☿ □ ⛢ 0:58
- 4 ☽ ☌ ⛢ 3:42
- ☿ ☌ P 6:31
- 5 ☽ □ ☿ 6:12
- 6 ☽ □ ♇ 10:25
- 7 ☽ □ ♄ 9:29
- ☿ ☍ ♇ 16:46
- 8 ♀ □ ♃ 6:55
- ☿ ☌ ⊕ 20:27
- ☽ ☍ ♃ 20:32
- ☽ □ ♀ 22: 8
- 9 ☽ ☍ ♂ 12:14
- ♀ ☌ A 16:29
- ☽ □ ♆ 17:10
- ☿ ☌ ♄ 19:40
- 10 ☽ □ ⛢ 18:39
- 12 ☽ ☌ ♇ 17:12
- 13 ☿ □ ♃ 9:17
- ☽ ☍ ♄ 13:48
- 14 ⊕ ☌ ♄ 18: 0
- ☽ □ ♃ 22:31
- 15 ♂ □ ♆ 0:20
- ☿ ☍ ♀ 9:48
- ☿ ☍ ♆ 15: 6
- ☽ ☌ ♀ 16:34
- ☿ □ ♂ 16:49
- ☽ ☌ ♆ 17:42
- ☽ □ ♂ 18:22
- ☽ ☍ ☿ 19: 7
- ☿ N ☊ 21:11
- 16 ♀ ☌ ♆ 3: 9
- ♀ □ ♂ 16:57
- ☽ ☍ ⛢ 19:47
- 18 ☿ ☌ ⛢ 19:53
- ☽ □ ♇ 23:13
- 19 ☽ □ ♄ 23:54
- 21 ☽ ☌ ♃ 16:22
- 22 ☽ □ ♆ 14:43
- ☽ ☌ ♂ 23:14
- 23 ☽ □ ♀ 14:31
- ☽ □ ⛢ 22:24
- 25 ☿ □ ♇ 20: 2
- 26 ♀ ☍ ⛢ 1:48
- ☽ ☍ ♇ 9:37
- ☽ □ ☿ 15:47
- 27 ☽ ☌ ♄ 12:50
- 29 ☽ □ ♃ 7: 7
- ☿ □ ♄ 15:33
- 30 ☽ ☍ ♆ 3:47
- ☽ □ ♂ 19:56
- 31 ☽ ☌ ⛢ 10: 1

SIDEREAL GEOCENTRIC LONGITUDES : JANUARY 31 Julian at 0 hours UT

DAY	☉	☽	☊	☿	♀	♂	♃	♄	♅	♆	♇
1 MO	11 ♑ 42	19 ♌ 31	22 ♉ 15R	16 ♐ 49	28 ♑ 27	26 ♓ 38	4 ♈ 51	22 ♊ 45R	13 ♌ 48R	26 ♑ 0	12 ♐ 3
2 TU	12 43	2 ♍ 19	22 7	17 52	29 42	27 16	4 58	22 41	13 46	26 2	12 5
3 WE	13 44	15 19	22 1	18 58	0 ♒ 57	27 55	5 4	22 36	13 44	26 4	12 7
4 TH	14 45	28 33	21 58	20 6	2 12	28 33	5 11	22 32	13 42	26 7	12 8
5 FR	15 45	12 ♎ 3	21 56	21 16	3 27	29 12	5 19	22 28	13 40	26 9	12 10
6 SA	16 46	25 51	21 57D	22 28	4 42	29 50	5 26	22 23	13 37	26 11	12 12
7 SU	17 47	9 ♏ 56	21 58	23 41	5 57	0 ♈ 28	5 33	22 19	13 35	26 13	12 14
8 MO	18 48	24 18	21 58R	24 57	7 12	1 7	5 41	22 15	13 33	26 16	12 16
9 TU	19 49	8 ♐ 56	21 56	26 13	8 26	1 45	5 49	22 11	13 31	26 18	12 18
10 WE	20 50	23 45	21 53	27 32	9 41	2 24	5 57	22 7	13 28	26 20	12 19
11 TH	21 51	8 ♑ 38	21 46	28 51	10 56	3 2	6 5	22 3	13 26	26 22	12 21
12 FR	22 51	23 27	21 37	0 ♑ 12	12 11	3 41	6 13	21 59	13 23	26 25	12 23
13 SA	23 52	8 ♒ 3	21 27	1 34	13 25	4 19	6 21	21 55	13 21	26 27	12 25
14 SU	24 53	22 19	21 17	2 57	14 40	4 58	6 30	21 51	13 19	26 29	12 26
15 MO	25 53	6 ♓ 11	21 7	4 22	15 55	5 36	6 39	21 48	13 16	26 32	12 28
16 TU	26 54	19 35	21 0	5 47	17 9	6 15	6 47	21 44	13 14	26 34	12 30
17 WE	27 55	2 ♈ 32	20 54	7 13	18 24	6 54	6 56	21 40	13 11	26 36	12 31
18 TH	28 55	15 5	20 51	8 41	19 38	7 32	7 5	21 37	13 9	26 38	12 33
19 FR	29 56	27 18	20 50	10 9	20 53	8 11	7 15	21 34	13 6	26 41	12 35
20 SA	0 ♒ 56	9 ♉ 17	20 50D	11 39	22 7	8 49	7 24	21 30	13 4	26 43	12 36
21 SU	1 57	21 8	20 51R	13 9	23 22	9 28	7 33	21 27	13 1	26 45	12 38
22 MO	2 57	2 ♊ 54	20 50	14 41	24 36	10 7	7 43	21 24	12 59	26 47	12 39
23 TU	3 58	14 42	20 47	16 13	25 51	10 45	7 53	21 21	12 56	26 50	12 41
24 WE	4 58	26 37	20 42	17 46	27 5	11 24	8 2	21 18	12 53	26 52	12 42
25 TH	5 59	8 ♋ 40	20 34	19 21	28 19	12 3	8 12	21 15	12 51	26 54	12 44
26 FR	6 59	20 56	20 23	20 56	29 34	12 41	8 22	21 13	12 48	26 56	12 45
27 SA	7 59	3 ♌ 25	20 11	22 32	0 ♓ 48	13 20	8 32	21 10	12 46	26 59	12 47
28 SU	9 0	16 8	19 57	24 9	2 2	13 58	8 43	21 8	12 43	27 1	12 48
29 MO	10 0	29 4	19 44	25 47	3 16	14 37	8 53	21 5	12 40	27 3	12 49
30 TU	11 0	12 ♍ 12	19 32	27 27	4 31	15 16	9 4	21 3	12 38	27 5	12 51
31 WE	12 0	25 31	19 23	29 7	5 45	15 54	9 14	21 1	12 35	27 8	12 52

INGRESSES :

1 ☽ → ♍ 19:41	19 ☉ → ♒ 1:37
2 ♀ → ♒ 5:38	☽ → ♉ 5:21
4 ☽ → ♎ 2:35	21 ☽ → ♊ 18: 4
6 ♂ → ♈ 6:17	24 ☽ → ♋ 6:46
☽ → ♏ 7: 8	26 ♀ → ♓ 8:28
8 ☽ → ♐ 9:23	☽ → ♌ 17:28
10 ☽ → ♑ 10: 4	29 ☽ → ♍ 1:43
11 ☿ → ♑ 20:27	31 ☽ → ♎ 8: 0
12 ☽ → ♒ 10:42	☿ → ♒ 12:38
14 ☽ → ♓ 13:12	
16 ☽ → ♈ 19:14	

ASPECTS & ECLIPSES :

1 ☽ N ☊ 5: 5	12 ☽ ☌ ♆ 4:50	18 ♀ □ ☊ 23: 8	29 ☽ ☍ ♀ 8:32
3 ☽ ☍ ♂ 23:59	♀ ☍ ♅ 22:39	19 ☉ □ ☽ 5:41	☿ ☌ ♆ 18:46
4 ☽ ☍ ♃ 11:57	13 ☽ ☍ ♅ 8:48	20 ☽ ☌ ☊ 23:25	31 ☉ ☍ ♅ 13:18
5 ☉ □ ☽ 7: 0	☽ ☌ ♀ 9:48	22 ☽ ☌ A 1:10	
☿ ☍ ♄ 22:37	☽ S ☊ 22:14	☽ ☍ ♇ 19:52	
7 ☽ ☌ ☋ 20: 7	15 ☉ ☌ ♆ 15:39	23 ☽ ☌ ♄ 13:22	
9 ☽ ☌ ♇ 5:28	16 ☿ □ ♂ 14: 7	25 ☽ ☍ ☿ 23:59	
☽ ☍ ♄ 21:22	☿ □ ♃ 18:43	26 ☽ ☍ ♆ 11:38	
10 ☽ ☌ P 4:28	17 ♂ ☌ ♃ 2:11	27 ☉ ☍ ☽ 9:25	
☽ ☌ ☿ 6:41	☽ ☌ ♃ 8:26	☽ ☌ ♅ 17:37	
11 ☉ ☌ ☽ 22:57	☽ ☌ ♂ 8:42	28 ☽ N ☊ 7: 0	

SIDEREAL HELIOCENTRIC LONGITUDES : JANUARY 31 Julian at 0 hours UT

DAY	Sid. Time	☿	♀	⊕	♂	♃	♄	♅	♆	♇	Vernal Point
1 MO	6:32: 4	2 ♎ 28	21 ♒ 28	11 ♋ 42	5 ♉ 26	16 ♈ 8	24 ♊ 47	12 ♌ 10	26 ♑ 28	11 ♐ 11	2♈37'39"
2 TU	6:36: 0	5 39	23 3	12 43	5 57	16 13	24 49	12 11	26 29	11 11	2♈37'38"
3 WE	6:39:57	8 46	24 39	13 44	6 28	16 19	24 52	12 12	26 29	11 11	2♈37'38"
4 TH	6:43:53	11 51	26 14	14 45	7 0	16 24	24 54	12 12	26 29	11 12	2♈37'38"
5 FR	6:47:50	14 52	27 49	15 46	7 31	16 30	24 56	12 13	26 30	11 12	2♈37'38"
6 SA	6:51:47	17 50	29 24	16 47	8 2	16 35	24 58	12 14	26 30	11 12	2♈37'38"
7 SU	6:55:43	20 47	0 ♓ 59	17 48	8 34	16 40	25 1	12 15	26 30	11 13	2♈37'38"
8 MO	6:59:40	23 40	2 35	18 49	9 5	16 46	25 3	12 15	26 31	11 13	2♈37'38"
9 TU	7: 3:36	26 32	4 10	19 49	9 36	16 51	25 5	12 16	26 31	11 13	2♈37'37"
10 WE	7: 7:33	29 23	5 45	20 50	10 7	16 57	25 7	12 17	26 32	11 14	2♈37'37"
11 TH	7:11:29	2 ♏ 11	7 21	21 51	10 38	17 2	25 10	12 18	26 32	11 14	2♈37'37"
12 FR	7:15:26	4 59	8 56	22 52	11 9	17 7	25 12	12 18	26 32	11 14	2♈37'37"
13 SA	7:19:22	7 45	10 31	23 53	11 40	17 13	25 14	12 19	26 33	11 15	2♈37'37"
14 SU	7:23:19	10 31	12 7	24 53	12 11	17 18	25 16	12 20	26 33	11 15	2♈37'37"
15 MO	7:27:16	13 16	13 42	25 54	12 42	17 24	25 19	12 21	26 33	11 15	2♈37'37"
16 TU	7:31:12	16 1	15 18	26 55	13 13	17 29	25 21	12 22	26 34	11 16	2♈37'36"
17 WE	7:35: 9	18 45	16 53	27 55	13 43	17 34	25 23	12 22	26 34	11 16	2♈37'36"
18 TH	7:39: 5	21 30	18 29	28 56	14 14	17 40	25 25	12 23	26 34	11 16	2♈37'36"
19 FR	7:43: 2	24 15	20 5	29 56	14 45	17 45	25 28	12 24	26 35	11 17	2♈37'36"
20 SA	7:46:58	27 0	21 40	0 ♌ 57	15 15	17 51	25 30	12 25	26 35	11 17	2♈37'36"
21 SU	7:50:55	29 46	23 16	1 57	15 46	17 56	25 32	12 25	26 35	11 17	2♈37'36"
22 MO	7:54:51	2 ♐ 33	24 52	2 58	16 16	18 1	25 34	12 26	26 36	11 18	2♈37'36"
23 TU	7:58:48	5 21	26 27	3 58	16 47	18 7	25 37	12 27	26 36	11 18	2♈37'36"
24 WE	8: 2:45	8 10	28 3	4 59	17 17	18 12	25 39	12 28	26 37	11 18	2♈37'35"
25 TH	8: 6:41	11 0	29 39	5 59	17 47	18 18	25 41	12 28	26 37	11 19	2♈37'35"
26 FR	8:10:38	13 53	1 ♈ 15	7 0	18 18	18 23	25 43	12 29	26 37	11 19	2♈37'35"
27 SA	8:14:34	16 47	2 51	8 0	18 48	18 28	25 46	12 30	26 38	11 19	2♈37'35"
28 SU	8:18:31	19 44	4 26	9 0	19 18	18 34	25 48	12 31	26 38	11 20	2♈37'35"
29 MO	8:22:27	22 42	6 2	10 0	19 48	18 39	25 50	12 32	26 38	11 20	2♈37'35"
30 TU	8:26:24	25 44	7 38	11 1	20 18	18 44	25 52	12 32	26 39	11 20	2♈37'35"
31 WE	8:30:20	28 49	9 14	12 1	20 48	18 50	25 54	12 33	26 39	11 21	2♈37'34"

INGRESSES :

6 ♀ → ♓ 9: 2
10 ☿ → ♏ 5:18
19 ⊕ → ♌ 1:24
21 ☿ → ♐ 2: 1
25 ♀ → ♈ 5:18
31 ☿ → ♑ 9: 9

ASPECTS (HELIOCENTRIC +MOON(TYCHONIC)) :

1 ☽ ☍ ♀ 4:12	7 ☽ □ ♅ 3:54	☽ ☍ ♅ 7: 7	☽ □ ♆ 22:33	27 ☽ ☌ ♅ 17:12
2 ☽ □ ♇ 16:25	♀ S ☊ 11: 5	♀ □ ♇ 10:55	20 ☽ □ ♅ 6:18	28 ☽ □ ♂ 6: 9
3 ☽ □ ♄ 17:23	8 ☽ □ ♀ 15:16	14 ♂ □ ♅ 7:15	☽ ☌ ♂ 12:36	29 ☽ □ ♇ 22:26
♂ ☌ ☊ 22:48	☿ □ ♆ 23:50	☿ □ ♅ 15:54	21 ☽ ☍ ☿ 23: 2	30 ☿ ☍ ♄ 1: 4
5 ☽ ☌ ☿ 6:18	9 ☽ ☌ ♇ 3:43	☿ ☍ ♂ 17:51	22 ♀ □ ♄ 10:58	31 ☽ □ ♄ 0:42
☽ ☍ ♃ 7:49	☿ ☌ ☋ 9:32	15 ☽ □ ♇ 9: 0	☽ ☍ ♇ 17: 5	☽ □ ☿ 7:40
☿ □ ⊕ 10:57	10 ☽ ☍ ♄ 2:13	☽ ☌ ♀ 15:11	23 ☽ ☌ ♄ 22: 3	⊕ ☌ ♅ 13: 2
☿ ☍ ♃ 13:30	11 ☽ □ ♃ 13:40	⊕ ☍ ♆ 15:39	24 ☽ □ ♀ 3:19	
⊕ □ ♃ 18:53	12 ☽ ☌ ♆ 5: 2	16 ☽ □ ♄ 10:37	25 ☿ ☌ ♇ 2:34	
6 ☽ □ ♆ 1: 8	☽ □ ☿ 23:23	17 ☿ ☌ A 6:57	☽ □ ♃ 19: 0	
☽ ☍ ♂ 21:36	13 ☽ □ ♂ 6:14	18 ☽ ☌ ♃ 5: 3	26 ☽ ☍ ♆ 10:59	

SIDEREAL GEOCENTRIC LONGITUDES : FEBRUARY 31 Julian at 0 hours UT

DAY	☉	☽	☊	☿	♀	♂	♃	♄	♅	♆	♇
1 TH	13 ♒ 0	9 ♎ 0	19 ♉ 17R	0 ♒ 48	6 ♓ 59	16 ♈ 33	9 ♈ 25	20 ♊ 59R	12 ♌ 32R	27 ♑ 10	12 ♐ 53
2 FR	14 1	22 39	19 14	2 30	8 13	17 11	9 36	20 57	12 30	27 12	12 55
3 SA	15 1	6 ♏ 28	19 13	4 14	9 27	17 50	9 47	20 55	12 27	27 14	12 56
4 SU	16 1	20 26	19 13	5 58	10 41	18 29	9 57	20 53	12 25	27 16	12 57
5 MO	17 1	4 ♐ 35	19 12	7 43	11 55	19 7	10 9	20 51	12 22	27 19	12 58
6 TU	18 1	18 52	19 10	9 30	13 9	19 46	10 20	20 50	12 19	27 21	12 59
7 WE	19 1	3 ♑ 16	19 5	11 18	14 22	20 25	10 31	20 48	12 17	27 23	13 1
8 TH	20 1	17 42	18 58	13 6	15 36	21 3	10 42	20 47	12 14	27 25	13 2
9 FR	21 1	2 ♒ 7	18 47	14 56	16 50	21 42	10 54	20 45	12 12	27 27	13 3
10 SA	22 1	16 22	18 35	16 47	18 4	22 20	11 5	20 44	12 9	27 29	13 4
11 SU	23 1	0 ♓ 23	18 23	18 40	19 17	22 59	11 17	20 43	12 6	27 31	13 5
12 MO	24 0	14 5	18 11	20 33	20 31	23 38	11 29	20 42	12 4	27 34	13 6
13 TU	25 0	27 24	18 1	22 27	21 45	24 16	11 41	20 42	12 1	27 36	13 7
14 WE	26 0	10 ♈ 20	17 54	24 22	22 58	24 55	11 53	20 41	11 59	27 38	13 8
15 TH	27 0	22 54	17 49	26 19	24 12	25 33	12 5	20 40	11 56	27 40	13 9
16 FR	27 59	5 ♉ 9	17 47	28 16	25 25	26 12	12 17	20 40	11 54	27 42	13 9
17 SA	28 59	17 10	17 46	0 ♓ 14	26 39	26 51	12 29	20 39	11 51	27 44	13 10
18 SU	29 59	29 2	17 46	2 13	27 52	27 29	12 41	20 39	11 49	27 46	13 11
19 MO	0 ♓ 58	10 ♊ 50	17 46	4 13	29 5	28 8	12 53	20 39	11 46	27 48	13 12
20 TU	1 58	22 40	17 44	6 13	0 ♈ 18	28 46	13 6	20 39D	11 44	27 50	13 13
21 WE	2 57	4 ♋ 37	17 40	8 14	1 32	29 25	13 18	20 39	11 42	27 52	13 13
22 TH	3 57	16 46	17 33	10 15	2 45	0 ♉ 3	13 30	20 39	11 39	27 54	13 14
23 FR	4 56	29 9	17 23	12 15	3 58	0 42	13 43	20 39	11 37	27 56	13 15
24 SA	5 56	11 ♌ 50	17 12	14 16	5 11	1 21	13 56	20 40	11 35	27 57	13 15
25 SU	6 55	24 49	17 0	16 16	6 24	1 59	14 8	20 40	11 32	27 59	13 16
26 MO	7 54	8 ♍ 5	16 48	18 15	7 37	2 38	14 21	20 41	11 30	28 1	13 16
27 TU	8 53	21 36	16 38	20 12	8 49	3 16	14 34	20 42	11 28	28 3	13 17
28 WE	9 53	5 ♎ 20	16 29	22 8	10 2	3 55	14 47	20 43	11 26	28 5	13 17

INGRESSES :

2 ☽ → ♏ 12:48
4 ☽ → ♐ 16:15
6 ☽ → ♑ 18:34
8 ☽ → ♒ 20:28
10 ☽ → ♓ 23:19
13 ☽ → ♈ 4:45
15 ☽ → ♉ 13:50
16 ☿ → ♓ 21: 6
18 ☉ → ♓ 0:30
☽ → ♊ 1:57
19 ♀ → ♈ 17:57
20 ☽ → ♋ 14:45
21 ♂ → ♉ 21:50
23 ☽ → ♌ 1:36
25 ☽ → ♍ 9:26
27 ☽ → ♎ 14:42

ASPECTS & ECLIPSES :

1 ☽ ☍ ♃ 0:44
☽ ☍ ♂ 13:57
3 ☉ □ ☽ 15:50
☽ ☌ ☋ 21:53
5 ☽ ☌ ♇ 14: 8
♀ □ ♇ 20:58
6 ☽ ☍ ♄ 3:16
☽ ☌ P 22:56
7 ☉ □ ☊ 1:37
☿ ☍ ♅ 12:45
8 ☽ ☌ ♆ 16:12
9 ☽ ☍ ♅ 16:52
10 ☽ ☌ ☿ 0:49
☽ □S ☊ 3:42
☉ ☌ ☽ 10:19
☿ □ ☊ 20:46
12 ♀ □ ♄ 3:37
☽ ☌ ♀ 12:40
14 ☽ ☌ ♃ 2:57
15 ☽ ☌ ♂ 5:26
☉ ☋S ☿ 17: 6
17 ☽ ☌ ☊ 1:12
18 ☉ □ ☽ 2: 5
♂ □ ♆ 10:52
☽ ☌ A 21:28
19 ☽ ☍ ♇ 4:47
☽ ☌ ♄ 19:54
22 ☉ □ π 2:33
☽ ☍ ♆ 21:37
23 ☿ □ ♇ 11:52
☽ ☌ ♅ 23:30
24 ☽ □N ☊ 9:50
25 ☉ ☍ ☽ 23:39
26 ☽ ☍ ☿ 21: 6
27 ☿ □ ♄ 6: 7
28 ☽ ☍ ♀ 8:55
☽ ☍ ♃ 16:35

SIDEREAL HELIOCENTRIC LONGITUDES : FEBRUARY 31 Julian at 0 hours UT

DAY	Sid. Time	☿	♀	⊕	♂	♃	♄	♅	♆	♇	Vernal Point
1 TH	8:34:17	1 ♑ 57	10 ♈ 50	13 ♌ 1	21 ♉ 18	18 ♈ 55	25 ♊ 57	12 ♌ 34	26 ♑ 39	11 ♐ 21	2♈37'34"
2 FR	8:38:14	5 8	12 26	14 1	21 48	19 1	25 59	12 35	26 40	11 21	2♈37'34"
3 SA	8:42:10	8 23	14 2	15 1	22 18	19 6	26 1	12 35	26 40	11 22	2♈37'34"
4 SU	8:46: 7	11 43	15 39	16 1	22 48	19 11	26 3	12 36	26 40	11 22	2♈37'34"
5 MO	8:50: 3	15 6	17 15	17 1	23 18	19 17	26 6	12 37	26 41	11 22	2♈37'34"
6 TU	8:54: 0	18 35	18 51	18 1	23 48	19 22	26 8	12 38	26 41	11 23	2♈37'34"
7 WE	8:57:56	22 9	20 27	19 1	24 17	19 28	26 10	12 38	26 42	11 23	2♈37'33"
8 TH	9: 1:53	25 48	22 3	20 1	24 47	19 33	26 12	12 39	26 42	11 23	2♈37'33"
9 FR	9: 5:49	29 33	23 40	21 1	25 17	19 38	26 15	12 40	26 42	11 24	2♈37'33"
10 SA	9: 9:46	3 ♒ 24	25 16	22 1	25 46	19 44	26 17	12 41	26 43	11 24	2♈37'33"
11 SU	9:13:43	7 22	26 52	23 1	26 16	19 49	26 19	12 42	26 43	11 24	2♈37'33"
12 MO	9:17:39	11 27	28 29	24 1	26 45	19 54	26 21	12 42	26 43	11 25	2♈37'33"
13 TU	9:21:36	15 39	0 ♉ 5	25 1	27 15	20 0	26 24	12 43	26 44	11 25	2♈37'33"
14 WE	9:25:32	19 59	1 42	26 1	27 44	20 5	26 26	12 44	26 44	11 25	2♈37'33"
15 TH	9:29:29	24 27	3 18	27 0	28 13	20 11	26 28	12 45	26 44	11 26	2♈37'32"
16 FR	9:33:25	29 3	4 55	28 0	28 43	20 16	26 30	12 45	26 45	11 26	2♈37'32"
17 SA	9:37:22	3 ♓ 48	6 31	29 0	29 12	20 21	26 33	12 46	26 45	11 26	2♈37'32"
18 SU	9:41:18	8 42	8 8	29 59	29 41	20 27	26 35	12 47	26 46	11 27	2♈37'32"
19 MO	9:45:15	13 45	9 44	0 ♍ 59	0 ♊ 10	20 32	26 37	12 48	26 46	11 27	2♈37'32"
20 TU	9:49:12	18 57	11 21	1 58	0 40	20 37	26 39	12 48	26 46	11 27	2♈37'32"
21 WE	9:53: 8	24 18	12 58	2 58	1 9	20 43	26 42	12 49	26 47	11 28	2♈37'32"
22 TH	9:57: 5	29 47	14 34	3 57	1 38	20 48	26 44	12 50	26 47	11 28	2♈37'31"
23 FR	10: 1: 1	5 ♈ 26	16 11	4 57	2 7	20 54	26 46	12 51	26 47	11 29	2♈37'31"
24 SA	10: 4:58	11 13	17 48	5 56	2 36	20 59	26 48	12 52	26 48	11 29	2♈37'31"
25 SU	10: 8:54	17 7	19 25	6 55	3 5	21 4	26 50	12 52	26 48	11 29	2♈37'31"
26 MO	10:12:51	23 9	21 1	7 55	3 34	21 10	26 53	12 53	26 48	11 30	2♈37'31"
27 TU	10:16:47	29 16	22 38	8 54	4 3	21 15	26 55	12 54	26 49	11 30	2♈37'31"
28 WE	10:20:44	5 ♉ 28	24 15	9 53	4 31	21 20	26 57	12 55	26 49	11 30	2♈37'31"

INGRESSES :

9 ☿ → ♒ 2:50
12 ♀ → ♉ 22:44
16 ☿ → ♓ 4:51
18 ⊕ → ♍ 0:18
♂ → ♊ 15:24
22 ☿ → ♈ 0:53
27 ☿ → ♉ 2:52

ASPECTS (HELIOCENTRIC +MOON(TYCHONIC)) :

1 ☽ ☍ ♀ 3:40
☽ ☍ ♃ 17:34
2 ☽ □ ♆ 6:59
3 ☽ □ ♅ 10:33
4 ☽ ☍ ♂ 4:10
5 ☽ ☌ ♇ 11:27
6 ☿ □ ♀ 3:19
☿ □ ♃ 5:29
♀ ☌ ♃ 8:15
☽ ☍ ♄ 12:10
8 ☽ □ ♃ 3: 5
☿ ☌ ♆ 5:50
☽ □ ♀ 8: 8
☿ □S ☊ 12: 3
☽ ☌ ♆ 14:58
☽ ☌ ☿ 18:11
9 ☽ ☍ ♅ 17:44
10 ☽ □ ♂ 16:37
♀ □ ♆ 21:40
11 ☽ □ ♇ 19:16
12 ☿ ☍ ♅ 7:17
☽ □ ♄ 22: 9
14 ☽ ☌ ♃ 18:42
15 ☽ □ ♆ 7:27
☿ ☍ ⊕ 17: 6
☿ □ ♂ 22: 3
☽ ☌ ♀ 23:26
16 ☽ □ ♅ 15: 9
17 ⊕ □ ♂ 9:46
18 ☽ ☌ ♂ 1:22
☿ □ ♇ 13:11
19 ☽ ☍ ♇ 1:14
☽ □ ☿ 10:28
20 ☽ ☌ ♄ 8: 3
♀ □ ♅ 21:55
21 ☿ □ ♄ 10:37
22 ☽ □ ♃ 7:56
☽ ☍ ♆ 19:27
24 ☽ ☌ ♅ 1:54
☽ □ ♀ 12:39
25 ☽ □ ♂ 15:34
☿ ☌ ♃ 16: 2
26 ☽ □ ♇ 6: 5
☿ □ ♆ 14:25
☿ ☌ ☊ 17:47
27 ☽ □ ♄ 9:20

SIDEREAL GEOCENTRIC LONGITUDES : MARCH 31 Julian at 0 hours UT

DAY	☉	☽	☊	☿	♀	♂	♃	♄	♅	♆	♇
1 TH	10 ♓ 52	19 ♎ 14	16 ♉ 24R	24 ♓ 2	11 ♈ 15	4 ♉ 33	15 ♈ 0	20 ♊ 44	11 ♌ 23R	28 ♑ 7	13 ♐ 18
2 FR	11 51	3 ♏ 14	16 21	25 54	12 28	5 11	15 13	20 45	11 21	28 8	13 18
3 SA	12 50	17 18	16 20	27 43	13 40	5 50	15 26	20 46	11 19	28 10	13 19
4 SU	13 49	1 ♐ 24	16 21D	29 28	14 53	6 28	15 39	20 47	11 17	28 12	13 19
5 MO	14 48	15 31	16 21R	1 ♈ 10	16 5	7 7	15 52	20 49	11 15	28 14	13 19
6 TU	15 47	29 39	16 20	2 48	17 18	7 45	16 5	20 50	11 13	28 15	13 20
7 WE	16 46	13 ♑ 45	16 18	4 21	18 30	8 24	16 18	20 52	11 11	28 17	13 20
8 TH	17 45	27 48	16 12	5 50	19 42	9 2	16 32	20 53	11 9	28 19	13 20
9 FR	18 44	11 ♒ 45	16 5	7 14	20 54	9 41	16 45	20 55	11 7	28 20	13 20
10 SA	19 43	25 33	15 56	8 33	22 6	10 19	16 58	20 57	11 5	28 22	13 21
11 SU	20 42	9 ♓ 9	15 46	9 46	23 19	10 57	17 12	20 59	11 3	28 23	13 21
12 MO	21 41	22 30	15 37	10 54	24 31	11 36	17 25	21 1	11 1	28 25	13 21
13 TU	22 40	5 ♈ 33	15 29	11 56	25 43	12 14	17 39	21 4	11 0	28 26	13 21
14 WE	23 39	18 18	15 24	12 51	26 54	12 52	17 52	21 6	10 58	28 28	13 21
15 TH	24 37	0 ♉ 46	15 20	13 41	28 6	13 31	18 6	21 8	10 56	28 29	13 21
16 FR	25 36	12 59	15 19	14 25	29 18	14 9	18 20	21 11	10 55	28 31	13 21R
17 SA	26 35	24 59	15 20D	15 2	0 ♉ 30	14 48	18 33	21 14	10 53	28 32	13 21
18 SU	27 33	6 ♊ 51	15 21	15 33	1 41	15 26	18 47	21 16	10 51	28 34	13 21
19 MO	28 32	18 40	15 22	15 58	2 53	16 4	19 1	21 19	10 50	28 35	13 21
20 TU	29 31	0 ♋ 31	15 22R	16 16	4 4	16 42	19 14	21 22	10 49	28 36	13 21
21 WE	0 ♈ 29	12 29	15 21	16 28	5 15	17 21	19 28	21 25	10 47	28 38	13 21
22 TH	1 28	24 39	15 19	16 34	6 27	17 59	19 42	21 28	10 46	28 39	13 20
23 FR	2 26	7 ♌ 6	15 14	16 34R	7 38	18 37	19 56	21 32	10 44	28 40	13 20
24 SA	3 25	19 52	15 8	16 28	8 49	19 16	20 10	21 35	10 43	28 41	13 20
25 SU	4 23	3 ♍ 0	15 2	16 16	10 0	19 54	20 24	21 38	10 42	28 43	13 20
26 MO	5 21	16 30	14 55	16 0	11 11	20 32	20 38	21 42	10 41	28 44	13 19
27 TU	6 20	0 ♎ 20	14 49	15 38	12 21	21 10	20 52	21 46	10 40	28 45	13 19
28 WE	7 18	14 27	14 45	15 13	13 32	21 49	21 5	21 49	10 38	28 46	13 19
29 TH	8 16	28 46	14 42	14 43	14 43	22 27	21 19	21 53	10 37	28 47	13 18
30 FR	9 14	13 ♏ 12	14 41	14 10	15 53	23 5	21 33	21 57	10 36	28 48	13 18
31 SA	10 12	27 41	14 42D	13 35	17 4	23 43	21 47	22 1	10 35	28 49	13 17

INGRESSES :

1 ☽ → ♏ 18:28
3 ☽ → ♐ 21:37
4 ☿ → ♈ 7:25
6 ☽ → ♑ 0:36
8 ☽ → ♒ 3:46
10 ☽ → ♓ 7:48
12 ☽ → ♈ 13:43
14 ☽ → ♉ 22:29
16 ♀ → ♉ 14: 5
17 ☽ → ♊ 10: 6
19 ☽ → ♋ 22:56
20 ☉ → ♈ 12: 2
22 ☽ → ♌ 10:22
24 ☽ → ♍ 18:34
26 ☽ → ♎ 23:26
29 ☽ → ♏ 2: 3
31 ☽ → ♐ 3:51

ASPECTS & ECLIPSES :

2 ☽ ☍ ♂ 3:30
☽ ☌ ☋ 22:21
3 ☉ □ ♇ 11:38
4 ☽ ☌ P 10:14
♀ ☌ ♃ 18:39
☽ ☌ ♇ 20:15
☉ □ ☽ 22:41
5 ☽ ☍ ♄ 8:59
7 ☉ □ Π 17:27
8 ☽ ☌ ♆ 0:52
☽ ☍ ♅ 22:54
9 ☽ □S ☊ 7:24
11 ♂ □ ♅ 3:33
☉ □ ♄ 7: 9
☉ ☌ ☽ 22:24
13 ☽ ☌ ☿ 12:53
☽ ☌ ♃ 23: 9
☉ □ Π 23:50
14 ☽ ☌ ♀ 18:15
15 ♀ □ ♆ 7:55
16 ☽ ☌ ♂ 2:27
☽ ☌ ☊ 4:39
17 ♂ ☌ ☊ 20:42
18 ☽ ☍ ♇ 13:10
☽ ☌ A 17:17
19 ☽ ☌ ♄ 5:23
☉ □ ☽ 21:46
22 ☽ ☍ ♆ 7:46
23 ☽ ☌ ♅ 6:53
☽ N□ ☊ 15:15
25 ♀ □ ♅ 13:59
27 ☉ ☍ ☽ 11: 0
28 ☽ ☍ ☿ 1:14
☽ ☍ ♃ 11:21
♀ ☌ ☊ 23:44
30 ☽ ☌ ☋ 2:27
☽ ☍ ♀ 4:50
☽ ☌ P 14:20
☽ ☍ ♂ 17: 7

SIDEREAL HELIOCENTRIC LONGITUDES : MARCH 31 Julian at 0 hours UT

DAY	Sid. Time	☿	♀	⊕	♂	♃	♄	♅	♆	♇	Vernal Point
1 TH	10:24:41	11 ♉ 43	25 ♉ 52	10 ♍ 52	5 ♊ 0	21 ♈ 26	26 ♊ 59	12 ♌ 55	26 ♑ 49	11 ♐ 31	2♈37'30"
2 FR	10:28:37	18 1	27 29	11 52	5 29	21 31	27 2	12 56	26 50	11 31	2♈37'30"
3 SA	10:32:34	24 19	29 6	12 51	5 58	21 37	27 4	12 57	26 50	11 31	2♈37'30"
4 SU	10:36:30	0 ♊ 37	0 ♊ 43	13 50	6 26	21 42	27 6	12 58	26 51	11 32	2♈37'30"
5 MO	10:40:27	6 53	2 20	14 49	6 55	21 47	27 8	12 58	26 51	11 32	2♈37'30"
6 TU	10:44:23	13 5	3 57	15 48	7 24	21 53	27 11	12 59	26 51	11 32	2♈37'30"
7 WE	10:48:20	19 12	5 34	16 47	7 52	21 58	27 13	13 0	26 52	11 33	2♈37'30"
8 TH	10:52:16	25 12	7 11	17 46	8 21	22 3	27 15	13 1	26 52	11 33	2♈37'30"
9 FR	10:56:13	1 ♋ 6	8 48	18 45	8 49	22 9	27 17	13 2	26 52	11 33	2♈37'29"
10 SA	11: 0:10	6 52	10 26	19 44	9 18	22 14	27 20	13 2	26 53	11 34	2♈37'29"
11 SU	11: 4: 6	12 29	12 3	20 43	9 46	22 20	27 22	13 3	26 53	11 34	2♈37'29"
12 MO	11: 8: 3	17 57	13 40	21 42	10 14	22 25	27 24	13 4	26 53	11 34	2♈37'29"
13 TU	11:11:59	23 16	15 17	22 40	10 43	22 30	27 26	13 5	26 54	11 35	2♈37'29"
14 WE	11:15:56	28 25	16 55	23 39	11 11	22 36	27 29	13 5	26 54	11 35	2♈37'29"
15 TH	11:19:52	3 ♌ 25	18 32	24 38	11 39	22 41	27 31	13 6	26 54	11 35	2♈37'29"
16 FR	11:23:49	8 15	20 9	25 37	12 8	22 46	27 33	13 7	26 55	11 36	2♈37'28"
17 SA	11:27:45	12 56	21 47	26 35	12 36	22 52	27 35	13 8	26 55	11 36	2♈37'28"
18 SU	11:31:42	17 28	23 24	27 34	13 4	22 57	27 37	13 8	26 56	11 36	2♈37'28"
19 MO	11:35:39	21 51	25 1	28 33	13 32	23 2	27 40	13 9	26 56	11 37	2♈37'28"
20 TU	11:39:35	26 7	26 39	29 31	14 0	23 8	27 42	13 10	26 56	11 37	2♈37'28"
21 WE	11:43:32	0 ♍ 14	28 16	0 ♎ 30	14 28	23 13	27 44	13 11	26 57	11 37	2♈37'28"
22 TH	11:47:28	4 14	29 54	1 28	14 56	23 19	27 46	13 12	26 57	11 38	2♈37'28"
23 FR	11:51:25	8 7	1 ♋ 31	2 27	15 24	23 24	27 49	13 12	26 57	11 38	2♈37'27"
24 SA	11:55:21	11 53	3 9	3 25	15 52	23 29	27 51	13 13	26 58	11 38	2♈37'27"
25 SU	11:59:18	15 33	4 46	4 23	16 20	23 35	27 53	13 14	26 58	11 39	2♈37'27"
26 MO	12: 3:14	19 7	6 24	5 22	16 48	23 40	27 55	13 15	26 58	11 39	2♈37'27"
27 TU	12: 7:11	22 36	8 1	6 20	17 16	23 45	27 58	13 15	26 59	11 39	2♈37'27"
28 WE	12:11: 8	26 0	9 39	7 18	17 44	23 51	28 0	13 16	26 59	11 40	2♈37'27"
29 TH	12:15: 4	29 19	11 17	8 17	18 12	23 56	28 2	13 17	27 0	11 40	2♈37'27"
30 FR	12:19: 1	2 ♎ 34	12 54	9 15	18 39	24 1	28 4	13 18	27 0	11 40	2♈37'27"
31 SA	12:22:57	5 45	14 32	10 13	19 7	24 7	28 7	13 18	27 0	11 41	2♈37'26"

INGRESSES :

3 ♀ → ♊ 13:22
☿ → ♊ 21:38
8 ☿ → ♋ 19:28
14 ☿ → ♌ 7:30
20 ⊕ → ♎ 11:49
☿ → ♍ 22:38
22 ♀ → ♋ 1:32
29 ☿ → ♎ 4:58

ASPECTS (HELIOCENTRIC +MOON(TYCHONIC)) :

1 ☽ ☍ ♃ 3:48
☿ □ ♅ 4:36
☽ □ ♆ 13: 2
⊕ □ ♇ 15:31
2 ☿ ☌ P 5:50
☽ □ ♅ 16:35
3 ☽ ☍ ☿ 21:36
☽ ☍ ♀ 22:41
4 ☿ ☌ ♀ 0:30
☽ ☍ ♂ 8:51
♀ ☌ ☊ 14:56
☽ ☌ ♇ 17:12
5 ☿ ☌ ♂ 0: 9
☿ ☍ ♇ 18: 0
☽ ☍ ♄ 19:47
6 ☿ □ ⊕ 12:40
7 ☽ □ ♃ 14: 6
☽ ☌ ♆ 22:24
8 ☿ ☌ ♄ 8:19
9 ♀ ☌ ♂ 0:14
☽ ☍ ♅ 2:12
10 ♀ ☍ ♇ 16:50
11 ☽ □ ♂ 1: 7
☽ □ ♇ 4:18
☽ □ ♀ 5:52
12 ☽ □ ♄ 8:58
☿ □ ♃ 20:27
13 ☿ ☍ ♆ 16:50
☿ N□ ☊ 20:27
14 ☽ ☌ ♃ 8:15
☽ □ ♆ 16:29
♂ ☍ ♇ 20:31
15 ☽ □ ☿ 8:34
16 ☽ □ ♅ 0:16
17 ☿ ☌ ♅ 1: 1
18 ⊕ □ ♄ 1:29
☽ ☍ ♇ 9:38
☽ ☌ ♂ 13: 7
19 ☽ ☌ ♀ 14:55
☽ ☌ ♄ 18:16
20 ♀ ☌ ♄ 15:54
21 ☽ □ ♃ 21:20
22 ☽ ☍ ♆ 4:28
23 ☽ ☌ ♅ 11:34
☿ □ ♇ 22:26
24 ♀ □ ⊕ 9:58
25 ☿ □ ♂ 6: 1
☽ □ ♇ 15:27
26 ☽ □ ♂ 0:33
☽ ☌ ☿ 6:10
☽ □ ♄ 19:55
27 ☽ □ ♀ 14:50
28 ☿ □ ♄ 14:32
☽ ☍ ♃ 15:52
☽ □ ♆ 21: 2
30 ☽ □ ♅ 0: 8
31 ☽ ☌ ♇ 23:17

SIDEREAL GEOCENTRIC LONGITUDES : APRIL 31 Julian at 0 hours UT											
DAY	☉	☽	☊	☿	♀	♂	♃	♄	♅	♆	♇
1 SU	11 ♈ 11	12 ♐ 6	14 ♉ 43	12 ♈ 57R	18 ♉ 14	24 ♉ 21	22 ♈ 2	22 ♊ 5	10 ♌ 35R	28 ♑ 50	13 ♐ 17R
2 MO	12 9	26 26	14 44	12 18	19 24	24 59	22 16	22 9	10 34	28 51	13 16
3 TU	13 7	10 ♑ 36	14 45	11 39	20 34	25 38	22 30	22 14	10 33	28 52	13 16
4 WE	14 5	24 37	14 45R	11 0	21 44	26 16	22 44	22 18	10 32	28 53	13 15
5 TH	15 3	8 ♒ 26	14 43	10 22	22 54	26 54	22 58	22 22	10 31	28 54	13 15
6 FR	16 1	22 3	14 40	9 46	24 4	27 32	23 12	22 27	10 31	28 55	13 14
7 SA	16 59	5 ♓ 27	14 36	9 11	25 14	28 10	23 26	22 31	10 30	28 55	13 13
8 SU	17 57	18 37	14 32	8 39	26 24	28 48	23 40	22 36	10 30	28 56	13 13
9 MO	18 55	1 ♈ 34	14 28	8 10	27 33	29 26	23 54	22 41	10 29	28 57	13 12
10 TU	19 53	14 16	14 25	7 45	28 43	0 ♊ 5	24 8	22 46	10 29	28 58	13 11
11 WE	20 51	26 45	14 22	7 24	29 52	0 43	24 23	22 51	10 28	28 58	13 10
12 TH	21 49	9 ♉ 2	14 22	7 7	1 ♊ 1	1 21	24 37	22 56	10 28	28 59	13 10
13 FR	22 47	21 7	14 22D	6 54	2 10	1 59	24 51	23 1	10 28	29 0	13 9
14 SA	23 44	3 ♊ 4	14 23	6 46	3 19	2 37	25 5	23 6	10 28	29 0	13 8
15 SU	24 42	14 54	14 24	6 42	4 28	3 15	25 19	23 11	10 27	29 1	13 7
16 MO	25 40	26 43	14 26	6 43D	5 37	3 53	25 33	23 16	10 27	29 1	13 6
17 TU	26 38	8 ♋ 34	14 27	6 48	6 45	4 31	25 47	23 22	10 27	29 2	13 5
18 WE	27 35	20 32	14 28	6 58	7 54	5 9	26 2	23 27	10 27D	29 2	13 4
19 TH	28 33	2 ♌ 41	14 28R	7 13	9 2	5 47	26 16	23 33	10 27	29 3	13 3
20 FR	29 31	15 6	14 27	7 32	10 10	6 25	26 30	23 38	10 27	29 3	13 2
21 SA	0 ♉ 28	27 52	14 26	7 55	11 18	7 3	26 44	23 44	10 27	29 3	13 1
22 SU	1 26	11 ♍ 1	14 25	8 23	12 26	7 41	26 58	23 50	10 28	29 4	13 0
23 MO	2 24	24 34	14 23	8 55	13 34	8 19	27 12	23 55	10 28	29 4	12 59
24 TU	3 21	8 ♎ 32	14 22	9 31	14 42	8 57	27 26	24 1	10 28	29 4	12 58
25 WE	4 19	22 53	14 21	10 10	15 49	9 35	27 40	24 7	10 29	29 4	12 57
26 TH	5 16	7 ♏ 31	14 20	10 54	16 56	10 13	27 54	24 13	10 29	29 5	12 56
27 FR	6 14	22 21	14 20D	11 41	18 4	10 51	28 9	24 19	10 29	29 5	12 55
28 SA	7 11	7 ♐ 14	14 21	12 32	19 11	11 29	28 23	24 25	10 30	29 5	12 54
29 SU	8 9	22 4	14 21	13 26	20 17	12 7	28 37	24 31	10 31	29 5	12 53
30 MO	9 6	6 ♑ 43	14 22	14 24	21 24	12 45	28 51	24 38	10 31	29 5	12 51

INGRESSES :

2 ☽ → ♑ 6: 1	21 ☽ → ♍ 3:57
4 ☽ → ♒ 9:18	23 ☽ → ♎ 9:24
6 ☽ → ♓ 14:12	25 ☽ → ♏ 11:43
8 ☽ → ♈ 21: 4	27 ☽ → ♐ 12:20
9 ♂ → ♊ 21: 9	29 ☽ → ♑ 12:57
11 ♀ → ♊ 2:47	
☽ → ♉ 6:18	
13 ☽ → ♊ 17:49	
16 ☽ → ♋ 6:39	
18 ☽ → ♌ 18:44	
20 ☉ → ♉ 12: 9	

ASPECTS & ECLIPSES :

1 ☽ ☌ ♇ 1:57	♀ ☌ ♂ 15: 7	☽ N□ ☊ 22:45	29 ☽ ☍ ♄ 4: 2
☽ ☍ ♄ 16:47	13 ☽ ☌ ♂ 23: 2	22 ♀ ☍ ♇ 11:53	30 ♂ ☍ ♇ 4: 4
2 ☉ ɓ ☿ 2:23	14 ☽ ☌ ♀ 0:34	24 ☽ ☍ ☿ 1:43	
3 ☉ □ ☽ 4:35	☽ ☍ ♇ 20:22	25 ☽ ☍ ♃ 8: 1	
4 ☽ ☌ ♆ 7:23	15 ☽ ☌ A 11:10	☉ ☍ ☽ 20: 4	
5 ☽ ☍ ♅ 3:39	☽ ☌ ♄ 16:56	☽ ●-● P 20:11	
☽ □S ☊ 10:59	☉ ☌ ♃ 20:19	26 ☽ ☌ ☋ 11: 3	
9 ☽ ☌ ☿ 12: 1	18 ☉ □ ☽ 15:11	27 ☽ ☌ P 11:44	
10 ☉ ☌ ☽ 11:37	☽ ☍ ♆ 16:51	28 ☽ ☍ ♂ 7: 9	
☽ ☌ ♃ 19:17	19 ☉ □ ♆ 12:21	☽ ☌ ♇ 9: 7	
12 ☽ ☌ ☊ 10:32	☽ ☌ ♅ 15: 4	☽ ☍ ♀ 20:53	

SIDEREAL HELIOCENTRIC LONGITUDES : APRIL 31 Julian at 0 hours UT											
DAY	Sid. Time	☿	♀	⊕	♂	♃	♄	♅	♆	♇	Vernal Point
1 SU	12:26:54	8 ♎ 53	16 ♋ 9	11 ♎ 11	19 ♊ 35	24 ♈ 12	28 ♊ 9	13 ♌ 19	27 ♑ 1	11 ♐ 41	2♈37'26"
2 MO	12:30:50	11 57	17 47	12 9	20 3	24 18	28 11	13 20	27 1	11 41	2♈37'26"
3 TU	12:34:47	14 58	19 25	13 7	20 30	24 23	28 13	13 21	27 1	11 42	2♈37'26"
4 WE	12:38:43	17 57	21 2	14 5	20 58	24 28	28 16	13 22	27 2	11 42	2♈37'26"
5 TH	12:42:40	20 53	22 40	15 4	21 25	24 34	28 18	13 22	27 2	11 42	2♈37'26"
6 FR	12:46:37	23 46	24 18	16 2	21 53	24 39	28 20	13 23	27 2	11 43	2♈37'26"
7 SA	12:50:33	26 38	25 55	17 0	22 21	24 44	28 22	13 24	27 3	11 43	2♈37'25"
8 SU	12:54:30	29 28	27 33	17 58	22 48	24 50	28 24	13 25	27 3	11 43	2♈37'25"
9 MO	12:58:26	2 ♏ 17	29 11	18 56	23 16	24 55	28 27	13 25	27 3	11 44	2♈37'25"
10 TU	13: 2:23	5 5	0 ♌ 48	19 54	23 43	25 0	28 29	13 26	27 4	11 44	2♈37'25"
11 WE	13: 6:19	7 51	2 26	20 51	24 10	25 6	28 31	13 27	27 4	11 44	2♈37'25"
12 TH	13:10:16	10 37	4 4	21 49	24 38	25 11	28 33	13 28	27 5	11 45	2♈37'25"
13 FR	13:14:12	13 22	5 41	22 47	25 5	25 16	28 36	13 28	27 5	11 45	2♈37'25"
14 SA	13:18: 9	16 7	7 19	23 45	25 33	25 22	28 38	13 29	27 5	11 45	2♈37'24"
15 SU	13:22: 6	18 51	8 57	24 43	26 0	25 27	28 40	13 30	27 6	11 46	2♈37'24"
16 MO	13:26: 2	21 36	10 34	25 41	26 27	25 33	28 42	13 31	27 6	11 46	2♈37'24"
17 TU	13:29:59	24 20	12 12	26 38	26 55	25 38	28 45	13 32	27 6	11 46	2♈37'24"
18 WE	13:33:55	27 6	13 50	27 36	27 22	25 43	28 47	13 32	27 7	11 47	2♈37'24"
19 TH	13:37:52	29 52	15 27	28 34	27 49	25 49	28 49	13 33	27 7	11 47	2♈37'24"
20 FR	13:41:48	2 ♐ 38	17 5	29 31	28 16	25 54	28 51	13 34	27 7	11 47	2♈37'24"
21 SA	13:45:45	5 26	18 42	0 ♏ 29	28 43	25 59	28 54	13 35	27 8	11 48	2♈37'24"
22 SU	13:49:41	8 16	20 20	1 27	29 11	26 5	28 56	13 35	27 8	11 48	2♈37'23"
23 MO	13:53:38	11 6	21 57	2 24	29 38	26 10	28 58	13 36	27 8	11 48	2♈37'23"
24 TU	13:57:35	13 59	23 35	3 22	0 ♋ 5	26 15	29 0	13 37	27 9	11 49	2♈37'23"
25 WE	14: 1:31	16 53	25 12	4 19	0 32	26 21	29 2	13 38	27 9	11 49	2♈37'23"
26 TH	14: 5:28	19 50	26 50	5 17	0 59	26 26	29 5	13 38	27 10	11 49	2♈37'23"
27 FR	14: 9:24	22 49	28 27	6 14	1 26	26 31	29 7	13 39	27 10	11 50	2♈37'23"
28 SA	14:13:21	25 50	0 ♍ 5	7 12	1 53	26 37	29 9	13 40	27 10	11 50	2♈37'23"
29 SU	14:17:17	28 55	1 42	8 9	2 20	26 42	29 11	13 41	27 11	11 50	2♈37'22"
30 MO	14:21:14	2 ♑ 3	3 19	9 7	2 47	26 47	29 14	13 42	27 11	11 51	2♈37'22"

INGRESSES :

8 ☿ → ♏ 4:29
9 ♀ → ♌ 12: 6
19 ☿ → ♐ 1:11
20 ⊕ → ♏ 11:55
23 ♂ → ♋ 19:41
27 ♀ → ♍ 22:52
29 ☿ → ♑ 8:20

ASPECTS (HELIOCENTRIC +MOON(TYCHONIC)) :

1 ♀ ☌ P 0:43	☿ □ ♀ 10: 5	☽ □ ♅ 8:46	19 ☽ ☌ ♅ 21: 2	27 ☽ □ ♀ 11: 2
☽ ☍ ♂ 12:55	7 ☿ □ ♆ 3:27	13 ☿ □ ♅ 0:58	20 ☽ ☌ ♀ 4:18	28 ☽ ☌ ♇ 7:25
2 ☿ ☌ ⊕ 2:23	☿ ☌ ☋ 8:42	14 ☽ ☍ ♇ 17:36	21 ♂ ☌ ♄ 9:42	29 ♀ N□ ☊ 0:19
☽ ☍ ♄ 2:58	☽ □ ♇ 11:22	15 ☿ ☌ A 6: 8	☽ □ ☿ 17:41	☿ ☍ ♄ 2: 7
3 ☽ □ ☿ 9:27	♀ ☍ ♆ 16:36	⊕ ☍ ♃ 20:19	22 ☽ □ ♇ 1:25	☽ ☍ ♄ 11:39
☽ ☍ ♀ 17: 2	8 ☽ □ ♂ 7:59	☽ ☌ ♂ 23:26	23 ☿ ☌ ♇ 5:54	☽ ☌ ☿ 14:12
☽ □ ♃ 23:45	☽ □ ♄ 18: 9	16 ☽ ☌ ♄ 4: 2	☽ □ ♄ 7:39	☽ ☍ ♂ 17:19
4 ☽ ☌ ♆ 4:10	10 ☽ ☌ ♃ 20:45	17 ⊕ □ ♆ 11:43	☽ □ ♂ 9: 4	30 ☿ ☍ ♂ 6:28
5 ☽ ☍ ♅ 8:40	11 ☽ □ ♆ 0:36	♀ ☌ ♅ 19:43	25 ☽ ☍ ♃ 5:44	
6 ♀ □ ♃ 5:31	☽ □ ♀ 12:44	18 ☽ □ ♃ 10:22	☽ □ ♆ 7: 2	
☿ ☍ ♃ 7:33	12 ☽ ☍ ☿ 4: 2	☽ ☍ ♆ 13: 3	26 ☽ □ ♅ 9:56	

SIDEREAL GEOCENTRIC LONGITUDES : MAY 31 Julian at 0 hours UT

DAY	☉	☽	☊	☿	♀	♂	♃	♄	⛢	♆	♇
1 TU	10 ♉ 3	21 ♑ 7	14 ♉ 22	15 ♈ 25	22 ♊ 30	13 ♊ 23	29 ♈ 5	24 ♊ 44	10 ♌ 32	29 ♑ 5	12 ♐ 50R
2 WE	11 1	5 ♒ 13	14 22	16 29	23 37	14 1	29 19	24 50	10 33	29 5R	12 49
3 TH	11 58	18 59	14 22R	17 36	24 43	14 39	29 33	24 56	10 33	29 5	12 48
4 FR	12 56	2 ♓ 26	14 22	18 46	25 49	15 16	29 46	25 3	10 34	29 5	12 46
5 SA	13 53	15 34	14 22	20 0	26 55	15 54	0 ♉ 0	25 9	10 35	29 5	12 45
6 SU	14 50	28 26	14 22D	21 16	28 0	16 32	0 14	25 16	10 36	29 5	12 44
7 MO	15 48	11 ♈ 2	14 22	22 35	29 6	17 10	0 28	25 22	10 37	29 5	12 43
8 TU	16 45	23 26	14 22	23 57	0 ♋ 11	17 48	0 42	25 29	10 38	29 4	12 41
9 WE	17 42	5 ♉ 39	14 22	25 21	1 16	18 26	0 56	25 36	10 39	29 4	12 40
10 TH	18 40	17 43	14 22R	26 49	2 20	19 4	1 10	25 43	10 40	29 4	12 39
11 FR	19 37	29 40	14 22	28 19	3 25	19 42	1 23	25 49	10 42	29 4	12 37
12 SA	20 34	11 ♊ 32	14 22	29 52	4 29	20 20	1 37	25 56	10 43	29 3	12 36
13 SU	21 32	23 21	14 21	1 ♉ 28	5 34	20 58	1 51	26 3	10 44	29 3	12 34
14 MO	22 29	5 ♋ 10	14 20	3 7	6 37	21 35	2 4	26 10	10 45	29 3	12 33
15 TU	23 26	17 2	14 19	4 48	7 41	22 13	2 18	26 17	10 47	29 2	12 32
16 WE	24 23	29 1	14 18	6 32	8 44	22 51	2 32	26 24	10 48	29 2	12 30
17 TH	25 21	11 ♌ 9	14 17	8 18	9 48	23 29	2 45	26 31	10 50	29 1	12 29
18 FR	26 18	23 32	14 16	10 7	10 50	24 7	2 59	26 38	10 51	29 1	12 27
19 SA	27 15	6 ♍ 14	14 16D	11 59	11 53	24 45	3 12	26 45	10 53	29 0	12 26
20 SU	28 12	19 18	14 17	13 53	12 55	25 23	3 26	26 52	10 55	29 0	12 24
21 MO	29 9	2 ♎ 47	14 18	15 49	13 57	26 0	3 39	26 59	10 56	28 59	12 23
22 TU	0 ♊ 6	16 43	14 19	17 48	14 59	26 38	3 52	27 7	10 58	28 58	12 21
23 WE	1 4	1 ♏ 4	14 20	19 49	16 1	27 16	4 6	27 14	11 0	28 58	12 20
24 TH	2 1	15 49	14 20R	21 52	17 2	27 54	4 19	27 21	11 2	28 57	12 18
25 FR	2 58	0 ♐ 50	14 19	23 56	18 2	28 32	4 32	27 28	11 4	28 56	12 17
26 SA	3 55	16 0	14 18	26 3	19 3	29 10	4 45	27 36	11 5	28 56	12 15
27 SU	4 52	1 ♑ 9	14 16	28 11	20 3	29 48	4 58	27 43	11 7	28 55	12 14
28 MO	5 49	16 8	14 13	0 ♊ 20	21 3	0 ♋ 25	5 11	27 51	11 9	28 54	12 12
29 TU	6 46	0 ♒ 49	14 11	2 29	22 2	1 3	5 25	27 58	11 11	28 53	12 11
30 WE	7 43	15 7	14 9	4 40	23 1	1 41	5 37	28 5	11 14	28 52	12 9
31 TH	8 40	28 59	14 7	6 51	24 0	2 19	5 50	28 13	11 16	28 52	12 8

INGRESSES :

1 ☽ → ♒ 15: 3
3 ☽ → ♓ 19:37
4 ♃ → ♉ 23:20
6 ☽ → ♈ 2:57
7 ♀ → ♋ 20: 2
8 ☽ → ♉ 12:50
11 ☽ → ♊ 0:39
12 ☿ → ♉ 1:56
13 ☽ → ♋ 13:30
16 ☽ → ♌ 1:58
18 ☽ → ♍ 12:17
20 ☽ → ♎ 19: 6
21 ☉ → ♊ 21:19
22 ☽ → ♏ 22:13
24 ☽ → ♐ 22:40
26 ☽ → ♑ 22: 9
27 ♂ → ♋ 7:54
☿ → ♊ 20:21
28 ☽ → ♒ 22:38
31 ☽ → ♓ 1:48

ASPECTS & ECLIPSES :

1 ♃ □ ♆ 0:58
☉ □ ⛢ 12: 1
☽ ☌ ♆ 13:29
2 ☽ ☍ ⛢ 9:13
☉ □ ☽ 10:47
☽ S ☊ 15:53
3 ♀ ☌ ♄ 5:28
5 ☉ ☌ ☊ 11:59
8 ☽ ☌ ☿ 1: 6
☽ ☌ ♃ 14:29
9 ☽ ☌ ☊ 17:18
10 ☉ ● A 1:54
☉ ☌ ☽ 2: 2
11 ☿ □ ♆ 11:29
12 ☽ ☍ ♇ 2: 8
☽ ☌ ♂ 18:51
13 ☽ ☌ A 0:43
☽ ☌ ♄ 5:32
☿ ☌ ♃ 6:29
14 ☽ ☌ ♀ 3:14
16 ☽ ☍ ♆ 0: 2
☽ ☌ ⛢ 23:21
17 ☽ N ☊ 6: 5
18 ☉ □ ☽ 5:41
☿ □ ⛢ 9:44
20 ☿ ☌ ☊ 5: 3
22 ♂ ☌ ♄ 22:10
23 ☽ ☍ ♃ 5: 2
☽ ☌ ☋ 21:36
24 ☽ ☍ ☿ 11:15
25 ☉ ☍ ☽ 3:35
☽ ☌ ♇ 18: 5
☽ ☌ P 18:51
26 ☽ ☍ ♄ 18:29
☽ ☍ ♂ 21:44
28 ☽ ☍ ♀ 8:31
☽ ☌ ♆ 20:48
29 ☽ ☍ ⛢ 17:23
☽ S ☊ 22:21
31 ☉ □ ☽ 18:34

SIDEREAL HELIOCENTRIC LONGITUDES : MAY 31 Julian at 0 hours UT

DAY	Sid. Time	☿	♀	⊕	♂	♃	♄	⛢	♆	♇	Vernal Point
1 TU	14:25:10	5 ♑ 15	4 ♍ 57	10 ♏ 4	3 ♋ 14	26 ♈ 53	29 ♊ 16	13 ♌ 42	27 ♑ 11	11 ♐ 51	2♈37'22"
2 WE	14:29: 7	8 30	6 34	11 1	3 41	26 58	29 18	13 43	27 12	11 51	2♈37'22"
3 TH	14:33: 4	11 49	8 11	11 59	4 8	27 3	29 20	13 44	27 12	11 52	2♈37'22"
4 FR	14:37: 0	15 13	9 48	12 56	4 35	27 9	29 23	13 45	27 12	11 52	2♈37'22"
5 SA	14:40:57	18 42	11 26	13 54	5 2	27 14	29 25	13 45	27 13	11 52	2♈37'22"
6 SU	14:44:53	22 16	13 3	14 51	5 29	27 19	29 27	13 46	27 13	11 53	2♈37'21"
7 MO	14:48:50	25 55	14 40	15 48	5 55	27 25	29 29	13 47	27 14	11 53	2♈37'21"
8 TU	14:52:46	29 40	16 17	16 46	6 22	27 30	29 32	13 48	27 14	11 53	2♈37'21"
9 WE	14:56:43	3 ♒ 32	17 54	17 43	6 49	27 36	29 34	13 48	27 14	11 54	2♈37'21"
10 TH	15: 0:39	7 30	19 31	18 40	7 16	27 41	29 36	13 49	27 15	11 54	2♈37'21"
11 FR	15: 4:36	11 35	21 8	19 38	7 43	27 46	29 38	13 50	27 15	11 54	2♈37'21"
12 SA	15: 8:33	15 47	22 45	20 35	8 9	27 52	29 40	13 51	27 15	11 55	2♈37'21"
13 SU	15:12:29	20 7	24 21	21 32	8 36	27 57	29 43	13 52	27 16	11 55	2♈37'21"
14 MO	15:16:26	24 36	25 58	22 29	9 3	28 2	29 45	13 52	27 16	11 55	2♈37'20"
15 TU	15:20:22	29 12	27 35	23 27	9 30	28 8	29 47	13 53	27 16	11 56	2♈37'20"
16 WE	15:24:19	3 ♓ 57	29 12	24 24	9 56	28 13	29 49	13 54	27 17	11 56	2♈37'20"
17 TH	15:28:15	8 51	0 ♎ 48	25 21	10 23	28 18	29 52	13 55	27 17	11 56	2♈37'20"
18 FR	15:32:12	13 54	2 25	26 18	10 50	28 24	29 54	13 55	27 17	11 57	2♈37'20"
19 SA	15:36: 8	19 7	4 1	27 15	11 16	28 29	29 56	13 56	27 18	11 57	2♈37'20"
20 SU	15:40: 5	24 28	5 38	28 13	11 43	28 34	29 58	13 57	27 18	11 57	2♈37'20"
21 MO	15:44: 2	29 58	7 14	29 10	12 10	28 40	0 ♋ 1	13 58	27 19	11 58	2♈37'19"
22 TU	15:47:58	5 ♈ 37	8 51	0 ♐ 7	12 36	28 45	0 3	13 58	27 19	11 58	2♈37'19"
23 WE	15:51:55	11 24	10 27	1 4	13 3	28 50	0 5	13 59	27 19	11 58	2♈37'19"
24 TH	15:55:51	17 18	12 3	2 1	13 29	28 56	0 7	14 0	27 20	11 59	2♈37'19"
25 FR	15:59:48	23 20	13 40	2 58	13 56	29 1	0 9	14 1	27 20	11 59	2♈37'19"
26 SA	16: 3:44	29 27	15 16	3 55	14 22	29 6	0 12	14 2	27 20	11 59	2♈37'19"
27 SU	16: 7:41	5 ♉ 39	16 52	4 53	14 49	29 12	0 14	14 2	27 21	12 0	2♈37'19"
28 MO	16:11:37	11 55	18 28	5 50	15 16	29 17	0 16	14 3	27 21	12 0	2♈37'18"
29 TU	16:15:34	18 12	20 4	6 47	15 42	29 22	0 18	14 4	27 21	12 0	2♈37'18"
30 WE	16:19:31	24 31	21 40	7 44	16 9	29 28	0 21	14 5	27 22	12 1	2♈37'18"
31 TH	16:23:27	0 ♊ 48	23 16	8 41	16 35	29 33	0 23	14 5	27 22	12 1	2♈37'18"

INGRESSES :

8 ☿ → ♒ 2: 2
15 ☿ → ♓ 4: 4
16 ♀ → ♎ 12: 0
20 ♄ → ♋ 18:19
21 ☿ → ♈ 0: 8
⊕ → ♐ 21: 5
26 ☿ → ♉ 2: 8
30 ☿ → ♊ 20:55

ASPECTS (HELIOCENTRIC +MOON(TYCHONIC)) :

1 ☽ □ ♃ 9:48
☽ ☌ ♆ 10:16
2 ☽ ☍ ⛢ 14:45
4 ☽ ☍ ♀ 15:17
☽ □ ♇ 17:11
♃ □ ♆ 17:31
⊕ □ ⛢ 20:31
5 ♀ □ ♇ 6:39
6 ☽ □ ♄ 1:56
☽ □ ♂ 13:51
7 ☿ ☌ ♆ 8:25
☿ □ ♃ 9:51
☿ S ☊ 11:15
8 ☽ □ ♆ 7:24
☽ ☌ ♃ 8: 0
☽ □ ☿ 17:49
9 ☽ □ ⛢ 16:11
11 ☿ ☍ ⛢ 12:58
12 ☽ ☍ ♇ 0:45
13 ☽ □ ♀ 2:21
☿ □ ⊕ 9:44
☽ ☌ ♄ 12:57
14 ☽ ☌ ♂ 8:10
15 ☽ ☍ ♆ 20:32
☽ □ ♃ 22:24
16 ♀ □ ♄ 9:35
17 ☽ ☌ ⛢ 5:23
☿ □ ♇ 14:45
19 ☽ □ ♇ 10:35
20 ☽ ☍ ☿ 15:37
☽ □ ♄ 19: 6
21 ☿ □ ♄ 0:11
☽ ☌ ♀ 8:46
☽ □ ♂ 16:46
22 ☽ □ ♆ 17:47
☿ ☍ ♀ 18:38
☽ ☍ ♃ 20:17
23 ☿ □ ♂ 7:18
☽ □ ⛢ 21: 4
25 ♀ □ ♂ 5:35
☿ □ ♆ 15:45
☿ ☌ ☊ 17: 3
☽ ☌ ♇ 17:39
☿ ☌ ♃ 22:38
26 ☽ ☍ ♄ 22:31
27 ☽ ☍ ♂ 22:32
28 ☽ □ ♀ 4:13
☿ □ ⛢ 8:11
☽ ☌ ♆ 18:16
☽ □ ♃ 21:35
29 ☿ ☌ P 5: 7
☽ ☍ ⛢ 22:14
31 ☽ □ ☿ 5:59
☽ □ ♇ 23:17

SIDEREAL GEOCENTRIC LONGITUDES : JUNE 31 Julian at 0 hours UT

DAY	☉	☽	☊	☿	♀	♂	♃	♄	♅	♆	♇
1 FR	9 ♊ 38	12 ♓ 25	14 ♉ 7	9 ♊ 2	24 ♋ 58	2 ♋ 57	6 ♉ 3	28 ♊ 20	11 ♌ 18	28 ♑ 51R	12 ♐ 6R
2 SA	10 35	25 27	14 8	11 12	25 56	3 35	6 16	28 28	11 20	28 50	12 5
3 SU	11 32	8 ♈ 8	14 9	13 22	26 53	4 12	6 29	28 36	11 22	28 49	12 3
4 MO	12 29	20 33	14 11	15 32	27 50	4 50	6 42	28 43	11 25	28 48	12 2
5 TU	13 26	2 ♉ 44	14 12	17 40	28 47	5 28	6 54	28 51	11 27	28 47	12 0
6 WE	14 23	14 45	14 13R	19 48	29 43	6 6	7 7	28 58	11 29	28 46	11 59
7 TH	15 20	26 40	14 12	21 54	0 ♌ 38	6 44	7 19	29 6	11 32	28 45	11 57
8 FR	16 17	8 ♊ 31	14 10	23 58	1 33	7 22	7 32	29 14	11 34	28 44	11 56
9 SA	17 15	20 20	14 6	26 1	2 28	8 0	7 44	29 21	11 37	28 42	11 54
10 SU	18 12	2 ♋ 9	14 1	28 3	3 22	8 37	7 56	29 29	11 39	28 41	11 53
11 MO	19 9	14 0	13 55	0 ♋ 3	4 16	9 15	8 9	29 37	11 42	28 40	11 51
12 TU	20 6	25 56	13 48	2 1	5 9	9 53	8 21	29 44	11 45	28 39	11 50
13 WE	21 3	7 ♌ 59	13 42	3 57	6 1	10 31	8 33	29 52	11 47	28 38	11 48
14 TH	22 0	20 10	13 37	5 51	6 53	11 9	8 45	0 ♋ 0	11 50	28 37	11 47
15 FR	22 58	2 ♍ 35	13 33	7 43	7 44	11 47	8 57	0 8	11 53	28 35	11 45
16 SA	23 55	15 14	13 31	9 34	8 34	12 25	9 9	0 15	11 56	28 34	11 44
17 SU	24 52	28 13	13 31D	11 23	9 24	13 3	9 21	0 23	11 58	28 33	11 42
18 MO	25 49	11 ♎ 35	13 31	13 10	10 13	13 40	9 32	0 31	12 1	28 32	11 41
19 TU	26 46	25 22	13 33	14 55	11 1	14 18	9 44	0 39	12 4	28 30	11 39
20 WE	27 43	9 ♏ 35	13 34	16 38	11 49	14 56	9 55	0 46	12 7	28 29	11 38
21 TH	28 41	24 12	13 33R	18 19	12 35	15 34	10 7	0 54	12 10	28 28	11 36
22 FR	29 38	9 ♐ 11	13 31	19 58	13 21	16 12	10 18	1 2	12 13	28 26	11 35
23 SA	0 ♋ 35	24 23	13 27	21 36	14 6	16 50	10 30	1 10	12 16	28 25	11 33
24 SU	1 32	9 ♑ 39	13 21	23 11	14 50	17 28	10 41	1 17	12 19	28 23	11 32
25 MO	2 29	24 48	13 14	24 45	15 33	18 6	10 52	1 25	12 22	28 22	11 31
26 TU	3 27	9 ♒ 41	13 7	26 17	16 16	18 44	11 3	1 33	12 25	28 21	11 29
27 WE	4 24	24 10	13 0	27 47	16 57	19 22	11 14	1 41	12 28	28 19	11 28
28 TH	5 21	8 ♓ 10	12 55	29 15	17 37	20 0	11 25	1 49	12 31	28 18	11 26
29 FR	6 18	21 41	12 52	0 ♌ 41	18 16	20 38	11 36	1 56	12 35	28 16	11 25
30 SA	7 16	4 ♈ 45	12 51	2 5	18 54	21 16	11 46	2 4	12 38	28 15	11 24

INGRESSES :

2 ☽ → ♈ 8:32
4 ☽ → ♉ 18:34
6 ♀ → ♌ 7:25
7 ☽ → ♊ 6:44
9 ☽ → ♋ 19:38
10 ☿ → ♋ 23:29
12 ☽ → ♌ 8: 7
14 ♄ → ♋ 0:34
☽ → ♍ 19: 3
17 ☽ → ♎ 3:13
19 ☽ → ♏ 7:54
21 ☽ → ♐ 9:20
22 ☉ → ♋ 9:21
23 ☽ → ♑ 8:49
25 ☽ → ♒ 8:18
27 ☽ → ♓ 9:53
28 ☿ → ♌ 12:31
29 ☽ → ♈ 15:11

ASPECTS & ECLIPSES :

1 ☉ ☌[S] ☿ 11:44
2 ☿ ☍ ♇ 9:34
3 ☉ ☍ ♇ 12:52
5 ♀ ☍ ♆ 0: 1
☽ ☌ ♃ 8:26
☽ ☌ ☊ 22:54
8 ☽ ☍ ♇ 6:55
☉ ☌ ☽ 17:11
9 ☽ ☌ A 6:52
☽ ☌ ☿ 13:58
☽ ☌ ♄ 18:32
10 ☽ ☌ ♂ 13:51
☿ ☌ ♄ 18:25
12 ☽ ☍ ♆ 5:25
☽ ☌ ♀ 19:48
13 ☽ ☌ ♅ 7:33
☽ □[N] ☊ 11:13
16 ☉ □ ☽ 17:22
♀ □ ♃ 21:54
18 ☿ ☌ ♂ 10:57
20 ☽ ☍ ♃ 0:35
☽ ☌ ☋ 6:35
♀ ☌ ♅ 10: 1
22 ☽ ☌ ♇ 3:47
♀ □ ☊ 4:46
23 ☽ ☌ P 4:24
☉ ☍ ☽ 10:23
☽ ☍ ♄ 10:44
☉ ☌ ♄ 16:54
24 ☽ ☍ ♂ 12:52
☽ ☍ ☿ 23:53
25 ☽ ☌ ♆ 5:40
26 ☽ ☍ ♅ 4:29
☽ □[S] ☊ 5:34
☽ ☍ ♀ 11:20
27 ☿ ☍ ♆ 8:35
30 ☉ □ ☽ 5: 6

SIDEREAL HELIOCENTRIC LONGITUDES : JUNE 31 Julian at 0 hours UT

DAY	Sid. Time	☿	♀	⊕	♂	♃	♄	♅	♆	♇	Vernal Point
1 FR	16:27:24	7 ♊ 4	24 ♎ 52	9 ♐ 38	17 ♋ 2	29 ♈ 38	0 ♋ 25	14 ♌ 6	27 ♑ 22	12 ♐ 1	2♈37'18"
2 SA	16:31:20	13 15	26 28	10 35	17 28	29 44	0 27	14 7	27 23	12 2	2♈37'18"
3 SU	16:35:17	19 22	28 4	11 32	17 54	29 49	0 30	14 8	27 23	12 2	2♈37'18"
4 MO	16:39:13	25 23	29 39	12 29	18 21	29 54	0 32	14 8	27 24	12 2	2♈37'18"
5 TU	16:43:10	1 ♋ 16	1 ♏ 15	13 27	18 47	0 ♉ 0	0 34	14 9	27 24	12 3	2♈37'17"
6 WE	16:47: 6	7 2	2 51	14 24	19 14	0 5	0 36	14 10	27 24	12 3	2♈37'17"
7 TH	16:51: 3	12 39	4 26	15 21	19 40	0 10	0 38	14 11	27 25	12 3	2♈37'17"
8 FR	16:55: 0	18 7	6 2	16 18	20 7	0 16	0 41	14 12	27 25	12 4	2♈37'17"
9 SA	16:58:56	23 25	7 37	17 15	20 33	0 21	0 43	14 12	27 25	12 4	2♈37'17"
10 SU	17: 2:53	28 34	9 13	18 12	20 59	0 26	0 45	14 13	27 26	12 4	2♈37'17"
11 MO	17: 6:49	3 ♌ 33	10 48	19 9	21 26	0 32	0 47	14 14	27 26	12 5	2♈37'17"
12 TU	17:10:46	8 23	12 24	20 7	21 52	0 37	0 50	14 15	27 26	12 5	2♈37'16"
13 WE	17:14:42	13 4	13 59	21 4	22 19	0 42	0 52	14 15	27 27	12 5	2♈37'16"
14 TH	17:18:39	17 36	15 34	22 1	22 45	0 48	0 54	14 16	27 27	12 6	2♈37'16"
15 FR	17:22:35	21 59	17 10	22 58	23 11	0 53	0 56	14 17	27 28	12 6	2♈37'16"
16 SA	17:26:32	26 14	18 45	23 55	23 38	0 58	0 59	14 18	27 28	12 6	2♈37'16"
17 SU	17:30:29	0 ♍ 21	20 20	24 52	24 4	1 3	1 1	14 18	27 28	12 7	2♈37'16"
18 MO	17:34:25	4 20	21 55	25 50	24 30	1 9	1 3	14 19	27 29	12 7	2♈37'16"
19 TU	17:38:22	8 13	23 30	26 47	24 57	1 14	1 5	14 20	27 29	12 7	2♈37'15"
20 WE	17:42:18	11 59	25 5	27 44	25 23	1 19	1 7	14 21	27 29	12 8	2♈37'15"
21 TH	17:46:15	15 39	26 40	28 41	25 49	1 25	1 10	14 22	27 30	12 8	2♈37'15"
22 FR	17:50:11	19 13	28 15	29 38	26 16	1 30	1 12	14 22	27 30	12 8	2♈37'15"
23 SA	17:54: 8	22 42	29 50	0 ♑ 35	26 42	1 35	1 14	14 23	27 30	12 9	2♈37'15"
24 SU	17:58: 4	26 6	1 ♐ 25	1 33	27 8	1 41	1 16	14 24	27 31	12 9	2♈37'15"
25 MO	18: 2: 1	29 25	3 0	2 30	27 35	1 46	1 19	14 25	27 31	12 9	2♈37'15"
26 TU	18: 5:58	2 ♎ 40	4 35	3 27	28 1	1 51	1 21	14 25	27 31	12 10	2♈37'15"
27 WE	18: 9:54	5 51	6 10	4 24	28 27	1 57	1 23	14 26	27 32	12 10	2♈37'14"
28 TH	18:13:51	8 58	7 45	5 22	28 53	2 2	1 25	14 27	27 32	12 10	2♈37'14"
29 FR	18:17:47	12 2	9 19	6 19	29 20	2 7	1 28	14 28	27 33	12 11	2♈37'14"
30 SA	18:21:44	15 3	10 54	7 16	29 46	2 13	1 30	14 28	27 33	12 11	2♈37'14"

INGRESSES :

4 ♀ → ♏ 5:10
☿ → ♋ 18:46
5 ♃ → ♉ 1:57
10 ☿ → ♌ 6:49
16 ☿ → ♍ 21:57
22 ⊕ → ♑ 9: 8
23 ♀ → ♐ 2:28
25 ☿ → ♎ 4:18
30 ♂ → ♌ 12:47

ASPECTS (HELIOCENTRIC +MOON(TYCHONIC)) :

1 ☿ ☍ ⊕ 11:44
☿ ☍ ♇ 19:13
2 ☽ □ ♄ 9:25
♀ □ ♆ 13:49
3 ⊕ ☌ A 8:41
⊕ ☌ ♇ 12:35
☽ □ ♂ 19:33
4 ♀ ☍ ♃ 3:56
☽ □ ♆ 13:26
☽ ☌ ♃ 18:31
☽ ☍ ♀ 20:36
☿ ☌ ♄ 21: 4
5 ☽ □ ♅ 22:48
8 ☽ ☍ ♇ 7:12
☿ ☌ ♂ 9:46
9 ☿ ☍ ♆ 18:38
☿ □[N] ☊ 19:46
☽ ☌ ♄ 21: 9
10 ☿ □ ♃ 9: 4
11 ☽ ☌ ♂ 15:31
12 ☽ ☍ ♆ 3: 0
☽ □ ♃ 9:25
13 ♀ □ ♅ 4:10
☿ ☌ ♅ 6:16
☿ □ ♀ 7:22
☽ ☌ ♅ 12:24
☽ □ ♀ 13:38
☽ ☌ ☿ 16: 1
15 ☽ □ ♇ 18: 6
17 ☽ □ ♄ 5: 4
18 ☽ □ ♂ 23:15
19 ☽ □ ♆ 3:37
☽ ☍ ♃ 10: 4
20 ☿ □ ♇ 0:57
☽ □ ♅ 7:54
21 ☽ ☌ ♀ 4:27
22 ☽ ☌ ♇ 4:41
☽ □ ☿ 20:34
23 ☽ ☍ ♄ 10:47
⊕ ☍ ♄ 16:54
24 ♀ ☌ ☋ 4:34
♂ ☍ ♆ 20:50
25 ☽ ☌ ♆ 4:20
☽ ☍ ♂ 4:33
☽ □ ♃ 11:13
☿ □ ♄ 14: 7
26 ☽ ☍ ♅ 7:46
☿ □ ⊕ 8:26
27 ☽ □ ♀ 23: 9
28 ☽ □ ♇ 7: 1
29 ☽ □ ♄ 17:56
30 ♀ ☌ ♇ 19:34

SIDEREAL GEOCENTRIC LONGITUDES : JULY 31 Julian at 0 hours UT

DAY	☉	☽	☊	☿	♀	♂	♃	♄	♅	♆	♇
1 SU	8 ♋ 13	17 ♈ 24	12 ♉ 52	3 ♌ 27	19 ♌ 31	21 ♋ 53	11 ♉ 57	2 ♋ 12	12 ♌ 41	28 ♑ 13R	11 ♐ 22R
2 MO	9 10	29 44	12 53	4 47	20 7	22 31	12 7	2 20	12 44	28 12	11 21
3 TU	10 8	11 ♉ 49	12 53R	6 6	20 41	23 9	12 18	2 27	12 48	28 10	11 20
4 WE	11 5	23 45	12 53	7 22	21 14	23 47	12 28	2 35	12 51	28 9	11 18
5 TH	12 2	5 ♊ 35	12 50	8 35	21 46	24 25	12 38	2 43	12 54	28 7	11 17
6 FR	13 0	17 23	12 45	9 47	22 16	25 3	12 48	2 51	12 58	28 5	11 16
7 SA	13 57	29 12	12 37	10 56	22 45	25 42	12 58	2 58	13 1	28 4	11 15
8 SU	14 55	11 ♋ 4	12 27	12 3	23 12	26 20	13 8	3 6	13 4	28 2	11 13
9 MO	15 52	23 2	12 16	13 7	23 38	26 58	13 18	3 14	13 8	28 1	11 12
10 TU	16 50	5 ♌ 6	12 4	14 9	24 2	27 36	13 28	3 21	13 11	27 59	11 11
11 WE	17 47	17 17	11 53	15 8	24 25	28 14	13 37	3 29	13 15	27 57	11 10
12 TH	18 45	29 38	11 43	16 5	24 46	28 52	13 47	3 37	13 18	27 56	11 9
13 FR	19 42	12 ♍ 9	11 35	16 58	25 5	29 30	13 56	3 44	13 22	27 54	11 8
14 SA	20 40	24 54	11 30	17 48	25 22	0 ♌ 8	14 5	3 52	13 25	27 53	11 7
15 SU	21 37	7 ♎ 53	11 27	18 35	25 37	0 46	14 14	3 59	13 29	27 51	11 6
16 MO	22 35	21 11	11 27	19 18	25 50	1 24	14 23	4 7	13 32	27 49	11 4
17 TU	23 33	4 ♏ 49	11 27D	19 58	26 1	2 2	14 32	4 14	13 36	27 48	11 3
18 WE	24 30	18 50	11 27R	20 34	26 11	2 41	14 40	4 22	13 40	27 46	11 2
19 TH	25 28	3 ♐ 14	11 25	21 6	26 17	3 19	14 49	4 29	13 43	27 44	11 1
20 FR	26 26	17 58	11 21	21 33	26 22	3 57	14 57	4 37	13 47	27 43	11 0
21 SA	27 23	2 ♑ 57	11 15	21 56	26 25	4 35	15 6	4 44	13 50	27 41	11 0
22 SU	28 21	18 4	11 6	22 15	26 25R	5 13	15 14	4 51	13 54	27 40	10 59
23 MO	29 19	3 ♒ 9	10 55	22 28	26 22	5 51	15 22	4 59	13 58	27 38	10 58
24 TU	0 ♌ 16	18 1	10 45	22 36	26 18	6 30	15 30	5 6	14 1	27 36	10 57
25 WE	1 14	2 ♓ 33	10 35	22 39R	26 11	7 8	15 37	5 13	14 5	27 35	10 56
26 TH	2 12	16 38	10 26	22 36	26 2	7 46	15 45	5 21	14 9	27 33	10 55
27 FR	3 10	0 ♈ 13	10 21	22 27	25 50	8 24	15 52	5 28	14 13	27 31	10 54
28 SA	4 8	13 20	10 17	22 13	25 36	9 3	16 0	5 35	14 16	27 30	10 54
29 SU	5 6	26 2	10 16	21 52	25 19	9 41	16 7	5 42	14 20	27 28	10 53
30 MO	6 4	8 ♉ 23	10 16	21 26	25 1	10 19	16 14	5 49	14 24	27 26	10 52
31 TU	7 2	20 28	10 16	20 54	24 40	10 58	16 21	5 56	14 27	27 25	10 51

INGRESSES :

2	☽ → ♉	0:31	23	☉ → ♌	17:10
4	☽ → ♊	12:40	24	☽ → ♓	19:44
7	☽ → ♋	1:37	26	☽ → ♈	23:36
9	☽ → ♌	13:53	29	☽ → ♉	7:38
12	☽ → ♍	0:42	31	☽ → ♊	19:12
13	♂ → ♌	18:55			
14	☽ → ♎	9:29			
16	☽ → ♏	15:35			
18	☽ → ♐	18:39			
20	☽ → ♑	19:17			
22	☽ → ♒	18:57			

ASPECTS & ECLIPSES :

3	☽ ☌ ♃	0:58		☿ □ ♃	4:45	19	☽ ☌ ♇	12:44	29	☉ □ ☽	19: 3
	☽ ☌ ☊	2: 8		☽ ☌ ♂	8:17	21	☽ ☍ ♄	2:51		♂ □ ☊	21:50
4	♅ □ ☊	7:29		☽ ☍ ♆	9:55		☉ ☍ ♆	7:15	30	☽ ☌ ☊	3:42
5	☽ ☍ ♇	11:35	10	☽ N□ ☊	13:33		☽ ☌ P	13:10		☽ ☌ ♃	15:42
	♃ ☌ ☊	18:41		♂ ☍ ♆	14: 8	22	☽ ☌ ♆	15:12			
6	☽ ☌ A	10:10		☽ ☌ ♅	16: 2		☉ ☍ ☽	17:26			
7	☽ ☌ ♄	7:43		☽ ☌ ☿	19:25	23	☽ ☍ ♂	4:31			
	♃ □ ♅	9:51	11	☽ ☌ ♀	14:18		☽ □S ☊	12:19			
8	☿ □ ☊	7:40	16	☉ □ ☽	2:41		☽ ☍ ♅	17:28			
	☉ ☌ ☽	8:24	17	☽ ☌ ☋	11:25	24	☽ ☍ ☿	7:32			
9	☿ ☌ ♅	0:10		☽ ☍ ♃	16:51		☽ ☍ ♀	13:29			

SIDEREAL HELIOCENTRIC LONGITUDES : JULY 31 Julian at 0 hours UT

DAY	Sid. Time	☿	♀	⊕	♂	♃	♄	♅	♆	♇	Vernal Point
1 SU	18:25:40	18 ♎ 2	12 ♐ 29	8 ♑ 13	0 ♌ 12	2 ♉ 18	1 ♋ 32	14 ♌ 29	27 ♑ 33	12 ♐ 11	2♈37'14"
2 MO	18:29:37	20 57	14 4	9 11	0 39	2 23	1 34	14 30	27 34	12 12	2♈37'14"
3 TU	18:33:33	23 51	15 38	10 8	1 5	2 29	1 36	14 31	27 34	12 12	2♈37'14"
4 WE	18:37:30	26 43	17 13	11 6	1 31	2 34	1 39	14 32	27 34	12 13	2♈37'13"
5 TH	18:41:27	29 33	18 48	12 3	1 57	2 39	1 41	14 32	27 35	12 13	2♈37'13"
6 FR	18:45:23	2 ♏ 22	20 22	13 0	2 24	2 45	1 43	14 33	27 35	12 13	2♈37'13"
7 SA	18:49:20	5 9	21 57	13 58	2 50	2 50	1 45	14 34	27 35	12 14	2♈37'13"
8 SU	18:53:16	7 56	23 32	14 55	3 16	2 55	1 48	14 35	27 36	12 14	2♈37'13"
9 MO	18:57:13	10 42	25 6	15 53	3 43	3 0	1 50	14 35	27 36	12 14	2♈37'13"
10 TU	19: 1: 9	13 27	26 41	16 50	4 9	3 6	1 52	14 36	27 36	12 15	2♈37'13"
11 WE	19: 5: 6	16 11	28 16	17 48	4 35	3 11	1 54	14 37	27 37	12 15	2♈37'12"
12 TH	19: 9: 2	18 56	29 50	18 45	5 1	3 16	1 56	14 38	27 37	12 15	2♈37'12"
13 FR	19:12:59	21 41	1 ♑ 25	19 43	5 28	3 22	1 59	14 39	27 38	12 16	2♈37'12"
14 SA	19:16:56	24 25	3 0	20 40	5 54	3 27	2 1	14 39	27 38	12 16	2♈37'12"
15 SU	19:20:52	27 11	4 34	21 38	6 20	3 32	2 3	14 40	27 38	12 16	2♈37'12"
16 MO	19:24:49	29 57	6 9	22 35	6 47	3 38	2 5	14 41	27 39	12 17	2♈37'12"
17 TU	19:28:45	2 ♐ 44	7 43	23 33	7 13	3 43	2 8	14 42	27 39	12 17	2♈37'12"
18 WE	19:32:42	5 32	9 18	24 31	7 39	3 48	2 10	14 42	27 39	12 17	2♈37'12"
19 TH	19:36:38	8 21	10 53	25 28	8 6	3 54	2 12	14 43	27 40	12 18	2♈37'11"
20 FR	19:40:35	11 12	12 27	26 26	8 32	3 59	2 14	14 44	27 40	12 18	2♈37'11"
21 SA	19:44:31	14 4	14 2	27 24	8 58	4 4	2 17	14 45	27 40	12 18	2♈37'11"
22 SU	19:48:28	16 58	15 37	28 21	9 25	4 9	2 19	14 45	27 41	12 19	2♈37'11"
23 MO	19:52:25	19 55	17 11	29 19	9 51	4 15	2 21	14 46	27 41	12 19	2♈37'11"
24 TU	19:56:21	22 54	18 46	0 ♒ 17	10 17	4 20	2 23	14 47	27 41	12 19	2♈37'11"
25 WE	20: 0:18	25 56	20 21	1 15	10 44	4 25	2 25	14 48	27 42	12 20	2♈37'11"
26 TH	20: 4:14	29 1	21 55	2 13	11 10	4 31	2 28	14 49	27 42	12 20	2♈37'10"
27 FR	20: 8:11	2 ♑ 9	23 30	3 10	11 36	4 36	2 30	14 49	27 43	12 20	2♈37'10"
28 SA	20:12: 7	5 21	25 5	4 8	12 3	4 41	2 32	14 50	27 43	12 21	2♈37'10"
29 SU	20:16: 4	8 36	26 39	5 6	12 29	4 47	2 34	14 51	27 43	12 21	2♈37'10"
30 MO	20:20: 0	11 56	28 14	6 4	12 55	4 52	2 37	14 52	27 44	12 21	2♈37'10"
31 TU	20:23:57	15 20	29 49	7 2	13 22	4 57	2 39	14 52	27 44	12 22	2♈37'10"

INGRESSES :

5	☿ → ♏	3:47
12	♀ → ♑	2:27
16	☿ → ♐	0:28
23	⊕ → ♒	16:58
26	☿ → ♑	7:34
31	♀ → ♒	2:49

ASPECTS (HELIOCENTRIC +MOON(TYCHONIC)) :

1	☽ ☍ ☿	1:34		☽ ☍ ♀	7: 1		♀ ☍ ♄	8:46		☽ ☍ ♄	22:54		☽ □ ☿	4:34
	☽ □ ♆	19:44		♂ □ ♃	23:47	14	☽ □ ♄	13:15	21	⊕ ☌ ♆	6:59	28	⊕ □ ♃	15: 4
2	☽ □ ♂	1:51	7	☽ ☌ ♄	5:12		☽ □ ♀	17: 5		☽ ☌ ♀	19:38	29	☽ □ ♀	1:22
	☽ ☌ ♃	5:16	9	☽ ☍ ♆	9: 7	16	♂ N□ ☊	10:27	22	♀ ☌ A	9: 5		☽ □ ♆	3:14
3	☽ □ ♅	5:24		☽ □ ♃	20: 1		☽ □ ♆	11:27		☽ ☌ ♆	15:16		♀ ☌ ♆	16:15
4	☿ □ ♆	7:13		☽ ☌ ♂	22: 3		☽ ☍ ♃	22: 3	23	☽ □ ♃	1:45		☽ ☌ ♃	17: 3
	☿ ☌ ☋	8: 0	10	☿ □ ♅	10:10	17	☽ □ ♂	4:16		☽ ☍ ♂	11: 4	30	☽ □ ♂	9:18
5	☽ ☍ ♇	13:30		☽ □ ♅	18:45		☽ □ ♅	16:59		☽ ☍ ♅	18:43		☽ □ ♅	12:50
6	☿ □ ♂	0:18		☽ □ ☿	21:14	19	☽ ☌ ☿	10:23	25	☽ □ ♇	16:35			
	☿ ☍ ♃	3:19	12	☿ ☌ A	5:25		☽ ☌ ♇	14:49	27	☿ ☍ ♄	2:38			
	♂ ☌ A	5:12	13	☽ □ ♇	0:11	20	☿ ☌ ♇	9:16		☽ □ ♄	4: 7			

SIDEREAL GEOCENTRIC LONGITUDES : NOVEMBER 31 Julian at 0 hours UT

DAY	☉	☽	☊	☿	♀	♂	♃	♄	⛢	♆	♇
1 TH	9 ♏ 16	4 ♎ 53	5 ♉ 14	0 ♐ 3	22 ♍ 50	11 ♎ 56	14 ♉ 3R	11 ♋ 36R	19 ♌ 6	26 ♑ 27	11 ♐ 55
2 FR	10 17	18 33	5 14	1 15	23 55	12 36	13 55	11 35	19 7	26 28	11 57
3 SA	11 18	2 ♏ 36	5 15	2 25	24 59	13 17	13 47	11 34	19 8	26 29	11 59
4 SU	12 19	16 57	5 15R	3 31	26 5	13 58	13 39	11 33	19 9	26 30	12 1
5 MO	13 20	1 ♐ 32	5 14	4 33	27 10	14 38	13 31	11 32	19 11	26 31	12 3
6 TU	14 21	16 14	5 13	5 32	28 16	15 19	13 22	11 30	19 12	26 32	12 5
7 WE	15 22	0 ♑ 57	5 12	6 26	29 22	16 0	13 14	11 29	19 13	26 33	12 7
8 TH	16 23	15 33	5 11	7 15	0 ♎ 28	16 40	13 6	11 27	19 14	26 34	12 9
9 FR	17 25	29 58	5 10	7 58	1 34	17 21	12 58	11 25	19 14	26 35	12 11
10 SA	18 26	14 ♒ 8	5 9	8 34	2 41	18 2	12 50	11 23	19 15	26 36	12 13
11 SU	19 27	28 1	5 9D	9 3	3 48	18 43	12 42	11 21	19 16	26 37	12 15
12 MO	20 28	11 ♓ 37	5 10	9 23	4 55	19 24	12 34	11 19	19 17	26 38	12 17
13 TU	21 29	24 58	5 11	9 34	6 2	20 4	12 26	11 17	19 17	26 39	12 19
14 WE	22 30	8 ♈ 3	5 12	9 35R	7 10	20 45	12 18	11 14	19 18	26 40	12 21
15 TH	23 31	20 54	5 14	9 25	8 18	21 26	12 10	11 12	19 19	26 42	12 23
16 FR	24 32	3 ♉ 33	5 14	9 4	9 26	22 7	12 2	11 10	19 19	26 43	12 25
17 SA	25 33	16 0	5 14R	8 31	10 34	22 48	11 54	11 7	19 20	26 44	12 27
18 SU	26 35	28 18	5 12	7 47	11 42	23 29	11 47	11 4	19 20	26 46	12 29
19 MO	27 36	10 ♊ 27	5 9	6 52	12 51	24 10	11 39	11 1	19 20	26 47	12 31
20 TU	28 37	22 28	5 5	5 47	14 0	24 51	11 31	10 58	19 20	26 48	12 33
21 WE	29 38	4 ♋ 23	5 1	4 34	15 9	25 32	11 24	10 55	19 21	26 50	12 35
22 TH	0 ♐ 39	16 15	4 56	3 15	16 18	26 14	11 17	10 52	19 21	26 51	12 37
23 FR	1 40	28 6	4 52	1 53	17 27	26 55	11 9	10 49	19 21	26 53	12 39
24 SA	2 42	10 ♌ 0	4 49	0 31	18 37	27 36	11 2	10 46	19 21	26 54	12 41
25 SU	3 43	22 0	4 47	29 ♏ 11	19 46	28 17	10 55	10 43	19 21R	26 56	12 44
26 MO	4 44	4 ♍ 11	4 46	27 55	20 56	28 58	10 48	10 39	19 21	26 57	12 46
27 TU	5 45	16 39	4 47D	26 47	22 6	29 40	10 42	10 36	19 21	26 59	12 48
28 WE	6 47	29 26	4 48	25 47	23 16	0 ♏ 21	10 35	10 32	19 21	27 0	12 50
29 TH	7 48	12 ♎ 38	4 50	24 57	24 26	1 2	10 29	10 28	19 20	27 2	12 52
30 FR	8 49	26 17	4 51	24 17	25 37	1 44	10 22	10 25	19 20	27 4	12 54

INGRESSES :

2 ☽ → ♏ 19:36	23 ☽ → ♌ 3:50
4 ☽ → ♐ 21:29	24 ☿ → ♏ 9: 4
6 ☽ → ♑ 22:27	25 ☽ → ♍ 15:47
7 ♀ → ♎ 13:56	27 ♂ → ♏ 11:49
9 ☽ → ♒ 0: 4	28 ☽ → ♎ 1: 2
11 ☽ → ♓ 3:28	30 ☽ → ♏ 6:24
13 ☽ → ♈ 9:11	
15 ☽ → ♉ 17:14	
18 ☽ → ♊ 3:20	
20 ☽ → ♋ 15: 9	
21 ☉ → ♐ 8:36	

ASPECTS & ECLIPSES :

1 ☽ ☌ ♂ 13: 5	9 ☽ (S) ☊ 8:44	19 ☽ ☍ ♇ 4: 7	☽ ☌ ☋ 14:40
3 ☽ ☌ ☋ 4:27	10 ☉ □ ☽ 7:57	21 ☽ ☌ ♄ 13: 9	☽ ☍ ♃ 23:47
☉ ● T 15:33	☽ ☍ ⛢ 8:48	☽ ☌ A 23:45	
☉ ☌ ☽ 15:43	☉ □ ⛢ 19:46	22 ☽ ☍ ♆ 21:31	
☽ ☍ ♃ 18:34	13 ☽ ☍ ♀ 22:13	♂ □ ♆ 22:41	
5 ☉ ☍ ♃ 3:35	15 ☽ ☍ ♂ 1: 4	23 ☉ ☌ ☿ 2: 8	
☽ ☌ ☿ 5:18	16 ☽ ☌ ☊ 3:13	☽ (N) ☊ 13:36	
☽ ☌ ♇ 17:12	☽ ☌ ♃ 16: 8	24 ☽ ☌ ⛢ 18:43	
☽ ☌ P 23:18	17 ♀ □ ♄ 11: 6	26 ☉ □ ☽ 1: 9	
7 ☽ ☍ ♄ 17:15	☉ ☍ ☽ 20:18	29 ☽ ☌ ♀ 22:44	
8 ☽ ☌ ♆ 18:19	18 ☽ ☍ ☿ 17:25	30 ☽ ☌ ♂ 9:50	

SIDEREAL HELIOCENTRIC LONGITUDES : NOVEMBER 31 Julian at 0 hours UT

DAY	Sid. Time	☿	♀	⊕	♂	♃	♄	⛢	♆	♇	Vernal Point
1 TH	2:30:37	3 ♒ 46	28 ♊ 45	9 ♉ 17	25 ♍ 30	13 ♉ 8	6 ♋ 5	16 ♌ 4	28 ♑ 17	12 ♐ 53	2♈36'57"
2 FR	2:34:33	7 45	0 ♋ 23	10 18	25 58	13 13	6 8	16 5	28 18	12 53	2♈36'57"
3 SA	2:38:30	11 50	2 0	11 19	26 27	13 18	6 10	16 6	28 18	12 53	2♈36'57"
4 SU	2:42:26	16 3	3 38	12 20	26 55	13 23	6 12	16 6	28 18	12 54	2♈36'57"
5 MO	2:46:23	20 24	5 15	13 21	27 24	13 29	6 14	16 7	28 19	12 54	2♈36'57"
6 TU	2:50:19	24 53	6 53	14 22	27 52	13 34	6 16	16 8	28 19	12 54	2♈36'56"
7 WE	2:54:16	29 30	8 30	15 23	28 21	13 39	6 19	16 9	28 20	12 55	2♈36'56"
8 TH	2:58:12	4 ♓ 15	10 8	16 24	28 50	13 44	6 21	16 9	28 20	12 55	2♈36'56"
9 FR	3: 2: 9	9 10	11 46	17 25	29 18	13 50	6 23	16 10	28 20	12 55	2♈36'56"
10 SA	3: 6: 6	14 14	13 23	18 26	29 47	13 55	6 25	16 11	28 21	12 56	2♈36'56"
11 SU	3:10: 2	19 27	15 1	19 27	0 ♎ 16	14 0	6 27	16 12	28 21	12 56	2♈36'56"
12 MO	3:13:59	24 49	16 38	20 28	0 45	14 5	6 30	16 12	28 21	12 56	2♈36'56"
13 TU	3:17:55	0 ♈ 19	18 16	21 29	1 14	14 11	6 32	16 13	28 22	12 57	2♈36'55"
14 WE	3:21:52	5 59	19 54	22 30	1 43	14 16	6 34	16 14	28 22	12 57	2♈36'55"
15 TH	3:25:48	11 46	21 31	23 32	2 11	14 21	6 36	16 15	28 22	12 57	2♈36'55"
16 FR	3:29:45	17 41	23 9	24 33	2 40	14 26	6 39	16 16	28 23	12 58	2♈36'55"
17 SA	3:33:41	23 43	24 47	25 34	3 9	14 31	6 41	16 16	28 23	12 58	2♈36'55"
18 SU	3:37:38	29 51	26 24	26 35	3 39	14 37	6 43	16 17	28 23	12 58	2♈36'55"
19 MO	3:41:35	6 ♉ 3	28 2	27 36	4 8	14 42	6 45	16 18	28 24	12 59	2♈36'55"
20 TU	3:45:31	12 19	29 40	28 37	4 37	14 47	6 47	16 19	28 24	12 59	2♈36'54"
21 WE	3:49:28	18 37	1 ♌ 17	29 39	5 6	14 52	6 50	16 19	28 25	12 59	2♈36'54"
22 TH	3:53:24	24 55	2 55	0 ♊ 40	5 35	14 58	6 52	16 20	28 25	13 0	2♈36'54"
23 FR	3:57:21	1 ♊ 13	4 33	1 41	6 5	15 3	6 54	16 21	28 25	13 0	2♈36'54"
24 SA	4: 1:17	7 28	6 10	2 42	6 34	15 8	6 56	16 22	28 26	13 0	2♈36'54"
25 SU	4: 5:14	13 39	7 48	3 43	7 3	15 13	6 58	16 22	28 26	13 1	2♈36'54"
26 MO	4: 9:10	19 46	9 25	4 45	7 33	15 19	7 1	16 23	28 26	13 1	2♈36'54"
27 TU	4:13: 7	25 46	11 3	5 46	8 2	15 24	7 3	16 24	28 27	13 1	2♈36'54"
28 WE	4:17: 4	1 ♋ 39	12 41	6 47	8 32	15 29	7 5	16 25	28 27	13 2	2♈36'53"
29 TH	4:21: 0	7 24	14 18	7 48	9 1	15 34	7 7	16 26	28 27	13 2	2♈36'53"
30 FR	4:24:57	13 0	15 56	8 50	9 31	15 40	7 10	16 26	28 28	13 2	2♈36'53"

INGRESSES :

1 ♀ → ♋ 18:23
7 ☿ → ♓ 2:34
10 ♂ → ♎ 10:43
12 ☿ → ♈ 22:37
18 ☿ → ♉ 0:35
20 ♀ → ♌ 5: 1
21 ⊕ → ♊ 8:24
22 ☿ → ♊ 19:21
27 ☿ → ♋ 17:13

ASPECTS (HELIOCENTRIC +MOON(TYCHONIC)) :

1 ☽ □ ♄ 2: 8	6 ☽ □ ♂ 19:37	☽ ☍ ♂ 11:52	19 ☽ ☍ ♇ 5: 2	☽ ☌ ⛢ 12:46	♀ ☌ ⛢ 7:33
2 ☽ □ ♆ 16:43	7 ☽ ☍ ♄ 8:48	☽ ☌ ☿ 17:12	♀ ☍ ♆ 5:24	♂ □ ♄ 19:51	
☿ □ ⊕ 19:58	☽ ☍ ♀ 13:57	☽ □ ♄ 21:15	20 ☿ ☌ ♃ 9:33	☿ ☍ ♇ 21:28	
3 ☿ □ ♃ 8:35	⊕ □ ⛢ 18:11	14 ☿ □ ♄ 2:29	☿ □ ⛢ 15:15	26 ☽ □ ♇ 17: 4	
☽ ☍ ♃ 18: 3	8 ☽ ☌ ♆ 21:16	15 ☽ □ ♀ 1:20	21 ☽ □ ♂ 1:30	28 ☽ □ ☿ 7:19	
☽ □ ☿ 21:53	9 ☿ □ ♇ 17:52	☽ □ ♆ 14: 8	☿ ☌ P 3:34	☽ □ ♄ 14: 2	
☽ □ ⛢ 22:35	☽ □ ♃ 23:38	16 ☽ ☌ ♃ 21: 6	☽ ☌ ♄ 4:56	☽ ☌ ♂ 17:15	
4 ☿ ☍ ⛢ 0:17	10 ☽ ☍ ⛢ 3:31	17 ☽ □ ⛢ 0:30	23 ☽ ☍ ♆ 0:38	☿ ☌ ♄ 22:49	
5 ⊕ ☌ ♃ 3:20	11 ♀ ☌ P 17:37	☿ □ ♀ 5:40	☿ ☌ ⊕ 2: 8	29 ☿ □ ♂ 7:31	
♀ ☌ ♄ 14:49	12 ☽ □ ♇ 2:20	☿ ☌ ☊ 15:29	☽ ☌ ♀ 15: 4	♀ □ ♃ 19:45	
☽ ☌ ♇ 18:34	13 ☿ ☍ ♂ 4:14	☿ □ ♆ 18:19	24 ☽ □ ♃ 10:23	30 ☽ □ ♆ 3:45	

SIDEREAL GEOCENTRIC LONGITUDES : MAY 32 Julian at 0 hours UT

DAY	☉	☽	☊	☿	♀	♂	♃	♄	⛢	♆	♇
1 TH	10 ♉ 46	12 ♊ 43	25 ♈ 50R	24 ♈ 12	2 ♉ 4	20 ♒ 44	25 ♉ 54	7 ♋ 26	15 ♌ 14	1 ♒ 17	14 ♐ 54R
2 FR	11 44	25 3	25 48	26 3	3 18	21 26	26 8	7 32	15 15	1 17	14 53
3 SA	12 41	7 ♋ 10	25 45	27 56	4 31	22 8	26 21	7 37	15 15	1 17R	14 52
4 SU	13 39	19 9	25 43	29 51	5 45	22 50	26 35	7 43	15 16	1 17	14 50
5 MO	14 36	1 ♌ 4	25 42	1 ♉ 49	6 58	23 32	26 48	7 48	15 17	1 17	14 49
6 TU	15 33	12 57	25 41	3 49	8 12	24 14	27 2	7 54	15 17	1 17	14 48
7 WE	16 31	24 54	25 41D	5 50	9 26	24 55	27 15	8 0	15 18	1 17	14 47
8 TH	17 28	6 ♍ 59	25 42	7 54	10 39	25 37	27 29	8 5	15 19	1 17	14 45
9 FR	18 25	19 18	25 43	9 59	11 53	26 18	27 43	8 11	15 20	1 17	14 44
10 SA	19 22	1 ♎ 53	25 45	12 6	13 6	27 0	27 56	8 17	15 21	1 16	14 43
11 SU	20 20	14 49	25 46	14 14	14 20	27 41	28 10	8 23	15 22	1 16	14 41
12 MO	21 17	28 7	25 46R	16 24	15 33	28 22	28 24	8 29	15 23	1 16	14 40
13 TU	22 14	11 ♏ 47	25 46	18 34	16 47	29 3	28 37	8 35	15 24	1 16	14 39
14 WE	23 11	25 48	25 44	20 45	18 0	29 44	28 51	8 41	15 25	1 15	14 37
15 TH	24 8	10 ♐ 6	25 41	22 57	19 14	0 ♓ 25	29 5	8 48	15 26	1 15	14 36
16 FR	25 6	24 36	25 37	25 8	20 28	1 6	29 19	8 54	15 28	1 14	14 34
17 SA	26 3	9 ♑ 11	25 33	27 20	21 41	1 47	29 32	9 0	15 29	1 14	14 33
18 SU	27 0	23 45	25 29	29 31	22 55	2 28	29 46	9 7	15 30	1 14	14 32
19 MO	27 57	8 ♒ 13	25 26	1 ♊ 42	24 8	3 8	0 ♊ 0	9 13	15 32	1 13	14 30
20 TU	28 54	22 31	25 25	3 51	25 22	3 49	0 13	9 19	15 33	1 13	14 29
21 WE	29 52	6 ♓ 35	25 25D	6 0	26 36	4 29	0 27	9 26	15 35	1 12	14 27
22 TH	0 ♊ 49	20 25	25 26	8 8	27 49	5 10	0 41	9 33	15 36	1 11	14 26
23 FR	1 46	4 ♈ 1	25 27	10 13	29 3	5 50	0 55	9 39	15 38	1 11	14 24
24 SA	2 43	17 23	25 29	12 18	0 ♊ 16	6 30	1 8	9 46	15 39	1 10	14 23
25 SU	3 40	0 ♉ 32	25 29R	14 20	1 30	7 10	1 22	9 53	15 41	1 9	14 21
26 MO	4 37	13 28	25 27	16 21	2 44	7 50	1 36	9 59	15 43	1 9	14 20
27 TU	5 34	26 12	25 24	18 20	3 57	8 29	1 50	10 6	15 45	1 8	14 18
28 WE	6 32	8 ♊ 45	25 19	20 17	5 11	9 9	2 3	10 13	15 46	1 7	14 17
29 TH	7 29	21 7	25 12	22 12	6 25	9 48	2 17	10 20	15 48	1 7	14 15
30 FR	8 26	3 ♋ 19	25 4	24 4	7 38	10 27	2 31	10 27	15 50	1 6	14 14
31 SA	9 23	15 23	24 56	25 55	8 52	11 7	2 44	10 34	15 52	1 5	14 12

INGRESSES :

2 ☽ → ♋ 9:45
4 ☿ → ♉ 1:46
☽ → ♌ 21:51
7 ☽ → ♍ 10:10
9 ☽ → ♎ 20:26
12 ☽ → ♏ 3:20
14 ☽ → ♐ 7: 5
♂ → ♓ 9: 4
16 ☽ → ♑ 8:54
18 ☿ → ♊ 5:17
☽ → ♒ 10:19
19 ♃ → ♊ 0:28
20 ☽ → ♓ 12:43
21 ☉ → ♊ 3:33
22 ☽ → ♈ 16:52
23 ♀ → ♊ 18:38
24 ☽ → ♉ 23: 1
27 ☽ → ♊ 7:12
29 ☽ → ♋ 17:25

ASPECTS & ECLIPSES :

1 ☽ ☍ ♇ 4:12
☿ ☌ ☊ 20:50
3 ☽ ☌ ♄ 0:53
4 ☽ N ☊ 13:11
☿ □ ♆ 17:32
☽ ☌ A 23:25
5 ☽ ☍ ♆ 0:27
☉ □ ⛢ 17:18
6 ☽ ☌ ⛢ 4:43
☉ □ ☽ 5:42
7 ☽ ☍ ♂ 0: 2
11 ☿ ☌ ♀ 2:27
☿ □ ⛢ 12:41
☽ ☌ ☋ 19:49
♀ □ ⛢ 20:33
12 ♂ □ ♃ 1:18
13 ☽ ☍ ♀ 9:26
☽ ☍ ☿ 13:49
☉ ☍ ☽ 19:14
14 ☽ ☍ ♃ 5:14
15 ☽ ☌ ♇ 7:27
☉ ☌S ☿ 23:10
16 ☽ ☌ P 22: 8
☽ ☍ ♄ 23:42
18 ☽ S ☊ 2:50
☿ ☌ ♃ 3: 3
☽ ☌ ♆ 12:21
19 ☽ ☍ ⛢ 12:14
☿ □ ♂ 23:19
20 ☉ □ ☽ 11:38
☽ ☌ ♂ 20:13
21 ☉ ☌ ♃ 19:42
24 ☽ ☌ ☊ 14:44
♀ ☌ ♃ 20:47
25 ☿ ☍ ♇ 0:10
27 ☽ ☌ ♃ 10:53
☽ ☌ ♀ 16:23
☉ ☌ ☽ 19:21
28 ☽ ☍ ♇ 10:39
29 ☽ ☌ ☿ 2:28
30 ☽ ☌ ♄ 14:17
31 ☽ N ☊ 19: 0

SIDEREAL HELIOCENTRIC LONGITUDES : MAY 32 Julian at 0 hours UT

DAY	Sid. Time	☿	♀	⊕	♂	♃	♄	⛢	♆	♇	Vernal Point
1 TH	14:28:10	29 ♒ 47	19 ♈ 49	10 ♏ 47	5 ♑ 2	28 ♉ 52	12 ♋ 47	18 ♌ 24	29 ♑ 23	13 ♐ 53	2♈36'32"
2 FR	14:32: 6	4 ♓ 33	21 25	11 44	5 40	28 57	12 49	18 25	29 23	13 53	2♈36'32"
3 SA	14:36: 3	9 28	23 1	12 42	6 17	29 2	12 51	18 26	29 23	13 54	2♈36'32"
4 SU	14:39:59	14 32	24 37	13 39	6 54	29 8	12 53	18 27	29 24	13 54	2♈36'32"
5 MO	14:43:56	19 45	26 14	14 36	7 32	29 13	12 56	18 27	29 24	13 54	2♈36'32"
6 TU	14:47:52	25 8	27 50	15 34	8 9	29 18	12 58	18 28	29 24	13 55	2♈36'32"
7 WE	14:51:49	0 ♈ 39	29 26	16 31	8 46	29 23	13 0	18 29	29 25	13 55	2♈36'31"
8 TH	14:55:46	6 19	1 ♉ 3	17 28	9 24	29 28	13 2	18 30	29 25	13 55	2♈36'31"
9 FR	14:59:42	12 7	2 39	18 26	10 1	29 33	13 4	18 30	29 26	13 56	2♈36'31"
10 SA	15: 3:39	18 2	4 16	19 23	10 39	29 38	13 7	18 31	29 26	13 56	2♈36'31"
11 SU	15: 7:35	24 5	5 52	20 20	11 16	29 43	13 9	18 32	29 26	13 56	2♈36'31"
12 MO	15:11:32	0 ♉ 12	7 29	21 17	11 54	29 49	13 11	18 33	29 27	13 57	2♈36'31"
13 TU	15:15:28	6 25	9 5	22 15	12 31	29 54	13 13	18 34	29 27	13 57	2♈36'31"
14 WE	15:19:25	12 41	10 42	23 12	13 9	29 59	13 15	18 34	29 27	13 57	2♈36'30"
15 TH	15:23:21	18 59	12 19	24 9	13 47	0 ♊ 4	13 18	18 35	29 28	13 58	2♈36'30"
16 FR	15:27:18	25 17	13 55	25 6	14 24	0 9	13 20	18 36	29 28	13 58	2♈36'30"
17 SA	15:31:15	1 ♊ 35	15 32	26 3	15 2	0 14	13 22	18 37	29 28	13 58	2♈36'30"
18 SU	15:35:11	7 50	17 9	27 0	15 40	0 19	13 24	18 37	29 29	13 59	2♈36'30"
19 MO	15:39: 8	14 1	18 45	27 58	16 17	0 24	13 26	18 38	29 29	13 59	2♈36'30"
20 TU	15:43: 4	20 7	20 22	28 55	16 55	0 30	13 29	18 39	29 29	13 59	2♈36'30"
21 WE	15:47: 1	26 7	21 59	29 52	17 33	0 35	13 31	18 40	29 30	14 0	2♈36'30"
22 TH	15:50:57	1 ♋ 59	23 36	0 ♐ 49	18 11	0 40	13 33	18 40	29 30	14 0	2♈36'29"
23 FR	15:54:54	7 44	25 13	1 46	18 48	0 45	13 35	18 41	29 31	14 0	2♈36'29"
24 SA	15:58:50	13 20	26 50	2 43	19 26	0 50	13 37	18 42	29 31	14 1	2♈36'29"
25 SU	16: 2:47	18 46	28 27	3 41	20 4	0 55	13 39	18 43	29 31	14 1	2♈36'29"
26 MO	16: 6:44	24 4	0 ♊ 4	4 38	20 42	1 0	13 42	18 44	29 32	14 1	2♈36'29"
27 TU	16:10:40	29 11	1 41	5 35	21 20	1 5	13 44	18 44	29 32	14 2	2♈36'29"
28 WE	16:14:37	4 ♌ 9	3 18	6 32	21 57	1 11	13 46	18 45	29 32	14 2	2♈36'29"
29 TH	16:18:33	8 58	4 55	7 29	22 35	1 16	13 48	18 46	29 33	14 2	2♈36'28"
30 FR	16:22:30	13 38	6 32	8 26	23 13	1 21	13 50	18 47	29 33	14 3	2♈36'28"
31 SA	16:26:26	18 9	8 9	9 23	23 51	1 26	13 53	18 47	29 33	14 3	2♈36'28"

INGRESSES :

1 ☿ → ♓ 1: 8
6 ☿ → ♈ 21:12
7 ♀ → ♉ 8:22
11 ☿ → ♉ 23:11
14 ♃ → ♊ 5:20
16 ☿ → ♊ 17:58
21 ⊕ → ♐ 3:22
☿ → ♋ 15:48
25 ♀ → ♊ 23: 5
27 ☿ → ♌ 3:52

ASPECTS (HELIOCENTRIC +MOON(TYCHONIC)) :

1 ☽ ☍ ♇ 2:14
2 ☽ ☍ ♂ 22: 7
3 ☽ ☌ ♄ 11:22
☿ □ ♇ 21: 1
4 ☽ □ ♀ 12:43
☽ ☍ ♆ 20:39
6 ☽ ☌ ⛢ 11: 7
♀ □ ♆ 23:36
7 ☽ □ ♃ 9: 0
8 ☽ □ ♇ 13:35
☿ □ ♂ 14:22
9 ⊕ □ ⛢ 2: 3
☿ □ ♄ 3:56
10 ☽ □ ♂ 17: 9
☽ □ ♄ 20:55
11 ☿ ☌ ☊ 14: 5
☿ □ ♆ 21: 1
12 ☽ □ ♆ 2:21
☽ ☍ ☿ 6:49
☽ ☍ ♀ 18:41
13 ☽ □ ⛢ 11:40
☿ ☌ ♀ 13:48
14 ♂ ☍ ♄ 4:15
☽ ☍ ♃ 7: 6
☿ □ ⛢ 22:29
15 ☿ ☌ P 2:11
☽ ☌ ♇ 6:25
☿ ☍ ⊕ 23:10
16 ☿ ☌ ♃ 18:48
17 ☽ ☍ ♄ 6:54
☽ ☌ ♂ 10: 3
18 ☽ ☌ ♆ 9:28
♀ □ ⛢ 22:10
☿ ☍ ♇ 23:52
19 ☽ ☍ ⛢ 17:28
☽ □ ♀ 19:55
20 ☽ □ ♃ 13:38
21 ☽ □ ♇ 12:48
⊕ ☍ ♃ 19:42
23 ☽ □ ☿ 11:26
☽ □ ♄ 17:11
24 ☿ ☌ ♄ 1:17
☽ □ ♂ 3:54
☽ □ ♆ 22: 8
25 ☿ ☍ ♂ 6:34
26 ☽ □ ⛢ 9:52
♀ ☌ ♃ 14:47
☿ N ☊ 16:47
27 ♀ ☌ ☊ 0:33
☿ ☍ ♆ 1:38
☽ ☌ ♃ 9:21
☽ ☌ ♀ 11:57
28 ☽ ☍ ♇ 10:12
30 ☽ ☌ ♄ 20:59
31 ☿ ☌ ⛢ 3:31
☽ ☍ ♂ 17:58

SIDEREAL GEOCENTRIC LONGITUDES : JUNE 32 Julian at 0 hours UT

DAY	☉	☽	☊	☿	♀	♂	♃	♄	♅	♆	♇
1 SU	10 ♊ 20	27 ♋ 19	24 ♈ 49R	27 ♊ 44	10 ♊ 6	11 ♓ 46	2 ♊ 58	10 ♋ 41	15 ♌ 54	1 ♒ 4R	14 ♐ 11R
2 MO	11 17	9 ♌ 11	24 43	29 30	11 20	12 24	3 12	10 48	15 56	1 3	14 9
3 TU	12 14	21 3	24 39	1 ♋ 14	12 33	13 3	3 25	10 55	15 58	1 2	14 8
4 WE	13 12	2 ♍ 58	24 36	2 57	13 47	13 42	3 39	11 2	16 0	1 1	14 6
5 TH	14 9	15 1	24 35	4 37	15 1	14 20	3 52	11 9	16 3	1 0	14 5
6 FR	15 6	27 18	24 36D	6 14	16 15	14 58	4 6	11 16	16 5	0 59	14 3
7 SA	16 3	9 ♎ 52	24 37	7 50	17 28	15 36	4 20	11 23	16 7	0 58	14 2
8 SU	17 0	22 48	24 37	9 24	18 42	16 14	4 33	11 31	16 9	0 57	14 0
9 MO	17 57	6 ♏ 10	24 37R	10 55	19 56	16 52	4 47	11 38	16 12	0 56	13 59
10 TU	18 54	20 0	24 34	12 24	21 10	17 29	5 0	11 45	16 14	0 55	13 57
11 WE	19 51	4 ♐ 15	24 30	13 51	22 23	18 6	5 14	11 53	16 17	0 54	13 56
12 TH	20 48	18 53	24 23	15 16	23 37	18 44	5 27	12 0	16 19	0 53	13 54
13 FR	21 46	3 ♑ 46	24 15	16 39	24 51	19 21	5 40	12 7	16 22	0 52	13 53
14 SA	22 43	18 47	24 7	17 59	26 5	19 57	5 54	12 15	16 24	0 50	13 51
15 SU	23 40	3 ♒ 45	23 59	19 17	27 18	20 34	6 7	12 22	16 27	0 49	13 50
16 MO	24 37	18 32	23 52	20 33	28 32	21 10	6 21	12 30	16 29	0 48	13 48
17 TU	25 34	3 ♓ 1	23 48	21 46	29 46	21 47	6 34	12 37	16 32	0 47	13 47
18 WE	26 31	17 10	23 46	22 56	1 ♋ 0	22 23	6 47	12 45	16 35	0 45	13 45
19 TH	27 28	0 ♈ 57	23 46D	24 4	2 14	22 58	7 0	12 52	16 37	0 44	13 44
20 FR	28 26	14 24	23 46	25 9	3 28	23 34	7 14	13 0	16 40	0 43	13 42
21 SA	29 23	27 31	23 47R	26 12	4 42	24 9	7 27	13 7	16 43	0 42	13 41
22 SU	0 ♋ 20	10 ♉ 23	23 46	27 12	5 55	24 44	7 40	13 15	16 46	0 40	13 39
23 MO	1 17	23 2	23 42	28 8	7 9	25 19	7 53	13 22	16 49	0 39	13 38
24 TU	2 15	5 ♊ 29	23 36	29 2	8 23	25 54	8 6	13 30	16 52	0 37	13 36
25 WE	3 12	17 47	23 27	29 53	9 37	26 28	8 19	13 38	16 55	0 36	13 35
26 TH	4 9	29 57	23 16	0 ♌ 40	10 51	27 2	8 32	13 45	16 58	0 35	13 34
27 FR	5 6	12 ♋ 1	23 3	1 23	12 5	27 36	8 45	13 53	17 1	0 33	13 32
28 SA	6 4	23 58	22 50	2 3	13 19	28 9	8 58	14 1	17 4	0 32	13 31
29 SU	7 1	5 ♌ 51	22 38	2 39	14 33	28 43	9 11	14 8	17 7	0 30	13 29
30 MO	7 58	17 42	22 28	3 11	15 47	29 16	9 24	14 16	17 10	0 29	13 28

INGRESSES :

1 ☽ → ♌ 5:25	21 ☽ → ♉ 4:35
2 ☿ → ♋ 6:50	☉ → ♋ 15:35
3 ☽ → ♍ 18: 2	23 ☽ → ♊ 13:23
6 ☽ → ♎ 5:12	25 ☿ → ♌ 3:42
8 ☽ → ♏ 13: 0	26 ☽ → ♋ 0: 5
10 ☽ → ♐ 16:54	28 ☽ → ♌ 12: 9
12 ☽ → ♑ 17:56	
14 ☽ → ♒ 17:58	
16 ☽ → ♓ 18:57	
17 ♀ → ♋ 4:31	
18 ☽ → ♈ 22:19	

ASPECTS & ECLIPSES :

1 ☽ ☍ ♆ 7:33	8 ☽ ☌ ☋ 3:18	15 ☽ ☍ ♅ 20:39	☽ N ☊ 21:46
☽ ☌ A 16:43	9 ☿ ☌ ♄ 12:26	18 ☽ ☌ ♂ 9:23	28 ☽ ☍ ♆ 13:12
☉ ☌S ♀ 20:37	11 ☽ ☍ ♃ 1:38	☉ □ ☽ 17:25	♀ ☌ ♄ 15: 6
2 ☽ ☌ ♅ 13:41	☽ ☌ ♇ 15:54	☿ □ ☊ 17:25	☽ ☌ ☿ 17:11
3 ♀ □ ♂ 20:15	12 ☉ ☍ ☽ 3:20	20 ☽ ☌ ☊ 17: 6	29 ☽ ☌ A 6:16
4 ♀ ☍ ♇ 6: 6	☽ ☍ ♀ 8:21	24 ☽ ☌ ♃ 5:10	☽ ☌ ♅ 22:54
♂ □ ♇ 14:50	13 ☽ ☍ ♄ 13:28	☽ ☍ ♇ 15:46	
☉ □ ☽ 22: 6	☽ ☌ P 18:33	25 ☿ ☍ ♆ 21:28	
☉ ☍ ♇ 22:23	☽ ☍ ☿ 22:36	26 ☉ ☌ ☽ 9: 2	
☽ ☍ ♂ 22:33	14 ☽ S ☊ 8:26	27 ☽ ☌ ♀ 0: 9	
5 ☉ □ ♂ 14:17	☽ ☌ ♆ 19:18	☽ ☌ ♄ 3:47	

SIDEREAL HELIOCENTRIC LONGITUDES : JUNE 32 Julian at 0 hours UT

DAY	Sid. Time	☿	♀	⊕	♂	♃	♄	♅	♆	♇	Vernal Point
1 SU	16:30:23	22 ♌ 31	9 ♊ 46	10 ♐ 21	24 ♑ 29	1 ♊ 31	13 ♋ 55	18 ♌ 48	29 ♑ 34	14 ♐ 3	2♈36'28"
2 MO	16:34:19	26 45	11 23	11 18	25 7	1 36	13 57	18 49	29 34	14 4	2♈36'28"
3 TU	16:38:16	0 ♍ 51	13 1	12 15	25 45	1 41	13 59	18 50	29 34	14 4	2♈36'28"
4 WE	16:42:13	4 49	14 38	13 12	26 23	1 46	14 1	18 50	29 35	14 4	2♈36'28"
5 TH	16:46: 9	8 41	16 15	14 9	27 1	1 51	14 4	18 51	29 35	14 5	2♈36'27"
6 FR	16:50: 6	12 27	17 52	15 6	27 39	1 57	14 6	18 52	29 36	14 5	2♈36'27"
7 SA	16:54: 2	16 6	19 30	16 3	28 17	2 2	14 8	18 53	29 36	14 5	2♈36'27"
8 SU	16:57:59	19 39	21 7	17 0	28 54	2 7	14 10	18 54	29 36	14 6	2♈36'27"
9 MO	17: 1:55	23 7	22 44	17 58	29 32	2 12	14 12	18 54	29 37	14 6	2♈36'27"
10 TU	17: 5:52	26 30	24 22	18 55	0 ♒ 10	2 17	14 15	18 55	29 37	14 6	2♈36'27"
11 WE	17: 9:48	29 49	25 59	19 52	0 48	2 22	14 17	18 56	29 37	14 7	2♈36'27"
12 TH	17:13:45	3 ♎ 3	27 37	20 49	1 26	2 27	14 19	18 57	29 38	14 7	2♈36'27"
13 FR	17:17:42	6 14	29 14	21 46	2 4	2 32	14 21	18 57	29 38	14 7	2♈36'27"
14 SA	17:21:38	9 21	0 ♋ 52	22 43	2 42	2 37	14 23	18 58	29 38	14 8	2♈36'26"
15 SU	17:25:35	12 25	2 29	23 40	3 20	2 42	14 26	18 59	29 39	14 8	2♈36'26"
16 MO	17:29:31	15 25	4 7	24 37	3 58	2 48	14 28	19 0	29 39	14 8	2♈36'26"
17 TU	17:33:28	18 23	5 44	25 35	4 36	2 53	14 30	19 1	29 39	14 9	2♈36'26"
18 WE	17:37:24	21 19	7 22	26 32	5 14	2 58	14 32	19 1	29 40	14 9	2♈36'26"
19 TH	17:41:21	24 13	8 59	27 29	5 52	3 3	14 34	19 2	29 40	14 9	2♈36'26"
20 FR	17:45:17	27 4	10 37	28 26	6 30	3 8	14 36	19 3	29 41	14 10	2♈36'25"
21 SA	17:49:14	29 54	12 14	29 23	7 8	3 13	14 39	19 4	29 41	14 10	2♈36'25"
22 SU	17:53:11	2 ♏ 43	13 52	0 ♑ 20	7 46	3 18	14 41	19 4	29 41	14 10	2♈36'25"
23 MO	17:57: 7	5 30	15 30	1 18	8 24	3 23	14 43	19 5	29 42	14 11	2♈36'25"
24 TU	18: 1: 4	8 16	17 7	2 15	9 2	3 28	14 45	19 6	29 42	14 11	2♈36'25"
25 WE	18: 5: 0	11 2	18 45	3 12	9 40	3 33	14 47	19 7	29 42	14 11	2♈36'25"
26 TH	18: 8:57	13 47	20 22	4 10	10 17	3 39	14 50	19 7	29 43	14 12	2♈36'25"
27 FR	18:12:53	16 32	22 0	5 7	10 55	3 44	14 52	19 8	29 43	14 12	2♈36'24"
28 SA	18:16:50	19 16	23 38	6 4	11 33	3 49	14 54	19 9	29 43	14 12	2♈36'24"
29 SU	18:20:46	22 1	25 15	7 1	12 11	3 54	14 56	19 10	29 44	14 13	2♈36'24"
30 MO	18:24:43	24 46	26 53	7 59	12 49	3 59	14 58	19 11	29 44	14 13	2♈36'24"

INGRESSES :

2 ☿ → ♍ 18:59
9 ♂ → ♒ 17:27
11 ☿ → ♎ 1:20
13 ♀ → ♋ 11:18
21 ☿ → ♏ 0:49
⊕ → ♑ 15:24

ASPECTS (HELIOCENTRIC +MOON(TYCHONIC)) :

1 ☽ ☍ ♆ 4:32	6 ☿ □ ♇ 10:42	13 ☽ □ ☿ 4:59	☿ ☌ ☋ 5: 1	☽ ☍ ♇ 16:56
♀ ☍ ⊕ 20:37	☿ □ ⊕ 23:38	♂ ☌ P 16: 5	♂ S ☊ 17:36	27 ☽ ☌ ♄ 5:43
2 ⊕ ☌ A 14:54	7 ☽ □ ♄ 8: 1	☽ ☍ ♄ 16:57	☿ □ ♆ 22: 6	☿ □ ♅ 22:55
☽ ☌ ♅ 19:30	8 ☽ □ ♂ 11:36	14 ☽ ☌ ♆ 17:24	21 ☽ □ ♆ 3:59	☽ ☌ ♀ 23:12
3 ☿ □ ♃ 5: 7	☽ □ ♆ 12:18	☽ ☌ ♂ 23:18	☽ ☍ ☿ 5:38	28 ☿ ☌ A 2:27
♀ ☍ ♇ 15:41	☿ □ ♀ 18:57	15 ☿ □ ♄ 16:12	☽ □ ♂ 18:48	☽ ☍ ♆ 11:36
☽ □ ♃ 21:34	9 ♂ ☌ ♆ 2:41	16 ☽ ☍ ♅ 0:46	22 ♀ ☌ ♄ 12:17	29 ☽ ☍ ♂ 13:32
4 ☽ ☌ ☿ 5:30	☽ □ ♅ 22: 9	☽ □ ♃ 23:45	☽ □ ♅ 16:27	30 ☽ ☌ ♅ 3: 0
⊕ ☌ ♇ 22: 6	10 ☽ ☍ ♃ 20:51	17 ☽ □ ♇ 18:49	23 ♀ ☌ P 10:32	☽ □ ☿ 18:40
☽ □ ♇ 22: 7	11 ☽ ☌ ♇ 16:14	19 ☽ □ ♀ 16:14	☽ ☌ ♃ 20: 4	
5 ☽ □ ♀ 2:47	12 ☽ ☍ ♀ 15:49	20 ☽ □ ♄ 0:23	24 ☿ □ ♂ 8:29	

SIDEREAL GEOCENTRIC LONGITUDES : JULY 32 Julian at 0 hours UT

DAY	☉	☽	☊	☿	♀	♂	♃	♄	♅	♆	♇
1 TU	8 ♋ 56	29 ♌ 33	22 ♈ 19R	3 ♌ 39	17 ♋ 1	29 ♓ 48	9 ♊ 37	14 ♋ 24	17 ♌ 13	0 ♒ 27R	13 ♐ 27R
2 WE	9 53	11 ♍ 27	22 14	4 3	18 15	0 ♈ 21	9 49	14 31	17 16	0 26	13 25
3 TH	10 50	23 28	22 11	4 22	19 29	0 53	10 2	14 39	17 19	0 24	13 24
4 FR	11 48	5 ♎ 42	22 10	4 36	20 43	1 24	10 15	14 47	17 22	0 23	13 23
5 SA	12 45	18 12	22 10	4 46	21 57	1 56	10 27	14 55	17 26	0 21	13 22
6 SU	13 43	1 ♏ 5	22 9	4 50	23 11	2 27	10 40	15 2	17 29	0 20	13 20
7 MO	14 40	14 24	22 8	4 49R	24 25	2 58	10 52	15 10	17 32	0 18	13 19
8 TU	15 37	28 12	22 4	4 43	25 39	3 28	11 4	15 18	17 36	0 17	13 18
9 WE	16 35	12 ♐ 29	21 58	4 32	26 53	3 58	11 17	15 25	17 39	0 15	13 17
10 TH	17 32	27 14	21 50	4 15	28 7	4 28	11 29	15 33	17 42	0 13	13 15
11 FR	18 30	12 ♑ 19	21 40	3 53	29 21	4 58	11 41	15 41	17 46	0 12	13 14
12 SA	19 27	27 35	21 29	3 26	0 ♌ 35	5 27	11 53	15 48	17 49	0 10	13 13
13 SU	20 25	12 ♒ 51	21 19	2 54	1 49	5 55	12 6	15 56	17 53	0 9	13 12
14 MO	21 22	27 55	21 10	2 17	3 3	6 24	12 18	16 4	17 56	0 7	13 11
15 TU	22 20	12 ♓ 40	21 4	1 36	4 17	6 52	12 30	16 12	17 59	0 5	13 10
16 WE	23 18	27 0	21 1	0 52	5 31	7 19	12 41	16 19	18 3	0 4	13 9
17 TH	24 15	10 ♈ 53	20 59	0 5	6 45	7 46	12 53	16 27	18 6	0 2	13 8
18 FR	25 13	24 20	20 59	29 ♋ 15	7 59	8 13	13 5	16 35	18 10	0 1	13 7
19 SA	26 11	7 ♉ 24	20 59	28 25	9 13	8 39	13 17	16 42	18 14	29 ♑ 59	13 6
20 SU	27 8	20 8	20 58	27 33	10 27	9 5	13 28	16 50	18 17	29 57	13 5
21 MO	28 6	2 ♊ 36	20 54	26 43	11 41	9 30	13 40	16 57	18 21	29 56	13 4
22 TU	29 4	14 53	20 48	25 54	12 55	9 55	13 51	17 5	18 24	29 54	13 3
23 WE	0 ♌ 2	27 0	20 38	25 8	14 10	10 20	14 3	17 13	18 28	29 52	13 2
24 TH	0 59	9 ♋ 1	20 27	24 25	15 24	10 43	14 14	17 20	18 32	29 51	13 1
25 FR	1 57	20 57	20 13	23 47	16 38	11 7	14 25	17 28	18 35	29 49	13 0
26 SA	2 55	2 ♌ 50	19 59	23 15	17 52	11 30	14 36	17 35	18 39	29 47	12 59
27 SU	3 53	14 42	19 46	22 48	19 6	11 52	14 47	17 43	18 42	29 46	12 58
28 MO	4 51	26 33	19 35	22 29	20 20	12 14	14 58	17 50	18 46	29 44	12 57
29 TU	5 49	8 ♍ 25	19 26	22 17	21 34	12 35	15 9	17 58	18 50	29 43	12 57
30 WE	6 47	20 22	19 20	22 12	22 48	12 56	15 20	18 5	18 54	29 41	12 56
31 TH	7 45	2 ♎ 26	19 16	22 16D	24 2	13 16	15 31	18 13	18 57	29 39	12 55

INGRESSES :

1	☽ → ♍ 0:55	18	♆ → ♑ 7:56
	♂ → ♈ 8:42		☽ → ♉ 10:19
3	☽ → ♎ 12:52	20	☽ → ♊ 18:56
5	☽ → ♏ 22: 0	22	☉ → ♌ 23:22
8	☽ → ♐ 3: 4	23	☽ → ♋ 5:58
10	☽ → ♑ 4:26	25	☽ → ♌ 18:15
11	♀ → ♌ 12:42	28	☽ → ♍ 6:59
12	☽ → ♒ 3:47	30	☽ → ♎ 19:10
14	☽ → ♓ 3:21		
16	☽ → ♈ 5: 7		
17	☿ → ♋ 2:22		

ASPECTS & ECLIPSES :

3	☽ ☍ ♂ 15:15	12	☽ ☌ P 1:10		♃ ☍ ♇ 2:56		♀ ☌ ♅ 15:59
4	☉ □ ☽ 12:45		☽ ☌ ♆ 4: 3	20	☉ i☌ ☿ 5:34	27	☽ ☌ ♅ 8:10
5	♀ □ ☊ 4: 7		☽ ☍ ♀ 5: 7	21	☽ ☍ ♇ 20:23		☽ ☌ ♀ 9:57
	☽ ☌ ☋ 7:26		☽ ☍ ☿ 8:53		☽ ☌ ♃ 21:56	31	☽ ☍ ♂ 21:50
7	☉ ☌ ♄ 14:27	13	☽ ☍ ♅ 7:59	22	☉ ☍ ♆ 20:17		
8	☽ ☍ ♃ 21:58		☿ ☌ ♀ 14:12	24	☽ ☌ ♄ 16:53		
9	☽ ☌ ♇ 1:17		☉ □ ☊ 19:27		☽ □N ☊ 22:32		
11	☽ ☍ ♄ 5:20	16	☽ ☌ ♂ 18:22	25	☽ ☌ ☿ 5:27		
	☉ ☍ ☽ 10:23	17	☿ ☍ ♆ 1:20		☽ ☍ ♆ 17:51		
	☽ □S ☊ 14:32		☽ ☌ ☊ 17:57	26	☉ ☌ ☽ 0:10		
	♀ ☍ ♆ 16:11	18	☉ □ ☽ 1:43		☽ ☌ A 12:34		

SIDEREAL HELIOCENTRIC LONGITUDES : JULY 32 Julian at 0 hours UT

DAY	Sid. Time	☿	♀	⊕	♂	♃	♄	♅	♆	♇	Vernal Point
1 TU	18:28:40	27 ♍ 31	28 ♋ 31	8 ♑ 56	13 ♒ 27	4 ♊ 4	15 ♋ 1	19 ♌ 11	29 ♑ 45	14 ♐ 13	2♈36'24"
2 WE	18:32:36	0 ♐ 17	0 ♌ 8	9 53	14 5	4 9	15 3	19 12	29 45	14 14	2♈36'24"
3 TH	18:36:33	3 4	1 46	10 51	14 43	4 14	15 5	19 13	29 45	14 14	2♈36'24"
4 FR	18:40:29	5 52	3 24	11 48	15 20	4 19	15 7	19 14	29 46	14 14	2♈36'24"
5 SA	18:44:26	8 42	5 1	12 46	15 58	4 24	15 9	19 14	29 46	14 15	2♈36'23"
6 SU	18:48:22	11 33	6 39	13 43	16 36	4 30	15 11	19 15	29 46	14 15	2♈36'23"
7 MO	18:52:19	14 25	8 17	14 40	17 14	4 35	15 14	19 16	29 47	14 15	2♈36'23"
8 TU	18:56:15	17 20	9 54	15 38	17 51	4 40	15 16	19 17	29 47	14 15	2♈36'23"
9 WE	19: 0:12	20 17	11 32	16 35	18 29	4 45	15 18	19 17	29 47	14 16	2♈36'23"
10 TH	19: 4: 9	23 17	13 10	17 33	19 7	4 50	15 20	19 18	29 48	14 16	2♈36'23"
11 FR	19: 8: 5	26 19	14 47	18 30	19 45	4 55	15 22	19 19	29 48	14 16	2♈36'23"
12 SA	19:12: 2	29 24	16 25	19 28	20 22	5 0	15 25	19 20	29 48	14 17	2♈36'22"
13 SU	19:15:58	2 ♑ 33	18 2	20 25	21 0	5 5	15 27	19 21	29 49	14 17	2♈36'22"
14 MO	19:19:55	5 45	19 40	21 23	21 37	5 10	15 29	19 21	29 49	14 17	2♈36'22"
15 TU	19:23:51	9 1	21 17	22 20	22 15	5 15	15 31	19 22	29 50	14 18	2♈36'22"
16 WE	19:27:48	12 21	22 55	23 18	22 53	5 20	15 33	19 23	29 50	14 18	2♈36'22"
17 TH	19:31:44	15 46	24 32	24 16	23 30	5 25	15 36	19 24	29 50	14 18	2♈36'22"
18 FR	19:35:41	19 15	26 10	25 13	24 8	5 31	15 38	19 24	29 51	14 19	2♈36'22"
19 SA	19:39:38	22 50	27 47	26 11	24 45	5 36	15 40	19 25	29 51	14 19	2♈36'21"
20 SU	19:43:34	26 30	29 25	27 9	25 23	5 41	15 42	19 26	29 51	14 19	2♈36'21"
21 MO	19:47:31	0 ♒ 16	1 ♍ 2	28 6	26 0	5 46	15 44	19 27	29 52	14 20	2♈36'21"
22 TU	19:51:27	4 9	2 39	29 4	26 37	5 51	15 46	19 27	29 52	14 20	2♈36'21"
23 WE	19:55:24	8 8	4 17	0 ♒ 2	27 15	5 56	15 49	19 28	29 52	14 20	2♈36'21"
24 TH	19:59:20	12 14	5 54	1 0	27 52	6 1	15 51	19 29	29 53	14 21	2♈36'21"
25 FR	20: 3:17	16 28	7 31	1 58	28 30	6 6	15 53	19 30	29 53	14 21	2♈36'21"
26 SA	20: 7:13	20 49	9 8	2 55	29 7	6 11	15 55	19 31	29 53	14 21	2♈36'21"
27 SU	20:11:10	25 18	10 46	3 53	29 44	6 16	15 57	19 31	29 54	14 22	2♈36'20"
28 MO	20:15: 7	29 56	12 23	4 51	0 ♓ 21	6 21	16 0	19 32	29 54	14 22	2♈36'20"
29 TU	20:19: 3	4 ♓ 43	14 0	5 49	0 59	6 26	16 2	19 33	29 55	14 22	2♈36'20"
30 WE	20:23: 0	9 38	15 37	6 47	1 36	6 31	16 4	19 34	29 55	14 23	2♈36'20"
31 TH	20:26:56	14 43	17 14	7 45	2 13	6 37	16 6	19 34	29 55	14 23	2♈36'20"

INGRESSES :

1	☿ → ♐ 21:29
	♀ → ♌ 21:56
12	☿ → ♑ 4:36
20	♀ → ♍ 8:43
	☿ → ♒ 22:17
22	⊕ → ♒ 23:12
27	♂ → ♓ 10:14
28	☿ → ♓ 0:19

ASPECTS (HELIOCENTRIC +MOON(TYCHONIC)) :

1	☽ □ ♃ 9:12	8	☽ ☍ ♃ 11: 1	15	☽ □ ♇ 2:41		☿ ☌ ♆ 21:25		☽ ☍ ♂ 8: 7
	♀ ☍ ♆ 18:11	9	☽ ☌ ♇ 2:55		♀ ☍ ♂ 23: 6	21	☽ ☌ ♃ 6:10		☽ ☍ ☿ 11:24
2	☽ □ ♇ 5:34		☽ ☌ ☿ 16: 0	16	☿ ☍ ♄ 22:49		♀ □N ☊ 10: 5		☽ □ ♃ 19:58
3	☿ ☍ ♃ 10:18	10	♂ ☍ ♅ 7:25	17	☽ □ ♄ 8:20		☽ ☍ ♇ 22:55	29	♀ □ ♇ 5:35
4	☽ □ ♄ 18:11	11	☽ ☍ ♄ 4:50		☽ □ ☿ 11:36	22	⊕ ☌ ♆ 20: 1		☿ □ ♃ 8:39
5	☽ □ ♆ 21:35	12	☽ ☌ ♆ 3:29	18	☽ □ ♆ 10: 3	24	♀ □ ♃ 1:50		☽ □ ♇ 11:58
6	☽ □ ♀ 11:33	13	☽ ☍ ♀ 9:12	19	☽ □ ♅ 22:39		☽ ☌ ♄ 13:45		☽ ☌ ♀ 12:58
	☿ ☌ ♇ 22:34		☽ ☍ ♅ 10:18	20	☿ ☌ ⊕ 5:34	25	☿ ☍ ♅ 16:51	30	☿ □ ♇ 22:28
7	☽ □ ♂ 5:14		☽ ☌ ♂ 13:29		☿ □S ☊ 7:29		☽ ☍ ♆ 18: 2	31	☿ ☍ ♀ 16:52
	☽ □ ♅ 8:34		♀ ☌ ♅ 19:25		☽ □ ♂ 10:33	27	☽ ☌ ♅ 9:47		
	⊕ ☍ ♄ 14:27	14	☽ □ ♃ 11:47		☽ □ ♀ 20:29	28	☿ ☌ ♂ 2:27		

SIDEREAL GEOCENTRIC LONGITUDES : AUGUST 32 Julian at 0 hours UT

DAY	☉	☽	☊	☿	♀	♂	♃	♄	♅	♆	♇
1 FR	8 ♌ 43	14 ♎ 41	19 ♈ 15R	22 ♋ 27	25 ♌ 17	13 ♈ 36	15 ♊ 41	18 ♋ 20	19 ♌ 1	29 ♑ 38R	12 ♐ 54R
2 SA	9 41	27 10	19 15D	22 47	26 31	13 55	15 52	18 28	19 5	29 36	12 54
3 SU	10 39	10 ♏ 0	19 16R	23 16	27 45	14 13	16 2	18 35	19 8	29 34	12 53
4 MO	11 37	23 13	19 15	23 52	28 59	14 31	16 13	18 42	19 12	29 33	12 53
5 TU	12 35	6 ♐ 53	19 13	24 36	0 ♍ 13	14 48	16 23	18 50	19 16	29 31	12 52
6 WE	13 33	21 3	19 8	25 28	1 27	15 4	16 33	18 57	19 20	29 30	12 51
7 TH	14 32	5 ♑ 40	19 1	26 28	2 41	15 20	16 43	19 4	19 23	29 28	12 51
8 FR	15 30	20 41	18 53	27 34	3 55	15 35	16 53	19 11	19 27	29 26	12 50
9 SA	16 28	5 ♒ 56	18 44	28 47	5 9	15 50	17 3	19 18	19 31	29 25	12 50
10 SU	17 26	21 15	18 35	0 ♌ 6	6 23	16 4	17 12	19 26	19 35	29 23	12 49
11 MO	18 25	6 ♓ 27	18 27	1 30	7 37	16 17	17 22	19 33	19 38	29 22	12 49
12 TU	19 23	21 22	18 22	2 59	8 52	16 29	17 32	19 40	19 42	29 20	12 49
13 WE	20 21	5 ♈ 53	18 19	4 33	10 6	16 41	17 41	19 47	19 46	29 19	12 48
14 TH	21 20	19 56	18 19	6 11	11 20	16 52	17 50	19 54	19 50	29 17	12 48
15 FR	22 18	3 ♉ 30	18 19D	7 52	12 34	17 2	17 59	20 1	19 54	29 16	12 48
16 SA	23 17	16 38	18 20	9 35	13 48	17 11	18 8	20 8	19 57	29 14	12 47
17 SU	24 15	29 23	18 20R	11 22	15 2	17 20	18 17	20 14	20 1	29 13	12 47
18 MO	25 14	11 ♊ 49	18 19	13 9	16 16	17 28	18 26	20 21	20 5	29 11	12 47
19 TU	26 12	24 2	18 15	14 59	17 30	17 35	18 35	20 28	20 9	29 10	12 47
20 WE	27 11	6 ♋ 4	18 9	16 49	18 44	17 41	18 43	20 35	20 12	29 9	12 47
21 TH	28 10	18 0	18 2	18 41	19 58	17 46	18 52	20 41	20 16	29 7	12 46
22 FR	29 8	29 52	17 53	20 32	21 12	17 51	19 0	20 48	20 20	29 6	12 46
23 SA	0 ♍ 7	11 ♌ 43	17 43	22 24	22 26	17 54	19 8	20 55	20 24	29 5	12 46
24 SU	1 6	23 35	17 34	24 16	23 40	17 57	19 16	21 1	20 27	29 3	12 46
25 MO	2 5	5 ♍ 30	17 26	26 8	24 54	17 59	19 24	21 8	20 31	29 2	12 46D
26 TU	3 3	17 29	17 20	27 59	26 8	18 0	19 32	21 14	20 35	29 1	12 46
27 WE	4 2	29 34	17 17	29 50	27 22	18 0R	19 40	21 20	20 38	28 59	12 46
28 TH	5 1	11 ♎ 47	17 15	1 ♍ 40	28 36	17 59	19 47	21 27	20 42	28 58	12 46
29 FR	6 0	24 10	17 15D	3 30	29 50	17 57	19 54	21 33	20 46	28 57	12 47
30 SA	6 59	6 ♏ 46	17 16	5 19	1 ♎ 4	17 55	20 2	21 39	20 49	28 56	12 47
31 SU	7 58	19 38	17 18	7 7	2 18	17 51	20 9	21 45	20 53	28 54	12 47

INGRESSES :

2 ☽ → ♏ 5:21	22 ☽ → ♌ 0:16
4 ☽ → ♐ 12: 0	☉ → ♍ 21: 6
♀ → ♍ 19:48	24 ☽ → ♍ 12:55
6 ☽ → ♑ 14:46	27 ☽ → ♎ 0:51
8 ☽ → ♒ 14:42	☿ → ♍ 2: 9
9 ☿ → ♌ 22:20	29 ♀ → ♎ 3:12
10 ☽ → ♓ 13:45	☽ → ♏ 11:10
12 ☽ → ♈ 14:10	31 ☽ → ♐ 18:53
14 ☽ → ♉ 17:43	
17 ☽ → ♊ 1:10	
19 ☽ → ♋ 11:52	

ASPECTS & ECLIPSES :

1 ☽ ☌ ☋ 8:51	☉ ☍ ☽ 17:36	21 ☽ N ☊ 0: 3	☽ ☍ ♂ 12: 3
3 ☉ □ ☽ 1:18	☽ ☍ ♅ 21:21	☽ ☌ ♄ 5:29	
5 ☽ ☌ ♇ 10:13	11 ☽ ☍ ♀ 2: 1	☿ ☌ ♅ 21:13	
☽ ☍ ♃ 16:22	12 ☉ ☌ ♅ 8:29	☽ ☍ ♆ 22:27	
6 ♄ □ ☊ 19:39	13 ☽ ☌ ♂ 18:37	22 ♂ ☌ ☊ 3:26	
7 ☽ S ☊ 21:10	☽ ☌ ☊ 21:11	☽ ☌ A 15: 4	
☽ ☍ ♄ 21:37	15 ♀ □ ♇ 4:30	23 ☽ ☌ ♅ 17:38	
8 ☽ ☍ ☿ 11:47	16 ☉ □ ☽ 13:27	24 ☽ ☌ ☿ 1:37	
☽ ☌ ♆ 13:47	18 ☽ ☍ ♇ 1:52	☉ ☌ ☽ 16:29	
9 ☽ ☌ P 11: 9	☽ ☌ ♃ 13: 6	26 ☽ ☌ ♀ 19: 9	
☿ ☍ ♆ 11:36	19 ♀ □ ♃ 23:46	28 ☽ ☌ ☋ 10:38	

SIDEREAL HELIOCENTRIC LONGITUDES : AUGUST 32 Julian at 0 hours UT

DAY	Sid. Time	☿	♀	⊕	♂	♃	♄	♅	♆	♇	Vernal Point
1 FR	20:30:53	19 ♓ 56	18 ♍ 51	8 ♒ 43	2 ♓ 50	6 ♊ 42	16 ♋ 8	19 ♌ 35	29 ♑ 56	14 ♐ 23	2 ♈ 36'20"
2 SA	20:34:49	25 19	20 28	9 41	3 27	6 47	16 11	19 36	29 56	14 24	2 ♈ 36'20"
3 SU	20:38:46	0 ♈ 50	22 5	10 39	4 4	6 52	16 13	19 37	29 56	14 24	2 ♈ 36'19"
4 MO	20:42:42	6 30	23 42	11 38	4 41	6 57	16 15	19 38	29 57	14 24	2 ♈ 36'19"
5 TU	20:46:39	12 19	25 18	12 36	5 18	7 2	16 17	19 38	29 57	14 25	2 ♈ 36'19"
6 WE	20:50:36	18 14	26 55	13 34	5 55	7 7	16 19	19 39	29 57	14 25	2 ♈ 36'19"
7 TH	20:54:32	24 17	28 32	14 32	6 32	7 12	16 21	19 40	29 58	14 25	2 ♈ 36'19"
8 FR	20:58:29	0 ♉ 25	0 ♎ 9	15 30	7 9	7 17	16 24	19 41	29 58	14 26	2 ♈ 36'19"
9 SA	21: 2:25	6 37	1 45	16 28	7 45	7 22	16 26	19 41	29 59	14 26	2 ♈ 36'19"
10 SU	21: 6:22	12 53	3 22	17 27	8 22	7 27	16 28	19 42	29 59	14 26	2 ♈ 36'18"
11 MO	21:10:18	19 11	4 58	18 25	8 59	7 32	16 30	19 43	29 59	14 27	2 ♈ 36'18"
12 TU	21:14:15	25 29	6 35	19 23	9 36	7 37	16 32	19 44	0 ♒ 0	14 27	2 ♈ 36'18"
13 WE	21:18:11	1 ♊ 47	8 11	20 22	10 12	7 42	16 35	19 44	0 0	14 27	2 ♈ 36'18"
14 TH	21:22: 8	8 2	9 48	21 20	10 49	7 48	16 37	19 45	0 0	14 28	2 ♈ 36'18"
15 FR	21:26: 5	14 13	11 24	22 19	11 25	7 53	16 39	19 46	0 1	14 28	2 ♈ 36'18"
16 SA	21:30: 1	20 18	13 0	23 17	12 2	7 58	16 41	19 47	0 1	14 28	2 ♈ 36'18"
17 SU	21:33:58	26 18	14 36	24 16	12 38	8 3	16 43	19 48	0 1	14 29	2 ♈ 36'18"
18 MO	21:37:54	2 ♋ 10	16 13	25 14	13 15	8 8	16 45	19 48	0 2	14 29	2 ♈ 36'17"
19 TU	21:41:51	7 54	17 49	26 13	13 51	8 13	16 48	19 49	0 2	14 29	2 ♈ 36'17"
20 WE	21:45:47	13 30	19 25	27 11	14 28	8 18	16 50	19 50	0 2	14 30	2 ♈ 36'17"
21 TH	21:49:44	18 56	21 1	28 10	15 4	8 23	16 52	19 51	0 3	14 30	2 ♈ 36'17"
22 FR	21:53:40	24 13	22 37	29 9	15 40	8 28	16 54	19 51	0 3	14 30	2 ♈ 36'17"
23 SA	21:57:37	29 21	24 13	0 ♓ 7	16 16	8 33	16 56	19 52	0 4	14 31	2 ♈ 36'17"
24 SU	22: 1:34	4 ♌ 18	25 49	1 6	16 53	8 38	16 59	19 53	0 4	14 31	2 ♈ 36'17"
25 MO	22: 5:30	9 7	27 24	2 5	17 29	8 43	17 1	19 54	0 4	14 31	2 ♈ 36'16"
26 TU	22: 9:27	13 46	29 0	3 4	18 5	8 48	17 3	19 55	0 5	14 32	2 ♈ 36'16"
27 WE	22:13:23	18 17	0 ♏ 36	4 3	18 41	8 53	17 5	19 55	0 5	14 32	2 ♈ 36'16"
28 TH	22:17:20	22 38	2 12	5 2	19 17	8 58	17 7	19 56	0 5	14 32	2 ♈ 36'16"
29 FR	22:21:16	26 52	3 47	6 1	19 53	9 3	17 9	19 57	0 6	14 33	2 ♈ 36'16"
30 SA	22:25:13	0 ♍ 58	5 23	7 0	20 29	9 8	17 12	19 58	0 6	14 33	2 ♈ 36'16"
31 SU	22:29: 9	4 56	6 58	7 59	21 4	9 14	17 14	19 58	0 6	14 33	2 ♈ 36'16"

INGRESSES :

2 ☿ → ♈ 20:23
7 ♀ → ♎ 21:52
☿ → ♉ 22:24
12 ☿ → ♊ 17:11
13 ♆ → ♒ 4:22
17 ☿ → ♋ 15: 3
22 ⊕ → ♓ 20:57
23 ☿ → ♌ 3: 8
26 ♀ → ♏ 15: 0
29 ☿ → ♍ 18:17

ASPECTS (HELIOCENTRIC +MOON(TYCHONIC)) :

1 ☽ □ ♄ 2:50	8 ♂ □ ♃ 6:23	13 ☽ ☍ ♀ 4:22	20 ♂ □ ♇ 1:21	☽ □ ♇ 18: 5
2 ☽ □ ♆ 5:13	☽ ☌ ♆ 14:39	☽ □ ♄ 18:14	☿ ☌ ♄ 14:42	26 ☽ ☍ ♂ 1:14
3 ☽ □ ♅ 17:33	9 ☽ □ ☿ 1:49	☿ ☌ ♃ 23: 4	☽ ☌ ♄ 21:43	♀ □ ♆ 16:13
4 ☽ □ ♂ 21: 7	☽ ☍ ♅ 21:34	14 ☿ □ ♂ 11:57	21 ☽ ☌ ☿ 3:27	27 ☿ ☌ ♅ 8:59
5 ☽ ☍ ♃ 0:14	10 ☿ □ ⊕ 20:32	☽ □ ♆ 17:44	☽ □ ♀ 7: 2	28 ☽ □ ♄ 10:25
☽ ☌ ♇ 12:51	11 ☿ ☌ P 1:24	15 ☿ ☍ ♇ 1: 0	☿ □ ♀ 13:23	29 ☽ □ ♆ 11:21
☿ □ ♄ 16:14	☽ □ ♃ 1:43	16 ☽ □ ♅ 5:52	22 ☽ ☍ ♆ 0:22	☽ ☌ ♀ 21: 0
6 ☽ □ ♀ 10:55	☿ □ ♅ 2: 1	17 ☽ ☌ ♃ 16:46	☿ N ☊ 16: 3	31 ☽ □ ♅ 0:36
7 ☿ ☌ ☊ 13:18	☽ ☌ ♂ 4:11	18 ☽ □ ♂ 2:55	23 ☿ ☍ ♆ 3:25	
☽ ☍ ♄ 17:11	☽ □ ♇ 12:47	☽ ☍ ♇ 5:11	☽ ☌ ♅ 16:30	
☿ □ ♆ 22:16	12 ⊕ ☍ ♅ 8:29	♀ □ ♄ 8:23	25 ☽ □ ♃ 6:30	

SIDEREAL GEOCENTRIC LONGITUDES : SEPTEMBER 32 Julian at 0 hours UT											
DAY	☉	☽	☊	☿	♀	♂	♃	♄	⛢	♆	♇
1 MO	8 ♍ 57	2 ♐ 51	17 ♈ 19	8 ♍ 55	3 ♎ 32	17 ♈ 47R	20 ♊ 15	21 ♋ 51	20 ♌ 57	28 ♑ 53R	12 ♐ 47
2 TU	9 56	16 25	17 19R	10 41	4 46	17 42	20 22	21 57	21 0	28 52	12 47
3 WE	10 55	0 ♑ 24	17 17	12 27	6 0	17 36	20 29	22 3	21 4	28 51	12 48
4 TH	11 55	14 46	17 14	14 12	7 14	17 29	20 35	22 9	21 8	28 50	12 48
5 FR	12 54	29 29	17 10	15 56	8 28	17 21	20 42	22 15	21 11	28 49	12 48
6 SA	13 53	14 ♒ 27	17 5	17 39	9 42	17 12	20 48	22 21	21 15	28 48	12 49
7 SU	14 52	29 33	17 0	19 21	10 55	17 2	20 54	22 27	21 18	28 47	12 49
8 MO	15 51	14 ♓ 36	16 57	21 3	12 9	16 52	21 0	22 32	21 22	28 46	12 50
9 TU	16 51	29 28	16 54	22 44	13 23	16 41	21 5	22 38	21 25	28 45	12 50
10 WE	17 50	14 ♈ 1	16 53	24 24	14 37	16 29	21 11	22 43	21 29	28 44	12 51
11 TH	18 49	28 9	16 53D	26 3	15 51	16 16	21 16	22 49	21 32	28 43	12 51
12 FR	19 49	11 ♉ 51	16 54	27 41	17 5	16 2	21 21	22 54	21 36	28 42	12 52
13 SA	20 48	25 6	16 56	29 19	18 18	15 48	21 26	22 59	21 39	28 41	12 52
14 SU	21 48	7 ♊ 56	16 57	0 ♎ 56	19 32	15 33	21 31	23 5	21 43	28 40	12 53
15 MO	22 47	20 26	16 58	2 32	20 46	15 17	21 36	23 10	21 46	28 39	12 54
16 TU	23 47	2 ♋ 40	16 58R	4 8	22 0	15 1	21 40	23 15	21 49	28 39	12 54
17 WE	24 47	14 42	16 56	5 43	23 14	14 44	21 45	23 20	21 53	28 38	12 55
18 TH	25 46	26 36	16 54	7 17	24 27	14 26	21 49	23 25	21 56	28 37	12 56
19 FR	26 46	8 ♌ 27	16 51	8 50	25 41	14 8	21 53	23 29	21 59	28 37	12 56
20 SA	27 46	20 19	16 48	10 23	26 55	13 49	21 56	23 34	22 2	28 36	12 57
21 SU	28 45	2 ♍ 13	16 45	11 56	28 8	13 30	22 0	23 39	22 6	28 35	12 58
22 MO	29 45	14 14	16 42	13 28	29 22	13 10	22 3	23 43	22 9	28 35	12 59
23 TU	0 ♎ 45	26 23	16 41	14 59	0 ♏ 36	12 50	22 7	23 48	22 12	28 34	13 0
24 WE	1 45	8 ♎ 40	16 40	16 29	1 49	12 30	22 10	23 52	22 15	28 34	13 1
25 TH	2 45	21 9	16 39D	17 59	3 3	12 9	22 13	23 57	22 18	28 33	13 2
26 FR	3 45	3 ♏ 49	16 40	19 28	4 17	11 48	22 15	24 1	22 21	28 33	13 3
27 SA	4 45	16 42	16 41	20 57	5 30	11 27	22 18	24 5	22 24	28 32	13 4
28 SU	5 45	29 48	16 42	22 25	6 44	11 6	22 20	24 9	22 27	28 32	13 5
29 MO	6 45	13 ♐ 10	16 43	23 53	7 57	10 45	22 22	24 13	22 30	28 31	13 6
30 TU	7 45	26 47	16 43	25 19	9 11	10 24	22 24	24 17	22 33	28 31	13 7

INGRESSES :

2	☽ → ♑	23:20
5	☽ → ♒	0:50
7	☽ → ♓	0:43
9	☽ → ♈	0:51
11	☽ → ♉	3:11
13	☽ → ♊	9: 5
	☿ → ♎	10: 8
15	☽ → ♋	18:44
18	☽ → ♌	6:52
20	☽ → ♍	19:31
22	☉ → ♎	5:57
	♀ → ♏	12:20
23	☽ → ♎	7: 6
25	☽ → ♏	16:48
28	☽ → ♐	0:21
30	☽ → ♑	5:36

ASPECTS & ECLIPSES :

1	☉ ⚻ ☿	1:22
	☉ □ ☽	11:44
	☽ ☌ ♇	17:39
2	☽ ☍ ♃	6:54
3	☿ □ ♇	4:46
4	☽ ⚼ ☊	4: 2
	☽ ☍ ♄	12:11
	☉ □ ♇	21:48
	☽ ☌ ♆	22:55
6	☽ ☍ ⛢	10:51
	☽ ☌ P	21: 6
7	♂ ☌ ☊	8:37
	☿ □ ♃	23: 9
8	☉ ☍ ☽	2: 8
	☽ ☍ ☿	11:40
10	☽ ☍ ♀	1: 6
	☽ ☌ ♂	4: 4
	☽ ☌ ☊	4:48
11	♀ ☍ ♂	6:55
	♀ ☍ ☊	20:37
13	☉ □ ♃	16:40
14	☽ ☍ ♇	9:25
15	☽ ☌ ♃	2:16
	☉ □ ☽	4:58
17	♀ □ ♄	2: 9
	☽ ⚺ ☊	4:30
	☽ ☌ ♄	17:30
18	☽ ☍ ♆	4: 5
19	☽ ☌ A	1:58
20	☽ ☌ ⛢	3:30
21	♀ □ ♆	8:40
	☿ ☍ ♂	20:15
23	☉ ☌ ☽	9:19
	☉ ● P	9:33
24	☿ ☍ ☊	2:44
	☽ ☍ ♂	7:11
	☽ ☌ ☋	15:23
	☽ ☌ ☿	17: 7
26	☽ ☌ ♀	0:57
28	☽ ☌ ♇	23:53
29	☿ □ ♄	5:50
	☽ ☍ ♃	16:19
30	☉ □ ☽	20:27

SIDEREAL HELIOCENTRIC LONGITUDES : SEPTEMBER 32 Julian at 0 hours UT											
DAY	Sid. Time	☿	♀	⊕	♂	♃	♄	⛢	♆	♇	Vernal Point
1 MO	22:33: 6	8 ♍ 48	8 ♏ 34	8 ♓ 58	21 ♓ 40	9 ♊ 19	17 ♋ 16	19 ♌ 59	0 ♒ 7	14 ♐ 34	2♈36'15"
2 TU	22:37: 3	12 33	10 9	9 57	22 16	9 24	17 18	20 0	0 7	14 34	2♈36'15"
3 WE	22:40:59	16 12	11 45	10 56	22 52	9 29	17 20	20 1	0 7	14 34	2♈36'15"
4 TH	22:44:56	19 45	13 20	11 55	23 27	9 34	17 23	20 1	0 8	14 35	2♈36'15"
5 FR	22:48:52	23 13	14 55	12 54	24 3	9 39	17 25	20 2	0 8	14 35	2♈36'15"
6 SA	22:52:49	26 36	16 31	13 53	24 38	9 44	17 27	20 3	0 9	14 35	2♈36'15"
7 SU	22:56:45	29 55	18 6	14 53	25 14	9 49	17 29	20 4	0 9	14 36	2♈36'15"
8 MO	23: 0:42	3 ♎ 9	19 41	15 52	25 49	9 54	17 31	20 5	0 9	14 36	2♈36'14"
9 TU	23: 4:38	6 19	21 16	16 51	26 25	9 59	17 33	20 5	0 10	14 36	2♈36'14"
10 WE	23: 8:35	9 26	22 51	17 50	27 0	10 4	17 36	20 6	0 10	14 37	2♈36'14"
11 TH	23:12:32	12 30	24 26	18 50	27 35	10 9	17 38	20 7	0 10	14 37	2♈36'14"
12 FR	23:16:28	15 30	26 1	19 49	28 11	10 14	17 40	20 8	0 11	14 37	2♈36'14"
13 SA	23:20:25	18 28	27 36	20 49	28 46	10 19	17 42	20 8	0 11	14 38	2♈36'14"
14 SU	23:24:21	21 24	29 11	21 48	29 21	10 24	17 44	20 9	0 11	14 38	2♈36'14"
15 MO	23:28:18	24 18	0 ♐ 46	22 48	29 56	10 29	17 47	20 10	0 12	14 38	2♈36'14"
16 TU	23:32:14	27 9	2 21	23 47	0 ♈ 31	10 34	17 49	20 11	0 12	14 39	2♈36'13"
17 WE	23:36:11	29 59	3 56	24 47	1 6	10 39	17 51	20 11	0 12	14 39	2♈36'13"
18 TH	23:40: 7	2 ♏ 47	5 31	25 47	1 41	10 44	17 53	20 12	0 13	14 39	2♈36'13"
19 FR	23:44: 4	5 35	7 6	26 46	2 16	10 49	17 55	20 13	0 13	14 40	2♈36'13"
20 SA	23:48: 1	8 21	8 41	27 46	2 51	10 54	17 57	20 14	0 14	14 40	2♈36'13"
21 SU	23:51:57	11 7	10 16	28 46	3 25	10 59	18 0	20 15	0 14	14 40	2♈36'13"
22 MO	23:55:54	13 52	11 50	29 46	4 0	11 5	18 2	20 15	0 14	14 41	2♈36'13"
23 TU	23:59:50	16 36	13 25	0 ♈ 45	4 35	11 10	18 4	20 16	0 15	14 41	2♈36'12"
24 WE	0: 3:47	19 21	15 0	1 45	5 9	11 15	18 6	20 17	0 15	14 41	2♈36'12"
25 TH	0: 7:43	22 6	16 35	2 45	5 44	11 20	18 8	20 18	0 15	14 42	2♈36'12"
26 FR	0:11:40	24 50	18 9	3 45	6 18	11 25	18 10	20 18	0 16	14 42	2♈36'12"
27 SA	0:15:36	27 36	19 44	4 45	6 53	11 30	18 13	20 19	0 16	14 42	2♈36'12"
28 SU	0:19:33	0 ♐ 22	21 19	5 45	7 27	11 35	18 15	20 20	0 16	14 43	2♈36'12"
29 MO	0:23:30	3 9	22 53	6 45	8 1	11 40	18 17	20 21	0 17	14 43	2♈36'12"
30 TU	0:27:26	5 57	24 28	7 45	8 36	11 45	18 19	20 22	0 17	14 43	2♈36'11"

INGRESSES :

7	☿ → ♎	0:38
14	♀ → ♐	12:16
15	♂ → ♈	2:44
17	☿ → ♏	0: 8
22	⊕ → ♈	5:47
27	☿ → ♐	20:50

ASPECTS (HELIOCENTRIC +MOON(TYCHONIC)) :

1	☿ ☍ ⊕	1:22
	☿ □ ♃	3:17
	⊕ □ ♃	9:16
	☽ ☍ ♃	11:35
	☽ □ ☿	14:41
	☽ ☌ ♇	20:45
2	☽ □ ♂	10:34
	☿ □ ♇	13:11
4	☽ ☍ ♄	4:18
5	☽ ☌ ♆	1: 3
	☿ ☍ ♂	7: 3
6	☽ □ ♀	3:39
	☽ ☍ ⛢	8:54
	⊕ □ ♇	17: 5
7	☽ □ ♃	16:25
	☽ □ ♇	23:59
8	♀ □ ⛢	5:59
	☽ ☌ ♂	18:49
9	☽ ☍ ☿	14:18
10	☽ □ ♄	6: 1
11	☽ □ ♆	3:29
12	☽ □ ⛢	14:55
	☿ □ ♄	17:38
13	☽ ☍ ♀	5:17
14	☽ ☌ ♃	4:43
	☽ ☍ ♇	12:47
15	♀ ☌ ☋	14:16
	☽ □ ♂	19:32
16	☿ ☌ ☋	4:20
17	☿ □ ♆	1:55
	☽ ☌ ♄	6:21
18	☽ ☍ ♆	7:19
	☽ □ ☿	16:23
19	☽ ☌ ⛢	23:50
21	♀ ☍ ♃	11:45
	☽ □ ♃	17:39
	☽ □ ♀	18:30
22	☽ □ ♇	0:52
23	☽ ☍ ♂	16:49
	♀ ☌ ♇	19:16
24	☿ ☌ A	1:47
	☿ □ ⛢	8:12
	☽ □ ♄	18:13
25	☽ □ ♆	17:18
27	☽ □ ⛢	6:41
28	☽ ☌ ☿	1:17
	☽ ☍ ♃	21:19
29	☽ ☌ ♇	2:45
	☽ ☌ ♀	19:25
30	☽ □ ♂	21:18

SIDEREAL GEOCENTRIC LONGITUDES : OCTOBER 32 Julian at 0 hours UT

DAY	☉	☽	☊	☿	♀	♂	♃	♄	♅	♆	♇
1 WE	8 ♎ 45	10 ♑ 40	16 ♈ 43R	26 ♎ 46	10 ♏ 25	10 ♈ 3R	22 ♊ 26	24 ♋ 21	22 ♌ 36	28 ♑ 31R	13 ♐ 8
2 TH	9 45	24 49	16 43	28 11	11 38	9 41	22 27	24 24	22 39	28 30	13 9
3 FR	10 45	9 ♒ 12	16 42	29 36	12 52	9 20	22 29	24 28	22 42	28 30	13 10
4 SA	11 45	23 46	16 42	1 ♏ 0	14 5	9 0	22 30	24 31	22 45	28 30	13 12
5 SU	12 45	8 ♓ 25	16 41	2 23	15 18	8 39	22 31	24 35	22 47	28 30	13 13
6 MO	13 46	23 5	16 41	3 45	16 32	8 19	22 31	24 38	22 50	28 30	13 14
7 TU	14 46	7 ♈ 38	16 41	5 6	17 45	7 59	22 32	24 41	22 53	28 30	13 15
8 WE	15 46	21 58	16 41D	6 26	18 59	7 40	22 32	24 44	22 55	28 29	13 17
9 TH	16 46	6 ♉ 0	16 41R	7 45	20 12	7 21	22 32	24 47	22 58	28 29	13 18
10 FR	17 47	19 41	16 41	9 3	21 25	7 2	22 32R	24 50	23 1	28 29D	13 19
11 SA	18 47	2 ♊ 58	16 41	10 20	22 38	6 44	22 32	24 53	23 3	28 29	13 21
12 SU	19 48	15 53	16 40	11 34	23 52	6 26	22 32	24 56	23 6	28 29	13 22
13 MO	20 48	28 28	16 40	12 48	25 5	6 9	22 31	24 58	23 8	28 30	13 24
14 TU	21 49	10 ♋ 45	16 40	13 59	26 18	5 53	22 30	25 1	23 10	28 30	13 25
15 WE	22 49	22 48	16 40D	15 8	27 31	5 37	22 29	25 3	23 13	28 30	13 26
16 TH	23 50	4 ♌ 44	16 40	16 14	28 44	5 21	22 28	25 5	23 15	28 30	13 28
17 FR	24 50	16 35	16 40	17 18	29 58	5 7	22 26	25 8	23 17	28 30	13 29
18 SA	25 51	28 27	16 41	18 19	1 ♐ 11	4 53	22 25	25 10	23 20	28 31	13 31
19 SU	26 51	10 ♍ 24	16 42	19 17	2 24	4 40	22 23	25 12	23 22	28 31	13 33
20 MO	27 52	22 30	16 43	20 10	3 37	4 28	22 21	25 13	23 24	28 31	13 34
21 TU	28 53	4 ♎ 47	16 44	20 59	4 50	4 16	22 18	25 15	23 26	28 32	13 36
22 WE	29 53	17 19	16 44R	21 43	6 3	4 5	22 16	25 17	23 28	28 32	13 37
23 TH	0 ♏ 54	0 ♏ 6	16 44	22 21	7 16	3 55	22 13	25 18	23 30	28 32	13 39
24 FR	1 55	13 8	16 43	22 53	8 29	3 46	22 10	25 20	23 32	28 33	13 41
25 SA	2 56	26 26	16 41	23 18	9 42	3 38	22 7	25 21	23 34	28 33	13 42
26 SU	3 57	9 ♐ 57	16 39	23 35	10 54	3 30	22 4	25 22	23 36	28 34	13 44
27 MO	4 57	23 40	16 36	23 43	12 7	3 23	22 1	25 23	23 37	28 35	13 46
28 TU	5 58	7 ♑ 33	16 34	23 42R	13 20	3 17	21 57	25 24	23 39	28 35	13 48
29 WE	6 59	21 33	16 32	23 31	14 33	3 12	21 53	25 25	23 41	28 36	13 49
30 TH	8 0	5 ♒ 40	16 31	23 9	15 45	3 8	21 49	25 26	23 42	28 36	13 51
31 FR	9 1	19 50	16 31D	22 36	16 58	3 5	21 45	25 27	23 44	28 37	13 53

INGRESSES :

2	☽ → ♒	8:41	22	☉ → ♏	2:34
3	☿ → ♏	6:55		☽ → ♏	23:49
4	☽ → ♓	10:13	25	☽ → ♐	6:23
6	☽ → ♈	11:23	27	☽ → ♑	10:59
8	☽ → ♉	13:40	29	☽ → ♒	14:22
10	☽ → ♊	18:34	31	☽ → ♓	17: 9
13	☽ → ♋	2:58			
15	☽ → ♌	14:27			
17	♀ → ♐	0:47			
18	☽ → ♍	3: 7			
20	☽ → ♎	14:42			

ASPECTS & ECLIPSES :

1	☽ S ☊	10:18	8	☉ ☍ ☊	21:47	17	☉ □ ♄	7: 8		☽ ☍ ♃	21: 8
	☉ ☍ ♂	22:57	9	☽ ☍ ☿	3:22		☽ ☌ ♅	13:37	28	☿ □ ♅	6:53
	☽ ☍ ♄	23:17	10	☽ ☍ ♀	3:25	20	☉ □ ♆	15:34		♀ ☌ ♇	9:21
2	☿ □ ♆	5:27	11	♀ □ ♅	8:21		☽ ☍ ♂	23: 0		☽ S ☊	15:25
	☽ ☌ ♆	6:11		☽ ☍ ♇	19:15	21	☽ ☌ ☋	22:54	29	☽ ☍ ♄	6:35
3	☽ ☍ ♅	22:19	12	☽ ☌ ♃	12:35	23	☉ ● P	1:19		☽ ☌ ♆	12: 0
5	☽ ☌ P	1:26	14	☽ N ☊	11:43		☉ ☌ ☽	1:37	30	☉ □ ☽	4:16
7	☽ ☌ ♂	0:34	15	☉ □ ☽	0: 1	24	☽ ☌ ☿	18:13	31	☽ ☍ ♅	6:35
	☽ ● T	12:45		☽ ☌ ♄	4:30	26	☽ ☌ ♀	1:51			
	☉ ☍ ☽	12:47		☽ ☍ ♆	11:26		☿ □ ♅	2:20			
	☽ ☌ ☊	15: 6	16	☽ ☌ A	19:32		☽ ☌ ♇	6:40			

SIDEREAL HELIOCENTRIC LONGITUDES : OCTOBER 32 Julian at 0 hours UT

DAY	Sid. Time	☿	♀	⊕	♂	♃	♄	♅	♆	♇	Vernal Point
1 WE	0:31:23	8 ♐ 47	26 ♐ 3	8 ♈ 45	9 ♈ 10	11 ♊ 50	18 ♋ 21	20 ♌ 22	0 ♒ 18	14 ♐ 43	2♈36'11"
2 TH	0:35:19	11 38	27 37	9 45	9 44	11 55	18 24	20 23	0 18	14 44	2♈36'11"
3 FR	0:39:16	14 30	29 12	10 45	10 18	12 0	18 26	20 24	0 18	14 44	2♈36'11"
4 SA	0:43:12	17 25	0 ♑ 46	11 46	10 52	12 5	18 28	20 25	0 19	14 44	2♈36'11"
5 SU	0:47: 9	20 22	2 21	12 46	11 26	12 10	18 30	20 25	0 19	14 45	2♈36'11"
6 MO	0:51: 5	23 22	3 56	13 46	12 0	12 15	18 32	20 26	0 19	14 45	2♈36'11"
7 TU	0:55: 2	26 24	5 30	14 46	12 34	12 20	18 34	20 27	0 20	14 45	2♈36'11"
8 WE	0:58:59	29 29	7 5	15 47	13 8	12 25	18 37	20 28	0 20	14 46	2♈36'10"
9 TH	1: 2:55	2 ♑ 38	8 40	16 47	13 41	12 30	18 39	20 28	0 20	14 46	2♈36'10"
10 FR	1: 6:52	5 50	10 14	17 47	14 15	12 35	18 41	20 29	0 21	14 46	2♈36'10"
11 SA	1:10:48	9 6	11 49	18 48	14 49	12 40	18 43	20 30	0 21	14 47	2♈36'10"
12 SU	1:14:45	12 27	13 24	19 48	15 22	12 45	18 45	20 31	0 21	14 47	2♈36'10"
13 MO	1:18:41	15 51	14 58	20 49	15 56	12 50	18 47	20 32	0 22	14 47	2♈36'10"
14 TU	1:22:38	19 21	16 33	21 49	16 29	12 55	18 50	20 32	0 22	14 48	2♈36'10"
15 WE	1:26:34	22 56	18 8	22 49	17 3	13 0	18 52	20 33	0 23	14 48	2♈36' 9"
16 TH	1:30:31	26 36	19 42	23 50	17 36	13 5	18 54	20 34	0 23	14 48	2♈36' 9"
17 FR	1:34:28	0 ♒ 23	21 17	24 51	18 10	13 10	18 56	20 35	0 23	14 49	2♈36' 9"
18 SA	1:38:24	4 16	22 52	25 51	18 43	13 15	18 58	20 35	0 24	14 49	2♈36' 9"
19 SU	1:42:21	8 15	24 26	26 52	19 16	13 20	19 1	20 36	0 24	14 49	2♈36' 9"
20 MO	1:46:17	12 21	26 1	27 53	19 49	13 25	19 3	20 37	0 24	14 50	2♈36' 9"
21 TU	1:50:14	16 35	27 36	28 53	20 22	13 30	19 5	20 38	0 25	14 50	2♈36' 9"
22 WE	1:54:10	20 57	29 11	29 54	20 55	13 35	19 7	20 38	0 25	14 50	2♈36' 8"
23 TH	1:58: 7	25 26	0 ♒ 45	0 ♉ 55	21 28	13 40	19 9	20 39	0 25	14 51	2♈36' 8"
24 FR	2: 2: 3	0 ♓ 5	2 20	1 55	22 1	13 45	19 11	20 40	0 26	14 51	2♈36' 8"
25 SA	2: 6: 0	4 51	3 55	2 56	22 34	13 50	19 14	20 41	0 26	14 51	2♈36' 8"
26 SU	2: 9:57	9 47	5 30	3 57	23 7	13 55	19 16	20 42	0 26	14 52	2♈36' 8"
27 MO	2:13:53	14 52	7 5	4 58	23 40	14 0	19 18	20 42	0 27	14 52	2♈36' 8"
28 TU	2:17:50	20 6	8 39	5 59	24 12	14 5	19 20	20 43	0 27	14 52	2♈36' 8"
29 WE	2:21:46	25 29	10 14	7 0	24 45	14 10	19 22	20 44	0 28	14 53	2♈36' 8"
30 TH	2:25:43	1 ♈ 1	11 49	8 0	25 17	14 15	19 24	20 45	0 28	14 53	2♈36' 7"
31 FR	2:29:39	6 41	13 24	9 1	25 50	14 20	19 27	20 45	0 28	14 53	2♈36' 7"

INGRESSES :

3	♀ → ♑	12:12
8	☿ → ♑	3:56
16	☿ → ♒	21:36
22	⊕ → ♉	2:24
	♀ → ♒	12:31
23	☿ → ♓	23:36
29	☿ → ♈	19:38

ASPECTS (HELIOCENTRIC +MOON(TYCHONIC)) :

1	☽ ☍ ♄	13: 7		☽ □ ♄	18:19	14	☽ □ ♂	11:56	19	☽ □ ♃	5:54	25	☽ □ ☿	23:33
	⊕ ☌ ♂	22:45	8	☽ □ ♆	14:15		☽ ☍ ♀	13:13		☽ □ ♇	8:49	26	☽ ☍ ♃	7: 2
2	☿ ☍ ♃	2:29	10	☽ □ ♅	1:26		☽ ☌ ♄	16: 5	21	☿ ☍ ♅	22:20		☽ ☌ ♇	8:38
	☽ ☌ ♆	9:11		⊕ □ ♄	22: 8		☿ □ ⊕	23: 0	22	☽ □ ♄	3:25		☿ □ ♃	19:55
3	☿ ☌ ♇	1:55	11	☽ ☌ ♃	18: 4	15	☽ ☍ ☿	0:21		☽ ☍ ♂	7: 7		☿ □ ♇	23:59
	☽ ☍ ♅	18:29		☽ ☍ ♇	21:55		♀ ☍ ♄	11:30		⊕ □ ♆	12:21	28	☽ ☍ ♄	20:15
5	☽ □ ♃	6: 9	12	☿ ☌ ♀	12:32		☽ ☍ ♆	15:13		♀ ☌ ♆	18:56	29	☽ □ ♂	5:39
	☽ □ ♇	10:21	13	☿ □ ♂	0:37	16	☿ S ☊	6:47	23	☽ □ ♆	0:36		☽ ☌ ♆	15:10
6	☽ □ ☿	0:35		♀ ☌ A	18:49	17	☿ ☌ ♆	0: 2		☽ □ ♀	1:23	30	☽ ☌ ♀	11:44
	☽ □ ♀	20: 3		☿ ☍ ♄	20:24		☽ ☌ ♅	8: 6		♀ □ ⊕	6:36	31	☽ ☍ ♅	1:33
7	☽ ☌ ♂	8:33		♀ □ ♂	22:40	18	♂ □ ♄	12: 2	24	☽ □ ♅	13:40			

SIDEREAL GEOCENTRIC LONGITUDES : NOVEMBER 32 Julian at 0 hours UT

DAY	☉	☽	☊	☿	♀	♂	♃	♄	⛢	♆	♇
1 SA	10 ♏ 2	4 ♓ 3	16 ♈ 32	21 ♏ 52R	18 ♐ 11	3 ♈ 2R	21 ♊ 41R	25 ♋ 27	23 ♌ 46	28 ♉ 38	13 ♐ 55
2 SU	11 3	18 16	16 34	20 58	19 23	3 0	21 36	25 27	23 47	28 39	13 57
3 MO	12 4	2 ♈ 26	16 35	19 54	20 36	2 59	21 31	25 28	23 49	28 40	13 59
4 TU	13 5	16 30	16 36R	18 42	21 48	2 59D	21 27	25 28	23 50	28 40	14 0
5 WE	14 6	0 ♉ 25	16 35	17 24	23 0	3 0	21 22	25 28	23 51	28 41	14 2
6 TH	15 7	14 8	16 33	16 2	24 13	3 1	21 16	25 28R	23 52	28 42	14 4
7 FR	16 8	27 36	16 29	14 39	25 25	3 4	21 11	25 28	23 54	28 43	14 6
8 SA	17 9	10 ♊ 47	16 24	13 18	26 37	3 7	21 5	25 28	23 55	28 44	14 8
9 SU	18 10	23 39	16 19	12 2	27 49	3 10	21 0	25 27	23 56	28 45	14 10
10 MO	19 11	6 ♋ 13	16 13	10 52	29 1	3 15	20 54	25 27	23 57	28 46	14 12
11 TU	20 12	18 32	16 8	9 51	0 ♑ 13	3 20	20 48	25 26	23 58	28 47	14 14
12 WE	21 13	0 ♌ 37	16 4	9 1	1 25	3 26	20 42	25 25	23 59	28 48	14 16
13 TH	22 14	12 32	16 2	8 21	2 37	3 32	20 36	25 25	24 0	28 49	14 18
14 FR	23 15	24 23	16 2D	7 52	3 49	3 40	20 29	25 24	24 1	28 51	14 20
15 SA	24 16	6 ♍ 14	16 2	7 35	5 1	3 48	20 23	25 23	24 1	28 52	14 22
16 SU	25 18	18 11	16 4	7 29	6 12	3 56	20 16	25 21	24 2	28 53	14 24
17 MO	26 19	0 ♎ 18	16 6	7 32D	7 24	4 6	20 9	25 20	24 3	28 54	14 26
18 TU	27 20	12 40	16 7	7 45	8 35	4 15	20 2	25 19	24 3	28 55	14 28
19 WE	28 21	25 21	16 6R	8 7	9 47	4 26	19 55	25 17	24 4	28 57	14 30
20 TH	29 22	8 ♏ 22	16 4	8 37	10 58	4 37	19 48	25 16	24 4	28 58	14 32
21 FR	0 ♐ 24	21 44	15 59	9 13	12 10	4 49	19 41	25 14	24 5	28 59	14 34
22 SA	1 25	5 ♐ 27	15 53	9 56	13 21	5 2	19 33	25 12	24 5	29 1	14 36
23 SU	2 26	19 27	15 45	10 44	14 32	5 15	19 26	25 10	24 6	29 2	14 38
24 MO	3 27	3 ♑ 40	15 37	11 37	15 43	5 28	19 19	25 8	24 6	29 4	14 40
25 TU	4 29	18 0	15 29	12 34	16 54	5 42	19 11	25 6	24 6	29 5	14 43
26 WE	5 30	2 ♒ 21	15 23	13 35	18 5	5 57	19 3	25 4	24 6	29 7	14 45
27 TH	6 31	16 40	15 19	14 40	19 15	6 12	18 55	25 2	24 6	29 8	14 47
28 FR	7 32	0 ♓ 52	15 17	15 47	20 26	6 28	18 48	24 59	24 6	29 10	14 49
29 SA	8 34	14 57	15 17D	16 57	21 36	6 44	18 40	24 57	24 6R	29 11	14 51
30 SU	9 35	28 53	15 18	18 10	22 47	7 1	18 32	24 54	24 6	29 13	14 53

INGRESSES :

2	☽ → ♈	19:52
4	☽ → ♉	23:16
7	☽ → ♊	4:19
9	☽ → ♋	12: 3
10	♀ → ♑	19:33
11	☽ → ♌	22:46
14	☽ → ♍	11:22
16	☽ → ♎	23:24
19	☽ → ♏	8:39
20	☉ → ♐	14:44
21	☽ → ♐	14:31
23	☽ → ♑	17:49
25	☽ → ♒	20: 3
27	☽ → ♓	22:31
30	☽ → ♈	1:56

ASPECTS & ECLIPSES :

1	☽ ☌ P	3:48	11	☽ ☌ ♄	13:39	21	☉ ☌ ☽	16:25	30	☽ ☌ ♂	14:27
3	☽ ☌ ♂	0:57		☽ ☍ ♆	20:23	22	☽ ☌ ♇	15:46			
	♀ ☍ ♃	17:21	12	☉ □ Π	17:29		☽ ☍ ♃	23:57			
4	☽ ☌ ☊	0:10	13	☽ ☌ A	16:32	23	♀ □ ☊	22:14			
6	☉ ☍ ☽	1:51		♀ □ ♂	20:30	24	☽ □S ☊	19:50			
	☽ ☍ ☿	3: 2		☉ □ ☽	21:29		☽ ☌ ♀	21:59			
	☉ ⊻ ☿	9:13		☽ ☌ ⛢	23:14	25	☽ ☍ ♄	11:50			
8	☽ ☍ ♇	6:13	14	☉ □ ⛢	18: 2		☽ ☌ ♆	18:34			
	☽ ☌ ♃	19: 2	17	☽ ☍ ♂	7:30		☽ ☌ P	20:37			
9	☽ ☍ ♀	8:44	18	☽ ☌ ☋	6:34	27	☽ ☍ ⛢	12:32			
10	☽ N□ ☊	19:19	20	☽ ☌ ☿	0:28	28	☉ □ ☽	12:13			

SIDEREAL HELIOCENTRIC LONGITUDES : NOVEMBER 32 Julian at 0 hours UT

DAY	Sid. Time	☿	♀	⊕	♂	♃	♄	⛢	♆	♇	Vernal Point
1 SA	2:33:36	12 ♈ 30	14 ♒ 59	10 ♉ 2	26 ♈ 22	14 ♊ 26	19 ♋ 29	20 ♌ 46	0 ♒ 29	14 ♐ 54	2♈36' 7"
2 SU	2:37:32	18 26	16 34	11 3	26 55	14 31	19 31	20 47	0 29	14 54	2♈36' 7"
3 MO	2:41:29	24 28	18 9	12 4	27 27	14 36	19 33	20 48	0 29	14 54	2♈36' 7"
4 TU	2:45:26	0 ♉ 37	19 44	13 5	28 0	14 41	19 35	20 49	0 30	14 55	2♈36' 7"
5 WE	2:49:22	6 49	21 19	14 6	28 32	14 46	19 38	20 49	0 30	14 55	2♈36' 7"
6 TH	2:53:19	13 5	22 54	15 7	29 4	14 51	19 40	20 50	0 30	14 55	2♈36' 6"
7 FR	2:57:15	19 23	24 30	16 8	29 36	14 56	19 42	20 51	0 31	14 56	2♈36' 6"
8 SA	3: 1:12	25 42	26 5	17 9	0 ♉ 8	15 1	19 44	20 52	0 31	14 56	2♈36' 6"
9 SU	3: 5: 8	1 ♊ 59	27 40	18 10	0 40	15 6	19 46	20 52	0 31	14 56	2♈36' 6"
10 MO	3: 9: 5	8 14	29 15	19 11	1 12	15 11	19 48	20 53	0 32	14 57	2♈36' 6"
11 TU	3:13: 1	14 25	0 ♓ 50	20 12	1 44	15 16	19 51	20 54	0 32	14 57	2♈36' 6"
12 WE	3:16:58	20 30	2 26	21 13	2 16	15 21	19 53	20 55	0 33	14 57	2♈36' 6"
13 TH	3:20:54	26 30	4 1	22 15	2 48	15 26	19 55	20 55	0 33	14 58	2♈36' 5"
14 FR	3:24:51	2 ♋ 22	5 36	23 16	3 20	15 31	19 57	20 56	0 33	14 58	2♈36' 5"
15 SA	3:28:48	8 6	7 12	24 17	3 51	15 36	19 59	20 57	0 34	14 58	2♈36' 5"
16 SU	3:32:44	13 41	8 47	25 18	4 23	15 41	20 1	20 58	0 34	14 59	2♈36' 5"
17 MO	3:36:41	19 7	10 22	26 19	4 55	15 46	20 4	20 59	0 34	14 59	2♈36' 5"
18 TU	3:40:37	24 23	11 58	27 20	5 26	15 51	20 6	20 59	0 35	14 59	2♈36' 5"
19 WE	3:44:34	29 30	13 33	28 22	5 58	15 56	20 8	21 0	0 35	15 0	2♈36' 5"
20 TH	3:48:30	4 ♌ 28	15 9	29 23	6 29	16 1	20 10	21 1	0 35	15 0	2♈36' 5"
21 FR	3:52:27	9 16	16 44	0 ♊ 24	7 0	16 6	20 12	21 2	0 36	15 0	2♈36' 4"
22 SA	3:56:23	13 55	18 20	1 25	7 32	16 11	20 14	21 2	0 36	15 1	2♈36' 4"
23 SU	4: 0:20	18 25	19 55	2 27	8 3	16 16	20 17	21 3	0 37	15 1	2♈36' 4"
24 MO	4: 4:17	22 47	21 31	3 28	8 34	16 21	20 19	21 4	0 37	15 1	2♈36' 4"
25 TU	4: 8:13	27 0	23 7	4 29	9 5	16 26	20 21	21 5	0 37	15 2	2♈36' 4"
26 WE	4:12:10	1 ♍ 6	24 42	5 30	9 37	16 31	20 23	21 6	0 38	15 2	2♈36' 4"
27 TH	4:16: 6	5 4	26 18	6 32	10 8	16 36	20 25	21 6	0 38	15 2	2♈36' 4"
28 FR	4:20: 3	8 55	27 54	7 33	10 39	16 41	20 27	21 7	0 38	15 3	2♈36' 3"
29 SA	4:23:59	12 40	29 30	8 34	11 10	16 46	20 30	21 8	0 39	15 3	2♈36' 3"
30 SU	4:27:56	16 19	1 ♈ 6	9 35	11 41	16 51	20 32	21 9	0 39	15 3	2♈36' 3"

INGRESSES :

3	☿ → ♉	21:37
7	♂ → ♉	17:49
8	☿ → ♊	16:24
10	♀ → ♓	11:19
13	☿ → ♋	14:16
19	☿ → ♌	2:20
20	⊕ → ♊	14:34
25	☿ → ♍	17:30
29	♀ → ♈	7:35

ASPECTS (HELIOCENTRIC +MOON(TYCHONIC)) :

1	☽ □ ♃	17:37	6	☿ ☌ ⊕	9:13		☽ ☌ ♄	2:36	18	☽ □ ♄	14:10	22	☽ ☌ ♇	16:25		☽ □ ♃	3: 7
	☽ □ ♇	18:19		☽ □ ⛢	11:53		☿ ☌ ♃	3:21		☿ N□ ☊	15:16		☽ ☍ ♃	18:31		☿ □ ♇	15:36
2	☿ □ ♄	4:22		☽ □ ♀	17:40		♀ □S ☊	13:13	19	☿ ☍ ♆	5: 9	23	☽ □ ♀	0:53	30	☿ □ ♃	3:37
3	☿ ☌ ☊	12:31	7	♃ ☍ ♇	0:25		⊕ □ ⛢	16:32		☽ □ ♆	9:44		☿ ☌ ⛢	14:27		☽ ☌ ♀	4:20
	☿ ☌ ♂	12:49		☿ ☌ P	0:37		☽ ☍ ♆	23:51		☽ □ ☿	12:35	25	☽ ☍ ♄	3:56			
	☿ □ ♆	23:33		☿ □ ⛢	5:33	12	☽ □ ♂	3:28		☽ ☍ ♂	20:26		☽ ☌ ♆	21: 6			
4	☽ □ ♄	5:19	8	☿ □ ♀	1:56	13	☽ ☌ ⛢	16:59		♀ □ ♇	21:46	26	☽ □ ♂	12:36			
	♀ ☍ ⛢	16:21		☽ ☍ ♇	7:41	15	☽ ☍ ♀	2:13	20	☿ □ ♂	11:12	27	☽ ☍ ⛢	7:29			
	☽ ☌ ♂	20:35		☽ ☌ ♃	7:52		☽ □ ♇	17:34		♀ □ ♃	13:44		☿ □ ⊕	12:14			
5	☽ □ ♆	0: 8		♂ □ ♆	17:19		☽ □ ♃	18:56		♂ ☌ ☊	21:49	28	☽ ☍ ☿	18:41			
	☽ ☌ ☿	20:34	11	☿ ☍ ♇	2: 6	17	☿ ☌ ♄	4:16		☽ □ ⛢	22:44	29	☽ □ ♇	0:10			

SIDEREAL GEOCENTRIC LONGITUDES : DECEMBER 32 Julian at 0 hours UT

DAY	☉	☽	☊	☿	♀	♂	♃	♄	♅	♆	♇
1 MO	10 ♐ 36	12 ♈ 39	15 ♈ 19	19 ♏ 24	23 ♑ 57	7 ♈ 18	18 ♊ 24R	24 ♋ 51R	24 ♌ 6R	29 ♑ 15	14 ♐ 55
2 TU	11 37	26 16	15 18R	20 40	25 7	7 36	18 16	24 48	24 6	29 16	14 57
3 WE	12 39	9 ♉ 44	15 16	21 58	26 17	7 54	18 8	24 46	24 6	29 18	14 59
4 TH	13 40	23 2	15 10	23 17	27 27	8 13	18 0	24 43	24 5	29 20	15 2
5 FR	14 41	6 ♊ 9	15 2	24 38	28 37	8 32	17 52	24 39	24 5	29 21	15 4
6 SA	15 42	19 3	14 51	25 59	29 46	8 52	17 44	24 36	24 5	29 23	15 6
7 SU	16 43	1 ♋ 44	14 40	27 22	0 ♒ 56	9 11	17 36	24 33	24 4	29 25	15 8
8 MO	17 45	14 11	14 27	28 45	2 5	9 32	17 27	24 30	24 4	29 27	15 10
9 TU	18 46	26 26	14 16	0 ♐ 10	3 14	9 53	17 19	24 26	24 3	29 29	15 12
10 WE	19 47	8 ♌ 29	14 7	1 35	4 23	10 14	17 11	24 23	24 2	29 30	15 14
11 TH	20 48	20 23	14 0	3 1	5 32	10 35	17 3	24 19	24 2	29 32	15 16
12 FR	21 50	2 ♍ 13	13 55	4 28	6 40	10 57	16 55	24 16	24 1	29 34	15 19
13 SA	22 51	14 2	13 53	5 55	7 49	11 19	16 47	24 12	24 0	29 36	15 21
14 SU	23 52	25 57	13 53	7 23	8 57	11 42	16 39	24 8	23 59	29 38	15 23
15 MO	24 53	8 ♎ 1	13 53D	8 52	10 5	12 5	16 31	24 4	23 59	29 40	15 25
16 TU	25 54	20 22	13 53R	10 21	11 13	12 28	16 23	24 0	23 58	29 42	15 27
17 WE	26 56	3 ♏ 3	13 52	11 51	12 21	12 51	16 15	23 56	23 57	29 44	15 29
18 TH	27 57	16 9	13 48	13 22	13 28	13 15	16 7	23 52	23 55	29 46	15 31
19 FR	28 58	29 42	13 41	14 52	14 36	13 39	16 0	23 48	23 54	29 48	15 33
20 SA	29 59	13 ♐ 41	13 31	16 24	15 43	14 4	15 52	23 44	23 53	29 50	15 35
21 SU	1 ♑ 0	28 3	13 20	17 56	16 50	14 29	15 44	23 39	23 52	29 52	15 37
22 MO	2 1	12 ♑ 42	13 8	19 29	17 56	14 54	15 37	23 35	23 51	29 54	15 40
23 TU	3 3	27 31	12 57	21 2	19 3	15 19	15 29	23 31	23 49	29 56	15 42
24 WE	4 4	12 ♒ 20	12 47	22 35	20 9	15 45	15 22	23 26	23 48	29 58	15 44
25 TH	5 5	27 1	12 40	24 10	21 15	16 11	15 15	23 22	23 47	0 ♒ 0	15 46
26 FR	6 6	11 ♓ 30	12 36	25 45	22 20	16 37	15 8	23 17	23 45	0 2	15 48
27 SA	7 7	25 41	12 34	27 20	23 26	17 3	15 0	23 13	23 44	0 4	15 50
28 SU	8 8	9 ♈ 35	12 34	28 56	24 31	17 30	14 54	23 8	23 42	0 7	15 52
29 MO	9 9	23 13	12 34	0 ♑ 33	25 36	17 57	14 47	23 3	23 41	0 9	15 54
30 TU	10 10	6 ♉ 34	12 32	2 10	26 40	18 24	14 40	22 59	23 39	0 11	15 56
31 WE	11 11	19 42	12 29	3 48	27 44	18 51	14 33	22 54	23 37	0 13	15 58

INGRESSES :

2	☽ → ♉ 6:36	21	☽ → ♑ 3:13
4	☽ → ♊ 12:42	23	☽ → ♒ 4: 1
6	♀ → ♒ 4:45	24	♆ → ♒ 22: 1
	☽ → ♋ 20:42	25	☽ → ♓ 4:54
8	☿ → ♐ 21:12	27	☽ → ♈ 7:23
9	☽ → ♌ 7: 4	28	☿ → ♑ 15:52
11	☽ → ♍ 19:29	29	☽ → ♉ 12: 8
14	☽ → ♎ 8: 6	31	☽ → ♊ 19: 4
16	☽ → ♏ 18:17		
19	☽ → ♐ 0:32		
20	☉ → ♑ 0:20		

ASPECTS & ECLIPSES :

1 ☽ ☌ ☊ 4:40	☽ ☌ ♄ 20: 5	20 ☽ ☌ ♇ 3:14	27 ♀ ☍ ♅ 6:27
♀ ☍ ♄ 17:51	9 ☽ ☍ ♆ 6: 3	☽ ☍ ♃ 3:39	☉ □ ☽ 21:15
4 ☽ ☍ ☿ 0:30	☽ ☍ ♀ 14:56	☽ ☌ ☿ 5: 8	28 ☽ ☌ ☊ 5:11
☿ □ ♅ 14:23	11 ☽ ☌ ♅ 7:22	21 ☉ ☌ ☽ 5:14	☽ ☌ ♂ 14:20
5 ☉ ☌ ♇ 9:13	☽ ☌ A 13:45	♃ ☍ ♇ 17: 0	
♀ ☌ ♆ 15:49	13 ☉ □ ☽ 19:26	22 ☽ S ☊ 0:41	
☽ ☍ ♇ 16:35	15 ☽ ☍ ♂ 8:12	☽ ☍ ♄ 17:33	
☉ ☍ ☽ 17:12	☽ ☌ ☋ 11:29	23 ☽ ☌ ♆ 3:55	
☽ ☌ ♃ 21:33	19 ♂ ☌ ☊ 1: 5	☽ ☌ P 8: 3	
7 ☉ ☍ ♃ 18: 0	☿ ☌ ♇ 10:58	24 ☽ ☌ ♀ 13:46	
8 ☽ N ☊ 0:31	☿ ☍ ♃ 16:14	☽ ☍ ♅ 18:41	

SIDEREAL HELIOCENTRIC LONGITUDES : DECEMBER 32 Julian at 0 hours UT

DAY	Sid. Time	☿	♀	⊕	♂	♃	♄	♅	♆	♇	Vernal Point
1 MO	4:31:52	19 ♍ 52	2 ♈ 41	10 ♊ 37	12 ♉ 11	16 ♊ 56	20 ♋ 34	21 ♌ 9	0 ♒ 39	15 ♐ 4	2♈36' 3"
2 TU	4:35:49	23 20	4 17	11 38	12 42	17 1	20 36	21 10	0 40	15 4	2♈36' 3"
3 WE	4:39:46	26 43	5 53	12 39	13 13	17 6	20 38	21 11	0 40	15 4	2♈36' 3"
4 TH	4:43:42	0 ♎ 1	7 29	13 40	13 44	17 11	20 40	21 12	0 40	15 5	2♈36' 3"
5 FR	4:47:39	3 15	9 5	14 41	14 14	17 16	20 43	21 12	0 41	15 5	2♈36' 2"
6 SA	4:51:35	6 25	10 41	15 43	14 45	17 21	20 45	21 13	0 41	15 5	2♈36' 2"
7 SU	4:55:32	9 32	12 17	16 44	15 16	17 26	20 47	21 14	0 42	15 6	2♈36' 2"
8 MO	4:59:28	12 36	13 53	17 45	15 46	17 31	20 49	21 15	0 42	15 6	2♈36' 2"
9 TU	5: 3:25	15 36	15 29	18 46	16 17	17 35	20 51	21 16	0 42	15 6	2♈36' 2"
10 WE	5: 7:21	18 34	17 5	19 48	16 47	17 40	20 53	21 16	0 43	15 6	2♈36' 2"
11 TH	5:11:18	21 30	18 42	20 49	17 17	17 45	20 56	21 17	0 43	15 7	2♈36' 2"
12 FR	5:15:15	24 23	20 18	21 50	17 48	17 50	20 58	21 18	0 43	15 7	2♈36' 2"
13 SA	5:19:11	27 14	21 54	22 51	18 18	17 55	21 0	21 19	0 44	15 7	2♈36' 1"
14 SU	5:23: 8	0 ♏ 4	23 30	23 52	18 48	18 0	21 2	21 19	0 44	15 8	2♈36' 1"
15 MO	5:27: 4	2 53	25 7	24 54	19 18	18 5	21 4	21 20	0 44	15 8	2♈36' 1"
16 TU	5:31: 1	5 40	26 43	25 55	19 49	18 10	21 6	21 21	0 45	15 8	2♈36' 1"
17 WE	5:34:57	8 26	28 19	26 56	20 19	18 15	21 9	21 22	0 45	15 9	2♈36' 1"
18 TH	5:38:54	11 12	29 56	27 57	20 49	18 20	21 11	21 22	0 45	15 9	2♈36' 1"
19 FR	5:42:50	13 57	1 ♉ 32	28 58	21 19	18 25	21 13	21 23	0 46	15 9	2♈36' 1"
20 SA	5:46:47	16 41	3 9	0 ♋ 0	21 49	18 30	21 15	21 24	0 46	15 10	2♈36' 0"
21 SU	5:50:44	19 26	4 45	1 1	22 19	18 35	21 17	21 25	0 47	15 10	2♈36' 0"
22 MO	5:54:40	22 11	6 22	2 2	22 48	18 40	21 19	21 26	0 47	15 10	2♈36' 0"
23 TU	5:58:37	24 55	7 58	3 3	23 18	18 45	21 22	21 26	0 47	15 11	2♈36' 0"
24 WE	6: 2:33	27 41	9 35	4 4	23 48	18 50	21 24	21 27	0 48	15 11	2♈36' 0"
25 TH	6: 6:30	0 ♐ 27	11 11	5 5	24 18	18 55	21 26	21 28	0 48	15 11	2♈36' 0"
26 FR	6:10:26	3 14	12 48	6 6	24 47	19 0	21 28	21 29	0 48	15 12	2♈36' 0"
27 SA	6:14:23	6 2	14 25	7 7	25 17	19 5	21 30	21 29	0 49	15 12	2♈35'59"
28 SU	6:18:19	8 52	16 2	8 8	25 47	19 10	21 32	21 30	0 49	15 12	2♈35'59"
29 MO	6:22:16	11 43	17 38	9 9	26 16	19 15	21 35	21 31	0 49	15 13	2♈35'59"
30 TU	6:26:13	14 35	19 15	10 10	26 46	19 20	21 37	21 32	0 50	15 13	2♈35'59"
31 WE	6:30: 9	17 30	20 52	11 11	27 15	19 25	21 39	21 33	0 50	15 13	2♈35'59"

INGRESSES :

3	☿ → ♎ 23:53
13	☿ → ♏ 23:24
18	♀ → ♉ 1: 2
20	⊕ → ♋ 0:10
24	☿ → ♐ 20: 6

ASPECTS (HELIOCENTRIC +MOON(TYCHONIC)) :

1 ☽ □ ♄ 13:56	8 ☽ ☌ ♄ 12:59	16 ☽ □ ♄ 1:25	☿ □ ♅ 17:24	29 ☽ □ ♆ 13:37
2 ⊕ ☌ P 6: 5	☿ ☍ ♀ 22: 3	☽ ☍ ♀ 13:51	22 ☿ ☍ ♂ 6:43	30 ☿ ☌ ♇ 5:11
☽ □ ♆ 7:47	9 ☽ ☍ ♆ 8:29	☽ □ ♆ 19:42	☽ ☍ ♄ 14: 1	31 ☽ ☌ ♀ 2:26
3 ☽ ☌ ♂ 6:29	10 ☽ □ ♂ 17:27	17 ☽ ☌ ☿ 12:37	23 ☽ ☌ ♆ 5:18	☽ □ ♅ 3:23
☽ □ ♅ 20:39	☿ □ ♄ 19:17	18 ☽ ☍ ♂ 8:40	☽ □ ♀ 18:59	♀ □ ♅ 10: 9
5 ⊕ ☍ ♇ 9:13	11 ☽ ☌ ♅ 1:49	☽ □ ♅ 9:21	24 ☽ ☍ ♅ 14:52	☽ ☌ ♂ 14:30
☽ ☍ ♇ 16:35	12 ♀ □ ♄ 10:11	♀ □ ♆ 12:24	☽ □ ♂ 19:22	☿ ☍ ♃ 16: 1
☽ ☌ ♃ 20:47	13 ☽ □ ♇ 2:11	19 ♂ □ ♅ 3:44	25 ☽ □ ☿ 6:59	
7 ⊕ ☌ ♃ 17:46	☿ ☌ ☋ 3:35	20 ☽ ☌ ♇ 2:30	26 ☽ □ ♇ 6:12	
☽ □ ☿ 19:53	☽ □ ♃ 7:54	☽ ☍ ♃ 8:10	☽ □ ♃ 12:42	
☽ □ ♀ 23:20	14 ☿ □ ♆ 5:40	21 ☿ ☌ A 1: 4	28 ☽ □ ♄ 21: 5	

SIDEREAL GEOCENTRIC LONGITUDES : JANUARY 33 Julian at 0 hours UT											
DAY	☉	☽	☊	☿	♀	♂	♃	♄	⛢	♆	♇
1 TH	12 ♑ 12	2 ♊ 38	12 ♈ 22R	5 ♑ 27	28 ♒ 48	19 ♈ 19	14 ♊ 27R	22 ♋ 49R	23 ♌ 36R	0 ♒ 15	16 ♐ 0
2 FR	13 13	15 23	12 12	7 6	29 52	19 47	14 21	22 45	23 34	0 17	16 2
3 SA	14 14	27 58	11 59	8 46	0 ♓ 55	20 15	14 15	22 40	23 32	0 20	16 3
4 SU	15 15	10 ♋ 23	11 45	10 27	1 58	20 43	14 9	22 35	23 30	0 22	16 5
5 MO	16 16	22 39	11 30	12 8	3 0	21 11	14 3	22 30	23 28	0 24	16 7
6 TU	17 16	4 ♌ 45	11 16	13 50	4 3	21 40	13 57	22 25	23 26	0 26	16 9
7 WE	18 17	16 43	11 4	15 33	5 4	22 9	13 51	22 20	23 25	0 28	16 11
8 TH	19 18	28 35	10 55	17 17	6 6	22 38	13 46	22 16	23 23	0 31	16 13
9 FR	20 19	10 ♍ 24	10 49	19 1	7 6	23 7	13 41	22 11	23 21	0 33	16 15
10 SA	21 20	22 12	10 45	20 47	8 7	23 36	13 36	22 6	23 18	0 35	16 17
11 SU	22 20	4 ♎ 5	10 44	22 33	9 7	24 5	13 31	22 1	23 16	0 37	16 18
12 MO	23 21	16 7	10 44D	24 19	10 6	24 35	13 26	21 56	23 14	0 40	16 20
13 TU	24 22	28 23	10 44R	26 7	11 6	25 5	13 21	21 51	23 12	0 42	16 22
14 WE	25 23	11 ♏ 1	10 43	27 55	12 4	25 35	13 17	21 46	23 10	0 44	16 24
15 TH	26 23	24 3	10 40	29 44	13 2	26 5	13 13	21 41	23 8	0 46	16 25
16 FR	27 24	7 ♐ 33	10 34	1 ♒ 33	14 0	26 35	13 9	21 37	23 5	0 49	16 27
17 SA	28 25	21 34	10 26	3 23	14 57	27 6	13 5	21 32	23 3	0 51	16 29
18 SU	29 25	6 ♑ 2	10 16	5 14	15 53	27 36	13 1	21 27	23 1	0 53	16 30
19 MO	0 ♒ 26	20 54	10 5	7 5	16 49	28 7	12 58	21 22	22 59	0 56	16 32
20 TU	1 26	6 ♒ 0	9 55	8 56	17 45	28 38	12 54	21 17	22 56	0 58	16 34
21 WE	2 27	21 11	9 45	10 48	18 39	29 9	12 51	21 13	22 54	1 0	16 35
22 TH	3 27	6 ♓ 16	9 39	12 39	19 33	29 40	12 48	21 8	22 51	1 2	16 37
23 FR	4 28	21 5	9 35	14 30	20 27	0 ♉ 11	12 46	21 3	22 49	1 5	16 39
24 SA	5 28	5 ♈ 34	9 34	16 21	21 19	0 43	12 43	20 58	22 47	1 7	16 40
25 SU	6 29	19 40	9 34D	18 11	22 11	1 14	12 41	20 54	22 44	1 9	16 42
26 MO	7 29	3 ♉ 22	9 34	20 0	23 3	1 46	12 39	20 49	22 42	1 12	16 43
27 TU	8 29	16 42	9 34R	21 48	23 53	2 17	12 37	20 45	22 39	1 14	16 45
28 WE	9 30	29 42	9 32	23 33	24 43	2 49	12 35	20 40	22 37	1 16	16 46
29 TH	10 30	12 ♊ 27	9 28	25 17	25 31	3 21	12 33	20 36	22 34	1 18	16 47
30 FR	11 30	24 57	9 21	26 58	26 19	3 53	12 32	20 31	22 32	1 21	16 49
31 SA	12 30	7 ♋ 17	9 12	28 35	27 6	4 25	12 31	20 27	22 29	1 23	16 50

INGRESSES :	
2 ♀ → ♓ 3: 4	21 ☽ → ♓ 13:59
3 ☽ → ♋ 3:53	22 ♂ → ♉ 15:26
5 ☽ → ♌ 14:32	23 ☽ → ♈ 14:41
8 ☽ → ♍ 2:52	25 ☽ → ♉ 18: 2
10 ☽ → ♎ 15:47	28 ☽ → ♊ 0:32
13 ☽ → ♏ 3: 5	30 ☽ → ♋ 9:46
15 ☿ → ♒ 3:34	31 ☿ → ♓ 21:39
☽ → ♐ 10:41	
17 ☽ → ♑ 14: 4	
18 ☉ → ♒ 13:48	
19 ☽ → ♒ 14:29	

ASPECTS & ECLIPSES :			
1 ☉ □ ☊ 3:25	8 ☽ ☌ A 6:56	☿ ☌ ♆ 14: 4	21 ☽ ☍ ⛢ 2:42
☽ ☌ ♃ 22: 2	☽ ☍ ♀ 16:41	16 ☽ ☍ ♃ 9:38	22 ☽ ☌ ♀ 22:52
2 ☽ ☍ ♇ 1:12	10 ☉ ☍ ♄ 16:51	☽ ☌ ♇ 15:22	24 ☽ ☌ ☊ 6:42
4 ☽ ☍ ☿ 0: 7	☿ ☍ ♄ 17:10	18 ☽ S☊ 6:47	♂ □ ♆ 20: 3
☽ N☊ 2:36	☉ ☌S ☿ 17:38	♀ □ ♇ 16:22	25 ☽ ☌ ♂ 21: 2
☉ ☍ ☽ 10:19	11 ☽ ☌ ☋ 13:19	19 ☽ ☍ ♄ 0:44	26 ☉ □ ☽ 7:56
☿ □ ☊ 16:12	12 ☿ □ ♂ 4:54	☉ ☌ ♆ 12:18	27 ☿ ☍ ⛢ 11:21
☽ ☌ ♄ 23:43	☉ □ ☽ 15:29	☽ ☌ ♆ 15:59	29 ☽ ☌ ♃ 0:12
5 ☽ ☍ ♆ 15:23	☽ ☍ ♂ 17:19	☉ ☌ ☽ 16:14	☽ ☍ ♇ 8:18
7 ♂ □ ♄ 8:27	14 ☉ □ ♂ 9:35	20 ☽ ☌ ☿ 5:16	31 ☽ N☊ 3:41
☽ ☌ ⛢ 13:28	15 ♀ □ ♃ 4: 4	☽ ☌ P 15: 7	

SIDEREAL HELIOCENTRIC LONGITUDES : JANUARY 33 Julian at 0 hours UT											
DAY	Sid. Time	☿	♀	⊕	♂	♃	♄	⛢	♆	♇	Vernal Point
1 TH	6:34: 6	20 ♐ 27	22 ♉ 29	12 ♋ 12	27 ♉ 44	19 ♊ 30	21 ♋ 41	21 ♌ 33	0 ♒ 50	15 ♐ 14	2♈35'59"
2 FR	6:38: 2	23 27	24 6	13 13	28 14	19 35	21 43	21 34	0 51	15 14	2♈35'59"
3 SA	6:41:59	26 29	25 43	14 14	28 43	19 40	21 45	21 35	0 51	15 14	2♈35'59"
4 SU	6:45:55	29 35	27 19	15 15	29 12	19 45	21 48	21 36	0 52	15 15	2♈35'58"
5 MO	6:49:52	2 ♑ 44	28 56	16 16	29 42	19 50	21 50	21 36	0 52	15 15	2♈35'58"
6 TU	6:53:48	5 56	0 ♊ 33	17 17	0 ♊ 11	19 55	21 52	21 37	0 52	15 15	2♈35'58"
7 WE	6:57:45	9 12	2 10	18 18	0 40	20 0	21 54	21 38	0 53	15 16	2♈35'58"
8 TH	7: 1:42	12 32	3 47	19 19	1 9	20 5	21 56	21 39	0 53	15 16	2♈35'58"
9 FR	7: 5:38	15 57	5 25	20 19	1 38	20 10	21 58	21 39	0 53	15 16	2♈35'58"
10 SA	7: 9:35	19 27	7 2	21 20	2 7	20 15	22 1	21 40	0 54	15 17	2♈35'58"
11 SU	7:13:31	23 2	8 39	22 21	2 36	20 20	22 3	21 41	0 54	15 17	2♈35'57"
12 MO	7:17:28	26 43	10 16	23 22	3 5	20 25	22 5	21 42	0 54	15 17	2♈35'57"
13 TU	7:21:24	0 ♒ 29	11 53	24 22	3 34	20 30	22 7	21 43	0 55	15 18	2♈35'57"
14 WE	7:25:21	4 22	13 30	25 23	4 3	20 35	22 9	21 43	0 55	15 18	2♈35'57"
15 TH	7:29:17	8 22	15 8	26 24	4 32	20 40	22 11	21 44	0 56	15 18	2♈35'57"
16 FR	7:33:14	12 28	16 45	27 24	5 1	20 45	22 14	21 45	0 56	15 19	2♈35'57"
17 SA	7:37:11	16 42	18 22	28 25	5 29	20 49	22 16	21 46	0 56	15 19	2♈35'57"
18 SU	7:41: 7	21 4	20 0	29 26	5 58	20 54	22 18	21 46	0 57	15 19	2♈35'56"
19 MO	7:45: 4	25 34	21 37	0 ♌ 26	6 27	20 59	22 20	21 47	0 57	15 20	2♈35'56"
20 TU	7:49: 0	0 ♓ 13	23 14	1 27	6 55	21 4	22 22	21 48	0 57	15 20	2♈35'56"
21 WE	7:52:57	5 0	24 52	2 27	7 24	21 9	22 24	21 49	0 58	15 20	2♈35'56"
22 TH	7:56:53	9 56	26 29	3 28	7 53	21 14	22 27	21 50	0 58	15 21	2♈35'56"
23 FR	8: 0:50	15 1	28 7	4 28	8 21	21 19	22 29	21 50	0 58	15 21	2♈35'56"
24 SA	8: 4:46	20 15	29 44	5 29	8 50	21 24	22 31	21 51	0 59	15 21	2♈35'56"
25 SU	8: 8:43	25 38	1 ♋ 22	6 29	9 18	21 29	22 33	21 52	0 59	15 22	2♈35'56"
26 MO	8:12:40	1 ♈ 10	2 59	7 29	9 46	21 34	22 35	21 53	0 59	15 22	2♈35'55"
27 TU	8:16:36	6 51	4 37	8 30	10 15	21 39	22 37	21 53	1 0	15 22	2♈35'55"
28 WE	8:20:33	12 40	6 14	9 30	10 43	21 44	22 40	21 54	1 0	15 23	2♈35'55"
29 TH	8:24:29	18 36	7 52	10 30	11 11	21 49	22 42	21 55	1 1	15 23	2♈35'55"
30 FR	8:28:26	24 39	9 29	11 30	11 40	21 54	22 44	21 56	1 1	15 23	2♈35'55"
31 SA	8:32:22	0 ♉ 47	11 7	12 31	12 8	21 59	22 46	21 56	1 1	15 24	2♈35'55"

INGRESSES :
4 ☿ → ♑ 3:13
5 ♂ → ♊ 15: 2
♀ → ♊ 15:43
12 ☿ → ♒ 20:55
18 ⊕ → ♌ 13:39
19 ☿ → ♓ 22:55
24 ♀ → ♋ 3:55
25 ☿ → ♈ 18:58
30 ☿ → ♉ 20:57

ASPECTS (HELIOCENTRIC +MOON(TYCHONIC)) :				
1 ☽ ☍ ♇ 23:42	☽ □ ♃ 20: 0	☽ ☍ ♂ 19:23	22 ☽ □ ♂ 2:40	28 ☽ ☌ ♂ 21:31
2 ☽ ☌ ♃ 8: 0	10 ⊕ ☌ ♄ 16:36	16 ☽ ☌ ♇ 13:23	☽ ☌ ☿ 8:54	29 ☽ ☍ ♇ 5:36
☽ ☍ ☿ 20:14	☿ ☍ ♄ 17:21	☽ ☍ ♀ 17:54	☽ □ ♇ 14:38	☿ □ ♄ 16:24
4 ☽ ☌ ♄ 22:23	☿ ☍ ⊕ 17:38	☽ ☍ ♃ 22:44	23 ☽ □ ♃ 0:22	☽ ☌ ♃ 18: 3
5 ♀ ☌ ♂ 16: 1	12 ☿ S☊ 6: 6	18 ☿ ☍ ⛢ 3:48	☿ □ ♇ 1:33	30 ☿ ☌ ☊ 11:51
☽ ☍ ♆ 16:16	☽ □ ♄ 11:46	♀ ☌ ♃ 14:14	☽ □ ♀ 13: 0	31 ☿ □ ♆ 0:55
6 ♀ ☌ ☊ 17: 9	13 ☿ ☌ ♆ 2:39	19 ☽ ☍ ♄ 2:17	24 ☿ □ ♃ 5:17	☽ ☌ ♀ 8:39
7 ☽ ☌ ⛢ 9:55	☽ □ ♆ 4:51	⊕ ☍ ♆ 12:18	25 ☽ □ ♄ 5: 0	
8 ☽ □ ♂ 5:25	☽ □ ☿ 5:49	☽ ☌ ♆ 15:59	☽ □ ♆ 19:47	
☽ □ ♀ 12:15	14 ☽ □ ⛢ 19:48	21 ☽ ☍ ⛢ 0:59	26 ☿ □ ♀ 10:50	
9 ☽ □ ♇ 9:55	15 ♀ ☍ ♇ 2:37	☿ □ ♂ 13: 3	27 ☽ □ ⛢ 9:31	

DAY	☉	☽	☊	☿	♀	♂	♃	♄	♅	♆	♇
1 SU	13 ♒ 30	19 ♋ 28	9 ♈ 1R	0 ♓ 9	27 ♓ 52	4 ♉ 58	12 ♊ 30R	20 ♋ 23R	22 ♌ 26R	1 ♒ 25	16 ♐ 52
2 MO	14 30	1 ♌ 32	8 50	1 38	28 37	5 30	12 29	20 19	22 24	1 27	16 53
3 TU	15 31	13 29	8 39	3 3	29 21	6 3	12 28	20 14	22 21	1 29	16 54
4 WE	16 31	25 22	8 30	4 21	0 ♈ 4	6 35	12 28	20 10	22 19	1 32	16 56
5 TH	17 31	7 ♍ 12	8 23	5 34	0 46	7 8	12 28	20 6	22 16	1 34	16 57
6 FR	18 31	19 0	8 18	6 40	1 27	7 40	12 28D	20 2	22 13	1 36	16 58
7 SA	19 31	0 ♎ 50	8 16	7 39	2 6	8 13	12 28	19 58	22 11	1 38	16 59
8 SU	20 30	12 45	8 16D	8 30	2 44	8 46	12 29	19 54	22 8	1 40	17 0
9 MO	21 30	24 49	8 17	9 14	3 21	9 19	12 29	19 51	22 6	1 43	17 2
10 TU	22 30	7 ♏ 5	8 19	9 49	3 57	9 52	12 30	19 47	22 3	1 45	17 3
11 WE	23 30	19 40	8 20	10 15	4 31	10 25	12 31	19 43	22 0	1 47	17 4
12 TH	24 30	2 ♐ 37	8 19R	10 33	5 4	10 59	12 32	19 40	21 58	1 49	17 5
13 FR	25 30	16 0	8 17	10 42	5 35	11 32	12 34	19 36	21 55	1 51	17 6
14 SA	26 29	29 52	8 14	10 42R	6 5	12 5	12 35	19 33	21 53	1 53	17 7
15 SU	27 29	14 ♑ 13	8 8	10 34	6 33	12 39	12 37	19 29	21 50	1 55	17 8
16 MO	28 29	28 59	8 2	10 18	7 0	13 12	12 39	19 26	21 47	1 58	17 9
17 TU	29 28	14 ♒ 5	7 56	9 54	7 24	13 46	12 41	19 23	21 45	2 0	17 10
18 WE	0 ♓ 28	29 20	7 52	9 23	7 48	14 19	12 43	19 20	21 42	2 2	17 11
19 TH	1 28	14 ♓ 35	7 48	8 46	8 9	14 53	12 46	19 17	21 40	2 4	17 12
20 FR	2 27	29 39	7 46	8 4	8 28	15 27	12 49	19 14	21 37	2 6	17 12
21 SA	3 27	14 ♈ 24	7 46D	7 17	8 45	16 1	12 51	19 11	21 34	2 8	17 13
22 SU	4 26	28 45	7 47	6 27	9 1	16 35	12 55	19 8	21 32	2 10	17 14
23 MO	5 26	12 ♉ 39	7 49	5 35	9 14	17 9	12 58	19 6	21 29	2 12	17 15
24 TU	6 25	26 7	7 50	4 41	9 25	17 43	13 1	19 3	21 27	2 14	17 15
25 WE	7 24	9 ♊ 11R	7 51R	3 48	9 34	18 17	13 5	19 1	21 24	2 16	17 16
26 TH	8 24	21 54	7 50	2 56	9 40	18 51	13 9	18 59	21 22	2 18	17 17
27 FR	9 23	4 ♋ 19	7 47	2 6	9 44	19 25	13 13	18 56	21 20	2 20	17 17
28 SA	10 22	16 32	7 44	1 19	9 46	20 0	13 17	18 54	21 17	2 21	17 18

INGRESSES :

1 ☽→♌ 20:56	22 ☽→♉ 2:8	
3 ♀→♈ 21:42	24 ☽→♊ 7:4	
4 ☽→♍ 9:23	26 ☽→♋ 15:35	
6 ☽→♎ 22:18		
9 ☽→♏ 10:12		
11 ☽→♐ 19:12		
14 ☽→♑ 0:13		
16 ☽→♒ 1:37		
17 ☉→♓ 12:43		
18 ☽→♓ 1:2		
20 ☽→♈ 0:34		

ASPECTS & ECLIPSES :

1 ☽☌♄ 1:47	12 ☽☍♃ 17:53	☽☌♀ 14:34
☽☍♃ 23:51	13 ☽☌♆ 1:55	23 ☉♂☿ 1:56
3 ☉☍☽ 4:27	14 ☿☌☊ 13:59	24 ☽☌♂ 8:17
☽☌♅ 17:50	15 ☽☍♄ 8:36	☉□☽ 20:25
4 ☽☌A 15:10	16 ☽☍♆ 4:46	25 ☽☌♃ 7:20
☽☍☿ 20:20	17 ☽☍♅ 12:2	☽☍♅ 15:12
7 ☽☍♀ 2:41	18 ☉☌☽ 1:54	27 ☽☌♅ 6:44
☽☌♇ 14:59	☽☌P 2:52	28 ☽☌♄ 4:41
9 ☉☍♅ 13:32	20 ☽☌☊ 13:8	
10 ☽☍♂ 5:36		
11 ☉□☽ 7:47		

DAY	Sid. Time	☿	♀	⊕	♂	♃	♄	♅	♆	♇	Vernal Point
1 SU	8:36:19	7 ♉ 0	12 ♋ 44	13 ♌ 31	12 ♊ 36	22 ♊ 4	22 ♋ 48	21 ♌ 57	1 ♒ 2	15 ♐ 24	2 ♈ 35'55"
2 MO	8:40:15	13 16	14 22	14 31	13 4	22 9	22 50	21 58	1 2	15 24	2 ♈ 35'54"
3 TU	8:44:12	19 34	16 0	15 31	13 32	22 14	22 53	21 59	1 2	15 25	2 ♈ 35'54"
4 WE	8:48:9	25 53	17 37	16 31	14 1	22 19	22 55	22 0	1 3	15 25	2 ♈ 35'54"
5 TH	8:52:5	2 ♊ 10	19 15	17 31	14 29	22 24	22 57	22 0	1 3	15 25	2 ♈ 35'54"
6 FR	8:56:2	8 25	20 53	18 31	14 57	22 29	22 59	22 1	1 3	15 25	2 ♈ 35'54"
7 SA	8:59:58	14 36	22 30	19 31	15 25	22 34	23 1	22 2	1 4	15 26	2 ♈ 35'54"
8 SU	9:3:55	20 41	24 8	20 31	15 53	22 38	23 3	22 3	1 4	15 26	2 ♈ 35'54"
9 MO	9:7:51	26 40	25 46	21 31	16 21	22 43	23 5	22 3	1 4	15 26	2 ♈ 35'53"
10 TU	9:11:48	2 ♋ 32	27 23	22 31	16 48	22 48	23 8	22 4	1 5	15 27	2 ♈ 35'53"
11 WE	9:15:44	8 16	29 1	23 30	17 16	22 53	23 10	22 5	1 5	15 27	2 ♈ 35'53"
12 TH	9:19:41	13 51	0 ♌ 39	24 30	17 44	22 58	23 12	22 6	1 6	15 27	2 ♈ 35'53"
13 FR	9:23:38	19 17	2 16	25 30	18 12	23 3	23 14	22 6	1 6	15 28	2 ♈ 35'53"
14 SA	9:27:34	24 33	3 54	26 30	18 40	23 8	23 16	22 7	1 6	15 28	2 ♈ 35'53"
15 SU	9:31:31	29 40	5 32	27 29	19 8	23 13	23 18	22 8	1 7	15 28	2 ♈ 35'53"
16 MO	9:35:27	4 ♌ 37	7 9	28 29	19 35	23 18	23 21	22 9	1 7	15 29	2 ♈ 35'53"
17 TU	9:39:24	9 25	8 47	29 29	20 3	23 23	23 23	22 10	1 7	15 29	2 ♈ 35'52"
18 WE	9:43:20	14 4	10 25	0 ♍ 28	20 31	23 28	23 25	22 10	1 8	15 29	2 ♈ 35'52"
19 TH	9:47:17	18 34	12 2	1 28	20 58	23 33	23 27	22 11	1 8	15 30	2 ♈ 35'52"
20 FR	9:51:13	22 55	13 40	2 27	21 26	23 38	23 29	22 12	1 8	15 30	2 ♈ 35'52"
21 SA	9:55:10	27 8	15 17	3 27	21 53	23 43	23 31	22 13	1 9	15 30	2 ♈ 35'52"
22 SU	9:59:7	1 ♍ 14	16 55	4 26	22 21	23 48	23 34	22 13	1 9	15 31	2 ♈ 35'52"
23 MO	10:3:3	5 12	18 32	5 26	22 49	23 53	23 36	22 14	1 9	15 31	2 ♈ 35'52"
24 TU	10:7:0	9 3	20 10	6 25	23 16	23 58	23 38	22 15	1 10	15 31	2 ♈ 35'51"
25 WE	10:10:56	12 48	21 48	7 25	23 44	24 2	23 40	22 16	1 10	15 32	2 ♈ 35'51"
26 TH	10:14:53	16 26	23 25	8 24	24 11	24 7	23 42	22 17	1 11	15 32	2 ♈ 35'51"
27 FR	10:18:49	19 59	25 3	9 23	24 38	24 12	23 44	22 17	1 11	15 32	2 ♈ 35'51"
28 SA	10:22:46	23 27	26 40	10 22	25 6	24 17	23 46	22 18	1 11	15 33	2 ♈ 35'51"

INGRESSES :

4 ☿→♊ 15:43
9 ☿→♋ 13:32
11 ♀→♌ 14:30
15 ☿→♌ 1:35
17 ⊕→♍ 12:34
21 ☿→♍ 16:43

ASPECTS (HELIOCENTRIC +MOON(TYCHONIC)) :

1 ☽☌♄ 6:37	7 ☽☍♂ 0:59	☽☍♆ 23:2	☿☌♅ 19:4	25 ♀☌♅ 7:0
☽☍♆ 23:0	☿☍♆ 3:16	13 ☽☍♂ 3:59	17 ☽☍♅ 12:44	☽□☿ 9:29
2 ☽□⊕ 5:38	♀☌♄ 7:45	♃☌♄ 4:27	19 ☿☌♃ 1:26	☽□♀ 11:55
☿☌P 23:56	8 ☿☌♃ 7:53	☿☌♄ 18:3	☽☌⊕ 10:27	☿□♂ 17:59
3 ♀☌P 3:8	☽☌♄ 20:35	♃☌♃? 23:4	☽☍♄ 14:18	♂☌♃ 20:14
☿□♇ 9:11	9 ☽☌♅ 2:9	14 ☿♂☊ 14:31	21 ☽☌♄ 15:13	26 ☽☌♃ 4:17
☽☌♅ 17:9	☽□♆ 12:18	15 ♀☌♅ 6:55	22 ☽□♆ 4:6	☽☌♂ 4:32
4 ☽□☿ 2:12	11 ☽□♅ 4:32	16 ☽☍♆ 3:24	23 ☿☌♅ 1:56	♀☌♅ 6:5
5 ☽☌♂ 15:24	12 ♀☍♆ 6:38	☽☍☿ 13:15	☽☍♀ 11:50	☿□♂ 13:29
☽□♆ 16:43		☽☍♀ 14:36	☽☍♅ 17:1	☽☌♄ 14:26
6 ☽□♃ 7:6				

SIDEREAL GEOCENTRIC LONGITUDES : MARCH 33 Julian at 0 hours UT											
DAY	☉	☽	☊	☿	♀	♂	♃	♄	♅	♆	♇
1 SU	11 ♓ 21	28 ♋ 34	7 ♈ 40R	0 ♓ 36R	9 ♈ 45R	20 ♉ 34	13 ♊ 21	18 ♋ 52R	21 ♌ 15R	2 ♒ 23	17 ♐ 19
2 MO	12 20	10 ♌ 30	7 35	29 ♒ 57	9 42	21 8	13 26	18 50	21 12	2 25	17 19
3 TU	13 19	22 21	7 31	29 22	9 37	21 43	13 30	18 48	21 10	2 27	17 20
4 WE	14 19	4 ♍ 11	7 27	28 53	9 29	22 17	13 35	18 47	21 8	2 29	17 20
5 TH	15 18	16 0	7 24	28 30	9 18	22 52	13 40	18 45	21 5	2 31	17 20
6 FR	16 17	27 52	7 23	28 12	9 5	23 26	13 45	18 43	21 3	2 32	17 21
7 SA	17 16	9 ♎ 48	7 22D	27 59	8 49	24 1	13 50	18 42	21 1	2 34	17 21
8 SU	18 14	21 50	7 23	27 52	8 31	24 36	13 56	18 41	20 58	2 36	17 22
9 MO	19 13	4 ♏ 2	7 24	27 51D	8 11	25 10	14 2	18 40	20 56	2 38	17 22
10 TU	20 12	16 26	7 26	27 55	7 48	25 45	14 7	18 38	20 54	2 39	17 22
11 WE	21 11	29 5	7 27	28 5	7 24	26 20	14 13	18 37	20 52	2 41	17 22
12 TH	22 10	12 ♐ 3	7 28	28 19	6 57	26 55	14 19	18 36	20 50	2 43	17 23
13 FR	23 9	25 23	7 28R	28 39	6 28	27 29	14 26	18 36	20 48	2 44	17 23
14 SA	24 7	9 ♑ 6	7 28	29 3	5 57	28 4	14 32	18 35	20 46	2 46	17 23
15 SU	25 6	23 13	7 27	29 31	5 25	28 39	14 39	18 34	20 44	2 47	17 23
16 MO	26 5	7 ♒ 44	7 26	0 ♓ 4	4 51	29 14	14 45	18 34	20 42	2 49	17 23
17 TU	27 3	22 33	7 24	0 41	4 16	29 49	14 52	18 34	20 40	2 50	17 23
18 WE	28 2	7 ♓ 36	7 23	1 22	3 40	0 ♊ 24	14 59	18 33	20 38	2 52	17 23
19 TH	29 1	22 42	7 23	2 6	3 3	1 0	15 6	18 33	20 36	2 53	17 23R
20 FR	29 59	7 ♈ 44	7 23D	2 54	2 25	1 35	15 13	18 33D	20 34	2 55	17 23
21 SA	0 ♈ 58	22 33	7 23	3 45	1 47	2 10	15 21	18 33	20 32	2 56	17 23
22 SU	1 56	7 ♉ 2	7 23	4 39	1 9	2 45	15 28	18 33	20 30	2 58	17 23
23 MO	2 55	21 6	7 24	5 37	0 31	3 20	15 36	18 34	20 29	2 59	17 23
24 TU	3 53	4 ♊ 43	7 24	6 37	29 ♓ 54	3 56	15 44	18 34	20 27	3 0	17 23
25 WE	4 51	17 54	7 25	7 40	29 17	4 31	15 52	18 35	20 25	3 2	17 23
26 TH	5 50	0 ♋ 42	7 25R	8 46	28 41	5 6	16 0	18 35	20 24	3 3	17 23
27 FR	6 48	13 9	7 24	9 54	28 6	5 42	16 8	18 36	20 22	3 4	17 22
28 SA	7 46	25 21	7 24	11 5	27 33	6 17	16 16	18 37	20 21	3 5	17 22
29 SU	8 45	7 ♌ 21	7 24D	12 18	27 0	6 53	16 25	18 38	20 19	3 7	17 22
30 MO	9 43	19 13	7 25	13 34	26 30	7 28	16 33	18 39	20 18	3 8	17 22
31 TU	10 41	1 ♍ 2	7 25	14 51	26 1	8 4	16 42	18 40	20 16	3 9	17 21

INGRESSES :

1 ☽ → ♌ 2:51	19 ☽ → ♈ 11:36
☿ → ♒ 21:45	20 ☉ → ♈ 0:19
3 ☽ → ♍ 15:31	21 ☽ → ♉ 12:16
6 ☽ → ♎ 4:18	23 ☽ → ♊ 15:36
8 ☽ → ♏ 16: 5	♀ → ♓ 20: 8
11 ☽ → ♐ 1:42	25 ☽ → ♋ 22:40
13 ☽ → ♑ 8: 9	28 ☽ → ♌ 9:16
15 ☽ → ♒ 11:17	30 ☽ → ♍ 21:54
☿ → ♓ 21:13	
17 ♂ → ♊ 7:16	
☽ → ♓ 11:54	

ASPECTS & ECLIPSES :

1 ☽ ☍ ♆ 7:40	♀ ☌ ☊ 20:46	☉ ● T 10:48	28 ☽ ☍ ♆ 15:28
2 ♂ □ ♅ 2:33	12 ☽ ☍ ♃ 4:10	☽ ☌ ♀ 15:49	30 ☽ ☌ ♅ 2:11
☽ ☌ ♅ 21:35	☽ ☌ ♇ 9:40	☽ ☌ ☊ 23:24	31 ☽ ☌ A 0:45
3 ☉ □ ♃ 4:45	☉ □ ☽ 19:42	21 ☉ [ь] ♀ 12:20	
☽ ☍ ☿ 13:39	13 ☽ [□S] ☊ 21:10	23 ☽ ☌ ♂ 22:31	
☽ ☌ A 15:35	14 ☽ ☍ ♄ 16:10	24 ☽ ☌ ♃ 20:11	
4 ☉ ☍ ☽ 22:25	15 ☽ ☌ ♆ 15:55	☽ ☍ ♇ 23: 1	
6 ☽ ☌ ☋ 19: 8	16 ☽ ☍ ♅ 20:57	26 ☉ □ ☽ 10:38	
☽ ☍ ♀ 22: 5	17 ☽ ☌ ☿ 13:35	☽ [N□] ☊ 12:51	
7 ☉ □ ♇ 2:21	18 ☽ ☌ P 13:41	27 ☽ ☌ ♄ 10:40	
10 ☽ ☍ ♂ 18:33	19 ☉ ☌ ☽ 10:43	☉ ☌ ☊ 14:56	

SIDEREAL HELIOCENTRIC LONGITUDES : MARCH 33 Julian at 0 hours UT											
DAY	Sid. Time	☿	♀	⊕	♂	♃	♄	♅	♆	♇	Vernal Point
1 SU	10:26:42	26 ♍ 49	28 ♌ 17	11 ♍ 22	25 ♊ 33	24 ♊ 22	23 ♋ 49	22 ♌ 19	1 ♒ 12	15 ♐ 33	2♈35'51"
2 MO	10:30:39	0 ♎ 8	29 55	12 21	26 0	24 27	23 51	22 20	1 12	15 33	2♈35'51"
3 TU	10:34:36	3 22	1 ♍ 32	13 20	26 28	24 32	23 53	22 20	1 12	15 34	2♈35'50"
4 WE	10:38:32	6 32	3 10	14 19	26 55	24 37	23 55	22 21	1 13	15 34	2♈35'50"
5 TH	10:42:29	9 38	4 47	15 18	27 22	24 42	23 57	22 22	1 13	15 34	2♈35'50"
6 FR	10:46:25	12 42	6 24	16 17	27 50	24 47	23 59	22 23	1 13	15 35	2♈35'50"
7 SA	10:50:22	15 42	8 1	17 16	28 17	24 52	24 2	22 23	1 14	15 35	2♈35'50"
8 SU	10:54:18	18 40	9 39	18 15	28 44	24 57	24 4	22 24	1 14	15 35	2♈35'50"
9 MO	10:58:15	21 35	11 16	19 14	29 11	25 2	24 6	22 25	1 15	15 36	2♈35'50"
10 TU	11: 2:11	24 29	12 53	20 13	29 38	25 7	24 8	22 26	1 15	15 36	2♈35'50"
11 WE	11: 6: 8	27 20	14 30	21 11	0 ♋ 5	25 12	24 10	22 27	1 15	15 36	2♈35'49"
12 TH	11:10: 5	0 ♏ 10	16 7	22 10	0 32	25 16	24 12	22 27	1 16	15 37	2♈35'49"
13 FR	11:14: 1	2 58	17 44	23 9	1 0	25 21	24 15	22 28	1 16	15 37	2♈35'49"
14 SA	11:17:58	5 46	19 21	24 8	1 27	25 26	24 17	22 29	1 16	15 37	2♈35'49"
15 SU	11:21:54	8 32	20 58	25 6	1 54	25 31	24 19	22 30	1 17	15 38	2♈35'49"
16 MO	11:25:51	11 17	22 35	26 5	2 21	25 36	24 21	22 30	1 17	15 38	2♈35'49"
17 TU	11:29:47	14 2	24 12	27 4	2 48	25 41	24 23	22 31	1 17	15 38	2♈35'49"
18 WE	11:33:44	16 47	25 48	28 2	3 15	25 46	24 25	22 32	1 18	15 39	2♈35'48"
19 TH	11:37:40	19 31	27 25	29 1	3 42	25 51	24 27	22 33	1 18	15 39	2♈35'48"
20 FR	11:41:37	22 16	29 2	0 ♎ 0	4 9	25 56	24 30	22 34	1 18	15 39	2♈35'48"
21 SA	11:45:34	25 1	0 ♎ 39	0 58	4 35	26 1	24 32	22 34	1 19	15 40	2♈35'48"
22 SU	11:49:30	27 46	2 15	1 57	5 2	26 6	24 34	22 35	1 19	15 40	2♈35'48"
23 MO	11:53:27	0 ♐ 33	3 52	2 55	5 29	26 11	24 36	22 36	1 20	15 40	2♈35'48"
24 TU	11:57:23	3 20	5 28	3 53	5 56	26 16	24 38	22 37	1 20	15 41	2♈35'48"
25 WE	12: 1:20	6 8	7 5	4 52	6 23	26 20	24 40	22 37	1 20	15 41	2♈35'47"
26 TH	12: 5:16	8 57	8 41	5 50	6 50	26 25	24 43	22 38	1 21	15 41	2♈35'47"
27 FR	12: 9:13	11 48	10 17	6 49	7 16	26 30	24 45	22 39	1 21	15 42	2♈35'47"
28 SA	12:13: 9	14 41	11 54	7 47	7 43	26 35	24 47	22 40	1 21	15 42	2♈35'47"
29 SU	12:17: 6	17 36	13 30	8 45	8 10	26 40	24 49	22 40	1 22	15 42	2♈35'47"
30 MO	12:21: 3	20 33	15 6	9 43	8 37	26 45	24 51	22 41	1 22	15 42	2♈35'47"
31 TU	12:24:59	23 33	16 42	10 41	9 3	26 50	24 53	22 42	1 22	15 43	2♈35'47"

INGRESSES :

1 ☿ → ♎ 23: 4
2 ♀ → ♍ 1:17
10 ♂ → ♋ 19:13
11 ☿ → ♏ 22:35
20 ⊕ → ♎ 0:10
♀ → ♎ 14:26
22 ☿ → ♐ 19:18

ASPECTS (HELIOCENTRIC +MOON(TYCHONIC)) :

1 ☽ ☍ ♆ 5:15	9 ☿ □ ♄ 21: 5	☽ ☌ ♆ 13:24	♀ ☌ ⊕ 12:20	28 ☿ ☌ ♇ 8:21
2 ☽ ☌ ♅ 23:58	10 ☽ □ ♅ 11:26	16 ☽ □ ☿ 7: 7	☽ □ ♆ 14:27	☽ ☍ ♆ 11:59
3 ♀ [N□] ☊ 2:36	11 ☿ ☌ ☋ 2:46	☽ ☍ ♅ 23:56	23 ☽ □ ♅ 2:36	30 ☽ ☌ ♅ 7: 3
☽ ☌ ♀ 21:36	♀ □ ♇ 16:27	17 ♀ □ ♃ 23:22	☽ ☍ ☿ 20:52	
4 ☽ □ ♇ 23: 7	12 ☽ ☌ ♇ 6:28	18 ☽ □ ♇ 12:47	24 ♀ □ ♂ 9:35	
5 ⊕ □ ♇ 6:42	☽ □ ♀ 8:24	19 ☿ ☌ A 0:15	☽ ☍ ♇ 19:53	
☽ □ ♃ 17:43	☿ □ ♆ 9:21	☽ □ ♃ 5: 1	25 ☽ ☌ ♃ 15:51	
☽ □ ♂ 23:55	☽ ☍ ♃ 23:57	☽ ☍ ♀ 8:23	26 ☽ ☌ ♂ 12:10	
7 ☽ ☌ ☿ 15:39	13 ☽ ☍ ♂ 10:14	☽ □ ♂ 18: 3	☽ □ ♀ 17:35	
8 ☽ □ ♄ 4:24	15 ☽ ☍ ♄ 1:49	20 ☿ □ ♅ 2:32	27 ⊕ □ ♂ 21:18	
☽ □ ♆ 18:31	⊕ □ ♃ 11: 3	21 ☽ □ ♄ 3:14	☽ ☌ ♄ 22:52	

SIDEREAL GEOCENTRIC LONGITUDES : APRIL 33 Julian at 0 hours UT

DAY	☉	☽	☊	☿	♀	♂	♃	♄	♅	♆	♇
1 WE	11 ♈ 39	12 ♍ 51	7 ♈ 25	16 ♓ 11	25 ♓ 35R	8 ♊ 39	16 ♊ 51	18 ♋ 41	20 ♌ 15R	3 ♒ 10	17 ♐ 21R
2 TH	12 37	24 43	7 26	17 33	25 10	9 15	17 0	18 42	20 14	3 11	17 20
3 FR	13 35	6 ♎ 41	7 26	18 58	24 48	9 50	17 9	18 44	20 13	3 12	17 20
4 SA	14 33	18 46	7 26R	20 24	24 28	10 26	17 18	18 45	20 11	3 13	17 19
5 SU	15 31	1 ♏ 2	7 25	21 52	24 10	11 2	17 27	18 47	20 10	3 14	17 19
6 MO	16 29	13 28	7 24	23 23	23 55	11 37	17 36	18 49	20 9	3 15	17 18
7 TU	17 27	26 8	7 23	24 55	23 42	12 13	17 46	18 51	20 8	3 16	17 18
8 WE	18 25	9 ♐ 1	7 22	26 29	23 31	12 49	17 55	18 53	20 7	3 17	17 17
9 TH	19 23	22 9	7 21	28 6	23 23	13 24	18 5	18 55	20 6	3 18	17 17
10 FR	20 21	5 ♑ 34	7 20	29 44	23 18	14 0	18 15	18 57	20 5	3 19	17 16
11 SA	21 19	19 15	7 19	1 ♈ 24	23 14	14 36	18 25	18 59	20 4	3 19	17 15
12 SU	22 17	3 ♒ 14	7 19D	3 7	23 14D	15 12	18 34	19 2	20 4	3 20	17 15
13 MO	23 15	17 29	7 20	4 51	23 15	15 48	18 45	19 4	20 3	3 21	17 14
14 TU	24 12	1 ♓ 58	7 21	6 37	23 19	16 24	18 55	19 7	20 2	3 22	17 13
15 WE	25 10	16 38	7 22	8 25	23 26	16 59	19 5	19 9	20 1	3 22	17 13
16 TH	26 8	1 ♈ 23	7 23	10 15	23 34	17 35	19 15	19 12	20 1	3 23	17 12
17 FR	27 6	16 8	7 22R	12 8	23 44	18 11	19 26	19 15	20 0	3 24	17 11
18 SA	28 3	0 ♉ 45	7 21	14 2	23 57	18 47	19 36	19 18	20 0	3 24	17 10
19 SU	29 1	15 7	7 19	15 58	24 12	19 23	19 47	19 21	19 59	3 25	17 9
20 MO	29 59	29 10	7 16	17 56	24 28	19 59	19 57	19 24	19 59	3 25	17 8
21 TU	0 ♉ 56	12 ♊ 49	7 13	19 55	24 47	20 35	20 8	19 27	19 59	3 26	17 7
22 WE	1 54	26 5	7 10	21 57	25 7	21 12	20 19	19 31	19 58	3 26	17 6
23 TH	2 52	8 ♋ 56	7 7	24 0	25 29	21 48	20 30	19 34	19 58	3 27	17 6
24 FR	3 49	21 27	7 6	26 5	25 53	22 24	20 41	19 38	19 58	3 27	17 5
25 SA	4 47	3 ♌ 40	7 5	28 12	26 18	23 0	20 52	19 41	19 58	3 27	17 4
26 SU	5 44	15 40	7 5D	0 ♉ 19	26 45	23 36	21 3	19 45	19 58	3 28	17 3
27 MO	6 42	27 32	7 6	2 28	27 14	24 12	21 14	19 49	19 58D	3 28	17 1
28 TU	7 39	9 ♍ 21	7 8	4 38	27 44	24 49	21 26	19 52	19 58	3 28	17 0
29 WE	8 37	21 11	7 10	6 49	28 15	25 25	21 37	19 56	19 58	3 28	16 59
30 TH	9 34	3 ♎ 7	7 11	9 1	28 48	26 1	21 49	20 0	19 58	3 29	16 58

INGRESSES :

2 ☽ → ♎ 10:37	22 ☽ → ♋ 7:14
4 ☽ → ♏ 21:59	24 ☽ → ♌ 16:45
7 ☽ → ♐ 7:15	25 ☿ → ♉ 20:22
9 ☽ → ♑ 14: 6	27 ☽ → ♍ 5: 0
10 ☿ → ♈ 3:49	29 ☽ → ♎ 17:44
11 ☽ → ♒ 18:29	
13 ☽ → ♓ 20:45	
15 ☽ → ♈ 21:44	
17 ☽ → ♉ 22:46	
20 ☉ → ♉ 0:30	
☽ → ♊ 1:27	

ASPECTS & ECLIPSES :

1 ☽ ☍ ☿ 7:38	☽ ☌ ♇ 15: 9	16 ☽ ☌ ☊ 9:43	24 ☽ ☍ ♆ 23:35
☿ □ ♃ 12:59	☽ ☍ ♃ 16:31	☽ ☌ ☿ 16:30	25 ☉ □ ☽ 2:24
☿ □ ♇ 20:14	10 ☽ ⊓S ☊ 3: 7	17 ☉ ☌ ☽ 19:14	26 ☽ ☌ ♅ 8:39
2 ☽ ☍ ♀ 0:53	☽ ☍ ♄ 23:32	19 ♂ ☌ ♃ 22: 8	27 ☿ □ ♆ 11: 2
3 ☽ ☌ ☋ 1:30	11 ☉ □ ☽ 3:50	20 ☿ □ ♄ 18:14	☽ ☌ A 16:34
☽ •☍ P 14:46	12 ☽ ☌ ♆ 0:11	21 ☽ ☍ ♇ 7:41	29 ☽ ☍ ♀ 14:54
☉ ☍ ☽ 14:56	13 ☽ ☍ ♅ 4:16	☽ ☌ ♃ 13:20	30 ☽ ☌ ☋ 8: 5
4 ♃ ☍ ♇ 4:18	14 ☿ ☌ ☊ 9:53	☽ ☌ ♂ 14:38	☉ S☋ ☿ 10:49
6 ☿ ☌ ♀ 7:14	15 ♂ ☍ ♇ 8:32	22 ☽ ⊓N ☊ 20:34	
8 ☽ ☍ ♂ 7:19	☽ ☌ ♀ 11: 9	23 ☉ □ ♆ 14:41	
☉ □ ♄ 11:45	☽ ☌ P 18:55	☽ ☌ ♄ 20:27	

SIDEREAL HELIOCENTRIC LONGITUDES : APRIL 33 Julian at 0 hours UT

DAY	Sid. Time	☿	♀	⊕	♂	♃	♄	♅	♆	♇	Vernal Point
1 WE	12:28:56	26 ♐ 35	18 ♎ 18	11 ♎ 40	9 ♋ 30	26 ♊ 55	24 ♋ 55	22 ♌ 43	1 ♒ 23	15 ♐ 43	2♈35'47"
2 TH	12:32:52	29 41	19 54	12 38	9 57	27 0	24 58	22 44	1 23	15 43	2♈35'46"
3 FR	12:36:49	2 ♑ 50	21 30	13 36	10 24	27 5	25 0	22 44	1 23	15 44	2♈35'46"
4 SA	12:40:45	6 2	23 6	14 34	10 50	27 10	25 2	22 45	1 24	15 44	2♈35'46"
5 SU	12:44:42	9 18	24 42	15 32	11 17	27 15	25 4	22 46	1 24	15 44	2♈35'46"
6 MO	12:48:38	12 39	26 18	16 30	11 44	27 19	25 6	22 47	1 25	15 45	2♈35'46"
7 TU	12:52:35	16 4	27 54	17 28	12 10	27 24	25 8	22 47	1 25	15 45	2♈35'46"
8 WE	12:56:32	19 34	29 30	18 26	12 37	27 29	25 11	22 48	1 25	15 45	2♈35'46"
9 TH	13: 0:28	23 9	1 ♏ 5	19 24	13 3	27 34	25 13	22 49	1 26	15 46	2♈35'45"
10 FR	13: 4:25	26 50	2 41	20 21	13 30	27 39	25 15	22 50	1 26	15 46	2♈35'45"
11 SA	13: 8:21	0 ♒ 37	4 17	21 19	13 57	27 44	25 17	22 50	1 26	15 46	2♈35'45"
12 SU	13:12:18	4 30	5 52	22 17	14 23	27 49	25 19	22 51	1 27	15 47	2♈35'45"
13 MO	13:16:14	8 29	7 28	23 15	14 50	27 54	25 21	22 52	1 27	15 47	2♈35'45"
14 TU	13:20:11	12 36	9 3	24 13	15 16	27 59	25 23	22 53	1 27	15 47	2♈35'45"
15 WE	13:24: 7	16 51	10 39	25 11	15 43	28 4	25 26	22 54	1 28	15 48	2♈35'45"
16 TH	13:28: 4	21 13	12 14	26 8	16 9	28 9	25 28	22 54	1 28	15 48	2♈35'44"
17 FR	13:32: 1	25 43	13 49	27 6	16 36	28 13	25 30	22 55	1 29	15 48	2♈35'44"
18 SA	13:35:57	0 ♓ 21	15 25	28 4	17 2	28 18	25 32	22 56	1 29	15 49	2♈35'44"
19 SU	13:39:54	5 9	17 0	29 1	17 29	28 23	25 34	22 57	1 29	15 49	2♈35'44"
20 MO	13:43:50	10 5	18 35	29 59	17 55	28 28	25 36	22 57	1 30	15 49	2♈35'44"
21 TU	13:47:47	15 10	20 10	0 ♏ 57	18 22	28 33	25 38	22 58	1 30	15 50	2♈35'44"
22 WE	13:51:43	20 25	21 45	1 54	18 48	28 38	25 41	22 59	1 30	15 50	2♈35'44"
23 TH	13:55:40	25 48	23 20	2 52	19 14	28 43	25 43	23 0	1 31	15 50	2♈35'44"
24 FR	13:59:36	1 ♈ 20	24 55	3 50	19 41	28 48	25 45	23 1	1 31	15 51	2♈35'43"
25 SA	14: 3:33	7 1	26 30	4 47	20 7	28 53	25 47	23 1	1 31	15 51	2♈35'43"
26 SU	14: 7:30	12 50	28 5	5 45	20 34	28 58	25 49	23 2	1 32	15 51	2♈35'43"
27 MO	14:11:26	18 46	29 40	6 42	21 0	29 2	25 51	23 3	1 32	15 52	2♈35'43"
28 TU	14:15:23	24 49	1 ♐ 15	7 40	21 26	29 7	25 54	23 4	1 32	15 52	2♈35'43"
29 WE	14:19:19	0 ♉ 58	2 50	8 37	21 53	29 12	25 56	23 4	1 33	15 52	2♈35'43"
30 TH	14:23:16	7 11	4 25	9 34	22 19	29 17	25 58	23 5	1 33	15 53	2♈35'43"

INGRESSES :

2 ☿ → ♑ 2:26
8 ♀ → ♏ 7:36
10 ☿ → ♒ 20: 9
17 ☿ → ♓ 22:11
20 ⊕ → ♏ 0:20
23 ☿ → ♈ 18:15
27 ♀ → ♐ 4:56
28 ☿ → ♉ 20:14

ASPECTS (HELIOCENTRIC +MOON(TYCHONIC)) :

1 ☿ ☍ ♃ 2:36	7 ☿ □ ⊕ 13:17	☽ □ ♀ 5: 2	☽ □ ♅ 13:18	26 ☽ ☌ ♅ 14:53
☽ □ ♇ 5:49	8 ☽ ☌ ♇ 12:23	☿ □ ♀ 13:51	21 ☿ □ ♇ 3: 3	27 ☽ □ ♀ 5: 0
2 ☽ □ ♃ 4:37	9 ♀ □ ♆ 5: 6	13 ☽ ☍ ♅ 8:58	☽ ☍ ♇ 5:22	☿ □ ♂ 9:34
☽ □ ☿ 13:32	☽ ☍ ♃ 9:49	14 ☽ □ ♇ 22:37	☽ □ ☿ 6:51	28 ☿ □ ♄ 4:13
3 ☽ □ ♂ 7:41	☿ ☍ ♄ 13:37	15 ⊕ □ ♄ 6:28	⊕ □ ♆ 13:53	♀ ☌ ☋ 6:54
4 ☽ ☌ ♀ 9:48	10 ☿ ⊓S ☊ 5:20	☽ □ ♃ 18:41	22 ☽ ☌ ♃ 4:44	☿ ☌ ☊ 11: 8
☽ □ ♄ 12:20	☽ ☍ ♂ 14:26	16 ☿ ☍ ♅ 9: 9	♀ □ ♅ 18:45	☽ □ ♇ 13:13
5 ☽ □ ♆ 0:43	11 ☿ ☌ ♆ 5:10	17 ☽ □ ♂ 0:46	23 ☿ □ ♃ 12:53	29 ☿ □ ♆ 2:15
♀ □ ♄ 5:34	☽ ☍ ♄ 10:26	☽ □ ♄ 15:22	☽ ☌ ♂ 20:27	☽ □ ♃ 16:15
☿ ☍ ♂ 16:24	☽ ☌ ♆ 20:57	18 ☽ □ ♆ 1:13	24 ☽ ☌ ♄ 8:25	30 ☿ ☍ ⊕ 10:49
6 ☽ □ ♅ 17:42	12 ☽ ☌ ☿ 2:59	19 ☽ ☍ ♀ 3:34	☽ ☍ ♆ 19:45	

SIDEREAL GEOCENTRIC LONGITUDES : MAY 33 Julian at 0 hours UT

DAY	☉	☽	☊	☿	♀	♂	♃	♄	⛢	♆	♇
1 FR	10 ♉ 31	15 ♎ 12	7 ♈ 10R	11 ♉ 12	29 ♓ 22	26 ♊ 37	22 ♊ 0	20 ♋ 5	19 ♌ 58	3 ♒ 29	16 ♐ 57R
2 SA	11 29	27 29	7 9	13 24	29 57	27 14	22 12	20 9	19 58	3 29	16 56
3 SU	12 26	10 ♏ 0	7 6	15 35	0 ♈ 34	27 50	22 23	20 13	19 59	3 29	16 55
4 MO	13 24	22 46	7 1	17 46	1 12	28 26	22 35	20 17	19 59	3 29	16 54
5 TU	14 21	5 ♐ 46	6 55	19 57	1 51	29 3	22 47	20 22	19 59	3 29	16 52
6 WE	15 18	19 1	6 49	22 6	2 31	29 39	22 59	20 26	20 0	3 29R	16 51
7 TH	16 16	2 ♑ 29	6 43	24 14	3 12	0 ♋ 15	23 11	20 31	20 0	3 29	16 50
8 FR	17 13	16 8	6 38	26 20	3 54	0 52	23 23	20 36	20 1	3 29	16 49
9 SA	18 10	29 58	6 35	28 25	4 37	1 28	23 35	20 40	20 2	3 29	16 47
10 SU	19 7	13 ♒ 58	6 34	0 ♊ 28	5 21	2 5	23 47	20 45	20 2	3 29	16 46
11 MO	20 5	28 5	6 34D	2 28	6 6	2 41	23 59	20 50	20 3	3 29	16 45
12 TU	21 2	12 ♓ 19	6 35	4 27	6 51	3 18	24 11	20 55	20 4	3 28	16 43
13 WE	21 59	26 38	6 36	6 24	7 38	3 54	24 23	21 0	20 5	3 28	16 42
14 TH	22 56	10 ♈ 58	6 36R	8 18	8 25	4 31	24 36	21 5	20 5	3 28	16 41
15 FR	23 54	25 18	6 35	10 10	9 14	5 7	24 48	21 11	20 6	3 28	16 39
16 SA	24 51	9 ♉ 32	6 31	12 0	10 2	5 44	25 0	21 16	20 7	3 27	16 38
17 SU	25 48	23 36	6 25	13 48	10 52	6 21	25 13	21 21	20 8	3 27	16 37
18 MO	26 45	7 ♊ 25	6 18	15 33	11 42	6 57	25 25	21 27	20 9	3 27	16 35
19 TU	27 43	20 56	6 10	17 15	12 33	7 34	25 38	21 32	20 11	3 26	16 34
20 WE	28 40	4 ♋ 6	6 1	18 55	13 24	8 11	25 50	21 38	20 12	3 26	16 33
21 TH	29 37	16 56	5 54	20 33	14 17	8 47	26 3	21 43	20 13	3 25	16 31
22 FR	0 ♊ 34	29 26	5 47	22 8	15 9	9 24	26 16	21 49	20 14	3 25	16 30
23 SA	1 31	11 ♌ 40	5 43	23 41	16 2	10 1	26 28	21 55	20 16	3 24	16 28
24 SU	2 28	23 40	5 41	25 11	16 56	10 38	26 41	22 0	20 17	3 24	16 27
25 MO	3 26	5 ♍ 32	5 41	26 38	17 51	11 15	26 54	22 6	20 18	3 23	16 25
26 TU	4 23	17 21	5 41D	28 3	18 45	11 51	27 7	22 12	20 20	3 22	16 24
27 WE	5 20	29 13	5 42	29 26	19 41	12 28	27 19	22 18	20 21	3 22	16 22
28 TH	6 17	11 ♎ 12	5 42R	0 ♋ 46	20 36	13 5	27 32	22 24	20 23	3 21	16 21
29 FR	7 14	23 22	5 40	2 3	21 33	13 42	27 45	22 30	20 25	3 20	16 19
30 SA	8 11	5 ♏ 49	5 36	3 17	22 29	14 19	27 58	22 36	20 26	3 20	16 18
31 SU	9 8	18 33	5 30	4 29	23 26	14 56	28 11	22 43	20 28	3 19	16 16

INGRESSES :

2 ♀ → ♈ 1:42
☽ → ♏ 4:51
4 ☽ → ♐ 13:24
6 ♂ → ♋ 13:50
☽ → ♑ 19:36
9 ☽ → ♒ 0: 2
☿ → ♊ 18:35
11 ☽ → ♓ 3:14
13 ☽ → ♈ 5:38
15 ☽ → ♉ 7:54
17 ☽ → ♊ 11: 3
19 ☽ → ♋ 16:26
21 ☉ → ♊ 9:41
22 ☽ → ♌ 1: 5
24 ☽ → ♍ 12:47
27 ☽ → ♎ 1:35
☿ → ♋ 10:12
29 ☽ → ♏ 12:51
31 ☽ → ♐ 21: 3

ASPECTS & ECLIPSES :

3 ☉ ☍ ☽ 4:59
☽ ☍ ☿ 12:45
5 ☿ □ ⛢ 0:31
☽ ☌ ♇ 20: 7
6 ☽ ☍ ♃ 7:13
☽ ☍ ♂ 19:53
7 ☽ □S ☊ 7:26
8 ☽ ☍ ♄ 7:48
9 ☽ ☌ ♆ 6: 2
10 ☉ □ ☽ 9:25
☽ ☍ ⛢ 10:21
☉ □ ⛢ 23:15
11 ♀ ☌ ☊ 15: 7
13 ☽ ☌ P 8:33
☽ ☌ ☊ 16:41
☽ ☌ ♀ 19:29
17 ♂ □ ☊ 2:34
☉ ☌ ☽ 4: 4
18 ☿ ☍ ♇ 14:25
☽ ☍ ♇ 16:11
☽ ☌ ☿ 16:27
19 ☽ ☌ ♃ 8:37
20 ☽ N□ ☊ 3:29
☽ ☌ ♂ 7:55
21 ☽ ☌ ♄ 9:10
22 ☽ ☍ ♆ 7:44
23 ☽ ☌ ⛢ 17:11
24 ☉ □ ☽ 19:21
25 ☿ ☌ ♃ 5: 3
☽ ☌ A 11: 1
27 ☽ ☌ ☋ 13: 1
28 ☉ □ Π 7: 6
☽ ☍ ♀ 20: 7
30 ♀ □ ♄ 3:19
31 ☿ □ ☊ 19: 7

SIDEREAL HELIOCENTRIC LONGITUDES : MAY 33 Julian at 0 hours UT

DAY	Sid. Time	☿	♀	⊕	♂	♃	♄	⛢	♆	♇	Vernal Point
1 FR	14:27:12	13 ♉ 27	6 ♐ 0	10 ♏ 32	22 ♋ 46	29 ♊ 22	26 ♋ 0	23 ♌ 6	1 ♒ 34	15 ♐ 53	2♈35'42"
2 SA	14:31: 9	19 45	7 35	11 29	23 12	29 27	26 2	23 7	1 34	15 53	2♈35'42"
3 SU	14:35: 5	26 4	9 10	12 27	23 38	29 32	26 4	23 7	1 34	15 54	2♈35'42"
4 MO	14:39: 2	2 ♊ 21	10 44	13 24	24 5	29 37	26 6	23 8	1 35	15 54	2♈35'42"
5 TU	14:42:59	8 35	12 19	14 21	24 31	29 42	26 9	23 9	1 35	15 54	2♈35'42"
6 WE	14:46:55	14 46	13 54	15 19	24 57	29 47	26 11	23 10	1 35	15 55	2♈35'42"
7 TH	14:50:52	20 52	15 29	16 16	25 24	29 51	26 13	23 11	1 36	15 55	2♈35'42"
8 FR	14:54:48	26 51	17 3	17 13	25 50	29 56	26 15	23 11	1 36	15 55	2♈35'41"
9 SA	14:58:45	2 ♋ 42	18 38	18 10	26 16	0 ♋ 1	26 17	23 12	1 36	15 56	2♈35'41"
10 SU	15: 2:41	8 26	20 13	19 8	26 43	0 6	26 19	23 13	1 37	15 56	2♈35'41"
11 MO	15: 6:38	14 0	21 47	20 5	27 9	0 11	26 21	23 14	1 37	15 56	2♈35'41"
12 TU	15:10:34	19 26	23 22	21 2	27 35	0 16	26 24	23 14	1 37	15 57	2♈35'41"
13 WE	15:14:31	24 42	24 57	22 0	28 1	0 21	26 26	23 15	1 38	15 57	2♈35'41"
14 TH	15:18:28	29 48	26 31	22 57	28 28	0 26	26 28	23 16	1 38	15 57	2♈35'41"
15 FR	15:22:24	4 ♌ 46	28 6	23 54	28 54	0 31	26 30	23 17	1 39	15 58	2♈35'41"
16 SA	15:26:21	9 33	29 40	24 51	29 20	0 35	26 32	23 18	1 39	15 58	2♈35'40"
17 SU	15:30:17	14 12	1 ♑ 15	25 48	29 47	0 40	26 34	23 18	1 39	15 58	2♈35'40"
18 MO	15:34:14	18 41	2 50	26 46	0 ♌ 13	0 45	26 37	23 19	1 40	15 58	2♈35'40"
19 TU	15:38:10	23 2	4 24	27 43	0 39	0 50	26 39	23 20	1 40	15 59	2♈35'40"
20 WE	15:42: 7	27 15	5 59	28 40	1 6	0 55	26 41	23 21	1 40	15 59	2♈35'40"
21 TH	15:46: 3	1 ♍ 20	7 33	29 37	1 32	1 0	26 43	23 21	1 41	15 59	2♈35'40"
22 FR	15:50: 0	5 18	9 8	0 ♐ 34	1 58	1 5	26 45	23 22	1 41	16 0	2♈35'40"
23 SA	15:53:57	9 9	10 43	1 32	2 24	1 10	26 47	23 23	1 41	16 0	2♈35'39"
24 SU	15:57:53	12 54	12 17	2 29	2 51	1 15	26 49	23 24	1 42	16 0	2♈35'39"
25 MO	16: 1:50	16 32	13 52	3 26	3 17	1 19	26 52	23 24	1 42	16 1	2♈35'39"
26 TU	16: 5:46	20 5	15 27	4 23	3 43	1 24	26 54	23 25	1 42	16 1	2♈35'39"
27 WE	16: 9:43	23 33	17 1	5 20	4 10	1 29	26 56	23 26	1 43	16 1	2♈35'39"
28 TH	16:13:39	26 55	18 36	6 17	4 36	1 34	26 58	23 27	1 43	16 2	2♈35'39"
29 FR	16:17:36	0 ♎ 13	20 11	7 14	5 2	1 39	27 0	23 28	1 44	16 2	2♈35'39"
30 SA	16:21:32	3 27	21 45	8 11	5 28	1 44	27 2	23 28	1 44	16 2	2♈35'38"
31 SU	16:25:29	6 37	23 20	9 9	5 55	1 49	27 4	23 29	1 44	16 3	2♈35'38"

INGRESSES :

3 ☿ → ♊ 15: 1
8 ☿ → ♋ 12:51
♃ → ♋ 18: 6
14 ☿ → ♌ 0:54
16 ♀ → ♑ 4:57
17 ♂ → ♌ 12: 9
20 ☿ → ♍ 16: 2
21 ⊕ → ♐ 9:32
28 ☿ → ♎ 22:22

ASPECTS (HELIOCENTRIC +MOON(TYCHONIC)) :

1 ☽ □ ♂ 15:21
☽ □ ♄ 21:10
☿ ☌ P 23:14
2 ☽ □ ♆ 7:52
☿ □ ⛢ 12:48
4 ☽ □ ⛢ 0:42
5 ☽ ☍ ☿ 9:43
☽ ☌ ♀ 13:32
☽ ☌ ♇ 18:24
☿ ☍ ♀ 19:25
6 ☿ ☍ ♇ 4:28
☽ ☍ ♃ 19:19
7 ♀ ☌ ♇ 6:41
8 ☿ ☌ ♃ 12:47
☽ ☍ ♂ 17:23
☽ ☍ ♄ 17:36
9 ♂ ☌ ♄ 0:55
☽ ☌ ♆ 2:48
10 ☽ ☍ ⛢ 15:45
12 ☽ □ ♇ 6: 5
☽ □ ♀ 20:50
13 ☽ □ ♃ 6:15
☿ ☌ ♄ 8: 6
☿ N□ ☊ 13:50
☿ ☌ ♂ 17: 0
14 ⊕ □ ⛢ 8: 9
☿ ☍ ♆ 8:47
15 ☽ □ ♄ 2: 1
☽ □ ♂ 6:15
☽ □ ♆ 10:40
16 ☽ □ ☿ 0: 3
♀ ☍ ♃ 14:42
☽ □ ⛢ 23:30
18 ☽ ☍ ♇ 15: 8
19 ☿ ☌ ⛢ 1:38
☽ ☌ ♃ 18: 5
20 ☽ ☍ ♀ 3:56
☿ □ ⊕ 10:42
21 ♂ ☍ ♆ 8:12
☽ ☌ ♄ 18:46
22 ☽ ☍ ♆ 4:22
☽ ☌ ♂ 5: 6
23 ♂ ☌ A 5: 3
☽ ☌ ⛢ 23:27
24 ☿ □ ♇ 20:29
25 ☽ □ ♇ 21:17
26 ☽ ☌ ☿ 7:51
♀ ☌ A 11:37
27 ☽ □ ♃ 4:36
28 ☽ □ ♀ 16:49
29 ☽ □ ♄ 7: 4
☿ □ ♃ 10:48
☽ □ ♆ 16:11
☽ □ ♂ 23:19
31 ☽ □ ⛢ 9: 7

SIDEREAL GEOCENTRIC LONGITUDES : JUNE 33 Julian at 0 hours UT

DAY	☉	☽	☊	☿	♀	♂	♃	♄	♅	♆	♇
1 MO	10 ♊ 5	1 ♐ 37	5 ♈ 22R	5 ♋ 38	24 ♈ 24	15 ♋ 33	28 ♊ 24	22 ♋ 49	20 ♌ 30	3 ♒ 18R	16 ♐ 15R
2 TU	11 2	15 0	5 12	6 43	25 22	16 10	28 37	22 55	20 32	3 17	16 13
3 WE	12 0	28 40	5 1	7 46	26 20	16 47	28 50	23 1	20 34	3 16	16 12
4 TH	12 57	12 ♑ 33	4 51	8 46	27 19	17 24	29 3	23 8	20 35	3 16	16 10
5 FR	13 54	26 36	4 43	9 43	28 18	18 1	29 16	23 14	20 37	3 15	16 9
6 SA	14 51	10 ♒ 44	4 36	10 36	29 18	18 38	29 29	23 21	20 39	3 14	16 7
7 SU	15 48	24 55	4 33	11 26	0 ♉ 17	19 15	29 43	23 27	20 41	3 13	16 6
8 MO	16 45	9 ♓ 5	4 31	12 12	1 17	19 52	29 56	23 34	20 44	3 12	16 4
9 TU	17 42	23 14	4 31D	12 55	2 18	20 29	0 ♋ 9	23 41	20 46	3 11	16 3
10 WE	18 39	7 ♈ 19	4 31R	13 34	3 19	21 6	0 22	23 47	20 48	3 10	16 1
11 TH	19 36	21 20	4 31	14 9	4 20	21 44	0 35	23 54	20 50	3 9	16 0
12 FR	20 34	5 ♉ 16	4 28	14 40	5 21	22 21	0 49	24 1	20 52	3 8	15 58
13 SA	21 31	19 5	4 22	15 7	6 23	22 58	1 2	24 8	20 55	3 6	15 57
14 SU	22 28	2 ♊ 44	4 14	15 30	7 25	23 35	1 15	24 14	20 57	3 5	15 55
15 MO	23 25	16 12	4 3	15 48	8 27	24 13	1 28	24 21	20 59	3 4	15 54
16 TU	24 22	29 26	3 51	16 1	9 30	24 50	1 42	24 28	21 2	3 3	15 52
17 WE	25 20	12 ♋ 23	3 39	16 10	10 32	25 27	1 55	24 35	21 4	3 2	15 51
18 TH	26 17	25 4	3 27	16 14	11 35	26 5	2 8	24 42	21 7	3 1	15 49
19 FR	27 14	7 ♌ 28	3 18	16 14R	12 39	26 42	2 22	24 49	21 9	2 59	15 48
20 SA	28 11	19 38	3 10	16 8	13 42	27 19	2 35	24 56	21 12	2 58	15 46
21 SU	29 8	1 ♍ 36	3 6	15 57	14 46	27 57	2 48	25 4	21 15	2 57	15 45
22 MO	0 ♋ 6	13 27	3 3	15 42	15 50	28 34	3 2	25 11	21 17	2 56	15 43
23 TU	1 3	25 15	3 2	15 22	16 54	29 12	3 15	25 18	21 20	2 54	15 42
24 WE	2 0	7 ♎ 6	3 2	14 58	17 58	29 49	3 28	25 25	21 23	2 53	15 41
25 TH	2 57	19 6	3 2	14 29	19 3	0 ♌ 27	3 42	25 32	21 25	2 52	15 39
26 FR	3 55	1 ♏ 19	3 0	13 56	20 7	1 4	3 55	25 40	21 28	2 50	15 38
27 SA	4 52	13 50	2 55	13 20	21 12	1 42	4 8	25 47	21 31	2 49	15 36
28 SU	5 49	26 43	2 49	12 41	22 18	2 20	4 22	25 54	21 34	2 47	15 35
29 MO	6 46	10 ♐ 0	2 40	12 0	23 23	2 57	4 35	26 1	21 37	2 46	15 34
30 TU	7 44	23 40	2 29	11 16	24 28	3 35	4 48	26 9	21 40	2 44	15 32

INGRESSES :

3	☽ → ♑	2:19
5	☽ → ♒	5:47
6	♀ → ♉	17: 3
7	☽ → ♓	8:36
8	♃ → ♋	7:52
9	☽ → ♈	11:31
11	☽ → ♉	14:54
13	☽ → ♊	19: 9
16	☽ → ♋	1: 2
18	☽ → ♌	9:29
20	☽ → ♍	20:46
21	☉ → ♋	21:40
23	☽ → ♎	9:37
24	♂ → ♌	6:52
25	☽ → ♏	21:26
28	☽ → ♐	6: 0
30	☽ → ♑	10:54

ASPECTS & ECLIPSES :

1	☉ ☍ ☽	16:24
2	☽ ☌ ♇	2: 9
3	☽ ☍ ♃	0:18
	☽ S ☊	10:53
	☽ ☍ ☿	17: 0
4	☽ ☍ ♂	8:41
	☽ ☍ ♄	18:14
5	☽ ☌ ♆	11:16
6	☽ ☍ ♅	16:49
7	☉ ☍ ♇	7:20
	☽ ☌ P	20:23
8	☉ □ ☽	13:56
9	☽ ☌ ☊	19:14
	♀ □ ♆	20:31
12	☽ ☌ ♀	0:10
	☉ □ Π	14:52
14	☽ ☍ ♇	23:27
15	♂ ☌ ♄	6:59
	☉ ☌ ☽	14: 2
16	☽ ☌ ♃	4:13
	☽ N ☊	7:59
	☉ □ Π	19:47
17	☽ ☌ ☿	7: 9
	☽ ☌ ♄	23:18
18	☽ ☌ ♂	2: 2
	☽ ☍ ♆	15:17
20	☽ ☌ ♅	3: 8
22	♃ □ ☊	2:51
	☽ ☌ A	5:34
23	☉ □ ☽	12:46
	☽ ☌ ☋	15:47
25	☉ □ ☊	1:47
26	☉ ☌ ♃	0:12
27	♀ □ ♅	7:13
	☽ ☍ ♀	15: 5
28	♂ ☍ ♆	17: 6
29	☽ ☌ ♇	9:49
30	☽ S ☊	14:56
	☽ ☍ ♃	19:24

SIDEREAL HELIOCENTRIC LONGITUDES : JUNE 33 Julian at 0 hours UT

DAY	Sid. Time	☿	♀	⊕	♂	♃	♄	♅	♆	♇	Vernal Point
1 MO	16:29:26	9 ♎ 44	24 ♑ 55	10 ♐ 6	6 ♌ 21	1 ♋ 54	27 ♋ 7	23 ♌ 30	1 ♒ 45	16 ♐ 3	2♈35'38"
2 TU	16:33:22	12 47	26 29	11 3	6 47	1 58	27 9	23 31	1 45	16 3	2♈35'38"
3 WE	16:37:19	15 48	28 4	12 0	7 14	2 3	27 11	23 31	1 45	16 4	2♈35'38"
4 TH	16:41:15	18 45	29 39	12 57	7 40	2 8	27 13	23 32	1 46	16 4	2♈35'38"
5 FR	16:45:12	21 41	1 ♒ 14	13 54	8 6	2 13	27 15	23 33	1 46	16 4	2♈35'38"
6 SA	16:49: 8	24 34	2 48	14 51	8 33	2 18	27 17	23 34	1 46	16 5	2♈35'38"
7 SU	16:53: 5	27 25	4 23	15 48	8 59	2 23	27 19	23 35	1 47	16 5	2♈35'37"
8 MO	16:57: 1	0 ♏ 15	5 58	16 45	9 25	2 28	27 22	23 35	1 47	16 5	2♈35'37"
9 TU	17: 0:58	3 3	7 33	17 43	9 52	2 33	27 24	23 36	1 48	16 6	2♈35'37"
10 WE	17: 4:55	5 51	9 8	18 40	10 18	2 37	27 26	23 37	1 48	16 6	2♈35'37"
11 TH	17: 8:51	8 37	10 43	19 37	10 44	2 42	27 28	23 38	1 48	16 6	2♈35'37"
12 FR	17:12:48	11 22	12 18	20 34	11 11	2 47	27 30	23 38	1 49	16 7	2♈35'37"
13 SA	17:16:44	14 7	13 52	21 31	11 37	2 52	27 32	23 39	1 49	16 7	2♈35'37"
14 SU	17:20:41	16 52	15 27	22 28	12 3	2 57	27 34	23 40	1 49	16 7	2♈35'36"
15 MO	17:24:37	19 37	17 2	23 25	12 30	3 2	27 37	23 41	1 50	16 8	2♈35'36"
16 TU	17:28:34	22 21	18 37	24 23	12 56	3 7	27 39	23 41	1 50	16 8	2♈35'36"
17 WE	17:32:30	25 6	20 12	25 20	13 22	3 12	27 41	23 42	1 50	16 8	2♈35'36"
18 TH	17:36:27	27 52	21 48	26 17	13 49	3 16	27 43	23 43	1 51	16 9	2♈35'36"
19 FR	17:40:24	0 ♐ 38	23 23	27 14	14 15	3 21	27 45	23 44	1 51	16 9	2♈35'36"
20 SA	17:44:20	3 25	24 58	28 11	14 42	3 26	27 47	23 45	1 51	16 9	2♈35'36"
21 SU	17:48:17	6 13	26 33	29 9	15 8	3 31	27 49	23 45	1 52	16 10	2♈35'35"
22 MO	17:52:13	9 3	28 8	0 ♑ 6	15 34	3 36	27 52	23 46	1 52	16 10	2♈35'35"
23 TU	17:56:10	11 54	29 43	1 3	16 1	3 41	27 54	23 47	1 53	16 10	2♈35'35"
24 WE	18: 0: 6	14 47	1 ♓ 18	2 0	16 27	3 46	27 56	23 48	1 53	16 11	2♈35'35"
25 TH	18: 4: 3	17 42	2 54	2 58	16 54	3 50	27 58	23 48	1 53	16 11	2♈35'35"
26 FR	18: 7:59	20 39	4 29	3 55	17 20	3 55	28 0	23 49	1 54	16 11	2♈35'35"
27 SA	18:11:56	23 39	6 4	4 52	17 47	4 0	28 2	23 50	1 54	16 12	2♈35'35"
28 SU	18:15:53	26 42	7 40	5 49	18 13	4 5	28 4	23 51	1 54	16 12	2♈35'35"
29 MO	18:19:49	29 47	9 15	6 47	18 40	4 10	28 7	23 52	1 55	16 12	2♈35'34"
30 TU	18:23:46	2 ♑ 56	10 50	7 44	19 6	4 15	28 9	23 52	1 55	16 12	2♈35'34"

INGRESSES :

4	♀ → ♒	5:21
7	☿ → ♏	21:51
18	☿ → ♐	18:31
21	⊕ → ♑	21:31
23	♀ → ♓	4:13
29	☿ → ♑	1:38

ASPECTS (HELIOCENTRIC +MOON(TYCHONIC)) :

2	☽ ☌ ♇	1:51
	♂ N ☊	9:12
	♀ ☍ ♄	10:11
	⊕ ☌ A	21:16
3	☽ ☍ ♃	5:55
4	☽ □ ☿	13:25
5	☽ ☍ ♄	1: 6
	♀ ☌ ♆	8:15
	☽ ☌ ♆	8:47
	☽ ☌ ♀	8:51
	☽ ☍ ♂	20: 9
6	☽ ☍ ♅	21:43
	☿ □ ♄	23: 9
7	☿ ☌ ☋	2: 2
	⊕ ☌ ♇	7: 3
8	☽ □ ♇	11:52
	☿ □ ♆	13: 7
9	☽ □ ♃	15:57
11	♀ ☍ ♂	0:33
	☽ □ ♄	10:34
	☽ □ ♆	18: 2
	☿ □ ♂	21:56
12	☽ □ ♂	10:34
	☽ ☍ ☿	13:13
	☽ □ ♀	13:45
	☿ □ ♀	18:50
13	☽ □ ♅	8: 0
14	☿ ☌ A	23:30
	☽ ☍ ♇	23:51
16	☽ ☌ ♃	6:48
	☿ □ ♅	11:43
18	☽ ☌ ♄	5: 5
	☽ ☍ ♆	13: 3
19	♀ ☍ ♅	5:23
	☽ ☌ ♂	13:49
20	☽ ☌ ♅	8:12
	☽ ☍ ♀	12:16
21	☽ □ ☿	12:15
22	☽ □ ♇	5:31
23	☽ □ ♃	17:11
24	♀ S ☊	6: 5
	☿ ☌ ♇	11:30
25	☽ □ ♄	17:31
26	⊕ ☍ ♃	0:12
	☽ □ ♆	1: 7
27	☽ □ ♂	7:41
	☽ □ ♅	18:42
28	☽ □ ♀	22:29
29	☽ ☌ ♇	10:59
30	☿ ☍ ♃	10: 6
	☽ ☍ ♃	18:15
	☽ ☌ ☿	20:36

GLOSSARY OF ESOTERIC CHRISTIANITY

This glossary of entries relating to Esoteric Christianity lists only some of the specialized terms used in the articles and commentaries of *Star Wisdom*. Owing to limited space, the entries are brief, and the reader is encouraged to study the foundational works of Rudolf Steiner for a more complete understanding of these terms.

Ahriman: An adversarial being identified by the great prophet Zarathustra during the ancient Persian cultural epoch (5067–2907 BC) as an opponent to the Sun God *Ahura Mazda* (obs.; "Aura of the Sun"). Also called Satan, Ahriman represents one aspect of the Dragon. Ahriman's influence leads to materialistic thinking devoid of feeling, empathy, and moral conscience. Ahriman helps inspire science and technology, and works through forces of sub-nature such as gravity, electricity, magnetism, radioactivity—forces that are antithetical to life. The influence of Ahriman's activity upon the human being limits human cognition to what is derived from sense perception, hardens thinking (materialistic thoughts), attacks the etheric body by way of modern technology (electromagnetic radiation, etc.), and hardens hearts (cold and calculating).

ahrimanic beings: Spiritual beings who have become agents of Ahriman's influences.

Angel Jesus: A pure immaculate Angelic being who sacrifices himself so that the Christ may work through him. This Angelic being is actually of the status of an Archangel, who has descended to work on the Angelic level to be closer to human beings and to assist them on the path of confrontation with evil.

Ascension: An unfathomable process at the start of which, on May 14 AD 33, Christ united with the etheric realm that surrounds and permeates the Earth with Cosmic Life. Thus began his cosmic ascent to the realm of the heavenly Father, with the goal of elevating the Earth spiritually and opening pathways between the Earth and the spiritual world for the future.

astral body: Part of the human being that is the bearer of consciousness, passion, and desires, as well as idealism and the longing for perfection.

Asuras: Fallen Archai (Time Spirits) from the time of Old Saturn, whose opposition to human evolution comes to expression through promoting debauched sexuality and senseless violence among human beings. So low is the regard that the Asuras have for the sacredness of human life, that as well as promoting extreme violence and debauchery (for example, through the film industry), they do not hold back from the destruction of the physical body of human beings. In particular, the activity of the Asuras retards the development of the consciousness soul.

bodhisattva: On the human level a bodhisattva is a human being far advanced on the spiritual path, a human being belonging to the circle of twelve great teachers surrounding the Cosmic Christ. One who incarnates periodically to further the evolution of the Earth and humanity, working on the level of an angelic, archangelic, or higher being in relation to the rest of humanity. Every 5,000 years, one of these great teachers from the circle of bodhisattvas takes on a special mission, incarnating repeatedly to awake a new human faculty and capacity. Once that capacity has been imparted through its human bearer, this bodhisattva then incarnates upon the Earth for the last time, ascending to the level of a Buddha to serve humankind from spirit realms. See also Maitreya Bodhisattva.

Central Sun: Heart of the Milky Way, also called the Galactic Center. Our Sun orbits this Central

Sun over a period of approximately 225 million years.

chakra: One of seven astral organs of perception through which human beings develop higher levels of cognition such as clairvoyance, telepathy, and so on.

Christ: The eternal being who is the second member of the Trinity. Also called the "Divine 'I AM,'" the Son of God, the Cosmic Christ, and the Logos–Word. Christ began to fully unite with the human vessel (Jesus) at the Baptism in the Jordan, and for 3½ years penetrated as the *Divine I AM* successively into the astral body, etheric body, and physical body of Jesus, spiritualizing each member. Through the Mystery of Golgotha Christ united with the Earth, kindling the spark of Christ consciousness (*Not I, but Christ in me*) in all human beings.

consciousness soul: The portion of the human soul in which "I" consciousness is awaking not only to its own sense of individuality and to the individualities of others, but also to its higher self—spirit self (Sanskrit: *manas*). Within the consciousness soul, the "I" perceives truth, beauty, and goodness; within the spirit self, the "I" becomes truth, beauty, and goodness.

crossing the threshold: a term applicable to our time, as human beings are increasingly encountering the spiritual world—in so doing, crossing the threshold between the sense-perceptible realm and non-physical realms of existence. To the extent that spiritual capacities have not been cultivated, this encounter with non-physical realms beyond the sense world signifies a descent into the subconscious (for example, through drugs) rather than an ascent to knowledge of higher worlds through the awaking of higher levels of consciousness.

decan: The zodiac of 360° is divided into twelve signs, each of 30°. A decan is 10°, thus one third of one sign or $1/36$ of the zodiac.

Devil: Another name for Lucifer.

dragon: As used in the Apocalypse of John, there are different appearances of the dragon, each one representing an adversarial being opposed to Michael, Christ, and Sophia. For example, the great red dragon of chapter 12 opposes Sophia, the woman clothed with the Sun (Sophia is the pure Divine-Cosmic Feminine Soul of the World). The imagery from chapter 12 of Revelation depicts the woman clothed with the Sun as pregnant and that the great red dragon attempts to devour her child as soon as it is born. The child coming to birth from the woman clothed with the Sun represents the Divine-Cosmic "I AM" born through the assistance of the pure Divine Feminine Soul of the World. The dragon is cast down from the heavenly realm by the mighty Archangel Michael. Cast down to the Earth, the dragon continues with attempts to devour the cosmic child (the Divine-Cosmic "I AM") coming to birth among humankind.

ego: The soul sheath through which the "I" begins to incarnate and to experience life on Earth (to be distinguished from the term *ego* used in Freudian and Jungian psychology). The terms *"I,"* and *soul* are sometimes used interchangeably in Spiritual Science. The ego maintains threads of integrity and continuity through memory, while experiencing new sensations and perceptions through observation and thinking, feeling, and willing. The ego is capable of moral discernment and also experiences temptation. Thus, it is often stated that the "I" comprises both a higher nature and the lower nature ("ego").

Emmerich, Anne Catherine (also "Sister Emmerich"): A Catholic stigmatist (1774–1824), whose visions depicted the daily life of Jesus, beginning some weeks before the event of the descent of Christ into the body of Jesus at the Baptism in the River Jordan and extending for a period of several weeks after the Crucifixion.

Ephesus: The area in Asia Minor (now Turkey) to which the Apostle John (also called John Zebedee, the brother of James the Greater) accompanied the Virgin Mary approximately three years after the death of Jesus Christ. Ephesus was a very significant ancient mystery center where cosmic mysteries of the East found their way into the West. Initiates at Ephesus were devoted to the goddess Artemis, known as "Artemis of Ephesus," whose qualities are more those of a Mother goddess than is the case with the Greek goddess Artemis, although there is a certain degree of overlap between Artemis and Artemis of Ephesus with regard to many of their respective characteristics. A magnificent Ionic mystery temple was built in honor of Artemis of Ephesus at a location close to the Aegean Sea. Mary's house, built by John, was located high up above, on the nearby hill known as Mount Nightingale, about six miles from the temple of Artemis at Ephesus.

etheric body: The body of life forces permeating and animating the physical body. The etheric body was formed during ancient Sun evolution. The etheric body's activity is expressed in the seven life processes permeating the seven vital organs. The etheric body is related to the movements of the seven visible planets.

Fall, The: A fall from oneness with spiritual worlds. The Fall, which took place during the Lemurian period of Earth evolution, was a time of dramatic transition in human evolution when the soul descended from "Paradise" into earthly existence. Through the Fall the human soul began to incarnate into a physical body upon the Earth and experience the world from "within" the body, perceiving through the senses.

Fifth Gospel: The writings and lectures of Rudolf Steiner based on new spiritual perceptions and insights into the mysteries of Christ's life on Earth, including the Second Coming of Christ—his appearance in the etheric realm in our time, beginning in the twentieth century.

Golgotha, Mystery of: Rudolf Steiner's designation for the entire mystery of the coming of Christ to the Earth. Sometimes this term is used more specifically to refer to the events surrounding the Crucifixion and Resurrection. In particular, the Crucifixion—the sacrifice on the cross—marked the birth of Christ's union with the Earth. Also referred to as the "Turning Point of Time," whereby at the Crucifixion Christ descended from the sphere of the Sun and became the "Spirit of the Earth."

Grail: An etheric chalice into which Christ can work to transform earthly substance into spiritual substance. The term *Grail* has many deep levels of meaning and refers on the one hand to a spiritual stream in service of Christ, and on the other hand to the means by which the human "I" penetrates and transforms evil into good. The power of transubstantiation expresses something of this process of transformation of evil into good.

Grail Knights: Those trained to confront evil and transform it into something good, in service of Christ. Members of a spiritual stream that existed in the past and continues to exist—albeit in metamorphosed form—in the present. Every human being striving for the good can potentially become a Grail Knight.

I AM: One's true individuality, that—with few exceptions—never fully incarnates but works into the developing "I" and its lower bodies (astral, etheric, and physical). The **Cosmic I AM** is the "I AM" of Christ, through which—on account of the Mystery of Golgotha—we are all graced with the possibility of receiving a divine spark therefrom.

Jesus: The pure human being who received the Christ at the Baptism in the River Jordan. *See also* **Nathan Jesus** and **Solomon Jesus**.

Jesus Christ: The Divine-Human being; the God-Man; the union of the Divine with the Human. The presence of the Cosmic Christ in the physical body of the human being called the Nathan Jesus during the 3½ years of the ministry.

Jesus of Nazareth: The name of the human being whose birth is celebrated in the Gospel of Luke, also referred to as the Nathan Jesus. When Jesus of Nazareth reached the age of twelve, the spirit of the Solomon Jesus (Gospel of Matthew) united with the body and sheaths of the pure Nathan Jesus. This union lasted for about 18 years, until the Baptism in the River Jordan. During these eighteen years, Jesus of Nazareth was a composite being comprising the Nathan Jesus and the spirit ("I") of the Solomon Jesus. Just before the Baptism, the spirit of the Solomon Jesus withdrew, and at the Baptism Jesus became known as "Jesus Christ" through the union of Christ with the sheaths of Jesus.

Jezebel: Wife of King Ahab, approximately 900 BC, who worked through the powers of black magic against the prophet Elijah.

Kali Yuga: Yugas are ages of influence referred to in Hindu cosmography, each yuga lasting a certain numbers of years in length (always a multiple of 2,500). The Kali Yuga is also known as the Dark Age, which began with the death of Krishna in 3102 BC (-3101). Kali Yuga lasted 5,000 years and ended in AD 1899.

Kingly Stream: Biblically, the line of heredity from King David into which the Solomon Jesus (Gospel of Matthew) was born. The kings (the three magi) were initiates who sought to bring the cosmic will of the heavenly Father to expression on the Earth through spiritual forces working from spiritual beings dwelling in the stars. The minds of the wise kings were enlightened by the coming of Jesus Christ.

Krishna: A cosmic-human being, the sister soul of Adam that over-lighted Arjuna as described in the Bhagavad Gita. The over-lighting by Krishna of Arjuna could be described as an incorporation of Krishna into Arjuna. An incorporation is a partial incarnation. The cosmic-human being known as Krishna later fully incarnated as Jesus of Nazareth (Nathan Jesus—Gospel of Luke).

Lazarus: The elder brother of Mary Magdalene, Martha, and Silent Mary. At his raising from the dead, Lazarus became the first human being to be fully initiated by Christ (see Lazarus–John).

Lazarus–John: At the raising of Lazarus from the dead by Christ, the spiritual being of John the Baptist united with Lazarus. The higher spiritual members of John (spirit body, life spirit, spirit self) entered into the members of Lazarus, which were developed to the level of the consciousness soul. *See also* **Presbyter John.**

Lucifer: The name of a fallen spiritual being, also called the Light-Bearer, who acts as a retarding force within the human astral body, as well as in the human sentient soul. Lucifer inflames egoism and pride within human beings, often inspiring genius and supreme artistry. Arrogance and self-importance are stimulated, without humility or sacrificial love. Lucifer stirs up forces of rebellion, but cannot deliver true freedom—only its illusion.

luciferic beings: Spiritual beings who have become agents of Lucifer's influences.

magi: Initiates in the mystery school of Zarathustra, the Bodhisattva who incarnated as Zoroaster (Zaratas, Nazaratos) in the sixth century BC and who, after he came to Babylon, became a teacher of the Chaldean priesthood. At the time of Jesus, the magi were still continuing the star-gazing tradition of the school of Zoroaster. The task of the magi was to recognize when their master would reincarnate. With their visit to the new-born Jesus child in Bethlehem (Gospel of Matthew), to this child who was the reincarnated Zarathustra–Zoroaster, they fulfilled their mission. The three magi are the "priest kings from the East" referred to in the Gospel of Matthew.

Maitreya Bodhisattva: The bodhisattva individuality that is preparing to become the successor of Gautama Buddha and will be known as the Bringer of the Good. This bodhisattva was incarnated in the second century BC as Jeshu ben Pandira, the teacher of the Essenes, who died about 100 BC. Rudolf Steiner indicated that Jeshu ben Pandira reincarnated at the beginning of the twentieth century as a great bodhisattva individuality to fulfill the lofty mission of proclaiming Christ's coming in the etheric realm, beginning around 1933: "He will be the actual herald of Christ in his etheric form" (lecture about Jeshu ben Pandira held in Leipzig on November 4, 1911). There are differing points of view as to who this individuality actually was in his twentieth century incarnation.

manas: Also called the spirit self; the purified astral body, lifted into full communion with truth and goodness by becoming the true and the good within the essence of the higher self of the human being. Manas is the spiritual source of the "I," and as it is the eternal part of the human being that goes from life to life, manas bears the human being's true "eternal name" through its union with the Holy Spirit. The "eternal name" expresses the human being's true mission from life to life.

Mani: The name of a lofty initiate who lived in Babylon in the third century AD. The founder of the Manichean stream, whose mission is the transformation of evil into goodness through compassion and love. Mani reincarnated as Parzival in the ninth century AD. Mani–Parzival is one of the leading initiates of our present age—the age of the consciousness soul (1414–3574). One of the highest beings ever to incarnate upon the Earth, he will become the future Manu beginning in the astrological Age of Sagittarius. This future Manu will oversee the spiritual evolution of a sequence of seven ages, comprising the seven cultural epochs of the Sixth Great Age of Earth evolution from the Age of Sagittarius to the Age of Gemini—lasting a total of 7 x 2,160 years (15,120 years), since each zodiacal age lasts 2,160 years.

Manu: Like the word Buddha, the word *Manu* is a title. A Manu has the task of spiritually overseeing one Great Age of Earth evolution, comprising seven astrological ages (seven cultural epochs)—lasting a total of 7 x 2,160 years (15,120 years), since each zodiacal age lasts 2,160 years. The present Age of Pisces (AD 215–2375)—with its corresponding cultural epoch (AD 1414–3574)—is the fifth epoch during the Fifth Great Age of Earth evolution. (Lemuria was the Third Great Age, Atlantis the Fourth Great Age, and since the great flood that destroyed Atlantis, we are now in the Fifth Great Age.) The present Manu is the exalted Sun-initiate who guided humanity out of Atlantis during the ancient flooding that destroyed the continent of Atlantis formerly in the region of the Atlantic Ocean—the Flood referred to in the Bible in connection with Noah. He is the overseer of the seven cultural epochs corresponding to the seven astrological ages from the Age of Cancer to the Age of Capricorn, following the sequence: Cancer, Gemini, Taurus, Aries, Pisces, Aquarius, Capricorn. The present Manu was the teacher of the Seven Holy Rishis who were the founders of the ancient Indian cultural epoch (7227–5067 BC) during the Age of Cancer. He is known in the Bible as Noah, and in the Flood story belonging to the Gilgamesh epic he is called Utnapishtim. Subsequently this Manu appeared to Abraham as Melchizedek and offered Abraham an agape ("love feast") of bread and wine. Jesus "was designated by God to be high priest in the order of Melchizedek" (Heb. 5:10).

Mary: Rudolf Steiner distinguishes between the Nathan Mary and the Solomon Mary (see corresponding entries). The expression "Virgin Mary" refers to the Solomon Mary, the mother of the child Jesus whose birth is described in the Gospel of Matthew.

Mary Magdalene: Sister of Lazarus, whose soul was transformed and purified as Christ cast out seven demons who had taken possession of her. Christ thus initiated Mary Magdalene. Later, she anointed Jesus Christ. And she was the first to behold the Risen Christ in the Garden of the Holy Sepulcher on the morning of his resurrection.

megastar: Stars with a luminosity greater than 10,000 times that of our Sun.

Nain, Youth of: Referred to in the Gospel of Luke as the son of the widow of Nain. The Youth of Nain—at the time he was twelve years old—was raised from the dead by Jesus. The Youth of Nain later reincarnated as the Prophet Mani (third century AD) and subsequently as the Grail King Parzival (ninth century AD).

Nathan Jesus: From the priestly line of David, as described in the Gospel of Luke. An immaculate and pure soul whose one and only physical incarnation was as Jesus of Nazareth (Nathan Jesus).

Nathan Mary: A pure being who was the mother of the Nathan Jesus. The Nathan Mary died in AD 12, but her spirit united with the Solomon Mary at the time of the Baptism of Jesus in the River Jordan. From this time on, the Solomon Mary—spiritually united with the Nathan Mary—was known as the Virgin Mary.

New Jerusalem: A spiritual condition denoting humanity's future existence that will come into being as human beings free themselves from the *maya* of the material world and work together to bring about a spiritualized Earth.

Osiris: *Osiris* and *Isis* are names given by the Egyptians to the preincarnatory forms of the spiritual beings who are now known as Christ and Sophia.

Parzival: Son of Gahmuret and Herzeloyde in the epic *Parzival* by Wolfram von Eschenbach.

Although written in the thirteenth century, this work refers to actual people and events in the ninth century AD, one of whom (the central figure) bore the name Parzival. After living a life of dullness and doubt, Parzival's mission was to seek the Castle of the Grail and to ask the question "What ails thee?" of the Grail King, Anfortas—moreover, to ask the question without being bidden to do so. Parzival eventually became the new Grail King, the successor of Anfortas. Parzival was the reincarnated prophet Mani. In the incarnation preceding that of Mani, he was incarnated as the Youth of Nain (Luke 7:11–15). Parzival is a great initiate responsible for guiding humanity during the Age of Pisces, which has given birth to the cultural epoch of the development of the consciousness soul (AD 1414–3574).

Pentecost: Descent of the Holy Spirit fifty days after Easter, whereby the cosmic "I AM" was birthed among the disciples and those individuals close to Christ. They received the capacity to develop manas, or spirit self, within the community of striving human individuals, whereby the birth of the spirit self is facilitated through the soul of the Virgin Mary. See also World Pentecost.

phantom body: The pure spiritual form of the human physical body, unhindered by matter. The far-distant future state of the human physical body when it has become purified and spiritualized into a body of transformed divine will.

Presbyter John: Refers to Lazarus–John, who moved to Ephesus about twenty years after the Virgin Mary died there. In Ephesus, John became a bishop. He is the author of the book of Revelation, the Gospel of St. John, and the Letters of John.

Risen One: The initial appearance of Christ in his phantom body (resurrection body), beginning with his appearance to Mary Magdalene on Easter Sunday morning. Christ frequently appeared to the disciples in his phantom body during the forty days leading from Easter to Ascension.

Satan: The traditional Christian name for Ahriman.

Serpent: Another name for Lucifer, but sometimes naming a combination of Lucifer and Ahriman: "The great dragon was hurled down—that ancient serpent called the devil, or Satan, who leads the whole world astray" (Rev. 12:9).

Shepherd Stream: Biblically, the genealogical line from David the shepherd through his son Nathan. It was into this line that the Nathan Jesus was born, whose birth is described in the Gospel of Luke. Rudolf Steiner describes the shepherds, who—according to Luke—came to pay homage to the newborn child, as those servants of pure heart who perceive the goodwill streaming up from Mother Earth. The hearts of the shepherds were kindled with the fire of Divine Love by the coming of the Christ. The shepherds can be regarded as precursors of the heart stream of humanity that now intuits the being of Christ as the spirit of the Earth.

Solomon Jesus: Descended from the genealogical line from David through his son Solomon. This line of descent is described in the Gospel of Matthew. The Solomon Jesus was a reincarnation of Zoroaster (sixth century BC). In turn, Zoroaster was a reincarnation of Zarathustra (6000 BC), the great prophet and founder of the ancient Persian religion of Zoroastrianism. He was a bodhisattva who, as the founder of this new religion that focused on the Sun Spirit Ahura Mazda, helped prepare humanity for the subsequent descent into incarnation of Ahura Mazda, the cosmic Sun Spirit, as Christ.

Solomon Mary: The wise mother of the Solomon Jesus, who adopted the Nathan Jesus after the death of the Nathan Mary. At the time of the Baptism of Jesus in the River Jordan, the spirit of the Nathan Mary united with the Solomon Mary. Usually referred to as the Virgin Mary or Mother Mary, the Solomon Mary bore witness at the foot of the cross to the Mystery of Golgotha. She died in Ephesus eleven years after Christ's Ascension.

Sophia: Part of the Divine Feminine Trinity comprising the Mother (counterpart of the Father), the Daughter (counterpart of the Son), and the Holy Soul (counterpart of the Holy Spirit). Sophia, also known as the Bride of the Lamb, is the Daughter aspect of the threefold Divine Feminine Trinity. To the Egyptians Sophia was known as Isis, who was seen as belonging to the starry realm surrounding the Earth. In the

Book of Proverbs, attributed to King Solomon, Sophia's temple has seven pillars (Proverbs 9:1). The seven pillars in Sophia's temple represent the seven great stages of Earth evolution (from ancient Saturn to future Vulcan).

Sorath: The great enemy of Christ who works against the "I" in the human being. Sorath is identified with the two-horned beast that rises up from the depths of Earth, as described in the book of Revelation. Sorath is the Sun Demon, and is identified by Rudolf Steiner as the Antichrist. According to the book of Revelation, his number is 666.

Sun Demon: Another name for Sorath.

Transfiguration: The event on Mt. Tabor where Jesus Christ was illumined with Divine Light raying forth from the purified etheric body of Jesus, which the Divine "I AM" of Christ had penetrated. The Gospels of Matthew and Luke describe the Transfiguration. The Sun-like radiance that shone forth from Jesus Christ on Mt. Tabor was an expression of the purified etheric body that had its origin during the Old Sun period of Earth evolution.

Transubstantiation: Sacramental transformation of physical substance—for example, the transubstantiation of bread and wine during the Mass to become the body and blood of Christ. During the Holy Eucharist the bread and wine are transformed in such a way that the substances of bread and wine are infused with the life force (body) and light (blood) of Christ. Thereby the bread and wine are reunited with their divine archetypes and are no longer "merely" physical substances, but are bearers on the physical level of a spiritual reality.

Turning Point of Time: Transition between involution and evolution, as marked by the Mystery of Golgotha. The descending stream of involution culminated with the Mystery of Golgotha. With the descent of the Cosmic Christ into earthly evolution, through his sacrifice on Golgotha an ascending stream of evolution began. This sacrifice of Christ was followed by the events of his Resurrection and Ascension, which were followed

in turn by Whitsun (Pentecost)—all expressing the ascending stream of evolution. This path of ascent was also opened up to all human beings by way of the power of the divine "I AM" bestowed—at least, potentially—on all humanity by Christ through his sacrifice on the cross.

Union in the Temple: The event of the union of the spirit of the Solomon Jesus with the twelve-year-old Nathan Jesus. This union of the two Jesus children signified the uniting of the priestly (Nathan) line and the kingly (Solomon) line—both lines descended from King David.

Whitsun: "White Sunday," or Pentecost. This holy day occurs on the seventh Sunday after Easter.

World Pentecost is the gradual event of cosmic revelation becoming human revelation as a signature of the end of the Dark Age (Kali Yuga). Anthroposophy (Spiritual Science) is a language of spiritual truth that could awake a community of striving human beings to the presence of the Holy Spirit and the founding of the New Jerusalem.

Zarathustra: The great teacher of the ancient Persians in the sixth millennium BC (around 6000 BC). In the sixth century BC, Zarathustra reincarnated as Zoroaster. He then reincarnated as the Solomon Jesus (6 BC–AD 12), whose birth is described in the Gospel of Matthew.

Zoroaster: An incarnation of Zarathustra. Zarathustra–Zoroaster was a bodhisattva. Zoroaster was a master of wisdom who lived in the sixth century BC. Among his communications as a teacher of wisdom was his specification as to how the zodiac of living beings in the heavens comes to expression in relation to the stars comprising the twelve zodiacal constellations. Zoroaster subsequently incarnated as the Solomon Jesus, whose birth is described in the Gospel of Matthew, to whom the three magi came from the East bearing gifts of gold, frankincense, and myrrh.

CITED WORKS AND RELATED READING

See also "Literature" (pages 8–10) for an annotated list of more books on Astrosophy.

Allen, Richard H. *Star Names and Their Meanings*. New York: Stechert, 1899. Currently in print: *Star Names: Their Lore and Meaning*. New York: Dover, 1963.

Andreev, Daniel. *The Rose of the World*. Trans. Jordan Roberts. Hudson, NY: Lindisfarne Books, 1997.

Anonymous. *Meditations on the Tarot: A Journey into Christian Hermeticism*. Trans. Robert Powell. New York: Tarcher/Penguin, 2002.

Collin, Rodney. *The Theory of Celestial Influence: Man, the Universe, and Cosmic Mystery*. New York: Penguin, 1993.

Dorsan, Jacques. *The Clockwise House System: A True Foundation for Sidereal and Tropical Astrology*. Trans. Lesley Spring. Great Barrington, MA: Lindisfarne Books, 2011.

——. *Retour au Zodiaque des Étoiles: Vous n'êtes pas né sous le signe que vous croyez* [*Return to the Stellar Zodiac: You're not the sign you think you are*]. Paris: Dervy-Livres, 1986.

Edwards, Ormond. *A New Chronology of the Gospels*. Edinburgh: Floris Books, 1972.

Fletcher, B. A. *The Aramaic Sayings of Jesus*. Hachette, UK: Hodder & Stoughton, 1967.

Fulcanelli. *The Mystery of the Cathedrals: And the Esoteric Interpretation of the Hermetic Symbols of the Great Work*. Trans. Daniel Bernardo. Jacksboro, TX: Sojourner, 2019.

Henning, W. B. *Zoroaster: Politician or Witch-doctor?* London: Cumberlege, 1951.

Hone, Margaret E. *The Modern Text-Book of Astrology*. Bel Air, MD: Astrology Classics, 1969.

Isaacson, Estelle. *Through the Eyes of Mary Magdalene*, 3 vols. Taos, NM: LogoSophia, 2012–2015.

Koepf, H. H., B. D. Pettersson, and W. Schaumann. *Biodynamic Agriculture: An Introduction*. New York: Anthroposophic Press, 1976.

Kolisko, Lili. *The Moon and the Growth of Plants*. London, 1938.

König, Karl. *The Human Soul*. New York: Anthroposophic Press, 1973 (current ed. Edinburgh: Floris Books, 2006).

Lewy, Hans. *Chaldaean Oracles and Theurgy: Mysticism, Magic and Platonism in the Later Roman Empire*. Paris: Études Augustiniennes, 1978

Manilius. *Astronomica*. Ed. & Trans. G. P. Goold. Cambridge, MA: Harvard University (Loeb Classical Library, no. 469), 1977.

Mayo, Jeff. *Astrology: A Key to Personality*. London: Hodder Stoughton, 1995.

McLaren Lainson, Claudia. *The Circle of Twelve and the Legacy of Valentin Tomberg*. Boulder: Windrose Academy, 2015.

Neugebauer, O. *A History of Ancient Mathematical Astronomy: Studies in the History of Mathematics and Physical Sciences* (3 vols.). New York: Springer, 1975.

Nowotny, K. A. *De occulta philosophia*. Graz, Austria: Akademische Druck- und Verlagsanstalt, 1967.

Pagan, Isabelle M. *From Pioneer to Poet, or the Twelve Great Gates: An Expansion of the Signs of the Zodiac Analyzed*. London: Theosophical Publishing, 1911.

Park, Joel Matthew (ed.). *Star Wisdom*, vols. 1–6. Great Barrington, MA/Spencertown, NY: Lindisfarne Books, 2019–2024.

Porphyry, *Vita Pythagorae*. Ed. Nauck (cited). See *The Life of Pythagoras*. Trans. K. S. Guthrie. Available at https://www.tertullian.org/fathers/porphyry_life_of _pythagoras_02_text.htm.

Powell, Robert A. *Cultivating Inner Radiance and the Body of Immortality: Awakening the Soul through Modern Etheric Movement*. Great Barrington, MA: Lindisfarne Books, 2012.

—— (ed.). *Journal for Star Wisdom*. Great Barrington, MA: SteinerBooks/Lindisfarne Books, 2010–2018.

——. *The Most Holy Trinosophia: The New Revelation of the Divine Feminine*. Great Barrington, MA: SteinerBooks, 2000.

——. *The Mystery, Biography, and Destiny of Mary Magdalene: Sister of Lazarus–John and Spiritual Sister of Jesus*. Great Barrington, MA: Lindisfarne Books, 2008.

——. *Prophecy Phenomena Hope: The Real Meaning of 2012: Christ and the Maya Calendar, an Update*. Great Barrington, MA: SteinerBooks, 2011.

——. *The Sophia Teachings: The Emergence of the Divine Feminine in Our Time.* Great Barrington, MA: Lindisfarne Books, 2007.

Powell, Robert A., and David Bowden. *Astrogeographia: Correspondences between the Stars and Earthly Locations: Earth Chakras and the Bible of Astrology.* Great Barrington, MA: SteinerBooks, 2012.

Powell, Robert A., and Kevin Dann. *The Astrological Revolution: Unveiling the Science of the Stars as a Science of Reincarnation and Karma.* Great Barrington, MA: SteinerBooks, 2010.

——. *Christ and the Maya Calendar: 2012 and the Coming of the Antichrist.* Great Barrington, MA: SteinerBooks, 2009.

Powell, Robert A., and Estelle Isaacson. *Gautama Buddha's Successor: A Force for Good in our Time.* Great Barrington, MA: SteinerBooks, 2013.

——. *The Mystery of Sophia: Bearer of the New Culture: The Rose of the World.* Great Barrington, MA: SteinerBooks, 2014.

Powell, Robert A., and Peter Treadgold. *The Sidereal Zodiac.* Tempe, AZ: AFA, 1985.

Robson, Vivian E. *The Fixed Stars and Constellations in Astrology.* Abingdon, MD: Astrology Classics (reprint of 1923 ed.), 2005.

Steiner, Rudolf. *According to Luke: The Gospel of Compassion and Love Revealed* (CW 114). Trans. Catherine E. Creeger. Great Barrington, MA: Anthroposophic Press, 2001.

——. *According to Matthew: The Gospel of Christ's Humanity* (CW 123). Trans. Catherine E. Creeger. Great Barrington, MA: Anthroposophic Press, 2002.

——. *Ancient Myths and the New Isis Mystery* (CW 180). Great Barrington, MA: SteinerBooks, 2018.

——. *The Apocalypse of St. John: Lectures on the Book of Revelation* (CW 104). Spring Valley, NY: Anthroposophic Press, 1985.

——. *Architecture as Peacework: The First Goetheanum, Dornach, 1914* (CW 287). Trans. Frederick Amrine. Great Barrington, MA: SteinerBooks, 2016.

——. *The Book of Revelation: And the Work of the Priest* (CW 346). Trans. Johanna Collis. Forest Row, UK: Rudolf Steiner Press, 1999.

——. *Calendar 1912–1913: The original book containing the calendar created by Rudolf Steiner for the year 1912–1913* (CW 40). Trans. Christopher Bamford. Great Barrington, MA: Anthroposophic Press, 2004.

——. *The Calendar of the Soul* (CW 40). Trans. Hans and Ruth Pusch. Spencertown, NY: SteinerBooks, 2023.

——. *The Challenge of the Times* (CW 186). Trans. Olin D. Wannamaker. Spring Valley, NY: Anthroposophic Press, 1979.

——. *Concerning the Astral World and Devachan* (CW 88). Trans. James H. Hindes. Great Barrington, MA: SteinerBooks, 2018.

——. *The Destinies of Individuals and of Nations* (CW 157). Trans. Anna R. Meuss. Hudson, NY: Anthroposophic Press, 1987.

——. *Esoteric Lessons 1904–1909: From the Esoteric School 1* (CW 266/1). Trans. James H. Hindes. Great Barrington, MA: SteinerBooks, 2007.

——. *Esoteric Lessons 1910–1912: From the Esoteric School 2* (CW 266/2). Trans. James H. Hindes. Great Barrington, MA: SteinerBooks, 2012.

——. *Esoteric Lessons 1904–1909: From the Esoteric School 3* (CW 266/3) Trans. Marsha Post. Great Barrington, MA: SteinerBooks, 2008.

——. *The Fall of the Spirits of Darkness* (CW 177). Trans. Frederick Amrine. Forest Row, UK: Rudolf Steiner Press, 1993.

——. *The Festivals and Their Meaning.* Forest Row, UK: Rudolf Steiner Press, 1996.

——. *Freemasonry and Ritual Work: The Misraim Service* (CW 265). Trans. John M. Wood. Great Barrington, MA: SteinerBooks, 2007.

——. *From Jesus to Christ* (CW 131). Forest Row, UK: Rudolf Steiner Press, 1994.

——. *Good and Evil Spirits: And their Influence on Humanity* (CW 102). Trans. Anna R. Meuss. Forest Row, UK: Rudolf Steiner Press, 2014.

——. *How Can Mankind Find the Christ Again? The Threefold Shadow-Existence of Our Time and the New Light of Christ* (CW 187). Spring Valley, NY: Anthroposophic Press, 1984.

——. *Human and Cosmic Thought* (CW 151). Trans. Charles Davy. Forest Row, UK: Rudolf Steiner Press, 2015.

——. *Interdisciplinary Astronomy: Third Scientific Course* (CW 323). Trans. Frederick Amrine. Great Barrington, MA: SteinerBooks, 2003.

——. *The Karma of Materialism: Aspects of Human Evolution* (CW 176). Trans. Rita Stebbing. Great Barrington, MA: SteinerBooks, 2022.

——. *Karmic Relationships: Esoteric Studies*, 8 vols. (CW 240). Forest Row, UK: Rudolf Steiner Press, 1982–2017.

——. *Materialism and the Task of Anthroposophy* (CW 204). Trans. Maria St. Goar. Hudson, NY: Anthroposophic Press, 1987.

——. *Occult Signs and Symbols* (CW 101). Spring Valley, NY: Anthroposophic Press, 1972.

——. *An Outline of Esoteric Science* (CW 13). Trans. Catherine E. Creeger. Hudson, NY: Anthroposophic Press, 1997.

——. *The Reappearance of Christ in the Etheric: A Collection of Lectures on the Second Coming of Christ.* Ed. Stephen E. Usher. Great Barrington, MA: SteinerBooks, 2022.

——. *The Search for the New Isis, the Divine Sophia.* See *Universal Spirituality and Human Physicality* (CW 202).

——. *Secret Brotherhoods and the Mystery of the Human Double* (CW 178). Trans. Johanna Collis. Forest Row, UK: Rudolf Steiner Press, 2004.

——. *Universal Spirituality and Human Physicality: Bridging the Divide: The Search for the New Isis and the Divine Sophia* (CW 202). Trans. Matthew Barton. Forest Row, UK: Rudolf Steiner Press, 2014.

Sucher, Willi. *The Drama of the Universe.* Larkfield, UK: Landvidi Research Centre, 1958.

——. *Isis Sophia I: Introducing Astrosophy.* Meadow Vista, CA: Astrosophy Research Center, 1999.

——. *Isis Sophia II: An Outline of a New Star Wisdom.* Meadow Vista, CA: Astrosophy Research Center, 1985.

——. *Star Journals II: Toward a New Astrosophy.* Meadow Vista, CA: Astrosophy Research Center, 2006.

Tomberg, Valentin. *Christ and Sophia: Anthroposophic Meditations on the Old Testament, New Testament, and Apocalypse.* Trans. R. H. Bruce. Great Barrington, MA: SteinerBooks, 2006.

——. *Studies on the Foundation Stone Meditation.* San Rafael, CA: LogoSophia, 2010.

Tradowsky, Peter. *Kaspar Hauser: The Struggle for the Spirit.* Forest Row, UK: Temple Lodge, 2012.

Van der Waerden, B. L. *Science Awakening.* Trans. A. Dresden. Leyden, Netherlands, 1974.

von Eschenbach, Wolfram. *Parzival: A Romance of the Middle Ages.* New York: Vintage Classics, 1961.

Wachsmuth, Guenther. *The Etheric Formative Forces in Cosmos, Earth and Man.* Ed. O. Wannamaker. London, New York: Anthroposophic Press, 1932.

——. *Kosmiche Aspekte von Geburt und Tod* (Cosmic aspects of birth and death). Dornach, 1956.

Weinreb, Friedrich. *Roots of the Bible: An Ancient View for a New Vision: The Key to Creation in Jewish Tradition.* Brooklyn, NY: Angelico, 2021.

Wiseman, D. J., et al. *Notes on Some Problems in the Book of Daniel.* London: Tyndale, 1965.

"They looked up, above all, to what is represented by the zodiac. And they regarded what the human being bears within as the spirit in connection with the constellations, the glory of the fixed stars, the spiritual powers whom they knew to be there in the stars."

Rudolf Steiner, *Karmic Relationships*, vol. 4, Sept. 12, 1924

THE CONTRIBUTORS

KRISZTINA CSERI (b. 1975) graduated as an economist and worked in the production and financial controlling field at various companies for twelve years. She started to work with astrology in 2002 and attended a course from 2004 until 2007. She became a student of Anthroposophy at Pentecost 2009, when a friend invited her to the anniversary celebration of Rudolf Steiner's "Budapest-lectures." Owing to the impact of that event, she soon left her financial career. She first encountered the work of Willi Sucher and Robert Powell in 2010. In 2012, with her husband she founded the Hungarian Sophia Foundation (www.szofia-magyarorszag.hu). They have a small publishing company and translate and distribute books on spiritual themes. Krisztina translated six books written by Robert Powell (and Kevin Dann) into Hungarian and finished translating *Meditations on the Tarot* into Hungarian in 2020. She is a mother of two little children and lives with her family in a village near Budapest. Email: krisztinacseri@hotmail.com.

FRED GETTINGS (1937–2013) was born in Yorkshire, England, and received an MA at Sussex University in 1969. He was listed by Marquis Who's Who as a notable writer of numerous books and a photographer.

NATALIA HAARAHILTUNEN studied singing and Anthroposophy at Snellman College from 1999 to 2003. She invited Robert Powell to Finland in both 2012 and 2013. She was the editor of *Starlight* from 2019 to 2021. In recent years, Natalia has been collaborating with Joel Park to develop the Footwashing service. Her interest toward Star Wisdom has been growing year by year, and lately she has been working with Krisztina Cseri. She welcomes emails: nataliah@olen.to.

JULIE HUMPHREYS has been a regular contributor to *Star Wisdom* and is the author of *Awakening to the Spiritual Archetypes in the Birth Chart*. An early interest in astrology lay dormant for more than three decades until she was introduced to the sidereal system, the works of Robert Powell and Valentin Tomberg, and the visions of Anne Catherine Emmerich. Julie offers a weekly "stargram" that appears in the Substack version of *Starlight*, the newsletter of the Sophia Foundation of North America.

JOEL MATTHEW PARK is a husband, father, and Christian Hermeticist based in Copake, New York. From 2011 to 2019 he was a life-sharing coworker at Plowshare Farm (a Camphill affiliate), farming and candle-making with people from a variety of countries, ages, and developmental backgrounds. During this time, he earned a certification in Social Therapy from the School of Spiritual Science through the Camphill Academy. He has been living and working in Camphill Village Copake since 2019. After a time devoted to elder care, he has become increasingly involved in teaching in the Camphill Academy, on topics such as Stargazing, the Karma of Vocation, Theosophy, the Human Soul, the Festival Year, and Philosophical Perspectives. Joel has been a student of Anthroposophy since 2008 and a Christian Hermeticist since 2010. In 2014, he met Phillip Malone; together, the two of them have been investigating the *Tarot of Marseilles* since 2016. Since then, Joel has led two retreats on "Tarot and the Art of Hermetic Conversation" (2017 and 2019). The fruits of Joel and Phillip's collaboration in this realm can be found at www.the-unknown-friends.com. In 2015, he joined the Grail Knighthood, a group-spiritual practice offered through the Sophia Foundation. Through this, he met Robert Powell, whose work he had been studying since 2009. Since then, Joel has been working actively with him to continue the karma research Robert began in 1977 and exemplifies in works such as *Hermetic Astrology,* volumes I and II, and *Elijah Come Again.* Joel's first contribution was to the *Journal for Star Wisdom* 2018, after which he became editor for the journal's continuation, the Star Wisdom series. The first volume of this series was published in November 2018. A selection of Joel's writings can be found on his website, Tree-House: www.treehouse.live.

ROBERT POWELL, PhD, is an internationally known lecturer, author, eurythmist, and movement therapist. He is founder of the Choreocosmos School of Cosmic and Sacred Dance, and cofounder of the Sophia Foundation of North America. He received his doctorate for his thesis *The History of the Zodiac,* available as a book from Sophia Academic Press. His published works include *The Sophia Teachings,* a six-tape series (Sounds True Recordings), as well as *Elijah Come Again: A Prophet for Our Time; The Mystery, Biography, and Destiny of Mary Madgalene; Divine Sophia—Holy Wisdom; The Most Holy Trinosophia and the New Revelation of the Divine Feminine; Chronicle of the Living Christ; Christian Hermetic Astrology; The Christ Mystery; The Sign of the Son of Man in the Heavens; Cultivating Inner Radiance and the Body of Immortality;* and the yearly *Journal for Star Wisdom* (previously *Christian Star Calendar*). He translated the spiritual classic *Meditations on the Tarot* and co-translated Valentin Tomberg's *Lazarus, Come Forth!* Robert is coauthor with David Bowden of *Astrogeographia: Correspondences between the Stars and Earthly Locations* and coauthor with Estelle Isaacson of *Gautama Buddha's Successor* and *The Mystery of Sophia.* Robert is also coauthor with Kevin Dann of *The Astrological Revolution: Unveiling the Science of the Stars as a Science of Reincarnation and Karma* and *Christ and the Maya Calendar: 2012 and the Coming of the Antichrist;* and coauthor with Lacquanna Paul of *Cosmic Dances of the Zodiac* and *Cosmic Dances*

of the Planets. He teaches a gentle form of healing movement: the sacred dance of eurythmy, as well as the Cosmic Dances of the Planets and signs of the zodiac. Through the Sophia Grail Circle, Robert facilitates sacred celebrations dedicated to the Divine Feminine. He offers workshops in Europe and Australia, and with Karen Rivers, cofounder of the Sophia Foundation, leads pilgrimages to the world's sacred sites: Turkey, 1996; the Holy Land, 1997; France, 1998; Britain, 2000; Italy, 2002; Greece, 2004; Egypt, 2006; India, 2008; Turkey, 2009; the Grand Canyon, 2010; South Africa, 2012; Peru, 2014; the Holy Land, 2016; and Bali, 2018. Visit www.sophiafoundation.org and www.astrogeographia.org.

RUDOLF STEINER (1861–1925) was born in the small village of Kraljevec, Austro-Hungarian Empire (now in Croatia), where he grew up. As a young man, he lived in Weimar and Berlin, where he became a well-published scientific, literary, and philosophical scholar, known especially for his work with Goethe's scientific writings. At the beginning of the twentieth century, he began to develop his early philosophical principles into an approach to systematic research into psychological and spiritual phenomena. Formally beginning his spiritual teaching career under the auspices of the Theosophical Society, Steiner came to use the term Anthroposophy (and spiritual science) for his philosophy, spiritual research, and findings. The influence of Steiner's multifaceted genius has led to innovative and holistic approaches in medicine, various therapies, philosophy, religious renewal, Waldorf education, biodynamic agriculture, education for special needs, the threefold social form, Goethean science, and the arts, including architecture, painting, sculpture, drama, speech, and eurythmy. In 1924, he reestablished the General Anthroposophical Society, which today has branches throughout the world. Rudolf Steiner died in Dornach, Switzerland.

EVENING MEDITATION

In the evening, meditate on the Earth as a great radiant green star
shining out into the cosmos, and allow your heart to speak:

May this prayer from my warm heart unite

With the Earth's Light that reveres the Christ-Sun,

That I may find Spirit in the Light of the Spirit,

Breath of the Soul in the World's Breath,

Human Strength in the Life of the Earth.

Given by Rudolf Steiner to Maud B. Monges of Spring Valley,
New York, March 9, 1924 (translated by Robert Powell)

Milton Keynes UK
Ingram Content Group UK Ltd.
UKHW050933011223
433587UK00001B/1